PROBLEM SOLVING, DECISION MAKING, AND PROFESSIONAL JUDGMENT

PROBLEM SOLVING, DECISION MAKING, AND PROFESSIONAL JUDGMENT

A GUIDE FOR LAWYERS AND POLICY MAKERS

PAUL BREST
LINDA HAMILTON KRIEGER

OXFORD
UNIVERSITY PRESS

OXFORD
UNIVERSITY PRESS

Oxford University Press, Inc., publishes works that further Oxford University's objective of excellence in research, scholarship, and education.

Oxford New York
Auckland Cape Town Dar es Salaam Hong Kong Karachi Kuala Lumpur Madrid
Melbourne Mexico City Nairobi New Delhi Shanghai Taipei Toronto

With offices in
Argentina Austria Brazil Chile Czech Republic France Greece Guatemala Hungary
Italy Japan Poland Portugal Singapore South Korea Switzerland Thailand
Turkey Ukraine Vietnam

Published by Oxford University Press, Inc.
198 Madison Avenue, New York, New York 10016

Library of Congress Cataloging-in-Publication Data

Brest, Paul
Problem solving, decision making, and professional judgment : a guide for lawyers and policymakers / Paul Brest, Linda Hamilton Krieger. — 1st ed.
p. cm.
Includes bibliographical references and index.
ISBN 978–0–19–536632–7 (pbk. : alk. paper)
1. Practice of law—Decision making. I. Krieger, Linda Hamilton, 1954– II. Title.
K346.B74 2010
320.6—dc22

2009052053

---

3 4 5 6 7 8 9

Printed in the United States of America on acid-free paper

Note to Readers
This publication is designed to provide accurate and authoritative information in regard to the subject matter covered. It is based upon sources believed to be accurate and reliable and is intended to be current as of the time it was written. It is sold with the understanding that the publisher is not engaged in rendering legal, accounting, or other professional services. If legal advice or other expert assistance is required, the services of a competent professional person should be sought. Also, to confirm that the information has not been affected or changed by recent developments, traditional legal research techniques should be used, including checking primary sources where appropriate.

(Based on the Declaration of Principles jointly adopted by a Committee of the American Bar Association and a Committee of Publishers and Associations.)

For Lee Ross, for his wisdom and generosity, his enormous contribution to social psychology and the study of judgment and decision making, and his leadership in demonstrating how insights from the empirical social sciences can be applied to improve, enrich, and ennoble our societies and ourselves.

CONTENTS

PART 1 INTRODUCTION TO PROBLEM SOLVING AND DECISION MAKING

ACKNOWLEDGMENTS

We began teaching a course in Problem Solving, Decision Making, and Professional Judgment in 1994, when Paul was Dean of Stanford Law School and Linda was a lecturer there.[1] The main motivation for developing the course was to provide law students with a foundation in the problem-solving skills that are a core part of the repertoire of excellent lawyers but are for the most part ignored by legal education. The development of the course was encouraged and supported by Charles T. Munger and by the Radcliffe Institute for Advanced Study at Harvard University, where Linda held a research fellowship during the 2004–2005 academic year.

We greatly appreciate the following contributions to this book. Iris Brest read and edited the revisions of each chapter more times than she would care to recall. Tom Griffiths wrote an initial draft of the statistics chapters; Brit Turnbull reviewed and corrected our revisions to these chapters, and then essentially wrote an entirely new version; Christopher Bryan, David Nussbaum, and Aner Sela helped develop and teach the first version of the book to include materials on public policy.[2] Alicia Thesing drafted the wastewater treatment plant problem in Chapter 4. Marc B. Victor provided great assistance with the decision tree problem in Chapter 15.[3] Rick Hanushek helped us develop the regression example in Chapter 6. Donna Shestowsky wrote an early draft of the material on social influence in Chapter 17. Jimmy Benjamin provided useful ideas for the decision-making chapters. Caeli Higney added material on program evaluation

1. Linda subsequently accepted a position at Boalt Hall, where she served as a professor of law from 1996 to 2009, and Paul became president of the William and Flora Hewlett Foundation (though he continues to teach a course on problem solving and decision making at Stanford). Linda is now a professor of law at the University of Hawai'i and a Senior Research Fellow at the Center for the Study of Law and Society at the University of California at Berkeley.

2. Chris contributed to the material on complexities of decision making (Chapter 13) and developed much of the material on persuasion through argument and priming (Chapter 18). Aner developed the material on metacognition in Chapter 9, and also worked on priming. Dave contributed to the material on belief revision in Chapter 10.

3. Marc Victor is an attorney and president of Litigation Risk Analysis, Inc., http://www.litigationrisk.com. He has performed decision-tree analyses on behalf of clients involved in complex, high-stakes litigation since the 1970s.

to Chapter 7. Kelly Spann contributed greatly to the material on scenario planning in Chapter 3. Chris Baker, Molly Elgin, Lauren Finzer, Bria Long, Daniela Rubio, and Tony Wang helped develop, edit, and cite-check various chapters. Chris Baker read the manuscript from cover to cover, and sharpened the statistics chapters and the portions of the teacher's manual accompanying them. Kathryn Segovia did amazing work on the page proofs.

We also want to thank Mahzarin Banaji, Maya Bar-Hillel, Ivan Barkhorn, Jonathan Baron, Max Bazerman, Jeremy Blumenthal, Jack Dovidio, Susan Fiske, Daniel Gilbert, Brent Harris, Richard Heckman, Tony Greenwald, Mark Kelman, Russell Korobkin, Varda Liberman, George Loewenstein, Sendhil Mullainathan, Danny Oppenheimer, Richard Revesz, Lee Ross, Barry Schwartz, Donna Shestowsky, Paul Slovic, Tom Steinbach, Jeff Strnad, George Taylor, Barbara Tversky, James Uleman, and Em Warren, who generously commented on the manuscript.

We are also grateful to Tom Bauch and Henry Hecht, who respectively cotaught the course with Paul at Stanford and Linda at Boalt Hall, and who contributed many ideas which found themselves in the book; to Liz Green, who took pleasure in finding quotidian as well as obscure journal articles and other readings; to Eric Brown, who corrected all allusions to professional sports; and to many Stanford and Boalt Hall law students who have been good-spirited experimental subjects as the materials have developed.

The citations make evident our indebtedness to Amos Tversky, Daniel Kahneman, and many social psychologists who developed and expanded the lines of inquiry they began.

PREFACE

Law schools prepare students for work as business dealmakers, litigators, legal services lawyers, city attorneys, public interest advocates, and corporate general counsel, among other careers. Schools of public policy prepare their graduates for careers in state, local, national, and international governments and in the nonprofit sector; their graduates carry out a vast range of activities including making and implementing policy, advocating for policy changes, and influencing the behavior of consumers, citizens, and businesses.

This book is concerned with a set of qualities and skills that we believe to be important across the entire range of careers that lawyers and policy makers pursue—skills that are also important in people's everyday lives as citizens and consumers. The qualities are sometimes defined in terms of judgment or practical wisdom; the skills in terms of problem solving and decision making.

> "Everyone complains about his memory; no one complains about his judgment."
>
> —La Rochefoucauld

The title of this book uses the terms problem solving and decision making in their conventional senses. It uses judgment in two quite different ways. In common parlance, the term implies good judgment—the capacity to assess situations shrewdly and to draw sound conclusions.[1] We hope that the book will contribute to improving readers' judgment in this sense. But we also draw heavily on the field of social science known as "judgment and decision making" (JDM), in which "judgment" refers mainly to the processes of empiricism—how one ascertains facts and makes predictions about the physical and social world.

Much JDM research asks how people actually come to judgments and make decisions; it focuses particularly on the systematic errors made by intuitive decision makers—all of us, much of the time. In addition to introducing basic analytic and quantitative tools of decision making, the book surveys the JDM literature in the hope that understanding these errors can at least sometimes help avoid them.

1. Anthony T. Kronman, The Lost Lawyer: Failing Ideals of the Legal Profession 72–73 (New York: Cambridge University Press, 1993).

The book is divided into four parts.

Part 1 is a once-over-lightly introduction to problem solving and decision making.

Because good decision making depends on accurate empirical knowledge, and because most important legal and policy decisions are based on probabilistic knowledge rather than certainties, **Part 2** introduces the basic concepts of statistics and identifies the systematic errors that bedevil intuitive empiricists.

Part 3 is about making decisions. Analogous to Part 2, it introduces the concepts and techniques of rational choice and then devotes considerable attention to systematic ways that intuitive decision makers deviate from models of rationality.

Part 4 considers how people's decisions and behavior can be guided or influenced—for better or worse—by individuals or groups. It asks how lawyers and policy makers can use the insights of social psychology and the JDM literature to counsel clients and improve decisions by citizens and consumers.

The last chapter briefly summarizes the material covered in the course and suggests how students can use the knowledge they have gained in the classroom to continue developing professional expertise over the course of a lifetime.

This book was originally intended for a stand-alone course, taught together with problems or "situational" case studies of the sort used in business and public policy schools and in some law schools as well.[2] The authors have used the text for comprehensive courses in law schools and public policy programs. As a stand-alone course, it should be of interest to students wishing to become better problem solvers and decision makers in any aspect of their work—including their everyday lives—as well as to those with an academic interest in statistics, decision making, JDM, and behavioral economics.

But the book also readily lends itself to being used in parts in conjunction with courses including ethics, counseling, and negotiation. Most clinical legal instructors begin with **Part 1** (Chapters 1–4) and then teach selected chapters. Chapters 5–8 offer an introduction to probability and statistics that can be taught as a stand-alone course for students (and by instructors) who have little appetite for the quantitative. For someone interested in teaching the core insights of the JDM literature, they are contained mainly in Chapters 9 and 10 and 12–16 with some snippets in the preceding chapters on probability and statistics.

The book focuses on individual decision makers who, in their roles as lawyers and policy makers, are required to take others' interests into account. While these professionals are often involved in negotiations and mediations, the book does not encompass game theory or negotiation as such. We have bitten off a big enough piece as it is, and hope that the book will provide a solid foundation for approaching this next level of complexity.

---

2. See, e.g., http://www.law.stanford.edu/casestudies/.

PART ONE

INTRODUCTION TO PROBLEM SOLVING AND DECISION MAKING

1. PROBLEM-SOLVING AND DECISION-MAKING PROCESSES
Deliberation, Intuition, and Expertise

A client with a problem consults a lawyer rather than, say, a psychologist, social worker, or business advisor because he believes that his problem has a significant legal dimension. But real-world problems seldom conform to the boundaries that define and divide different disciplines, and it is a rare client who wants his lawyer to confine herself strictly to "the law." Rather, most clients expect their lawyers to integrate legal considerations with other aspects of their problem. Solutions are often constrained or facilitated by the law, but finding the *best* solution—that is, a solution that addresses *all* of the client's concerns—often requires more than technical legal skills. Indeed, it often turns out that no solution is ideal in all respects, and that analyzing *trade-offs* is itself an important nonlegal problem-solving skill.

Reflecting this reality, an American Bar Association report on the ten "fundamental lawyering skills" that new lawyers should acquire places "problem solving" at the very top of the list—even before legal analysis.[1] At their best, lawyers serve as society's general problem solvers, skilled in avoiding as well as resolving disputes and in facilitating public and private ordering. They help clients approach and solve problems flexibly and economically, not restricting themselves to the decision frames that "legal thinking" tends to impose on a client's needs. Good lawyers bring more to bear on a problem than legal knowledge and lawyering skills. They bring creativity, common sense, practical wisdom, and that most precious of all qualities, good judgment.

Designing and implementing public policy—whether done by lawyers or people with other professional backgrounds—call for the same attributes. While counseling and litigating focus on the individual client's interests, policy making is intrinsically concerned with many individuals and institutions with different and often clashing interests. Understanding and accommodating competing, even incommensurable, interests and designing policies that will change behaviors in desired ways are among the policy maker's fundamental skills.

This chapter inquires into the nature of problem solving and decision making, both in general and more particularly in lawyers' work with individual clients and policy makers' work in government agencies and nonprofit organizations. To illustrate problems in both domains, we begin with some vignettes from

1. Robert MacCrate, Legal Education and Professional Development—An Educational Continuum (St. Paul, West Publishing, 1992).

a day in the professional life of two characters: Luis Trujillo, a partner at a mid-sized law firm in Orange County, California; and Christine Lamm, the director of a county environmental protection agency.

1.1 A DAY IN THE LIFE OF A PROBLEM-SOLVING LAWYER

It is an ordinary, if busy, work day for Luis Trujillo. On arriving at his office, he finds on his calendar an initial consultation with a long-standing client at 9:00 a.m., a noon meeting with Karen Moore, a friend from law school, and an afternoon conference with one of the firm's associates to discuss the strategy in a breach of contract action, which the associate has been handling under Trujillo's mentorship.

Trujillo's nine o'clock meeting is with Jack Serrano, owner of Terra Nueva Properties, a real estate development company that builds and manages low and moderate income rental housing projects in the Orange County area. Serrano takes great pride in his company's reputation for providing family-friendly, affordable housing. Until now, the company has enjoyed good relationships with its tenants and with local, state, and federal government agencies. In all of his many years in business, Serrano has never been involved in litigation.

Serrano arrives for his meeting with Trujillo in a state of obvious distress. He is carrying a copy of the local newspaper, with a front-page story about a wave of illnesses suffered by his tenants, allegedly the result of a polyurethane foam product used to insulate the apartments. The article quotes tenants as saying that the walls of the apartments smell bad, "like chemicals," and it is accompanied by a photo of tenants holding a piece of insulation at arm's length. The article also contains graphic descriptions of the tenants' physical ailments and is accompanied by yet another photo—this one of a lawyer and grim-faced residents of Terra Nueva, captioned "Foam Insulation Syndrome Downs Local Residents—Tenants to File Class Action Lawsuit." The article quotes a report of a consumer organization saying that similar outbreaks of "foam insulation syndrome" have occurred elsewhere in the country.[2] We return to Trujillo's meeting with Jack Serrano later in this and subsequent chapters.

Trujillo does pro bono work for the Los Angeles Volunteer Legal Services Association (VLSA). After finishing his meeting with Serrano, he turns to a memorandum from VLSA concerning mass firing of employees, without notice, when a small manufacturing plant decided to move its operations to Mexico.

2. For an example of how life immitates hypothetical problems, see Leslie Wayne, *Chinese Drywall Linked to Corrosion*, New York Times, November 23, 2009, http://www.nytimes.com/2009/11/24/business/energy-environment/24drywall.html?scp=1&sq=chinese%20drywall&st=cse.

The terminations do not appear to violate either federal or state statutes, but Trujillo has the germ of an idea of how to deal with this (to which we will return in Chapter 3).

Trujillo's musings are interrupted by a phone call from the front desk, alerting him that Karen Moore has arrived and is headed back to his office. Moore is a vice president for Big-Mart, a chain of discount department stores in the region. Trujillo has helped negotiate many real estate contracts for Big-Mart, which has grown quickly to have over thirty stores. Trujillo and Moore spend most of the time discussing a complex deal involving a new location. But toward the end of the lunch, Moore presents a quite different problem.

On Trujillo's advice some years ago, Big-Mart has done regular internal audits to ensure that it is in compliance with the law, rather than await regulatory actions or litigation.[3] She reports that the human resources director has taken an extensive look at Big-Mart's employment records, and has discovered an unsettling disparity between the salaries of male and female assistant managers. The average male assistant manager makes $39,257 a year, while the average woman makes $38,528—a disparity of $729.

Trujillo wonders whether the disparity might be due to other factors, such as seniority or education. Resolving this question will require the statistical analysis of Big-Mart's employment data, something we will defer to Part 2 of the book.

Later in the day, Trujillo meets with Anna Wilkins, a recent law school graduate and new associate at the firm. Before turning to the main point of the meeting, a breach of contract case, Trujillo mentions an incident in a trial in a tort case—the first trial in which she ever acted as lead counsel. Anna had been about to object to a question on the ground that it called for hearsay, when Trujillo tugged at her sleeve and indicated that she should let it pass. Wilkins says that she has since checked her recollection of the law. The response would certainly have been inadmissible, and she wonders why Trujillo stopped her from objecting. "You're absolutely right on the law," he says, "but we're really not contesting that particular factual issue. Moreover, we had been making quite a few objections, and the judge was communicating her increasing irritation to the jury."

They then discuss the breach of contract case that Wilkins is handling for the firm. The firm's client, Clyde Evers, has sued Newport Records, a small recording company. Newport refuses to pay for accounting software that Evers customized and installed, saying that the software does not do what Evers said it would do. The amount due is $600,000.

---

3. See Thomas D. Barton, Preventive Law and Problem Solving: Lawyering for the Future (Lake Mary, FL: Vandeplas Publishing, 2009).

Yesterday, Wilkins received a phone call from Evers, who seemed upset that nothing had happened since the case was filed quite a long time ago, and asked her whether she couldn't hasten its resolution.

Based on her knowledge of summary judgment from her Civil Procedure class in law school, her reading of the contract (which disclaims any warranty of performance), and her study of the relevant law concerning warranties, Wilkins believes that Evers can win on summary judgment and proposes to file a motion to that effect. After examining the case file, Trujillo introduces Wilkins to the practical realities of summary judgment practice in the state courts.

Trujillo explains that even though a motion for summary judgment could theoretically bring about a quick disposition of the case, it could have untoward consequences. The judge before whom the motion is likely to be argued views summary judgment—especially for plaintiffs—with considerable skepticism.

It is true that the contract disclaims any warranty of performance. But it appears that Evers had made extravagant oral representations about what the software would do. Even if those representations are not formally binding, they may bias the judge further against summary judgment once he learns of them.

Moreover, the law requires that warranty disclaimers be in a particular typeface, which is somewhat different from the disclaimer in the contract with Newport. The judge might regard the difference as inconsequential and grant summary judgment; or he might have the jury determine whether or not the defendant actually read and understood the disclaimer.

And there is yet another problem. The defendant claims that after a brief trial period it stopped using Evers' software and purchased an off-the-shelf product instead. If the written disclaimer of warranty is ineffective, Newport may have a claim against Evers for breach of warranty. But the statute of limitations on this claim—which is much shorter than the statute of limitations governing Evers' claim—is about to run out. The defendant's lawyer, a local sole practitioner not known for high-quality work, probably hasn't been focusing on the case; but the motion may lead him to pay attention and file the claim.

What's more, Trujillo explains, the cost of litigating the motion for summary judgment will not be insubstantial. If the motion is denied, Evers' costs would be greatly increased. Even if the motion is granted, Newport Records will likely appeal, with attendant costs and the possibility of still having to go to trial.

"Hmmm, I take your points," says Wilkins. "We'll just have to wait until the case comes to trial." But Trujillo responds, "Not so fast. Did Evers give you any indication *why* he was upset that the case wasn't progressing? Surely you discussed the time frame with him at an earlier point." Wilkins replies that Evers mentioned that he was anxious to have the funds from the judgment to invest in a new venture.

Trujillo then asks Wilkins whether she can think of any available options beside moving for summary judgment and waiting for trial, and eventually they discuss the pros and cons of approaching Newport Records' lawyer with a settlement offer.

1.2 A DAY IN THE LIFE OF A PROBLEM-SOLVING POLICY MAKER

Christine Lamm received a joint degree in law and public policy only ten years ago. A deputy administrator in the county's environmental protection agency, she was catapulted into the role of acting administrator of the department upon the sudden departure of her boss two years ago. Last year, with some misgivings based on her lack of experience and her tendency to do everything "by the book" in an overly deliberative manner that did not always take political realities into account, the mayor formally appointed her head of the department. She serves in that capacity "at the pleasure" of the mayor, meaning that she can be removed by the mayor at will.

Lamm begins the day by continuing to work on a complex project involving the siting of a wastewater treatment plant in Edenville. But the work is interrupted (and will not be resumed until Chapter 4) by an urgent phone call from Paula Henderson, the mayor's chief of staff, about the Terra Nueva affair. The mayor saw the same newspaper articles that brought Serrano to Luis Trujillo's office that morning, and he wants something done about the foam insulation problem "ASAP." Henderson asks Lamm to draft a set of proposed regulations banning use of polyurethane foam insulation in new construction and renovation projects in the county.

Lamm listens anxiously to Henderson's request, mindful that her continued employment turns on her ability to remain in the mayor's good graces. But Lamm doesn't just have her job to worry about; she feels personally and professionally committed to approaching the foam insulation problem at Terra Nueva in a manner consistent with principles of sound public policy making. Quickly calculating how best to mediate between these two sets of concerns, Lamm explains to Henderson that, under the state's Administrative Procedures Act, any regulatory initiative banning the foam insulation will have to be premised on agency findings—arrived at using scientifically acceptable methods—that the foam was in fact causing harm. After a rather pointed response, underscoring the mayor's desire to act decisively in response to requests from community groups that had long supported him, Henderson agrees with Lamm's suggestion that she convene a working group to investigate the causal connection between the insulation product and the symptoms experienced by Terra Nueva residents.

After getting off the phone with Henderson, Lamm decides to take a walk to clear her head, and to give a maintenance worker access to her office to repair a light above her desk. When she returns, she notices that her computer screen is dark, and recalls that she had a number of word-processing and spreadsheet documents open when she left. Grumbling to herself that the last thing she needs on a stressful day like this is a bunch of lost work, she checks the electric plug, thinking, "I'll bet the maintenance guy accidentally unplugged it when he moved my desk; that sort of thing has happened to me before." She checks under her desk where the electrical socket is located. "It's plugged in, but it seems a bit loose," she thinks. "I'll jiggle it." In the process, the plug comes completely out of the socket, and the background sound of the hard drive and fan, which she had not noticed until then, suddenly goes silent. The computer had not been off before, but it is now. On further inspection, Lamm discovers that the screen was dark because the cable connecting the computer to the monitor had come loose. Now she in fact has lost some work.

1.3 DEFINING PROBLEM SOLVING AND DECISION MAKING

As these vignettes suggest, in their day-to-day work, lawyers and public policy makers are constantly working to solve problems, either alone or in collaboration with others. The qualities they need to do this well are sometimes defined in terms of judgment or practical wisdom, the skills in terms of problem solving and decision making.

The academic and professional literatures provide a variety of definitions of the term *problem*. For example, Charles Kepner and Benjamin Tregoe define a problem as a situation where "something has gone wrong."[4] This definition captures at least two of the situations described above. "Something has gone wrong" at Jack Serrano's Terra Nueva apartments, and something "went wrong" with Christine Lamm's computer.

More broadly, law professor Gerald Lopez defines a "problem" as a situation in which "the world we would like varies from the world as it is."[5] Correspondingly, Lopez defines *problem solving* as "trying to move the world in the desired direction."[6] This definition aptly describes Christine Lamm's project for siting the wastewater treatment plant. It also describes the situation presented by VLSA's potential case on behalf of the laid-off woodworkers. From the laid-off workers' perspective, "the world they would like" is one with a legally enforceable right to reasonable notice of pending layoffs, if not protection from the layoffs themselves. However, "the world as it is" apparently provides no such claim. Crafting a novel legal theory, and then persuading a judge to apply it and provide a remedy, represents an effort to "move the world in the desired direction."

Problems also include situations where nothing has gone wrong yet, but where there is reason to believe that if some action is not taken, something *may*

---

4. Charles H. Kepner and Benjamin B. Tregoe, The New Rational Manager viii (Princeton: Princeton, 1981).

5. Gerald P. Lopez, *Lay Lawyering* 32 UCLA Law Review, 2 (1984).

6. *Id.*

go wrong in the future. Problem solving in these cases calls for the deployment of strategies calculated to head off foreseeable future problems. Much of lawyers' work in their roles as counselors, deal makers, estate planners, and legislative drafters involves anticipating and avoiding problems that might arise. That's why Trujillo recommended that Big-Mart do a regular legal audit—the equivalent of an annual physical exam. To take another example, the standard lease agreement that Trujillo had drafted years ago for Jack Serrano tries to anticipate various things that might "go wrong" with a particular tenancy—persistent loud parties disturbing to neighbors, chronically late or unpaid rent, undesirable subletting arrangements, to name a few. Part of Trujillo's craft as a lawyer involves his ability to anticipate problems of this sort and to work into the lease agreement mechanisms through which Serrano can address them quickly, effectively, and at the lowest possible cost. Unless anticipated ahead of time, a "something may go wrong" problem can easily become a "something has gone wrong" problem.

To accommodate problems of these various types, we adopt a more inclusive definition of the term *problem*, similar to that suggested by Allen Newell and Herbert Simon: a "problem" is any situation in which the state of affairs varies, or may in the future vary, from the desired state, and where there is no obvious way to reach the desired state.[7] For example, we will see in Chapter 4 that there is no single obvious solution to Christine Lamm's problem of where to site the wastewater treatment plant.

Newell and Simon define the conceptual area between the existing and desired states of affairs as a *problem space*. To solve a problem is to navigate through the problem space—through the virtual area between the actual or potential unsatisfactory state and the desired state. We can represent this conception of a problem and the problem solving process in the following way, as shown in Figure 1.1.

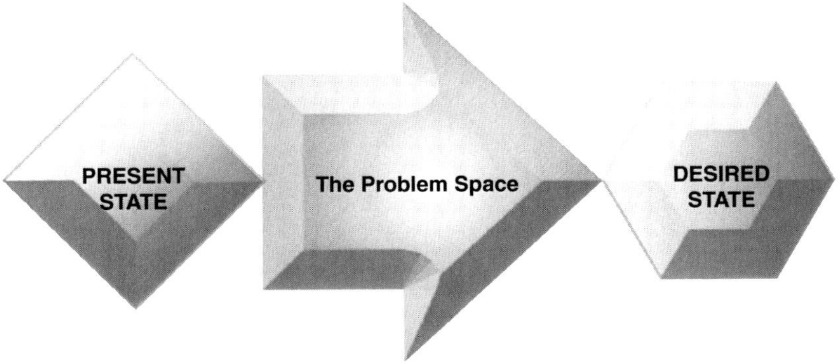

FIGURE 1.1 THE PROBLEM SPACE.

7. Allen Newell and Herbert A. Simon, Human Problem Solving (Englewood Cliffs, NJ: Prentice Hall, 1972).

Problem solving often requires solving a number of constituent subproblems. For this reason, the problem space can be viewed as containing a number of segmented paths, one or more of which leads from the initial state to the desired state—if the problem is solvable at all. Each of the nodes located along these paths represents a decision point—a point at which the problem solver must choose between different available courses of action. In most situations, there is more than one possible pathway through a problem space. Sometimes these present themselves as distinct options at the outset. At other times, a single pathway branches off into different directions partway through the traverse. Either way, problem space navigation is almost always multinodal. Moving from one node to the next requires making a decision, as the graphic in Figure 1.2 illustrates.

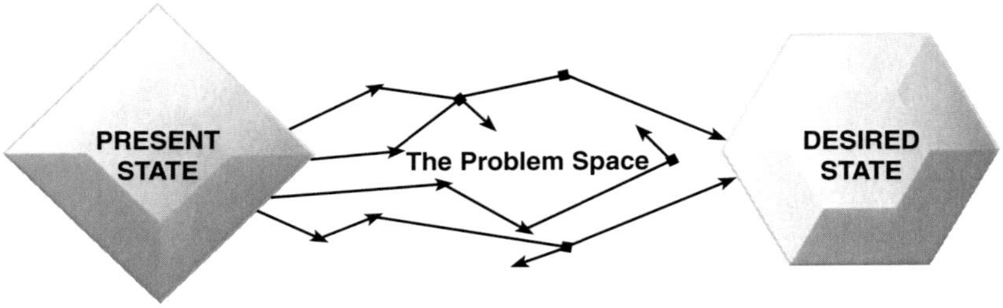

FIGURE 1.2 NAVIGATING THE PROBLEM SPACE.

The various pathways through a problem space may not be equally satisfactory. Some pathways that appear promising at the outset may ultimately prove to be dead ends. Some are inferior because they demand the expenditure of excessive resources, or create new problems even while solving the original one, or because they compromise other objectives. Problem solving is thus subject to what Newell and Simon term *path constraints*. A completely satisfactory solution is a path that leads through the problem space *and* is consistent with all relevant constraints.

The process described by Newell and Simon can be analogized to an expedition by explorers who must cross uncharted territory to get to their desired destination. The explorers may take one path, only to have to backtrack after discovering that it ends at a steep cliff. They may take another and encounter a wide river. How to cross the river in effect poses an ancillary problem, which must be solved to continue the journey. As for path constraints, the explorers might be vegetarians, or might have mores that preclude them from traveling on the Sabbath, which could hinder their progress toward the destination but nevertheless must be taken into account.

If "problem solving" consists of "trying to move the world in the desired direction," it must ultimately eventuate in a *decision*—a "commitment to a course of action that is intended to produce a satisfying state of affairs."[8] In terms of the preceding discussion, decision making involves choosing a particular pathway across the problem space that lies between the actual and desired states of affairs. The "best" solution to a problem is one that satisfies, to the greatest extent possible, the broadest range of objectives, including constraints, implicated by the problem.

1.4 DELIBERATIVE AND INTUITIVE PROBLEM SOLVING AND DECISION MAKING

There are essentially two distinct, but complementary, approaches to problem solving and decision making. One relies on analysis or deliberation, the other on intuition. While intuition is pervasive, deliberation is relatively rare because, among other things, it requires considerable cognitive energy. Deliberative decision making is informed by intuition at the same time as it corrects for the limitations and biases of pure intuition. Intuition can also be informed by deliberation, as happens in the development of expertise. While the processes of intuition are largely opaque to the decision maker, deliberation is transparent. For this reason, among others, we begin with deliberation.

1.4.1 Deliberative Processes

An ideal deliberative model of decision making consists of the following steps or elements:

1. State, or "frame," the problem to be solved;
2. Identify and prioritize the relevant values, interests, and objectives;
3. Identify and resolve major uncertainties concerning the cause of the problem;
4. Generate a range of plausible solutions or alternative courses of action;
5. Predict the consequences of the courses of action and assess their impact on the relevant interests or objectives;
6. Select the course of action that optimizes the interests or objectives to be served (i.e., make a decision);
7. Implement, observe, and learn from the outcome of the decision.

The process is recursive, beginning with the need to frame the problem in terms of the interests involved and to consider the interests in the context of the particular problem. After completing step 5, a decision maker would be wise to review the earlier steps, not just because he may have accidentally omitted

---

8. J. Frank Yates, Elizabeth S. Veinott, and Andrea L. Patalano, *Hard Decisions, Bad Decisions: On Decision Quality and Decision Aiding*, *in* EMERGING PERSPECTIVES ON JUDGMENT AND DECISION RESEARCH 13–63 (Sandra L. Schneider and James Shanteau eds., New York: Cambridge University Press, 2003).

something, but because the concreteness of positing solutions can reframe objectives and his conception of the overall problem.

1.4.1.a Framing the Problem Problem solvers sometimes go about solving the wrong problem because they do not frame the issues adequately. They may mistake symptoms of a problem for the problem itself, or define the problem too narrowly, or define the problem in terms of a ready solution without taking account of the objectives they are actually trying to achieve. Some lawyers might immediately frame Jack Serrano's problem solely as defending against the potential class action suit. By contrast, as we will see in Chapter 2, Trujillo will help Jack Serrano consider the problem at Terra Nueva from a variety of different perspectives, resisting the temptation to adopt the first problem frame that comes to mind.

1.4.1.b Identifying Interests and Objectives The German philosopher Friedrich Nietzsche is reputed to have said, "To forget one's purpose is the commonest form of stupidity."

The best frame for a problem is the one that incorporates the broadest possible range of purposes, interests, objectives, and values implicated by the situation. For this reason, the second step in deliberative problem solving entails a thoroughgoing specification of all relevant interests and objectives, not just those most readily brought to mind. For example, Jack Serrano obviously has an interest in minimizing his legal liability to tenants of Terra Nueva. But he may have other interests, such as his reputation in the community and his ongoing relations with tenants. Because of Christine Lamm's responsibilities as county environmental administrator, concerns for the tenants' health predominate, but they must be balanced against other economic and social interests.

Anna Wilkins thought that a summary judgment motion was the solution to Evers's problem in Newport Records—getting the matter resolved quickly. But this was a solution to a problem she did not fully understand, and could not understand without asking her client *why* he was so anxious to have his case resolved. In considering where to site the waste treatment plant, Christine Lamm will also have to understand her various stakeholders' interests with considerable specificity.

Sometimes, a client may come to a lawyer without a clear sense of his underlying objectives and interests, but with his mind set on a particular solution. In these situations, a good lawyer will slow down the client and help him identify all his interests and objectives before generating, let alone selecting among, alternative courses of action.

1.4.1.c Diagnosing Causes While the causes of some problems are perfectly clear, many others call for analysis or diagnosis. For example, in responding to the situation at Terra Nueva, both Trujillo and Lamm must consider whether Serrano's tenants' distress is really being caused by the foam insulation. It is possible that their symptoms result from or are heightened by a different cause. With respect to gender inequities at Big-Mart, Trujillo's partner will need to determine whether the difference in Big-Mart's compensation of male and female assistant managers is statistically significant and, if so, whether it is attributable to gender or to some other variable. As Christine Lamm worked her way through her "dead computer" problem, she had to determine or, in any event, should have determined, whether the dark monitor screen resulted from an unplugged power cord or from some other cause.

Just as a physician who misdiagnoses the underlying cause of a set of symptoms is likely to prescribe an unhelpful, or even harmful, treatment, so too may a lawyer or policy maker take useless or counterproductive actions based on an inadequate analysis of the facts. Section 2.5 introduces issues of empirical analysis, which are then considered in detail in Part 2.

1.4.1.d Developing Alternatives The best problem frame is not necessarily the first to come to mind, and this is true of potential solutions or courses of action as well. Problem solving often benefits from a period of divergent thinking about different possible solutions, rather than from rapid convergence on the first seemingly attractive strategic option that sashays by. We examine the generation of alternative courses of action in Chapter 3.

1.4.1.e Evaluating Alternatives Once a variety of potential solutions or courses of action have been generated, a deliberative problem solver proceeds to evaluate them. In this phase, the problem solver must predict the consequences of each plausible option, and then assess the consequences in light of his client's objectives.

We take a first look at evaluating alternatives in Chapter 4, and continue to explore these issues throughout the rest of the book.

1.4.1.f Choosing and Implementing a Course of Action Eventually the problem-solving process comes to a conclusion and a decision must be made. Quite often, this requires making trade-offs among competing interests—a process introduced in Chapter 4 and explored further in Part 3. As implementation progresses, the selected solution is monitored, adjusted if necessary, and reviewed to see what can be learned from the experience of its selection and implementation.

* * *

1.4.2 Divergent and Convergent Thinking

The deliberative approach to problem solving combines elements of *divergent* and *convergent* thinking. Divergent thinking expands the range of perspectives, dimensions, and options related to a problem. Convergent thinking eliminates possible alternatives through the application of critical analysis, thereby eventually reducing the number of options that remain open. Divergent thinking conceives; convergent thinking critiques. Divergent thinking envisions; convergent thinking troubleshoots, fine tunes, selects, and implements.

As the following figure suggests, you can think of divergent thinking as two lines emerging from a common point and then moving away from each other, and of convergent thinking as two lines coming together from different directions on a single point, as shown in Figure 1.3.

Figure 1.4 illustrates how the model of deliberative problem solving just described above combines elements of divergent and convergent thinking.

Early in the process, when a problem is being framed, when interests and objectives are being identified, and when alternative solutions are being generated, divergent thinking can bring a great deal of value to the problem-solving endeavor. Divergent thinking enables us to conceptualize the problem from a wide variety of perspectives, so as to permit consideration of the broadest possible array of potential solutions. Divergent thinking helps identify the full range of interests implicated by a particular decision. And divergent thinking inspires innovation in coming up with solutions to the problem. Later in the process, convergent thinking comes into play in analyzing causation, evaluating options, choosing which course of action to implement, and implementing and monitoring the choice.

1.5 INTUITIVE PROCESSES IN PROBLEM SOLVING AND DECISION MAKING

> *Intuition or know-how . . . is neither wild guessing nor supernatural inspiration, but the sort of ability we use all the time as we go about our everyday tasks.*
> —Hubert and Stuart Dreyfus, Mind Over Machine[9]

"Most of a person's everyday life is determined not by their conscious intentions and deliberate choices but by mental processes that are put into motion by features of the environment that operate outside of conscious awareness and guidance."[10] Most of the time we solve problems without coming close to the conscious, step-by-step analysis of the deliberative approach. In fact, attempting to approach even a small fraction of the problems we encounter in a full, deliberative manner would bring our activities to a screeching halt. Out of necessity, most of problem-solving is intuitive. In contrast with the deliberative model of decision making, intuitive decisions rely on a process "that somehow produces an answer, solution, or idea without the use of a conscious, logically defensible step-by-step process."[11] Intuitive responses "are reached with little apparent

---

9. Hubert Dreyfus and Stuart Dreyfus, Mind Over Machine: The Power of Human Intuitive Expertise in the Era of the Computer 29 (New York: Free Press, 1986).

10. John Bargh and Tanya Chartrand, *The Unbearable Automaticity of Being*, 54 American Psychologist 462 (1999).

11. Kenneth Hammond, Human Judgment and Social Policy: Irreducible Uncertainty, Inevitable Error, Unavoidable Injustice 60 (New York: Oxford University Press, 1996).

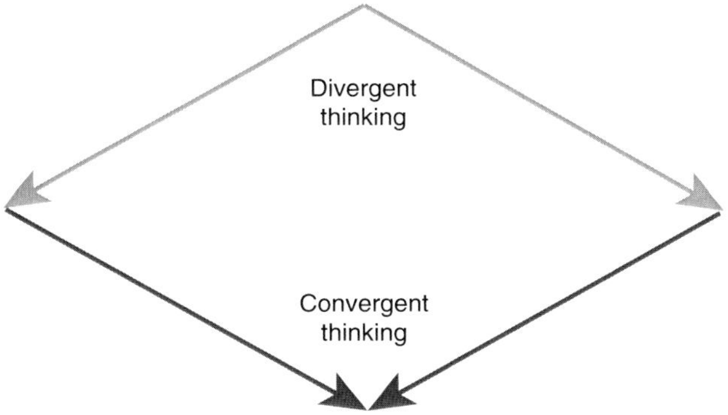

FIGURE 1.3 DIVERGENT AND CONVERGENT THINKING.

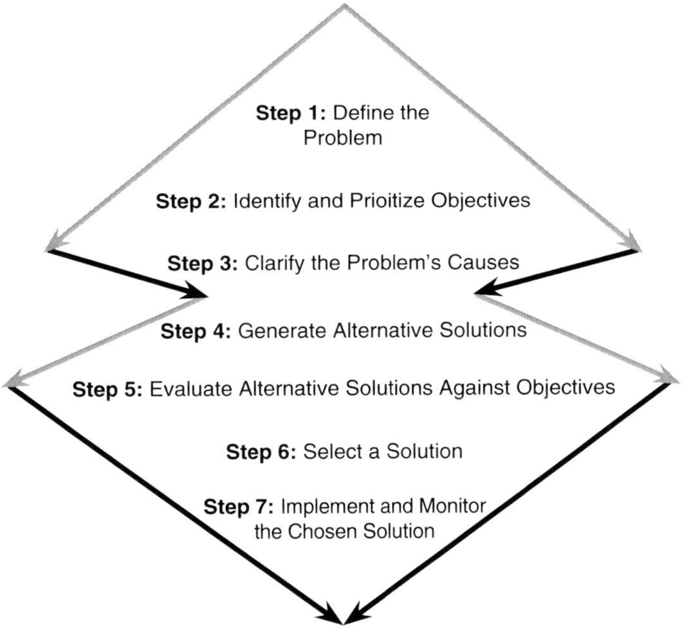

FIGURE 1.4 DIVERGENT AND CONVERGENT ELEMENTS IN FORMAL PROBLEM SOLVING.

effort, and typically without conscious awareness. They involve little or no conscious deliberation."[12]

1.5.1 Recognition-Primed Decision Making

Experts employ intuition—often informed by deliberation and reflection on past decisions—through a strategy that Gary Klein calls *recognition-primed decision making*.[13] According to this model, experience in the world gives us myriad problem *schemas*—mental maps that allow us to immediately "size up" a situation, see it as an example of a problem prototype, understand its meaning, and know what action to take.[14] If the problem does not have an obvious solution, then rather than systematically generate and compare a number of options (as in the deliberative model), we evaluate a plausible option through "mental simulation"—by imagining ourselves carrying it out.[15] If this does not seem to lead to a good outcome, we evaluate another possible option.[16]

A problem schema often supplies the problem solver with a prefabricated agenda for thought and action. It tells her what features of the problem situation are important, what additional information, if any, is needed, and what action she needs to take to reach a solution. The decision maker can then execute the solution, often automatically, without conscious deliberation or thought. As this description implies, many problem schemas have stock solutions, stored in the mind as part of the schema itself.

> The [chess] grand masters . . . use their intuition to recognize the promising moves that they should examine more closely. They shift to an analytic mode by looking at the moves they will play out in the context of the game, and rely on their ability to mentally simulate what will happen if they play a move. In the course of these mental simulations, some of the moves drop out because they are found to contain weaknesses. By the end of the mental simulations, the grand masters are usually left with only a single move they find playable.
> — GARY KLEIN, INTUITION AT WORK 75 (2003).

12. ROBIN HOGARTH, EDUCATING INTUITION 14 (Chicago: University of Chicago Press, 2001).

13. GARY KLEIN, SOURCES OF POWER: HOW PEOPLE MAKE DECISIONS 17 (Cambridge: MIT Press, 1998).

14. *Id.* at 17, 89.

15. *Id.* at 20, 21.

16. In the process of solving the problem, we may even change our understanding of the goal we are pursuing. *See* KLEIN, 122.

Recognition-primed decision making describes the mode of operation of, say, an experienced firefighter deciding on how to make his way safely into a burning building, or a doctor or nurse responding to a medical crisis. Klein describes the response of two nurses working in a neonatal intensive care unit.[17]

Darlene had been working with premature infants for a long time; Linda was an experienced nurse, but new to this unit. Linda was responsible for an infant whose temperature had dropped slightly several times during her watch; each time, she turned up the temperature in the isolette. She also noticed that the place in the baby's heel where a medical technician had taken a blood sample was still bleeding a bit, and attributed it to a sloppy procedure. When Darlene saw the baby, something "just looked funny." After doing a quick physical, she woke up the duty physician, saying that she thought the baby had sepsis. If they had awaited the results of a blood culture before putting the baby on antibiotics, it would probably have been too late. Darlene's experience enabled her to see a pattern which was not available to Linda—and also to respond. As Klein writes:

> A "pattern" is a set of cues that usually chunk together, so that if you see a few of the cues you can expect to find the others. When you notice a pattern you may have a sense of familiarity—yes, I've seen that before! As we work in any area, we accumulate experiences and build up a reservoir of recognized patterns. The more patterns we learn, the easier it is to match a new situation to one of the patterns in our reservoir . . .
>
> Once we recognize a pattern, we gain a sense of situation: We know what *cues* are going to be important and need to be monitored. We know what types of *goals* we should be able to accomplish. We have a *sense* of what to expect next. And the patterns include routines for responding. . . . If we see a situation as typical then we can recognize the typical way to react. [18]

1.5.2 The Role of Schemas and Scripts

Schematic processing is not only the key to recognition-primed decision making, but to navigating the everyday world. Every person, object, and situation we encounter is unique, but to treat them as such would be impossible. Were we to treat every experience as sui generis, we would fast be inundated by an unmanageable complexity that would overwhelm our cognitive capabilities. To function at all, we must radically simplify our experience of the world.

In a classic article entitled *On Perceptual Readiness*, cognitive psychologist Jerome Bruner observed that when we perceive a stimulus from our environment, our first task is to fit that information into some existing knowledge structure

---

17. Gary Klein, *A Case Study of Intuition*, *in* INTUITION AT WORK: WHY DEVELOPING YOUR GUT INSTINCTS WILL MAKE YOU BETTER AT WHAT YOU DO 3–9 (New York: Doubleday, 2002).

18. *Id.* at 11, 12–13.

represented in memory.[19] Perception is given meaning only when filtered through and incorporated into preexisting cognitive elements, such as schemas.[20]

As people learn through experience, they organize their acquired knowledge into an interconnected web of associations. A schema represents an individual's accumulated knowledge, beliefs, experiences, and affective orientations toward the schematized construct. The schema activation process is automatic. We do not see an object consisting of four upright legs topped by a square platform and backed by a vertical plane; we see a "chair." The "chair" schema is automatically activated by the incoming visual information. This perception happens unintentionally, outside of conscious awareness, through a process that is not readily interrupted and that interferes little with other ongoing mental activity.[21]

A schema imposes meaning on the inherently ambiguous information supplied by raw perception. Once a schema is activated, we implicitly expect incoming information to be consistent with its elements.[22] Schematic processing is both inevitable and a pervasive source of errors of judgment. Our need to impose order on the world leads us to see patterns even where they do not exist, and schemas lie at the core of inaccurate stereotypes based on race, sex, and other factors.

A *script* is a schema consisting of a sequence of social interactions in which you are an actor or observer.[23] Richard Nisbett and Lee Ross analogize a script to a cartoon strip, in which each scene depicts a basic social action; for example, a restaurant script might involve entering, ordering, eating, paying, and leaving. "The importance of scripts . . . lies in the speed and ease with which they make events (or secondhand accounts of events) readily comprehensible and predictable. Their potential cost . . . is the possibility of erroneous interpretations, inaccurate expectations and inflexible modes of response."[24]

---

19. Jerome Bruner, *On Perceptual Readiness*, 64 PSYCHOLOGICAL REVIEW, 123–152 (1958).

20. Eleanor Rosch, *Principles of Categorization* (1978), *in* FROM READINGS IN COGNITIVE SCIENCE: A PERSPECTIVE FROM PSYCHOLOGY AND ARTIFICIAL INTELLIGENCE 312–22 (Allan Collins and Edward E. Smith eds., San Mateo, CA: Morgan Kaufmann Publishers, 1988); ZIVA KUNDA, SOCIAL COGNITION (Cambridge: MIT Press, 1999); RICHARD E. NISBETT AND LEE ROSS, HUMAN INFERENCE: STRATEGIES AND SHORTCOMINGS OF SOCIAL JUDGMENT (Englewood Cliffs, NJ: Prentice Hall, 1980); SUSAN FISKE AND SHELLEY TAYLOR, SOCIAL COGNITION (2d ed. Columbus, OH: McGraw-Hill, 1991); C. NEIL MACRAE ET AL., STEREOTYPES AND STEREOTYPING (New York: Guilford Press, 1996). Fiske and Taylor define a *schema* as a "cognitive structure that represents knowledge about a concept or type of stimulus, including its attributes and the relations among those attributes."

21. Laraine Winter, James Uleman, and Cathryn Cunniff, *How Automatic Are Social Judgments?*, 49 JOURNAL OF PERSONALITY AND SOCIAL PSYCHOLOGY 904–17 (1985).

22. KUNDA, SOCIAL COGNITION: MAKING SENSE OF OTHER PEOPLE 18–21 (Cambridge, MA: MIT Press, 1999).

23. *See* ROGER C. SCHANK AND ROBERT P. ABELSON, SCRIPTS, PLANS, GOALS, AND UNDERSTANDING (Hillsdale, NJ: Erlbaum, 1977); NISBETT AND ROSS, *supra* at 34.

24. NISBETT AND ROSS, *supra* at 34–35.

Christine Lamm's response to the computer problem provides an example of schematic processing in everyday life. The sight of her dark computer screen activated a "dead computer" schema, which she had developed as a result of earlier experiences with computers and with other electrical appliances. Once activated, the "dead computer" schema spontaneously supplied a causal theory (electrical cord unplugged), a thumbnail narrative accompanying the causal theory (cord unplugged by the window cleaner), and a solution: "plug in the cord." This intuitive process was virtually self-executing and required very little cognitive exertion. In nontechnical terms, Lamm was just "sizing up the situation."

Schemas and scripts play a role in a lawyer's deciding whether to object to a question put to a witness at trial. The process is more reflexive than reflective: A lawyer instinctively calls out "objection!" and often only formulates a rationale while rising to address the court. Anna Wilkins' and Luis Trujillo's different reactions to the question that called for hearsay flowed from different schemas or scripts. For Wilkins, the question triggered a hearsay schema, based on the rules of evidence she had learned in law school. Trujillo intuitively placed the rules in the broader script of a trial narrative that would be helpful to the client's case.

Beyond these particular examples, lawyers and policy makers are constantly called upon to engage in what Karl Weick has called "sensemaking."[25] They must size up or interpret situations—for example, a complex financial transaction—with a keen eye for anomalies, for what might go wrong. Recognizing patterns without allowing oneself to become trapped by them is an essential part of this task.

1.5.3 The Role of Affect

The heart has its reasons that reason does not understand.
—Blaise Pascal

Intuitive problem solving and decision making depends not only on the essentially mental processes of recognizing patterns, but on affect as well. In recent years, researchers have given increasing attention to the role of affect in decision making—ranging from a "faint whisper of emotion to strong feelings of fear and dread, to visceral drives such as hunger and sexual need."[26] Thomas Hoving writes that the art historian, Bernard Berenson

---

25. Karl Weick, Sensemaking in Organizations: Foundations for Organizational Science (Thousand Oaks, CA: Sage Publications, 1995).

26. Paul Slovic et al., *The Affect Heuristic, in* Heuristics and Biases: The Psychology of Intuitive Judgment 397–420 (Thomas Gilovich, Dale Griffin, and Daniel Kahneman eds., New York: Cambridge University Press, 2002). The authors define *affect* as "the specific quality of 'goodness' or 'badness' (1) experienced, as a feeling state (with or without consciousness) and (2) demarcating a positive or negative quality of a stimulus."

> sometimes distressed his colleagues with his inability to articulate how he could see so clearly the tiny defects and inconsistencies in a particular work that branded it either an unintelligent reworking, or a fake. In one case, in fact, Berenson was able to say only that his stomach felt wrong. He had a curious ringing in his ears. He was struck by a momentary depression. Or he felt woozy and off balance.[27]

American soldiers in Iraq and Afghanistan with expertise in detecting roadside improvised explosive devices (IEDs) describe affective responses preceding conscious thought. On an unusually quiet morning in Mosul, a sergeant saw a car with the windows rolled up and a couple of children inside, and warned a soldier not to approach the car. "My body suddenly got cooler; you know, that danger feeling."[28] A moment later, the car exploded. (See Section 10.5.2 for the sergeant's explanation of this intuition.)

In a laboratory experiment by Antonio Damasio and his colleagues, participants were allowed to gamble by choosing cards from several decks, some of which had been stacked against them. Well before the participants could articulate why they disliked these decks, they showed physiological signs of tension when choosing from them.[29]

Without emotions, our decision-making processes would be overwhelmed by the burdens of cognition. "The action of biological drives, body states, and emotions may be an indispensable foundation for rationality . . . Rationality is probably shaped and modulated by body signals, even as it performs the most sublime distinctions and acts accordingly."[30] Emotions and reasoning exist in a delicate balance, however, and (as we discuss in Chapter 16) emotions can sometimes overwhelm reasoning to our detriment.

Affect plays an important role in many lawyers' activities—not just under pressure in the course of a trial, but in the relative calm of one's office. Consider Luis Trujillo's trying to assess the candor of a witness, or someone he is negotiating with, or, indeed, his client. Or consider Christine Lamm's dealing with upset tenants at Terra Nueva and how her sense of her own professional responsibilities is implicated in how she handles their problem. Among other things, the

---

27. THOMAS HOVING, FALSE IMPRESSIONS: THE HUNT FOR BIG TIME ART FAKES 19–20 (New York: Simon & Schuster, 1996). For a discussion of the role of intuition in the discovery of another art fraud, *see* MALCOLM GLADWELL, BLINK: THE POWER OF THINKING WITHOUT THINKING 3–17 (New York: Little Brown, 2005).

28. Benedict Carey, *In Battle, Hunches Prove to be Valuable*, NEW YORK TIMES, July 28, 2009, http://www.nytimes.com/2009/07/28/health/research/28brain.html?pagewanted=2&_r=1&hp.

29. Antoine Bechara, Hanna Damasio, Daniel Tranel, Antonio R. Damasio, *Deciding Advantageously Before Knowing the Advantageous Strategy*, 275 (5304) SCIENCE 1293–95 (Feb. 28, 1997).

30. ANTONIO DAMASIO, DESCARTES' ERROR 200 (New York: G.P. Putnam's Sons, 1994).

skilled professional must be able to differentiate between her own emotions and those of clients and others. This capacity is a component of so-called *emotional intelligence*.[31] Like many of the other skills of intuition, these capacities are best improved through reflective experience and practice.

1.6 THE INTERACTION OF INTUITION AND DELIBERATION

1.6.1 The Two-Systems Model of Cognition

The two models of decision making described above exemplify what psychologists and cognitive scientists—following the pathbreaking work of Amos Tversky and Daniel Kahneman—have described as a *dual process* or *two-systems model of cognition*. "System 1 quickly proposes intuitive answers to judgment problems as they arise, and System 2 monitors the quality of these proposals, which it may endorse, correct, or override. The judgments that are eventually expressed are *intuitive* if they retain the hypothesized initial proposal without much modification."[32] Kahneman and Shane Frederick summarize the two systems in this chart in Table 1.1.

TABLE 1.1 THE TWO-SYSTEMS MODEL OF INFORMATION PROCESSING

System 1 (intuitive)	System 2 (reflective)
Process Characteristics	
Automatic	Controlled
Effortless	Effortful
Associative	Deductive
Rapid, parallel	Slow, serial
Process opaque	Self-aware
Skilled action	Rule application
Content on which Processes Act	
Affective	Neutral
Causal properties	Statistics
Concrete, specific	Abstract
Prototypes	Sets

31. *See* DANIEL GOLEMAN, EMOTIONAL INTELLIGENCE: WHY IT CAN MATTER MORE THAN IQ (10th Anniversary Edition New York: Bantam, 2006); John D. Mayer, Peter Salovey, and David Caruso, *Models of Emotional Intelligence*, *in* HANDBOOK OF INTELLIGENCE 396–420 (Robert Sternberg ed., 2d ed. New York: Cambridge University Press, 2000).

32. Daniel Kahneman and Shane Frederick, *Representativeness Revisited: Attribute Substitution in Intuitive Judgment*, *in* HEURISTICS AND BIASES: THE PSYCHOLOGY OF INTUITIVE JUDGMENT, *supra* at 49.

Kahneman and Frederick suggest that "System 2 endorsements of intuitive judgments are granted quite casually under normal circumstances." They give the example of this puzzle: "A bat and a ball cost $1.10 in total. The bat costs $1 more than the ball. How much does the ball cost?"

> Almost everyone we ask reports an initial tendency to answer "10 cents" because the sum of $1.10 separates naturally into $1 and 10 cents, and 10 cents is about the right magnitude. Many people yield to this immediate impulse. The surprisingly high rate of errors in this easy problem illustrates how lightly System 1 monitors the output of System 2: people are not accustomed to thinking hard, and are often content to trust a plausible judgment that quickly comes to mind.

At very least, the two systems provide useful metaphors for the different ways that people process information. Moreover, there is considerable evidence that they map onto different physical parts of the brain. Especially when the problem has any affective component, System 1 activities take place in the amygdala and possibly the orbitofrontal cortex; System 2 activities take place in the lateral prefrontal cortex—an area of the brain that is associated with reasoning and that is much larger in human beings than in any other species.[33]

1.6.2 The Limits of Deliberation: Bounded Rationality

Problem solving and decision making in professional contexts and in everyday life call for a mixture of intuition and deliberation—of System 1 and System 2 processes. The predominance of intuitive decision making is an inevitable aspect of the human condition of limited cognitive ability and time—what Herbert Simon has called the condition of *bounded rationality*.[34]

We solve thousands of little problems and make thousands of decisions every day. Given God-like cognitive powers and infinite time, we could apply a deliberative model to all of these actions. But under conditions of bounded rationality, we rely mostly on intuitive decision making. Indeed, we do not think of most events as decisions at all; they are just something we "do." Even when we are self-conscious about decision making and employ something resembling the deliberative model, we seldom seek to optimize the outcomes of a decision. This would require taking into account and ranking every criterion relevant to our

---

33. Samuel M. McClure et al., *Conflict Monitoring in Cognition-Emotion Competition, in* THE HANDBOOK OF EMOTION REGULATION 204–26 (James J. Gross ed., New York: Guilford, 2006); Matthew D. Lieberman, *Reflexive and Reflective Judgment Processes: A Social Cognitive Neuroscience Approach, in* SOCIAL JUDGMENTS: IMPLICIT AND EXPLICIT PROCESSES 44–67 (Joseph P. Forgas et al. eds., New York: Cambridge University Press, 2003).

34. HERBERT A. SIMON, MODELS OF MAN: SOCIAL AND RATIONAL 204–05 (New York: John Wiley & Sons, 1957); JAMES G. MARCH AND HERBERT A. SIMON, ORGANIZATIONS 140–41 (New York: John Wiley & Sons, 1958).

satisfaction with the outcome. Rather, to use Simon's evocative neologism, we *satisfice*,[35] opting for a reasonably good outcome—often the first that meets some threshold of satisfaction—rather than devoting excessive cognitive energy to seeking the very best.

In both professional and personal contexts, then, human decision making is a continual intermixture of intuitive and deliberative processes, with the consideration of all interests, options, and constraints seldom, if ever, being fully pursued. When the stakes are high and the variables ascertainable, it often makes sense to follow a relatively deliberative route. For example, it makes more sense to articulate your criteria and engage in comparison shopping for an apartment or automobile than for an ice cream cone. But sometimes, even though the stakes are high, time is limited and one has no choice but to rely on recognition-primed, intuitive decision making. As Justice Oliver Wendell Holmes famously remarked in a self-defense case, "Detached reflection cannot be demanded in the presence of an uplifted knife."[36] Consider the on-the-spot decisions demanded of firefighters, police officers, and, for that matter, trial lawyers.

What Herbert Simon writes of judgment by managers applies as well to that of lawyers and policy makers:

> It is a fallacy to contrast "analytic" and "intuitive" styles of management. Intuition and judgment—at least good judgment—are simply analyses frozen into habit and into the capacity for rapid response through recognition. Every manager needs to be able to analyze problems systematically (and with the aid of the modern arsenal of analytical tools provided by management science and operations research). Every manager needs also to be able to respond to situations rapidly, a skill that requires the cultivation of intuition and judgment over many years of experience and training. The effective manager does not have the luxury of choosing between "analytic" and "intuitive" approaches to problems. Behaving like a manager means having command of the whole range of management skills and applying them as they become appropriate.[37]

Kenneth Hammond and Berndt Brehmer have suggested that judgment takes place on a cognitive continuum:

> The *analytical* end of the continuum is characterized by a form of thinking that is explicit, sequential, and recoverable. That is, it consists of a series of steps that transform information according to certain rules . . . [which] can be reported by the thinker . . . *Intuitive* thinking, on the other hand, is implicit,

35. Simon, *supra* note 34.

36. Brown v. United States, 256 U.S. 335, 343 (1921).

37. Herbert A. Simon, *Making Management Decisions: The Role of Intuition and Emotion*, 1 Academy of Management Executive 57 (Feb. 1987).

> nonsequential, and nonrecoverable. Usually, the thinker can report no more than the outcome of his thinking . . . Most instances of thinking will have both intuitive and analytic components. We will refer to this composite as *quasi-rational* thought.[38]

Most real-world problem solving and decision making is quasi-rational in this sense. One's initial "take" on almost any problem is essentially intuitive. Most problems come to our attention as a result of some trigger, which activates one or more schemas. As a result, we approach a problem with an intuitive grasp of the interests involved; an initial, spontaneously generated hypothesis about its cause; and a corresponding, also spontaneously generated, proposal for its solution. The difference between deliberative and intuitive decision-making processes lies in where our thought processes go from there—on how systematically and deliberatively we navigate through the problem space.

Consider Luis Trujillo's approach to the question whether to seek summary judgment in the Newport Records case. As an experienced litigator, Trujillo's summary judgment schema is embedded in a larger civil litigation script, which includes settlement as well as pretrial or posttrial judgment as a means by which clients' cases are brought to successful conclusion.

Each of the factors Trujillo considers (e.g., the opposing counsel's and judge's reactions to the motion) is a problem-solving exercise in itself, which he approaches largely intuitively rather than through a sustained process of inferential reasoning. As Gary Blasi (from whom we borrowed the Newport Records problem) notes, Trujillo does not retrieve all the irrelevant details of the past summary judgment-related experiences, but rather the "action scripts" he extracted from them. If these scripts had names, they might carry labels like "passive-acting opposing counsel provoked to prepare case," or "state court judge denies legally meritorious summary judgment motion because of general negative attitude toward summary adjudication."[39] Trujillo's consideration of the consequences likely to follow from filing the motion also involves mental simulation—imagining what happens if the judge denies or grants it.

Trujillo's handling of the Newport Records situation also reflects elements of a deliberative problem-solving approach. Note, for example, that he did not simply accept the manner in which Wilkins structured the decision to be made: "should we file a motion for summary judgment or wait for trial?" Rather, he reframed the decision as: "given the client's current objectives, what is the best course of action to take at this time?" He explicitly assesses two alternative

---

38. Kenneth R. Hammond and Berndt Brehmer, *Quasi-Rationality and Distrust: Implications for International Conflict, in* Human Judgment and Social Interactions (Leon Rappoport and David A. Summers eds., New York: Holt, 1973).

39. Gary L. Blasi, *What Lawyers Know: Lawyering Expertise, Cognitive Science, and the Functions of Theory,* 45 Journal of Legal Education 313, 355 (1995).

courses of action (moving for summary judgment and doing nothing), and concludes that one is superior to the other. While he reaches this conclusion intuitively and quickly, he confirms his hypothesis more systematically in the discussion with Wilkins. Then, recognizing that neither solution meets all of the client's objectives, Trujillo broadens the problem frame—a strategy characteristic of more deliberative problem-solving processes.

As Hubert and Stuart Dreyfus note, "when time permits and much is at stake, detached deliberative rationality . . . can enhance the performance of even the intuitive expert. . . . [S]uch deliberation tests and improves whole intuitions."[40] Note also—and this is an important element of interaction between lawyers and their clients as well as associates—that the very fact of discourse with Wilkins forces Trujillo to articulate intuitive judgments, a process which tends to move decision making toward analysis and deliberation.

1.6.3 The Necessity and Limits of Intuition

If employing the deliberative model takes too much time—more, really, than we could spend on most decisions—the intuitive model makes a virtue of "jumping to conclusions." It offers a degree of efficiency without which we could not cope with the myriad problems and decisions we encounter daily in our personal and work lives. Trying the most ready-to-mind solution first (such as checking a computer's power cord when the screen is blank) often proves successful and costs far less in time and cognitive effort than taking a more deliberative approach.

However, reliance on mental shortcuts may lead the intuitive decision maker to overlook significant aspects of problems—as in Christine Lamm's analysis of and "solution" to her computer problem—and to consider an impoverished set of potential solutions—as in Anna Wilkins' selection of a summary judgment motion as the obvious response to a client's desire to have his case move quickly to conclusion. Avoiding this error requires, among other things, taking the time to acquire a better understanding of the situation and the client's objectives, and to consider the range of alternatives that might be employed to achieve them.

We return to the strengths and limitations of intuitive judgment throughout the book.

1.7 PROFESSIONAL PROBLEM SOLVING AND THE NATURE OF EXPERTISE

Analysis and intuition work together in the human mind. Although intuition is the final fruit of skill acquisition, analytic thinking is necessary for beginners learning a

40. Hubert Dreyfus and Stuart Dreyfus, Mind Over Machine: The Power of Human Intuitive Expertise in the Era of the Computer 40 (New York: Free Press, 1986).

new skill. It is also useful at the highest levels of expertise, where it can sharpen and clarify intuitive insights.

—Hubert and Stuart Dreyfus, Mind Over Machine[41]

What is the relationship between expertise and the two models of problem solving outlined above? Experts and others with proficiency in a subject often rely heavily on intuition, but their intuitions are usually informed and complemented by deliberation.

Before turning to expertise, consider the various nonprofessional activities in which you have *know-how, competence,* or *proficiency*—for example, crossing the street, driving a car, cooking, or playing or watching a sport. Although expertise denotes a proficiency (whether in medicine, law, or poker) that sets someone apart from most fellow citizens, we develop competence in these activities of everyday life much as an expert does in a professional domain—through observation, education, mentorship, and feedback from experience. Recall, if you can, the transition from novice to proficient actor—when you learned how to drive, for example—as you moved from approaching each activity deliberatively, often with conscious reference to rules or procedures, to (for the most part) just "doing it."

Both everyday competences and expertise are domain-specific. You can be an expert chef and have no idea what's going on in a football game. In *Life on the Mississippi*, Mark Twain writes:

> Give a man a tolerably fair memory to start with, and piloting will develop it into a very colossus of capability. But only in the matters it is daily drilled in. A time would come when the man's facilities could not help noticing landmarks and soundings, and his memory could not help holding on to them with grip of a vise; but if you asked the same man at noon what he had had for breakfast, it would be ten chances to one that he could not tell you. Astonishing things can be done with the human memory if you will devote it faithfully to one particular line of business.[42]

In what may be one of the earliest texts to connect judgment and expertise, Twain goes on to describe other qualities that an expert must have:

> A pilot must have a memory; but there are two higher qualities which he must also have. He must have good and quick judgment and decision, and a cool, calm courage that no peril can shake. Give a man the merest trifle of pluck to start with, and by the time he has become a pilot he cannot be unmanned by any danger a steamboat can get into; but one cannot quite say

41. *Id.* at xiv.

42. Mark Twain, Life on the Mississippi 116–17 (New York: Penguin Classics, 1883: 1962).

> the same for judgment. Judgment is a matter of brains, and a man must start with a good stock of that article or he will never succeed as a pilot.[43]

In a study of nurses' development of expert judgment, Patricia Brenner quotes this description of a novice nursing student:[44]

> I gave instructions to the new graduate, very detailed and explicit instructions: When you come in and first see the baby, you take the baby's vital signs and make the physical examination and you check the I.V. sites, and the ventilator and make sure that it works, and you check the monitors and alarms. When I would say this to them, they would do exactly what I told them to do, no matter what else was going on. . . . They couldn't choose which one was the most important. . . . They couldn't do for one baby the things that were most important and then go to the other baby and do the things that were the most important, and leave the things that weren't as important until later on. . . . If I said, you have to do these eight things, . . . they did these things, and they didn't care if their other kid was screaming his head off. When they did realize, they would be like a mule between two piles of hay.

Hubert and Stuart Dreyfus note that the solution for the student is a set of hierarchical decision-making rules, spelling out priorities. As she develops expertise, however, these largely give way to an intuitive sense of the situation.

What does an expert professional, like Luis Trujillo, bring to problem solving in a particular domain that a nonexpert would be unable to provide? Drawing on Newell and Simon's metaphor of problem solving as navigation across a virtual problem space, an expert possesses special navigational knowledge or skill with respect to problems of a particular type. Experts often know about pathways through a problem space of which nonexperts are unaware. Though several paths may look promising at the outset, an expert may be better able to predict which ones will prove to be dead ends or worse.

Thus, a person might hire an expert to navigate a particular type of problem space for the same reasons that a novice group of explorers would hire a guide rather than set out entirely by themselves. An experienced guide has the ability to "read" the terrain, finding likely routes and avoiding perils that would be invisible to the novice. Indeed, in law, medicine, and some other domains, only a licensed professional is permitted to guide another person across a problem space.

Consider Luis Trujillo's expertise in serving as a guide for his client, Jack Serrano, with respect to the complaints of the tenants at Terra Nueva. Trujillo

---

43. *Id.* at 118–19. We are grateful to James Shanteau, Mark Twain on Expertise, http://mail.sjdm.org/pipermail/jdm-society/2007-August/003168.html, for this quotation.

44. Patricia Brenner, From Novice to Expert: Excellence and Power in Clinical Nursing Practice 23 (Upper Saddle River, NJ: Pearson Higher Education, 1984), *quoted in* Dreyfus and Dreyfus.

must know the substantive law and relevant procedural rules bearing on the threatened suit whether or not it is filed. Such knowledge is necessary background to considering other means of resolving the problem. If Trujillo does not know the law in this particular area, he has the expertise to research and learn it. (This ability to do legal research is an area of expertise initially acquired at law school and then honed on the job.)[45]

By the same token, in considering the siting of the wastewater treatment plant, Christine Lamm will combine procedural knowledge (likely acquired in public policy school) about how to structure decisions of this sort with substantive knowledge (probably acquired on the job) of the factors relevant to the decision. And in addressing the Terra Nueva problem, it is possible that both Trujillo and Lamm will need to acquire knowledge about medicine, epidemiology, and the properties of polyurethane foam—to understand the connections between exposure to the insulation and the claimed illnesses. They won't have time to—and won't need to—acquire the extensive knowledge that would make them either intuitive or sophisticated analytic problem solvers in these domains; rather, they will have to rely on other experts.

Trujillo and Lamm and the scientific experts on whom they may call differ from laypersons not merely in the quantity of domain-specific knowledge, but in the quality of its cognitive organization. Experts possess large sets of particular schemas, which describe the attributes of domain-relevant problems and contain solutions to them.[46] The development of professional expertise entails learning many increasingly nuanced expert schemas. Once learned, these schemas enable the expert to recognize recurring patterns, rapidly draw inferences from them, and execute effective responsive interventions.

Robin Hogarth asserts that the essential difference between experts and novices is that they process knowledge differently. Not surprisingly, his description bears a strong resemblance to Gary Klein's description of recognition-primed decision making:[47]

> First, experts acquire habits that help them process more information. They learn to counteract limitations in short-term or working memory and are able to "chunk" information more effectively. In other words, despite facing normal limitations on memory, experts find ways of restructuring information so that they can take more into account . . . For example, whereas a medical student might see a patient's symptoms as several different items of

45. *See* Gary Marchant and John Robinson, *Is Knowing the Tax Code All It Takes to be a Tax Expert? On the Development of Legal Expertise*, *in* Tacit Knowledge in Professional Practice 3–20 (Robert Sternberg and Joseph Horvath eds., Mahwah, NJ: Lawrence Erlbaum, 1999).

46. Kurt Van Lehn, *Problem Solving and Cognitive Skill Acquisition*, *in* Foundations of Cognitive Science 527, 545–46 (Michael I. Posner ed., Cambridge: MIT Press, 1989).

47. Hogarth, Educating Intuition, *supra* at 158.

information, the experienced physician may recognize the same information as an instance of a pattern of symptoms, that is, a specific disease.

Second, experts and novices use different problem-solving strategies. Novices tend first to identify a specific goal and then work backward through the details of the problem to find a way to reach that goal. Experts, however, tend first to take in the details of the problem they face, then determine (through a process of recognizing similarities) the general framework that best fits the data, and, finally, work forward from that framework to explore possible solutions (goals). The process that novices follow (working backward) is more deliberate; the process that experts follow (working forward) is more intuitive. Not surprisingly, experts solve problems faster than novices.

In summary, professional expertise involves the development and deployment of an information-rich, schematically organized mental database, which enables the expert to extract key elements from a complex informational array and to match those elements with an existing expert schema stored in memory. Once this match has occurred and the relevant schema has been activated, the schema supplies the expert with a great deal of substantive and procedural information. This information can then be used either intuitively, or through a more deliberative approach, to identify problem-relevant goals and objectives, generate alternative courses of action, accurately predict the consequences associated with those courses of action, and select and then implement the course of action most likely to realize the identified interests and goals.

1.8 LAWYERS AND POLICY MAKERS AS EXPERTS

To understand just what sort of expertise lawyers and policy makers possess, consider these examples of the kinds of tasks they are called upon to perform:

- An appellate lawyer seeks to influence the course of the law by persuading a court that common-law doctrines prohibiting race discrimination by common carriers should prohibit sexual orientation discrimination by landlords.
- A public health administrator is asked by the mayor to develop a set of initiatives to address the disproportionate rate of asthma-related deaths of minority children in a large city in California.
- A company's general counsel works with its president and chief operating officer to develop a procedure for responding to sexual harassment claims if any should arise; or responds to the crisis occasioned by a particular accusation of harassment.
- A business lawyer identifies risks involved in a movie deal, including other parties' incentives to behave strategically, and structures the transaction so as to mitigate the risks to his client.

- The executive director of a community foundation is asked by her board of directors to develop a plan for grant making over the next five years to reduce teen-age obesity in the community.
- An administrator at the U.S. Fish and Wildlife Service seeks to develop and implement a plan to reintroduce wolves to an area of Montana in which ranchers have traditionally opposed such initiatives.
- A lobbyist for a coalition of marine preservation groups seeks the enactment of legislation banning the use of sonar in or near areas frequented by humpback and gray whales.
- The Governor of American Samoa, an elected official, designs a response to strikes at the two major U.S.-owned tuna packing plants in the territory. The strikers demand that American Samoa no longer be exempted from the minimum wage provisions of the Fair Labor Standards Act; the tuna companies threaten to pull out of American Samoa if the workers don't return and the existing exemptions aren't kept in place.
- An environmental lawyer representing a local government agency negotiates an agreement with neighboring jurisdictions involving the quality of drinking water in their common watershed.

Lawyers arguably bring three different kinds of professional expertise to these diverse tasks: (1) knowledge about the law, legal institutions, and legal actors; (2) knowledge about particular substantive domains; and (3) expertise in problem solving as such. Policy makers bring similar forms of expertise to their work, though their process-related knowledge tends to focus more on legislative and administrative domains rather than those involving judicial institutions.

1.8.1 Lawyers' Knowledge About the Law, Legal Institutions, and Actors

In the first of these vignettes, the lawyer's task of persuading an appellate court to extend settled case law to a new area calls for creative problem solving with respect to both analogical reasoning and advocacy. The task draws on the skills of doctrinal analysis, legal research, writing, and advocacy—many of which play a background role in the other tasks as well. The vignettes also highlight other kinds of legal expertise, such as knowing how to influence judges, juries, administrative officers, and other actors in the legal system.

1.8.2 Policy Makers' Knowledge about Legislative and Administrative Institutions and Processes

In various other of these scenarios, public policy makers must use their knowledge of legislative and administrative and regulatory processes to design workable policies, and to navigate the often complex processes by which they are adopted and implemented.

1.8.3 Expertise in Other Substantive Domains

In addition to knowledge of the legal and policy institutions, many of the tasks outlined in the vignettes draw on experience beyond the domains of law and public policy making as such. The general counsel relies on her sense of how organizations function; and in her crisis prevention mode, she must know how to deal with the press, the public, and investors as much as with legal actors. The same can be said of the Governor of American Samoa. He must know how the U.S. legislative process works, but he must also know how to mediate between angry workers and indignant corporate representatives to resolve a conflict that, if not suitably settled, may do serious harm to both the Samoan economy and its social fabric. The environmental lawyer negotiating for the local government agency must not only be familiar with state and federal water law; she must also know a good deal about water quality standards, hydrology, and other relevant areas of science and technology. The executive director of the community foundation will need to learn a great deal about the behaviors that lead to teen obesity and which local organizations have effective strategies to change those behaviors.

Sometimes, the lawyer's or policy maker's knowledge merely shadows expertise possessed by others, such as an organization's chief operating officer, accountants, or consulting scientists. Sometimes, however, the lawyer or policy maker may have a broader perspective than his or her clients or constituents do—simply by virtue of having encountered analogous problems in other spheres. For example, over a professional lifetime, a good transactional lawyer develops a sense for what can go wrong with a deal and how to guard against it. A policy maker working with administrative agencies and legislatures develops both general know-how about the processes and knowledge about particular officials.

1.8.4 Problem-Solving Expertise

A fundamental premise of this book is that lawyers and policy makers can develop problem-solving expertise applicable to a range of unfamiliar substantive domains. Whether or not this can be tested empirically, you will at least have some intuitions about this by the time you finish the book.

* * *

The materials that follow combine what might be termed positive and negative approaches to problem solving. On the positive side, they provide some of the basic tools necessary for sound and creative problem solving. On the negative or cautionary side, they survey cognitive, social, and motivational phenomena that distort people's perceptions of reality, and impede their understanding and pursuit of their own or their client's goals.

2. FRAMING PROBLEMS, IDENTIFYING OBJECTIVES, AND IDENTIFYING PROBLEM CAUSES

A problem well put is half solved.
—John Dewey[1]

Chapter 1 introduced a model of problem solving that moves systematically through a number of steps leading up to the selection of the particular course of action that the decision makers believe is best-calculated to solve the problem at hand. These steps include:

1. State, or "frame," the problem to be solved;
2. Identify and prioritize the relevant values, interests, and objectives;
3. Identify and resolve major uncertainties concerning the cause of the problem;
4. Generate a range of plausible solutions or alternative courses of action;
5. Predict the consequences of the courses of action and assess their impact on the relevant interests or objectives.
6. Select the course of action that optimizes the interests or objectives to be served (make a decision);
7. Implement, observe, and learn from the outcome of the decision.

In this chapter, we take a closer look at the first several steps, which reflect John Dewey's view that "a problem well put is half solved."

2.1 THE DECISION CONTEXT AND PROBLEM FRAMES

The frame in which one views a problem or decision is a function of the *decision context*,[2] which is determined both by the values, interests, or objectives at stake and by the authority of the decision maker. People may address the same problem in different decision contexts. For Frank Serrano and his lawyer, Luis Trujillo, litigation determines the initial context for addressing the problem at Terra Nueva, but the broad range of possible stakeholders and interests suggest the possibility of different or broader decision contexts as well.

---

1. John Dewey, Logic: The Theory of Inquiry (New York: Holt, Rinehart, and Winston, 1938).

2. Ralph Keeney, Value-Focused Thinking: A Path to Creative Decisionmaking 30 (Cambridge: Harvard University Press, 1992).

Christine Lamm's decision context for Terra Nueva is circumscribed by the scope of her official authority. For example, while Serrano might (in principle) offer to address the tenants' complaint by lowering their rent, this option is not available to Lamm. Of course, the decision context for a public official is often subject to interpretation or even to legal contest. The U.S. Environmental Protection Agency determined that, while the Clean Air Act authorized the regulation of conventional local pollutants, the agency lacked authority to treat carbon dioxide as a pollutant. In *Massachusetts v. EPA*, the Supreme Court reversed this decision.

Ralph Keeney gives an example of how decision contexts constrain the consideration of potentially valuable solutions to problems:

> Suppose that a utility company is required to spend $1 billion to reduce the probability of a major accident at a nuclear power plant in the event of a large earthquake. The main reason is to minimize radiation danger to the residents of a nearby town. But suppose there is evidence that such an earthquake would probably destroy the town. Indeed, it may be the case that parts of the town would be destroyed by earthquakes or other events that would not damage the nuclear plant with its current protection standards. An alternative that used $200 million from the utility to improve safety in town and the town's ability to respond to disasters might be much better for the town's residents than the $1 billion spent on the plant. It would also lead to lower utility rates for the company's customers.[3]

In actuality, though, the limited jurisdictions of agencies—limitations that serve other legitimate ends—are likely to frustrate such tradeoffs: the authority to regulate nuclear power plants and to take other means to ensure the town's safety probably reside in different agencies—perhaps even different governments.

2.2 PROBLEM FRAMING

The major constraints on creative problem solving do not arise from jurisdictional limitations on decision contexts, but from human psychology. Chapter 1 introduced the concept of "schemas," which structure people's perception of the environment. We schematize problems in the same ways that we schematize everything else. Problem schemas, also referred to as "problem frames," serve important cognitive functions. They enable us to perform a wide range of problem-solving tasks intuitively, with little expenditure of cognitive resources. But like all knowledge structures, problem frames have a potential downside

3. *Id.* at 205.

as well. They can cause us to over-simplify or otherwise misconstrue a problem, leading to an inferior solution strategy.

Problem frames set boundaries on our thinking, defining what is "inside" and what is "outside" the scope of the problem situation. They not only tell us how to describe the problem, but also indirectly indicate what goals, objectives, and solutions to consider.

A particular frame inevitably provides only one of a number of possible views of reality and implicitly blocks the consideration of alternative perspectives with other possible solutions. When you are viewing a situation through a particular frame, though, it seems to provide a complete picture of reality. Indeed, the frame is often invisible: You have the illusion that you're seeing the world "just as it is," and it is difficult to imagine that there could be another way to view it. To use another analogy, seeing a problem within a particular frame is like walking down one of a number of paths that do not converge, with the result that your understanding of the problem and hence the solutions to it become path-dependent—just as some technological practices (video recording formats, operating systems) can become path-dependent—and crowd out valuable, even superior alternatives.

We have just used two different metaphors to illustrate the same phenomenon. Does one or the other resonate more with you? Can you think of yet another one? The metaphors we bring to a situation have a powerful framing effect, and people's framing of the same situation with different metaphors is a ready source of misunderstanding and conflict. Do you view attending the university as a consumer's purchase of a commodity or as becoming a member of a community? Do you view joining a law firm or a government agency as essentially transactional or as joining a family? Do you view negotiation as a game, a war, or a collaboration? (Might professional negotiators get stuck in a particular frame themselves?)

Frames make a difference to outcomes. There's the old story of one monk who asks the abbot, "May I smoke while I pray?" while another monk asks "May I pray while I smoke?" Though we don't have a reliable account of the abbot's responses, it's a good guess that the second monk had a better chance of getting permission. In an experiment by Varda Liberman, Steven M. Samuels, and Lee Ross, American college students, Israeli pilots, and their flying instructors played a Prisoner's Dilemma–type game in which they had the choice of cooperating or defecting. In all the groups of participants, those who were told that the exercise was called the "Wall Street Game" were more likely to defect than those who were told it was called the "Community Game."[4]

4. Varda Liberman, Steven M. Samuels, and Lee Ross, *The Name of the Game: Predictive Power of Reputations versus Situational Labels in Determining Prisoner's Dilemma Game Moves*, 30 Personality and Social Psychology Bulletin 1175–85 (2004).

Framing plays an important role in public discourse and, therefore, in public policy making. As linguist George Lakoff notes, "People use frames—deep-seated mental structures about how the world works—to understand facts. . . It is impossible to think or communicate without activating frames, and so which frame is activated is of crucial importance."[5] The application of this observation is commonplace in contemporary politics. Consider the use of "death tax" or "estate tax" to refer to a tax on the transfer of wealth upon the death of wealthy Americans. Or consider framing legislation designed to protect lesbians and gay men against employment discrimination as "special rights for gays" or "guarantees of employment opportunity for all Americans." These rhetorical tactics work because they activate cognitively compelling frames, which predispose people toward particular preferences and judgments.

We sometimes frame problems in terms of particular *time horizons*, focusing either on the near term or long term, but not on both. It often requires less cognitive effort to think of the near term because one needs to do less "mental simulation" and there are fewer uncertainties. Moreover, a short-term outcome that is laden with either positive or negative affect is likely to be more salient than one in the distance. On the other hand, one can be so focused on long-term goals that one ignores more immediate considerations: Consider someone who takes a clerkship with a known tyrant of a judge because of its (supposed) résumé value.

In short, because they do so much cognitive "work," problem frames are enormously powerful. You cannot avoid viewing problems through frames, but with effort you can become aware of how you are framing a situation and whether there are alternatives. Understanding the origins of your frames is a good start. Asking how other stakeholders in the situation might frame it can only broaden your horizons and reduce possible conflict.

In any event, as the epigraph from John Dewey suggests, effective problem solving begins with effective problem framing. We begin the chapter by exploring common pitfalls involved in framing problems and suggest a variety of techniques for developing better problem frames. We then work on specifying the goals or objectives implicated in a problem and show their relationship to the way the problem is framed. Finally, we outline the empirical task of identifying the causes that may underlie a problem.

2.3 PROBLEM-FRAMING PITFALLS

People often solve the wrong problem. They may mistake symptoms of a problem for the problem itself, define the problem too narrowly, or define the problem in

---

5. George Lakoff, Thinking Points: Communicating Our American Values and Vision 10 (New York: Farrar, Staus & Giroux, 2006).

terms of one particularly salient, but not necessarily optimal, solution. Problem framing can occur automatically with little or no conscious, considered thought. Experts, who "over-learn" reoccurring problem frames as part of their professional training, are particularly susceptible to automatic problem framing.

The most common problem-framing errors can be divided into three broad groups:

1. defining the problem in terms of one salient potential solution;
2. mistaking a salient symptom of the problem for the deeper problem itself; and
3. defining a multidimensional problem unidimensionally, often as a result of "expert," or otherwise automatic, problem-framing processes.

We consider each of these in turn.

2.3.1 Framing by Solution

There's an anecdote about a farmer who drives to a neighbor's house to pick up some bags of chicken feed. Finding no one home and the feed bags left neatly stacked by the neighbor's barn door, the farmer drives up beside the barn and loads the feed into the truck bed. As he is about to get back into his truck's cab, he sees that his front left tire is flat—and then remembers that he has no jack in the truck. Feeling no small measure of exasperation, the farmer begins the long walk to the nearest gas station, without noticing that the barn's hay-lift pulley was perfectly positioned to lift the front of his truck.[6] The farmer erred in framing his problem too narrowly. Specifically, he confused the problem ("How can I lift my truck?") with one particularly salient solution ("Find a jack!").

Like the farmer in this story, clients and their lawyers are prone to "framing by solution." A client often comes to a lawyer with only a vague sense of his underlying objectives, but with his mind set on a particular solution. Consider our farmer again. Several years after the flat tire incident, he and his wife decide that they want to retire. They ask their lawyer to transfer ownership of the farm to their three children as equal partners. Specifically, they tell the lawyer that they want her to draft them a grantor retained income trust (GRIT) that during their lifetimes transfers ownership of the farm to their children. They have a friend who did this, they explain, and they hear that the technique minimizes estate tax liability, which is of great concern to family farmers.

The lawyer informs the couple that the tax laws have changed so that a GRIT will not achieve these ends. Moreover, in the course of the consultation, she learns that two of the children play different roles in running the farm, reflecting their different interests and talents, and that the third child has moved to New York City and has not been involved in the farm at all. The lawyer points out that

6. Jacob Getzels, *Problem Finding and the Invention of Solutions*, 9 Journal of Creative Behavior 12, 15–16 (1975).

the trust and tax issues are relatively minor compared to questions about how the children will participate harmoniously in running the farm and share in its profits (or losses). She knows from experience with other family businesses that whatever stability in family relations may exist while the parent is actively running the enterprise often dissolves upon the parent's retirement or death. The clients' problem frame—"how do we set up a GRIT?"—failed to capture important dimensions of their actual problem: How should we structure our estate plan to best provide for our children? Helping her clients develop a better problem frame was an important aspect of the lawyer's job.

The most powerful protection against shallow, solution-based problem frames is the deceivingly simple question, "*Why?*" For example, by asking the clients what they want to accomplish, the lawyer leads her clients to reframe their problem as, "How can I best provide for the needs of our family after our deaths?" Once the problem frame is expanded past the false boundaries drawn by the presumed solution of drafting a particular instrument, the utility of other interventions becomes apparent. By asking "why" until a client's deepest practical goals and objectives are recognized, a lawyer can assist her client in solving the right problem.

Ralph Keeney provides a good example from the realm of public policy, involving the decision of how to transport hazardous material to a distant waste dump:

> One objective may be to minimize the distance the material is transported by trucks. The question should be asked, "Why is this objective important?" The answer may be that shorter distances would reduce both the chances of accidents and the costs of transportation. However, it may turn out that shorter transportation routes go through major cities, exposing more people to the hazardous material, and this may be recognized as undesirable. Again, for each objective concerning traffic accidents, costs, and exposure, the question should be asked, "Why is this important?" For accidents, the response may be that with fewer accidents there would be fewer highway fatalities and less exposure of the public to hazardous material. And the answer to why it is important to minimize exposure may be to reduce the health impacts of the hazardous material. To the question, "why is it important to reduce health impacts?" the response may be that it is simply important. This indicates that the objective concerning impacts on public health is a candidate to be a fundamental objective in the decision context.[7]

2.3.2 Symptoms vs. Problems

Most people do not go through their lives looking for problems to solve. Solving problems requires time, attention, money, and other resources that most citizens and officials would rather expend in other ways. As a result, many of the problems

7. Keeney, *supra* at 66.

that lawyers and policy makers face are situations where something has "gone wrong" rather than opportunities to keep things from going wrong or, better yet, to improve the world. The uproar over Terra Nueva is the trigger that gets the immediate attention of Luis Trujillo and Christine Lamm. Because the events are vivid, consequential, and emotionally freighted, it is easy to experience the trigger as the problem itself. But this is not necessarily so. The trigger may just be the symptom of a deeper problem.

Of course, this does not mean that the symptom should be ignored. More often than not, the issue that triggered the problem demands attention. The mistake is in failing to identify the relationship between the trigger and the deeper, often multidimensional, state of affairs that gave rise to the problem.

Consider the following example. In 1992, an undercover investigation by the California Department of Consumer Affairs caught Sears Auto Centers systematically defrauding customers by selling them unnecessary repairs. A parallel investigation in the State of New Jersey uncovered a similar pattern of fraudulent sales activity by Sears Auto Centers located there. After initially denying that anything improper had occurred, Sears eventually admitted that "mistakes had occurred" and paid many millions of dollars to settle the two matters. If Sears's problem were defined as "resolving the enforcement actions at the lowest feasible cost," the multimillion dollar settlements might well be viewed as a successful solution.[8]

However, consumer advocates and eventually Sears itself defined the problem differently. The problem was not just the state enforcement actions or even the fraudulent sales themselves. A deeper problem, and the cause of these symptoms, lay in Sears's management practices, which encouraged dishonest behavior. These practices included the imposition of mandatory repair-dollars-per-hour quotas on mechanics, the use of a commission-based compensation system, and the deployment of high-stakes contests—all designed to encourage employees to maximize repair sales. Seen through this lens, the fraudulent behaviors and the enforcement actions themselves were symptoms of a deeper problem involving Sears's management and compensation practices. Solving the problem required changing these practices, as well as resolving the lawsuits.

As this example suggests, effective problem framing often requires careful thinking about the causal antecedents that gave rise to a particular problem trigger:

1. Generate an initial statement of the problem—an "initial frame statement."
2. Identify the "trigger" that instigated the problem-solving procedure in the first place.

8. Clifton Brown, *Sears Auto Centers*, The Department of Accountancy, University of Illinois at Urbana-Champaign (2000), http://www.business.uiuc.edu/ce%2Dbrown/accy304spg01/Downloads/Sears%20Auto%20Centers.pdf.

3. Identify the situation or context in which the problem trigger occurred. Assess the relationship between the trigger and this situation or context, asking such questions as:
   a. Is the trigger the whole problem, or is it part of a larger, deeper, or multidimensional problem?
   b. What are the trigger's causal antecedents, and which, if any, of them are within my control?
   c. If I solve the trigger problem, but do nothing else, what might happen?
   d. What did my initial frame statement overlook?
4. Reframe the problem as necessary, incorporating additional aspects of the deeper problem uncovered in these steps.

2.3.3 Automatic Problem Framing and the Pitfalls of Expert Problem Frames

Problem solving often occurs automatically, through the intuitive activation and application of well-learned problem schemas. In these situations, some salient aspect of the problem activates a stored representation of "problems-of-this-type" residing in memory. Once activated, the schema directs the problem solver's attention to whatever information the schema contains. This may include a ready-made problem frame, a set of plausible solutions, and an information search blueprint, telling the schema-holder what type of unknown information is relevant to solving the problem and how to go about obtaining and using that information to select the most effective solution strategy.

Experts, including lawyers and specialized policy makers, are particularly susceptible to automatic problem framing. The process of developing professional expertise entails learning sets of "expert frames." These frames efficiently capture aspects of the situation that are relevant to the professional's particular area of expertise. But they are inevitably rather narrow, often failing to capture important dimensions of the problem as it is actually experienced by clients, citizens, and other stakeholders.

Lawyers tend to frame problems differently from the way their clients do because they approach the problem with different schematic mind sets. The lawyer hears the client's story through the filters provided by the lawyer's expert schemas. These tell him which aspects of the client's narrative are important and which are not. They direct the lawyer to follow up on certain subjects, asking additional questions and probing for detail, and to cut the client short when she dwells too long on "irrelevant" matters. In this way, aspects of the situation that the client subjectively experiences as important may become invisible to the lawyer, and the entire matter may head in a direction that poorly serves the client's interests, broadly conceived.[9]

9. Conversely, the client may come to the lawyer wanting a legal solution, but having a mistaken impression of the nature of applicable legal constraints. Because he is

Consider the different ways in which the problem at Frank Serrano's Terra Nueva apartments might be framed. If Serrano had consulted a stereotypic "hardball" litigator, the lawyer might have conceptualized the problem simply as being "sued" by the tenants and the solution as winning a decisive victory in court.

But the lawsuit may be only one aspect of a multidimensional problem. Serrano has been the subject of a front page news story that, he worries, may be followed by others. With his reputation at stake, Serrano does not just have a lawsuit problem, but a public relations problem as well—a problem that could be exacerbated by a no-holds-barred litigation defense strategy. And what about Serrano's relationships with his company's various stakeholders and constituencies: tenants, community activists, financial backers, regulators, and his contractors and suppliers?

Though successfully defending Serrano against the suit will constitute an important element of a successful outcome, these other aspects of the situation may also be important to Serrano. If he is to do his job well, Trujillo must act as a good counselor as well as a skilled litigator. He must also help Serrano identify nonlegal aspects of the situation that he may experience as important problems now or in the future.

A good lawyer understands that, even though it was the client's identification of the problem as a "legal" one that brought him to the office, a purely legal frame may be too narrow. But a lawyer who reflects on his or her own professional development will be aware of the forces that induce such framing. Professional expertise often works like a kind of zoom lens, focusing in on one small portion of a broad landscape, revealing its features in great detail. This focus—an intentional myopia—facilitates the accurate, efficient, and effective identification of problems and the rapid deployment of interventions designed to solve them. But it can also lead the expert to miss important features of the larger picture, with significant collateral consequences for what lies beyond his field of vision.

The solution to this dilemma is not to abandon the schemas that lie at the core of the lawyer's professional expertise. After all, it was because of this expertise that the client walked in the door. Optimal problem framing in lawyer-client collaborations requires a "both/and" rather than an "either/or" approach—an

---

unfamiliar with the law and lacks a robust set of expert legal schemas, the client may in fact misframe his problem. The client may dwell on material that he erroneously believes to be pertinent to the legal frame. He may frame his problem in terms of an ineffective or unavailable solution. He may resist his lawyer's efforts to direct the conversation toward subject matters that the lawyer knows are relevant to the proper framing of the legal problem, or he may be reluctant to provide in sufficient detail information that the lawyer knows is important.

approach that enables the lawyer-client team to view the problem from a variety of different perspectives.

2.4 IDENTIFYING INTERESTS AND OBJECTIVES

The idealized model of problem solving (set out in Chapter 1 and at the beginning of this chapter) first defines the nature of the problem and then identifies client objectives. But the problem definition is inextricably bound up with the those objectives. Since problems often implicate a number of different objectives, the best problem frame makes room for consideration of all of them.

In the following discussion, we use *objectives* and *goals* synonymously to refer to relatively concrete aspects of the client's or other stakeholders' desired outcomes. *Interests* are somewhat more general or abstract than objectives and somewhat more concrete than *values*. These concepts are not separated by bright lines, but lie on a continuum. It is useful to bear in mind that someone's actual experience of a solution as a "success" or a "failure" will be driven by both concrete and more intangible factors, ranging from monetary gains or losses on one side of the spectrum to fidelity to philosophical, religious, or spiritual values on the other.

2.4.1 Multidimensional Frames and the Process of Framing-by-Objectives

To identify the entire range of interests and objectives affected by a particular problem, it is helpful to view the situation from the standpoint of all its potential stakeholders and constituencies. We refer to this process as a *stakeholder analysis*. Identifying the interests of stakeholders other than himself does not imply that an individual is or should be altruistic—he may or may not be. Rather, the analysis ensures the consideration of all external factors that could affect resolution of the problem at the same time as it helps canvass the client's own interests.

A problem's trigger draws attention only to those objectives most closely associated with it. In Serrano's case, the trigger may be the threat of a lawsuit. The most salient objective is avoiding or winning the lawsuit or, at least, minimizing its financial costs. But looking at the problem from the perspectives of other actors (as shown in Figure 2.1) conduces to a more complete articulation of the interests at stake:

The stakeholder analysis will help Serrano and Trujillo systematically consider what actions should be taken to:

1. minimize Serrano's financial exposure, taking into account both potential liability in the lawsuit and costs of defense;
2. minimize damage to Serrano's reputation;
3. minimize damage to Serrano's relationships with government regulators, financial backers, present and potential business partners, current tenants, and prospective tenants;

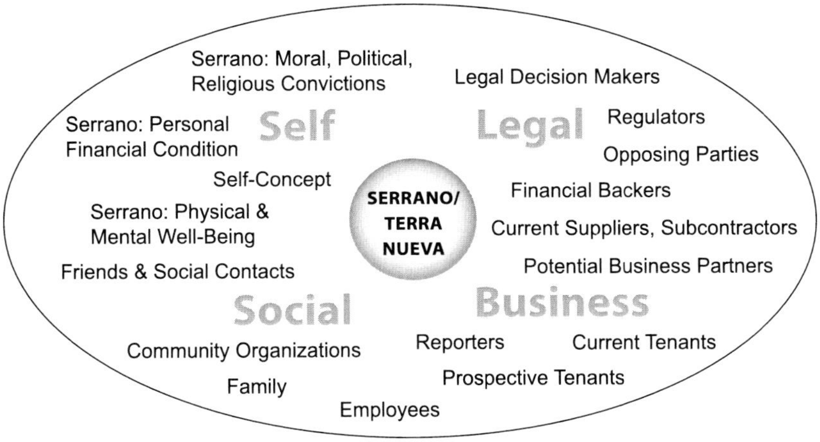

FIGURE 2.1 STAKEHOLDER ANALYSIS.

4. minimize psychological stress on Serrano and others in his family and business; and
5. "do right" by anyone who has actually been injured by materials used in the homes.

Problem: Sketch a "stakeholder analysis" for Christine Lamm in addressing the Terra Nueva matter.

2.4.2 Underspecification of Objectives: Causes, Consequences, and Corrective Strategies

There are many reasons why decision makers may underspecify the interests and objectives implicated by a particular problem. We have discussed the problem of "superficial" or "shallow" objectives, illustrated by the story of the farmer with the flat tire. The farmer underspecified his objectives by treating one possible means of solving his problem as the end itself. We have also seen how expert schemas—for example, that of the hardball litigator—can lead to ignoring interests that do not come within the ambit of a professional's conception of a problem.

Social norms, fear of embarrassment, or other social constraints may also interfere with the full specification of client goals and objectives. Jack Serrano may be truly concerned about the possibility that residents in his housing units are being physically harmed. He may be experiencing disturbing feelings of fear, self-doubt, or shame. But something about the litigation context tends to submerge litigants' concern for others—particularly opposing parties. Perhaps we automatically think of litigation as the "Wall Street Game," or even as the "War Game." Many lawyers may feel that it is not their place to raise other-regarding objectives and interests unless the client does so first. But unless the lawyer provides an opening for the consideration of these issues, the client is apt to avoid them too, implicitly assuming that they are irrelevant or inappropriate.

Hidden or submerged objectives do not disappear simply because they were never explicitly identified. But if they are not identified, they are less likely to be achieved. Under these circumstances, the client may feel dissatisfied with an outcome, even if it achieved all overtly specified goals.

Stakeholder analysis suggests that the client may himself comprise a variety of different "stakeholders." A client's various "selves" may have differing, even competing interests in a particular problem situation. Serrano's social self, his emotional self, his financial self, and his ethical/religious self may all have "stakes," or interests, in the Terra Nueva situation. These interests may compete and even conflict with each other. For example, if Serrano were only concerned with mitigating legal liability, his lawyer might take steps that would damage his relationship with tenants, suppliers, regulators, and others. The conflicts may be essentially *intrapersonal* as well as strategic. For example, strong empathy with the tenants or a desire to apologize may compromise the possibility of an ultimate victory in the courts. Likewise, a legal victory might leave Serrano wracked with guilt or shame.

In summary, the optimal framing of a problem requires a thoroughgoing identification of all the important objectives implicated by the situation. Here is a checklist for going about this:

1. Construct a list of stakeholders and then view the problem situation from each stakeholder's perspective.
2. Identify the objectives pertaining to the client's relationship with each stakeholder.
3. Imagine the best outcome for each stakeholder and identify exactly what it is about that outcome you would like to achieve.
4. Imagine the worst outcome for each stakeholder and identify exactly what it is about that outcome you want to avoid. (People often find it difficult to think about worst-case scenarios.[10])
5. Watch out for "shallow" objectives, resulting from the confusion of means with ends. Deepen these by asking, "Why?" until you cannot go back any further (without becoming unconstructively existential or just annoying).
6. Allow for the surfacing of objectives that may be difficult to discuss in the particular social context in which decision making is occurring. If the client is an individual, consider the whole person, and make the lawyer-client

10. Karen A. Cerulo, Never Saw it Coming: Cultural Challenges to Envisioning the Worst (2006); Lee Clarke, *Thinking About Worst-Case Thinking*, 78 Sociological Inquiry 154 (2008).

relationship as safe a space as possible for the discussion of sensitive, personal issues.

7. Stay open to the possibility that additional objectives will emerge as problem solving continues, particularly as various alternative courses of action are being considered. If a particular course of action causes unexplained discomfort, that may signal the presence of an overlooked interest, objective, or an as yet unidentified path constraint.

Given the constraints of bounded rationality (see Section 1.6.2), "human beings have unstable, inconsistent, incompletely evoked, and imprecise goals at least in part because human abilities limit preference orderliness."[11] An individual's objectives may only emerge with clarity during the process of deciding how to pursue them.[12] None of this diminishes the value of being as clear as possible about one's objectives from the outset. However, it does suggest that as the problem-solving or decision-making process proceeds, one should be open to new objectives coming into sight and to a revised understanding of their relationships and relative priorities.

2.5 IDENTIFYING PROBLEM CAUSES

In many problem situations, solving a problem effectively requires accurately diagnosing its causes.

Causal analysis often takes place at the intuitive end of the problem-solving continuum—and often successfully so, notwithstanding Christine Lamm's computer fiasco. Developing accurate intuitions for analyzing causes is a crucial aspect of acquiring expertise in a domain—though even within their specialties, experts often follow up their intuitive causal hypotheses with more deliberative diagnostic procedures. In any event, expertise is *domain specific*. The physician with fabulous skills in diagnosing medical problems may have no intuitions whatever about why her car stalls on the way to work.

Yet the nature of many lawyers' and policy makers' work requires them to engage in problem solving in a wide variety of substantive domains, and this requires developing a general sense of how to analyze causal relations. General problem-solving skills include both a positive and what might be called a precautionary component. On the positive side are structured analytical techniques designed to assist causal reasoning. The precautionary components consist of awareness of errors that the intuitive empiricist is prone to make. The remainder

11. James March, *Bounded Rationality, Ambiguity, and the Engineering of Choice*, 9 Bell Journal of Economics 598 (1978).

12. John W. Payne, James R. Bettman, and Eric J. Johnson, The Adaptive Decision Maker 10 (New York: Cambridge University Press, 1993).

of this section introduces one positive analytic technique developed by Charles Kepner and Benjamin Tregoe[13] and touches briefly on some of the errors of the intuitive empiricist. We continue both subjects in Part 2, with an exploration of statistical techniques that can assist in attributing causation and with a deeper examination of the cognitive biases and heuristics that can impede sound empirical judgments.

Recall the conversation between Christine Lamm's and Paula Henderson, the mayor's chief of staff. Lamm has suggested putting together a working group of public health professionals whose task it will be to determine whether the foam insulation that the mayor proposes to ban is, in fact, making Terra Nueva's tenants sick. In the following scenario, Lamm is conducting an initial meeting with Marsha Yamamoto, who works at the Division of Environmental and Occupational Medicine at the County's Department of Public Health, and Sam Cooke, a toxicologist from the State Department of Occupational and Environmental Safety, who has conducted preliminary interviews with Jack Serrano and various of his employees and contractors. Lamm sets the meeting's agenda.

LAMM: I've called this meeting to figure out what we know and what information we are going to need to determine whether the foam insulation, or anything else in the apartments, is actually making the tenants sick. Before I initiate a formal rule-making process geared toward proposing a countywide ban on the use of the material, I want to be sure that we have some reason to believe that the insulation is actually causing harm. I know that the mayor is concerned about the political angle here, but our concern is the science, not the politics.

YAMAMOTO: Before we start, I think you should see this morning's *Gazette*. Poor Jack Serrano now has the United Electrical Workers after him as well. That's going to make the mayor even more edgy.

LAMM: Why in the world would the UEW be interested in this?

YAMAMOTO: You recall the new factory that United Semiconductor built a year ago? Well, it turns out that many of their employees were relocated from the company's Valley View plant, and many moved into Serrano's newest apartments—into units 5 and 6. A couple of months ago, the union began trying to organize the employees. It held a meeting in the community hall at Terra Nueva. One of my assistants went to the meeting and saw their leaflets, which said something about workers' health. Maybe they think that showing concern for the tenants at Terra Nueva will be helpful in organizing the factory.

13. Charles H. Kepner and Benjamin B. Tregoe, The New Rational Manager (2d ed. Princeton: Princeton Research Press, 1997). For a similar approach, *see* Dean K. Gano, Apollo Root Cause Analysis (2d ed. Yakima, WA: Apollonian Publications, 2003).

In any event, the article says that the UEW surveyed families in the new buildings and that 40 percent have reported headaches, dizziness, or rashes developing since they moved into their apartments. The union claims that this is "overwhelming evidence" that the foam insulation is causing the sickness. I should add that the article does not say whether the UEW had heard complaints before it did the survey.

LAMM: By the way, didn't I read in the documents we got from the mayor's office that all of the affected Terra Nueva residents live in units 5 and 6? What can you tell me about those units?

YAMAMOTO: They were finished and people started moving into them a year ago.

COOKE: I talked yesterday to one of Serrano's people, who said that the manufacturer who supplied the insulation that they used for the older apartments had raised his prices so much that the contractor bought the insulation for the new units from another company. Apparently, it's a completely new product. Serrano was among the first developers in the county to use it. He told me that it did have a sort of "chemical" smell when it was installed—lots of synthetics do—but it wore off pretty quickly.

LAMM: Well, that's interesting. Do you know if there are any other differences in the materials used in the new apartments—for example, carpets or paint?

COOKE: I'm pretty sure that there aren't.

YAMAMOTO: Let me just say that if 40 percent of the Terra Nueva tenants are sick, that's a pretty strong argument in favor of there being a problem with the insulation. I am also mindful that there have been similar reports of "foam insulation syndrome" in other parts of the country.

COOKE: Well, hold on a minute, Marsha. My guess is that if you asked anyone if they had had headaches, dizziness, or rashes at some point, 40 percent or more would say yes. If there was something wrong with the foam insulation, it should be making *everyone* in those units sick. And we don't know anything about the other units. I recall reading an article about people throughout Europe getting sick from Perrier water after they learned that it contained a tiny trace of some chemical. The company withdrew the so-called "contaminated" bottles, but the whole thing turned out to be mass hysteria. Clusters of illnesses of this sort often turn out to be illusions.

In my view, there isn't any solid evidence in the toxicology literature supporting the theory that this particular product causes illness of this type. Where I sit right now, particularly after doing some interviews last week, I don't think the problem is the foam insulation, or the union for that matter.

In my purely personal opinion, I wonder whether this whole thing may in fact be a tactic by the tenants' association. When I talked to Serrano last week, he mentioned that, because his costs had risen, he raised rents at Terra Nueva a couple of months ago. The new rents will go into effect the first of next year. He told me that the tenants' association presented tremendous opposition to the rent hikes and that the association's president is one of the named plaintiffs in new lawsuit.

LAMM: Forty percent of the tenants may be a lot or a little. But we really don't know enough to come to any conclusions yet. We don't even know whether the apartments with the new product have the same insulation as the ones in the reports of so-called "foam insulation syndrome"—whatever that is. These are things we need to explore.

At this point, all we have is some different theories about what's going on. So let's step back and walk through this systematically. I'm going to suggest that we follow these steps:

1. Define the problem;
2. Specify the problem's "what," "where," "when," and "extent";
3. Spot distinctions and identify changes responsible for the distinction;
4. Identify causal theories for further testing.

2.5.1 Define the Problem

LAMM (continued): Before we try to identify the *cause* of the problem, let's begin with the problem itself. To generalize, a "gone-wrong" problem involves a deviation from some standard or norm. Here, the norm is health and the deviation is the tenants' sicknesses.

Initially, I had thought that the problem was "tenants experiencing headaches, dizziness, and rashes." But we don't want to jump to any conclusions. So at this point it's probably best to describe the problem as *reports* that tenants are experiencing these symptoms. We don't know what the tenants are actually experiencing, or what questions are being asked to elicit information, or how accurate the surveys are. Notice, by the way, that headaches, dizziness, and rashes are pretty amorphous symptoms. We may need to come back to that issue later. Anyway, let's move on to step 2.

2.5.2 Specify the Problem's "What," "Where," "Extent," and "When"

LAMM (continued): The next step is to a get a clear sense both of what the problem *is* and what the problem *is not*. Let me draw a chart showing what we know in these respects and also what we don't know.

The *what* is whether there are reports of illnesses. The *where*, so far as we know, are the new units. And the *extent* is 40 percent of the residents who report having symptoms—40 percent of those surveyed. But we don't know

TABLE 2.1 THE PROBLEM AT TERRA NUEVA

	Is	Is not
What	Reports of headaches, dizziness, or rashes	
Where	Units 5 & 6 (new units)	[What about the other units?]
Extent	40% of those surveyed in those units	[60% did not report symptoms?]
When	Since 1 year	Before
	After new units built	Before
	After United Semiconductor employees moved in	Before
	After rent increase announced	Before
	Before union began organizing?	After?

how many tenants were surveyed, or who they were, or how the survey was conducted—let alone anything about the health of tenants in the other units.

YAMAMOTO: What difference does that make if this many people are sick?

LAMM: That's a good question, Marsha. It's easy to get fixated on where the problem is. But you can't really begin to unpack the causes of the problem until you know where it *isn't*. Suppose, just for the sake of argument, that lots of the tenants in the old units, with older insulation, also report the symptoms. There could still be a problem. But it wouldn't be the problem that the tenants, the mayor, and now half the county thinks it is—the new insulation. That's why we need to learn more about how the tenants in the other units are doing—and also to be sure we know what kinds of insulation their apartments have.

Just to finish my chart, let's talk about the *when* of the reports. We really don't know when any of the tenants first *experienced* these symptoms, but for the moment, let's say it's a year ago—it doesn't seem as if it could have been any earlier than that. That will give us a baseline for some other "whens": the symptoms were reported after the new units were built, after United Semiconductor employees moved in, and after the rent increase was announced. We don't know whether the first reports were made before the union organizing campaign, although it seems likely they were—otherwise, why would the union have conducted the survey; still, we need to check this out.

2.5.3 Spot Distinctions and Identify Changes Responsible for the Distinction

LAMM (continued): Now let me add a column about anything that seems distinctive about what *is* and is *not* and about anything else noteworthy:

TABLE 2.2 THE PROBLEM AT TERRA NUEVA ANNOTATED

	Is	Not	Distinctive, noteworthy, questions, notes
What	Reports of headaches, dizziness, or rashes		Illness reports [Actual symptoms?]
Where	Units 5 & 6 (new units)	[What about the other units?]	(1) New insulation [though not sure about whether some older units have the same insulation] (2) plaintiffs live here
Extent	40% of those surveyed in those units	[60% did not report symptoms?]	[How many people were surveyed? Who was surveyed? What about the other units?]
When	Since 1 year	Before	
	After new units built	Before	New units
	After United Semiconductor employees moved in	Before	United Semi employees move in
	After rent increase announced	Before	Rent increase affected all tenants (not just those in new units)
	Before union organizing?	After?	Doesn't seem causally related—but check whether reports had been made before survey

With respect to the *what,* the reports of illness obviously are distinctive. With respect to the *where,* the fact that the known complaints come from people living in the new units is distinctive. The particular insulation used in their apartments may be distinctive, but we really don't know for sure. The *whens* seem most interesting. The complaints only began after the new units were built, after the United Semiconductor employees moved in, and after the announcement of the rent increase. But it is at least noteworthy that, though the rent increase affects all the tenants, the only people complaining of illness are in the new units. We need to check out if the symptoms were reported before the union-organizing campaign.

YAMAMOTO: If so, that eliminates the union as the cause of the whole mess.

LAMM: Probably so—though we can't discount the fact that the union may be distorting or exaggerating the extent of the problem.

2.5.4 Identify Hypotheses for Further Testing

LAMM (continued): In any event, we end up with a number of possible ideas about what's going on at Terra Nueva. But let me suggest that we spend our time and, I'm afraid, some of the county's resources, focusing on one question in particular: whether there is a causal connection between any materials in the Terra Nueva apartments and the tenants' reported headaches, dizziness, and rashes. To the extent we have a clear answer to this, it will affect any other theories of what's going on.

In addition to doing some research, including contacting the manufacturer to see whether there have been other problems of this sort, we will need to learn about any differences in insulation and other materials in the newer and older units that could be related to the tenants' sicknesses. And we need to bring an epidemiologist to conduct a study that clearly specifies the symptoms the tenants may be experiencing and collects data on those symptoms appearing in tenants living in the new units and in those living in the old units.

2.5.5 Attributing Causation

The discussion about what's actually going on at Terra Nueva illustrates a number of issues relevant to the process of attributing causation, and we note some others as well.

1. Think about what has changed with respect to any context or environment that might explain the problem. When attempting to identify a problem's causes, specify the problem both with respect to what, where, and when it *is*, and what, where, and when it might reasonably have been but *is not*. Comparisons between, say, where and when the problem happened and where and when else it *might* have happened but didn't can be instructive.
2. Inferences of causation often depend on assessing probabilities. Yet when assessing probabilities, one's attention often (and often misleadingly) focuses on particularly vivid descriptions of risks—a tendency encompassed by what the psychologists Amos Tversky and Daniel Kahneman call the *availability heuristic*. In this case, individual tenants' stories and front-page newspaper reports of "foam insulation syndrome" occurring elsewhere in the country provide a vivid explanation for the situation at Terra Nueva. The statistical analysis that Christine Lamm and her colleagues will undertake will be pallid by comparison. We will do the statistics in Chapter 5, and discuss the availability heuristic and some other phenomena that tend to distort judgments of probability in Chapter 9.
3. People also tend to make judgments about causation based on the degree to which they perceive a resemblance between the cause and effect.

For example, it is more intuitive that bad-smelling foam insulation, rather than odorless material, would cause the symptoms reported by Terra Nueva residents. This is one aspect of the phenomenon that Tversky and Kahneman called the *representativeness heuristic,*[14] which we will discuss later as well (See Section 8.3).

4. People doing intuitive statistical analysis tend to focus on cases where the putative cause (foam insulation) and effect (illness) occur together. But as we will see in Part 2, one usually cannot draw valid statistical conclusions without taking account of cases where the possible "cause" exists but the "effect" does not occur (foam insulation but no illness), where the "cause" is absent but the "effect" occurs (no foam insulation, but tenants feel ill), and where neither occurs (no foam, no sickness). For instance, if it turned out that 40 percent of the tenants in the foam-free units reported illness, it would seriously undermine the theory that the foam caused the illness.
5. Be open to considering every plausible causal theory at the beginning of the deliberative process, and don't get fixated on any particular one. With respect to each plausible theory, consider how to go about testing its soundness. (Resist the common tendency to overvalue information that would confirm a favored theory at the expense of information that could disconfirm it.)
6. Correlation does not entail causation. The incidence of shark attacks is positively correlated with ice-cream sales at the beach. Which causes which? What might cause both?
7. One factor alone may not have caused the effect; it may result from the confluence of several causes. Some of these may be background conditions that were present before and after the particular effect, or present in difference places or circumstances where the effect did not occur. But they may still be but-for causes of the effect.
8. Acquiring information to test causal theories is often expensive, and the cost of obtaining the information itself must be balanced against the costs of making decisions without it.

2.5.6 Problem

Toward the end of the discussion, Christine Lamm remarked, "There's something bothering me that I can't quite put my finger on." It sounds as if she has in mind yet another hypothesis for the sicknesses at Terra Nueva. What might it be—and how would you go about testing it?

---

14. Daniel Kahneman and Shane Frederick, *Representativeness Revisited: Attribute Substitution in Intuitive Judgment, in* HEURISTICS AND BIASES, THE PSYCHOLOGY OF INTUITIVE JUDGMENT 49 (Thomas Gilovich, Dale Griffin, and Daniel Kahneman eds., New York: Cambridge University Press, 2002).

2.6 MOVING THE WORLD IN THE DESIRED DIRECTION THROUGH STRATEGIC PLANNING

Terra Nueva and the examples given so far in this chapter demonstrate decision-making strategies to use when something has gone wrong. But lawyers and policy makers also have opportunities to be proactive in problem solving, to move the world in a desired direction. Strategic planning—whether by state or local governments, nonprofit organizations, or foundations—is a classic case of forward-looking problem solving.

Here we provide an example of strategic planning by the William and Flora Hewlett Foundation. Unlike governments, which often implement strategies through their own agencies and personnel, grant-making foundations do so through grants to nonprofit organizations. However, a foundation cannot know what grants to make to what organizations until it has established its own goals and determined strategies for achieving them.

Note to students: While the discussion of goals, barriers, outcomes, and targets fits within the theme of Chapter 2, much of the rest of the materials concern the choice among alternatives, and fits better with Chapter 4 or elsewhere. To present a coherent story, we present all aspects of the strategic plan here rather than divide it among several chapters.

Since its establishment in 1967, the Hewlett Foundation's concerns have included preserving the natural heritage of the American West. In 2009, the Foundation's Environment Program engaged in a strategic planning process for this area of its grant-making.[15] The Foundation was willing to devote approximately $125 million over five years to achieve its goals in the West, with the hope that this would be matched by other donors interested in the region. The total commitment, though fairly large by philanthropic standards, pales in comparison to the magnitude of the problems addressed. Hence the need for great clarity and focus in goals and strategies.

Scope of work. The Foundation began by defining the geographic scope of its work. Bounding its definition of the American West from "the uplift on the eastern edge of the Rocky Mountains to the Pacific coast" (as shown in Figure 2.2) made it possible to establish clear goals for the region and analyze the barriers to achieving them.

Goals. There are many possible goals related to protecting the natural heritage of the American West, from preserving iconic landscapes to ensuring the viability of farming and ranching communities. The Hewlett Foundation envisioned "an ecologically vibrant West where the landscape is unspoiled and people and wildlife thrive." Since functioning natural systems underpin this vision, the

15. The planning was done by foundation staff members, led by Environment Program Director Tom Steinbach, with the assistance of Ivan Barkhorn and staff from the Redstone Strategy Group, LLC.

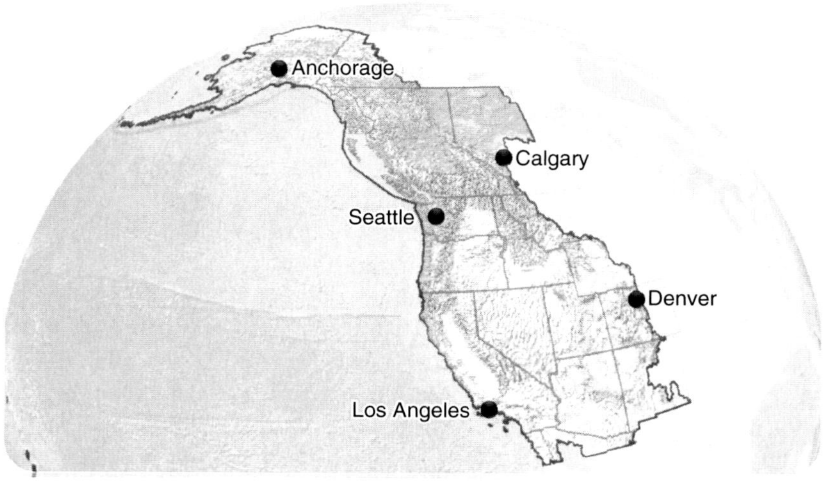

FIGURE 2.2 ECOLOGICAL SCOPE.

Foundation made its ultimate goal ensuring the "ecological integrity" of the West, meaning that natural systems would function close to the way they would in the absence of human activity (see Figure 2.3).

Barriers. The next step in the Foundation's strategic planning process was to identify the barriers to achieving ecological integrity in the West. These barriers in effect describe the problems the Foundation would need to solve to reach its goals.

The Foundation's research and experience showed that current and emerging human uses in the West, in addition to bringing economic benefits, can pose

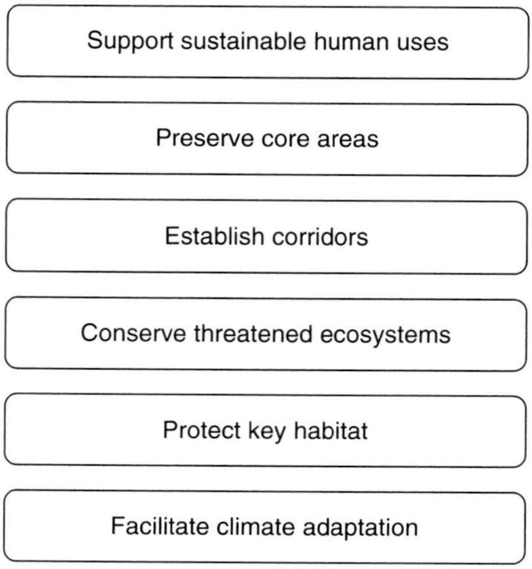

FIGURE 2.3 THE ELEMENTS OF ECOLOGICAL INTEGRITY.

threats to ecological integrity. Leading threats include unplanned population growth, resource extraction, and human-induced climate change. Rapidly increasing population and per capita consumption in the West have led to the use and development of formerly unoccupied lands. This has sometimes fragmented habitats and blocked species' migration routes, threatening their survival. Agricultural and urban areas can also place increasing demands on freshwater supplies, which may have negative impacts on species and ecosystems. Current methods of resource extraction can create health and environmental problems. In the face of these pressures, some policies critical to ensure responsible stewardship of the West needed strengthening or improved enforcement to ensure the ecological integrity of the region.

Outcomes and targets. Analysis of these problems led the Foundation to specify four key measurable targets[16] in achieving its goal of ecological integrity in the West:

1. Land conservation improved for 150 million acres.
2. Water and riparian conservation improved for 2400 river miles.
3. Fossil fuel development reduced on 85 million acres, and renewable use/energy efficiency increased by 100 thousand gigawatt hours per year.
4. Lasting support for conservation created in each of the West's four major ecological zones.

Each of these key outcomes ties back to the Foundation's overall goal and is based on analyses of the barriers to achieving that goal. For example, the target for improving land conservation emerged from the Foundation's recognition of two key problems:

- On private land, increasing population, tourism, energy development, and division of large spaces into suburban "ranchettes" created challenges to ecological integrity.
- Land management plans for the public land that makes up over 85 percent of the West sometimes prioritized human use and resource extraction over ecological integrity.

Setting goals, analyzing problems, and developing strategies to solve them was an iterative process. Measurable targets were established to enable the Foundation to track its progress and amend its strategies as necessary. Throughout the planning process, program staff remained aware of the costs of collecting information. They attempted to strike a balance between optimizing grant-making decisions based on the best information available and working to obtain better information.

Multiple stakeholders. Recall Serrano's analysis of the stakeholders in the Terra Nueva problem. The Hewlett Foundation's strategic planning also took

16. These targets were specified in much greater detail than appears in this overview.

into account that it is only one of many stakeholders concerned with the American West. The frame through which the Foundation's Environment Program views the problems facing the West sometimes differs from that of state and federal policy makers, businesses, citizens, interest groups, and other organizations. A collaborative approach to strategic planning drew on the knowledge and resources of these stakeholders and set the groundwork for future collaboration with them.

Advocacy. Foundations and the nonprofit organizations they support have various tools for achieving their goals, including providing direct services (supporting public parks, for example), basic and applied research, and policy advocacy. Advocacy, typically based on applied research, was a major strategy for achieving the goals of the Foundation and its grantees in Western conservation.[17] for example, improving land conservation requires policy changes that create new protected areas and improve management and planning of existing protected lands. The Foundation's grantees, aware of the high cost of purchasing land, found it important to advocate for federal and state funding and incentives for private conservation.

Understanding the many stakeholders in the West is essential to building constituencies supportive of Western conservation. Although other stakeholders' priorities do not necessarily overlap completely with the Foundation's, the Foundation was able to identify opportunities for collaboration with other funders and interest groups. For example, hunters and anglers share the Foundation's interest in expanding land protections that help ensure both more enjoyable sporting and greater ecological integrity.

Stakeholders include governments as well as private interests. After eight years of stalled policy progress at the national level during the Bush administration, the political environment became more favorable to conservation in 2009. The Foundation's advocacy strategies appropriately changed to respond to the Obama administration's conservation-minded Secretaries of Agriculture, Energy, and Interior, and to greater interest in conservation at local levels.

Comparing alternative courses of action. The next step in the Environment Program's strategic planning was to generate and compare different possible courses of action to achieve the outcomes it desired. The Foundation's analysis of the problem led it to embrace a combination of broad West-wide policy changes and work in specific regions, such as the Alberta Tar Sands, where the extraction of oil is particularly damaging to the environment.

Within this broad approach, the Foundation sought the optimal way to maximize the impact of its grants in improving the ecological integrity of the West.

17. Federal law provides constraints on certain activities defined as "attempts to influence legislation," but the kind of advocacy in which the foundation and its grantees engaged is fully compatable with those constraints.

Although we defer a full discussion of the concept of *expected return* until Part 3 of the book, we preview it here in order to complete this example of strategic planning.

An expected return framework helps estimate the effectiveness of dollars spent on particular grant-making strategies in achieving the Foundation's goals. Quantitative expected return analysis involved multiplying estimates of the benefit an intervention would have if it succeeded by the likelihood that it will succeed, and dividing by the costs of the intervention to the Foundation (see Figure 2.4). The expected return for each promising project could thus be compared, and the most cost-effective ones chosen.

Benefit is a monetizable measure of the progress a specific set of grants would make toward the Foundation's overall goal. In this case, the benefit was the number of acres improved multiplied by what expert interviews and scientific studies indicated would be the magnitude of improvement in ecological integrity produced by the grant.

The ***likelihood of success*** is the estimated probability of a particular intervention succeeding. Interviews with stakeholders and experts, and polls by the League of Conservation Voters helped the Foundation calculate likelihoods of success for particular policy changes in the various political jurisdictions encompassed by the West.

For the denominator, the Foundation considered the ***cost*** to the Foundation of achieving the desired outcome. For a strategy to be cost-effective, the cost must be less than the benefit times the likelihood of success—ideally a great deal less. The higher the calculated expected return, the greater the Foundation's "bang for the buck." The Foundation's main costs were the amounts of its grants and the staff resources needed to make and monitor the grants and facilitate collaborations among stakeholders.

A rough comparison of the expected return of various strategies helped the Foundation choose among different possible investments to achieve its conservation goals. The expected return framework helped staff set clear targets and make quantitative comparisons. Staff complemented the rough assumptions necessary for the calculations with continual internal review and external feedback to select the combination of strategies that would most cost-effectively achieve the Program's desired outcomes.

$$\boxed{\textbf{Expected return}} = \frac{\textbf{Benefit}\ \text{(area-adjusted integrity improvement)} \times \textbf{Likelihood of success}\ (\%)}{\textbf{Cost}\ (\$)}$$

FIGURE 2.4 EXPECTED RETURN.

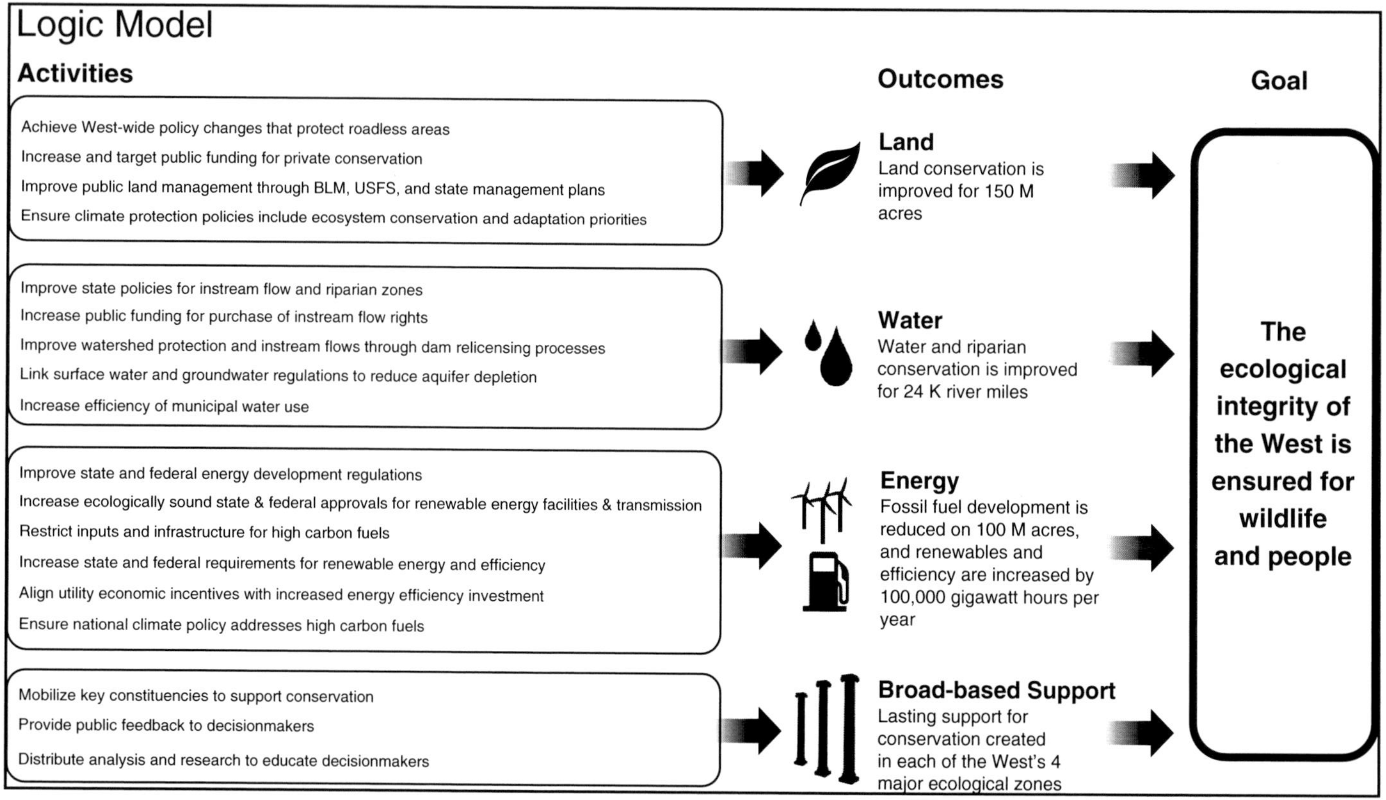

FIGURE 2.5 A STRATEGY, OR LOGIC MODEL, TO ACHIEVE ECOLOGICAL INTEGRITY.

The Strategic Plan, or Logic Model. Figure 2.5 shows the core of the strategic plan, sometimes called a *logic model*, which connects the specific activities the Foundation supports to its outcomes and targets, and ultimately to the goal of ensuring the ecological integrity of the West. As the preceding discussion indicates, a strategic plan is developed by working backward from the general goal to more specific outcomes and then to the activities necessary to produce those outcomes. Of course, a strategy is only a working hypothesis that must remain flexible to seize high-return opportunities and respond to unanticipated threats to critical habitat or migration corridors. Although details of the strategy were modified in the light of changing circumstances within a year of its adoption, it continues to provide the framework for the Foundation's work in the American West.

Targets, grantmaking, monitoring, and evaluation. Foundation staff determined outcome metrics for each of the activities and outcomes—some of which are measurable on an annual basis, others of which may take a number of years to assess.

Having identified the activities necessary to work toward the goal, Foundation staff then identify the organizations that can carry out the activities. Staff members engage in due diligence, make grants, monitor organizations' performance, and evaluate progress toward their goals.

We will discuss the need for feedback in decision making later in the book. For now, suffice it to say that feedback is vital to any decision maker's long-term effectiveness. Monitoring and evaluation will help the Foundation respond to changing conditions and problems as they arise. The Foundation's explicit metrics and targets are helpful in measuring the contribution of each grant to achieving its overall goal. A rigorous evaluation of the program as a whole will document successes and lessons learned for use in the next round of strategic planning.

Returning to the overall topic of this chapter, the Hewlett Foundation's strategic plan for the West provides an illustration of how analyzing the problems to be solved, examining relevant interests, and comparing the consequences of different courses of action can guide proactive attempts to move the world in a certain desired direction.

3. GENERATING ALTERNATIVES
Creativity in Legal and Policy Problem Solving

In Chapters 1 and 2, we explored the first three steps in a formal model of problem solving. These steps included problem framing, the specification and prioritization of relevant interests and objectives, and the identification of major uncertainties concerning the problem's causes. We also saw in Chapter 1 that not all problems occur in the present tense. Some will emerge in a future that we can anticipate and plan for more or less effectively. With any problem, present or future, the first three steps in a formal approach are followed by a fourth, involving the generation of potential solutions. In this chapter, we consider this fourth step in more detail, first in the context of present problems, then in the context of problems that may emerge in the future. Finally, we consider barriers to the effective generation of alternative solutions and suggest some possible ways to overcome them.

More than any other aspect of problem solving, the generation of alternatives is associated in popular consciousness with the notion of creativity, which we explore in this chapter. As will become clear, however, creativity is implicated at almost every step of the problem-solving process. At its core, creativity is a *stance*. It is about being a "chooser," not merely a "picker."

3.1 "PICKERS" AND "CHOOSERS": PROBLEM-SOLVING FRAMES OF MIND

In *The Paradox of Choice*, Barry Schwartz draws a distinction between "choosers" and "pickers." A chooser is someone who thinks actively before making a decision. She reflects on what is important to her in life, what is important about a particular decision, and what the decision's short- and long-term consequences might be. As importantly, after surveying the most readily apparent solutions, a chooser may conclude that perhaps none is satisfactory, and that if she wants a better alternative, she will have to create it.[1]

1. Barry Schwartz, The Paradox of Choice: Why More Is Less 75 (New York: HarperCollins, 2004).

"Pickers," on the other hand, are "relatively passive selectors from whatever is available. With a world of choices rushing by like a music video," Schwartz observes, "all a picker can do is grab this or that and hope for the best."[2]

As Schwartz's description suggests, what separates choosers from pickers is the ability to pause and reflect about a problem before taking action. Generally speaking, people are uncomfortable with an unsolved problem and, as a result, may reflexively seize upon the first plausible solution that comes to mind. A chooser can forbear from this sort of reflexive "picking" long enough to think expansively about the values, goals, and objectives implicated by a problem, a process we considered in Chapter 2. She is able to do two other things described in Chapter 2: she can view the problem from multiple perspectives, and she can think systematically about its causes.

Choosers are able to resist the urge to jump at the first solution that comes to mind. This is more difficult than it might seem. As we saw in Chapter 1, many decisions result from the spontaneous application of problem schemas. Schemas supply a standard problem frame, a set of apparently relevant interests and objectives, and one or two stock solutions. In this sort of recognition-primed problem solving, only those solutions that are schematically associated with the problem are even considered. Over time, as a person responds to a particular type of problem with a stock solution, that response can become deeply habituated, even if it fails to yield optimal solutions. And if this response pattern is common to a community of experts—lawyers or administrative officials, for instance—the response can come to be viewed as normative.

For these reasons, striking out beyond a preset solution to a schematized problem can be unsettling. The same is true of novel problems, for which no standard solution has yet been developed. In such situations, "pickers" may feel confused and anxious, which may increase the tendency to seize at the first plausible solution that presents itself.

Choosers, on the other hand, are able to cope with the indeterminacy accompanying an unsolved problem. In the empty space between problem recognition and the selection of an alternative solution, a chooser can think more systematically, and ultimately decide more successfully, about how best to frame the problem, about the goals, values, and interests it implicates, about its causes, and about its potential solutions. It is this last subject—the generation of alternative courses of action—to which our attention now turns.

---

2. *Id.* at 224.

3.2 FRAMEWORKS FOR GENERATING SOLUTIONS TO PRESENT PROBLEMS

3.2.1 Basic Principles

In his work on "lateral thinking,"[3] Edward deBono observes that, much of the time, we "satisfice" in solving problems, that is, abandon the search for alternatives as soon as the first plausible solution comes to mind. On the upside, this saves cognitive energy and time. The downside, of course, is that the first solution that comes to mind may not be very good. Another downside is that if no solution comes readily to mind we may prematurely conclude that the problem is unsolvable and abandon the effort to solve it. Seeing no obvious way to reach a desired goal, we simply conclude that, "It can't be done."

To avoid these pitfalls, we need to train ourselves to "leave the problem open" long enough to generate a rich range of alternative solutions.[4] In this respect, we agree with law professor Tom Barton, who writes:

> [P]roblems are likely to be solved better—more reliably, more durably, more respectfully and with fewer side-effects—where a diversity of alternative procedures is available to approach the problem . . . The more dimensions of a problem have been considered in advance of applying a solution, the more comprehensive and better the solution is likely to be.[5]

Unfortunately, life provides no guarantee that problem solvers will generate a rich set of alternative solutions, nor any assurance that those alternatives will circumvent well-worn ruts. Here are some pedestrian ways to think about increasing the likelihood that a full complement of alternatives will be identified. We describe prospects for enhancing creativity later in the chapter.

3.2.2 Different Kinds of Alternatives

In Chapter 2, we considered the variety of interests and objectives that a person might have in relation to a problem or decision. One way of stretching your

---

3. EDWARD DEBONO, LATERAL THINKING: CREATIVITY STEP BY STEP (New York: Harper & Row, 1970).

4. One note of caution is warranted here. Both the quality of decisions and decision makers' subjective sense of satisfaction with their decisions can be impaired by the desire to "leave doors open," that is, to avoid committing to a particular course of action. For a discussion of this problem, *see* Jiwoong Shin and Dan Ariely, *Keeping Doors Open: The Effect of Unavailability on Incentives to Keep Options Viable*, 50 MGMT. SCI. 575 (2004); Daniel T. Gilbert and Jane E. J. Ebert, *Decisions and Revisions: The Affective Forecasting of Changeable Outcomes*, 82 J. PERSONALITY & SOC. PSYCHOL. 503 (2002).

5. Thomas D. Barton, *Conceiving the Lawyer as Creative Problem Solver*, 34 CAL. W. L. REV. 267, 269 (1998).

ability to generate different types of alternatives is to use these interests and objectives to generate potential solutions of two sorts: [6]

1. solutions that maximize the achievement of the most important among many objectives, even at the expense of the others; and
2. solutions that simultaneously satisfy several important objectives, even if no one solution is optimal for any one of them.

Taking the first step before the second helps keep your aspirations high and may lead to solutions that achieve secondary as well as primary. As we describe in greater detail in Chapter 12 (on trade-offs), it is not always possible to "have it all," but you cannot know unless you have thought about alternative solutions long enough to try.

3.2.3 Buying Information and Time

An ideal solution solves an entire problem in all of its aspects. But many problems have no "silver bullet" solution that satisfies all the interests at stake. More importantly, early in one's thinking about a problem, one may not have sufficient time, information, or "maneuvering room" to devise an optimal solution. Sometimes, it seems, the world won't wait for us to generate and evaluate a rich set of alternatives. If we don't decide quickly, the world may decide for us.

Under these circumstances, it is worth considering various types of information-buying or time-buying alternatives. That "alternatives exclude"[7] is a fact of life. But one can sometimes delay the inevitable, and this can conduce to better outcomes down the road. Here are some examples.

3.2.3.a Information-Gathering Alternatives Consider steps that will gather essential information without (significantly) compromising ultimate solutions.

One productive way to gather more information is to study the people involved in a problem. For example, product design engineers spend endless hours determining what will work for consumers. They map the users' behavior, ask them to keep journals, interview diverse groups of users, and seek out people who have never seen a particular product before to ask for their reaction.[8] They do this with the understanding that a useful technological innovation is only one step toward adoption.

Like engineers, good lawyers seek to understand what will actually assist clients and be persuasive to legal decision makers. Lawyers will read a judge's opinions in order to better understand how he or she approaches issues. In general, studying the people involved in a problem may provide cues as to what

---

6. *See* JOHN HAMMOND, RALPH, KEENEY, AND HOWARD RAIFFA, SMART CHOICES: A PRACTICAL GUIDE TO MAKING BETTER DECISIONS (Boston, MA: Harvard Business School Press, 1999).

7. JOHN GARDNER, GRENDEL 159 (New York: Knopf, 1971).

8. Bruce Nussbaum, *This is the IDEO Way*, BUSINESS WEEK, May 17, 2008.

solutions should look like, and whether they will pass the approval of gatekeepers.

Think of some information-gathering alternatives that Luis Trujillo or Christine Lamm might devise after being confronted with the problem at Terra Nueva discussed in the previous chapters.

3.2.3.b Time-Buying Alternatives Especially when faced with a stress-inducing problem, many of us are inclined to follow the adage, "Don't just sit there, do something!" and follow a "fire, ready, aim" process. But, some problems take care of themselves over time. How often have you made a doctor's appointment, only to have the symptoms disappear before entering the waiting room? Even those problems that are likely to persist may require time for analysis, information gathering, consultation, and the generation and evaluation of an alternative course of action. In these circumstances, consider first alternatives that will buy you time—again, without (significantly) compromising ultimate solutions. What might Luis Trujillo advise Jack Serrano to do in this respect in the face of public controversy and the threat (or actuality) of suit?

One important way that people keep their options open over time is, well, to buy options—not financial options (to purchase securities at a particular price), but real options, where the underlying asset is not a financial instrument. William Hamilton writes:[9]

> An essential characteristic of all options is asymmetry in the distribution of returns—greater upside potential than downside exposure. This results from opportunities to terminate the investment or otherwise limit negative outcomes while taking future actions to exploit positive outcomes fully . . . In concept, real options are quite similar to financial options because they both create the flexibility, but not the requirement for further action, as the future unfolds.
>
> If you have ever made a non-refundable deposit on any purchase, you have purchased a real option.[10]

Cass Sunstein suggests that certain government policies can be understood to create societal options against irreversible harms. Sunstein writes:

> [W]here a decision problem is characterized by (1) uncertainty about future costs and benefits of the alternatives, (2) prospects for resolving or reducing the uncertainty with the passage of time, and (3) irreversibility of one or more

9. *See* William F. Hamilton, *Managing Real Options, in* WHARTON ON MANAGING EMERGING TECHNOLOGIES 271 (George S. Day, Paul J. Schoemaker, and Robert E. Gunther eds., 2000).

10. Joseph Grundfest and Peter Huang have analyzed the litigation process in terms of the plaintiff's buying a series of options to continue litigating. REAL OPTIONS AND THE ECONOMIC ANALYSIS OF LITIGATION: A PRELIMINARY INQUIRY (1996).

of the alternatives, an extra value, an option value, properly attaches to the reversible alternative(s)."[11]

Richard Posner uses the option concept to describe prudential responses to the problem posed by climate change. He argues that we cannot afford to wait to mitigate catastrophic climate change; making cuts in greenhouse gas emissions now "can be thought of as purchasing an option to enable global warming to be stopped or slowed at some future time at a lower cost."[12]

3.2.4 Divergent Thinking and the Generation of Alternatives

In Chapter 1, we introduced the concepts of "divergent" and "convergent" thinking, derived from the work of Joy Paul Guilford.[13] Divergent thinking involves the generation of multiple potential solutions to a problem. Convergent thinking posits or evaluates those solutions.

Experts often approach problems in a "convergent" manner—that is, they focus attention and effort on a relatively narrow range of frames, objectives and options. Convergent thinking is an essential cognitive skill. But optimal problem solving also includes divergent thinking, which expands the range of options, perspectives, and elements that are considered. Divergent thinking conceives; convergent thinking critiques. Divergent thinking envisions; convergent thinking troubleshoots, fine tunes, selects, and implements. Both are required for good decision making.

In Section 1.4.2, we suggested that you can think of divergent thinking as two lines emerging from a common point and then moving away from each other, and of convergent thinking as two lines closing in from different directions on a single point. We also suggested that a fully deliberative problem-solving process combines elements of both. Divergent thinking makes its greatest contribution when a problem is being framed, when interests and objectives are being identified, and when alternative solutions are being generated for later evaluation. It also plays an important role in generating alternative hypotheses about the causes of a problem. Divergent thinking enables us to conceptualize a problem from a wide variety of perspectives. It is generative.

It is useful to think about divergent thinking in relation to schematic information processing, which we introduced in Section 1.5.2. In a sense, divergent thinking takes the thinker beyond the particular schematic framework triggered by his initial take on a problem and helps him think *across* a variety of interconnected schemas. For this reason, it is useful then to think of divergent thinking as

---

11. Cass Sunstein, Worst-Case Scenarios 179 ff (Cambridge: Harvard University Press 2007), *quoting* Anthony C. Fisher, Uncertainty, Irreversibility, and the Timing of Climate Change Policy 9 (2001), http://www.pewclimate.com/docUploads/timing_fisher.pdf, *quoted in* Worst-Case Scenarios.

12. Richard Posner, Catastrophe: Risk and Response 161–62 (New York: Oxford University Press, 2005), *quoted in* Worst-Case Scenarios.

13. Joy Paul Guilford, *Creativity*, 15 American Psychologist 444–54 (1950).

"panschematic," combining elements of different but somehow related schemas in nonhabituated ways. This sort of thinking does not always come easily.

3.2.5 On Possibilities and Path Constraints

Without lifting your writing implement from the paper, draw four or fewer straight lines connecting all nine dots in Figure 3.1 below.[14]

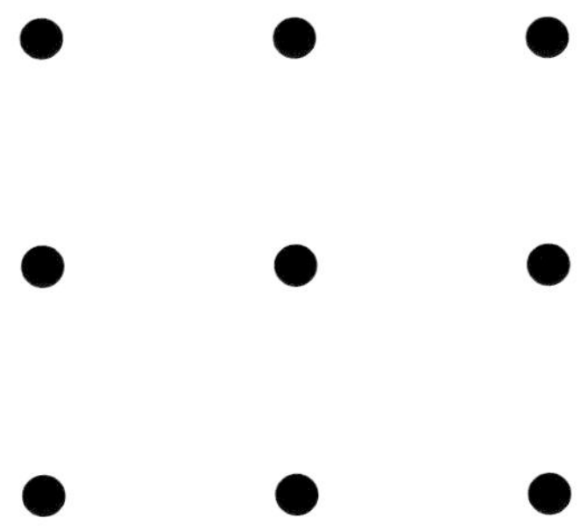

FIGURE 3.1 THE NINE DOT PROBLEM.

How did you go about trying to solve the problem? Most people try drawing lines that pass through the dots and remain within the imaginary square they constitute—and then they give up. They implicitly assume that the problem has a path constraint that, in fact, it does not have—the rule, "Don't go outside the dots." Who knows where we learned this tacit rule—perhaps from childhood games of "connect the dots," from the injunction to "color inside the lines," or from the fact that we are used to seeing objects in (more or less literal) frames. In any event, it then becomes a limiting frame for solving the problem.[15]

For present purposes, we use the nine-dot problem to illustrate an important point about the generation of alternative courses of action. It is often easier to assume the *presence* of path constraints that limit a problem's potential solutions than it is to recognize their *absence*. Indeed, the very process of structuring a problem may create path constrains. We will say more about this later in the chapter.

3.3 CREATIVITY IN PROFESSIONAL PROBLEM SOLVING

Judge Richard Posner has bemoaned that "only in law is 'innovation' a pejorative."[16] Georgetown University law professor Carrie Menkel-Meadow has

---

14. We are not sure who created the Nine Dot Problem. We found it in James L. Adams, Conceptual Blockbusting: A Guide to Better Ideas 24–25 (Reading MA: Basic Books, 3rd ed., 1986).

15. You can find the "classic" solution (and several other wicked ones as well) in James Adams' book (*supra*) or on any number of Web sites.

16. U.S. v. McKinney, 919 F.2d 405, 421 (7th Cir. 1990) (Posner, J., concurring).

asked, "Is it possible to speak of legal *creativity* or is the phrase itself an oxymoron?"[17] Not only is it possible, but it is commonplace in the professions, ranging from law to policy making to medicine and engineering.

3.3.1 An Opening Scenario

Recall that our intrepid problem-solving lawyer, Luis Trujillo, does volunteer work for the Los Angeles Volunteer Legal Services Association (VLSA). The Association's director has sent him a memorandum outlining a potential pro bono employment case. After having been led to believe that their employer was doing extremely well financially, and that their jobs were secure, twenty woodworkers at a custom furniture plant in nearby Anaheim had suddenly been terminated after the plant's owners decided to move manufacturing operations to Vietnam to take advantage of cheaper labor costs there. The plant's employees, who were not unionized, had come to work one day, been gathered into a meeting room, and told that they no longer had jobs. They got no advance notice, no severance pay . . . nothing. The manager gave them their final paychecks, including unpaid wages and vacation pay, told them to gather up their personal property, and had them escorted off the premises by security guards.[18]

Had the company employed more people the terminations would have been covered by the federal WARN Act, which requires advance notice of pending mass layoffs, or an equivalent amount in severance pay. Absent special rules of this sort, California's employment at-will doctrine, codified in California Labor Code Section 2922, presents a seemingly insurmountable obstacle to recovery of any sort of monetary relief—even relief in the nature of severance benefits. Section 2922 is generally interpreted by human resources professionals and employment lawyers to mean that, absent an enforceable contract providing otherwise (e.g., an individual contract or a collective bargaining agreement), employment can be terminated at any time, for any reason, so long as the reason is not itself illegal. As a technical legal matter, employees are not legally entitled to the customary "two weeks' notice" of popular imagination. Lawyers at the VLSA, who frequently advise newly terminated workers about the "at-will" rule, see no way around the problem. But before giving up, the director wants Trujillo's firm to consider whether there might be some novel legal theory under which the laid-off workers might obtain a remedy.

Trujillo, whose practice focuses on real estate, construction, and commercial matters, and who knows very little about employment law, takes a quick look at the relevant Labor Code section. It provides, in relevant part, that "[a]n

17. Carrie Menkel-Meadow, *Aha? Is Creativity Possible in Legal Problem Solving and Teachable in Legal Education?*, 6 Harv. Negotiation L. Rev. 97–144, at 125 (2001).

18. This scenario is based on an analogous case litigated by one of the authors in the early 1980s. Carson v. Atari, Inc., California Superior Court, County of Santa Clara, No. 53073 (1982).

employment, having no specified term, may be terminated at the will of either party on notice to the other." Trujillo is puzzled. He knows that, under the Uniform Commercial Code, "notice" of termination of a contract involving continuing or successive performance of no specified duration is interpreted as meaning "reasonable" notice. He wonders why the rule should be any different for employment contracts. Checking the annotations, and doing a quick Westlaw search, he finds, to his amazement, only two dusty old commercial contract cases—one from 1902 and the other from 1905—that interpret "notice" to mean "reasonable notice." But with those two old cases as precedent, and with arguments by analogy, the theory might work. Or, it might not. But in any event, Trujillo's problem sets the stage for thinking about creativity in legal problem solving—and beyond.

3.3.2 Creativity: Working Definitions

Howard Gardner, whose work on multiple intelligences has profoundly influenced education theory and practice, defines *creativity* in the following way:

> People are creative when they can solve problems, create products or raise issues in a domain in a way that is initially novel but is eventually accepted in one or more cultural settings . . . [A] work is creative if it stands out at first in terms of its novelty but ultimately comes to be accepted within a domain. The acid test of creativity is simple: In the wake of a putatively creative work, has the domain subsequently been changed?[19]

Harvard Business School professor Theresa Amabile's definition sounds many of the same themes, when she writes that a product is considered creative to the extent that experts in a domain consider it "both a novel response and an appropriate, useful, correct, or valuable response to an open-ended task."[20]

Notice what these two definitions have in common: they both acknowledge that creative solutions are not only *novel*, they are also *effective*. So, as Yale psychologist Robert Sternberg observes, "Creativity is the ability to produce work that is novel (that is, original, unexpected), high in quality, and appropriate (that is, useful, meets path constraints)."[21]

Along the same lines, Jerome Bruner notes that a creative solution to a problem tends to produce in the knowing observer a sense of "effective surprise."[22]

---

19. Howard Gardner, Intelligence Reframed: Multiple Intelligences for the 21st Century 116–17 (New York: Basic Books, 1999).

20. Beth A. Hennessey and Theresa M. Amabile, The *Conditions of Creativity, in* The Nature of Creativity: Contemporary Psychological Perspectives 11, 14 (Robert J. Sternberg ed., New York: Cambridge University Press, 1988).

21. Robert J. Sternberg, Wisdom, Intelligence, and Creativity Synthesized 89 (New York: Cambridge University Press, 2003).

22. Jerome S. Bruner, On Knowing: Essays for the Left Hand 18 (Cambridge, MA: Harvard University Press, 1962).

What makes the solution effective is that it solves the problem. What makes the solution surprising is that it differs from the stock alternative(s) spontaneously triggered by the relevant problem schema. Most of the time, creative solutions grow out of *some* established schema or combination of schemas. They involve old things combined in new ways, or new things combined in old ways. A break with the past makes the solution novel, but it is often continuity with the past that makes it effective.

In this regard, notice that Luis Trujillo's idea about a potential solution to the Anaheim woodworkers' problem did not exactly come out of "legal left field." The concept of "reasonable notice" that he proposed to introduce into employment law had deep roots in commercial law. This illustrates a number of important points about how creativity operates in professional fields.

3.3.3 Creativity and Cross-Fertilization

During the 1950s and 1960s, writer Arthur Koestler[23] studied humor, literature, and biology to develop insights into the nature of creativity. He used the following joke to illustrate one of those insights:

> Question: Where does a general keep his armies?
>
> Answer: In his sleevies.

What makes the joke funny, Koestler suggested, is essentially the same attribute that makes an idea creative: the unexpected juxtaposition of two self-consistent, but habitually incompatible frames of reference. In the joke, the words "general" and "armies" evoke a military frame of reference, which brings with it a set of associations centering on adult masculinity, seriousness, and all things martial. Laughter results when that frame unexpectedly intersects with another that involves juvenile talk, body parts, and clothing.

Creativity, in Koestler's view, involves a process of "bisociation," in which two self-consistent but habitually dissociated frames of reference are brought together, so that a construct from one is used productively in another. The idea can be illustrated by Figure 3.2, in which each of two frames of reference is represented as a discrete plane. Ordinarily, the planes are dissociated and do not intersect. The creative act brings them together. The line at which the two planes then intersect is the zone of bisociation, where creative ideas emerge.

Luis Trujillo's way of thinking about the Anaheim woodworkers' problem illustrates Koestler's insight. Whether or not employment and commercial contracts might seem to represent closely associated frames of reference, legal doctrines have developed in very different ways in the two domains. The legal requirement of reasonable notice of termination is as foreign to employment contract law as it is taken for granted in commercial law. Relatively few lawyers

---

23. Arthur Koestler, The Act of Creation (London: Hutchinson, 1964).

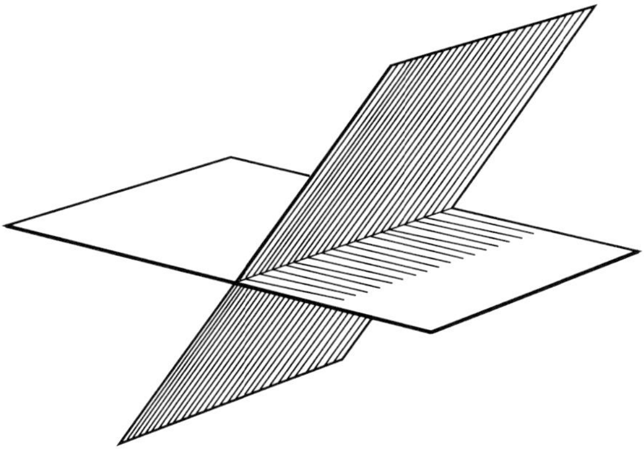

FIGURE 3.2 BISOCIATION.

practice in both areas. For these lawyers, employment law and commercial law represent discrete areas of specialization involving "habitually incompatible frames of reference." In such situations, the solution to a problem that might seem intractable to an employment lawyer habituated to a doctrinal framework in which "notice" has not been equated with "reasonable notice," might appear quite obvious to a lawyer habituated to doctrines in commercial law, in which it has.

Many of the legal innovations we recognize as "creative" derived from this kind of cross-fertilization between separate doctrinal or disciplinary domains. Consider, for example, the warranty of habitability in landlord tenant law. The concept of a "warranty" was originally unknown to the common law of real property. In fact, the principle of *caveat emptor* stood in direct opposition to the notion that an interest in real property might come with an implied warranty of any kind.[24] To solve a persistent social problem occasioned by informational asymmetries between landlords and tenants, disparate levels of market sophistication, and other sources of bargaining inequality, lawyers eventually persuaded courts to take the warranty concept from contract law and graft it onto landlord tenant law.[25]

A similar process, through which a construct taken from one legal domain is introduced to solve a problem in another, is illustrated by Charles Reich's

---

24. *See, e.g.*, Clifron v. Montague, 40 W. Va. 207 (1985); Walsh v. Schmidt, 206 Mass. 405 (1919); and Daly v. Wise, 132 N.Y. 306 (1892) (applying the principle of caveat emptor).

25. *See, e.g.*, Green v. Superior Court, 10 Cal. 3d 616 (1974); Javins v. First Nat'l Realty Corp., 138 App. D.C. 369 (1970); Lemle v. Breedon, 51 Haw. 426 (1969) (abrogating the doctrine of caveat emptor and imposing an implied warranty of habitability in landlord tenant transactions).

landmark 1964 *Yale Law Journal* article, *The New Property*.[26] In *The New Property*, Reich urged that statutory entitlements to government benefits, such as Aid to Families with Dependent Children or Medicaid, should be viewed as a species of personal property, of which a person could not be deprived without due process of law. Any first year law student who has read *Goldberg v. Kelly* in Civil Procedure has seen the fruits of this innovation: Reich's idea provided the basis for decades of work protecting social welfare beneficiaries from the arbitrary, capricious, or otherwise unfair denial or deprivation of public benefits.

Sometimes, a legal innovation can result from the cross-fertilization of a particular legal subject matter area with an idea from an entirely different discipline, such as economics. Consider in this regard the First Amendment metaphor of the "marketplace of ideas," emerging from Justice Oliver Wendell Holmes' dissent in *Abrams v. United States.* Although Holmes did not use this phrase himself, Justice William Brennan later drew on the opinion to write:

> [T]he ultimate good desired is better reached by free trade in ideas—that the best test of truth is the power of the thought to get itself accepted in the competition of the market . . . [27]

Here, a principle drawing its persuasive appeal and normative force from the domain of laissez faire economics was applied to the completely different domain of free speech.

Law, public policy, and business contain many additional examples of innovative solutions to seemingly intractable legal problems. Consider these, many of which were self-consciously devised by lawyers, social advocates, and entrepreneurs:[28]

- elimination of the privity requirement (that a manufacturer was only liable to the purchaser of a product) in product liability;
- recovery of compensatory damages for emotional distress;
- the creation of a common law, and later of a constitutional "right to privacy";
- joint custody;
- same-sex marriage;
- condominiums, cooperatives, the corporation;
- pornography as a violation of civil rights;
- sexual harassment as a violation of sex discrimination laws;
- truth and reconciliation commissions;
- the joint venture;
- the "poison pill" as a response to a threatened hostile takeover; and
- the political action committee (PAC) and its successors.

---

26. Charles A. Reich, *The New Property*, 73 YALE L.J. 733, 785 (1964).
27. Abrams v. United States, 250 U.S. 616, 631 (Holmes, J. dissenting).
28. Menkel-Meadow, *supra* at 125.

As Carrie Menkel-Meadow notes, many of these ideas have come about by the creative reading or misreading of legal words and concepts—by "expanding, aggregating, disaggregating, rearranging and altering existing ideas and concepts, borrowing or translating ideas from one area of law to another or from other disciplines, and . . . by use of redesign or architecture of words and concepts to build both new legal theories at the abstract level and new institutions at the practical level."[29]

In making this observation, Menkel-Meadow's view harmonizes with that of psychologist Mihály Csikszentmihalyi, who suggests that creativity often involves crossing the boundaries of different domains, combining elements of one with elements of another to create something new. "An intellectual problem," he suggests, "is not restricted to a particular domain. Indeed, some of the most creative breakthroughs occur when an idea that works well in one domain gets grafted onto another and revitalizes it."[30] In legal problem solving, as in many other domains, innovation entails a kind of *conceptual blending*, a process in which the problem solver combines two or more organizing conceptual frames to create a distinctly new frame that does not merely hybridize its constituent elements, but also generates its own emergent structure.[31]

3.3.4 Creativity, Expertise, and Critical Thinking

Creative individuals take problems that others see in one way and recast them as something different and new.[32] The preceding discussion suggests that bringing the perspectives from a diversity of subject areas and ways of thinking about problems—e.g., law, economics, science, and engineering—may be an effective way to generate a range of innovative solutions. Approaching a problem from interdisciplinary perspectives supports the exercise of three cognitive skills or techniques that Theresa Amabile suggests lie at the core of creativity:

1. the ability to "break set," that is, to diverge from one's habitual way of thinking about a particular problem;
2. the ability to "break script," or diverge from group norms about how a particular type of problem "should" be solved; and
3. the ability to view problems from a variety of vantage points.

---

29. *Id.*

30. Mihaly Csikszentmihalyi, Creativity: Flow and the Psychology of Discovery and Invention 88 (HarperPerennial 1996).

31. George H. Taylor, *Law and Creativity*, *in* Philosophy and American Law 81 (Francis J. Mootz III ed., New York: Cambridge University Press, 2009); Gilles Fauconnier and Mark Turner, The Way We Think: Conceptual Blending and the Mind's Hidden Complexities (New York: Basic Books, 2002).

32. *Id.* at 255.

Taken together, these three points caution against increasing levels of specialization in the teaching and practice of many professional disciplines.

At the same time, for creativity to be effective, it depends on expertise *within* a domain. From the standpoint of the creator, innovation is necessarily linked to what has come before. And from the perspective of its users, a product or practice must be rooted in a domain in order for it to be understood or recognized as useful. Thus, the creative problem solver must have expertise in the domain in which the problem arises, because even the most radically novel product or practice tends to be grounded in one or more domains.[33] For example, in our hypothetical scenario, it is the fact that the "reasonable notice" idea is rooted in commercial law that made it intelligible to Luis Trujillo. Those same roots will increase the odds that a court will find the argument persuasive.

So professional creativity often requires mastery of a domain in question—in Trujillo's case, a knowledge of substantive law combined with skill in legal analysis and research. Paradoxically, however, the fact that Trujillo was *not* a specialist in employment law, but rather in commercial law and real estate, may have helped him identify potential solutions to the no-notice problem that might have evaded an employment law specialist. Thus, while domain knowledge is essential, specialization can sometimes actually constrain the generation of alternative solutions to commonly encountered problems. Not only are specialists likely to approach a problem with a pre-scripted set of expert frames and solutions, they may lack the exposure to concepts, tools, or principles from other fields that might be adapted to solve problems arising in their own.

3.3.5 The Movement Between Convergent and Divergent Thinking

Isolated moments of creativity have little effect unless they are part of an overall process that includes convergent as well as divergent phases. Innovative ideas are seldom self-executing; their execution often requires critical, strategic, and analytical thinking—all of which require convergent thought. For a good problem solver, creative and critical thinking are transient mindsets that are deployed synchronically during a problem-solving process.[34] People move between these phases in the blink of an eye—or less.

Though they occur in convergent or evaluative phases as well,[35] moments of inspiration and creative insight are most common in divergent phases, which permit breaking away from familiar patterns. The divergent phase is rich with

---

33. SHARON BALIN, ACHIEVING EXTRAORDINARY ENDS: AN ESSAY ON CREATIVITY (Dordrecht: Kluwer Academic, 1988).

34. Raymond S. Nickerson, *Dimensions of Thinking: A Critique*, *in* DIMENSIONS OF THINKING AND COGNITIVE INSTRUCTION: IMPLICATIONS FOR EDUCATIONAL REFORM (VOL. I) 495–509 (Beau Fly Jones and Loma Idol eds., Hillsdale, NJ: Erlbaum, 1990).

35. Joy P. Guilford *Transformation: Abilities or Functions*, 17 JOURNAL OF CREATIVE BEHAVIOR 75–86 (1983).

metaphors going back to Greek mythology, in which one was possessed by a Muse during moments of creativity. Indeed, the creative work was seen as flowing from the Muse herself. The creator was merely a conduit through which the Muse's creation passed, and he was always at peril of her abrupt withdrawal.[36] Later, the Muses were joined by the "daemon," a spirit that lived in, and could suddenly depart from, the writer's pen. Wrote Rudyard Kipling, "When your Daemon is in charge, do not think consciously. Drift, wait, and obey."[37]

William James both captured and exaggerated the dichotomy of the phases when he contrasted everyday thinking with creative states. In everyday thinking:

> The force of habit, the grip of convention, hold us down on the Trivial Plane; we are unaware of our bondage because the bonds are invisible, their restraining action below the level of awareness. They are the collective standards of value, codes of behavior, matrices with built-in axioms which determine the rules of the game, and make most of us run, most of the time, in the grooves of habit—reducing us to the status of skilled automata which Behaviorism proclaims to be the only condition of man.[38]

In a creative state:

> Instead of thoughts of concrete things patiently following one another in a beaten track of habitual suggestion, we have the most rarefied abstractions and discriminations, the most unheard of combination of elements, the subtlest associations of analogy; in a word, we seem suddenly introduced into a seething cauldron of ideas, where everything is fizzling and bobbing about in a state of bewildering activity, where partnerships can be joined or loosened in an instant, treadmill routine is unknown, and the unexpected seems only law.[39]

The Jamesian dichotomy continues in much of the popular literature, which regards critical thinking as dour, constrained, and mechanical, while creativity is unconstrained, fanciful, undisciplined, and free-spirited.[40] Alex Osborn, the

---

36. *See generally* PENELOPE MURRAY, GENIUS: THE HISTORY OF AN IDEA (Oxford, UK: Blackwell, 1989).

37. Rudyard Kipling, *Working Tools* (1937), *in* THE CREATIVE PROCESS: A SYMPOSIUM 161–63 (Brewster Ghislin ed., Berkeley, CA: The University of California Press, 1985).

38. WILLIAM JAMES, TALKS TO TEACHERS ON PSYCHOLOGY 64 (New York: Henry Holt, 1908).

39. William James, *Great Men, Great Thoughts, and the Environment*, 46 ATLANTIC MONTHLY 441–59 at 456 (1880).

40. *See, for example*, ROGER VON OECH, A WHACK ON THE SIDE OF THE HEAD: HOW YOU CAN BE MORE CREATIVE (New York: Warner Books, 1983); PAUL SLOANE, THE LEADER'S GUIDE TO LATERAL THINKING SKILLS: UNLOCKING THE CREATIVITY AND INNOVATION IN YOU AND YOUR TEAM (2d ed. Philadelphia, PA: Kogan Page, 2006).

advertising executive who created the technique of "brainstorming," contrasted the "creative mind" as an idea generator that works through free association with the "judicial mind," which functions logically and acts as a filter. In Osborn's view, creative people are creative because they are able to "turn off" their judicial minds, allowing free association to occur.[41] These stereotypes capture the spirit of convergent and divergent thinking, and they may be helpful in freeing people to let their minds roam. But effective creativity requires both modes of thinking.

A similar dichotomy is often drawn between expertise and creativity, with the view that expertise carries with it preconceptions about how a problem *should* be approached that stifle "out-of-the-box" thinking.[42] Too much knowledge is said to impede creativity.[43] Yet, as we have mentioned, effective creativity often calls for domain-specific knowledge that mainly experts possess. The synthesis of these dichotomies requires acknowledging the value of expertise at the same time as it counsels against overspecialization in the teaching and practice of law, public policy, or any other discipline.

3.3.6 A Confluence Approach to Creativity—And the Skills It Requires

Most contemporary researchers view creativity as requiring a confluence of skills, mindsets, and abilities. The following taxonomy draws on the findings of Theresa Amabile and Robert Sternberg:[44]

Intellectual skills. These include the abilities to generate ideas that are novel, high in quality, and task appropriate; to recognize which of one's ideas are worth pursuing and which are not; to "think about thinking," particularly in relation to how problems are defined; and to persuade others in the field to accept one's ideas.

Self-governance skills. These include planning, self-monitoring, and the evaluation of one's thought processes and products.

Intrinsic task motivation.[45] Intrinsic motivation conduces to creativity, while extrinsic motivation may inhibit it.[46] Sternberg writes that "people rarely do truly

---

41. ALEX F. OSBORN, APPLIED IMAGINATION (New York: Scribner, 1953).

42. EDWARD DEBONO, NEW THINK: THE USE OF LATERAL THINKING IN THE GENERATION OF NEW IDEAS 228 (New York: Basic, 1968).

43. Robert W. Weisberg, *Creativity and Knowledge: A Challenge to Theories, in* HANDBOOK OF CREATIVITY 226–50, 226 (R. J. Sternberg ed., New York: Cambridge University Press, 1999).

44. Robert J. Sternberg and Linda A. O'Hara, *Creativity and Intelligence, in* HANDBOOK OF CREATIVITY, *supra* at 255.

45. TERESA M. AMABILE, CREATIVITY IN CONTEXT 83–127 (Boulder, CO: Westview, 1996).

46. For a summary of this research, *see* Mary Ann Collins and Teresa M. Amabile, *Motivation and Creativity, in* HANDBOOK OF CREATIVITY, *supra* at 297. Mihalyi Csikszentmihalyi, *The Domain of Creativity* (1990), *in* THEORIES OF CREATIVITY 190–214 (Mark A. Runco & Robert S. Albert eds., Newbury Park, CA: Sage). HOWARD GARDNER, CREATING MINDS: AN ANATOMY

creative work in an area unless they really love what they are doing and focus on the work rather than the potential rewards."[47]

Individual traits. Sternberg notes that some people find it easier than others "to transit back and forth between conventional and unconventional thinking."[48] Certain personality traits may be positively correlated with creative production.[49] These include a preference for moderate risk-seeking, willingness to tolerate ambiguity, persistence, and self-efficacy, as well as an attraction to complexity and aesthetic orientation. Bucking the crowd to "break script" requires self-confidence, independence, and persistence, as well as communicative skill.

3.3.7 The Individual, the Domain, and the Field

We agree with those theorists and researchers who argue that the acid test of creativity is whether, in the wake of a putatively creative work, the domain into which it is introduced has been changed.[50] For creative ideas to succeed in a domain, they must be accepted by "gatekeepers," who are empowered to make decisions about what should or should not be included in the domain.[51] In the art world, these gatekeepers include critics, publishers, gallery owners, buyers, and funders. In law, they include clients, other lawyers, administrative officials, legislators, and judges. In public policy, they include government officials, legislators, citizens, and nonprofit organizations.

Referring to our story of Trujillo and the woodworkers, imagine how opposing counsel or a skeptical judge might respond to Trujillo's attempt to graft the Uniform Commercial Code's construction of "notice" as "reasonable notice" onto California's at-will employment rule. Anyone familiar with the rough and tumble of state court motion practice can easily envision Trujillo's opposing

---

OF CREATIVITY SEEN THROUGH THE LIVES OF FREUD, EINSTEIN, PICASSO, STRAVINSKY, ELIOT, GRAHAM, AND GANDHI (New York: Basic, 1993).

47. ROBERT J. STERNBERG, WISDOM, INTELLIGENCE, AND CREATIVITY SYNTHESIZED, 108 (New York: Cambridge University Press, 2003).

48. *Id.* at xv. By the same token, Joy Paul Guilford posits that what we define as "thinking" comprises five different mental operations (cognition, memory, divergent thinking, convergent thinking, and evaluation), which act on four categories of content (figurative, symbolic, semantic, behavioral) to produce intellectual products. Creativity depends on cognitive flexibility—the thinker's ability to break apart different configurations of preexisting products and combine them in original ways. *See generally* JOY PAUL GUILFORD, THE NATURE OF HUMAN INTELLIGENCE (New York: McGraw-Hill, 1969).

49. For a summary of the relevant research, *see* Timothy I. Lubart, *Creativity*, *in* THINKING AND PROBLEM SOLVING 290–332 (Robert J. Sternberg ed., 1994); ROBERT J. STERNBERG AND TIMOTHY I. LUBART, DEFYING THE CROWD: CULTIVATING CREATIVITY IN A CULTURE OF CONFORMITY (New York: Free Press, 1995).

50. HOWARD GARDNER, INTELLIGENCE REFRAMED: MULTIPLE INTELLIGENCES FOR THE 21ST CENTURY 116-17 (New York: Basic Books, 1999).

51. Emma Policastro and Howard Gardner, *From Case Studies to Robust Generalizations: An Approach to the Study of Creativity*, *in* HANDBOOK OF CREATIVITY, *supra* at 213–25.

counsel rising to the podium in response to Trujillo's proffered interpretation and remarking with a wry smile, "Well, Your Honor, the plaintiffs' legal theory in this case is . . . how shall I say? . . . 'creative.'" It would not be a compliment.

The point is that for a creative idea to spark innovation, others in the domain or field must be persuaded of its merit. Thus, successful creators are also entrepreneurs, who are able not only to generate new ideas but to sell them to others.[52]

Along these lines, Robert Sternberg has set out what he calls a *propulsion theory* of creative contributions,[53] which describes how creative ideas can propel a field forward. On a continuum of impact, these include ideas that:

- move a field forward in the same direction it was going, but extend it into new subject matter areas. Consider in this regard the reach of neo-classical economics into law during the 1980s;
- move a field forward in the same direction in which it was heading, but stretch further and faster than others in the field were ready to go. If eventually accepted, such ideas are said to have been "ahead of their time;"
- re-orient a field, so that it moves in a different direction than previously;
- move a field backward to an earlier point and proceed forward from there in a new direction;
- propose that a field has reached an impasse, and should move in a different direction "from an entirely new point in the multidimensional space of contributions."[54]

Consider these two significant innovations, the first of which has become an integral part of legal doctrine and the second not:

- Joseph Sax's work developing public trust doctrine in the law of takings.[55] Prior to Sax's contribution, property rights were conceived as implicating only activities occurring within the property's physical boundaries. Accordingly, limiting those activities was viewed as a "taking" of a right appertaining to ownership. Sax, however, urged courts to view property

52. For more on this point, *see* Robert J. Sternberg, Wisdom, Intelligence, and Creativity Synthesized (2003), *supra* at 21, 101–09.

53. Robert J. Sternberg, *A Propulsion Model of Types of Creative Contributions*, 3 Review of General Psychology, 83–100 (1999); Robert J. Sternberg, James C. Kaufman, and Jean E. Pretz, The Creativity Conundrum: A Propulsion Model of Kinds of Creative Contributions (New York: Psychology Press, 2002).

54. Robert J. Sternberg, Wisdom, Intelligence, and Creativity Synthesised, *supra*at 138.

55. Joseph L. Sax, *The Public Trust Doctrine in Natural Resource Law: Effective Judicial Intervention*, 68 Mich. L. Rev. 471 (1970); Joseph Sax, *Takings and the Police Power*, 74 Yale L. J. 36 (1964).

rights quite differently, in a way that recognized the interconnectedness among different uses on various pieces of property. "Once property is seen as an interdependent network of competing uses, rather than as a number of independent and isolated entities," Sax observed, "[m]uch of what was formerly deemed a taking is better seen as an exercise of the police power in vindication of what shall be called 'public rights.'"[56]

- The concept of "market share" or "enterprise" liability was first applied in product liability cases involving the antimiscarriage drug diethylsilberstol (DES), which can cause vaginal cancer in female children. Prior to the California Supreme Court's decision in *Sindell v. Abbott Laboratories*,[57] plaintiffs who were harmed by DES but did not know which of numerous drug manufacturers had produced the particular medication their mothers took were unable to obtain a remedy in tort, as they could not establish causation. In *Sindell*, the court rejected this requirement and held that a plaintiff could recover from any of the major manufacturers in proportion to their share of the market for the drug during the relevant time period. The entire concept of actual causation, derived from the common law of tort, was replaced with the concept of market share, taken from economics and business. The "market share" approach was subsequently rejected by the same court, and by others as well.[58]

Mihály Csikszentmihalyi and other scholars have proposed a "systems approach" to creativity, which emphasizes the relationship among an individual, a performance domain, and a field. The *domain* is a related set of bodies of knowledge—in law, for example, constitutions, judicial doctrines, legislative enactments, administrative regulations, and rules of procedure. A *field* is the people who exercise influence or control over the domain,

A domain supplies an individual working within it with a set of interrelated rules, patterns, and representations—the "old," if you will. The creative individual draws on information in a domain and transforms or extends it, putting it to some new use. Creativity occurs when the individual generates an idea that modifies these rules, patterns, and representations in some way, creating "the new." However, most such ideas are quickly forgotten, much in the same way in which most genetic mutations are "forgotten" by evolution. Novel ideas are not incorporated into the domain unless they are accepted by the gatekeepers who

56. Joseph L. Sax, *Takings, Private Property, and Public Rights*, 81 YALE L. J. 149, 151 (1971).

57. Sindell v. Abbott Laboratories, 163 Cal. Rptr. 132, 607 P.2d 924 (1980).

58. Brown v. Superior Court, 751 P.2d 470 (Cal. 1988); Hymowitz v. Eli Lilly and Co., 539 N.E.2d 1069 (N.Y. 1989).

constitute the field. Once the new ideas are accepted, the domain preserves and transmits them to other individuals.[59]

These relationships are illustrated by Figure 3.3.[60]

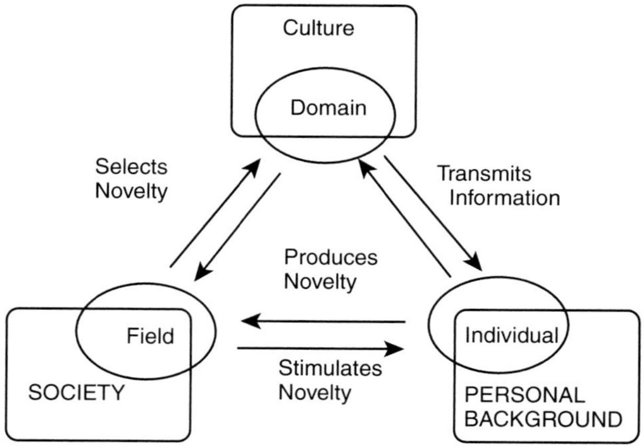

FIGURE 3.3 DOMAIN, FIELD, AND INDIVIDUAL.

The systems approach emphasizes that creativity cannot be understood as existing independently from the environment in which it operates. Creativity necessarily involves an interaction between the individual, the domain in which she works, the field that evaluates her work products, and the broader culture in which all three are embedded.

Indeed, since whether a novel idea becomes a creative contribution depends, in large measure, on its reception in the field into which it is injected, then one can speak of creative *fields* as well as creative *individuals*. It is interesting to speculate when and why particular fields, such as law and public policy, are more or less open to creative ideas.

3.4 PROBLEMS IN THE FUTURE TENSE: SCENARIO PLANNING

So far, we have focused on solving problems that occur pretty much in the present. But individuals, corporations, nonprofit organizations, and governments are often called upon to act today to solve problems that lie in the future. As in the case of our farmer's estate planning problem in Chapter 2, the future

---

59. Mihály Csikszentmihalyi, *Society, Culture, and Person: A Systems View of Creativity* (1988), *in* The Nature of Creativity 325–39 (Robert J. Sternberg ed., New York: Cambridge University Press , 1988).

60. Figure 3.3 is from Mihály Csikszentmihalyi, *Implications of a Systems Perspective for the Study of Creativity*, *in* Handbook of Creativity, *supra* at 13–35, 315.

may be as near as the next generation. In addressing problems of energy and climate change, the future may involve generations not yet born.

One major barrier to solving such problems creatively is people's tendency to anchor their thinking in the present and make only incremental adjustments as they contemplate the future. One tool for overcoming this barrier is scenario planning.[61]

3.4.1 What Are Scenarios? How Are They Used?

Scenarios are alternative descriptions of different possible futures that help decision makers consider the implications of these future possibilities for planning and decision making today. Scenario planning helps decision makers expand their conceptions of what is possible and imagine a broader range of futures than might otherwise be considered.[62] It is a creative tool rather than a forecasting instrument. The scenario planning firm, Global Business Network (GBN), a member of the Monitor Group, suggests that the technique can be used as:[63]

- *a decision tool* – "future proofing" a portfolio of activities and proposed actions;
- *a prioritization tool* – determining where and how to allocate finite resources;
- *a testing tool ("wind tunnel")* – using multiple "settings" to strengthen an existing strategy, innovation, initiative, or priority;
- *an oversight tool* – adding perspective and insight to other planning processes;
- *an integrative tool* – applying judgment to complexity for making sense of the world;
- *a generative tool* – producing innovative ideas, programs, products, and services;
- *a timing tool* – reacting appropriately (i.e., neither overreacting nor underreacting);
- *a scanning tool* – monitoring for deeper shifts in the external environment;
- *a proactive tool* – combating reactive demands; taking affirmative steps to prepare for the future;
- *a conversation tool* – talking about difficult issues in a safe (hypothetical) way.

Scenario planning has been used by governments, businesses, and entire industries. Here we consider their use by policy makers to enable safe and

61. Much of our discussion is based on the work of the Global Business Network (GBN), a member of the Monitor Group.

62. DIANA SCEARCE AND KATHERINE FULTON, WHAT IF? THE ART OF SCENARIO THINKING FOR NONPROFITS 11 (Global Business Network, 2004).

63. Erik Smith, *Chapter 5: Using a Scenario Approach: From Business to Regional Futures*, *in* ENGAGING THE FUTURE: FORECASTS, SCENARIOS, PLANS AND PROJECTS 85 (Cambridge: Lincoln Institute of Land Policy, 2007).

productive dialogues among diverse stakeholders considering challenging or contentious policy issues.[64]

For example, in 2002, the Great Valley Center (GVC),[65] a nonprofit organization that supports community sustainability and regional progress in California's Central Valley, used scenarios to help engage citizens in thinking about the future of this huge region that runs from Redding in the north to Bakersfield in the south. Working with GBN, the Great Valley Center engaged citizens and experts in exploring how development issues, including traffic congestion, access to quality education, land use policy, agriculture, and regional industry, might evolve over the coming twenty-five years. Four scenarios were developed, as shown in Figure 3.4.[66]

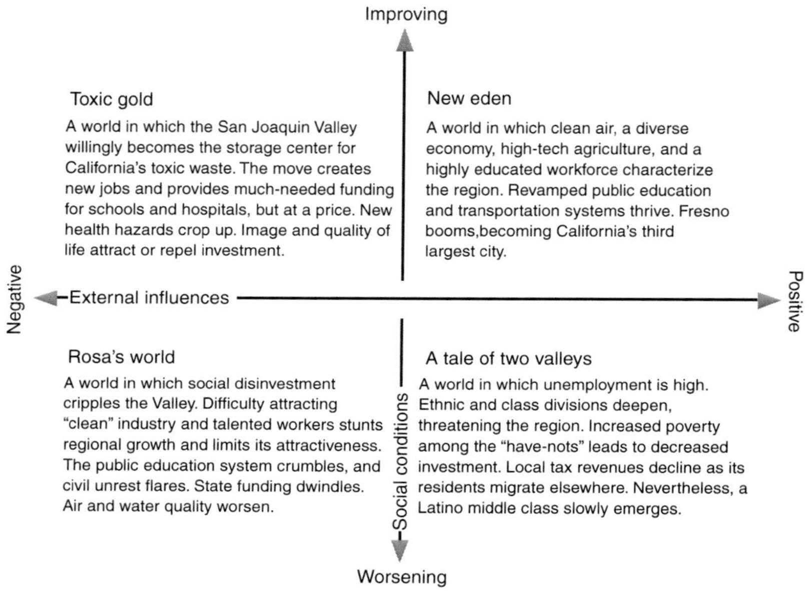

FIGURE 3.4 SCENARIOS FOR CALIFORNIA'S CENTRAL VALLEY.
Global Business Network, a member of the Monitor Group.[67]

Materials illustrating these scenarios were broadly disseminated through electronic and print media.[68] Citizens and students in this conservative and increasingly multiethnic region discussed a number of issues, including its

64. Smith 85–93.

65. *Great Valley Center & Casey Family Programs* examples have been adapted and paraphrased from SCEARCE, et al.

66. SCEARCE 73–76.

67. *Id.* 76.

68. Hosley, David, President, Great Valley Center, personal interview, Nov. 21, 2008.

racial and economic divisions, with the goal of catalyzing regional change.[69] Although it is too early to discern the effects of the exercise, GVC was sufficiently optimistic to launch a new scenario initiative, "The Great Valley in 2020," including publication of a workbook for use by nonprofits and other organizations to guide their scenario-planning efforts.[70]

Scenarios were also employed in a 2002 strategic planning effort by Casey Family Programs, a nonprofit organization dedicated to providing and improving foster care. The organization was struggling to clarify its strategy and mission. A then-rising stock market had dramatically increased Casey's endowment, inspiring the organization to consider what success for the organization would look like ten years down the road. Two critical uncertainties were considered:

- "How will U.S. society and government evolve over the next 10 years? Will citizens become more/less actively involved in social issues and supportive of an interventionist government?
- What role will technology play in fostering community?"[71]

Scenario workshops yielded the results shown in Figure 3.5.

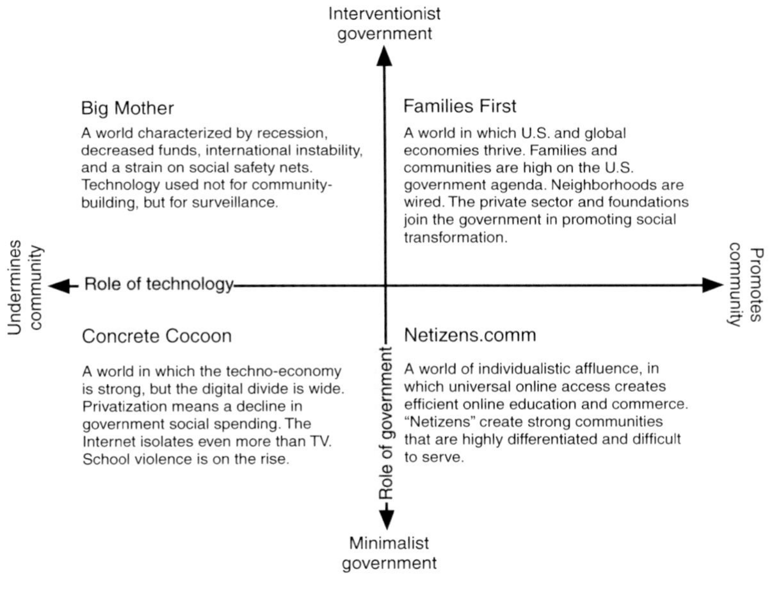

FIGURE 3.5 SCENARIOS RELEVANT TO FOSTER CARE.
Global Business Network, a member of the Monitor Group.[72]

69. SCEARCE 73–76.
70. Hosley, David, President, Great Valley Center, personal interview, Nov. 21, 2008.
71. SCEARCE 67.
72. *Id.*

As it turned out, key aspects of the *Big Mother* scenario did in fact unfold. This scenario encompassed international geopolitical crises, increasing nationalism, and an economic downturn—none of which was generally expected in 2002. Chiemi Davis, Casey's senior director of strategic planning and advocacy, reports that "because of the scenario work . . . we now consider ourselves much better prepared for the current economic and cultural realities."[73] GBN notes that the Casey Foundation "saw the potential threat in a bleak scenario, like *Big Mother*, and prepared accordingly." [74]

3.4.2 Why Use Scenarios?

Many decision makers assume that the future will closely resemble the present. Scenarios challenge this assumption by imagining how the future world might plausibly be dramatically different, with the goal of assessing various decision alternatives in possible futures. The scenarios are not grounded principally in a continuation of past trends or data. Rather, they involve plausible visions of the ways that relevant uncertainties might evolve in the future. Most of these uncertainties are driven primarily by forces beyond the control of the decision maker.

Diana Scearce and Katherine Fulton of GBN note that the goal of scenario planning is not to predict the future, but rather "to arrive at a deeper understanding of the world in which . . . you operate, and to use that understanding to inform your strategy and improve your ability to make better decisions today and in the future."[75] Rather than being predictions, projections, or forecasts,[76] scenarios are more like simulations or war games, allowing decision makers to imagine the outcome of their choices in differing worlds. By challenging a "business-as-usual" vision of the future, scenarios can help counterbalance a number of biases described in later chapters, including confirmation bias and other judgmental errors, overconfidence, dogmatism, belief perseverance, and groupthink.

3.4.3 Key Principles of Scenario Planning

Three key principles form the foundation of scenario planning:[77]

- *Taking the long view*: Rather than considering potential near-term changes, scenario planning is often used to imagine how large-scale, systemic changes may affect the future that strategic plans are designed to address, five, ten or even twenty years from now.

---

73. *Id.*
74. *Id.*
75. *Id.* 7.
76. George A. Goens, *Beyond Data: The World of Scenario Planning. Constructing Plausible Plots in a World that Defies Linear Logic,* April 2001, http://www.aasa.org/publications/saarticledetail.cfm?ItemNumber=3761.
77. Smith 83.

- *Thinking from the outside in*: Rather than focusing on factors under our control, scenario planning explores how events beyond our control might affect the future.
- *Including multiple perspectives*: Scenario planning helps overcome myopic visions of the future, and forces policy makers to think more openly about what the future might bring.

In developing a scenario, planners must determine an appropriate *time frame* based on when the most important effects of the decision will play out. The relevant horizon for policy decisions may be as long as several decades. Planners must also identify key future *uncertainties*, including external drivers—a process that can be aided by considering emerging social, technical, economic, environmental, and political (STEEP) trends.

After prioritizing key uncertainties, participants can begin to *brainstorm future scenarios*. This is conceptually challenging. An almost infinite variety of scenarios are possible—after all, almost anything could happen in the future. To remain useful, the exercise must be bounded. A useful set of scenarios generally will have quite different implications for decision making (though it would be noteworthy and important if radically different scenarios led to identical decisions for an organization or polity). In selecting scenarios for consideration, planners seek out scenarios that are:

- *Plausible*. The scenario must be believable.
- *Relevant* to the key strategic issues and decisions at hand. If the scenario would not cause a decision maker to act differently compared to another scenario, there is little use in considering it.
- *Challenging* to today's conventional wisdom. It should make one think about different possibilities and options.
- *Divergent from each other*. Together, the scenarios should "stretch" the thinking about the future environment, so that the decisions take account of a wider range of issues.
- *Balanced*. It is useful to ensure that a group of scenarios strike a good psychological balance between challenges and opportunities, risks, and upside potential.[78]

Once a compelling set of scenarios is identified, it is useful to identify "leading indicators" to serve as warning signs that a given scenario is unfolding.

3.4.4 Drawbacks of Scenario Planning

Whatever their benefits, the vividness and detail of scenarios can contribute to judgmental biases—particularly those related to the *availability heuristic*—that

78. *Id*. 84.

mislead participants about the probability that a particular scenario will occur.[79] Scenario planners work to weave together vivid storylines; their storytelling often entails "unpacking" a scenario into its component parts to illustrate how a given set of events could converge to result in such an outcome. But vivid stories about how a particular event might unfold make its occurrence seem more likely than it may actually be.[80] And the unpacking process can contribute to a logical error in which participants' assessments of the probability of events that are mutually exclusive and collectively exhaustive add up to more than 100 percent.[81] Scenario-thinking thus may impair predictive accuracy by inspiring forecasters to "attach excessive probabilities to too many possibilities."[82]

3.5 BARRIERS TO CREATIVE PROBLEM SOLVING—AND OVERCOMING THEM

Earlier in this chapter, we used the nine-dot problem as a way to illustrate one common obstacle to the generation problem solutions—imagining nonexistent path constraints.

Most people are not able to solve the nine-dot problem at all. By contrast, we do come up with solutions to most of our personal and professional problems—though we have a tendency to adopt the first plausible alternative that comes to mind, so long as it seems "good enough." Such "satisficing" often makes sense: We have many little problems to solve in the course of a day. However, even when a particular situation warrants giving more thought to possible solutions, we tend not to systematically consider a range of alternatives. We are constrained by cognitive, social and emotional, practical, and personal factors. We consider a number of these here.

3.5.1 Cognitive Process Constraints

Because problem schemas often include a stock solution, the triggering of a particular problem schema also tends to trigger a pre-scripted solution, which, because of its close cognitive association with the problem trigger, comes "first to mind" and strikes us as particularly promising or apt. We tend to adopt this default solution, and, if we consider alternatives at all, they tend to be incremental, altering the stock solution in small ways rather than significantly broadening the range of potential solutions we consider.

---

79. *See* Philip E. Tetlock, Expert Political Judgment: How Good Is It? How Can We Know? The Limits of Open Mindedness 194, 196 (Princeton and Oxford: Princeton University Press, 2005); Section 9.6, *infra*.

80. Daniel Reisberg, Cognition: Exploring the Science of the Mind 386–87 (New York: W.W. Norton Press, 2001).

81. *Id.* 197.

82. *Id.* 201.

Specialization often exacerbates this tendency. As the quotation from William James cited in Section 3.3.5 suggests, specialization of any kind tends to create "grooves of habit." As an expert encounters more and more problems of a particular type, he may become increasingly susceptible to the rote application of a narrow range of solutions. With increasing expertise in his own field and without exposure to others, he may become less adept at borrowing concepts from different frameworks and adapting them to solve a problem within his own field.

3.5.2 Social Constraints

In *Conceptual Blockbusting*, Stanford University engineering Professor James Adams presents readers with the problem illustrated in Figure 3.6.

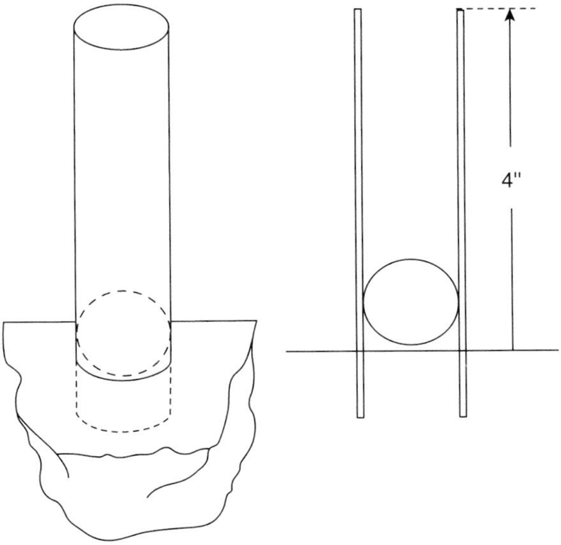

FIGURE 3.6 THE PING PONG BALL IN THE PIPE.

Imagine that a steel pipe is imbedded in the concrete floor of a bare room. The inside diameter of the tube is .06 inches larger than the diameter of a ping pong ball, and, in fact, a ping pong ball is resting on the concrete floor at the bottom of the pipe. You are one of a group of six people in the room, in which you also find a carpenter's hammer, a chisel, a box of cereal, a file, a wire coat hanger, a monkey wrench, a light bulb, and one hundred feet of clothesline. You must find a way to get the ping pong ball out of the pipe without damaging the ball, the tube, or the floor.[83]

83. ADAMS, *supra* at 54.

Despite its obvious effectiveness, Adams observes, few people presented with this problem propose to solve it by having the people present pee into the pipe, thus floating the ping pong ball to the top of the tube where it can easily be retrieved. Few if any people would even think of this solution, let alone propose it, because, as Adams notes, urination is a private activity, at least in our society.[84]

Though somewhat atypical, Adams' scenario illustrates another class of impediments to the generation of a robust set of alternative solutions—social conformity effects. We don't want to make fools of ourselves or offend the sensibilities of others in our social environment—and proposing untested ideas about alternative approaches to a problem can be risky. Social norms tend to develop around recurring problems, providing a relatively small set of "acceptable" candidate solutions. Fearing disapproval, or perhaps not wanting to offend someone—often a person in authority—who has already proposed a plausible, more "traditional" solution, may keep us from even imagining, let alone suggesting a new approach. Indeed, pursuing solutions that violate social norms may be perceived as somehow "cheating," even if the solution does not violate any explicit rules applicable to the problem itself.

We do not know whether lawyers and policy makers are more or less susceptible to social conformity constraints than anyone else. But lawyers are often viewed—by themselves as well as by others—as conservative, risk-averse, and precedent-bound. Deviation from the "tried and true" can easily slip into deviation from the applicable "standard of practice." Such deviations may, at least under some circumstances, subject a lawyer not only to ridicule, but also to malpractice liability or bar discipline. In like fashion, the public accountability of policy makers and the constrained routines of bureaucrats often promote risk-averse behavior and inhibit taking creative approaches to solving problems.

While some professional school courses—probably more in public policy than in law—encourage students to be creative problem solvers, much of the core curriculum trains students to be more comfortable criticizing ideas than creating them. The tendency to criticize ideas prematurely inhibits the generation of a rich and varied array of potential solutions or alternative courses of action. Risk aversion, fear of breaking the rules or making a mistake, and an implicit belief that there is one right answer to every problem all combine with our general discomfort with an unsolved problem to tend us toward quick convergence on one, or at most a small set, of stock, safe solutions.

3.5.3 Practical Constraints

Deliberative, process-conscious problem-solving procedures take time. This holds as true for the generation of alternative solutions as it does for the framing of the client's problem, the identification of goals and objectives, and the

84. By the way, based on informal empirical observations, men are not more likely to solve this problem than women.

resolution of causal uncertainty. Often, people do not have as much undistracted time as they need to work on any particular problem, and this may prevent even the best-intentioned problem solver from generating a range of options before selecting a solution for implementation.

Even when time is available, our ability to generate alternative solutions may be constrained by knowledge deficits. Helping a client generate alternative solutions requires knowledge about the particular practical context—whether in business, government, the nonprofit sector, or the client's personal or professional life—in which the problem has arisen. A field's institutionalized practices often provide both the building blocks for potential solutions and obstacles around which a successful solution must navigate. Professionals must understand these if they are to generate practical, rather than merely imaginative, alternatives.

3.5.4 Personal Constraints

As with many other of their "multiple intelligences,"[85] individuals differ in their capacities for instrumental creativity. The differences may be rooted in differing needs for certainty and tolerance of ambiguity, in different levels of comfort with offering ideas that may be rejected, and simply in the capacity for imagination.

There is considerable speculation on how these capacities develop, or do not, and on how they can be improved. Without rejecting any possibilities—from psychological counseling to solving lots of puzzles and brainteasers—we suspect that repeatedly being challenged to solve practical problems in law and related domains is likely to improve professionals' capacities in this respect, whatever their differing starting points. It also seems apparent that particular environments are more or less conducive to the risk-taking that accompanies exposing one's ideas to others. It falls to research not yet conducted to determine whether law and public policy students can develop better creative problem-solving skills through transactional case studies (of the sort taught in business schools), simulated exercises, and reflective clinical practice.

3.6 SUMMARY: GENERATING BETTER ALTERNATIVES

It also remains unclear whether the various techniques for enhancing creativity hawked by any number of "how-to" books can systematically be employed to improve the problem-solving abilities of lawyers and policy makers. But in summary, we offer a number of helpful ideas, gleaned from the trade literature and the work of academic researchers.

Perhaps most significantly, if necessity is the mother of invention, overwork makes for effective birth control, creating the ideational equivalent of China's

---

85. *See* Howard Gardner, Intelligence Reframed, *supra*.

"one child" policy. The generation of a broad range of potential solutions to any given problem appears to benefit from:

- time to ruminate and let problems percolate in the unconscious mind;
- permission to sit for a while with an unsolved problem. In the quest for creativity, idleness may prove a virtue.
- awareness of the constraints that schematic expectancies and other pre-scripted responses implicitly impose on our thinking;
- the ability to go beyond the frames and schemas automatically triggered by a problem of a particular sort; and
- willingness to at least temporarily eschew evaluation, reserve judgment, and postpone evaluative scrutiny of potential alternative solutions.

Here are a few practical guidelines for applying these general principles to specific problem-solving situations:

1. Focus individually on each of the objectives identified earlier in the problem-solving process and, with respect to each one, ask, "How could it be achieved?"
2. Generate at least three ideas for each identified objective before moving on to the next.
3. Question the constraints you have imposed on possible solutions to the problem.
4. Think about analogous problems in other fields or disciplines and ask whether there is some device from those fields or disciplines that might be adapted to solve the problem.
5. Consult with people with knowledge sets other than your own to get their ideas about potential solutions.
6. Generate a number of potential solutions before critiquing or choosing any one of them.

We close the chapter with a problem, which you can use to stretch your thinking about the topics we have covered here.

Luis Trujillo and his client, Jack Serrano, do not yet have enough information to have any confidence in the causes of the problems at Terra Nueva. Yet, they need to act quickly. If the newspaper report is accurate, a class action suit has already been filed against Serrano. Remember that defending the suit is not necessarily Serrano's only interest. He may also be concerned with his reputation; with his relationships with government regulators, financial backers, present and potential business partners, current tenants, and prospective tenants; with dealing with his and his family's psychological stress; and with "doing right" by anyone who has actually been injured by materials used in the homes.

Generate a list of actions that Serrano might take within the next days or weeks to address these or any other interests you think he might have.

4. CHOOSING AMONG ALTERNATIVES

Having thought through a variety of alternative strategies that may achieve your objectives, it's time to make the decision. Sometimes, the process up to this point will lead inexorably to a single choice. Often, however, you may be faced with competing interests or objectives or competing strategies for achieving them—as Jack Serrano is, for example, in trying to decide how to respond to his tenants' complaints.

4.1 SPECIFYING THE CONSEQUENCES OF ALTERNATIVES

The first step toward choosing among several plausible alternatives is to be clear about the consequences of choosing each one. The alternatives facing Serrano are fraught with uncertainties, including how others will react to any actions he takes. Before tackling such complexities, consider how you might assess the consequences of alternatives in a simpler case—perhaps one closer to your own experience. Suppose that you are considering renting an apartment, and that you have four major criteria:

- *Cost.* The lower the rent, the better.
- *Size.* You need at least two rooms, and three (one of which would serve as a guest room) would be ideal.
- *Proximity to the campus.* The closer the better.
- *Neighborhood.* You'd like to live in a safe, attractive neighborhood.

You have now seen a number of apartments that seem plausible candidates. How might you describe them in terms of these criteria?

Cost is the simplest and most readily quantifiable. When you think about size, you realize it's not just the number of rooms, but their dimensions. The guest room is really tiny—all right for an occasional out-of-town friend, but your mother might give you a hard time when she visits. (On the other hand, that may keep her visits reasonably short.)

With respect to proximity, the apartment is not really within walking distance of the campus, but there's a bus stop just in front of your door; also it seems like a fairly short bike ride. But does the bus go directly to campus, or do you have to transfer? Would biking require you to ride on a busy commercial street with no bike lanes? The neighborhood looks pretty nice during the daytime, but you haven't been there at night when the jazz nightclub across the street is open. Also, now that you think about it, you haven't seen a supermarket anywhere nearby.

This little scenario suggests a number of *general guidelines* for specifying the consequences of a potential decision.[1]

- Describe the consequences of the highest-ranked alternatives in terms of each of your interests or objectives.
- Wherever possible, describe the consequences quantitatively; this will facilitate the comparison with other (existing or possible) alternatives. Make sure that the quantity captures all the dimensions of an interest (e.g., size of the rooms as well as number; commute time to campus as well as distance.)
- Don't disregard consequences that can't be quantified, such as the quality of the neighborhood or the safety of the bike ride. As Einstein famously said: "Not everything that counts can be counted, and not everything that can be counted counts."
- Gather data about the consequences. If you've only seen the neighborhood during the daytime or on weekends, go there on an evening or weekday.
- Pretend that you have already chosen an alternative, and imagine a day in your life from morning to night. Engage in such "mental simulation" with a number of alternatives, not just your favorite. Otherwise, you may become too committed to one choice and have difficulty imagining the others.
- Be open to new interests or objectives coming to mind. Even when you follow a deliberative model, the processes are recursive, with subsequent steps reminding you of lacunae in earlier ones.

After engaging in the process with all plausible alternatives, one of them may so obviously *dominate* others—that is, be better in some respects and at least as good in all others—that the decision is inescapable. (Also, an alternative may be obviously dominated by others, so you can eliminate it from consideration.) The interesting decisions, though, are ones where there is no one obvious choice.

Note that this little exercise makes at least two implicit simplifying assumptions: (1) that there are no significant risks or uncertainties in how the future will unfold, and (2) that you are pretty good at predicting how you will feel about the decision once you actually begin living with it. In fact, real-world decision making tends to be more complex in both of these respects. But we'll leave that for part 3 of the book.

---

1. We are indebted to John Hammond, Ralph, Keeney, and Howard Raiffa, Smart Choices: A Practical Guide to Making Better Decisions (1999) for some of the guidelines.

4.2 THE SPECTRUM OF DECISION-MAKING PROCESSES[2]

Underlying every decision is an implicit metadecision of how much effort to devote to the decision and what processes to employ for making it. The objective of the metadecision is to minimize the sum of the costs of making the decision and the costs of suboptimal outcomes. Cass Sunstein and Edna Ullman-Margalit catalog these decision-making costs, which include time, money, unpopularity, anxiety, boredom, agitation, anticipated ex post regret or remorse, feelings of responsibility for harm done to self or others, injury to self-perception, guilt, and shame.[3]

Sunstein and Ullman-Margalit also catalog a mixture of decision processes, to which we add a few of our own:

Intuition. Not only are most of the myriad decisions that we make every day done intuitively, but intuition continues to play a role even when we attend to the decision-making process. Intuition often gives us an *affective* or emotional response to an alternative we are considering. Negative affect, including just an uneasy feeling, provides a warning of a problem with the choice, even when the problem is hidden from our consciousness. To fail to attend to this signal is to invite a poor decision.

Intuition is a double-edged sword, however, and it can mislead. Suppose that you are considering renting an apartment. One apartment seems pretty nice, albeit expensive, and you are quite taken with the real estate agent who recommended it to you. Though your feelings about the realtor may unconsciously spill over to the apartment, they are unlikely to improve your satisfaction with the apartment in the long run. Indeed, every salesperson worth her salt will use techniques to make you feel positive toward her and hence toward the transactional experience.[4] We'll have a lot more to say about the interplay of intuition and deliberation in later chapters.[5]

Heuristics. In Section 1.6.1 we described the two-systems model of judgment and decision making. System I heuristics, or mental shortcuts, allow people to make myriad judgments about probability, causation, and other matters with little or no cognitive effort. Although heuristics often lead to good outcomes, they can also mislead. For example, in the Terra Nueva problem, a foul-smelling

---

2. We are indebted to Cass Sunstein and Edna Ullman-Margalit, *Second-Order Decisions*, 110 Ethic 5–11 (October 1999) for stimulating our thinking about these issues and categorizing decision-making strategies.

3. *Id.* 12.

4. *See* Robert Cialdini, Influence: Science and Practice ch. 16 (Boston: Pearson/Allyn & Bacon, 2000).

5. For some general readings on the subject, *see* Better Than Conscious? Decision Making, the Human Mind, and Implications for Institutions (Christoph Engel and Wolf Singer eds., 2008); H. Plessner et al., Intuition in Judgment and Decision Making (2008).

odor might evoke images or feelings of illness. Whether or not this is generally accurate, it would be best to check it out with some conscious System II analysis before making an important decision based on the linkage.

Routines. Routines are patterns of behavior that one follows regularly and without thought: for example, swallowing vitamin pills with one's morning coffee or taking a particular route to work. Most bureaucracies and other organizations depend on routinized ways of doing things—new employees are taught to do it that way because "that's the way it is done." A routine may be the result of past deliberation, but present actors do not necessarily advert to its rationale and may not even know what it is.

Rules. A rule specifies the outcome of a decision given the existence of certain facts. Rules have low decision-making costs and constrain discretion. Many government regulations take the form of rules: "Maximum speed limit, 65 miles per hour" and "No bicycle riding in the playground." Rules typically are both over- and under-inclusive and therefore entail some individually suboptimal decisions—traffic conditions may be such on a particular stretch of highway that 75 miles per hour is perfectly safe, but don't waste your time arguing this to the highway patrol officer or the judge. Self-imposed rules—for example, "never have second helpings"—are often designed to avoid succumbing to temptations.

Even though a rule does not call for deliberation by the immediate decision maker, it does require that someone has deliberated in advance to create the rule.

Checklists

Checklists, of the sort used by airplane pilots, are similar to rules or presumptions. In 1935, the so-called "Flying Fortress" often crashed on take-off until the military realized that this four-engine aircraft was so complex that pilots needed to rely on a checklist rather than their intuition. Recent studies suggest that using a checklist can make a huge difference in critical medical care. For example, by checking off five simple steps in putting catheters into patients—from washing hands with soap to putting a sterile dressing over the site—physicians and nurses could dramatically reduce the number of infections. Atul Gawande, *Annals of Medicine: The Checklist*, New Yorker, December 10, 2007.

Presumptions and rules of thumb. A presumption is a rule that can be rebutted under special circumstances that cannot be specified in advance; in effect, it shifts the burden of proof, requiring you to justify—to yourself or others—why you are deviating from the rule. In personal life, you might have a presumption against eating second helpings, which could be overcome if it would be rude to your host. A common example from law practice is: "Never ask a witness a question on cross-examination unless you know the answer yourself." An environmental regulation might prohibit discharging more than a certain amount of a pollutant unless the business can prove that it isn't feasible to keep the discharge below the limit.

Presumptions of this sort permit quick, nondiscretionary decisions. They can also allow for a gradual learning curve. People new to an organization or field of practice may adhere to them strictly and loosen the constraints as they develop more experience.

Business Rules of Thumb

In the course of researching this chapter, we came across these examples from a book on business rules of thumb, modestly subtitled, *Words To Live By And Learn From That Touch Every Aspect Of Your Career*:

- Throw a tantrum within the first ten minutes of the negotiating (from a sports consultant).
- Never hire a salesman you'd want your daughter to marry.
- Don't order drinks served with a paper umbrella.

Seth Godin and Chip Conley, Business Rules of Thumb (Warner Books 1987).

Like a rule, a presumption may be the result of someone's deliberation beforehand. Unlike a rule, a presumption calls for a degree of deliberation at the time of its application—enough deliberation to determine whether the circumstances justify rebutting the presumption.

Standards. A standard leaves it to the individual decision maker and those who will review her judgment to apply a norm such as "reasonableness," "excessiveness," or "competency" to a particular situation. For example, in addition to setting particular speed limits, California law provides that "No person shall drive a vehicle upon a highway at a speed greater than is reasonable or prudent having due regard for weather, visibility, the traffic on, and the surface and width of, the highway."[6] Depending on whether the norms of reasonableness, etc., are well defined by practice and precedent, a standard may require more or less deliberation.

Small steps. A decision maker may proceed by taking small, reversible steps and observing their consequences, rather than making a big decision in one fell swoop. This is akin to the use of time-buying options, discussed in Section 3.2.3.

6. People v. Huffman, 88 Cal. App. 4th Supp. 1, 106 Cal. Rptr.2d 820 (2000).

Sunstein and Ullman-Margalit give the examples of Jane living with Robert before deciding whether to marry him, and observing of the Anglo-American common law tradition of deciding cases on as narrow a ground as possible.[7]

Delegation. Rather than make the decision yourself, you can delegate the responsibility to another individual or agency. A client may ask her lawyer to make a decision on her behalf; an administrative official may be required to delegate a decision to an agency.

Random processes. In addition to providing a fair way to resolve some interpersonal disputes, a random process like flipping a coin can quickly resolve *intra*personal disputes when you are faced with two equally attractive options and the choice doesn't justify further analysis.

4.3 DELIBERATIVE, NONCOMPENSATORY DECISION-MAKING STRATEGIES

Under a noncompensatory decision-making strategy, a strength in one attribute (e.g., the rent is very low) does not compensate for a weakness in another (e.g., the apartment has only two rooms).

Elimination by aspects (EBA) is a paradigmatic noncompensatory procedure. The decision maker identifies relevant attributes, assigning each a minimum threshold. She then assesses the alternatives in terms of the first attribute, eliminating alternatives that do not meet the threshold. If several alternatives remain, she evaluates them in terms of the next attribute, and so on. Ideally, but not inevitably in practice, the attributes are ordered in terms of their importance. EBA is cognitively pretty easy, and people make many decisions ranging from choosing restaurants and vacation destinations to buying cars using variations of EBA—often "quick and dirty" approximations.

Sometimes the threshold will follow inexorably from your values or needs—for example, a vegetarian would eliminate meat dishes in a restaurant before choosing among options for her entrée. But many thresholds are more matters of preference—for example, fresh rather than farm-raised salmon. If no available alternative meets your thresholds, you would reduce some of them and go through the procedure again.

What happens when several alternatives meet the threshold depends on your rule for stopping the search. For example, one of us (Paul) has a simple strategy for shopping for a suit. He has two attributes—whether he likes it and whether it is available in his size. When he sees the first suit that meets these thresholds he stops the search. To be sure, there may be even nicer suits in the store (let alone the wonderful suits in other stores), but all decision making involves a trade-off between the costs of decision making, including time and cognitive effort on the one hand and accuracy on the other—and he does not like shopping for clothes.

---

7. Sunstein and Ullman-Margalit, *supra*.

To understand how EBA works and see its limitations, let's consider the housing example in greater detail. Suppose that you are considering thirteen rental apartments, and that you rank the four major attributes in this order: cost, size, proximity to the campus, and neighborhood, with cost being the most important. You then determine a specific acceptability threshold for each attribute. For example, you cannot spend more than $1500 a month, and you need at least 600 square feet of space. Under EBA, you eliminate, say, eight apartments that have monthly rents greater than $1500. Of the five apartments remaining, you eliminate two studios with 575 square feet of floor space.

Each of the three remaining apartments costs about $1300 a month and has about 800 square feet of space. One is located in the more cosmopolitan downtown center—an eight-minute commute to campus; the two others are virtually adjacent to one another in a smaller, more suburban neighborhood north of the town—also an eight-minute commute to campus. Though the atmospheres and amenities of the two neighborhoods differ, each is pleasant, safe, and attractive in its own way.

EBA helped whittle thirteen choices down to three, all of which are satisfactory. But notice that the procedure can lead to a suboptimal outcome if the thresholds for the first several attributes were based on preferences rather than absolute necessities. Perhaps you eliminated an apartment that was a bit too expensive but that was so great in all other respects that it would have justified stretching your budget. This is an inherent limitation of any noncompensatory procedure.

Along similar lines, EBA may allow others to manipulate your rankings for their own interests. Amos Tversky provides this parodic example from an actual television commercial:

> "There are more than two dozen companies in the San Francisco area which offer training in computer programming." The announcer puts some two dozen eggs and one walnut on the table to represent the alternatives, and continues: "Let us examine the facts. How many of these schools have on-line computer facilities for training?" The announcer removes several eggs. "How many of these schools have placement services that would help you find a job?" The announcer removes some more eggs. "How many of these schools are approved for veteran's benefits?" This continues until the walnut alone remains. The announcer cracks the nutshell, which reveals the name of the company and concludes: "That's all you need to know in a nutshell."[8]

Suppose that you can attend the classes in person and would prefer to do so, that you are seeking training to advance in your current job, that you are not a veteran, etc. Perhaps the best instructors teach at places that lack all of the attributes touted by the commercial. In such a case, the EBA methodology outlined above would lead you far astray from your ideal outcome. EBA is only

8. Amos Tversky, *Elimination by Aspects: A Theory of Choice*, 79 Psychological Review 281 (1972).

useful if the aspects to be assessed are important to your decision-making process and if they are ordered in terms of their importance.

Fast and Frugal Heuristics

Gerd Gigerenzer and his colleagues argue that, in making factual judgments, people use "fast and frugal heuristics" similar to EBA. For example, in estimating the relative size of two cities, if we recognize the name of one but not the other, we will employ the "recognition heuristic" to conclude that if we recognize one city but not another, the recognized city is larger. Gigerenzer asserts that, in general, we tend to make judgments based on a single cue and only look to another as a tie-breaker if it doesn't produce a result. More generally, under the *take the best* heuristic, the decision maker tries cues in order, one at a time, searching for a cue that discriminates between the two objects in question. For example, "when inferring two professors' salaries, the [professorial] rank cue might be tried first. If both professors are of the same rank (say both associate professors), then the gender cue might be tried. If one of the professors is a woman and the other is a man, then we might say that the gender cue 'discriminates.' Once a discriminating cue is found, it serves as the basis for an inference, and all other cues are ignored. For instance, if gender discriminates between two professors, the inference is made that the male earns a higher salary, and no other information about years of experience or highest degree earned is considered."[9]

There is little doubt that people, in fact, often use simplifying decision procedures in making factual judgments as well as decisions. But there is serious controversy whether we employ only one cue at a time and, more fundamentally, whether fast and frugal heuristics tend to produce accurate judgments.[10]

4.4 COMPENSATORY PROCEDURES

As we mentioned, noncompensatory decision procedures such as EBA can yield outcomes that seem somewhat arbitrary. For example, if your highest priority in voting for a candidate for public office is her position on gun control, then a noncompensatory procedure may eliminate candidates who have the "wrong"

9. Gerd Gigerenzer, Peter M. Todd, and the ABC Research Group, Simple Heuristics that Make Us Smart 99 (New York: Oxford University Press, 1999).

10. *See, e.g.*, Daniel M. Oppenheimer, *Not So Fast! (and Not So Frugal!): Rethinking the Recognition Heuristic*, 90 Cognition B1 (2003); Mark G. Kelman, The Heuristics Debate: Its Nature and Its Implications for Law and Policy (Oxford University Press, forthcoming 2010).

position on this issue but who hold positions that you agree with on many other issues. Also, a noncompensatory procedure does not account well for your intensity of preferences. Unless gun control matters to you more than all other issues together, you may not be choosing the candidate who best reflects your interests.

In fact, most decisions invite making trade-offs among competing interests or objectives. For example, you might trade off the candidate's position on gun control with her position on other social and economic issues that you deem important. In choosing the apartment, you might be willing to trade off the rental price for proximity. One can approach making trade-offs by (1) giving *reasons* for one's choices or (2) assigning quantitative *values* to different attributes of the things being chosen.

4.4.1 Reason-Based Decision Strategies

Consider Charles Darwin's approach to trade-offs in these notes on a scrap of paper with the heading, "This is the question," as shown in Table 4.1.[11]

TABLE 4.1 DARWIN'S PROS AND CONS OF MARRIAGE

MARRY	Not MARRY
Children—(if it please God)—constant companion (friend in old age) who will be interested in one, object to be beloved and played with—better than a dog anyhow—Home, and someone to take care of house—Charms of music and female chit-chat. These things are good for one's health. Forced to visit and receive relations but *terrible loss of time*. My God, it is intolerable to think of spending one's whole life, like a neuter bee, working, working and nothing after all.—No, no won't do.—Imagine living all one's day solitarily in a smoky dirty London House.—Only picture to yourself a nice soft wife on a sofa with good fire, and books and music perhaps—compare this vision with the dingy reality of Grt. Marlboro' St.	No children (no second life) no one to care for one in old age. . . . Freedom to go where one liked—Choice of Society and *little of it*. Conversation of clever men at clubs—Not forced to visit relatives, and to bend in every trifle—to have the expense and anxiety of children—perhaps quarreling. Loss of time—cannot read in the evenings—fatness and idleness—anxiety and responsibility—less money for books, etc.—if many children, forced to gain one's bread. (But then it is very bad for one's health to work too much.) Perhaps my wife won't like London; then the sentence is banishment and degradation with indolent idle fool—

11. Charles Darwin, The Autobiography of Charles Darwin, 1809–1882, 232–33 (Nora Barlow ed., New York: Norton, 1969). *Quoted in* Gerd Gigerenzer, Peter M. Todd, and the ABC Research Group, *supra*, at 7.

At the bottom of the first column, Darwin wrote: "Marry—Marry—Marry Q.E.D.," though he also noted, "There is many a happy slave."[12]

The Importance that We (Sometimes) Attribute to Reasons

You are about to take the bar examination. If you pass the exam, you will celebrate with a week's vacation in Hawaii. If you fail the exam, you will console yourself with a week's vacation in Hawaii. Your travel agent says that you can lock in low airline fares now, and that the fares are sure to rise if you wait. Will you book the vacation now, or wait until you receive the results of the exam? In a study by Eldar Shafir, Itamar Simonson, and Amos Tversky, most students chose to pay the additional cost and wait. They wanted to choose the vacation for the "right" reason, which couldn't be known in advance.[13]

Darwin was applying a reason-based compensatory decision-making strategy—giving reasons for the pros and cons of the decision without explicitly assigning any weights to the criteria. In a letter to Joseph Priestly, Benjamin Franklin develops a pro-and-con approach into a somewhat more quantitative strategy:[14]

> When . . . difficult cases occur, they are difficult, chiefly because while we have them under consideration, all the reasons pro and con are not present to the mind at the same time; but sometimes some set present themselves, and at other times another, the first being out of sight. Hence the various purposes or inclinations that alternately prevail, and the uncertainty that perplexes us.
>
> To get over this, my way is to divide half a sheet of paper by a line into two columns; writing over the one pro, and over the other con. Then during three or four days' consideration, I put down under the different heads short hints

12. Note, by the way, the role of images, scenarios, and affect in Darwin's list-making. Recall Antonio Damasio's description of the role of affect in decision making in Section 1.5.3. As it turned out, Darwin married his cousin, Emma Wedgewood, in 1839, and they had ten children, many of them notable in their own right. Twenty years later, he published *On the Origin of Species by Means of Natural Selection.*

13. Eldar Shafir, Itamar Simonson, and Amos Tversky, *Reason-Based Choice,* 49 COGNITION (1993).

14. Benjamin Franklin to Joseph Priestly, September 19, 1772. At the time, Priestly was happily preaching and conducting scientific experiments. When offered the position of librarian to Lord Shelburne, he asked Franklin for advice. Rather than advise on the merits, Franklin offered a method of decision making.

> of the different motives, that at different times occur to me, for or against the measure.
>
> When I have thus got them all together in one view, I endeavor to estimate their respective weights; and where I find two, one on each side, that seem equal, I strike them both out. If I find a reason pro equal to two reasons con, I strike out the three. If I judge some two reasons con, equal to some three reasons pro, I strike out the five; and thus proceeding I find at length where the balance lies; and if, after a day or two of further consideration, nothing new that is of importance occurs on either side, I come to a determination accordingly.
>
> And, though the weight of reasons cannot be taken with the precision of algebraic quantities, yet when each is thus considered, separately and comparatively, and the whole lies before me, I think I can judge better, and am less liable to make a rash step, and in fact I have found great advantage from this kind of equation, in what may be called moral or prudential algebra.

Franklin's procedure of canceling the pros and cons of a decision is a rough approximation of quantifying the strength and importance of the attributes involved in the decision. Franklin seemed to have in mind a yes-no decision about whether to take a particular action. But you could extend his procedure to deciding among multiple alternatives, such as the choice among apartments. If you are choosing between two apartments, write down the pros and cons of each and do the cancellation. If you are choosing among more than two, you might begin with what appear to be relatively strong and weak candidates, then see if you can eliminate the weak one, and put another in its place.[15]

Almost surely, Darwin and Franklin did not think their processes would determine their decisions rather than inform their intuitions. But this is by no means a useless project. Indeed, as we suggest below, even when one uses a more quantitative process, it is always useful to perform an intuitive "reality check" at the end.

4.4.2 Quantitative Decision Strategies

> *"Value-focused thinking involves starting at the best and working to make it a reality. Alternative-focused thinking is starting with what is readily available and taking the best of the lot."*[16]

---

15. In Smart Choices, *supra*, Hammond, Keeney, and Raiffa describe how one can extend this procedure to handle multiple alternatives simultaneously.

16. Ralph L. Keeney, Value-Focused Thinking: A Path to Creative Decisionmaking 6 (Cambridge: Harvard University Press, 1992).

Consider these two policy decisions:[17]

1. A mayor must decide whether to approve a major new electric power generating station and, if so, where to locate it. There is need for more electricity, but a new station would worsen the city's air quality, and the mayor is concerned with the effects that his actions will have on:
   - the residents' health
   - their economic conditions
   - their psychological state
   - the economy of the city and the state
   - carbon dioxide and other greenhouse gas emissions
   - businesses
   - local politics
2. A city is considering alternative approaches to addressing a growing problem of drug addiction, which is thought to be responsible for a growing crime rate and the city's deterioration. The city's goals include:
   - reduce the number of addicts
   - reduce costs to the city
   - reduce crimes against property and persons
   - improve the quality of life and health of addicts
   - improve the quality of life of the city's residents
   - reduce organized crime
   - safeguard civil liberties and civil rights

Even if there were only two possible locations for the power plant and two possible strategies for dealing with the drug addiction problem, the number of interests involved would make it difficult to use Darwin's or Franklin's approach. With multiple locations or strategies, the problems become very complex.

4.5 A SUBJECTIVE LINEAR MODEL: SITING A WASTEWATER TREATMENT PLANT

In fact, there are a variety of sophisticated quantitative techniques for addressing the trade-offs among multiple objectives.[18] They are rooted in Multi-Attribute Utility Theory (MAUT) and are taught in decision analysis courses in business, engineering, and public policy schools. Here, we shall introduce a rather simple approach, sometimes called a *subjective linear model*. The model is *subjective* because the weightings and ratings ultimately depend on the decision maker's preferences—whether as an individual acting on her own behalf or as an agent

---

17. Ralph L. Keeney and Howard Raiffa, Decisions with Multiple Objectives: Preferences and Value Tradeoffs 1–2 (New York: Cambridge University Press, 1993).

18. *See* Keeney and Raiffa; Keeney, Value-Focused Thinking.

acting on behalf of a public, private, or nonprofit entity. It is *linear* because preferences are aggregated simply through addition.

Although simple both in concept and use, the subjective linear model is quite robust and will take you quite a way toward solving even complex problems. We will illustrate it with an example.

The mayor of Edenville has asked Christine Lamm to staff a task force on siting a wastewater treatment plant. The city's current wastewater treatment plant no longer meets the demands of its growing population. To further complicate the problem, the majority of the population growth is occurring in the northern outskirts of Edenville, far away from the city's only current treatment plant in south central Edenville. While the houses in this formerly rural area are currently served by septic systems, the projected growth will require connections to sewer lines.

Lamm considers the options broadly:

(1) Expand/upgrade the existing plant with new technology to make it more efficient, and construct new pipelines to the north.
(2) Select a site for a new wastewater treatment plant, preferably in the north.

This problem pits several competing interests—environmental, economic, and political—against each other.

The expansion/upgrade option may be less expensive and less contentious, and will also solve the immediate problem by increasing capacity enough to meet current needs with more efficient technology. However, the siting of a new facility may better serve the city's longer term needs if growth trends continue. And, a new facility may be able to benefit more from new technology that allows not only better treatment, but also reduced energy consumption. However, the community's only reference point is the current plant, a smelly, outdated eyesore, blamed for the blight in south central Edenville. If not handled carefully, the proposal of a new facility is likely to stir up public opposition of the usual NIMBY (not in my backyard) variety. Lamm, while cognizant of the political expediency of the upgrade option, has an intuitive preference for a new facility that would serve the growing community's long term interests. Lamm would also like to see if she can incorporate some of her mayor's green initiatives into the wastewater treatment plant solution.

Lamm decided to conduct the decision process in a highly transparent manner with community outreach and public involvement. She believes that early and regular public involvement is likely to result in the best outcome, to produce the best project site and design, to encourage public buy-in from various stakeholders, and to reduce the likelihood of litigation. She met with her staff to prepare a list of objectives for the site selection to be discussed at the first public meeting.[19]

19. For the assertion that objectives-based thinking is superior to alternative-based thinking, *see* KEENEY 29–52.

1. Meet long-term capacity needs.
2. Incorporate green initiatives.
3. Provide truck access that minimizes traffic through residential neighborhoods.
4. Site the plant in proximity to source and treated water release locations to minimize pump stations.
5. Minimize costs.

She directed her staff to prepare a fact sheet on "Our Growing Need for Water Solutions" that will explain the city's current capacity crisis. She requested that staff explain that the need for additional wastewater treatment capacity in north Edenville is due to that community's surging growth, which has strained the current plant. Quality wastewater treatment is critical to protect public health and the environment, including threatened and endangered species. A new or improved plant is essential for further development in the north part of the city. The existing wastewater treatment plant is burdened by high operating costs due to overloading, failing equipment, and operating problems, resulting in excessive energy use.

Lamm's staff posted the fact sheet on the city's Web site, placed the "Water Solutions" issue on the next city council meeting's agenda, and invited the public to attend this important meeting. At the city council meeting, the staff presented their preliminary list of objectives and submitted them for public comment. Several community members presented additional concerns, which the staff framed as community objectives.

Community objectives:

1. Maintain/improve high water quality.
2. Dedicate adequate land for odor containment and screening.
3. Reduce impacts of construction, traffic, noise.
4. Maintain property values.

The interested parties who spoke during the public comment period included a community organizer on behalf of the south central residents to express her community's frustration with the odors and noise of the current plant and to argue for a northern site as the only equitable location given that the population growth is centered in the north. New northern residents spoke against the siting of a new facility in the north due to concerns about property values, odors, and compatibility with the residential community. (Residents were skeptical about a city engineer's statement that odors were contained by filtering air emissions from the plant's exhaust.)

Residents from the neighboring city to the north, Pleasantville, expressed concern that siting a new facility at its border would negatively impact their community. Several environmentalists stressed the need for cleaner, greener technology at the plant, possible initiatives for reduction of wastewater through recycled water, and the importance of exceeding clean water regulations to ensure the best water quality for the community.

Lamm asked the staff to incorporate the public comments, accepted the additional (community) objectives, and directed the staff to post the "Shared Objectives" list on the city's Web site. She hoped that, by generating a list of shared objectives, she would incorporate early community input while still retaining the ultimate decision-making power.

In continuing with this example, we shall use the term *alternatives* to describe the things to be chosen among (e.g., possible sites for wastewater treatment plant). And we shall call the features (e.g., capacity, costs) that make an alternative more or less attractive *attributes*, criteria, or aspects. By definition, a decision involves two or more alternatives. Most difficult decisions involve several attributes.

Lamm's decision procedure involves these steps:

1. Identify the major attributes affecting the decision.
2. Identify the alternatives or options facing the decision maker.
3. Evaluate (objectively or subjectively, as the case may be) the attributes for each alternative.
4. Translate the evaluations into normalized values.
5. Aggregate the evaluations for each alternative and compare the alternatives.
6. Perform a reality check.

4.5.1 Identify the Major Attributes Affecting the Decision

The attributes flow from Lamm's objectives. She directs her staff to translate the shared objectives into attributes for the site selection, and they produce the following list:

1. *Adequate size*: Site size with sufficient area usable for long-term capacity needs, odor containment, and screening.
2. *Environmental impacts*: Minimize real and perceived impacts on air (odors), land, water, and endangered species.
3. *Low traffic impacts*: Truck access that minimizes traffic through residential neighborhoods.
4. *Low land costs*: Minimize costs, inexpensive land, efficient planning, and construction.
5. *Low pipeline lengths and costs*: Minimize costs of wastewater transportation, including pumping stations; keep site proximate to growing sewage sources and proximate to treated water release location; and minimize costs of pipelines.
6. *Compatibility*: Ensure compatibility with surrounding land uses, and design plant to integrate with neighboring uses.

Lamm decides to treat *"greenness"* as a *decision opportunity* to be discussed later rather than as a specific attribute. In the final trade-off analysis, she will look for opportunities to incorporate positive enhancements like habitat restoration, hiking trails, and rooftop gardens.

4.5.2 Identify the Alternatives or Options Facing the Decision Maker

Lamm's staff then evaluates the most promising of the available sites, considering demolition of existing structures, the presence of hazardous materials, zoning regulations, impacts on adjacent property values, compatibility with neighboring activities, downstream uses, wetlands, and endangered species. Based on this analysis, the staff prepares a list of four alternatives, as shown in Figure 4.1, including one alternative for the expansion/upgrade option:

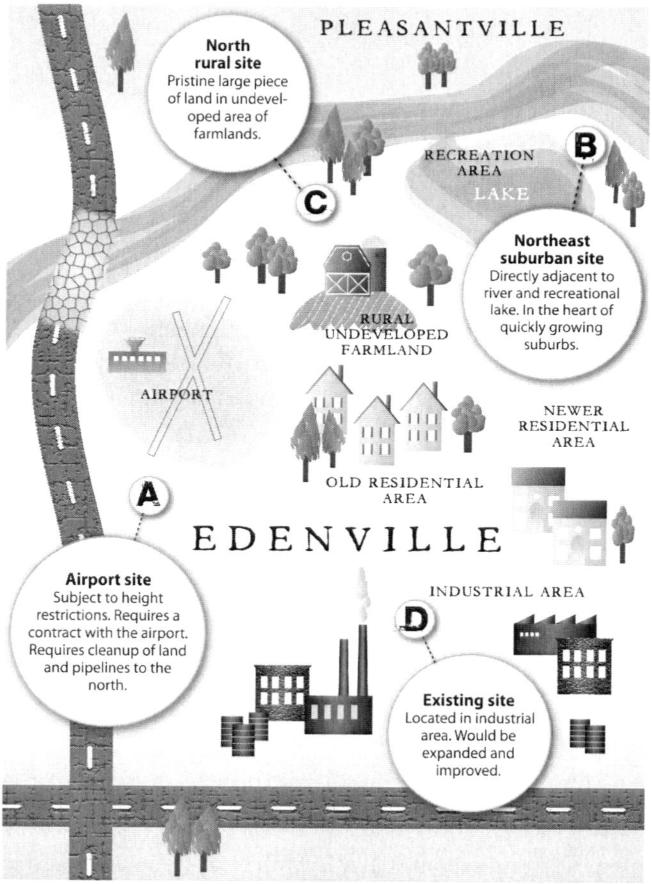

FIGURE 4.1 EDENVILLE.

- *Site A.* Airport site. This site, directly adjacent to the Edenville Municipal Airport, is in the outer, western section of Edenville. This site would be subject to height restrictions imposed by flight paths maintained by the airport and would necessitate a contract with the airport. Initial cleanup of land and pipelines to the north would be required.
- *Site B.* Northeast suburban site. This site is directly adjacent to a river that feeds into a lake that is used for recreational activities. It is in the heart of the quickly growing northern suburban land.
- *Site C.* Outermost north rural site. This site features a pristine piece of large land in the northernmost section of Edenville. This area mostly contains farmlands and is not yet impacted by development pressures.
- *Site D.* Expansion/upgrade of existing site. This major expansion option would transport sewage from the growing population center in outer Edenville to the existing, large wastewater treatment plant in south central Edenville by laying pipelines through neighborhoods. The existing plant would be greatly expanded and equipped with new technology to make it more efficient.

4.5.3 Evaluate (Objectively or Subjectively, as the Case May Be) the Attributes for Each Alternative

Lamm considers each alternative in turn:

- *Site A.* The airport area, which is not residential but industrial, presents a site compatible with the plant. The flight paths would likely be easy to accommodate. However, this site, while politically optimal, requires a large economic investment in the cleanup of the land due to illegal dumping and existing structures. Because of its location, this site would also require costly pipelines to the north.
- *Site B.* This site is located optimally for proximity to influent sources, since it is at the heart of the growing residential community. It will reduce the number of pump stations involved. However, it is also greatly impacted by development pressures, making any land expensive and limiting the size of any facility. Similarly, the recreational character of the adjacent area makes industrial use of this site problematic. Also, the downstream recreational uses would require that the quality of the effluent from the waste treatment plant be fairly high.
- *Site C.* This site provides the most space, with the capacity to screen the plant. It sits high on hill, however, and would affect the view for the population in north Edenville. Also, the site is the habitat of some small animals, an issue which may be raised by environmental organizations.
- *Site D.* This expansion/upgrade option includes a lower capital cost for treatment facilities and avoids the need to site new treatment facilities. This option is attractive because most community members prefer the maximum

use of the existing wastewater treatment plant before siting a new one. With investment in new technology, the upgraded plant could make use of existing infrastructure for space-efficient increase of treatment capacity and effluent quality. However, the disadvantages are the costly pipelines, technology investment, size limits, and environmental justice issues.

Lamm first creates a chart using qualitative words to describe the values of the attributes for each possible site as shown in Table 4.2.

TABLE 4.2 WASTEWATER TREATMENT PLANT: QUALITATIVE DESCRIPTION OF ATTRIBUTES

Site	Size	Enviro Impacts	Traffic Impacts	Land Cost	Pipeline Lengths	Compatible
A	Good	Very good	Good	Poor, due to cleanup	Good	Very good
B	Good	Poor	Poor	Very poor	Ideal	Poor
C	Very good	Poor	Poor	Very good	Very good	Okay
D	Poor	Very good	Good	Very good	Poor	Okay

4.5.4 Translate the Evaluations into Normalized Values

Using a 100-point grade scale where the highest score is 100, she then translates her evaluation of the attributes into rankings on this scale, as shown in Table 4.3. Once she begins to use numbers, she makes finer gradations than when she used words. For example, Lamm thinks that both the Site A and Site B provide adequate sized land, but she gives the airport site a slight edge.

TABLE 4.3 WASTEWATER TREATMENT PLANT: QUANTITATIVE DESCRIPTION OF ATTRIBUTES

Site	Size		Enviro Impacts		Traffic Impacts		Land Cost		Pipeline Lengths		Compatible	
		Score		Score		Score		Score		Score		Score
A	Good	80	Very good	90	Good	85	Poor, due to cleanup	60	Good	75	Very good	90
B	Good	75	Poor	60	Poor	60	Very poor	50	Ideal	100	Poor	60
C	Very good	100	Poor	50	Poor	50	Very good	95	Very good	90	Okay	65
D	Poor	50	Very good	85	Good	80	Very good	100	Poor	50	Okay	70

She then sums up the score of the attributes for each site, as shown in Table 4.4

TABLE 4.4 WASTEWATER TREATMENT PLANT: AGGREGATE EVALUATIONS

Site	Size	Enviro Impacts	Traffic Impacts	Land Cost	Pipeline Lengths	Compatible	Total
A	80	90	85	60	75	90	**480**
B	75	60	60	50	100	60	**405**
C	100	50	50	95	90	65	**450**
D	50	85	80	100	50	70	**435**

4.5.5 Aggregate the Evaluations for Each Alternative and Compare the Alternatives

Site A has the highest score, followed at a distance by Site C.

4.5.6 Perform a Reality Check

Finally, Lamm thinks again about each of the site options—especially the top two scores—and asks whether the decision in favor of the Site A (airport site) makes "gut sense." After all, the procedure is only designed to aid her in making and explaining or justifying an essentially subjective decision—to help her clarify her thinking by disaggregating the factors involved in the decision.

Her procedure makes some simplifying assumptions. It assumes that the attributes are essentially independent of each other.[20] This is not always the case. For example, the pipeline lengths might be related to environmental impacts.[21]

4.5.7 Weight the Attributes: A Possible Additional Step

The procedure also assumes that each of the attributes—size, environmental impacts, etc.—is equally valuable. In fact, Lamm might believe that some of these are more important than others and want to weight the decision process accordingly. She could therefore add one more wrinkle to this procedure before undertaking the reality check. She could rank the attributes in importance and

---

20. *See, e.g.*, Paul Kleindorfer, Howard Kunreuther, and Paul Schoemaker, Decision Sciences: An Integrative Perspective 137–39 (New York: Cambridge University Press, 1993).

21. There are multi-attribute decision approaches that are designed to reflect the fact that some of our preferences are nonlinear. Indeed, through a process known as conjoint analysis, it is possible to assess an individual's utility for two or more attributes and determine trade-offs without engaging in the rather abstract weighting process that Christine Lamm engaged in. *See* Jonathan Baron, Thinking and Deciding 340 (3rd ed. New York: Cambridge University Press, 2000).

assign percentages to each one so that percentages all add up to 100 percent, with (say) these results:

Size	20%
Enviro Impacts	15%
Traffic Impacts	15%
Land Cost	5%
Pipeline Lengths	20%
Compatible	25%

At this point, Lamm would multiply each attribute's normalized value by its weight (step 4 above), as shown in Table 4.5.

TABLE 4.5 WASTEWATER TREATMENT PLANT: WEIGHTED ATTRIBUTES

Site	Size (20%)		Enviro Impacts (15%)		Traffic Impacts (15%)		Land Cost (5%)		Pipeline Lengths (20%)		Compatible (25%)	
	Score	Score x weight	Score	Score x weight	Score	Score x weight	Score	Score x weight	Score	Score x weight	Score	Score x weight
A	80	16	90	13.5	85	12.75	60	3	75	15	90	22.5
B	75	15	60	9	60	9	50	2.5	100	20	60	15
C	100	20	50	7.5	50	7.5	95	4.75	90	18	65	16.25
D	50	10	85	12.75	80	12	100	5	50	10	70	17.5

She would then sum up and compare the final scores for each firm, as shown in Table 4.6.

TABLE 4.6 WASTEWATER TREATMENT PLANT: AGGREGATE WEIGHTED SCORES

Site	Size (20%)	Enviro Impacts (15%)	Traffic Impacts (15%)	Land Cost (5%)	Pipeline Lengths (20%)	Compatible (25%)	Total
	Score x weight	Score x weight	Score x weight	Score x weight	Score x weight	Score x weight	
A	16	13.5	12.75	3	15	22.5	**82.75**
B	15	9	9	2.5	20	15	**70.5**
C	20	7.5	7.5	4.75	18	16.25	**74**
D	10	12.75	12	5	10	17.5	**67.25**

Even with this weighted adjustment, Site A and Site C still lead the choices, confirming the earlier unweighted findings.

Is the additional step worthwhile? The calculations don't take much effort, but if you put yourself in Lamm's shoes or, more accurately, in her head, you may find it difficult to assign weights to the attributes and may be left feeling that the weightings are pretty arbitrary. In fact, there are some useful strategies for determining a decision maker's weightings.[22] But it turns out that a simple non-weighted process works pretty well, even for complex decisions.[23]

In any event, a subjective linear model has clear advantages over noncompensatory procedures for making decisions with multiple alternatives and attributes. Though it may be tedious, it is computationally simple. It is especially useful when a decision must be based on a number of different people's input, because it tends to make the potential differences in their desires or values explicit.

4.5.8 Decision Opportunities[24]

Bearing in mind that the choices are now very close in value and that assessing the risks associated with the initial project costs and likely delays at Site A is extremely difficult, Lamm reviews her options in light of a consideration she shelved earlier—making the wastewater treatment plan "green." She always thought that this would be a benefit. She could have included it in the formal analysis, but left it out because it was not a high public priority. But she can now use it as a tie-breaker.

It is clear that Site C provides the more green opportunities as compared to Site A. Its large, pristine space, affords great potential for hiking trails and other compatible recreational uses, rooftop gardens, community educational center, and beautiful views, which should assuage the neighboring city's fears. Lamm enjoys the idea of turning an undesirable project into a landmark and community asset. She decides to include several other green initiatives to help allay the environmental concerns regarding development in Edenville's valued open space. She would like to impose green construction requirements, like solar panels, on the building. She would also like to incorporate community-wide wastewater reduction measures, such as incentives for Edenville residents to install low-flow toilets, to help allay the environmental concerns of developing the open space. With this vision in mind and her growing discomfort with the likely hassles of Site A, Lamm now confidently pursues Site C as the preferred option.

---

22. For example, under the process of *conjoint analysis* mentioned in a previous footnote, one would determine Lamm's utility function by interrogating her about many hypothetical trade-offs.

23. *See* Section 10.5.1; Robyn Dawes, *The Robust Beauty of Improper Linear Models in Decision Making*, 39 AMERICAN PSYCHOLOGIST 571–82 (1979).

24. For a description of decision opportunities, *see* KEENEY, VALUE-FOCUSED THINKING, 241–67.

4.6 SUMMARY: THE FEATURES OF DIFFERENT DECISION-MAKING STRATEGIES

Table 4.7 summarizes the salient features of some of the different decision-making strategies outlined above. "Transparency" refers to how clearly one can articulate and explain the basis for the decision—which are predicates for discussing it with others and justifying it to them.[25]

TABLE 4.7 CHARACTERISTICS OF DIFFERENT DECISION-MAKING STRATEGIES

Method	What Sorts of Decisions	Quality	Effort	Transparency
Rules, presumptions	Repetitive	Varies	Low	High
Intuition, heuristics	All	Varies	Low	Very low
Noncompensatory	All	Moderate	Moderate	Moderate to high
Compensatory	All	High	High	High

Most decisions about which lawyers are asked to counsel clients are not of the repetitive sort that would permit using rules. And although clients may sometimes ask a lawyer for her "gut reaction," good counseling usually calls for a transparent process in which the client's interests and the extent to which alternatives satisfy them are articulated and discussed.

The range of public policy decisions is huge, with many being rule-based or amenable to formal decision-making processes and others calling for on-the-spot assessments that preclude formalization. The administrative law scholar Thomas O. McGarity writes of two different ways of thinking about administrative decision making:[26]

> Although the goal of rational agency decisionmaking seems unexceptional, its proponents had in mind a very ambitious agenda. They meant to interject a new and very different way of thinking into a firmly entrenched bureaucratic culture. Following the conventional nomenclature, we may label this new kind of thinking "comprehensive analytical rationality." The term "comprehensive" suggests that this kind of thinking ideally explores all possible routes to the solution of a problem. The term "analytical" implies that it

25. The table is based on J. Edward Russo and Paul J.J. Schoemaker, Winning Decisions 155 (New York: Doubleday, 2002).

26. Thomas O. McGarity, Reinventing Rationality—The Role of Regulatory Analysis in the Federal Bureaucracy 6–7 (New York: Cambridge University Press, 1991).

attempts to sort out, break down, and analyze (quantitatively, if possible) all of the relevant components of a problem and its possible solutions. The term "rationality" captures the pride that its proponents take in its objectivity and the dispassion with which it debates the pros and cons of alternative solutions without regard to whose ox is being gored. In practice, comprehensive analytical rationality has been dominated by the paradigms of neoclassical micro-economics.

This kind of rationality contrasts sharply with the thinking that has traditionally dominated the rulemaking process in most regulatory agencies, which I shall refer to as "techno-bureaucratic rationality." I use the term techno-bureaucratic to distinguish the thinking that dominates highly technical rulemaking activities that must grapple with highly complex (and often unresolvable) issues of science, engineering, and public policy. Some of the existing models of bureaucratic thinking, such as Lindblom's perceptive "muddling through" model, are relevant to bureaucratic programs that have highly technical, scientific, and engineering components. I use the word "rationality" because, unlike many students of regulation, I do not believe that this kind of thinking is irrational per se. Techno-bureaucratic rationality is a rationality built on a unique understanding of the regulatory universe that is born out of frustrating hands-on experience with unanswerable questions of extraordinary complexity. It is, in a sense, a "second best" rationality that recognizes the limitations that inadequate data, unquantifiable values, mixed societal goals, and political realities place on the capacity of structured rational thinking, and it does the best that it can with what it has.

All things being equal—that is, given sufficient time, cognitive capacity, and patience—value-based decision making is more transparent and seems more likely to satisfy stakeholders' long-run needs than its alternatives. But all things are seldom equal. People appropriately tend to reserve full-fledged decision value-based models (of which we have provided the most simple example) for a very limited number of important decisions, where it is plausible to quantify or at least ordinally rank the attributes of each alternative.

PART TWO

MAKING SENSE OF AN UNCERTAIN WORLD

Life is the art of drawing sufficient conclusions from insufficient premises.
—Samuel Butler

Most issues that lawyers and policy makers encounter involve uncertainties. We may be uncertain about what happened in the past: what caused the tenants' rashes and other symptoms at Terra Nueva? And we are inevitably uncertain about what will happen in the future: what is the likelihood that a particular approach to eradicating malaria will actually work? How much do we need to reduce greenhouse gas emissions to prevent the earth's temperature from rising more than 2 degrees, and what will happen if it does rise more?

Part 2 is devoted to *judgment* in the empirical sense of how one ascertains or predicts facts about the physical and social worlds in situations of uncertainty. It focuses mainly on the past—on whether a particular event or phenomenon occurred and on understanding its nature. Often—as in the case of assessing liability for a tort or crime—the past is of legal interest in its own right. And almost always understanding what occurred in the past is essential to making forward-looking decisions. For example, the decision whether to ban the use of a putatively toxic product will be based on evidence about what happened to people who were (or were not) exposed to it in the past.

THE CHALLENGES OF DETECTING CORRELATION AND IMPUTING CAUSATION

Whether one's interest is backward- or forward-looking, the central question is usually one of *causation*. Sometimes, causation can be established directly through observation of the event—for example, an eyewitness saw the defendant's car run into the plaintiff's. In these situations, while there may be conflicting evidence, the fundamental paradigm is a Newtonian model of cause and effect. In many other cases, though, the evidence is essentially of a probabilistic nature. For example, even in the absence of knowledge of the process by which a supposed toxic substance causes illness, causation may be hypothesized based on the correlation of many instances of the putative cause (exposure to a pesticide) and effects (illnesses) and the exclusion of other possible causes. By the same token, predicting the consequences of most decisions is a probabilistic enterprise that requires taking into account various uncertainties.

Correlation by no means entails causation, but correlation is usually a necessary condition for inferring and imputing causation. Many if not most of the empirical judgments made by lawyers, policy makers, and individuals in their personal decisions involve detecting correlation between events in order to make judgments about causation.[1] On what data can they base their conclusions?

The examples from Terra Nueva and Big-Mart to be considered in Chapters 5 and 6 involve fairly large datasets—large enough that we can use statistical techniques to understand relationships between supposed independent variables or predictors and dependent or outcome variables. By contrast, in our everyday professional and personal lives we must often make assessments of correlation based on relatively small samples in situations that do not provide very good information or allow for generalization. Often, we depend on feedback from our own experiences. Consider these situations:

- *Multiple and not necessarily clearly defined outcome variables.* Consider the number of indicators of what constitutes a good employee or a good public policy decision and the number and vagueness of the attributes of "goodness" in these contexts.
- *Multiple and ambiguous predictors.* Consider the number of factors that go into an employer's predicting whether candidates will perform well on the job, or a trial lawyer's predicting whether prospective jurors will be inclined toward, or at least not biased against, her client.
- *Feedback only on positive decisions.* The employer and trial lawyer never see the performance of the candidates they rejected, and thus never have the opportunity to learn whether they would have been satisfactory.
- *No feedback at all.* One of the authors met a diagnostic radiologist at a party. The radiologist examines X-rays and MRIs and then communicates his conclusions to orthopedists. Asked (not entirely innocently) whether the orthopedists then tell him whether his diagnoses were correct, he responded that they often do not.
- *Delayed feedback.* Contrast the feedback available to a meteorologist who forecasts the daily weather with that available to most employers, lawyers, and policy makers.
- *Self-fulfilling prophecies and treatment effects.* Having hired the candidate, the employer has a vested interest in having him succeed and may act to make

1. Richard Nisbett and Lee Ross, Human Inference: Strategies and Shortcomings of Social Judgment (Englewood Cliffs, NJ: Prentice Hall, 1980)

that happen. Consider the not uncommon situated where a teacher believes that a student will succeed or fail and, as a result of the "Pygmalion effect," helps make the prediction true. A famous series of experiments on the determinants of worker productivity at the Western Electric Company's Hawthorne plant showed that productivity was increased by virtually any intervention that made the workers feel important and valued—the so-called *Hawthorne effect.*[2]

THE LENS MODEL

The "lens" model, first proposed by Egon Brunswik, and later developed by Kenneth Hammond, Robin Hogarth, and others,[3] provides a particularly helpful way of conceptualizing the tasks of empirical inquiry under conditions of uncertainty. The model assumes that there is a "real world" out there—we'll call it the *environment*—and that it is the observer's task to use available evidence, or indicators, to discover it.[4] We offer our own, slightly revised version as shown in Figure A.

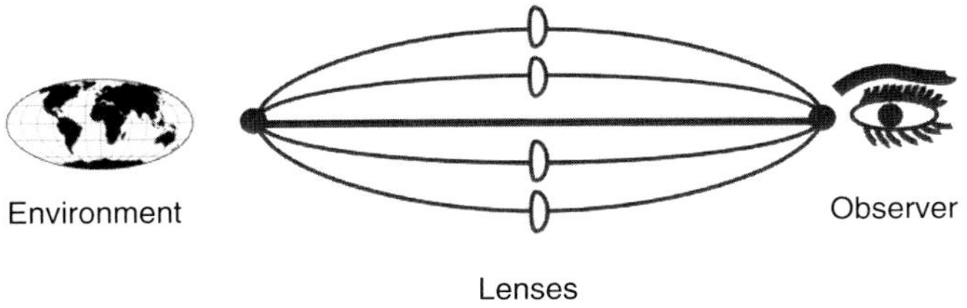

FIGURE A THE LENS MODEL.

2. Richard Herbert Franke and James D. Kaul, *The Hawthorne Experiments: First Statistical Interpretation*, 43 AMERICAN SOCIOLOGICAL REVIEW 623–643 (1978).

3. KENNETH R HAMMOND, HUMAN JUDGMENT AND SOCIAL POLICY: IRREDUCIBLE UNCERTAINTY, INEVITABLE ERROR, UNAVOIDABLE INJUSTICE (New York: Oxford University Press, 2000). ROBIN HOGARTH, HUMAN JUDGEMENT AND SOCIAL CHOICE (2d ed. New York: John Wiley & Sons, 1987).

4. While this is inconstant with the wildest version of postmodernism, it is entirely consistent with the notion that reality is "socially constructed"—that is, that there is no one right or universal way to describe things, events, or phenomena. One need only look at the contemporary debates over abortion to see two very different views about what it means to be a "person," with vastly different moral and legal implications for terminating its existence. In the end, though, the question whether someone did in fact terminate its existence (whatever the disagreement about the nature of the "it") is a fact subject to empirical study—a fact that can be known with some degree of certitude.

On the left side is the environment, or real world. One can think of the lines emanating from the environment as *indicators* of its actual features or characteristics. A fundamental characteristic of the environment is that it is *probabilistic*—that is, the real world is accessible only through what Hammond terms *multiple fallible indicators*: The relationship between the real world and its indicators cannot be represented by strict functional rules, but only as probabilities.[5]

On the right side is the observer's *perception* of reality, or judgment, as he or she seeks to integrate those multiple fallible indicators into a coherent understanding of the real world. But perception inevitably takes place through lenses, depicted in the center—lenses that can be more or less distorted.

To use a simple perceptual example: You're waiting on a corner to meet your friend Karen for lunch. You see an object in motion on a sidewalk. The light reflecting off the object (the left side of the lens diagram) shows its features, its gait, and its apparel. As it gets closer, you discern a human being . . . a woman . . . Karen. You wave to her. But as she gets still closer, you realize that it's not Karen after all, but a stranger. What happened? The characteristics were ambiguous—-multiple fallible indicators. Moreover, your perception of those indicators was not "neutral"—for example, it incorporated whatever schemas were active in your mind at the time: you were supposed to meet Karen at this very time and place and therefore expected that the person would be her.

In many legal applications, the person making the ultimate judgment—let's say a judge hearing a civil case—will not have direct access to the event but must rely on reports of others' perceptions. For example, suppose that a judge is trying to determine whether Donna sideswiped Patricia's car while it was parked at the supermarket. Donna denies being at the scene. An eyewitness testifies that she saw Donna graze the car and drive off. An expert testifies that paint scratched onto Patricia's car matches that of Donna's. The lens model applies not only to each witness's recollection of what he or she observed, but also to the judge's perception of the statements of each witness. Consider the many ambiguities in the evidence and the opportunities for distortion both in people's initial perception and in their recollection. (One might think of the adversary model,

---

5. Hogarth, *supra* at 10. For all practical purposes, it does not matter whether the uncertainty is inherent in the environment or only reflects our limited access to the environment (as it really is). In either case, we are saddled with the lack of certainty.

Hammond notes that the indicators can be fallible on two dimensions: the accuracy of information or the accuracy of the cue or indicator reflecting the information. Using the term "ecological" to refer to its relationship to the environment, or real world, he writes: "Accuracy of *information* can be described in terms of its *ecological reliability*; the accuracy of a *cue* or *indicator* is described as its *ecological validity*." For example, while wind direction may have a high ecological validity for predicting rain, holding up one's finger to the wind is unreliable compared to a wind gauge. Hammond, *supra* at 170.

including rules of evidence and direct and cross examination, as designed to help the judge identify those distortions.)

Finally, consider Christine Lamm's task of determining whether the polyurethane foam caused the illnesses supposedly experienced by the tenants of Terra Nueva Properties. Epidemiological data concerning the relationship between exposure to the foam and illness are nothing but a bunch of fallible indicators, which can only be effectively sorted out through statistical methods. Any conclusion will be explicitly couched in term of the probability of a relationship existing.

THE ROLES OF INTUITION AND ANALYSIS IN EMPIRICAL JUDGMENT

The goal of factual judgment is to understand some aspect of the world as it really is. We make thousands of such judgments a day, most of them unconsciously and intuitively. Only on a highly selective basis do we engage in conscious analysis. When you are about to cross the street and see a car only in the far distance, you don't give it a second thought—perhaps not even a first thought. Yet if the car is close to the intersection, you may consciously consider whether you can safely cross before it arrives. In Chapter 1, we broadly considered the roles of intuition and analysis in professional decisions. Here we focus particularly on their role in making empirical or factual judgments. In this regard, it is helpful to consider the traditional stages of the *scientific method*.[6]

1. Observing phenomena,
2. speculating to form hypotheses,
3. testing the hypotheses, and
4. generalizing to create a rule or set of objective criteria, typically of the form: *if cause then effect.*

To invoke Hans Reichenbach's useful distinction, the first two stages concern the process of scientific *discovery* while the latter two concern the process of scientific *justification*.[7] (Consider the analogy to the processes of divergent and convergent thinking discussed in the preceding chapters.) As Richard Wasserstrom put it:[8]

---

6. This description, though highly conceptualized and oversimplified, in effect sets out the ground rules for empirical inquiry and proof. For a more nuanced and sophisticated discussion, *see* Hugh G. Gauch, Jr., Scientific Method in Practice (Cambridge: Cambridge University Press, 2002).

7. Hans Reichenbach, Experience and Prediction (Chicago: University of Chicago Press, 1938).

8. Richard A. Wasserstrom, The Judicial Decision: Toward a Theory of Justification 25–28 (Stanford, CA: Stanford University Press, 1961). Wasserstrom draws

> One kind of question asks about the manner in which a decision or conclusion was reached; the other inquires whether a given decision or conclusion is justifiable. . . .
>
> Consider: . . . A scientist who has discovered a vaccine which purportedly provides complete immunization against cancer informs the scientific community that he hit upon this particular chemical combination in the following manner. He wrote down 1,000 possible chemical combinations on separate pieces of paper, put them all into a big hat, and pulled out the pieces at random. . . . The scientist has announced how he arrived at the conclusion that this chemical formula might immunize against cancer, but of course he has not answered the question of whether the vaccine will in fact immunize. . . . Whether this formula is an effective vaccine is a quite different one. Furthermore, if *ex hypothesi* the vaccine were effective, it certainly would not be rejected because of the way in which the scientist selected it for testing. . .

The example is not purely hypothetical. Friedrich August Kekulé von Stradonitz, who is credited with discovering the structure of benzene, said that it came to him in a dream of a snake eating its own tail.

Intuition is critical to the second of the four stages of the process, and it also plays roles in observation, hypothesis testing, and generalization.[9]

Part 2 considers essentially three questions. First, what are, in effect, "best practices" for engaging in these processes in a formal, analytic way? Second, in what ways do people systematically deviate from these practices, and with what consequences? And finally, what, if any, useful generalizations can one make about the roles of intuition and analysis in empirical judgment?

---

the analogy between these two processes and an appellate judge's developing intuitions about the correct decision in a case from justifying the decision. The former is analogous to the speculative process of developing a hypothesis under the scientific method, while the latter is analogous to the process of testing and generalizing a hypothesis. He writes that "to insist—as many legal philosophers appear to have done—that a judicial opinion is an accurate description of the decision process there employed if and only if it faithfully describes the procedure of discovery is to help guarantee that the opinion will be found wanting. But if the opinion is construed to be a report of the justificatory procedure employed by the judge, then the not infrequent reliance on such things as rules of law and rules of logic seems more plausible."

9. The process is often recursive, with testing and generalizing leading to new observations and hypotheses. Hence Michael Polanyi's description of a mathematician's work as an alternation between intuition and analysis. MICHAEL POLANYI, PERSONAL KNOWLEDGE: TOWARDS A POST-CRITICAL PHILOSOPHY 130–31 (New York: Harper & Row, 1964).

THE ROLE OF STATISTICS IN LAW, POLICY, AND CITIZENSHIP

Statistical thinking will one day be as important for good citizenship as the ability to read and write.
—H.G. Wells[10]

I keep saying that the sexy job in the next 10 years will be statisticians. And I'm not kidding.
—Hal Varian, chief economist, Google[11]

The "best practices" for testing empirical hypotheses are rooted in statistics. Examples of statistics abound in legal disputes, some of which involve major issues of public policy. The evidence in *Anne Anderson v. W.R. Grace & Co.*, made famous by *A Civil Action*, involved alleged correlations between drinking water from contaminated wells and childhood leukemia in Woburn, Massachusetts. Statistical evidence has played a central role in litigation concerning asbestos, silicone breast implants, electromagnetic radiation from cell phones, and autism putatively caused by the mercury preservative in childhood vaccines. In *Castenada v. Partida*,[12] the Supreme Court relied on statistical analysis of the correlation between Mexican Americans in the population and on grand juries to conclude that Mexican Americans were systematically excluded from grand jury service. In *Hazelwood Independent School District v. United States*,[13] the Court applied a similar analysis to determine whether the school district discriminated in the hiring of African American teachers.

Beyond their professional identities, lawyers and policy makers are citizens, consumers, and community leaders. If nothing else, basic concepts of probability and statistics will improve their understanding of newspaper articles on health, the environment, and many other subjects and give them a healthy skepticism about claims made by advocates, businesses, and governments.

This hardly entails that every lawyer, policy maker, and citizen must be a statistician. But it does suggest that you should grasp the fundamental concepts of probability and statistics—to understand how a statistician thinks about the empirical world. Possessing this basic knowledge will alert you to issues you might otherwise miss and, just as important, provide you with an informed skepticism about causal claims. Such knowledge will help you know

---

10. Oscar Wilde went even further, to write that "it is the mark of an educated man to be moved by statistics." *But see* Joseph Stalin: "The death of one man is a tragedy; the death of a million is a statistic."

11. Steve Lohr, *For Today's Graduate, Just One Word: Statistics*, New York Times, Aug. 5, 2009.

12. 430 U.S. 482 (1977).

13. 33 U.S. 299 (1977).

when to seek expert advice, and will enable you to communicate with experts. Moreover—referring back to the "two systems" of judgment described in Section1.6.1—there is reason to believe that a grasp of probability and statistics will reduce the "intuitive" statistician's errors. The evidence indicates that "even very brief" statistical training has "profound effects on people's reasoning in their everyday lives[14] and mitigates the biases of unmediated System I processes.[15]

The following chapters are premised on the belief that understanding the fundamental concepts is more important than being able to do complex calculations. Our goal, essentially, is to help you become a savvy consumer of statistics and strengthen your empirical intuitions. If nothing else, the chapters should demystify some statistical concepts and terms that you encounter in reading scholarly articles, legal opinions, and newspapers.

---

14. Richard Nisbettt, David Krantz, Christopher Jepson, and Ziva Kunda, *The Use of Statistic Heuristics in Everyday Inductive Reasoning, in* Thomas Gilovich, Dale Griffin, and Daniel Kahneman, HEURISTICS AND BIASES: THE PSYCHOLOGY OF INTUITIVE JUDGMENT 520, 528, 529 (New York: Cambridge University Press, 2002)

15. Franca Agnoli, "*Development of Judgmental Heuristics and Logical Reasoning: Training Counteracts the Representativeness Heuristic*" 6 *Cognitive Development* 195 (1991); Franca Agnoli & David H. Krantz, "*Suppressing Natural Heuristics by Formal Instruction: The Case of the Conjunction Fallacy*," 21 *Cognitive Psych*. 515 (1989). See also Peters, et al., Numeracy and Decision Making, 17 Psychological Science 407 (2006).

5. INTRODUCTION TO STATISTICS AND PROBABILITY

This chapter introduces statistical thinking and its application to law and public policy. At the end of the chapter, you can find a glossary with definitions of the numerous terms we discuss. Our main example will involve the tenants' complaints of illnesses possibly caused by foam insulation in the apartments at Terra Nueva (discussed in Chapter 1). Before turning to this example, though, we provide a brief introduction to probability.

5.1 PROBABILITY

A natural way of expressing beliefs about events that may or may not occur is with ideas of chance. You might say that the odds of a certain candidate winning an election are 3 to 1, or that he or she has a 75 percent chance of winning. In making these statements, you are expressing your beliefs in terms of the **probability** (or chance) of a particular event. The language of probability is an effective way to communicate the strength of beliefs in cases where we are not sure about an outcome but have some intuition on which to base our thoughts. In these situations of uncertainty, as well as situations in which the involvement of chance is more explicit, we use probabilistic notions to express our knowledge and beliefs.

5.1.1 Random Variables

A **variable** can take on either quantitative or categorical (qualitative) values. **Quantitative** variables are characteristics like *height, grade point average (GPA)*, and *number of years of education*, which take on a range of numbers. **Categorical** (or **qualitative**) variables are attributes, such as *gender* or *occupation*, that have two or more distinct categories.

A simple example of a variable is the result of a coin toss, which can take on the values "heads" and "tails." A **random variable** is a variable whose value is determined at least in part by chance. Chance, or randomness, comes from factors we do not know about or cannot determine. If one knew the way the coin was facing to begin with, the amount, direction, and placement of the force on the coin, and the relevant physics equations, one could likely determine on which side the coin would land. In that case, the variable would be **deterministic**. However, not being able to determine these things, we consider the outcome random.

If we tossed a coin ten times, we might see four heads, five tails, and then another heads: HHHHTTTTTH, for example. These results are called realized values, realizations, or instances of the random variable *coin toss*.

5.1.2 The Foundations of Probability

An **event** is a possible outcome of a random variable. It can be one particular realization or a set (range) of them: for example, a coin coming up heads or a candidate winning an election. For an event A, we write the probability of A occurring as $P(A)$. Thus we would write the probability of seeing heads as a result of a coin flip as *P(heads)*. In the Terra Nueva example, we would write the probability of a randomly-chosen resident having a rash as *P(rash present)*.

The formal theory of probability adopts a simple standard: probabilities are real numbers between 0 and 1. Thus odds of 3:1 in favor of an event and a 75 percent chance of its occurrence are both equivalent to the probability of that event being 0.75.

The entire mathematical treatment of probability follows from three axioms:

1. For an event A, $P(A)$ is a number between 0 and 1.
2. If A is certain to happen, then $P(A) = 1$. If it is certain not to happen, then $P(A) = 0$.
3. If A and B are **mutually exclusive events**, then $P(A \text{ or } B) = P(A) + P(B)$.

The third axiom tells us how to calculate probabilities for events that cannot occur together. For example, if we flip a coin we will get either heads or tails. These are mutually exclusive events—we cannot get both heads and tails at the same time from this one coin. So the third axiom entails: *P(heads* or *tails)* = *P(heads)* + *P(tails)*. Since we know that we are certain to have either heads or tails,[1] we can apply the second axiom and know that *P(heads* or *tails)* = 1. And we can go on to work out that *P(heads)* + *P(tails)*=1, or equivalently, *P(tails)* = 1 - *P(heads)*.

When two events, like heads and tails, are mutually exclusive and we are certain one or the other must occur, the events are called **complements** of each other. The complement of an event A is often written "~A" and read "not A." Using the same reasoning as above for a more general case, we can use the axioms to show the probability of A not occurring:

$$P(\sim A) = 1 - P(A)$$

This is called the **complement rule**.

1. This example assumes that *heads* and *tails* are not only mutually exclusive but *jointly exhaustive*: i.e., one and only one of them must occur. If we wanted to factor in the possibility that a coin could land and remain on its edge, the formula would be somewhat more complicated: *P(heads* or *tails* or *edge)* = 1. Therefore, *P(tails)* = 1 – *P(heads)* – *P (edge)*.

5.1.2.a Odds We just said that "the odds of a candidate winning an election are 3:1" is equivalent to "the candidate has a 75 percent chance (or a probability of 0.75) of winning." Odds of 3 to 1 means that the event is likely to occur about 3 times for every time it does not, that is, 3 out of 4 times, which can be represented as ¾ = 0.75. In terms of probabilities, the **odds** of an event are the ratio of the probability that it will happen to the probability that it will not:

Odds of event A = P(A)/P(~A).
We know from the complement rule that P(~A) = 1 - P(A), so
Odds of event A = P(A)/(1 - P(A)).

In this case, the ratio of the probability of the event—P(win) = 0.75—to the probability that it does not occur—P(lose) = 0.25—is 3:1.

5.1.2.b Meaning of Probabilities: Frequentism vs. Subjectivism What does it mean to say, "The probability of the coin landing on heads is 0.5?" There are two ways to define probabilities, **frequentism** and **subjectivism**. A frequentist would define the probability of heads as the relative frequency of heads if the coin were tossed infinitely many times. After many many tosses, 50 percent of them will have landed on heads and 50 percent on tails, so each probability is 0.5.

On the other hand, a subjectivist would say that the probability of a coin landing on heads represents how likely this event seems, possibly based on some evidence. For example, she might examine the coin and conclude that there is no evidence that it is weighted to make heads more likely than tails or vice versa, so the two events must have equal probabilities.

5.2 PROBABILITY DISTRIBUTIONS

From the axioms in 5.1.2, we saw that the probabilities of mutually exclusive and jointly exhaustive events sum to 1. In flipping a coin, $P(heads) + P(tails) = 1$. The same holds with more than two mutually exclusive events. When tossing a die, we can consider the random variable of what number lands facing up, with possible values 1, 2, 3, 4, 5, and 6. Then $P(1) + P(2) + P(3) + P(4) + P(5) + P(6) = 1$.

With any random variable, a total probability of 1 is *distributed* among all possible values. If we represented the total probability of 1 with a dollar in coins, those coins would be distributed over the possible values, with, 50¢ on heads and 50¢ on tails. In the die toss, 1/6, or about 17 cents, would be on each number 1–6. In these examples, the probability happens to be distributed evenly, but this doesn't have to be the case: imagine a die weighted so that the "6" came up more than 1/6 of the time.

Like a set amount of money ($1) or a set number of die faces, there is a set amount of probability (1), and it is distributed (not always evenly) over the mutually exclusive events. How it is distributed over the events is called the *probability distribution* of a random variable. Every random variable has a probability distribution. The probability distribution for the random variable *coin flip* is 0.5 on heads and 0.5 on tails. The probability distribution for the random variable *die toss* is 1/6 on each of the numbers 1 through 6 (see Figure 5.1(a)). When you are about to toss a die, you do not know which side will come up on top, but you might know the probability distribution.

5.3 POPULATION DISTRIBUTION VS. EMPIRICAL DISTRIBUTION: THE AIM OF STATISTICS

We can display the probability distribution of a discrete quantitative or ordered categorical random variable in a histogram. The probability distribution of *die toss*, in which each side of the die has an equal probability of 1/6 (about 0.17) of facing up, is displayed in Figure 5.1(a).

Suppose we tossed a die 100 times and obtained the following **frequencies**, the number of times each event occurs:

Side Up	Frequency
1	11
2	19
3	22
4	19
5	11
6	18

Dividing these by the total number of tosses, 100, we obtain the **relative frequencies**, which are displayed in Figure 5.1(b). The relative frequency of an event is the proportion of total opportunities on which it actually occurs, i.e., the ratio of the number of times the event occurs (its frequency) to the total number of times it could have occurred. In this case, for example, the die came up a 4 in 19 times out of a possible 100, so the relative frequency of the event that it comes up a 4 is 19/100 = 0.19.

The difference between Figure 5.1(a) and 5.1(b) is key to statistics. Figure 5.1(a) represents the probability distribution, which is the same for every die toss. Figure 5.1(b), on the other hand, results from just one experiment of one hundred tosses. Each of these one hundred realizations came from one die toss, with the probability distribution shown in Figure 5.1(a). For another experiment of one hundred tosses, the result would be slightly different, because it depends on chance.

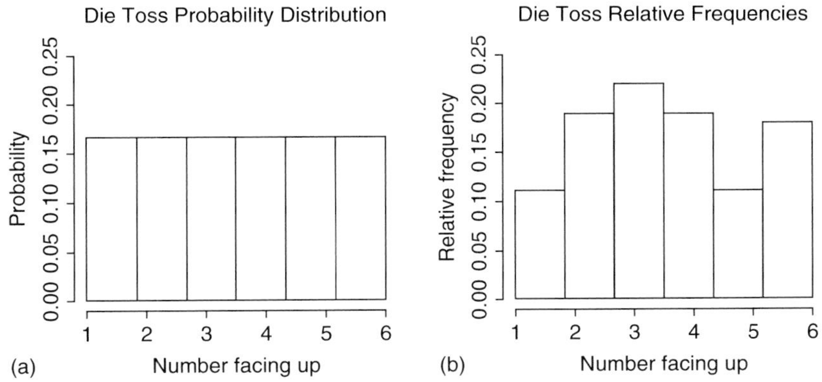

FIGURE 5.1 (A) AND (B) PROBABILITY DISTRIBUTION AND RELATIVE FREQUENCIES FOR DIE TOSS.

The distribution in Figure 5.1(b)—the relative frequencies in our sample—is called the **empirical distribution**, because it is based on what we observed in the sample.

Imagine the empirical distribution of a sample size of one—that is, the relative frequency distribution from just one toss. It would have one bar of height 1.0 and no other bars, very different from the probability distribution. The larger the number of tosses, the closer Figure 5.1(b) will look to Figure 5.1(a). After infinitely many tosses, Figure 5.1(b) will look just like Figure 5.1(a). In fact, in the frequentist interpretation of probability, that is how Figure 5.1(a) is defined.[2]

Therefore, we can call Figure 5.1(a) the **population distribution**, the relative frequencies among infinitely many tosses. *Population distribution* refers to the same thing as *probability distribution*. However, the term "population distribution" emphasizes the frequentist view that each realization is picked from a population.

5.3.1 The Aim of Statistics

In the case of a die toss, we happen to know the population distribution, since it is reasonable to assume equal probabilities for the six sides. In most real-world situations, however, the population distribution is unknown. In fact, it is what we are looking for. **The aim of statistics is to work backward—using only the observed sample, such as what gave us Figure 5.1(b), to infer properties of the population distribution, such as Figure 5.1(a).**

2. Subjectivist might disagree with this frequentist interpretation of Figure 5.1(a). Instead, they might say that the distribution is uniform due to the symmetry of the die, an argument that avoids imagining impossible experiments of infinitely many tosses and instead emphasizes the current state of one's knowledge.

It is worth pausing for a moment to emphasize this point. Recall the **lens model** discussed in the introduction to Part 2: you can never know the real world directly, but can only estimate it through multiple fallible indicators. In this sense, the *die toss* random variable is completely atypical because (assuming that it's a perfect die) we know that its population distribution is 1/6 for each possible value.

In summary then:

- **Population distribution**: The true distribution of the population will never be known. We estimate its characteristics by studying our sample, but these estimates will probably be a little bit off the truth—a different random sample of the same size will usually have resulted in slightly different estimates.
- **Empirical distribution**: The distribution of events within our random sample from the population is called the empirical distribution.

5.4 THE POPULATION AND EMPIRICAL DISTRIBUTION AT TERRA NUEVA

Recall the Terra Nueva problem discussed in Chapter 1. The survey to determine the incidence of rashes included 453 residents. We know the *empirical* distribution of the incidence of rashes of those who live in apartments with and without foam insulation. But these are fallible indicators of the population distribution, which cannot be known directly.[3] The task of statistics is to inform us how good an estimate of the population we can make based on the sample. The purpose of statistical inference is not to determine whether the foam insulation caused a rash in these particular 453 individuals; it is to use the sample to infer whether foam insulation is related to rash in the general population of Terra Nueva.

5.4.1 Contingency Tables

The Terra Nueva problem involves two categorical variables: We will use *insulation* to represent the variable indicating whether an apartment has the foam insulation. The *insulation* variable takes on the two values: "foam" and "not foam." We will use *rash* to represent the variable indicating whether the residents of an apartment have a rash. The *rash* variable takes on the values "absent" and "present." As a shorthand, we'll just use *foam* to mean foam = present and *rash* to mean rash = present.

---

3. In this particular instance, it might have been feasible to sample the entire actual population of Terra Nueva. However, in most real-world situations, from environmental hazards to public opinion polls, this isn't possible or cost-effective. In any event, as a conceptual matter, statistics assumes that the actual population is infinite—all possible past, future, and present tenants of Terra Nueva.

The typical format for depicting two categorical variables is called a **contingency table** because, as we will see later, it can be used to determine whether one variable is contingent on the other. In Table 5.1, in each of four **cells** is a frequency, the number of members of the sample that fall into that cell's joint categories.

TABLE 5.1 BASIC CONTINGENCY TABLE

		Rash	
		Present	*Absent*
Insulation	*Foam*	foam & rash	foam & no rash
	Not Foam	not foam & rash	not foam & no rash

This is a two-by-two contingency table. In other circumstances, we might have used three or more categories for *rash*—none, mild, and severe. (The categories are not inherent in a quality but are chosen based on what is relevant to the problem at hand.) In any event, the categories are *mutually exclusive and collectively exhaustive* (MECE): each apartment can either have foam or not, and each tenant can either have a rash or not—and there are no other possibilities.

We can populate each cell with the probability that any two of the variables occur together. The contingency table in Table 5.2 also shows the **marginal probability**—"marginal," because it is shown in the margin of the confluence of each variable; for example, the top right margin shows the probability that an apartment has foam; the bottom left margin shows the probability that a tenant of that apartment has a rash. Based on the principles discussed in Section 5.1.2, the total probability (bottom right) must sum to 1.0.

TABLE 5.2 CONTINGENCY TABLE WITH MARGINAL PROBABILITIES

		Rash		
		Present	*Absent*	Marginal
Insulation	*Foam*	P(foam & rash)	P(foam & no rash)	P(foam)
	Not Foam	P(not foam & rash)	P(not foam & no rash)	P(not foam)
	Marginal	P(rash)	P(no rash)	1.0

5.4.1.a The (*Unknowable*) Population Distribution The Terra Nueva complex consists of 465 units total (12 vacant). 279 (60 percent) of the units have foam insulation and 186 (40 percent) do not. With many families, including children, the complex has over 1000 residents, of whom we have surveyed 453.

Let's suppose that when a new tenant comes to Terra Nueva, she chooses or is assigned to an apartment without anyone's taking into account the insulation type. So for each tenant, the variable *insulation* has a probability distribution of 0.6 on "foam" and 0.4 on "not foam." That is, there's a 60 percent chance she is placed in a foam apartment and a 40 percent chance she's placed in a no-foam apartment. As just mentioned, these are the marginal distributions of the variable *insulation*, and appear in the right-most column of Table 5.3:

TABLE 5.3 THE (UNKNOWABLE) POPULATION DISTRIBUTION

Probabilities		*Rash*		
		Present	*Absent*	Marginal
Insulation	*Foam*	**0.25**	**0.35**	0.60
	Not Foam	**0.15**	**0.25**	0.40
	Marginal	0.40	0.60	1.00

We cannot know the actual population distribution of *rash*, but—only because your authors have invented the example—we can tell you that, among the population under consideration, a person moving into Terra Nueva has a 40 percent chance of developing a rash. Therefore, the marginal distribution of *rash* is 0.6 on "absent" and 0.4 on "present," as displayed in the bottom row of the probability table.

Again, only because we have constructed the microcosm of Terra Nueva, we can tell you that the probability that a randomly-chosen resident both inhabits an apartment with foam insulation and develops a rash— *P(rash & foam)*—is 0.25. (Even our omniscience has its limits: we can't tell you whether the rash is caused by the foam, but only that we observe both events happening together 25 percent of the time.) Because the marginal distributions have already been determined, the other three bold probabilities in the table are set to make each row and column add up to the correct marginal probability. The four bold numbers comprise the **joint distribution** of the two variables *insulation* and *rash*. Just as each pair of marginal probabilities sums to 1, the four joint probabilities sum to 1.

5.4.1.b The (Known) Empirical Distribution

Usually, the probabilities of having a rash with or without foam (Table 5.3) are unknown. They cannot be discerned directly but only based on the sample of the 453 residents of Terra Nueva who were surveyed. The population (of all 1000 residents) is equivalent to the infinitely many die tosses it would take to obtain an empirical distribution like Figure 5.1(a); the sample (of 453 surveyed residents) is analogous to the sample of 100 die tosses it took to obtain the empirical distribution of Figure 5.1(b). Suppose that the survey of Terra Nueva's residents has yielded the following information (Table 5.4):

TABLE 5.4 THE EMPIRICAL DISTRIBUTION IN NUMBERS

Observed Frequencies — *Rash*

Insulation		*Present*	*Absent*	Total
	Foam	**120**	**149**	269
	Not Foam	**63**	**121**	184
	Total	183	270	453

In some situations, one might want to display the data as proportions of the total—that is, as relative frequencies. Table 5.5 displays the same information as Table 5.4, but in relative frequencies. (Note that the format of the table resembles that of the (unknowable) probability distribution of the population from which it sampled. Table 5.3 is analogous to Figure 5.1(a), while Table 5.5 is analogous to Figure 5.1(b).)

(A different sample of tenants would almost surely have produced slightly different numbers than the sample represented in Tables 5.4 and 5.5).

TABLE 5.5 THE EMPIRICAL DISTRIBUTION IN RELATIVE FREQUENCIES

Observed Relative Frequencies: — *Rash*

Insulation		*Present*	*Absent*	Total
	Foam	**0.26**	**0.33**	0.59
	Not Foam	**0.14**	**0.27**	0.41
	Total	0.40	0.60	1.00

5.5 ESTIMATING PROBABILITIES

Our goal is to use the frequencies we observe in this sample of residents to **estimate** the probabilities, i.e., the relative frequencies in the total population. For example, in our sample of 453 residents, we see that 120 had both a rash and foam insulation, giving a relative frequency of 0.26. But a sample is always a fallible representation of the population. That is, an estimate is almost inevitably somewhat off from the true probability. How can we know how closely (or not) the relative frequencies of the sample approximate it?

We begin with a discussion of the concept of sampling, and then turn to the concepts of conditional probability and independence. Finally we discuss the matter of hypothesis testing—and in particular ascertaining the independence (or not) of having a rash and living in a foam-insulated apartment.

5.5.1 Sampling

Like pollsters before an election, lawyers and policy makers often are interested in the characteristics of a large population but lack the time or resources to measure or survey every member of that population. This leads us to choose a smaller **random sample** from the population and take the relevant measurements of those in the sample.

Often, investigators take a **simple random sample**, which means that each population member has an equal chance of being in the sample. From the information on the sample, we use statistics to infer a conclusion about the entire population.

Population -> Sampling -> Sample -> Inference -> Conclusions about population.

For pollsters, the population of interest consists of all voters in the region of interest. A simple poll might survey a random sample of, say, 1000 likely voters from the population of all voters in the region, then use **statistical inference** to predict the outcome of the election. However, if the sample was not chosen at random and therefore is not representative of the population as a whole, the conclusions may be incorrect. This is a problem called **selection bias** or **sampling bias**; examples are in the "Surveys" box. (In reality, pollsters do not always use simple random sampling and often instead use complex formulas based on knowledge about party registration, past elections, etc.)

You may have noticed that such predictions come with a "margin of error." That's because the sample does not exactly reflect the entire population from which it is drawn. In the next chapter, we'll discuss the characteristics of the sample that determine its margin of error.

Surveys

Efforts to obtain random samples, especially in surveys, are subject to practical pitfalls. Three presidential polls provide a good illustration. The 1936 *Literary Digest* poll that erroneously predicted that Alfred Landon would defeat Franklin Roosevelt by a large margin was biased in two ways: it had a selection bias by using lists of automobile owners and telephone subscribers to poll voters; but in 1936 only the relatively affluent had cars and phones. It also had a nonresponse bias: as it turned out, Landon voters were more likely to return the questionnaire. The 1948 misprediction that Thomas Dewey would defeat Harry Truman was based partly on the fact that more of the interviewers were Republicans than Democrats and that, consciously or not, they made their leaning known to the respondents, who told them what they wanted to hear. Exit polls that erroneously favored John Kerry over George W. Bush in some precincts in the 2004 presidential election may have been due to (youthful) Kerry voters' greater willingness to respond to the interviewers, which in turn may have been due to the interviewers' relative youth.

HANS ZEISEL AND DAVID KAYE, PROVE IT WITH FIGURES: EMPIRICAL METHODS IN LAW AND LITIGATION 103–04 (New York: Springer-Verlag, 1997); Evaluation of Edison/Mitofsky Election System 2004 prepared by Edison Media Research and Mitofsky International for the National Election Pool (NEP), Jan. 19, 2005, http://www.exit-poll.net/faq.html. *See generally* Fritz Scheuren, "What is a Survey," http://www.whatisasurvey.info/.

5.6 CONDITIONAL PROBABILITY AND INDEPENDENCE

In Section 5.4.1, we discussed marginal and joint probabilities. Recall that marginal probabilities are those (in the margins of the contingency table) that give the probability for a single variable, regardless of what the other variable equals, such as $P(foam) = 0.6$ and $P(rash) = 0.4$, while joint probabilities are those in the center of the table, such as $P(foam \;\&\; rash) = 0.25$.

In this section, we introduce **conditional probability**. A conditional probability is the probability that event A will occur if we know that B has occurred. It is written

$$P(A|B)$$

and is stated: "the probability of A *given* B."

For example, suppose you are flying from San Francisco to Cedar Rapids via Chicago. We can talk about the probability of your catching the flight from

Chicago to Cedar Rapids *given* that your flight from San Francisco leaves on time—or given that it is thirty minutes late.

Conditional probabilities tell us the probability distribution of one variable when another variable is known. In the Terra Nueva case, one might want to know the probability of a tenant's having a rash, *given* that she lives in an apartment with foam insulation. We represent this conditional probability formally by

$$P(rash|foam)$$

As noted above, the "|" is read "given," so this is stated as: "the probability that the tenant has a rash, given that she lives in an apartment with foam insulation."

Although this probability does not appear in Table 5.3, it can be calculated from those that are. Because we know the insulation is foam, we focus only on the top row. The conditional probability is that fraction of the total probability of the top row (0.60) for which a rash is present. That is,

$$P(rash|foam) = 0.25 \,/\, 0.60 = 0.42$$

One way to think about this is in terms of frequencies: Imagine that there are 1000 people total. Six hundred of them have foam insulation. And of those 600, 250 have a rash. So, of the group with foam insulation, the fraction with a rash is 250/600 = 0.42—that is, 42 percent of those with foam insulation have a rash. More generally, we can write this calculation as:

$$P(rash\ present|foam) = P(foam\ \&\ rash)/P(foam)$$

Is $P(rash|foam)$ the same as $P(foam|rash)$? Or to put the question more generally, is $P(A|B)$ the same as $P(B|A)$? Absolutely not! Consider the difference between $P(pregnant|woman)$ and $P(woman|pregnant)$.

Bush Voters and Moral Values

Correction: The Mail of January 3rd contained the incorrect statistic that four-fifths of Bush voters identified moral values as the most important factor in their decision. In fact, four-fifths of those identifying moral values as the most important factor of their decision were Bush voters. New Yorker, Feb. 14–21, 2005, 38.

5.6.1 Independence

Conditional probabilities are used to express information about how knowledge of one variable influences our knowledge of another. Often, we want to know if two variables are, or are not, related to each other. In the language of probability theory, we can ask whether or not two variables are **independent**.

Formally, we say that two events are independent of each other if $P(A/B) = P(A)$—which also implies that $P(B/A) = P(B)$. This means that the probability of A happening does not change, regardless of whether B happens or not, and vice versa. This matches up well with the intuitive notion of independence: If we say that two things are independent, we usually mean that they have no effect on one another. In the example above, is the probability of your catching the flight from Chicago to Cedar Rapids independent of the fact that your flight from San Francisco left on time? Is it independent of the fact that the flight number is the same as the month and day of your birth?

In the Terra Nueva case, if *insulation* and *rash* were independent, then being in an apartment with foam would not make it any more or less likely that a resident would develop a rash. In terms of conditional probabilities, the probability of having a rash given that one lives in a foam-insulated apartment would be identical to the probability of having a rash given that one lives in *any* apartment, or $P(rash/foam) = P(rash)$. Based on the calculations in the previous subsection, does this seem to be true?[4] We'll find out in a while.

In gambling, events are supposed to be statistically independent. For example, subsequent spins of a roulette wheel should give numbers that are completely unrelated to previous spins. If this were not the case, a player could use the result of previous spins to improve his or her chances of winning, to the detriment of the casino. By the same token, subsequent tosses of a coin are also independent: the information that the last toss produced a head tells you nothing about the expected outcome of the next toss.

A convenient consequence of independence is that when two variables are independent, the probability that an event involving one and an event involving the other both occur is the product of the marginal probabilities. If the first spin and the second spin of a roulette wheel are independent, then the probability that the ball lands on red on the first and on black on the second is

$$P(first\ spin = red\ \&\ second\ spin = black) = P(first\ spin = red) * P(second\ spin = black)$$

Similarly, if getting a rash were independent of one's type of insulation, then the joint probability that a Terra Nueva resident has foam insulation and a rash would be

$$P(rash\ \&\ foam) = P(rash) * P(foam)$$

4. Without knowing a tenant's insulation type, her chance of having a rash is the marginal probability, 0.40. When we learn that her apartment has foam insulation, however, the chance increases to 0.42. So *insulation* and *rash* are not independent.

In our case, in particular, this would be 0.6*0.4 = 0.24. If *rash* and *insulation* were independent, and we selected a Terra Nueva resident at random, there would be a 24 percent chance that the resident had both foam insulation and a rash.

In general, *if events A and B are independent,*

$$P(A \& B) = P(A) * P(B)$$

This is called the **multiplication rule** for independent events.

Problem: When rolling a pair of dice, what is the probability of rolling a double six?

The idea of independence is essential to statistics. The existence of a dependency between two variables means that those variables are related. Much of the practice of statistics involves attempting to find relationships among variables, and to quantify the strength of those relationships. These tasks correspond to testing whether variables are independent and measuring the extent to which they deviate from independence.

5.7 RANDOMNESS, INDEPENDENCE, AND INTUITION

Schemas are an essential part of the human situation. "We are predisposed to see order, pattern, and meaning in the world, and we find randomness, chaos, and meaninglessness unsatisfying. Human nature abhors a lack of predictability and the absence of meaning.

—Thomas Gilovich.[5]

Much psychological research has examined how good people are at detecting relationships or their absence. It turns out that people often neglect the implications of statistical independence when evaluating the probability of events being produced by a random process.

5.7.1 Illusory Correlation

As a consequence of our schematic perception and desire to impose order on reality, we sometimes see the correlations that we expect to see even where they do not exist—especially when there is a plausible explanation for the correlation. For example, a study of arthritis patients showed that they were virtually certain that their pain was correlated with the weather, when the actual correlation was close to zero.[6] In another experiment, done at a time when many psychologists

5. Thomas Gilovich, How We Know What Isn't So: The Fallibility of Human Reason in Everyday Life, 9 (New York: The Free Press, 1991).

6. Donald A. Redelmeier and Amos Tversky, *On the Belief that Arthritis Pain Is Related to the Weather*, 93 Proceedings of the National Academy of Sciences 2895 (1999).

diagnosed psychiatric disorders by interpreting a patient's drawings in a "Draw-a-Person" Test, Lauren J. Chapman and Jean P. Chapman surveyed clinicians and found considerable agreement about what characteristics of the drawing were characteristic of particular disorders—for example, strongly dependent people emphasize the mouth, paranoids emphasize the eyes, and impotent men draw men with broad shoulders. Psychologists' beliefs in these correlations were strong, despite robust evidence that the correlations were no stronger than random.[7]

Richard Nisbett and Lee Ross observe that in the contest between expectations or theory and evidence or data, "expectations based on a priori theories or on semantic connotations overwhelm the influence of data that do not coincide with expectations or even refute them."[8]

5.7.2 The Illusion of Control

The winner of the Spanish lottery, who bought a lottery ticket ending in 48, when asked why he chose that number, explained that for 7 nights in a row he dreamed of the number 7, and since 7 times 7 equal 48, he knew that would be the lucky number.[9]

Related to illusory correlation, people also manifest what Ellen Langer has termed the **illusion of control**—acting as if they exercise control over events that are in fact matters of chance.[10] For example, some gamblers throw the dice softly to get low numbers and hard to get high numbers; people playing a game of chance will bet more against an opponent who looks like a "schnook" than one who seems competent; and people who choose a lottery ticket demand a higher price to sell it than those given a lottery ticket at random. In some of these cases, a misunderstanding of chance may be combined with a desire or need for personal efficacy—the drive to master one's environment begins early in infancy, and the sense of not being in control can be stressful and debilitating—or with a tendency to believe that if we desired an outcome and it occurred, we must have been responsible for bringing it about.[11]

---

7. Lauren J. Chapman and Jean P. Chapman, *Genesis of Popular But Erroneous Psycho-Diagnostic Observations*, 72 Journal of Abnormal Psychology 193–204 (1967); Lauren J. Chapman and Jean P. Chapman, *Illusory Correlation as an Obstacle to the Use of Valid Diagnostic Signs*, 74 Journal of Abnormal Psychology 271–80 (1969).

8. Richard Nisbett and Lee Ross, Human Inference: Strategies and Shortcomings of Social Judgment 97 (Englewood Cliffs, NJ: Prentice Hall, 1980).

9. Stanley Meisler (1977), *cited in* Reid Hastie and Robyn Dawes, Rational Choice in an Uncertain World 154 (Thousand Oaks, CA: Sage Publishing, 2001).

10. Ellen J. Langer, *The Illusion of Control*, 32 Journal of Personality and Social Psychology 311 (1975).

11. Ellen. J. Langer and Jane Roth, *Heads I Win, Tails It's Chance: The Illusion of Control as a Function of the Sequence of Outcomes in a Purely Chance Task*, 34 Journal of Personality and Social Psychology 191–98 (1975); Ellen J. Langer, *The Illusion of Control*, *in* Judgment

The illusion of control is a special case of illusory correlation—involving the correlation between one's own actions and an outcome. The foundations for the illusion of control lie in people's tenuous understanding of probability and the difficulties of assessing correlations between putative causes and effects, especially when the environment does not lend itself to accurate feedback. The illusion may arise from the apparent connection between *intending* an outcome and having the outcome occur—an instance of both the availability heuristic (one's own action is readily brought to mind) and the representative heuristic (the similarity between the intention and the outcome).[12]

There is ample experimental evidence that even bright, well-educated people engage in "magical thinking" in which, for example:

> One grumbles bitterly about Grandma just before she falls and breaks a hip or expressed anger toward the greedy landlord the day before he is arrested for tax evasion. Without a shred of evidence about who caused their troubles, one may still feel implicated. . . . [T]he sense may range from an outright belief in personal responsibility for the bad outcome to a nagging feeling of responsibility that persists despite the rational belief that one is not actually responsible. In any case, the inference involves an erroneous perception of causality.[13]

> There are thirty-nine categories of work that are prohibited on the Sabbath. Category No. 27, Kindling a Fire, also rules out the "kindling" of anything electrical, including a television. It was Friday, May 6, 1994: Game Four of the Stanley Cup conference semifinals between the Rangers and the Washington Capitals was scheduled for that Saturday afternoon. I had decided to switch on the television Friday afternoon—before Sabbath began, at sundown—and just leave it on until Sabbath ended, twenty-five hours later. This wasn't, technically, "being in the spirit of the Sabbath," but it wasn't technically a sin, and the Rangers were

UNDER UNCERTAINTY: HEURISTICS AND BIASES (Daniel Kahneman, Paul Slovic, and Amos Tversky eds., New York: Cambridge University Press, 1982). *See also* Paul Presson and Victor Benassi, *Illusion of Control: A Meta-Analytic Review*, 11 JOURNAL OF SOCIAL BEHAVIOR AND PERSONALITY (1996); SHELLEY TAYLOR, POSITIVE ILLUSIONS 26 (1989).

12. *See* Suzanne Thompson, Wade Armstrong, and Craig Thomas, *Illusions of Control, Underestimations, and Accuracy: A Control Heuristic Explanation*, 123 PSYCHOLOGY BULLETIN 113 (1998); NISBETT AND ROSS, *supra* at 136–37. In Section 13.5, we will discuss research indicating that positive illusions, such as the illusion of control, are adaptive because they increase motivation and persistence. http://www.answers.com/topic/illusion-of-control.

13. Emily Pronin et al., *Everyday Magical Powers: The Role of Apparent Mental Causation in the Overestimation of Personal Influence*, 91 JOURNAL OF PERSONALITY AND SOCIAL PSYCHOLOGY 218 (2006).

very likely nine victories away from winning the Stanley Cup for the first time in fifty-four years.

. . . I switched on the television, turned down the volume, and draped a bath towel over the screen to hide from the neighbors the flickering blue light of our moral weakness.

"Do you really think that if you turn on the TV on Sabbath God will make the Rangers lose?" Orli asked.

Her naiveté astounded me.

"I don't think He will. I know He will."

Shalom Auslander, *Personal History*, NEW YORKER, Jan. 15, 2007, PG38.

5.7.3 The Gambler's Fallacy

The **gambler's fallacy** is the belief that, after a run of several of the same event (same color, number, side of a coin or die, etc.), that event becomes less likely than otherwise on the following trial. For example, an empirical study of roulette players in a casino showed that the longer the streak of outcomes of a particular type (e.g., black), the more likely a player was to bet against the streak.[14] Similarly, people tend not to bet on a recent winning lottery number.

Underlying the gambler's fallacy is the belief that, after seeing a run of tails in a sequence, the next toss is more likely to result in a head: it does not reflect the fact that the outcomes of the bets, or the tosses of the coin, are independent. For independent events, the probabilities of different outcomes do not change as a consequence of the results seen so far.

The gambler's fallacy can be seen as a misapplication of the frequentist interpretation of probability. The fact that a fair coin produces heads with probability 0.5 does not mean that for every finite number of tosses, half of the outcomes are guaranteed to be heads. Those who commit the gambler's fallacy explain it with the idea that after a number of tails, the coin must come up heads in order to "balance out" the sequence. The phenomenon is often attributed to the **representativeness heuristic**, mentioned briefly at the end of Chapter 2 and described in more detail in Section 8.3. In this case, sequences containing approximately equal numbers of heads and tails are representative of those produced by a fair coin. Seeing a head after a sequence of tails makes the

14. Rachel Croson and James Sundali, *The Gambler's Fallacy and the Hot Hand: Empirical Data from the Casinos*, 30 JOURNAL OF RISK AND UNCERTAINTY 195 (2005).

sequence more representative of a fair coin than seeing another tail, so people give it a higher probability.[15]

The other side of the gambler's fallacy coin, so to speak, is the belief that an individual is sometimes on a winning streak, so that random sequences are interpreted as other than random. For example, the roulette study mentioned above indicated that players made more "outside" bets (bets on red/black, odd/even, or groups of numbers) when they had previously won on outside bets and more inside bets (bets on particular numbers) when they had previously won on inside bets.[16] The notion that athletes exhibit periods of unusually good play—the "hot hand," "streak shooting," or being "in the zone"—may be an example of this fallacy.

There is a considerable debate about whether and when players actually have a hot hand. The psychologists Thomas Gilovich, Robert Vallone, and Amos Tversky recorded a professional basketball teams' statistics for an entire season and concluded that, in fact, players' shots were independent.[17] The researchers did not argue that an individual can *never* be "in the zone"; only that their study indicated that claims of this sort were unfounded. Sports fans, including scholars of judgment and decision making as well as our own students, strongly resist this finding. For example, an article on *Bowlers' Hot Hands* criticized the basketball study on the ground that it did not control for several confounding influences and presented evidence that most bowlers actually have a higher proportion of strikes after bowling a certain number of consecutive strikes than after consecutive nonstrikes.[18]

Our apparently poor intuitions about randomness may also help provide insight into another psychological phenomenon—the idea of meaningful coincidence. Seemingly unlikely events catch our attention and often appear in newspapers. Scott Plous gives an example of two men sharing the same surname, the same model of car and even exactly the same car keys, both being in a shopping center on the same time on April Fool's Day, and managing to confuse their cars.[19]

---

15. This argument was made by Amos Tversky and Daniel Kahneman, *Belief in the Law of Small Numbers*, 76 Psychological Bulletin 105–10 (1971).

16. An inside bet is made within the 36 numbers of the roulette table, for example, on a single number or on two or four adjacent numbers. An outside bet is, say, red or black, odd or first 12. The correlations were small but statistically significant at $p < 0.05$.

17. Thomas Gilovich, Robert Vallone, and Amos Tversky, *The Hot Hand in Basketball: On the Misperception of Random Sequences*, 17 Journal of Personality and Social Psychology 295–314 (1985).

18. Reid Dorsey-Palmateer and Gary Smith, *Bowlers' Hot Hands*, 58 American Statistician 38 (2004).

19. Scott Plous, The Psychology of Judgment and Decision Making 154 (New York: McGraw Hill, 1993).

Similar chains of strange co-occurrences can be found discussed in many books, and the Internet provides several sites dedicated to recording coincidences.[20]

By not noticing the multitude of uninteresting events that take place, we underestimate the number of opportunities that have been available for an interesting (and unlikely) coincidence to occur. A one-in-a-million chance will often arise when given a million opportunities, and if we do not notice those opportunities we can be surprised when it does arise.

Similar sorts of phenomena account for many of the strange coincidences that we encounter. Statisticians Persi Diaconis and Fred Mosteller, who have investigated coincidences in detail, discuss a newspaper article about a woman who won the New Jersey lottery twice within four months. This seems very unlikely, but Diaconis and Mosteller estimate the probability of something like this happening to somebody in the United States to be as high as one in thirty.[21]

5.8 TESTING HYPOTHESES—AND THE CONCEPT OF STATISTICAL SIGNIFICANCE

Hypothesis testing allows us to determine whether an apparent empirical relationship is large enough to make us confident that it reflects a real relationship in the population, not just in the random sample we chose. Hypothesis testing allows us to use the sample we have to reach a conclusion about the relationship between the two variables in the whole population. It involves:

- hypothesizing that there is no real underlying relationship between the two variables;
- calculating a measure of how unlikely our sample data would be if, in fact, there were no relationship; and then
- determining whether the data are extreme enough to justify rejecting the null hypothesis and concluding that there is a relationship.

Step 1) State the two hypotheses of the test:

- The **null hypothesis** is the default hypothesis—typically that there is no relationship—that we would believe in the absence of sufficient evidence against it. We need evidence to reject the null hypothesis. Typically, it states that there is *no* relationship between two variables. In the Terra Nueva case, the null hypothesis is that *insulation* and *rash* are independent.
- The **alternative hypothesis** is the scenario that we might suspect is the case but require evidence to conclude that it is. Typically, it states that

---

20. *For example, see* http://go.to/coincidences/.

21. Persi Diaconis and Frederick Mosteller, *Methods of Studying Coincidences*, 84 Journal of the American Statistics Association 853–61 (1989).

two variables are related. In the Terra Nueva case, the alternative hypothesis is that *insulation* and *rash* are not independent but rather are related such that *rash* is more likely given the presence of *insulation*.

We test the hypotheses by comparing the observed relative frequencies (Table 5.5) to the relative frequencies that we would expect if insulation and rash were independent. We can calculate the latter using the multiplication rule, as shown below.

The question is, how far apart do those two tables have to be to convince us that the null hypothesis is false?

The two tables will almost certainly be somewhat different. But is the difference small enough to be chalked up to chance or is the difference **statistically significant**? A hypothesis test allows us to reach a conclusion about the entire population based only on our sample data.

Step 2) Set the level of the test.

Since we have only a sample with which to test our hypothesis, it is possible that we will make an error. In fact, we can distinguish two kinds of errors that can result from performing a hypothesis test. There are two possible states of the world: a relationship between two variables exists, or it does not. And there are two possible conclusions we can draw: that a relationship exists, or that it does not. In the case where no relationship exists, but we conclude that one does, we have made a **Type I error**. In the case where a relationship exists but we conclude that it does not, we have made a **Type II error**.

A good way to think about the difference between Type I and Type II errors is in the context of medical diagnosis. A medical test can give two different kinds of erroneous results: it can return a positive result when the patient does not have the condition tested for (a false positive), or it can return a negative result when a patient actually has the condition tested for (a miss). Both of these errors can have important consequences for the patients involved, and medical researchers try to develop tests that avoid making them. In statistics, false positives are called Type I errors and misses are called Type II errors. (See Table 5.6.)

TABLE 5.6 TYPE I AND TYPE II ERRORS

	Test suggests relationship (rejects null)	Test does not suggest relationship (does not reject null)
Relationship exists (alternative is true)	Hit	Miss **(Type II error)**
No relationship (null is true)	False positive **(Type I error)**	Correct negative

In hypothesis testing in science, policy, and law, it is typical to err on the side of avoiding Type I errors. There are at least two motivations for this.

First, it is important to make sure that false findings of relationships do not readily make their way into the scientific literature. Second, the probability of making a Type I error is easy to quantify. For a Type I error to occur, the null hypothesis must be true. Since the null hypothesis is more clearly defined than the alternative (which could be any number of possible relationships), it is easier to calculate probabilities of events occurring under the null hypothesis.

The significance **level** of a hypothesis test is the highest probability of Type I error that is acceptable. Often, the level—sometimes referred to as **alpha level** and denoted by the Greek letter α (alpha)—is chosen to be 0.05. So, even if the null hypothesis is true, we expect to reject it one out of twenty times. For example, if we conduct twenty well-designed experiments to determine whether a supposedly toxic substance in fact causes harm, on average one of them will suggest that it causes harm even if the substance is in fact harmless.

The value $\alpha = 0.05$ is arbitrary, but it is accepted by convention in many disciplines. In some cases, where we want the probability of a Type I error to be reduced, it is appropriate to use a more stringent alpha level, such as $\alpha = 0.01$, 0.001, or 0.0001. One context in which people are very careful with the alpha level is where they are conducting many statistical tests at once. We pointed out above that, even if no relationship existed, about 1 in 20 tests would conclude statistical significance at the $\alpha = 0.05$ level. This is called the problem of **multiple testing** or **multiple comparisons**. To reduce the chance of making at least one Type I error among several tests, one could make the α level more stringent (i.e., smaller) for each test or, better yet, use an approach based on Bayes' Theorem (discussed in Section 8.5).

The choice of the alpha level also has implications for the probability of a Type II error. All things being equal, the probability of making a Type II error will increase as α decreases—if you are more stringent about the values of a statistic that you will allow to count as evidence against the null hypothesis, it becomes more difficult to reject the null hypothesis, and the probability of a Type II error rises accordingly. The choice of an alpha level reflects a compromise between producing a lot of Type I errors and a lot of Type II errors.

You might think of the different burdens of proof in civil and criminal cases as different balances between Type I and Type II errors. If the alternative hypothesis is that the defendant is liable, the civil standard requiring a "preponderance" of the evidence manifests a very slight preference against Type I errors, and the criminal standard of "beyond a reasonable doubt" manifests a very strong preference against Type I errors, erring on the side of letting the guilty go free rather than convicting an innocent person.

In the Terra Nueva problem we will set the level to the customary $\alpha = 0.05$.

Step 3) Suppose that the null hypothesis is true.

The main idea of a statistical hypothesis test is to find how extreme the sample data would be if the null hypothesis were true.

The null hypothesis is that *insulation* and *rash* are independent. Supposing independence is true, and using the observed marginal relative frequencies as estimates of the marginal probabilities, the multiplication rule gives us the estimate:

$$P(foam \,\&\, rash) = P(foam) * P(rash) = 0.59 * 0.40 = 0.24$$

We can do the same calculation for the other combinations of *insulation* and *rash*: *foam &not rash*, *not foam & rash*, and *not foam & not rash*, and present them in a new table of the relative frequencies *expected* under the null hypothesis. (See Table 5.7.)

TABLE 5.7 EXPECTED RELATIVE FREQUENCIES

Expected Relative Frequencies: *Rash*

Insulation		*Present*	*Absent*	Total
	Foam	**0.24**	**0.35**	0.59
	Not Foam	**0.16**	**0.25**	0.41
	Total	0.40	0.60	1.00

To express the expected distribution in terms of (absolute) frequencies, we multiply the relative frequencies by the total number of residents in our sample, 453. This gives us the following frequencies expected under the null hypothesis of independence, as shown in Table 5.8.

TABLE 5.8 EXPECTED ABSOLUTE FREQUENCIES

Expected Frequencies *Rash*

Insulation		*Present*	*Absent*	Total
	Foam	**109**	**160**	269
	Not Foam	**74**	**110**	184
	Total	183	270	453

Step 4) Calculate how far the data are from what would be expected under the null hypothesis.

Let us compare the *observed* frequencies with the frequencies *expected* under the null hypothesis of independence, as shown in Table 5.9.

TABLE 5.9 OBSERVED VERSUS EXPECTED FREQUENCIES

Observed

		Rash	
		Present	*Absent*
Insulation	*Foam*	120	149
	Not Foam	63	121

Expected

		Rash	
		Present	*Absent*
Insulation	*Foam*	109	160
	Not Foam	74	110

In our sample, the upper left and lower right cells contain frequencies (of 120 and 121) higher than their expected frequencies (of 109 and 110). Consequently, in the lower left and upper right cells, the observed frequencies are lower than what is expected under independence. The further from the expected frequencies the observed frequencies are, the further from independent the variables appear to be. Here are the differences in frequencies between observed and expected, as shown in Table 5.10.

TABLE 5.10 OBSERVED MINUS EXPECTED FREQUENCIES

Obs–Exp

		Rash	
		Present	*Absent*
Insulation	*Foam*	11	−11
	Not Foam	−11	11

A hypothesis test determines whether these differences between observed and expected frequencies are large enough to indicate a relationship between *insulation* and *rash*.

In a 2-by-2 table, the four differences will always have the same magnitude, with the cells along one diagonal negative and the cells along the other diagonal positive. This is because the four marginal frequencies are the same for both observed and expected tables, so each row and column of Table 5.10 has to sum to 0.

So the difference from what's expected under independence is 11 in each cell, not 0. But is 11 large enough to allow us to conclude a relationship in the population?

To determine whether the data are extreme enough to justify the conclusion that there is a relationship, we calculate the probability, if independence were true, that the difference would be 11 or greater. This probability is called the **p-value** of the test. If the p-value is small (specifically, smaller than our chosen significance level of 0.05), then these data are quite extreme to be due only to chance—quite improbable if independence were true—and we conclude that a relationship exists, i.e., that the data are statistically significant.

The p-value can be calculated by a computer program or found in a table. While we're not going to go into the details here, it is calculated using the **chi-squared test** (pronounced "kai squared") for a relationship between two qualitative variables.

For our data, with a sample of 453 and a difference in each cell of 11, the p-value is 0.03. That is, if insulation and rash were independent, there would be a 3 percent chance that the difference in each cell were 11 or greater. This is quite improbable—0.03 is less than the level we set of 0.05—allowing us to conclude that a relationship between insulation and rash exists.

Step 5) State your conclusion.

Because this result would be very unlikely if insulation and rash were independence true, we are justified in rejecting the null hypothesis and concluding that there likely is a relationship between insulation type and the absence or presence of a rash.

5.8.1 What Null Hypothesis Statistical Testing Is and Is Not

We have just reviewed the technique called null hypothesis statistical testing (NHST) as applied to two qualitative variables (foam insulation and rash). We will examine its application to other sorts of variables in the next chapter. It is important to emphasize that NHST asks the question: "given that the null hypothesis (H^0) is true, what is the probability of getting these (or more extreme data)," and *not*: "given these data, what is the probability that the null hypothesis is true."[22] P *(data| H_0)* is as radically different from P(*H_0|data*) as *P(pregnant|woman)* and *P(woman|pregnant)*.[23] Even experts sometimes get this wrong, and for an

22. *See* Jacob Cohen, *The Earth is Round (p <.05)*, 49 Am. Psychol. 997 (1994).

23. In Section 8, we will examine Bayes Theorem, which in principle can convert P (*data| H^0*) into P(*H^0|data*). But it requires assigning a value P(*H^0*), the probability of the null hypothesis prior to the experiment, which is often not known.

understandable reason: we really want to know the answer to the second question, which tells us how big a deal we can make of the data.

In general, this does not pose a problem when the results of a study turn out to be statistically significant. The concern, rather, is that NHST may produce too many misses (Type II errors), where a real effect goes unnoticed. We will return to this issue in Section 7.6.

5.8.2 Intuitions about Hypothesis Testing

An expert on organizational behavior is conducting a study of what factors conduce to a company's long-term success. He selects fifty companies that have thrived over many decades and identifies a number of factors—involving mission, organizational structure, leadership, and the like—that are present in all or most of them. The approach is sometimes called **selection on the dependent variable** because it only examines cases where the particular outcome (successful companies) that presumably depends on other factors (e.g., leadership) occurs. Is it sound?

Consider the broader question of which cells of a 2-by-2 contingency table (such as that involved in the Terra Nueva case) you need to test a hypothesis of independence. (See Table 5.11.)

TABLE 5.11 WHICH CELLS OF A CONTINGENCY TABLE ARE IMPORTANT?

		Rash	
		Present	*Absent*
Insulation	*Foam*	A	B
	Not Foam	C	D

- Cell A. To what extent do the putative cause and effect happen together? This can be phrased either as (1) when the putative cause occurs, to what extent does the effect also occur?, or (2) when the effect occurs, to what extent did the putative cause occur? Most people find it intuitively obvious that this cell is necessary.
- Cell B. To what extent does the putative cause occur when the effect does not? Consider the possibility that many Terra Nueva residents who live in apartments with foam insulation do not have a rash.
- Cell C. To what extent does the effect occur even when the putative cause is absent? Consider the possibility that many Terra Nueva residents have a rash even though they do not live in apartments with foam insulation.
- Cell D. To what extent did neither the putative cause nor the effect occur? Though less obvious, this cell is needed as well, as we describe immediately below.

Consider these two possible scenarios, in which cells A, B, and C are identical, as shown in Table 5.12.

TABLE 5.12 THE NECESSITY OF THE "NO-NO" CELL

		Rash	
		Present	*Absent*
Insulation	*Foam*	100	12
	Not Foam	20	0

		Rash	
		Present	*Absent*
Insulation	*Foam*	100	12
	Not Foam	20	100

In the first scenario, 100 percent of the 20 residents of apartments *without* foam have rashes, compared to 89 percent of residents of apartments with foam (100 out of 112)—so it appears that living in an apartment with foam is safer than living in an apartment without foam. In the second, only 17 percent (20 out of 120) of residents of apartments without foam have rashes.

Which cells were missing in the study of successful companies—and how does this affect your confidence in its conclusions?

The Sports Illustrated Cover Jinx

A week after he was featured on the cover of the very first issue of Sports Illustrated, Major League Baseball player Eddie Mathews, suffered an injury that forced him to miss seven games, giving rise to the notion that being on the cover "jinxed" an athlete. In 2002, the editors reviewed all 2456 magazine covers to find that 37 percent of the featured athletes suffered "measurable and fairly immediate" negative consequences. Alexander Wolf, *That Old Black Magic*, SPORTS ILLUSTRATED, Jan. 21, 2002, 50–61.

How would you determine whether there was actually a Sports Illustrated cover jinx?

5.9 CANCER CLUSTERS, THE TEXAS SHARPSHOOTER, AND MULTIPLE TESTING

A seemingly high incidence of a disease among those exposed to a possible causative agent often gives rise to the victims' belief—and often to a class action suit alleging—that the agent is the cause of the disease. This was the case with the association of childhood leukemia with contaminated drinking water in Woburn, Massachusetts (the subject of the book and film, *A Civil Action*); the association of respiratory disease with contaminated drinking water in Hinkley, California (the subject of the film *Erin Brockovich*); the association of connective tissue diseases with silicone breast implants; and the association of brain cancer with electromagnetic radiation from electric power lines, microwave ovens, and cellular telephones.

The first indication of an environmentally caused disease has often been a pattern of instances of the disease coupled with the putative disease-causing agent. For example, a Turkish physician noticed many cases of myeloid leukemia among hatters. He investigated this and correctly deduced that it was because of their heavy use of benzene as a cleaning fluid. Similar patterns link the inhalation of asbestos with malignant mesothelioma; mothers' use of DES during pregnancy with their daughters' vaginal cancer; and smoking with lung cancer. If this is so, ask the British epidemiologists Ravi Maheswaran and Anthony Staines, why are scientists so skeptical about cancer clusters (regions with unusually high cancer rates at some time)?[24] They answer:[25]

> [B]ecause, in practice, the yield has been very disappointing given the resources and energy expended. In addition, it is fraught with technical difficulties.
>
> The poor yield is well documented. The Centers for Disease Control in Atlanta investigated 108 cancer clusters over 22 years but found no clear cause for any of them.
>
> A major problem with cluster investigation is the choice of boundaries used to define the cluster. The suspicion of a cluster usually begins with the identification of a group of cases of cancer. The boundaries defining this cluster, for example the geographical area and time frame, are determined later. This process defines the population from which the cancer cases arose. The tighter the boundaries are drawn, the higher the cancer rate will be. This has been described as the "Texas sharpshooter" procedure, where the sharpshooter first empties his gun into the barn door and then carefully draws the

---

24. Laypersons may have a different view than experts. *See* Phil Brown, *Popular Epistemology and Toxic Waste Contamination: Law and Professional Ways of Knowing*, 33 HEALTH AND SOCIAL BEHAVIOUR 267 (1992).

25. Ravi Maheswaran and Anthony Staines, *Cancer Clusters and Their Origins*, 7 CHEMISTRY AND INDUSTRY 254–256 (1997).

target around the bullet holes.

For example, three cases of leukemia over a year in a small town are not surprising. But what if these three cases can be linked in some way, say the subjects live in the same neighborhood, go to the same church or used to go to school together? Although this can seem alarming, it is almost always possible to define boundaries that will create a disease cluster—or that will make a cluster disappear. It is not possible to do a conventional statistical analysis in such a situation.

Maheswaran and Staines also discuss the problem of multiple comparisons (which we introduced in Section 5.8):

> A further statistical problem is that of multiple comparisons. If, for example, rates for several cancers are examined, perhaps in several age groups, it is likely that a "statistically significant" elevated rate will be found. It isn't just researchers searching through large databases who do this. Members of the public or media may also inadvertently make multiple comparisons if they are on the lookout for something unusual. Indeed, this is the origin of many reported cancer clusters . . .

Our readiness to see clusters of diseases is another instance of our intuitions about randomness discussed in Section 5.7—the intuition that in eight tosses of a fair coin HHTHTHTT is more likely than the sequence HHHHHHHH. Here is a randomly generated list of 48 0's and 1's:

0 1 0 1 1 0 0 0 1 0 0 1 0 0 1 1 1 0 1 1 1 0 1 0 1 1 1 1 0 0 0 1 0 1 1 1 0 1 1 1 1 1 1 1 1 0 1 0 1

Note that there is a run of eight 1's, completely by chance. This is analogous to a cancer cluster with no environmental cause specific to the geographical area. To people in that area, it looks alarming, but actually, such variation occurs by chance.

Suppose that the average annual incidence of a particular form of cancer is 1 percent, and suppose that a neighborhood has 1000 residents. On average, we would expect 10 residents of the neighborhood to be diagnosed in a year. The population of the United States is 293,000,000, so one can draw borders to define 293,000 neighborhoods of 1000 residents each. Simply as a matter of chance, some neighborhoods will have zero cases of cancer and some will have 50.

When conducting many tests, we should expect to see at least a few statistically significant results by chance, and should correct our methods to take this into account. If we are not keeping track of all of the possible tests we could have conducted, our statistical analyses will be skewed in favor false positive results (Type I errors). If we use appropriately conservative statistical tests, keeping track of the number of tests we have conducted, and still find statistically significant results, then it seems that further inquiry is warranted. The further inquiry might be of an epidemiological nature—for example, looking at the cancer rates in other places with similar drinking water contamination. Or it might involve controlled experiments with laboratory animals—also essentially statistical. Finally, it might involve learning how the chemical alters genes to produce the cancer.

Multiple testing, along with various biases, can affect the power, and even validity, of studies that have statistically significant results. In the provocatively titled, *Why Most Published Research Findings Are False*,[26] John Ioannidis notes that the hotter a scientific field (with more scientific teams involved), the less likely the research findings are to be true. He argues that the possibilities for improvement lie mainly in taking account of the prestudy odds of the truth of the relationship that the study is testing. We will consider the notion of prior probability in the introduction to Bayesian statistics in Section 8.5. But consider these possible determinants:

- data from previous experimental studies;
- data from previous epidemiological or other observational studies;

Legal Problem

A plaintiffs' law firm that specializes in toxic and related torts has a particular interest in cancers putatively caused by strong electromagnetic fields. It has been monitoring one hundred neighborhoods near large transformer stations. One of those neighborhoods recently reported what appears to be a high incidence of brain tumors in children. After informing several of the unfortunate families of their legal rights and being retained by them, the firm undertook a well-designed survey, which showed a statistically significant incidence of brain tumors. Does this raise any concerns for you as a statistically astute observer of the legal system?

- knowledge about the mechanics of causality—e.g., the effects of a particular chemical on cell division;
- general social, economic, or scientific theories—e.g., the general effects of incentives and deterrents;
- an expert's informed intuition;
- common (uninformed) intuitions.

26. John P. A. Ioannidis, *Why Most Published Research Findings Are False*, 2 PLoS MED e124 (2005).

5.10 GLOSSARY

Conditional probability, P(A|B)	The probability that A will occur given than B has occurred
Independence	Events A and B are independent when P(A|B) = P(A) and P(B|A) = P(B)
Random sample	A subset of a population, chosen by a random mechanism
Simple random sample	A subset of a population, chosen by a random mechanism in which each population member has an equal chance of being chosen
Sampling bias (selection bias)	The amount by which an estimate is off from the population parameter it is estimating due to the way the sample was chosen from the population
Statistical inference	Making conclusions about a population based upon a sample from it
Variable	A characteristic that can take on more than one value
Quantitative variable	A variable that takes on numerical values
Qualitative or categorical variable	A variable that can be any of a number of categories
Random variable	A variable whose value is determined by chance

6. SCORES, DOLLARS, AND OTHER QUANTITATIVE VARIABLES

6.1 CONTINUOUS VARIABLES

The Terra Nueva problem involved two qualitative variables—foam insulation and rash. Many of the issues that concern policy makers and lawyers involve quantitative variables as well. Sometimes, policy makers may just need a picture of a population—for example, the age distribution of residents of the United States. Sometimes, they may want to compare two different populations—for example, the income of men and women holding the same job. This would involve one qualitative variable (sex) and one quantitative variable (income). And policy makers often are concerned about the relationship between two quantitative variables, say the relationship between per-pupil expenditure and academic achievement.

We introduce the statistical concepts underlying such studies by trying to learn whether Big-Mart is discriminating against female assistant managers by paying them lower wages than their male counterparts. We will look at the relationship between wage and gender at the Big-Mart stores, as well as other relevant information, to help determine this issue.

6.1.1 Central Tendency

Suppose that you were head of Big-Mart's human resources division, and were asked for information about all assistant managers' salaries. If you could communicate only a single number, what would it be? Most likely you would provide information relating to the **central tendency** of a sample of salaries. This means a number that indicates a salary that is somehow typical of the population. There are three commonly used descriptive statistics that describe the central tendency of quantitative distributions—the mean, the median, and the mode.

The **mean** is the average. So if you pulled five assistant managers' files at random, and their salaries were $36,857, $37,532, $39,774, $40,830, $42,797, the mean salary of these employees would be (36,857 + 37,532 + 39,774 + 40,830 + 42,797)/5 = $39,558.

The mean is a good way to indicate the central tendency of a set of data, and is the statistic most often used to describe quantitative variables. However, it is sensitive to **outliers**. An outlier is an observation that is very different from the other observations. Outliers can be the result of data entry errors, or they may reflect an aspect of the population unrelated to your concern. Consider the assistant manager in our small sample with a salary of $42,797. If the clerk doing data entry mistook the four for a nine in that survey answer, the mean would change from $39,558 to $49,558, a $10,000 increase just as a result of the change in that single salary. Or his salary might be atypically high because he was the boss's son.

In cases in which it is important to avoid the effects of outliers, the **median** is a better measure of central tendency. The median is the number that falls in the middle of the observations, when they are ordered by magnitude. (If there are an even number of observations, the median is the average of the two observations that fall in the middle when the scores are ordered.) So, for our five salaries, the median is $39,774. You can see why the median will not be strongly affected by outliers—the values of the extreme scores are not involved in the calculation. Thus, the change in one salary that would lead to a $10,000 increase in the mean would have no effect on the median. The median is often used in reports of housing prices, since, in a neighborhood of mostly homes worth less than $500,000, just one multimillion dollar home could increase the mean by thousands.

In some cases it is useful to consider the **mode** of a set of data. The mode is the value that occurs the most times. The term has the same origin as "mode" in fashion—the most popular number.

6.1.2 Dispersion, Variance, and Standard Deviation

So, if you were allowed to report only one piece of information about a set of salaries, some measure of central tendency would be a good candidate. What would be your choice for a *second* piece of information? Central tendency neglects an important aspect of a set of numbers, its **dispersion**. For example, the set of five salaries given above have a mean of $39,558. But the same mean might have come from a set of five in which three employees earn $19,550 and the other two earn $69,570, or from a set of five in which all five earn $39,558. Dispersion is how spread out the data are. The former set has large dispersion, while the latter has small (actually zero) dispersion. Paying attention to dispersion lets us discriminate between bunched and spread data.

Figure 6.1 shows two sets of data. Which has greater dispersion?

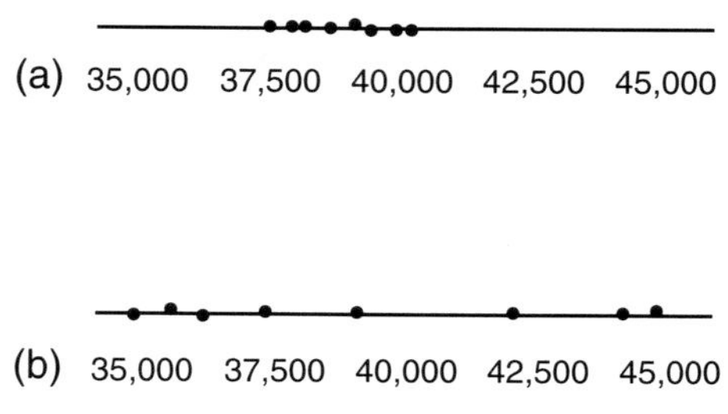

FIGURE 6.1 EXAMPLES OF DISPERSION.

When the mean is used to measure central tendency, the **standard deviation (SD)** is usually used to measure the dispersion. The standard deviation of a population is an indication of the amount by which the numbers differ from the mean.

How do we determine the standard deviation? We want to know how far the five salaries deviate from the mean salary. Since we do not know the population mean,[1] we estimate it with the mean of our sample of five, $39,558. For example, by subtracting $39,558 from each of our five salaries, on the high side we have what is shown in Table 6.1(a).

TABLE 6.1(a) DEVIATION OF HIGH SALARIES FROM THE MEAN

Salary	39,774	42,797	40,830
Deviation	216	3239	1272

And on the low side, we have what is shown in Table 6.1(b).

TABLE 6.1(b) DEVIATION OF LOW SALARIES FROM THE MEAN

Salary	36,857	37,532
Deviation	-2701	-2026

Because by definition the mean is in the middle, the average of the deviations themselves will always be zero. To get a useful measure of the amount of dispersion in the sample we need to make the numbers positive and give extra weight to those observations further from the mean. To do so, we square each observation's deviation from the mean and then take the average of all those deviations, which is 5,888,960.[2]

This gives the **variance**, which is a calculation of how far the data points deviate from the mean. But because we squared each deviation, the value of the

1. See Section 5.3.

2. Actually, we take a kind of average in which, instead of dividing by the number of data points (denoted N), we divide by one less than that (N-1), in this case 4. $(216^2 + 3239^2 + 1272^2 + (-2701)^2 + (-2026)^2)/4 = 5{,}888{,}960$. Why N-1? We want to average the squared deviations of the five salaries from the population mean, but, since it is unknown, we are using the sample mean instead. The sample mean is calculated from our same sample of five salaries, so it will be especially close to these particular five salaries. That is, because it is calculated from this particular sample, the sample mean is closer to the sample values than is the population mean. Therefore, the deviations we calculate will be smaller than the deviations we really want, the deviations from the population mean. In order to make up for this, we increase the estimate slightly by decreasing the denominator of the average, from N to N-1.

variance is entirely incommensurate with salaries. Therefore, we take the square root of the variance to get the **standard deviation**, in this case $\sqrt{5{,}888{,}960}$ = \$2,427.

A small standard deviation indicates that scores vary little around the mean, while a large standard deviation means that they vary a lot.

6.1.2.a A Sample of One Hundred Salaries with a Mean of \$38,627 For reasons we will come to below, a sample of only five assistant managers' salaries is usually too small to do useful statistical analyses. Therefore, we based the rest of the chapter on a sample of one hundred salaries, described in the Appendix (Section 6.4). Whereas our sample of five salaries had a mean of \$39,558, the sample of one hundred has a mean of \$38,627. The standard deviation for the large sample turns out to be \$1,800. If you wonder why the samples might have different means, stay tuned.

6.1.3 Normal Distributions

In Section 5.2, we introduced the concept of probability distributions for qualitative variables. Quantitative variables also have probability distributions. While qualitative variable have discrete amounts of probability (e.g., 0.5 on heads, 0.5 on tails), the probability distribution of a quantitative variable is a continuous function of the possible values of the variable.

A common probability distribution of quantitative variables is the **normal distribution**, whose graph is the bell curve. Height, weight, and many other natural phenomena tend to be characterized by a normal distribution.

Although not inevitable, it is not unusual for the salaries of a group of employees to be normally distributed. If you were to take the sample of one hundred assistant managers and plot their salaries on the vertical axis, you would end up with approximately a bell curve. This would be the empirical distribution of *salary* (analogous to Figure 5.1(b)). If you knew *all* the Big-Mart assistant managers' salaries, you would have the population distribution of *salary* (analogous to Figure 5.1(a)), which would even more closely approximate the normal distribution. Figure 6.2 shows a normal distribution of the salaries of all Big-Mart assistant managers.

One important quality of a normal distribution is that its mean, median, and mode are all the same. To find the mean, draw a vertical line down from its peak to the horizontal axis.

Another property of a normal distribution is the *68/95/99.7 rule*: 68 percent of the population fall within a range that is one standard deviation to the left and one standard deviation to the right of the mean, 95 percent fall within two standard deviations to either side, and 99.7 percent fall within three standard deviations to either side. This is true, regardless of how large or small the standard deviation is—that is, regardless of the population's dispersion.

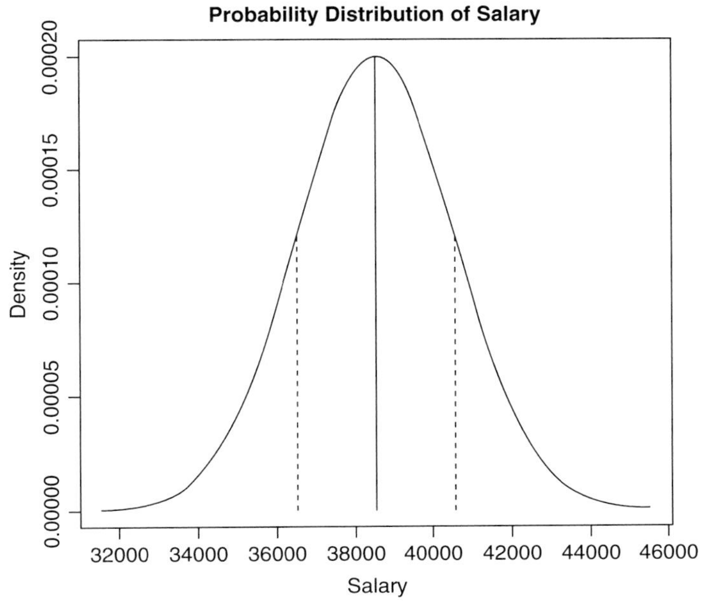

FIGURE 6.2 THE POPULATION DISTRIBUTION OF ASSISTANT MANAGERS' SALARIES.

So if the salaries of Big-Mart assistant managers are normally distributed, and you sample a salary at random, the probability is about 0.68 that it will be within 1 SD, or \$1,820, of the mean, and 0.95 that it will be within 2 SD, or \$3,640.

A competitor of Big-Mart is the Bulls-eye chain of stores. As a check on your understanding of the idea of standard deviation, consider Figure 6.3. Panel (a) displays the probability distribution of *salary* among Big-Mart assistant

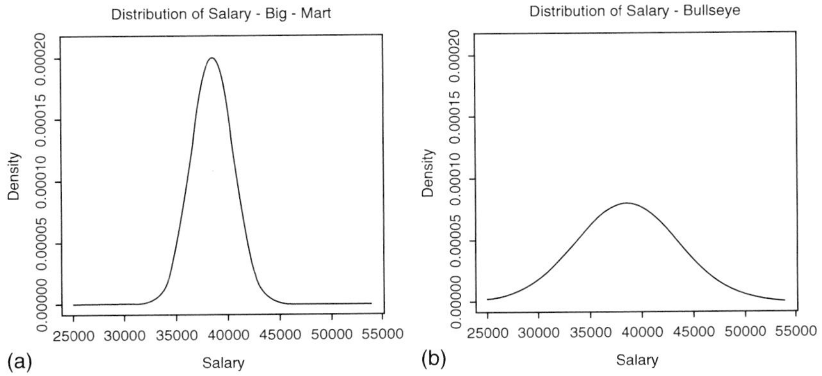

FIGURE 6.3 (A) AND (B) DISTRIBUTIONS OF SALARIES HAVING THE SAME MEAN BUT DIFFERENT STANDARD DEVIATIONS.

managers (the same as Figure 6.2 but graphed on a different horizontal scale), and panel (b) displays the probability distribution of *salary* among Bulls-eye assistant managers. Bulls-eye assistant managers have the same mean salary as do Big-Mart assistant managers. Which population distribution has the greater standard deviation?

The standard deviation tells how useful the mean of the sample of salaries is in estimating the mean of the population of assistant managers' salaries. If we could look at a second number (after the sample mean) describing the distribution of salaries, the standard deviation would be a good choice.

You can visualize the bell shape of a normally distributed curve as an upside-down bowl. Since the inside of the bowl is facing down, we say that there the curve is **concave downward**. On the left and right sides of the curve, it is the shape of a part of a right-side-up bowl. The inside of the bowl faces up, and this part of the curve is called **concave upward**. An **inflection point** of a curve is a point at which the curve switches from being concave up to concave down or vice versa. In a normal distribution, there are two inflection points, and they are each exactly one SD away from the mean. Using this fact is a good way to get a rough idea of the SD when you have only a graph of the probability distribution.

6.1.4 Estimating the Population Mean

As in Terra Nueva, we have data on only a sample of the total population. The mean of the sample is our best estimate of the mean of the population. But how precise is the estimate?

The statistic describing the precision of an estimate is its **standard error (SE)**. The SE of the sample mean is the SD of its **sampling distribution**. To understand this new term, consider:

Recall that the sample mean of the one hundred Big-Mart salaries is $38,627. We want an idea of how far off this estimate is from the true population mean. Suppose that we now take ninety-nine more samples of one hundred managers each, and calculate the mean of each of these hundred samples. The distribution of these hundred means—which are likely not to be all the same—is the **sampling distribution**. This distribution is always normal distribution (even if the samples themselves are not), and it will always have a smaller SD than most of the samples on which it is based. The distribution might look like Figure 6.4.

The mean of means, the peak of the sampling distribution, is not likely to be hugely different from the mean of our first sample. But the standard error—the SD of the sampling distribution—will be much smaller than the SD of this one sample.

Why so? When you take a mean of each sample, you are getting rid of some of the variation. Accordingly, the variation of the means of a bunch of samples is likely to be smaller. Another way to think about it is to ask yourself which would be easier to guess: the salary of the next assistant manager chosen at random, or

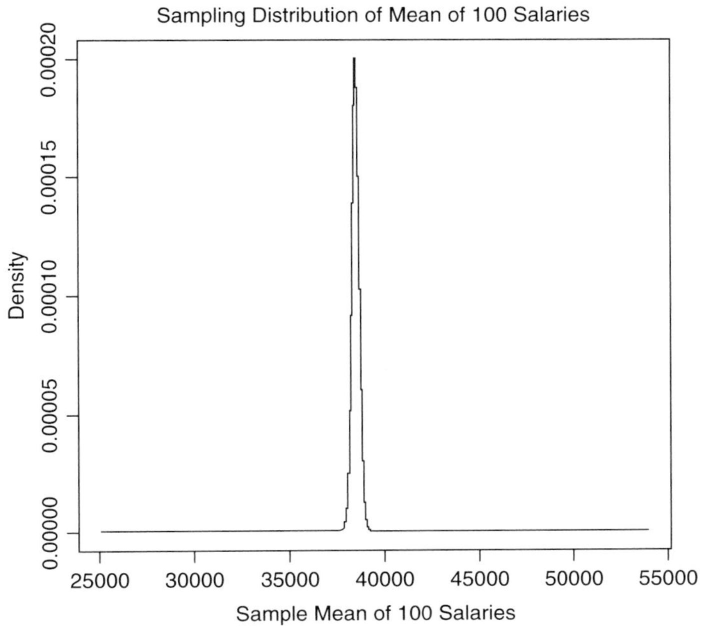

FIGURE 6.4 SAMPLING DISTRIBUTION OF THE MEAN OF 100 SALARIES.

the mean of the next one hundred salaries chosen at random? In the mean of 100, an extreme score is likely to be canceled out when combined with the other 99. On the other hand, it is quite possible that one randomly chosen salary will be extreme.

So how far from the population mean is any sample mean likely to be? Rather than take a hundred different samples, you can just use this formula to calculate its standard error (SE)—

$$SE = \frac{SD}{\sqrt{N}}$$

—where SD is the standard deviation of the sample and N is the size of the sample. The smaller the SE, the better an estimate our sample mean is of the mean of the population.

Looking at the denominator, you'll see that the larger the sample, the smaller the standard error—though the SE only decreases by the square root of the size of the sample. As we obtain more and more observations, the distribution of the sample mean becomes tighter and tighter about the population mean, the standard error decreases, and the precision with which a sample mean estimates the population mean increases.

Why is the mean of a larger sample a more precise estimate of the population mean than the mean of a small sample? Let's go back to the discussion of categorical variables early in the previous chapter. Suppose that you didn't know anything about the mechanics of coin tosses or dice rolls: how much information does one toss of a coin that lands on heads, or one roll of a die that lands on four, provide about the chances of coins coming up heads or dice landing on four? What about two tosses or rolls? What about a thousand? So, too, the mean of the sample of many salaries provides a better estimate than the mean of a sample of one, or even five.

Looking at the numerator, you'll see that the smaller the standard deviation of the sample, the smaller the SE. Recall that the standard deviation of a sample is a measure of the dispersion of the items in the sample, in this case the dispersion of salaries. Which is more dispersed: a sample of the population of Big-Mart assistant managers or a sample of Big-Mart employees (including everyone from cleaning staff to executives)? And which population mean would you be better able to estimate from their respective samples of one hundred: the population of Big-Mart assistant managers or the population of all Big-Mart employees?

Notice that the formula for determining SE does not take account of the size of the population from which the sample is taken. Our confidence in the relationship between the sample mean and the population mean is based solely on the size and standard deviation of the sample and not on the proportion of the sample to the population as a whole. If this seems counterintuitive, consider: as long as a pot of soup is well stirred, one sip is all you need to taste the soup—no matter what the size of the pot.

In our example, using the formula above, the SE of the sample mean is $\$1820/\sqrt{100} = \$182$.

Another common way to indicate our confidence in the estimate is to report a range, called a **confidence interval**, around it that is likely (often with 95 percent probability) to cover the true mean. (The confidence interval is the same as the margin of error in a public opinion poll.)

Because the sampling distribution of the sample mean is normally distributed, we are 68 percent confident that the sample mean is within one SE of the population mean, and 95 percent confident that it is within two SEs. The smaller the SE, the smaller the confidence interval.

Thus, using our estimated SE of $182, we can be about 95 percent confident that the mean score for the population is within $364 of our estimate:

$$\$38{,}627 \pm 2 * \$182,$$

i.e., between $38,263 and $38,991. In other words, the estimate of $38,627 has a margin of error of 2 * $182 = $364.[3]

---

3. More precisely, there is a 95 percent chance that the sample mean is within 1.96 standard errors of the population mean. A more precise estimate of the 95 percent confidence interval for the population mean is therefore $38,627 ± 1.96 * $182.

Sample vs. Population Mean

Though it is generally true that one never knows the population mean and must estimate it from the sample, *Sears, Roebuck, and Co. vs. City of Inglewood* (Los Angeles Superior Court, 1955) provides a rare counterexample. The City of Inglewood imposed a half-percent sales tax on sales made by stores to residents living within the city limits. Sears sued to recover taxes erroneously imposed on nonresidents. Sears retained a statistician, who randomly sampled 33 out of the 826 business days during the period at issue, and examined sales slips from each of those 33 days. Based on the mean overpayments on these days, the expert estimated that the total overpayment was $28,250 with a 95 percent confidence interval between $24,000 and $32,400. The judge refused to accept the estimate and required Sears to prove its refund claim on each individual transaction rather than on the sample information. Subsequently, a complete audit of all transactions over the entire 826 days was performed and the actual refund amount was determined to be $26,750.22—well within the confidence interval.

R. Clay Sprowls, *The Admissibility of Sample Data Into a Court of Law: A Case History*, 4 UCLA L. Rev. 222 (1957).

6.1.5 Intuitions about Sample Size and Variability

As the preceding discussion indicates, estimates vary less when we have more observations. We just relied on your intuitions to show this. But studies by Daniel Kahneman and Amos Tversky indicate that this is not intuitively obvious to many people. Kahneman and Tversky[4] gave the following problem to Stanford undergraduates:

> A certain town is served by two hospitals. In the larger hospital about 45 babies are born each day, and in the smaller hospital about 15 babies are born each day. As you know, about 50% of all babies are boys. The exact percentage of baby boys, however, varies from day to day. Sometimes it may be higher than 50%, sometimes lower. For a period of 1 year, each hospital recorded the days on which more than 60% of the babies born were boys. Which hospital do you think recorded more such days?
>
> Take a moment to write down your answer before reading on.

An extreme outcome is more likely to occur in a small sample, because an average pulled from a small sample has the potential to be much more affected by an unusual pattern of births and consequently has higher variance. You can think

4. Daniel Kahneman and Amos Tversky, *Subjective Probability: A Judgment of Representativeness*, 3 Cognitive Psychology 430–454 (1972).

about this in the terms that we presented above: for each day, we compute an estimate of the probability of a boy being born. This estimate is in fact the mean of a set of observations, where each observation corresponds to a birth and is either 1 (if a boy was born) or 0 (if a girl was born). The standard error of the mean of 45 observations is less than that of the mean of 15 observations, so the confidence interval on the percentage of boys born is tighter for the large hospital. Hence we would expect more days with 60 percent boys from the smaller hospital.

The students' responses are shown in Table 6.2. Only 20 percent of the respondents answered correctly:

TABLE 6.2 ESTIMATES OF BOY BABIES BORN IN LARGE AND SMALL HOSPITALS

Response	Frequency
Larger hospital	12
Smaller hospital	10
About the same (within 5%)	28

Kahneman and Tversky found several other circumstances in which people fail to comprehend the relationship between sample size and variance, and explained this failure in terms of the **representativeness heuristic** (discussed in Section 8.3), in which people intuitively assign a probability to an event according to its similarity to the processes that are supposed to produce it. A heuristic is an unconscious mental shortcut that substitutes for conscious analysis. In this case, if the process is known to produce boys and girls with equal probabilities, the heuristic suggests that any random sample of births will produce an equal number.

The **availability heuristic** (described in Section 9.6) can also affect people's intuitive inferences from small samples. In an experiment, students were significantly more influenced by personally hearing two or three fellow students evaluate a particular course than by the mean course evaluations based on a sample of "dozens of previous students."[5]

6.1.6 Comparing Two Groups: Testing for a Relationship Between One Quantitative Variable (*salary*) and One Categorical Variable (*sex*)

So far we have examined a sample of one hundred assistant managers at Big-Mart to ask how confident we could be that the mean of their salaries reflects the mean of the population of all assistant managers. Here we build on this scaffolding to compare two groups of assistant managers: men and women.

5. Eugene Borgida and Richard E. Nisbett, *The Differential Impact of Abstract vs. Concrete Information on Decisions*, 7 J. Applied Social Psychology 258 (1977).

In particular, we would like to know whether male and female assistant managers at Big-Mart have different salaries, on average.

The human resources director of Big-Mart was motivated to ask this question when, in reviewing the sample of one hundred assistant managers, which includes forty-nine men and fifty-one women, she noticed that the groups had different mean salaries:

mean salary of males: \$39,257,
mean salary of females: \$38,528.

Thus, in our sample, on average, male assistant managers make \$729 more than female assistant managers.

While males have a slightly higher mean in our sample, we need a statistical test to determine whether this is just due to the chance involved in sampling from the population, or whether there is a real difference in the population. Thus, we need to address the question whether, in the whole population of Big-Mart assistant managers, there is a relationship between *salary* and *sex*—whether we can say with sufficient confidence that the curves for the population of male and female assistant managers also diverge.

We engage in the process of hypothesis testing that we used to determine whether there was a relationship between foam insulation and rashes in Terra Nueva. We'll go through the same five steps as before.

Step 1) State the hypotheses of the test:

- The **null hypothesis** indicates that there is no relationship between two variables—that the two curves have the same mean (Figure 6.5). It is what we set out to reject.

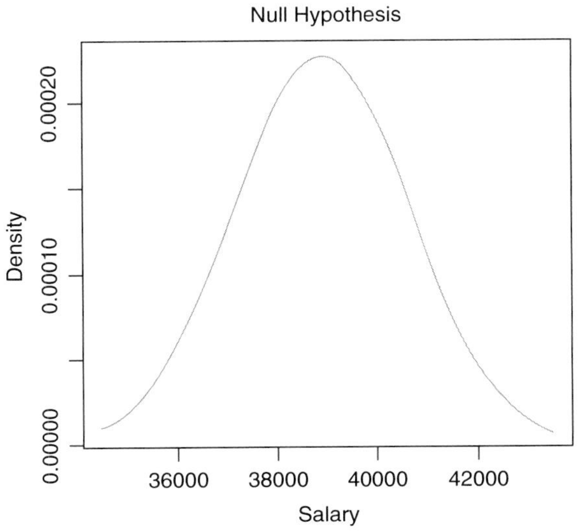

FIGURE 6.5 NULL HYPOTHESES.

- The **alternative hypothesis** is that there *is* a relationship between two variables—that the two curves have different means. Figure 6.6 shows one of myriad possible alternative hypotheses. (One rationale for null hypothesis testing is that there is only one null hypothesis.)

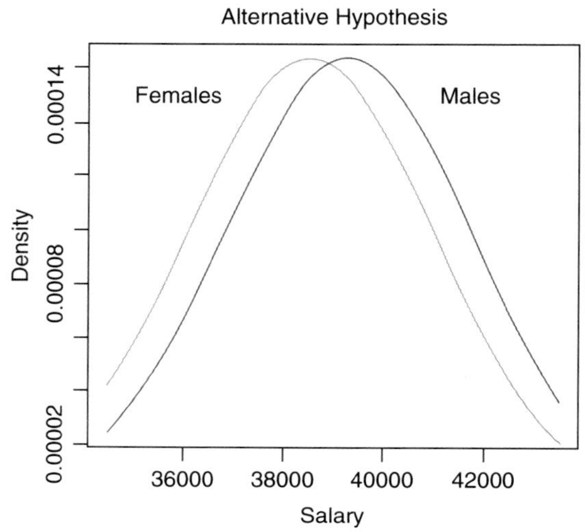

FIGURE 6.6 ALTERNATIVE HYPOTHESES.

In our example, the null hypothesis is that there is no relationship between male and female assistant managers' salaries.

Step 2) Set the level of the test. Let's set it at $\alpha = 0.05$, meaning that we are willing to allow a 5 percent chance that we conclude statistical significance even if no relationship exists.

Step 3) Suppose that the null hypothesis is true. The main idea of a statistical hypothesis test is to find how extreme the sample data would be if the null hypothesis were true.

Step 4) Calculate how extreme the sample data are. How likely or unlikely would it be to see a difference in mean salaries of at least $729 in a random sample if that difference were $0 in the population? We calculate this probability with the t-test (using statistical software).[6] While we won't show the calculation here, the probability (the p-value) of having data this extreme is 0.03. In other

6. The t-test considers the difference of $729 relative to the variance of the data, and compares it to the t-distribution, a probability distribution like the normal distribution but that varies according to the size of the sample.

words, under the null hypothesis of no salary difference in the population, there would be a 3 percent chance that, in samples like ours, the mean salaries of the two groups would differ by at least $729.

Step 5) State your conclusion. If the p-value is less than the alpha level, we reject the null hypothesis in favor of the alternative. In our case, the p-value is 0.03. This means that, under the null hypothesis of no relationship between *sex* and *salary*, only 3 percent of samples would be more extreme than ours. Since this is less than 5 percent (the level of Type I error we were willing to tolerate) we can reject the null hypothesis. We conclude that there is a relationship between *sex* and *salary*.

So we have concluded that there is a statistically significant difference between the salaries of male and female assistant managers at Big-Mart. But can we conclude that Big-Mart is discriminating based on sex in setting salaries? Perhaps there is another variable that explains the difference. We explore this possibility in Section 6.2.7.b below.

6.2 REGRESSION

In Section 5.6, we encountered the definition of independence between variables.

- If variables are **independent**, the value of one of them provides no information about the value of the other. For example (so far as we know), the days of the week on which people are born provides no information about their height or weight.
- If variables are **not independent**, differences in one correspond to differences in the other. For example, *height* and *weight* are related: taller individuals tend to be heavier.

Much of statistics is concerned with whether, how, and how much variables are related.

In this section, we look at the relationship between two quantitative variables. We use an example from an important realm of public policy: education. In particular, we will look at the relationship between a state's *spending* on public education and *student achievement* as measured by scores on the NAEP (National Assessment of Educational Progress) test.[7]

7. Each state's NAEP scores aggregated from individual student scores, using sampling methods discussed in the preceding chapters. Tests are administered to a random sample of students in schools that themselves are chosen to be representative of schools and students in their states selected to participate. NAEP typically selects 3000 students in approximately 100 schools in each state for each grade and subject.

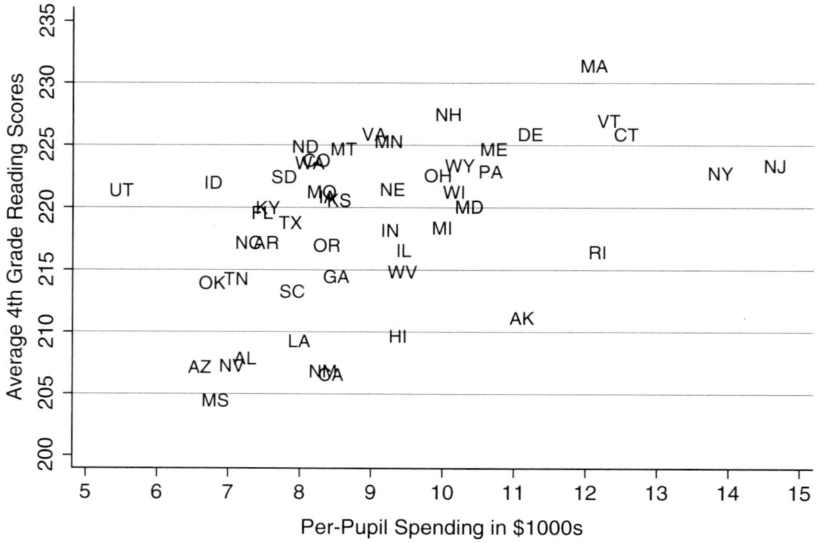

FIGURE 6.7 SCATTERPLOT OF SCHOOL SPENDING AND READING SCORES.

6.2.1 Line of Best Fit

A good way to gauge the relationship between two quantitative variables, such as per-pupil *spending* and *achievement*, is to produce a **scatterplot**. This is a graph with one variable along each axis, with each instance of data represented by a point. Figure 6.7 shows the relationship between states' per-pupil spending in public education and fourth grade reading achievement. The horizontal (X) axis measures per-pupil spending, ranging from $4,000 to $12,000. The vertical (Y) axis measures NAEP reading test scores, on a scale that ranges from 200 to 235.

In this scatterplot, each point represents one state. For example, looking at the leftmost datapoint, Utah spends $5475 per pupil and its average fourth graders score is 221.3. Moving to the right, Idaho, Oklahoma, Arizona, and Mississippi spend in the mid to high $6000s per pupil, and have average reading scores ranging from 222 to 204.

Looking at the scatterplot is a good way to get an idea of the relationship between two quantitative variables. In this section we will use statistics to assess **linear** relationships. If two variables vary linearly with each other, the rate of change of one compared to the other is constant. For example, if *achievement* and *spending* are linearly related, then, if *spending* increases by a certain amount, achievement will increase by some constant amount. If the variables are linearly related, the points cluster around a straight line, and the tighter their clustering the stronger the relationship.

A large number of relationships relevant to law and policy are approximately linear—at least in the range of interest. For example, income may increase linearly with years of higher education, and the number of crimes in a particular neighborhood may decrease linearly as the number of police patrols in the neighborhood increases.

When studying two quantitative variables, we often consider one the **predictor** or **independent variable** and the other the **outcome**, **response**, or **dependent**

Nonlinear Relationships

Nonlinear relationships are also common. For example, the number and severity of traffic accidents increases with the speed at which vehicles are traveling, but the increase is geometric (i.e., based on a power of the speed)—rather than arithmetic. In this case, the relationship would not be shown by a line, but by an upward-sloping curve. Or consider the relationship between *room temperature* and productivity in the workplace. A scatterplot of points with horizontal position indicating temperature and vertical position indicating productivity might have a ∩ (inverted U) shape, with low productivity values at both extremes and high productivity in the middle.

In cases where the relationships between the variables are *monotonic*—that is, the slope of the curve does not change direction—the variables sometimes can be transformed to make their relationship linear. For example, the radius of a circle and its area are not linearly related, but the radius is linearly related to the square root of the area. Other functions commonly used to linearize a relationship are the square, the logarithm, and the reciprocal.

variable. When constructing a scatterplot, it is conventional to put the predictor on the horizontal (or x) axis and the outcome on the vertical (or y) axis.

In our example, we would like to predict students' achievement when we know the state's per-pupil spending, so *spending* is the predictor and *achievement* is the outcome. If these two variables are linearly related, we can describe their relationship with the **line of best fit**, also called the **regression line**. This is the line that gives the best prediction of the dependent variable when the independent variable is known. Figure 6.8 shows the line of best fit for the relationship between *spending* and *achievement*.

To predict a state's level of student achievement when we know its per-pupil spending, we would find the point on the line directly above the known value of *spending*, and its height would be our guess of *achievement*. For example, if we

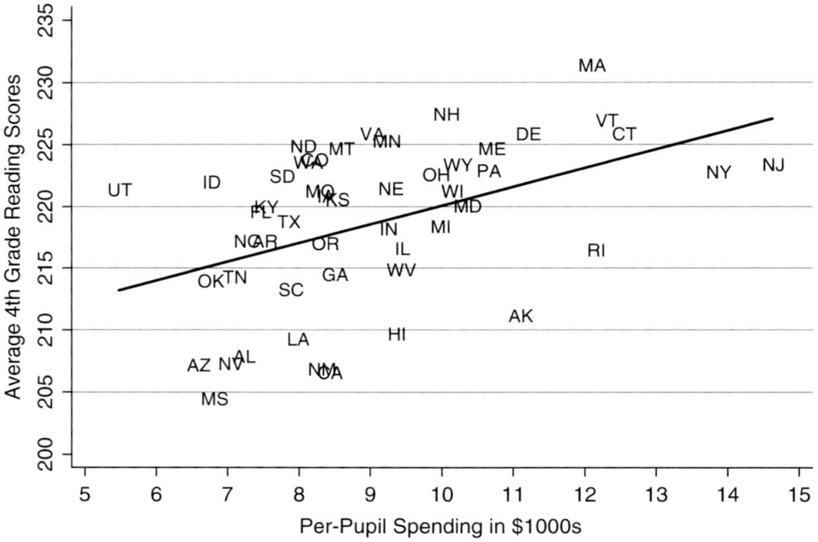

FIGURE 6.8 REGRESSION OF READING SCORES ON SPENDING.

know that a state spends $10,000 per pupil, our best guess is that its students would have an average NAEP score of about 220.

Often the response (such as *achievement*) is represented by the letter y and the predictor (such as *spending*) by x. The line of best fit is then represented by the **regression equation**, which is also the general equation for a line:

$$y = a + bx.$$

Because we can use this line to predict the response when we know the predictor, it is also called the **prediction equation**. In our example:

Predicted achievement = $a + b$ * *spending.*

- a is the **intercept**—the height at which the line of best fit intercepts, or crosses, the vertical axis at $0 per pupil. This is not shown in Figures 6.7 and 6.8; it is off the chart to the left. In this purely hypothetical case, a is 205—a state's average predicted achievement score if the predictor, per-pupil expenditure, were $0. (Since $0 is outside the range of the data, we would not venture to make that prediction; although the relationship between spending achievement appears linear in the range of the data we do not have evidence that it is linear elsewhere, and it is dangerous to make extrapolations outside the range of the actual data.)

- b is the **slope** of the line—the amount the line goes up for each unit it goes right. b is also called the **coefficient** of x. 1.5 is the slope of this regression line. With an increase in spending of $1000, the predicted average score increases by 1.5.
- x is the **predictor**, in this case *spending*.
- y is the predicted outcome, in this case *achievement*.

While x and y vary from state to state, a and b represent constant numbers.

If b is positive, the line slopes up, so the outcome increases when the predictor increases. If b is negative, the line slopes down, so the outcome decreases when the predictor increases. a and b can be calculated by any statistical computer program.

If the slope (b) equaled zero, we would have a horizontal line, which would correspond to no relationship between the predictor and the outcome. In our example, no matter how much was spent, we would not change our prediction of achievement.

In our example, if spending increases by $1000, the predicted outcome y (*achievement*) increases by 1.5 points on the NAEP test. So our regression equation is

*Predicted achievement = 205+ 1.5 * spending (in thousands).*

For example, if a state spends $8000 per pupil, our best guess is that its fourth graders will on average score 217 on the reading test. You can observe this by looking at the regression line in Figure 6.7.

The difference between a data point's observed outcome and its predicted outcome is called the **error** of the prediction. In Figure 6.7, we can see that California spends $8,417 per pupil, and its students score 206.5 on average. But the line of best fit predicts that students in a state with $8,417 of spending per pupil will achieve scores of 217.7 on average. The difference of 11.2 is the error of that observation.

The line of best fit is the line that minimizes the sum of the squared errors over all observations in the sample. (Squaring each error ensures that it is positive and weights those observations that are further away.)

6.2.2 Correlation

Another way of saying that two variables are linearly related is to say that they are **correlated.** The **correlation coefficient** (or **correlation**), denoted r, of two variables indicates the strength of the linear relationship.

r has the same sign (positive, negative, or zero) as b, so, like b, it is positive when the line of best fit slopes up (when the outcome increases with an increase in the predictor) and is negative when the line slopes down (when the outcome decreases with an increase in the predictor). However, the magnitudes of b and r are generally not equal.

- b is the amount by which y increases for a one-unit increase in x. Two states that differ in *spending* by $1000 differ in predicted *achievement* by b.

- *r* is the number of standard deviations that *y* increases for a one SD increase in *x*. In this case $r = 0.46$.

Recall the discussion of SD earlier in Section 6.1.2. We won't do the calculations here, but in this example, one SD in spending = $1,934, and one SD in test scores is 6.45. So two states that differ in *spending* by one SD ($1,934) differ in predicted *achievement* by *r* SDs, or 3.0.

r is always between -1 and 1. Unlike *b*, *r* is not affected by the scale of the variables. If *spending* were measured in dollars instead of thousands of dollars, *b* would be 1000 times smaller, but *r* is the same no matter what the scale.

The correlation coefficient thus reflects two aspects of a linear relationship: direction and strength.

> *Direction*: A positive correlation coefficient indicates a positive linear relationship, in which the two variables increase and decrease together. A negative correlation coefficient indicates a negative linear relationship, in which, as one variable increases, the other variable decreases. In this case, the regression line would slope downward from left to right and we say that the variables are **inversely** or **negatively correlated**. (What is an example of two inversely correlated variables?)
>
> *Strength:* The correlation coefficient (*r*) also describes the strength of this relationship: for a weak relationship, the correlation coefficient is small (close to 0), while a stronger relationship will be reflected in a larger (closer to 1 or -1) correlation coefficient. When two variables have a large correlation coefficient, we say that they are **highly correlated**.

Let's look at the extremes of *r* in the context of the NAEP reading score example. Recall that $b = 0$ whenever $r = 0$. So if *spending* and *achievement* were not correlated, the data points would be scattered randomly on the scatterplot, and the line of best fit would be a horizontal line at the average achievement among all fifty states, i.e., 217, as shown approximately in Figure 6.9. (Samples being what they are, our effort to randomize did not quite succeed. What does Figure 6.9 actually suggest about the correlation?

This means that per-pupil spending gives us no information at all about reading achievement.

At the other extreme, suppose $r = 1$. Then we would say that *spending* and *achievement* were **perfectly correlated**. As is evident in Figure 6.10, if you know a state's per-pupil expenditure, you can predict exactly its fourth grade reading scores.

6.2.3 Regression to the Mean

The name **regression** was coined by Francis Galton, who developed the concept while exploring the relationship between the heights of fathers and sons. Galton, a cousin of Charles Darwin, was keenly interested in the nature of heredity and explored its implications in a number of domains. When examining the heights

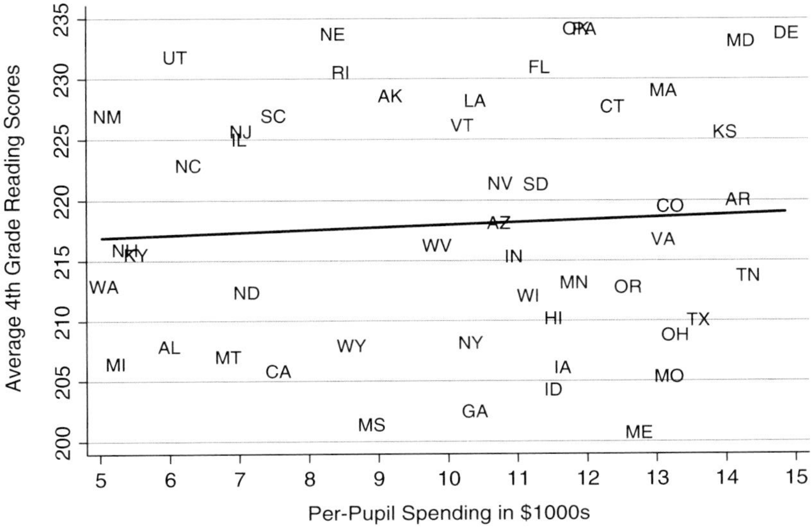

FIGURE 6.9 REGRESSION OF READING SCORES ON SPENDING WITH (ALMOST) NO CORRELATION.

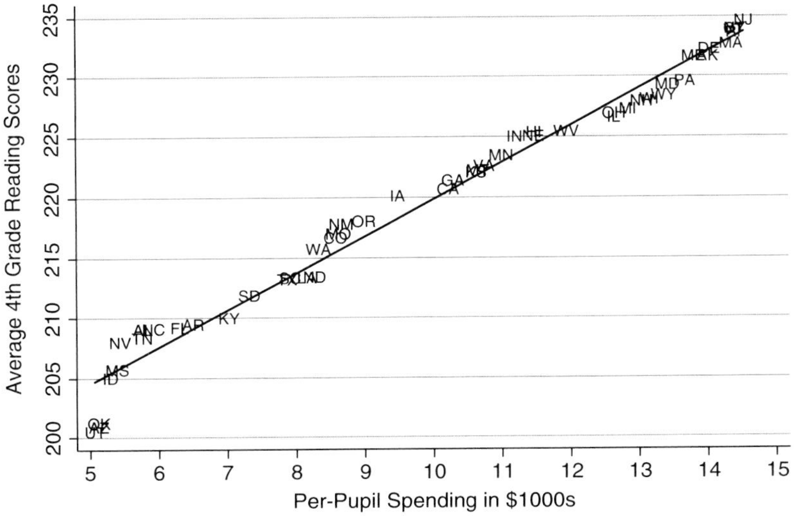

FIGURE 6.10 REGRESSION OF READING SCORES ON SPENDING WITH PERFECT CORRELATION.

of men in successive generations, Galton found that while tall fathers tended to have reasonably tall sons, the sons were seldom as tall as their fathers. Likewise, very short fathers had reasonably short sons, but the sons were unlikely to be as short as their fathers. Because it seemed like the children's heights were moving away from the heights of their fathers, and towards the mean height, Galton dubbed this phenomenon **regression to the mean**.

6.2.3.a Regression and Chance Galton came to understand that this process is not due to a characteristic unique to heredity, but to the involvement of chance. Regression to the mean is a consequence of the fact that some chance is involved in determining the height of an individual, i.e., that r is not equal to 1 or -1. By **chance** in this context, we mean anything that is not explained by the predictor (*father's height*), for example, mother's height or nutrition—that is, chance comprises both factors that we don't know about and factors that we know about but are not considering.

To see how the involvement of chance produces regression to the mean, consider a case in which chance alone determines the outcome. Imagine that you telephone two numbers selected from the phone book at random, and ask the people at the other end to tell you their height. The first person you speak to reports his height as 6'2". Do you expect the next person to be of similar height, or closer to the average height of people in the phone book?

When chance is the only process involved, it is intuitive that an extreme event—like a very tall person—is likely to be followed by something less extreme. Moderate outcomes are just more probable. But the same phenomenon holds even when there is a relationship between pairs of events, as there is between the heights of fathers and sons. While heredity contributes to determining a son's height, so do several other factors. Having a tall father pulls the son's height toward the tall end, but chance pulls it toward the middle. Consequently, regression to the mean takes place.

Just as factors other than a father's height determine the height of his son, so do many factors besides a state's per-pupil expenditures determine fourth grade reading scores. Consider that states may differ in families' average education and average income, and that these factors may also play a role in student achievement.

6.2.4 Intuitions about Regression

Regression to the mean is not intuitively obvious, and even people trained in statistics can fail to recognize and interpret it. Kahneman and Tversky[8] gave the following problem to graduate students in psychology:

> The instructors in a flight school adopted a policy of consistent positive reinforcement recommended by psychologists. They verbally reinforced each

8. Daniel Kahneman and Amos Tversky, *On the Psychology of Prediction*, 80 Psychological Review 237–251 (1973).

successful execution of a flight maneuver. After some spending with this training approach, the instructors claimed that contrary to psychological doctrine, high praise for good execution of complex maneuvers typically resulted in a decrement of performance on the next try. What should the psychologist say in response?

Because performance on flight maneuvers is variable—especially among novice pilots—a pilot who does exceptionally well on one maneuver is likely to do less well on the next, regardless of the instructor's response. By the same token, a pilot who does exceptionally poorly on one maneuver is likely to do better on the next. The quality of any particular student's flight maneuvers may look like a normal distribution, with his own mean score defining the center, and exceptionally good and bad performances lying in the tails.

Though trained in statistics, none of the graduate students attributed the phenomenon to regression to the mean. Rather, they thought that verbal reinforcement might not work for pilots or that positive reinforcement led to the pilots' overconfidence, and some doubted that the flight instructors had accurately perceived the phenomenon.

More generally, people tend to engage in nonregressive predictions. An early experiment by Kahneman and Tversky showed that subjects' predictions of a student's grade point average (GPA) based on (a) the student's grades in percentile form, (b) her success on a mental concentration task, and (c) a measure of her sense of humor—variables that ranged from highly predictive to entirely unpredictive—showed almost no regressiveness in any of the conditions.[9]

In this and similar studies, the subjects were given information that they believed (whether or not extravagantly) to be diagnostic, i.e., predictive. When diagnostic predictors are combined with predictors that subjects believe to be nondiagnostic, this has the effect of diluting the diagnostic predictors and producing more regressive predictions. For example, the strength of the prediction that a social work client who had sadomasochistic thoughts was likely to be a child abuser diminished when subjects were also informed that the client "fixes up cars in his spare time." This is not due to any enlightenment about the regression phenomenon, but more likely to the operation of the **representativeness heuristic**, which made a person who fixes cars as well as having sadomasochistic thoughts seem less typical of a child abuser than one who only has sadomasochistic thoughts.[10] (Other statistical and logical errors caused by the representativeness heuristic are discussed in Section 8.3.)

---

9. Richard E. Nisbett and Lee Ross, Human Inference: Strategies and Shortcomings of Social Judgment (Englewood Cliffs, NJ: Prentice-Hall, 1980).

10. Richard E. Nisbett, Henri Zukier, and Ronald E. Lemley, *The Dilution Effect: Nondiagnostic Information Weakens the Implications of Diagnostic Information*, 13 Cognitive Psychology 248 (1981). Nisbett and Ross, 154–55.

The *winner's curse* refers to the phenomenon that, in an auction with many bidders and high variance in their estimates of the value of the commodity, the winning bidder will overestimate the value of the commodity and pay too much for it. This may occur, for example, when oil companies bid for exploration rights, or baseball teams bid for free agents, or companies compete to acquire another company.

Richard Harrison and Max Bazerman link the winner's curse to regression to the mean.[11] Imagine two normally distributed curves, one showing bidders' estimates of the value of the auctioned item and the other showing their actual bids. Assume that the midpoint of the estimate curve is the actual value of the item. The average bid will be lower than the average estimate, since people will bid less rather than more than their estimate of the value of the item. The winning bid will, by definition, be above the mean of bids, and will reflect one of the highest estimations of the item's value.This concept is illustrated in Figure 6.11.

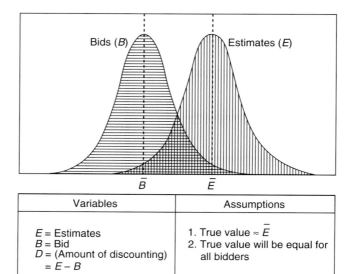

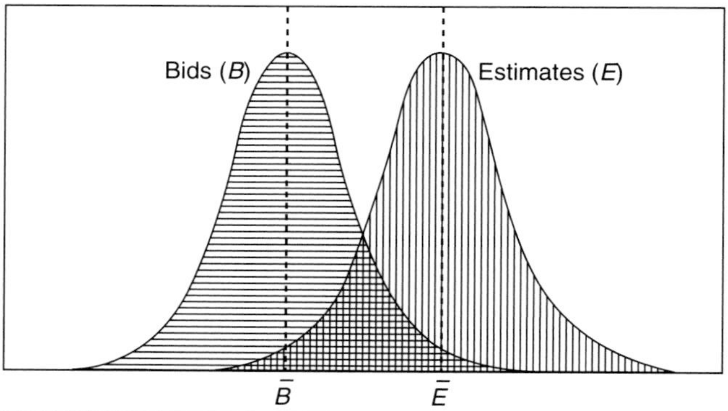

Variables	Assumptions
E = Estimates B = Bid D = (Amount of discounting) = $E - B$	1. True value ≈ $\bar{E}$ 2. True value will be equal for all bidders

FIGURE 6.11 THE WINNER'S CURSE[12] COPYRIGHT © 1995, REPRINTED BY PERMISSION.

11. J. Ricardo Harrison and Max H. Bazerman, *Regression to the Mean, Expectation Inflation, and the Winner's Curse in Organizational Contexts*, in NEGOTIATION AS A SOCIAL PROCESS 69 (Roderick Moreland Kramer and David M. Messick eds., 1995). They draw on an earlier paper by Bazerman and William E. Samuelson, *I Won the Auction But Don't Want the Prize*, 27 JOURNAL OF CONFLICT RESOLUTION 618–634 (1983).

12. *Id.*

By much the same psychology that people engage in nonregressive predictions, bidders at an auction tend not to adjust their estimates downward. And, in the same way, it leads to inflated expectations and systematic disappointment.

Later chapters of the book will discuss biases—in addition to the representativeness heuristic— that may contribute to inflated expectations and to the possibilities for debiasing.

6.2.5 Determining How Much of the Variance in the Outcome Can Be Explained by the Predictor

To recapitulate what we have learned about regression thus far: Suppose we wanted to predict the average reading achievement of a particular state's fourth graders. If we knew nothing about that state's per-pupil spending, our best prediction would be the mean achievement of all fifty states' averages. However, if we knew its per-pupil spending, and had determined a linear relationship between *spending* and *achievement*, we could use this information to improve our prediction. Instead of predicting the mean achievement, represented by a horizontal line on the scatterplot, we would predict the achievement of the point on the line of best fit directly above the state's *spending*. Since this uses additional relevant information, it is likely to be a better prediction, closer to the state's true achievement.

In addition to knowing the strength of the correlation between the two variables, you may be interested in knowing the explanatory power of the predictor, that is, how much of variation of the data can the predictor variable account for. For example, how much of the variation in the height of sons can be accounted for by their fathers' height? How much of the variation in states' fourth grade reading scores can be accounted for by state spending? The more we can account for, the better we understand this piece of the world and the better we—as individuals or policy makers—can use the information for decision making.

Recall the discussion of variance and standard deviation in Section 6.1.2: The deviation of a typical data point from its prediction is measured by the sample's variance (or, alternatively, by its standard deviation, which is the square root of the variance). We calculated the **total variance** of the sample. The total variance is also called the **variance around the mean**, because it is the average of the squared errors, where the error of an observation is its distance from the sample mean.

While the line of best fit provides the best prediction of how a change in one variable will affect another, there are many errors—points that are not on the line of best fit.

Based on the data, we can estimate **the variance around the line of best fit**. Instead of averaging the squared differences between state achievements and the mean achievement, we average the squared errors, where the errors are the vertical distances of the observations from the line of best fit; that is, the differences between each sample member's (state's) observed outcome and its predicted outcome based on its spending (see Figure 6.8). These errors are generally smaller than the errors from the sample mean, so the average of their squares will be smaller. In other words, the variance around the line of best fit is smaller than the variance around the mean. This is because the regression line captures some of the systematic changes in one variable as a function of the other.

The difference between these two variances is referred to as the variance **accounted for by** or **explained by** the predictor, here *spending*. In other words, the total variance of the outcome consists of two parts:

$$\frac{\text{Total varianceof outcome}}{\text{(around its mean)}} = \frac{\text{Variance of outcome}}{\text{explained by predictor}} + \frac{\text{Variance of outcome}}{\text{due to chance}}$$

This is called the **analysis of variance (ANOVA)** equation. The better the predictor, the larger the proportion of the total variance it explains. This proportion is therefore used as a measure of the usefulness of a predictor and is called the **coefficient of determination**:

$$\text{Coefficient of determination} = \frac{\text{Variance explained by predictor}}{\text{Total variance of outcome around its mean}}$$

The coefficient of determination answers the question: by what percentage does taking the predictor into account decrease the variance in the outcome?

It turns out that the coefficient of determination is r^2—the square of the correlation coefficient discussed above. r^2 is the percentage by which knowing the value of the predictor decreases the variance of the outcome. The greater r^2, the more the predictor accounts for or explains the outcome.

If the variance around the line of best fit is small compared to the total variance, then r^2 is large, signifying a strong linear relationship. At the extreme, an r^2 of 1 (r of 1 or -1) means that all of the variance in the outcome can be explained by the predictor: knowing the value of the predictor, you will know exactly the value of the outcome. A small r^2, on the other hand, signifies a weak linear relationship: using the line of best fit instead of the outcome mean does not decrease the variance by much. An r^2 of 0 means that taking the predictor into account does not decrease the variance, or improve the prediction, at all.

In our example, the correlation between a state's per-pupil spending and its students' fourth grade reading achievement is 0.46. Thus, *spending* accounts for about $0.46^2 = 0.21$, that is, 21 percent of the variance in *achievement*.

	r	r2
Aspirin and reduced risk of heart attack	0.02	0.0004
Chemotherapy and surviving breast cancer	0.03	0.0009
Calcium intake and bone mass in post-menopausal women	0.08	0.0064
Ever smoking and subsequent incidence of lung cancer within 25 years	0.08	0.0064
Alcohol use during pregnancy and subsequent premature birth	0.09	0.0081
Effect of nonsteriodal anti-flammatory drugs (e.g., ibuprofen) on pain reduction	0.14	0.0196
Gender and weight for U.S. adults	0.26	0.0676
ECT for depression and subsequent improvement	0.29	0.0841
Sleeping pills and short-term improvement in chronic insomnia	0.3	0.09
Age and episodic memory	0.33	0.1089
Elevation above sea level and lower daily temperatures in the U.S.	0.34	0.1156
Viagra and improved male sexual functioning	0.38	0.1444
Age and reasoning	0.4	0.16
Weight and height for U.S. adults	0.44	0.1936
Age and speed	0.52	0.2704
Gender and arm length	0.55	0.3025
Nearness to equator and daily temperature in the U.S.	0.6	0.36
Gender and height for U.S. adults	0.67	0.4489

Timothy Salthouse, "Cognitive Research and Aging" (workshop on neuroeconomics and aging, Stanford University, Stanford, CA, March 31, 2006).

FIGURE 6.12 SOME EXAMPLES OF CORRELATION STRENGTHS.

Does an r^2 of 0.21 strike you as large or small? Correlations considerably smaller than this are not at all unusual in the realms of medicine, science, and social science, and can be quite meaningful. A correlation of 0.23 ($r^2 = 0.05$) between administration of the antiretroviral drug AZT and the survival of AIDS patients represented a reduction of deaths from 61.5 percent to 38.5 percent, and led to the termination of the clinical trials so that the control group could receive the drug as well.[13]

In your own personal life, would you take seriously the fact that eating certain foods, or smoking, accounts for 21 percent of the variance in your chance of developing heart disease?

13. Paul Slovic and Ellen Peters, *The Importance of Worldviews in Risk Perception*, 3 Risk Decision and Policy 165–170 (1998), *citing* Robert Rosenthal, *How Are We Doing in Soft Psychology*, 45 American Psychologist 775–7 (1990).

6.2.6 Statistical Significance and Hypothesis Testing

The NAEP reading scores are based on a sample of pupils in a sample of schools, and it is possible that a correlation between *spending* and *achievement* in the sample does not indicate a correlation in the population. It is possible that the correlation in the sample is a result of chance; so we need a way to test whether the relationship we see in the sample is statistically significant. The approach to hypothesis testing is not essentially different from that discussed in the previous chapter.

Step 1) State the two hypotheses of the test.

Recall from Section 6.2.1 that we represent the line of best fit with the regression equation—

$$y = a + bx$$

—where x represents the predictor (*spending*), y the outcome (*achievement*), and a the intercept of the line and b its slope. A slope of 0, or equivalently a correlation coefficient r of 0, would indicate that there was no linear relationship between x and y. This gives us our null hypothesis: $b = 0$. Our alternative hypothesis is: $b \neq 0$.

The slope of the line of best fit of our sample was 1.5, not 0. But if we had randomly chosen a different set of students from different schools, our b might have been 0 or even negative. To learn whether b is *significantly* different from 0, we do a hypothesis test.

Step 2) Set the level of the test.

We set the level to the customary $\alpha = 0.05$.

Step 3) Suppose that the null hypothesis is true.

The value $b = 1.5$ per $1000 spent is specific to our sample. Suppose in the population, $b = 0$, i.e., there is no true linear relationship between spending and average score. In the sample, we still would observe a slope not exactly 0, because of chance. We want to know: how likely or unlikely would it be to observe (in the sample) a slope as large as $b = 1.5$?

Step 4) Calculate how extreme the sample data are, compared to what we would expect. How likely or unlikely would the observed measurements be if the null hypothesis were true?

In this example, if the true (population) value of b were 0 (no linear relationship), the probability that the sample value of b is 1.5 or greater (or –1.5 or less) is 0.001. This is calculated (with statistical software) using the t-test for a regression line slope, which considers the observed b (1.5) relative to the estimated variance and compares it to the t distribution.

Step 5) State your conclusion.

Since the above probability is quite small (less than our set level of 0.05), we are justified in rejecting the null hypothesis, and we conclude that there is a linear relationship between a state's per-pupil spending and its fourth graders' reading achievement.

6.2.7 Multiple Regression

Thus far, we examined linear regression of a quantitative outcome on one quantitative predictor. This is called **simple linear regression**. But if a single variable accounts for only some portion of the variance of the data, perhaps we can improve our prediction by taking account of other variables. In Galton's study, for example, we might improve our prediction of sons' heights by taking account not only their fathers' height, but their mothers' as well.

When we consider more than one variable that might affect the outcome, we use **multiple regression**. The predictive variables collectively are called the **explanatory variables**. With two explanatory variables, for example, the multiple regression equation is

$$y = a + b_1x_1 + b_2x_2.$$

In our example, the regression equation is of the form

$$\textit{Predicted height} = a + (b_1 * \textit{father's height}) + (b_2 * \textit{mother's height}).$$

As in simple regression, the coefficient of a variable in multiple regression is the amount by which the predicted outcome would increase if that variable were to increase by 1. But in multiple regression, it is that amount, *assuming that all of the other explanatory variables remain constant.*

In our effort to predict reading achievement, we might regress on another variable in addition to spending:

$$\textit{Predicted achievement} = a + (b_1 * \textit{spending}) + (b_2 * \textit{another variable}).$$

What might you hypothesize as other variables that could account for a part of the variance of average reading achievement among the states? As its name implies, multiple regression analysis can look at any number of variables at the same time.

6.2.7.a Using Multiple Regression Analysis in Employment Discrimination Cases Multiple regression analysis is a common tool in determining whether an employer is discriminating based on sex, race, or another forbidden characteristic. Recall that in Section 6.16, we concluded that there was a statistically significant difference between the salaries of male and female assistant managers at Big-Mart. But perhaps something other than gender accounts for the difference. For example, (1) salaries may be based on management experience, and (2) male assistant managers may, on average, be more experienced than females. Regression analysis can test both of these hypotheses.

The same personnel files that contain employees' salaries also have information about their experience. A simple regression of *salary* on number of months of management *experience* would determine whether the salaries of the sample of one hundred assistant managers correlated with their experience, and we would then test whether the correlation was sufficiently strong to justify rejecting the null hypothesis that there is no correlation in the population of assistant managers as a whole.

Let us suppose that there is a statistically significant correlation between the employees' months of management experience and their salaries. So now we need to know whether the difference between the sample of male and female employees' salaries remains statistically significant when one controls for differences in their experience. This would involve doing a multiple regression of *salary* on both *gender* and *experience*, obtaining a regression equation of the form

$$y = a + b_1x_1 + b_2x_2,$$

or

$$\textit{Predicted salary} = a + (b_1 * \textit{gender}) + (b_2 * \textit{experience}).$$

The problem is that *gender* is a categorical variable. We cannot plug "male" and "female" in for x_1. We need to use numbers.

The solution is to use the numbers 0 and 1. It is arbitrary which category is assigned which number; let's say we represent females by 0 and males by 1. Our variable is then a **dummy**, or **indicator variable**, a variable that can take on only the values 0 and 1, according to a condition. Here the condition is whether the applicant is male. An indicator variable is represented by an *I* followed by the condition in parentheses. Our new variable is

$$x_1 = I(\textit{male}) \begin{array}{l} = 1 \text{ if the individual is male} \\ = 0 \text{ if the individual is female} \end{array}$$

Using this indicator variable for x_1, our regression equation is

$$\textit{Predicted salary} = a + b_1 * I(\textit{male}) + b_2 * \textit{experience}.$$

Then, for a female with (say) 20 months of experience, we predict her salary to be

$$\textit{Predicted salary} = a + b_1 * 0 + b_2 * 20 = a + b_2 * 20.$$

For a male with 20 months of experience, we predict his salary to be

$$\textit{Predicted salary} = a + b_1 * 1 + b_2 * 20 = a + b_1 + b_2 * 20.$$

So a male and a female of equal experience are predicted to differ in salary by b_1 dollars. If b_1 turns out to be positive, the male has higher predicted salary. If it is negative, the female has higher predicted salary. Finally, if $b_1 = 0$, there is no difference in predicted salary between males and females when we have controlled for experience.

6.2.7.b Using Multiple Regression in Other Domains of Public Policy Multiple regression analysis plays an important role in many areas of policy. Here are just a few examples:

- In the famous Supreme Court case of *McCleskey v. Kemp*, the appellant, who was sentenced to death, claimed that there was discrimination in imposing the death penalty based on the race of the crime's victim. David Baldus, a law professor at the University of Iowa, ran a regression on a large number of death penalty cases. The indicator of *receiving the death penalty*[14] was regressed on the indicator of the *victim being Black*. As covariates, he included *race of defendant*, *method of killing*, *motive*, and *defendant's criminal history*. The victim's race turned out to be significant in the direction suggesting that those who killed Whites were more likely to be sentenced to death than were those who killed Blacks.[15]
- An analysis by John Donohue and Steven Levitt suggests that the nationwide legalization of abortion in 1973 led to a reduction in crime rates two decades later—presumably the result of fewer unwanted and poorly cared-for children. Among other things, the scholars looked at crime data in states where abortion was legal before *Roe v. Wade*, correlations between a state's abortion and crime rates, and correlations between age and crime.[16]
- In *More Guns, Less Crime: Understanding Crime and Gun-Control Laws* (1998), John R. Lott used regression analysis to argue that citizens' possession of guns reduced the amount of violent crime—presumably through the deterrent effect on those contemplating assaults. Ian Ayres, John Donohue, and Steven Levitt have argued that the analysis does not support this conclusion and, indeed, that the data show the opposite.[17] (The dispute also illustrates the relative opaqueness of econometric analyses as compared to, say, randomized controlled studies, and a layperson's difficulty in following technical arguments about the assumptions underlying the former.
- Lawrence A. Greenfeld, whom President Bush named in 2001 to lead the Bureau of Justice Statistics, lost his job in 2005 after refusing to suppress

14. Often, when the outcome is categorical, the more advanced method of logistic regression is used instead of ordinary regression.

15. *See* Adam Liptak, *Death Penalty Found More Likely When Victim Is White*, New York Times, Jan. 8, 2003.

16. John J. Donohue III and Steven D. Levitt, *The Impact of Legalized Abortion on Crime*, 116 Quarterly Journal of Economics 136–44 (2001).

17. *See* Ian Ayres and John J. Donohue III, *Shooting Down the "More Guns Less Crime" Hypothesis*, 55 Stanford Law Review 1193 (2001); Steven D. Levitt and Stephen J. Dubner, Freakonomics 130–134 (New York: HarperCollins Publishers, 2005).

an analysis that showed that, although White, Black, and Hispanic drivers are stopped by police at about the same rate, Hispanic drivers were searched or had their vehicles searched by the police 11.4 percent of the time and Blacks 10.2 percent of the time, compared with 3.5 percent for White drivers; and Blacks and Hispanics were also subjected to force or the threat of force more often than Whites.[18]

- Many Supreme Court Justices have urged Congress to increase the salaries of federal judges, arguing (in Justice Alito's words) that "eroding judicial salaries will lead, sooner or later, to less capable judges and ultimately to inferior adjudication." In *A Skeptical Response to the Judicial Salary Debate,* Stephen Choi, G. Mitu Gulati, and Eric Posner used multiple regression analyses to find the absence of any correlation between salaries and performance in the highest courts of the fifty states. For proxies for performance, the scholars measured *effort* in terms of the number of pages of opinions published, *skill* by citations by out-of-state judges and law journals, and *independence* by disagreement with fellow judges with the same political party affiliation.[19]

While multiple regression analysis has great power, it is subject to many of the same limitations as simple regression analysis: multiple regression can measure the strength only of relationships that are linear or that can be "linearized"; it is sensitive to outliers, and (unless the explanatory variables are carefully manipulated in an experiment, instead of just observed) it cannot prove the existence of causal relationships. As we will discuss in Section 7.2.1, there could be a so-called **confounding variable** that you didn't measure that influences the ones you did measure. To eliminate confounding variables, one must conduct **randomized controlled experiments** (discussed in Sections 7.3.1 and 7.3.5).

6.3 GLOSSARY

Central tendency measures	Mean (average), Median (middle), Mode (most common)
Coefficient of determination (r^2)	The amount of total variance explained by the predictor
Confidence Interval	A range of numbers in a sample that are, say, 95 percent likely to encompass the population mean
Correlation	A linear relationship between two variables
Correlation coefficient (r)	The strength of the linear relationship between two variables

18. Eric Lichtblau, *Profiling Report Leads to a Demotion,* New York Times, Aug. 24, 2005.
19. Http://papers.ssrn.com/sol3/papers.cfm?abstract_id=1077295.

Dispersion	How spread out the data are. (See Variance and Standard Deviation)
Empirical distribution	The distribution of the sample
Independence	Where the value of the so-called predictor or dependent variable provides no information about the outcome, response, or independent variable
Line of best fit	A straight line that best describes the relationship between the predictor and response variables
Multiple regression analysis	Linear regression analysis that takes into account more than one predictor variable
Normal distribution	A specific bell-shaped curve with the mean, median, and mode all at the center point
Regression analysis	A technique for determining correlation between two or more continuous variables
Regression to the mean	The tendency of extreme predictor variables to produce responses that are less extreme (i.e., closer to the mean)
Sampling distribution	The distribution of the sample mean
Scatterplot	A collection of datapoints showing the predictor and outcome values for each item
Standard deviation (SD)	A measure of the dispersion or variance of a sample. Square root of variance
Standard error (SE)	The standard deviation of the sampling distribution
Variance	Squared deviation of data points from the mean

6.4 APPENDIX

BIG-MART EMPLOYEE SALARIES BY MONTHS OF EXPERIENCE AND SEX

ID	MOE	SEX	SAL	ID	MOE	SEX	SAL	ID	MOE	SEX	SAL
1	67	M	39435	35	40	F	39492	69	37	F	40253
2	60	F	39028	36	46	F	39589	70	55	M	38728
3	46	M	39055	37	60	F	40966	71	43	F	38662
4	82	M	39345	38	51	M	38010	72	21	F	36672
5	31	M	39889	39	38	F	36843	73	67	F	39497
6	47	F	37224	40	84	F	43140	74	50	M	37684
7	60	M	40468	41	69	M	40097	75	70	M	42339
8	49	M	39304	42	54	F	39636	76	27	M	36193
9	27	M	36988	43	75	F	41645	77	38	M	39632
10	47	F	38453	44	46	M	40843	78	65	F	41166
11	4	F	35855	45	42	F	36688	79	39	M	37685
12	45	F	36917	46	38	F	36254	80	14	F	35413
13	29	F	34965	47	33	F	37486	81	39	F	35719
14	43	F	35391	48	65	M	40923	82	48	F	37141
15	44	M	38901	49	48	F	37572	83	61	M	41842
16	61	M	38581	50	20	M	37740	84	44	F	38788
17	49	M	38544	51	81	M	40460	85	74	F	37753
18	55	F	37720	52	26	F	38531	86	29	M	38877
19	44	F	39473	53	58	F	37724	87	54	M	38677
20	63	F	39147	54	46	F	39188	88	59	F	40387
21	31	F	36349	55	53	M	39628	89	60	F	37749
22	64	F	40668	56	45	M	40427	90	62	M	38093
23	60	M	41882	57	52	M	36545	91	46	M	35393
24	59	F	41261	58	42	M	38764	92	54	M	38157
25	51	M	38867	59	36	F	37931	93	44	M	39142
26	66	F	40186	60	63	M	40507	94	13	F	37532
27	53	F	40777	61	54	M	39292	95	74	M	39670
28	38	F	38910	62	58	M	38789	96	25	M	38273
29	46	M	36527	63	70	M	42989	97	40	F	37270
30	74	M	41168	64	64	M	39730	98	64	M	40559
31	47	F	39965	65	45	M	39462	99	63	F	38539
32	60	M	41698	66	30	F	38294				
33	73	F	40113	67	64	F	39655				
34	46	F	39335	68	82	M	40697				

7. INTERPRETING STATISTICAL RESULTS AND EVALUATING POLICY INTERVENTIONS

The primary use of statistics in science, policy, and law is to throw light upon the causal relationships that might exist between two or more variables. In this chapter we consider some of the ways in which statistics interacts with scientific reasoning, as well as some psychological findings that suggest caution in moving from statistical to causal conclusions. Much of the chapter focuses on evaluating the outcomes of policy interventions, and we also consider efforts to understand underlying social phenomena of concern to policy makers.

Recall that the introduction to Part 2 introduced the "lens" model, under which the real world can only be perceived through multiple fallible indicators. This chapter is concerned largely with identifying, separating, and giving appropriate weight to those indicators in order to establish the existence (or nonexistence) of causal relationships. One way in which this is done is through evaluation activities aimed at assessing the conceptualization, design, implementation and utility of social intervention programs.[1]

There are a number of different ways in which we use evaluation in policy making. Oftentimes, policy makers will oversee the design of a particular social program or select from among different types of interventions that use different assessment designs. Thus, it is important for policy makers to understand potential design flaws and the advantages and disadvantages of different types of program evaluation. More importantly, perhaps, is the ability for a policy maker to understand how to analyze impact assessments, compare different evaluations, think critically about the utility of such evaluations and make judgments about the inferences that can be drawn from them.

7.1 MEASURING IMPACT: CORRELATION VS. CAUSATION

Policy makers often design, support, and evaluate health and social programs designed to improve people's lives. How can they learn whether the programs actually achieve their intended effects?

The critical issue in impact evaluation is whether or not a program produces more of an effect or outcome than would have occurred either without the intervention or with an alternative intervention. Common among all approaches to

1. Peter H. Rossi and Howard E. Freeman, Evaluation: A Systematic Approach 19 (Beverly Hills: Sage Publications, 1985).

FIGURE 7.1 CORRELATION VS. CAUSATION http://xkcd.com/552/.
Source: Reprinted by permission of xkcd.

evaluating impact are the goals of establishing (1) that a particular intervention is *correlated* with the outcome, and (2) that the intervention *causes* the outcome—for example, establishing that the rate of malaria infections in a village goes down (1) *when* residents use bed nets and (2) *because* they use bed nets.

Imagine that we conducted a study of drowning deaths in Florida and discovered that the number of drowning deaths in a given month was highly correlated with ice cream sales for that month.[2] We could develop a number of possible

> A man rode the Fifth Avenue bus to work every day. And every day, when the bus stopped at Forty-Second Street, he opened the window and threw the sports section of the newspaper into a litter basket. After many years, the bus driver asked why he did this, and the man replied: "I do it to keep the elephants off Fifth Avenue." "But there aren't any elephants on Fifth Avenue," said the bus driver, to which the man responded: "See, it works!"

explanations for this correlation. (a) It could be that eating ice cream causes drowning, with more people developing cramps in the water and thus not being able to swim. (b) It could also be that drowning causes people to buy ice cream, as friends and family of the victims seek to console themselves by eating. (c) Or it could be that there is some other variable that causes both drowning and ice cream consumption—for example, the average temperature in a given month.

---

2. This example comes from Ewart Thomas, to whom the authors are also grateful for less direct influences.

Further testing could tease these explanations apart, but the observation of a correlation is consistent with all three causal scenarios.

A *causal diagram* represents the causal process that results in a correlation of interest. The three scenarios listed above as possible explanations of the correlation between drowning deaths and ice cream sales are diagramed in Figure 7.2. A solid arrow indicates a hypothesized causal relationship in the arrow's direction. A dashed line, on the other hand, emphasizes that, while a correlation exists between two variables, we are not hypothesizing any causation. When one variable, such as *temperature*, is related to two other variables (*drownings* and *ice cream sales*), a correlation appears between those two variables. But *correlation does not imply causation.*

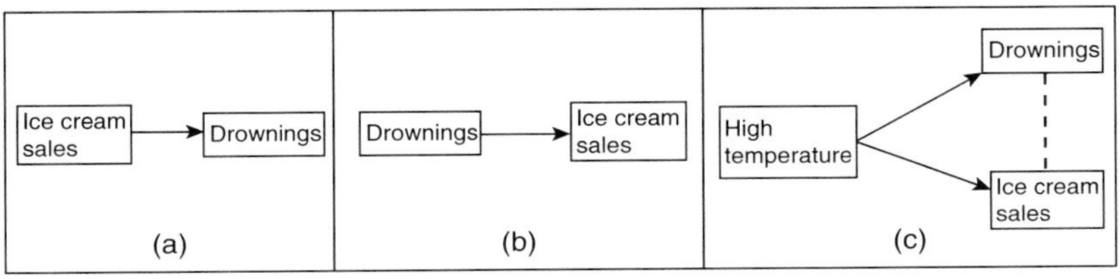

FIGURE 7.2 A CAUSAL DIAGRAM OF ICE CREAM SALES AND DROWNINGS.

Scenarios (a) and (b) of Figure 7.2 show alternative causal hypotheses. Scenario (c) implies that *temperature* may be a *confounding* or *lurking variable.* Confounding is the situation in which a variable you are *not* studying (here *temperature*) is related to both the variables you are studying (here *ice cream sales* and *drownings*). Data show a correlation between the variables you are interested in, but a third lurking variable may actually be causing both.

Consider, for example, a health survey of 21,101 Finns that indicated that pet owners were more likely to suffer from illnesses that included high blood pressure, high cholesterol, ulcers, depression, kidney disease, and being overweight. Did owning a pet cause these diseases? Did having these diseases cause people to own pets? Alternatively:

> Pets seem to be part of the lives of older people who have settled down and experienced an increase in the number of illnesses, whereas young healthy single people have no time, need, or possibility for a pet. Associations of pet ownership with disease indicators were largely explained with socio-demographic factors. Characteristics were those that bring forward the background of poor health in epidemiological investigations: male gender, low level of education, life without a couple relationship, and poor social standing.[3]

3. Leena K. Koivusilta and Ansa Ojanlatva, *To Have or Not To Have a Pet for Better Health?*, 1 PLoS ONE e109 (2006), doi:10.1371/journal.pone.0000109 (2006).

7.2 ESTABLISHING CAUSATION

Establishing what the outcome actually was and its correlation with the intervention is often hard enough. For example, in attempting to evaluate the outcome of the bed net program, it may be difficult to gather the data necessary to establish a baseline of malaria infections and then to track the number of infections over time. Establishing causation is usually more difficult, because even if there is a change, it may be due to factors other than the intervention being studied (introduction of bed nets): perhaps the weather was drier than usual, thus producing fewer mosquitoes, or perhaps other antimalaria interventions were introduced at the same time.

A *gross outcome* is all the changes that occur from time point A, before program implementation, and time point B, after implementation.

Gross Outcome = Effects of intervention (net outcome) + Effects of extraneous and confounding factors + Design effects.[4]

Implementation of bed net program

A---> B

(no bed nets) (bed nets fully distributed)

In the above intervention, the gross outcome would consist of all changes that occurred during the implementation period, including the changes in malaria infection rates attributable to the program, as well as changes resulting from other factors, such as a change in the weather or other variables that could have also reduced malarial infection rates.

What we ultimately care about is the *net outcome*, or the effects that are attributable to the intervention itself. As we see above,

Net Outcome = Gross Outcome – Effects of extraneous and confounding factors – Design effects.

Therefore, it is important to identify and, if possible, measure the effects that are not related to the intervention that may influence the gross outcome.

7.2.1 Confounding Effects

There are a number of different types of confounding variables that could influence the relationship between two given variables of interest. Such confounding factors could either (a) be the actual cause of the correlation, or (b) influence the causation such that the gross outcome must be reduced by the effect attributable to the interfering factor.

The different (general) kinds of confounding variables that policy makers and evaluation designers should be aware of include:

4. Rossi and Freeman, *supra* at 191.

- endogenous change: environmental effects such as temperature;
- secular trends: long-term trends in the community of interest such as a decline in birthrates or increased employment;
- interfering events: a short-term event such as an earthquake or a war; and
- maturational trends: especially relevant when evaluating change in young children.

Additionally, one must be aware of *uncontrolled selection biases*, meaning that some people may be more likely than others to participate in the program under evaluation, which will in turn influence the outcome. Common uncontrolled selection biases include self-selection and differential attrition.

Self-selection is especially relevant in voluntary programs, where some people may be more likely to volunteer for the given treatment than others. Take for instance a charter school such as the well-known KIPP (Knowledge is Power Program) program (an evaluation of KIPP is described in Section 7.4). KIPP admits students randomly from a pool of those who wish to attend. But to be in the pool, students or parents must be motivated to sign up. Such motivation may make these children significantly different from their counterparts in public schools whose parents did not try to enroll them in KIPP. Thus, when comparing the educational outcomes between KIPP and non-KIPP students, one must take into account these possible self-selection biases.

There are similar processes at work that lead to *differential attrition* in program participation. It is very rare that all program participants complete treatment, and individuals who drop out of the program may be significantly different than those who continue participating. For instance, children who find the KIPP program too demanding and unrewarding may be the most likely to drop out. Thus, the consequence of attrition is often that those who may have needed the program the least and were more likely to have changed on their own are the ones who are most likely to remain in the program.[5] One can easily imagine how such attrition can skew evaluation results if not properly accounted for.

Different types of controls and evaluation designs are aimed at reducing and accounting for the impact of these confounding variables. As we will see in our discussion below, some are better than others at achieving this goal.

7.2.2 Design Effects

Design effects are effects that are attributable to the evaluation itself or flaws in the evaluation design. These include errors that could spring from the measurement tool itself, as well as errors resulting from the simple process of measuring.

Measurement reliability refers to how prone to error the given measuring instrument is. In other words, its describes the extent to which an instrument produces results that vary from one administration to another when applied to

---

5. *Id.* 194.

the same object. Some measurements, such as the measurement of height and weight through standard instruments, have a high degree of reliability. Others, such as surveys that rely on subjects' responses to written or oral questions, are more prone to unreliability because of the inherent ambiguity in language and interviewer differences in their administration of the survey. In most cases, it is not possible to eliminate unreliability completely, although it is possible to make adjustments in results that take unreliability into account.

Even if a measuring procedure produces consistent results and is therefore deemed reliable, it will not be valid if it does not measure what it is intended to measure.

Measurement validity depends on whether there is a consensus that the measure is valid among the appropriate stakeholders, such as members of the scientific community. For example, the effectiveness of the bed net program could be measured by a number of alternative measures, including (1) self-reported malarial infection rates, (2) hospital visits related to malaria, or (3) professional surveys of malarial infection rates. A good outcome measure is generally one that may be feasibly employed, given the constraints of time and budget, and that is directly related to the goals of the program.

The process of conducting an evaluation in and of itself can also influence the outcome of the evaluation. This can happen through what is known as the Hawthorne or placebo effect. The *Hawthorne Effect* stems from a famous experiment, in which efforts to discover whether changes in factory lighting intensity would improve worker productivity disclosed that *any* change had that effect.[6] Researchers concluded that the effect was the result of the experiment itself—workers interpreted their participation in the experiment as a sign that the firm was interested in their personal welfare, and thus were motivated to work harder. In medical experiments, the Hawthorne Effect is known as the *placebo effect*, and refers to the fact that subjects may be as much affected by the knowledge that they are receiving treatment as by the treatment itself. For example, in some experiments testing the effectiveness of pain relievers, the control groups receiving sugar pills (unbeknownst to them) reported a decrease in pain levels.

The *Pygmalion Effect* refers to the fact that expectations can also influence outcomes. An experiment by Robert Rosenthal and Lenore Jacobson found that if teachers were led to expect enhanced performance from some children rather than others, then those children did indeed perform better.[7] The experiment confirmed the researchers' hypothesis that biased expectancies could essentially affect reality and create self-fulfilling prophecies as a result. Policy makers and evaluators should be especially aware of such effects where treatment is

---

6. Fritz J. Roethlisberger and William J. Dickson, Management and the Worker (Cambridge, MA: Harvard University Press, 1939).

7. Robert Rosenthal and Lenore Jacobson, Pygmalion in the Classroom (expanded edition New York: Irvington, 1992).

delivered in a non-neutral manner, such as by an individual whose personal biases could influence the way in which treatment is administered.

7.3 REDUCING UNWANTED EFFECTS THROUGH CONTROLS

Confidence in the results of evaluations and other empirical studies not only requires identifying various confounding factors and potential design flaws, but using controls. Here we discuss four important kinds of controls:

- Randomized controls—the "gold standard" of evaluation, in which participants are randomly assigned either to the treatment (or experimental) group—those who receive the intervention—or to a control group.
- Constructed controls—a major form of *quasi-experimental* evaluation, in which the treatment and control groups are constructed to be similar to each other.
- Reflexive controls—in which one looks at the same population before and after the intervention.
- Statistical controls—in which multiple regression analysis is used to control for suspected confounding factors.

The approaches other than randomized controls are sometimes called *observational studies,* because the experimenters merely observe the populations they are studying.

7.3.1 Randomized Controlled Studies

Randomized controlled studies are employed by randomly assigning program participants to either a treatment group or a control group. Here it is important to ensure that every person in the target population has the same chance as any other person of being selected into either group. The goal is not that the control and treatment groups be perfectly comparable. Rather, the goal is complete randomization such that because the experimental and control groups differ from one another only by chance, whatever processes or confounding factors that may be competing with the treatment to produce outcomes are present in both groups to the same extent, except for chance variations. Thus, because we are comparing the treatment group to a control group that has been exposed to the same confounding factors, we do not need to worry about how such effects have potentially skewed our results.

After collecting data on the two groups' outcomes, you compare the measures to see if there are sufficiently large—statistically significant—differences between the two. As we saw in Chapters 5 and 6, statistical significance is a function of the magnitude of the differences and the size of the groups. Too small a sample may make it difficult to draw any conclusions one way or the other. But if you find statistically significant differences, you can conclude that the intervention had an impact because the random assignment controlled for other factors. The main drawbacks to randomized controlled studies are that they are expensive to perform and difficult to replicate.

The U.S. Food and Drug Administration requires that most new pharmaceutical products be subject to randomized controlled studies before being introduced into the market. Participants in clinical trials receive either the new drug (the treatment) or a control (a placebo, or conventional treatment if there is one), and researchers analyze whether the health of those receiving the new drug improves more—or less—than the health of those in the control group.

Randomized controlled studies are not mandated for social interventions, and they are seldom done due to time and expense constraints. But when feasible, they can provide essential insights into the actual effects of social programs.[8] In 2005, the U.S. Department of Health and Human Services published the *National Head Start Impact Study*, a randomized controlled study analyzing the impact of the Head Start program on a variety of measures of children's social and cognitive development.[9] The study employed random controls and found that Head Start had limited effects on the social and cognitive development of participating children. This conclusion contradicted many previous Head Start studies, which had relied on constructed or statistical controls.

7.3.2 Constructed Controls

When using *constructed controls* a group of untreated or differently treated targets are selected by nonrandom methods to be as comparable as possible in crucial respects to the targets constituting the intervention group. This process is often known as *matching*. The success of this control depends on how closely the constructed group resembles the intervention group in all essential characteristics. For instance, if we were using a constructed control for an evaluation of a prekindergarten program we would try to select a nontreatment group that matched our prekindergarteners in terms of age, race, socio-economic status, language spoken at home, parental education level, and any other factors that we thought might affect early childhood learning.

However, it is important to note that some characteristics—such as motivation and parental attitudes about education—would be difficult to "match," and that not controlling for such factors could influence the outcome. In a 1969

---

8. The Coalition for Evidence-Based Policy maintains an excellent Web site on social programs that work: http://www.evidencebasedprograms.org.

9. U.S. Department of Health and Human Services, Administration for Children and Families, "Head Start Impact Study: First Year Findings: (Washington, DC: U.S. Department of Health and Human Services, 2005), *available at* http://www.acf.hhs.gov/programs/opre/hs/impact_study/.

evaluation of the Head Start program,[10] first-graders who had participated in Head Start were compared with first-graders of comparable backgrounds in the same or nearby schools who had not participated. The study was widely criticized, however, because it did not control for differences in environmental circumstances.

The use of matching techniques has increased greatly in the last decade, with some researchers going as far as to argue that matching "mimic[s] randomization."[11] However, economists are more skeptical about the use of techniques, finding that matching performs well only under specific data conditions.[12] The critiques of the use of matching in observational and quasi-experimental studies are discussed below.

7.3.3 Reflexive Controls

With *reflexive controls*, or a "before and after" approach, targets are compared to themselves, before the intervention took place. Such a technique may be required in large, full-coverage programs in which it is impossible to define randomized or constructed controls or locate nonparticipants. This may also be an appropriate technique where it is reasonable to believe that the targets remain identical in relevant ways before and after the intervention. Reflexive control designs, however, are highly vulnerable to incorrect estimation of net effects because they do not control for confounding factors such as maturational effects, secular trends, and interfering events.

The so-called "broken windows" theory of crime reduction provides a famous example of the problem of before-after studies: New York's zero-tolerance policy for vandalism and other petty crimes in the 1990s was claimed to have resulted in a significant reduction of all crimes, including felonies. But it turned out that crime rates declined simultaneously, and to approximately the same extent, in other U.S. cities that had not adopted this approach. The decline might have resulted from the waning of the crack epidemic, or the increase in the number of drug offenders in prisons (and therefore not on the streets), or the general

---

10. Victor G. Cicerelli et al., The Impact of Head Start : An Evaluation of the Effects of Head Start on Children's Cognitive and Affective Development. (Athens: Westinghouse Learning Corporation and Ohio University, 1969).

11. Debbie L. Hahs-Vaughn and Anthony J. Onwuegbuzie, *Estimating and Using Propensity Score Analysis with Complex Samples*, 75 Journal of Experimental Education 31 (2006).

12. Multiple studies conclude that matching only performs well in data that satisfy three criteria: 1) treatment and comparison groups come from identical sources, 2) individuals in both groups live in the same geographical area, and 3) "the data contain a rich set of variables that affect both" the outcome and the probability of being treated. Jeffrey Smith, and Petra Todd, *Does Matching Overcome LaLonde's Critique of Nonexperimental Estimators?*, 125 Journal of Econometrics 309 (2005).

demographic decline in the number of young males.[13] Here, simple observation of the correlation between implementation and declining crime rates was not enough to establish causation.

7.3.4 Statistical Controls

Rather than matching participants with nonparticipants, a researcher can also use *statistical controls* to adjust for statistical differences between the two groups. This can be done in cross-sectional surveys, using the techniques of multiple regression analysis to control for potentially confounding differences among individuals. For example, in the study (mentioned in Section *6.2.7.a*) that concluded that killers of white victims were more likely to receive the death penalty than killers of Black victims, statistical techniques were used to control for the method of killing, motive, and defendant's criminal history.

7.3.5 The Advantages and Drawbacks of Different Methods

As noted above, observational designs are vulnerable to confounding. For example, a large cross-sectional study in the 1990s found that hormone replacement therapy (HRT) for postmenopausal women reduced the risk of heart disease.[14] But a later randomized controlled trial found that HRT actually increased the risk of heart attacks.[15]

The later study randomly assigned 16,608 postmenopausal women to groups of roughly equal size and gave one group the hormone combination and the other a placebo. It turned out that the original studies had not controlled for the fact that women on HRT "were also more likely to see a doctor (which is how they were put on hormone therapy in the first place), and probably more likely to exercise and to eat a healthful diet, than women who were not taking the drug."[16] Thus, the relationship wasn't that taking hormones made women healthy, it was that healthy women took hormones.

Even when the investigator controls for every known potential confounder, there always could be more confounders that the investigator did not think of or that were difficult or expensive to measure. It has been suggested that, in the studies that found a decreased heart attack risk in subjects on HRT, the culprit confounder was a variable representing lifestyle—including diet and exercise,

---

13. The literature on this theory is nicely summarized in *Wikipedia*, s.v. "Fixing Broken Windows," http://en.wikipedia.org/wiki/Fixing_Broken_Windows (last visited June 30, 2008).

14. Jane Brody, *New Therapy for Menopause Reduces Risks*, NEW YORK TIMES, Nov. 18, 1994.

15. Gina Kolata with Melody Petersen, *Hormone Replacement Study: A Shock to the Medical System*, NEW YORK TIMES, July 10, 2002.

16. Susan M. Love, *Preventive Medicine, Properly Practiced*, NEW YORK TIMES, July 16, 2002.

frequency of doctor visits, and other less tangible aspects of attention to one's health. Variables like these, even if thought of, may be too vaguely defined to control for completely. The suspected confounding in these studies is represented in Figure 7.3.

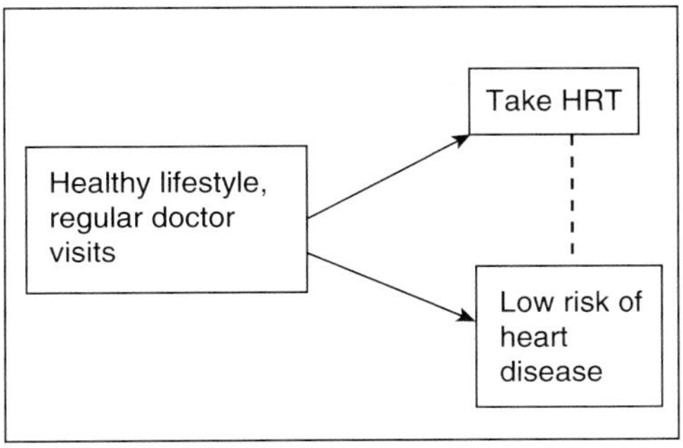

FIGURE 7.3 A CAUSAL DIAGRAM OF HEALTH LIFESTYLE, HRT, AND HEART DISEASE.

When subjects are randomly assigned to treatment (exposure) or placebo (no exposure) groups, effects of confounders disappear. Because *exposure* to HRT is randomly assigned, it cannot be correlated with any other characteristics of the subjects. The two groups are almost exactly the same in their characteristics; there is very little chance that a systematic difference (such as *diet* or *exercise behavior*) exists between them. (Some known confounders, such as *age*, are often purposely balanced between the groups, to avoid the possibility of a difference occurring by chance in the randomization.)

Even where the available data set is extensive, with a "rich" set of covariates and samples lending itself to very precise matching between the experimental and control groups, selection bias can still sneak in. Kevin Arceneaux, Alan Gerber, and Donald Green demonstrate this by comparing estimates generated by matching to an experimental benchmark in a voter mobilization experiment.[17]

Based on a large-scale randomized field experiment, the authors developed an experimental benchmark measurement of the effect of get-out-the-vote phone calls on people's voting behavior. Using random assignment, the average treatment effect on receiving a get-out-the-vote phone call on voter turnout was estimated to be 1.98 percentage points. The effect on the placebo group (which received calls encouraging them to buckle up their seat belts) was

17. Kevin Arceneaux, Alan S. Gerber, and Donald P. Green, 2004-04-15 "Comparing Experimental and Matching Methods using Two Large-Scale Field Experiments on VoterMobilization" *Paper presented at the annual meeting of the The Midwest Political Science Association, Palmer House Hilton, Chicago, Illinois Online* 2009-05-26 from http://www.allacademic.com/meta/p83115_index.html.

0.95 percentage points. The researchers then compared treated individuals to untreated individuals with matching techniques. The treatment and placebo groups were exactly matched to control groups such that the comparison groups shared exactly the same descriptive statistics on important characteristics such as past voting behavior and age. Using matching, the average effect of a get-out-the vote phone call was estimated to be 7.53 percentage points—over three times the estimate derived from a randomized experiment. Even more surprisingly, the matching experiment also suggested that the buckle-up calls raised voter turnout by 5.36 percentage points.

What accounts for the stark difference between the randomized experimental and the matching results? The authors conclude that the variation occurred because the treated individuals who were matched with untreated individuals were people who actually answered calls from a commercial phone bank, and were more likely to have elevated voting tendencies, even after controlling for past voting habits and other demographic characteristics. While it was impossible to control for this selection bias in the matching experiment, the randomized experiment did just that.

As evidenced by the above comparisons, randomized controlled experiments are vastly preferable to observational studies based only on statistical controls. In fact, many scientists and statisticians believe that one can never infer causality from an observational study. But observational studies are often our only choice in situations where the phenomena in question have already occurred or where it is not feasible to conduct a controlled experiment. The analysis of legal claims, as well as many natural sciences, including astronomy, geology, and paleontology, depend primarily on observational studies. Even issues of public health are not always susceptible to randomized controlled studies. An article in the *British Medical Journal* entitled *Parachute Use to Prevent Death and Major Trauma Related to Gravitational Challenge: Systematic Review of Randomised Controlled Trials* concluded:[18]

> As with many interventions intended to prevent ill health, the effectiveness of parachutes has not been subjected to rigorous evaluation by using randomised controlled trials. Advocates of evidence based medicine have criticised the adoption of interventions evaluated by using only observational data. We think that everyone might benefit if the most radical protagonists of evidence based medicine organised and participated in a double blind, randomised, placebo controlled, crossover trial of the parachute.

In any event, developing and testing hypotheses requires not merely quantitative skills, but good empirical intuitions in order to posit possible correlates and to identify and weed out confounding variables. Legal issues involving

18. Gordon C. S. Smith and Jill P. Pell, *Parachute Use to Prevent Death and Major Trauma Related to Gravitational Challenge: Systematic Review of Randomised Controlled Trials*, 327 British Medical Journal 1459–61 (2003).

FIGURE 7.4 PARACHUTES REDUCE THE RISK OF INJURY AFTER GRAVITATIONAL CHALLENGES, BUT THEIR EFFECTIVENESS HAS NOT BEEN PROVED WITH RANDOMIZED CONTROLLED STUDIES.
Source: Reproduced from Gordon C. S. Smith and Jill P. Pell, *Parachute Use to Prevent Death and Major Trauma Related to Gravitational Challenge: Systematic Review of Randomised Controlled Trials*, 327 British Medical Journal 1459. © 2003. Reprinted with permission from BMJ Publishing Group Ltd.

employment discrimination and toxic torts of the sort illustrated in the Big-Mart and Terra Nueva examples are typical. Thus, the lawyer's or policy maker's task—or the statistician's task under their guidance—is to determine correlation and often to attribute causation based on the relationship of plausible independent variables (the *insulation* in a tenant's apartment) with a dependent variable of interest (the *presence of illness*).

7.4 SOME FURTHER EXAMPLES OF PROGRAM EVALUATION

In formulating interventions in uncharted areas, policy makers may have little choice but to rely on the intuitions of experts and practitioners in the field. But intuitions about social change are notoriously inaccurate.

Consider the work of Dr. Joan McCord, a criminologist who evaluated programs for troubled youth.[19] Her best-known work was a longitudinal study comparing participants in programs that provided mentoring, health care

19. Douglas Martin, *Joan McCord, Who Evaluated Anticrime Efforts, Dies at 73*, New York Times, March 1, 2004.

services, and summer camp to high-risk boys with a control group of similar youths. She found that boys in the program were more likely to become criminals, have employment and marital problems, and become alcoholics than those in the control group. The evidence contradicted not only the expected outcome but also the participants' own belief that they had benefited from the program. (Dr. McCord hypothesized that the boys in the treatment group may have felt that they were given the attention because something was wrong with them, making it a self-fulfilling prophecy—the Hawthorne Effect at work.) She found similar paradoxical effects from a "just say no" drug education program and from Scared Straight, a program designed to deter young people from following a criminal path.

Thus, even (perhaps especially) when intuitions strongly support a particular intervention, it is important to evaluate its actual impact. In this section, we look at some cases where evaluation has demonstrated pretty conclusively that an intervention works or that it doesn't work and where it has been inconclusive.

The Good. The Abdul Latif Jameel Poverty Action Lab (J-PAL), a research center at the Massachusetts Institute of Technology, specializes in conducting randomized controlled studies in developing countries. J-PAL randomly assigned girls in Kenya either to a group that was promised merit-based scholarships and a cash grant for school supplies if they scored well on academic exams, or to a control group. It turned out that just being eligible for scholarships led the girls to think of themselves as "good students" and led to higher academic grades. In fact, both student and teacher attendance improved in eligible schools, and even boys showed improved test scores.[20]

In 2004–2005, SRI International employed a cross-sectional approach in evaluating the outcomes of the Bay Area KIPP (Knowledge is Power Program) charter schools, whose "pillars" include high expectations, parental choice, long school days, autonomous school leaders, and a relentless focus on results. (Although a randomized controlled study is now under way, KIPP and its sponsors also wanted this early, formative assessment of its impact to detect any

20. Michael Kremer, Edward Miguel, and Rebecca Thornton, "Incentives to Learn" (NBER Working Paper No. 10971, National Bureau of Economic Research, 2004, http://www.nber.org/papers/w10971). Another experiment by J-PAL demonstrates the failure of an intervention to achieve its intended goals, though it certainly did some good along the way. In a randomized controlled study to determine whether reducing the incidence of parasitic worms among children could lead to better attendance and, consequently, higher test scores, J-PAL administered low-cost deworming drugs to children at randomly chosen schools in a poor, densely settled farming region near Lake Victoria. The drugs worked well: after one year only 27 percent of children in treatment schools had moderate to heavy worm infections, compared with 52 percent of children in control schools. The effects on schooling, though, were minimal at best: though attendance rates in treatment schools were 7 to 9 percent higher than in control schools, the test scores of children in intervention and control schools were not significantly different.

obvious need for midcourse corrections.) Using two standard state tests, the SAT and CST, experimenters tracked KIPP students' achievement over two years and compared their achievement with that of students in comparable California schools. The report explains the limits of the methodology:

> In an ideal world we would make two comparisons as a basis for determining if KIPP students are performing better than if they were not attending KIPP schools. The first would be to compare achievement growth of KIPP students to their growth trajectory prior to KIPP. However, this requires individual student data for several years prior to enrollment in KIPP that is not publicly available. . . . The second would be to compare KIPP students' achievement with that of a comparison group of students, defined based on KIPP school waitlists (which do not yet exist), or matching students in the district based on demographic characteristics. Again, this comparison requires access to student-level data for both KIPP and non-KIPP students.[21]

With these limitations, the report noted:

> The spring 2005 CST data indicate that the overall percentage of students performing at a proficient level or above is consistently higher for KIPP schools than for comparable schools in the district—in some cases dramatically so. Similarly, when comparing students in KIPP schools to all students in the state, more fifth graders in two of the five KIPP schools scored at or above proficient in ELA (English language arts) than students statewide; in three of five KIPP schools, the percentage of fifth-grade students who scored at or above proficient in math was higher than the state average. Likewise, in three of the four KIPP schools with sixth-grade scores, a higher percentage of sixth-grade students reached proficiency in math and ELA compared to the state as whole. In the one KIPP school with seventh-grade scores, the percent proficient in both ELA and math exceeded the state average.

Although not conclusive, the size of the differences was great enough to strongly support the hypothesis that the KIPP approach made a real difference in children's academic outcomes—sufficient to justify continuing and even expanding the program while conducting more precise studies.

The Bad. The next best thing to learning that a social intervention succeeds, is determining conclusively that it does not succeed—so that funders will seek better options rather than pouring money down the drain. A famous example of a demonstrably ineffective intervention is the Drug Abuse Resistance Education (DARE) program, which sought to prevent youth substance abuse through classroom instruction. Randomized controlled studies of the DARE program

21. SRI International, Bay Area KIPP Schools, "A Study of Early Implementation: First Year Report 2004–05" (Menlo Park, Calif.: SRI International, 2006), *available at* http:// policyweb.sri.com/cep/publications/KIPPYear_1_Report.pdf.

consistently showed that students in treatment and control groups had the same rates of both short- and long-term drug use.[22]

In another case, the evaluation firm Mathematica Policy Research Inc. was commissioned to conduct a randomized controlled evaluation of federal abstinence education initiatives designed to prevent teen pregnancy. Mathematica worked with four different states to randomly assign schools either to receive or not to receive abstinence education, and then analyzed students' self-reported sexual activity rates. The results, released in 2007, show that students whose schools received abstinence programs were just as likely to be sexually active as students whose schools did not.[23] James Wagoner, the president of Advocates for Youth, said of the results: "After 10 years and $1.5 billion in public funds these failed abstinence-only-until-marriage programs will go down as an ideological boondoggle of historic proportions."[24]

The Inconclusive. In 1997, the New York City Voucher Experiment randomly assigned two thousand low-income families with K–4 students to either a treatment group or a control group. Families in the treatment group received school vouchers for private-school tuition, worth $1400 per child per year, for four years,[25] while families in the control group did not receive vouchers. After three years, researchers administered math and reading tests to students in each group and analyzed the results. It turned out that vouchers did not significantly affect children's test scores in the aggregate, though they had a small positive impact on the test scores of African Americans.[26]

The voucher experiment did not show that vouchers are ineffective. Rather, methodological problems, especially the small sample size, made it hard to draw a conclusion one way or the other.[27] Given the difficulty of designing and implementing studies of social interventions, you should be prepared for inconclusive

---

22. Cheryl L. Perry et al., *A Randomized Controlled Trial of the Middle and Junior High School D.A.R.E. and D.A.R.E. Plus Programs*, 157 Archives of Pediatrics and Adolescent Medicine 178–184 (2003).

23. Christopher Trenholm et al., "Impacts of Four Title V, Section 510 Abstinence Education Programs: Final Report," report prepared by Mathematica Policy Research Inc. for the U.S. Department of Health and Human Services, April 2007.

24. Advocates for Youth, "10-Year Government Evaluation of Abstinence-Only Programs Comes Up Empty," news release, April 13, 2007, http://www.advocatesforyouth.org/news/press/041307.htm.

25. Social Programs That Work, "New York City Voucher Experiment," http:// www.evidencebasedprograms.org/Default.aspx?tabid=143 (last visited June 30, 2008).

26. *See* Alan Krueger and Pei Zhu, *Another Look at the New York City School Voucher Experiment*, 47 American Behavioral Scientist 658–99 (2003); and Institute of Education Sciences, National Center for Education Evaluation and Regional Assistance, "Evaluation of the DC Opportunity Scholarship Program: Impacts After One Year," http://ies.ed.gov/ncee/pubs/20074009 (last visited June 30, 2008).

27. William G. Howell, book review, *Data Vacuum*, 2 Education Next (2002), *available at* http://www.hoover.org/publications/ednext/3366891.html.

results much of the time. This can happen, for example, because samples that were originally of reasonable size diminish as a result of attrition—for example, families in the control group move away and the experimenters lose track of them. Or the control group coincidentally could receive some interventions from another source—whether similar to or different from the "treatment" group.[28]

Unfortunately, many negative and inconclusive results never see daylight—the former, for reasons of motivation; the latter, for lack of interest. There is also a strong bias in many scholarly fields against publishing statistically insignificant results. But even knowing about inconclusive results is useful, since a subsequent study may be able to learn from the first and remedy some of the defects that prevented a clearer outcome.

7.4.1 The Connecticut Crackdown on Speeding: A Legal Policy Case Study

A classic article on confounding variables and other methodological problems in assessing the effects of legal policy changes is Donald Campbell's and H. Lawrence Ross's study of the effect of the State of Connecticut's decision to impose draconian penalties—suspension of licenses—for speeding offenses in 1956.[29] Governor Abraham Ribicoff announced the policy during the last week of 1955, a year that had a record number of 324 deaths caused by car accidents. As shown in Figure 7.5, a year later, the number of deaths had declined to 284, and the Governor stated: "With the saving of forty lives . . ., a reduction of 12.3 percent from the 1955 motor vehicle death toll, we can say the program is definitely worthwhile."

"Not so fast," in effect responded Campbell and Ross, in an article that details the problems of observational, or quasi-experimental studies. Consider these alternative explanations:

- *Rival hypotheses.* Was the speeding crackdown the only plausible change between 1955 and 1956 that might have contributed to the reduction of traffic fatalities? Consider that 1956 might have had an unusually mild winter or been an unusually dry year. Perhaps that's the year that Connecticut instituted medevac services? Or perhaps the decline from one year to the next is part of a long-term trend caused by improved automobile or highway safety?
- *Measurement changes.* Though not likely in this example, someone conducting series studies any time should be alert to possible changes in measurement or reporting. Here are some examples from other domains:

28. *See, for example,* Paul T. Decker, Daniel P. Mayer, and Steven Glazerman, "The Effects of Teach for America on Students: Findings from a National Evaluation" (Princeton, N.J.: Mathematica Policy Research Inc., 2004), *available at* http://www.mathematica-mpr.com/publications/pdfs/teach.pdf.

29. Donald Campbell and H. Lawrence Ross, *The Connecticut Crackdown on Speeding: Time-Series Data in Quasi-Experimental Analysis,* 33 Law & Society Review 33–54 (1968).

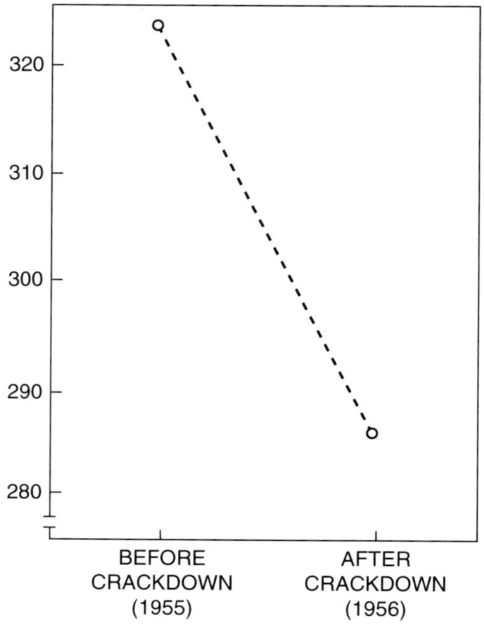

FIGURE 7.5 DECLINE IN FATAL CAR ACCIDENTS FROM 1956 TO 1957.
Source: Reprinted by permission of Wiley-Blackwell.

Campbell and Ross refer to a dramatic increase in suicide statistics in nineteenth-century Prussia when record keeping was transferred from the local police to national civil service. For some more recent examples: What some dermatologists have thought to be a drastic increase in melanoma may just be an increase in people's being screened for skin cancer.[30] And there is considerable uncertainty about the extent to which an apparent epidemic of autism reflects an actual increase in the syndrome rather than a more capacious definition of this diagnostic category.[31] While the air traffic controllers' union believes that an increase in near-misses is the result

30. *See* Gina Kolata, *Melanoma Is Epidemic. Or Is It*, New York Times, Aug. 9, 2005. "They found that since 1986, skin biopsies have risen by 250 percent, a figure nearly the same as the rise in the incidence of early stage melanoma. But there was no change in the melanoma death rate. And the incidence of advanced disease also did not change, the researchers found."

31. Tina Kelley, *An Autism Anomaly, Partly Explained*, New York Times, Feb. 18, 2007; Graham Lawton, *The Autism Myth*, New Scientist, Aug. 13, 2005.

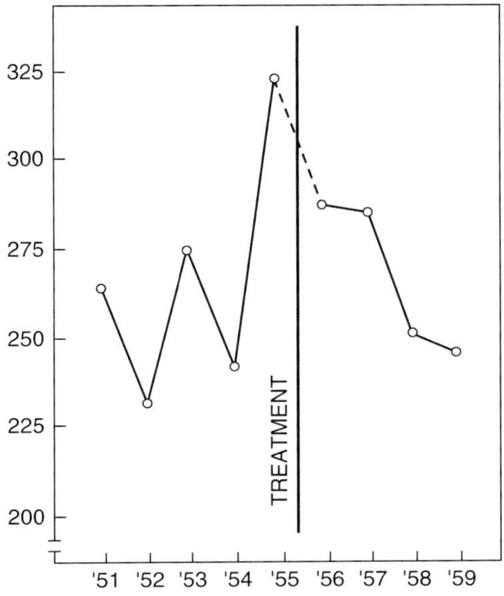

FIGURE 7.6 FATAL CAR ACCIDENTS, 1951–1959.
Source: Reprinted by permission of Wiley-Blackwell.

of understaffing, FAA officials suggest that it is error detection rather than the actual error rate that has increased.[32]

- *Variability, sample size, and regression.* Consider Figure 7.6, which shows the history of Connecticut traffic fatalities for several years before and after the speeding crackdown. Note that there is significant variation from year to year. In effect, one year may constitute too small a sample on which to base the conclusion that the crackdown had any effect. Consider also that the governor instituted the crackdown because of the extraordinarily high fatality rate during 1955. What does the phenomenon of regression to the mean predict about the rate in 1956?

When undertaking before/after observational studies, it is useful to simulate a control group by examining similar situations where there was no intervention. Similar trends in those situations provide a clue that an independent variable other than the intervention may have been at work.

As shown in Figure 7.7, Campbell and Ross compared Connecticut to four nearby "control states"—New York, New Jersey, Rhode Island, and Massachusetts.

32. Matthew Wald, *Errors in the Air and a Battle on the Ground*, NEW YORK TIMES, Aug. 13, 2005.

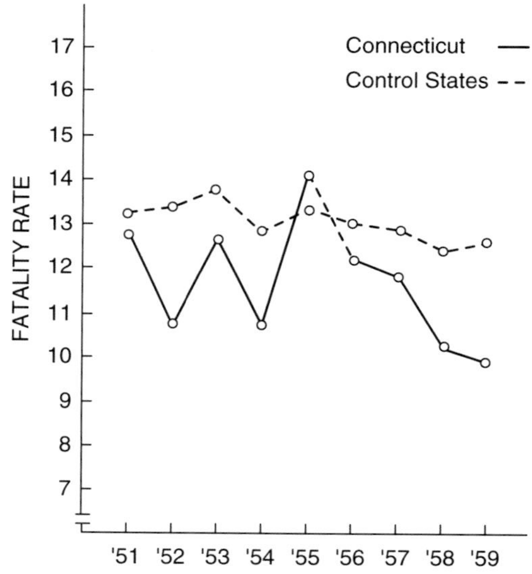

FIGURE 7.7 FATAL CAR ACCIDENTS IN CONNECTICUT AND NEARBY STATES, 1951–1959.
Source: Reprinted by permission of Wiley-Blackwell.

(Why do you suppose the combined data for those four states is much smoother than for Connecticut?).

Although the comparison lends some support to the Governor's causal hypothesis, Campbell and Ross mention the possibility that there may have been some *diffusion*—a tendency for the intervention in the experimental group to affect the control group. Also, there is some doubt whether the differences are statistically significant.[33]

This underscores one of the central points of this chapter: purported causal relationships must be viewed with caution. One must be wary about making decisions based on evidence derived from observational or quasi-experimental studies. While randomized controlled experiments are subject to less potential errors and do a better job of proving causality, such experiments are rarely available. Thus, the policy maker must use common sense and basic statistical knowledge to identify potential confounding factors and design effects that could influence the observational study's outcome and make decisions about causality accordingly.

---

33. The analysis of significance in this context is complex. Using a one-tailed test, G.V. Glass, found significance at somewhere between $p < 0.05$ and $p < 0.07$. Gene V. Glass, *Analysis of Data on the Connecticut Speeding Crackdown as a Time-Series Quasi-Experiment*, 55 Law & Society Review 55–76 (1968).

7.5 THE SIGNIFICANCE OF STATISTICAL SIGNIFICANCE[34]

7.5.1 Effect Size

Most end users of statistical analyses are ultimately interested in the strength or magnitude of the relationship between variables—in how large an *effect* a change in one variable has on another: Is there just a small or a large difference in the number of reported illnesses of Terra Nueva residents who live in apartments with and without foam insulation? Do the salaries of male and female assistant managers at Big-Mart differ by a few dollars or a few hundred? Does spending additional $100 per pupil have a big or a small effect on achievement?

The correlation coefficient (r), discussed in Section 6.2.2, *is* an indication of effect size, and effect size can be inferred from other statistical tests as well. But recall from our discussions of hypothesis testing that effect size is only one component of *statistical significance*, which also depends on the size (and variance) of the samples. To find a statistically significant difference in the symptoms of residents with and without foam insulation means that we are probably right to reject the null hypothesis and conclude that there is some correlation, but it does not say how great the correlation is. Meeting a more demanding level of significance (say, 0.001 rather than 0.5) tells you that it's more likely that differences revealed by the survey of a sample of the population actually reflects the population, but it does not tell you that the effect size is greater. Knowing with near certainty that the tenants living in apartments with foam insulation have seventeen headaches a year when those in apartments without the insulation have sixteen is unlikely to wow a jury or energize the mayor to take action.

7.5.2 Meta-Analysis

The Terra Nueva, Big-Mart, and education examples in the preceding chapters showed statistically significant effects of sufficient magnitude to be of legitimate interest to various stakeholders. But it is possible for a real effect to be masked because the sample is too small. Apart from applying a less demanding significance level—which trades off Type II for Type I errors—is there anything to be done? In situations where a number of experiments have been done to study essentially the same phenomenon, medical and social scientists sometimes use the statistical technique of *meta-analysis* to aggregate and analyze information from a variety of existing studies. Meta-analysis can increase the effective sample size and thus reveal an effect that was not statistically significant in a single study.

34. *See generally* Jeremy A. Blumenthal, *Meta-Analysis: A Primer for Legal Scholars*, 80 Temple L. Rev. 201, 209–10 (2007); John E. Hunter and Frank L. Schmidt, *Cumulative Research Knowledge and Social Policy Formulation: The Critical Role of Meta-Analysis*, 2 Psychol. Pub. Pol'y & L. 324, 342–43 (1996).

For example, the American Public Health Association undertook a meta-analysis of studies evaluating teen smoking prevention programs,[35] which examined ninety-four studies of different programs. The studies were initially evaluated for methodological rigor and placed into categories based on strength of methodology. Researchers then focused analysis on the studies with stronger methodologies in order to get more accurate results. The meta-analysis concluded that programs that incorporate attention to social norms and social reinforcement are more successful than those that try to convince teens to abstain from smoking by giving them reasons.

Meta-analysis has strong proponents. But it also has critics, who note, among other things, the dangers of relying on studies that are poorly designed or implemented, the difficulty of aggregating studies of interventions that differ from each other, and the susceptibility of meta-analysis to publication bias—the fact that studies showing statistically significant results are more likely to be published than those that do not.[36] Without professing expertise, we believe that these vulnerabilities can be controlled for sufficiently to make meta-analysis a valuable tool.

7.5.2.a Practical Importance: The Representation of Effect Size How do you interpret the statement that people with high cholesterol can reduce their risk of death by 22 percent by taking statins, or that an arthritis pain-reliever increases one's chance of a heart attack by 30 percent?

A particular drug could halve or double your risk of a dreaded outcome, but the difference might be between a risk of 0.001 and 0.002 or between 0.1 and 0.2. A more useful way to report and think about risk is *incremental risk*, where a difference between 0.001 and 0.002 entails an incremental risk of 0.001 or one per thousand and the difference between 0.1 and 0.2 entails an incremental risk of 0.1, or of 100 per thousand. Another way to describe risk is the *number needed to expose* to observe one added death: the first risk would be described as 1000 needed to expose per additional death, and the second, much more serious risk, is only 10 needed to expose per additional death.

Unfortunately, most media accounts of the benefits or dangers of particular pharmaceuticals do not make clear what statistic they are using.

7.6 EXPERIMENTAL DESIGN AND EXTERNAL VALIDITY

We have already discussed some experiments—mostly by Amos Tversky and Daniel Kahneman—designed to understand how people deal intuitively with statistical problems, and the remainder of the book describes a variety of

35. http://www.pubmedcentral.nih.gov/articlerender.fcgi?artid=1694752.

36. For an excellent review of the pros and cons of meta-analysis, as well as description of its techniques, *see* Blumenthal, *supra*.

experiments on judgment and decision making. For this reason alone, it is worth spending some time considering the value and limitations of such experiments. This will also provide an opportunity to review some of the concepts developed in the preceding chapters.

7.6.1 Within-Subject vs. Between-Subjects Experiments

A number of the empirical studies discussed so far are essentially surveys that do not involve comparison groups—for example, a survey to determine respondents' intuitions about the variance of the sex of babies born in hospitals with many or fewer births. But, as in the Big-Mart and Terra Nueva examples, we are often interested in comparing two groups.

Suppose that you are trying to learn which of two different sneakers, the Zephyr or the Rapido, enables an athlete to run faster. You could do a within-subject experiment with, say, ten athletes, first getting their average time in a 100-yard dash with the Zephyr and then with the Rapido. Or you could do a between-subjects experiment with two groups of (say) ten athletes each running the 100-yard dash.[37] The within-subjects experiment has the practical advantage that it only requires ten subjects and the statistical advantage that the average differences between the two runs does not reflect different abilities of the two groups. On the other hand, it may be difficult to replicate the experimental condition for the within-subject experiment. For example, if the same ten people run the 100-yard dash with the Rapido right after having run with the Zephyr, a difference in the time may reflect their exhaustion from the first run; if they do it the next day, the track conditions may be different.

Many if not most of the studies reported in this book are between-subjects experiments, because exposure to the first condition would bias subjects' response to the second. For example, in Section 10.1 we will describe the phenomenon of *anchoring*, where subjects' estimation of a quantity—say, the number of cities in the United States—is influenced by an arbitrary number given them before they answer the question. One group might be asked, "How many cities are there in the United States—is it greater or fewer than 100?" while a second group would be asked, "How many cities are there in the United States—is it greater or fewer than 1 million?" It is not hard to imagine that someone who has already answered the first question may give a different answer to the second than someone who starts fresh with the second.

Between-subjects experiments always raise the possibility that different results reflect differences between the two groups of subjects. As discussed earlier, however, random assignment of subjects to sufficiently large groups minimizes the likelihood of this error.

---

37. The example is taken from DAVID W. MARTIN, DOING PSYCHOLOGY EXPERIMENTS (5th ed. Belmont: Thomson Brooks/Cole, 2000).

7.6.2 External Validity: Generalizability

The preceding chapters have been concerned with *internal validity*—with whether a change in a dependent variable is attributable to a change in the hypothesized independent variable or to some other confounding variable. But even a well-designed study with statistically significant results may present a question of *external validity*—whether those results can be generalized to other situations. The question can arise in both randomized controlled experiments and observational studies—though in somewhat different ways.

Although the subjects of the paradigmatic clinical trial are randomly assigned to the treatment and control groups, they are nonetheless drawn from a population which itself is seldom a random sample of the population of all possible users of the pharmaceutical. For example, some medicines have different effects on people of different races and ethnicities,[38] but not all clinical trials include representative samples of ethnic groups. Observational studies have these problems as well—for example, a drug prevention program that is very successful in a wealthy suburban high school may have little impact in a poor urban high school, or vice versa. And observational studies are particularly susceptible to the additional problem of confounding discussed in Section 7.2.1.

By contrast to statistical hypothesis testing, establishing the external validity of a study is more an art than a science, relying on knowledge or intuition about whether differences between the group studied and the population to which the study might be generalized are likely to make any difference in outcomes.

It is instructive to look at the problem of external validity with respect to psychological studies concerning people's intuitions about statistics and other matters of judgment and decision making. We have already discussed some findings, and the rest of the book will report on many more. To say that these findings have internal validity is to say that the studies are well designed and implemented and that the results are statistically significant. But this does not entail external validity.

One psychological finding, known as *prospect theory*, has been particularly criticized in this respect. Prospect theory underlies much contemporary behavioral economics, and we will describe its implications in Chapters 14 and 15.[39] Here we are interested not in the substance of the theory, but in the methodological problems of generalizing experimental findings to explain people's behavior in

38. For example, on March 2, 2005, the Food and Drug Administration required that the cholesterol drug Crestor be relabeled to add a caution that starter doses should be reduced in Asian Americans and some other patients. A clinical trial found that levels of Crestor in Asian patients were double those of Caucasians taking the same dose, increasing the chance of muscle damage. Asians, it seemed, did not metabolize the drug at as rapid a rate, causing it to stay in their systems longer.

39. *See also* Charles R. Plott and Kathryn Zeiler, *The Willingness to Pay/Willingness to Accept Gap, the "Endowment Effect," Subject Misconceptions and Experimental Procedures for Eliciting Valuations*, 95 AMERICAN ECONOMIC REVIEW 530–45 (2004), who argue that a major series of laboratory experiments were infected by confounding variables.

the real world.[40] Law professor Chris Guthrie's defense of the theory addresses issues that apply to many other psychological experimental findings:[41]

> Critics typically worry about three external validity factors: the subjects who participate in the experiments, the lack of incentives they face, and the simplicity of experimental designs versus the complexity of decision making in the real world.
>
> **Subjects.** Critics often contend that experimental work lacks external validity because the participants in these studies are typically undergraduates (often enrolled in introductory Psychology classes). Although undergraduates differ from other members of the population in terms of age, education level, life experience, and so on, psychologists have found that they are in fact a fairly good proxy for "real people." Generally speaking, expert decision makers exhibit the same decision-making patterns as undergraduates. Moreover, many of the participants in the prospect theory studies identified in this article were not undergraduates but rather adults with expertise relevant to the domain being studied. For example, law students and federal magistrate judges participated in some of the litigation studies; licensed physicians participated in the medical treatment study; executive MBA students participated in some of the tax studies; and corporate managers participated in some of the managerial decision-making studies.
>
> **Incentives.** When making decisions in the real world, people generally have incentives to "get it right." Some critics suggest that this could mean that real-world decision makers are more "rational" than participants in experimental studies. Although real-world incentives might induce decision makers to take more care with their decisions, they do not appear to induce rational decision-making patterns. In one rather impressive illustration of this, Steven Kachelmeier and Mohamed Shehata conducted decision-making studies in China where the researchers could afford to offer substantial monetary incentives relative to local salaries. In one experimental condition, for instance, the researchers were able to offer subjects an amount roughly comparable to three months' worth of income. Despite these substantial monetary incentives, Kachelmeier and Shehata found that the participants, just like their uncompensated counterparts in American universities, behaved consistent with prospect theory. In short, incentives do not magically induce people to behave in accord with rational choice theory.[42]

---

40. Chris Guthrie, *Prospect Theory, Risk, Preference, and the Law*, 97 Nw. U.L. Rev. 1115 (2003).

41. *Id.* at 1156–59. (The excerpt is based on the text of Guthrie's article but does not adhere strickly to it.) Reprinted by special permission of Northwestern University School of Law, Northwestern University Law Review.

42. *See also* Colin Camerer and Robin Hogarth, *The Effects of Financial Incentives in Experiments: A Review and Capital-Labor-Production Framework*, 7 Journal of Risk and

Experimental Environment. Critics also contend that it is inappropriate to draw inferences about the complicated world we inhabit based on responses to simple hypotheticals presented in a controlled setting. Experimental work in cognitive psychology is generally designed to isolate the effects of one particular phenomenon. The fact that psychologists (and others who do similar work) construct problems that are often quite simplistic does not mean, however, that these problems do not illuminate behavior in the real world.

Lending credence to the external validity of this experimental work is the fact that many of the prospect theory-based observations reported here are confirmed by real-world empirical evidence. For example, Rachlinski found evidence of framing in litigated cases; analyses of tax-returns support the prospect-theory account of taxpayer compliance; several corporate law studies of real-world decisions corroborate the prospect-theory account of managerial decision making; and studies of settlement rates after the adoption of comparative fault in Arkansas support the prospect-theory view of the relative advantages of comparative fault over contributory negligence.

These and other concerns about the external validity of prospect-theory analyses are certainly legitimate. Prospect theory analyses typically rely on experimental work conducted in the lab with college students. Extrapolating from such experimental results should be done with some care. Nonetheless, the available evidence suggests that external validity concerns about subjects, the incentives they face, and the laboratory context are often overstated. Prospect theory has received substantial attention from proponents and opponents alike, and its empirical findings have withstood this scrutiny.

Granting the limitations of both laboratory experiments and observational studies, the best of both worlds involves randomized controlled studies conducted in natural settings. The Poverty Action Lab at MIT, mentioned above, is one of a small but growing number of organizations doing this.

UNCERTAINTY 3–42 (1999), reviewing seventy-four experiments to conclude that "incentives sometimes improve performance, but often don't. . . . [T]he data shows that higher levels of incentives have the largest effects in judgment and decision tasks. Incentives improve performance in easy tasks that are effort-responsive, like judgment, prediction, problem-solving, recalling items from merely or clerical tasks. Incentives sometimes hurt when problems are too difficult or when simple intuition or habit provides an optimal answer and thinking harder makes things worse. In games, auctions, and risky choices the most typical result is that incentives do not affect mean performance, but incentives often reduce variance in responses." The authors note that no replicated study has made rationality violations disappear purely by raising incentives.

8. EXPLAINING AND PREDICTING ONE-TIME EVENTS

Up to this point, we have been using statistics to look for regularities in situations in which there are many similar events—an employer's setting the wages of employees, many residents' being exposed (or not) to foam insulation in their apartments. Statistical analysis of this sort plays an important role not just in law and public policy but also in many other aspects of people's personal and professional lives.

In this chapter, we are interested in the probability that an event will occur one time. We begin by reviewing our treatment of conditional probability begun in Chapter 5, and then turn to Bayesian (or subjectivist) statistics, which is a quite different approach from the frequentist approach explored thus far.

Note to Students: This chapter derives, uses, and transforms a number of formulas, which readers who haven't done math for a while may find daunting. It's not essential that you remember any of them—only that you understand the basic concepts of probability they express.

8.1 CALCULATING CONDITIONAL PROBABILITIES (A REVIEW)

Recall that a conditional probability is the probability that event A will occur, given that event B has occurred. It is written

$$P(A|B)$$

and is read: "the probability of A given B." For example, in the Terra Nueva case, *P(rash present|foam)* is "the probability of having a rash given that the tenant lives in an apartment with foam insulation." We repeat the contingency table for Terra Nueva in Table 8.1. In view of the focus of this chapter, we'll use its synonym of **probability table**.

In Chapter 5, we found that:

$$P(\textit{rash present}|\textit{foam}) = P(\textit{foam \& rash present})/P(\textit{foam})$$

which turns out to be $0.25/0.60 = 0.42$.

Here is a generalized probability table, as shown in Table 8.2. (The symbol "~" (tilde) means "not.")

Remember that the probabilities in the margins of the table, such as P(A), are called **marginal probabilities**. The probability P(A & B) is called a **joint probability**.

TABLE 8.1 PROBABILITY TABLE FOR TERRA NUEVA

Insulation \ *Rash*	*Present*	*Absent*	Marginal
Foam	P(foam & rash)	P(foam & no rash)	P(foam)
Not Foam	P(not foam & rash)	P(not foam & no rash)	P(not foam)
Marginal	P(rash)	P(no rash)	1.0

Probabilities:

Insulation \ *Rash*	*Present*	*Absent*	Marginal
Foam	**0.25**	**0.35**	0.60
Not Foam	**0.15**	**0.25**	0.40
Marginal	0.40	0.60	1.00

To generalize the calculation above, the **conditional probability** of event B given A is the joint probability of A and B divided by the marginal probability of A:

$$P(B|A) = \frac{P(A \& B)}{P(A)}$$

While joint probabilities are symmetric—P(A & B) = P(B & A)—conditional probabilities are not: $P(A|B) \neq P(B|A)$. As we see in the formula, the denominator for determining P(B|A) is P(A), the row marginal, but the denominator for determining P(A|B) would be P(B), the column marginal.

$$P(A|B) = \frac{P(A \& B)}{P(B)}$$

TABLE 8.2 GENERALIZED PROBABILITY TABLE

A \ *B*	*B*	*~B*	Total
A	P(A & B)	P(A & ~B)	P(A)
~A	P(~A & B)	P(~A & ~B)	P(~A)
Total	P(B)	P(~B)	1.00

In the Terra Nueva example, we have

$$P(\textit{rash present}|\textit{foam}) = P(\textit{foam \& rash present})/P(\textit{foam}) = 0.25/0.60 = 0.42$$

$$P(\textit{foam}|\textit{rash present}) = P(\textit{foam \& rash present})/P(\textit{rash present}) = 0.25/0.40 = 0.625$$

While the former is the proportion of foam-insulation residents who have a rash, the latter is the proportion of rash-afflicted tenants whose premises have foam insulation.

8.2 THE PROBABILITY OF CONJUNCTIVE EVENTS

In *People v. Collins*, an interracial couple was prosecuted for robbery.[1] Here are the facts, as summarized by the Supreme Court of California:

> On June 18, 1964, about 11:30 a.m. Mrs. Juanita Brooks, who had been shopping, was walking home along an alley in the San Pedro area of the City of Los Angeles. She was pulling behind her a wicker basket carryall containing groceries and had her purse on top of the packages. She was using a cane. As she stooped down to pick up an empty carton, she was suddenly pushed to the ground by a person whom she neither saw nor heard approach. She was stunned by the fall and felt some pain. She managed to look up and saw a young woman running from the scene. According to Mrs. Brooks the latter appeared to weigh about 145 pounds, was wearing "something dark," and had hair "between a dark blond and a light blond," but lighter than the color of defendant Janet Collins' hair as it appeared at trial. Immediately after the incident, Mrs. Brooks discovered that her purse, containing between $35 and $40, was missing. About the same time as the robbery, John Bass, who lived on the street at the end of the alley, was in front of his house watering his lawn. His attention was attracted by "a lot of crying and screaming" coming from the alley. As he looked in that direction, he saw a woman run out of the alley and enter a yellow automobile parked across the street from him. He was unable to give the make of the car. The car started off immediately and pulled wide around another parked vehicle so that in the narrow street it passed within six feet of Bass. The latter then saw that it was being driven by a male Negro, wearing a mustache and beard. At the trial Bass identified the defendant as the driver of the yellow automobile. However, an attempt was made to impeach his identification by his admission that, at the preliminary hearing, he testified to an uncertain identification at the police lineup shortly after the attack on Mrs. Brooks, when defendant was beardless.

1. People v. Collins, 68 Cal.2d 319, 66 Cal Rptr. 497, 438 P.2d 33 (1968).

In his testimony Bass described the woman who ran from the alley as a Caucasian, slightly over five feet tall, of ordinary build, with her hair in a dark blond ponytail and wearing dark clothing. He further testified that her ponytail was "just like" one which Janet had in a police photograph taken on June 22, 1964.

At the trial an expert testified as to the probability of the occurrence of the physical characteristics of the defendants and the car:

Partly yellow automobile	0.1
Man with mustache	0.25
Girl with ponytail	0.1
Girl with blond hair	0.33
Negro man with beard	0.1
Interracial couple in car	0.0001

The expert assumed that these six characteristics were independent, and calculated that there was only one chance in 12 million that any couple possessed all of these distinctive characteristics.

8.2.1 The Probability of Dependent Conjunctive Events

Even assuming the accuracy of the expert's assessments of the probability of the occurrence of each of the six events in the Los Angeles area, he was incorrect in assuming their independence. In reversing the convictions, the Supreme Court of California noted that there was some likely "overlap" in being a man with a mustache (0.25) and being a Negro man with a beard (0.1).

If these were independent, you would just use the multiplication rule as described below in 8.2.2. But it's pretty obvious that they are not. Let's assume that a survey of the region shows that for every 10 men with mustaches, 9 have beards. How do we calculate the probability of a man's having both a mustache and a beard, P(mustache & beard)?

If we take the conditional probability formula in Section 8.1,

$$P\,(B\,|A) = \frac{P(A\,\&\,B)}{P(A)}$$

and multiply both sides by P(A), we get the equivalent equation[2]

$$P(A\&B) = P(A)\,P(B\,|A)$$

2. By the same token, multiplying the formula for P(A|B) by P(B) on both sides, would give $P(A\&B) = P(B)P(A|B)$.

So, we can calculate the joint probability of the events A and B, P(A & B), using the marginal probability of A and the conditional probability of B given A, or the marginal probability of B and the conditional probability of A given B.

In our example,

$$P(\textit{mustache} \,\&\, \textit{beard}) = P(\textit{mustache})\, P(\textit{beard} \mid \textit{mustache})$$

If for every 10 men with mustaches, 9 have beards, then

$$P(\textit{beard} \mid \textit{mustache}) = 0.9$$

Thus:

$$\begin{aligned} &P(\text{mustache \& beard}) \\ &= P(\text{mustache})\, P(\text{beard} \mid \text{mustache}) \\ &= 0.25 * 0.9 \\ &= 0.225 \end{aligned}$$

> What American president had a beard but no mustache? Look at a $5 bill.

8.2.2 Conjunctive Independent Events

Recall that two events are independent if knowledge about one does not change one's belief about the probability of the other. That is, A and B are independent if P(B|A) = P(B) and P(A|B) = P(A). If all the relevant events are independent, the formulas in Section 8.2.1 for joint probabilities become

$$P(A \,\&\, B) = P(A)P(B)$$

This is the multiplication rule for independent events. Under the Collins expert's mistaken view that mustache and beard are independent,

$$\begin{aligned} P(\textit{mustache} \,\&\, \textit{beard}) &= P(\textit{mustache})\, P(\textit{beard}) \\ &= 0.1 * 0.25 \\ &= 0.025 \end{aligned}$$

Noting that the expert's assumption of independence made it seem less likely that a randomly chosen man would have both a beard and a mustache, and thus more likely that the accused couple was at the scene of the event than the facts justified. The Supreme Court of California reversed the convictions.[3]

---

3. The court also noted that the expert's conclusions about the probabilities of the particular events were not supported by evidence. The court did not address the accuracy of the eyewitness identification—e.g., *P(beard|witness says beard)*—which is presented in the taxicab problem in Section 8.5.

8.2.3 Intuitions about Conjunctions

Suppose that Luis Trujillo has a brief due in a complex case, and has assigned its three major sections to three associates. Based on past experience and the amount of work to be done, he estimates that these are the probabilities that they will complete their sections by next Friday:

- Amy: 0.9
- Bill: 0.8
- Cindy: 0.9

If events A, B, and C are independent of each other, you obtain their joint probability by multiplying the (marginal) probabilities:

$$P(A \,\&\, B \,\&\, C) = P(A) * P(B) * P(C) = 0.65$$

Are you surprised at how low this result is? People tend to overestimate the probability of **conjunctive** events—multipart events in which each stage or component needs to be successful for the entire strategy to be successful. This leads to unwarranted optimism about the likelihood of the success of multistage plans (e.g., developing and launching a new product) or about the *un*likelihood of the *failure* of complex, interactive systems (e.g., a nuclear power plant).

Kahneman and Tversky explain this tendency in terms of **anchoring and adjustment**, which we will discuss in more detail in Section 10.1. In brief, people tend to focus on the probability of success of any one part or stage of the multipart event. They "anchor" their estimation of the overall probability on this number, and make insufficient adjustment for the other stages.

National Intelligence Estimates

The simplest, easiest, cheapest and most powerful way to transform the quality of intelligence would be to insist that analysts attach two little numbers to every report they file.

The first number would state their confidence in the quality of the evidence they've used for their analysis: 0.1 would be the lowest level of personal/professional confidence; 1.0 would be—former CIA director George Tenet should pardon the expression—a "slam dunk," an absolute certainty.

The second number would represent the analyst's own confidence in his or her conclusions. Is the analyst 0.5— the "courage of a coin toss" confident—or a bolder 0.75 confident in his or her analysis? Or is the evidence and environment so befogged with uncertainty that the best analysts can offer the National Security Council is a 0.3 level of confidence?

These two little numbers would provoke intelligence analysts and intelligence consumers alike to think extra hard about analytical quality, creativity and accountability. Policy makers could swiftly determine where their analysts had both the greatest—and the least—confidence in their data and conclusions. Decision-makers could quickly assess where "high confidence" interpretations were based on "low-confidence" evidence and vice versa.

Michael Schrage, *What Percent Is 'Slam Dunk'?"* WASHINGTON POST, Feb. 20, 2005, editorial.

8.3 THE CONJUNCTION FALLACY AND THE REPRESENTATIVENESS HEURISTIC

One consequence of the law of total probability is that the joint probability of two events must always be less than or equal to the probability of one of those events. P(A & B) can never be greater than just P(A) or just P(B).

One of the most famous results in the judgment and decisionmaking (JDM) research suggests that people do not obey the law of total probability: they sometimes give more probability to the conjunction of two events than they give to the two events on their own. This is called the **conjunction fallacy**.[4]

Perhaps the most common context in which people succumb to the conjunction fallacy is where the conjunction of two events seems intuitively more plausible than one of the events alone. For example, read the paragraph below:

> Linda is 31 years old, single, outspoken and very bright. She majored in philosophy. As a student, she was deeply concerned with issues of discrimination and social justice, and also participated in anti-nuclear demonstrations.
>
> Now, rate the following options in order of likelihood:
>
> 1. Linda is a teacher in an elementary school.
> 2. Linda is active in the feminist movement.

4. The example below, and any other examples in this section given without references, are from studies described in detail in Amos Tversky and Daniel Kahneman, *Judgments Of and By Representativeness*, quoted in JUDGMENT UNDER UNCERTAINTY: HEURISTICS AND BIASES (Daniel Kahneman, Paul Slovic and Amos Tversky eds., New York: Cambridge University Press, 1982) [hereafter, HEURISTICS AND BIASES] The conjunction fallacy is discussed further in Amos Tversky and Daniel Kahneman, *Extensional Versus Intuitive Reasoning: The Conjunction Fallacy in Probabilistic Judgment*, 90 PSYCHOLOGICAL REVIEW 293–315 (1983).

3. Linda is a bank teller.
4. Linda is a bank teller and active in the feminist movement.

How did you order the options? Many people rate option 4 as more likely than option 3. Since the event described in option 4 is the conjunction of options 2 and 3, the law of total probability says that we should never rate option 4 as more probable than option 3. If your intuitions and logic are in conflict, you're in good company. The eminent biologist Stephen Jay Gould wrote: "Knowledge of the truth does not dislodge the *feeling* that Linda is a feminist bank teller: I know [the right answer], yet a little homunculus in my head continues to jump up and down, shouting at me—'but she can't just be a bank teller; read the description.'"[5]

Daniel Kahneman and Amos Tversky explain the conjunction fallacy in the "Linda problem" in terms of the **representativeness heuristic**. The description of Linda is very similar to what we might expect for somebody who is active in the feminist movement, but not at all similar to our stereotypical idea of a bank teller. But since the description of Linda also seems more similar to a feminist bank teller than to that of an ordinary bank teller, the representativeness heuristic leads us to commit the conjunction fallacy. In effect, the description leads one to assign too low a probability that Linda is merely a bank teller, or too high a probability that she is a feminist bank teller.

Kahneman and Tversky describe representativeness as "an assessment of the degree of correspondence between a sample and a population, an instance and a category, an act and an actor, or, more generally between an outcome and a model." Under the representativeness heuristic, "probability judgments (the likelihood that X is a Y) are mediated by assessments of resemblance (the degree to which X 'looks like' Y)."[6] In Chapter 1, we mentioned that the representativeness heuristic could lead people to attribute causes to phenomena that resemble the effect (smelly foam insulation causes distressing physical symptoms).

Determining correct probabilistic solutions is a very challenging task. Daniel Kahneman and Shane Frederick write: "When confronted with a difficult question people often answer an easier one instead, usually without being aware of the substitution."[7] We substitute the target attribute (the *likelihood* that Linda is

5. *Quoted in* Daniel Kahneman and Shane Frederick, *Representativeness Revisited: Attribute Substitution in Intuitive Judgment* (Aug. 2001), in HEURISTICS AND BIASES, *supra* at 103. The "Linda" problem and the representativeness heuristic more generally have spawned a considerable critical (and defensive) literature. *See id.*; Barbara Mellers, Ralph Hertwig and Daniel Kahneman, *Do Frequency Representations Eliminate Conjunction Effects*, 12 PSYCHOLOGY SCIENCE 269 (2001).

6. Daniel Kahneman and Shane Frederick, *Representativeness Revisited: Attribute Substitution in Intuitive Judgment*, *in* HEURISTICS AND BIASES, *supra* at 49.

7. *Id.*

a feminist bank teller) with the heuristic attribute (Linda's *resemblance* to a feminist bank teller).

8.3.1 Explanation Through Narrative

Jerome Bruner writes:[8]

> There are two modes of cognitive functioning, two modes of thought, each providing distinctive ways of ordering experience, of constructing reality. . . . They differ radically in their procedure for verifications. A good story and a well-formed argument are different natural kinds. Both can be used as means for convincing another. Yet what they convince *of* is fundamentally different: arguments convince one of their truth, stories of their lifelikeness. The one verifies by eventual appeal to procedures for establishing formal and empirical proof. The other establishes not truth but verisimilitude.

Which of these scenarios seems more likely?[9]

Scenario A: A war involving the United States and North Korea.

Scenario B: A situation in which neither side intends to attack the other side, but a war between the United States and North Korea occurs against the background of U.S. efforts to isolate North Korea economically; it is triggered by the U.S. Navy's seizure of a North Korean ship containing a shipment of missiles followed by massive movement of North Korean troops near the DMZ.

Many people choose the second and more detailed scenario, despite the fact that providing more details actually decreases the probability of the scenario. As Tversky and Kahneman observed, "as the amount of detail in a scenario increases, its probability can only decrease steadily, but its representativeness and hence its apparent likelihood may increase." They conclude that people's reliance on representativeness "is a primary reason for the unwarranted appeal of detailed scenarios and the illusory sense of insight that such constructions often provide."[10] (This is a potential hazard of of scenario planning, discussed in Section 3.4.)

This should not be surprising, given the role that stories or narratives play in our lives. Narratives are part and parcel of our schematic ordering of experience (see Section 1.5.2.); it is through narratives that we understand and

---

8. Jerome Bruner, Actual Minds Possible Worlds 11 (Boston, MA: Harvard University Press, 1986).

9. This is an updated version of an example described in Scott Plous, The Psychology of Judgment and Decision Making (New York: McGraw Hill, 1993).

10. Amos Tversky and Daniel Kahneman, *Judgments of and by Representativeness*, in Heuristics and Biases, *supra* at 98.

explain the world. In this respect, consider Table 8.3 (which provides its own narrative).

TABLE 8.3 DETAILS, PROBABILITY, AND VERISIMILITUDE

Question	Never	Once or twice	More than twice
How often has this happened to you: Waking up paralyzed with a sense of a strange person or presence or something else in the room?	87	36	21
How often has this happened to you: Waking up paralyzed?	124	12	8

Poll conducted by Robin Dawes and Matthew Mulford. In KENDRICK FRAZIER, BARRY KARR, AND JOE NICKELL, THE UFO INVASION: THE ROSWELL INCIDENT, ALIEN ABDUCTIONS, AND GOVERNMENT COVERUPS (1997)

In a study of jury decision making, Nancy Pennington and Reid Hastie suggest that, given a number of possible competing versions of the facts, jurors will select the "best story," with their confidence being determined by several factors:[11]

- *coverage*—how well the story accounts for all the evidence;
- *coherence*—which consists of:
  - *consistency*—the absence of internal contradictions,
  - *plausibility*—correspondence with the decision maker's knowledge of what typically happens in the world, and
  - *completeness*—the story's inclusion of relevant causes, psychological states, actions, goals, consequences;
- *uniqueness*—the absence of good alternative competing stories.

Notice that a number of these criteria of confidence depend on detailed rather than parsimonious data. We share Pennington and Hastie's belief that the same criteria are germane to explanations in many domains beyond the courtroom. Persuasion often consists less of convincing others of the logic of one's argument than having them replace their narrative construction of reality with your own.[12] And the richer and more detailed the story, the more persuasive. In these respects, Scenario B in the North Korean conflict is far superior to A.

---

11. NANCY PENNINGTON AND REID HASTIE, INSIDE THE JUROR: THE PSYCHOLOGY OF JUROR DECISION MAKING (New York: Cambridge University Press, 1993). *See The Story Model for Juror Decision Making* and *A Theory of Explanation-Based Decision Making.*

12. *See* HOWARD GARDNER, CHANGING MINDS ch. 4 (Boston, MA: Harvard Business School, 2004); JEROME BRUNER, MAKING STORIES (Boston, MA: Harvard University Press,

The phenomenon (illustrated by the Linda and Korean War examples) in which the sum of the probabilities of necessary components of an outcome are greater than the probability of the outcome or, indeed, greater than 1.0, is (somewhat confusingly) called *subadditivity*. We can think of at least one kind of situation where subadditivity makes sense. Imagine a jury determining whether or not a defendant committed homicide. It has inconclusive evidence (1) of his presence at the crime scene, and (2) about his motivation to kill the deceased. A juror might rationally conclude that the defendant was more likely to kill the victim with some particular motive than to think that he killed him at all, with no motive given.[13]

Generally, though, subadditivity is simply a logical error. A set of experiments by Craig Fox and Richard Birke suggests how the phenomenon may bias a lawyer's advice to a client.[14] For example, when asked (in 1997) to predict the outcome of Paula Jones's suit against Bill Clinton, lawyers who were given the two options of the case ending in verdict or no verdict assigned a probability of 0.2 to the former and 0.75 to the latter. When given the options of a verdict, settlement, dismissal, immunity, or withdrawal of the suit, the probability of a verdict remained at 0.2, but the nonverdict probabilities summed to 1.29. "[U]npacking the description of an event into more detailed description of disjoint components will generally yield a higher judged probability" because it draws one's attention to each component.

Fox and Birke asked lawyers to advise the plaintiff's counsel whether to accept an offer of settlement in a personal injury case. All of the subjects were given the identical scenario detailing what the plaintiff must prove to prevail at trial, but for one group, these were described as necessary to establish "liability," while for the other they were described in terms of the elements of a torts claim: "duty, breach, and causation." Seventy-four percent of the second group (compared to 52 percent of the first group) recommended settling—because unpacking the elements made the difficulty of proof seem greater. As Fox and Birke note, an attorney's advice might flip depending on whether she was predicting whether a client would "prevail" or "lose."

To mitigate the bias, Fox and Birke suggest that attorneys (1) consider multiple formulations of the probability of the event at various levels of specificity; (2) make an effort to explicitly consider all possible scenarios while ensuring that the all the probabilities sum to 100 percent; and (3) base their predictions on good base rate data (See Section 8.5).

2002); ANTHONY G. AMSTERDAM AND JEROME BRUNER, MINDING THE LAW (Boston, MA: Harvard University Press, 2002).

13. MARK G. KELMAN, THE HEURISTICS DEBATE: ITS NATURE AND ITS IMPLICATIONS FOR LAW AND POLICY (Oxford University Press, forthcoming 2010).

14. Craig R. Fox and Richard Birke, *Forecasting Trial Outcomes: Lawyers Assign Higher Probabilities to Possibilities that Are Described in Greater Detail*, 26 LAW AND HUMAN BEHAVIOR 159 (2002).

More broadly, since Kahneman and Tversky demonstrated the existence of the conjunction fallacy, psychologists have explored ways of thinking about probabilistic information that help us to avoid making representativeness errors. In particular, Gerd Gigerenzer and his research group have argued that the best way not to get confused by probabilities is to turn them into more concrete quantities. A particularly effective method is to express the probabilities in frequencies and consider one variable at a time. For example, out of 1000 people, how many are bank tellers? Say the number of bank tellers is about ten. Then how many of those bank tellers are feminists? Maybe two or three? By phrasing the probabilities explicitly in terms of frequencies, and thinking about one variable at a time, it becomes very hard to think that there could be more feminist bank tellers than there are bank tellers in total.[15]

8.4 THE PROBABILITY OF DISJUNCTIVE EVENTS

In Section 8.2, we calculated a joint probability—the probability that event A *and* event B happen. Here we discuss the probability that event A *or* event B happens. In ordinary discourse, "A or B" can mean either "A or B but not both" or it can mean "A or B or both." In probability, we always take *or* to have the latter meaning. Another way this can be stated is "at least one of A and B."

For example, if you throw a pair of dice, what's the probability of getting at least one ace? Let A represent the event that the first die is an ace and B the event that the second die is an ace. Then the probability of getting at least one ace is:

$$P(A \text{ or } B) = P(A) + P(B) - P(A \,\&\, B)$$

To understand this formula, consider the Venn diagram of Figure 8.1. The area of the circle on the left represents P(A). The area of the circle on the right represents P(B). If we were to add these two areas, we would be double-counting the area of the shaded region, which represents P(A&B) (in the example, the probability that both dice are aces). Therefore, we subtract the area of the shaded region to obtain the total area.

In the dice example, since there are 6 sides of a die, P(A) = 1/6 and P(B)=1/6. Because the two tosses are independent, P(A & B) = P(A)P(B) = (1/6)(1/6) = 1/36. Therefore, the probability of getting at least one ace is

$$P(A \text{ or } B) = P(A) + P(B) - P(A \,\&\, B) = 1/6 + 1/6 - 1/36 = 11/36 = 0.31$$

15. Gerd Gigerenzer, Adaptive Thinking: Rationality in the Real World 250 (Oxford: Oxford University Press, 2000). A complete discussion of the consequences of using frequencies for probabilistic reasoning is given in Gerd Gigerenzer and Ulrich Hoffrage, *How to Improve Bayesian Reasoning Without Instruction: Frequency Formats,* 102 Psychological Review 684–704 (1995).

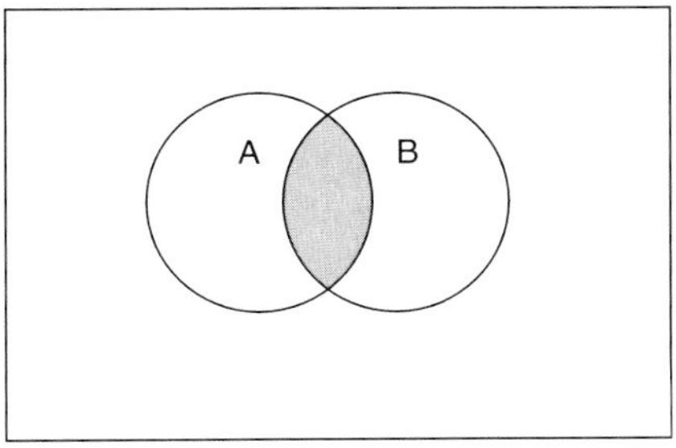

FIGURE 8.1 VENN DIAGRAM OF EVENTS A AND B.

or 31 percent.

If two events are mutually exclusive—that is, it is impossible for both to happen—the circles in the Venn diagram will not intersect. In this case, P(A & B) = 0, so the formula simplifies to

$$P(A \text{ or } B) = P(A) + P(B)$$

(This is Axiom 3 in Section 5.1.2) For example, what is the probability that the toss of a single die will result in an ace or a deuce? Since these events are mutually exclusive, we just add their probabilities: 1/6 + 1/6 = 1/3 = 0.33 or 33 percent.

Whenever you are interested in the probability that *at least one* of a number of events will happen, summing all the probabilities and subtracting all the overlaps can be tedious. There's a simpler way to calculate the probability of at least one of the events occurring. Consider this example:

> It is late in the afternoon in California and you must send a signed document to someone in New York, who must have it by 9 a.m. the next morning.[16] You can send the document simultaneously through three overnight services, each of which costs about $20, with these probabilities of getting the document to the destination on time:
>
> - AirFast: 0.9
> - BeThere!: 0.8
> - Chronos: 0.8
>
> Alternatively, you can give it to a courier who will take it with him on the red-eye, at a cost of $2000. Before deciding whether to opt for this high-cost

16. The example comes from Amir D. Aczel, Chance: A Guide to Gambling, Love, the Stock Market, and Just about Everything Else (New York: Thunder's Mouth Press, 2004).

option, you would like to know the probability of the document getting to New York on time if you send three signed copies, one with each service.

We are interested in the probability that at least one of these services will deliver on time. Let A represent the event that AirFast is on time, B the event that BeThere! is on time, and C the event that Chronos is on time. We want to find P(A or B or C) Instead of adding the probabilities and adjusting for the various overlaps, we notice that *the event that at least one happens is the complement of the event that none happen*. Recall that the probability of an event A's complement is $P(\sim A) = 1 - P(A)$ In this case,

$$P(A \text{ or } B \text{ or } C) = 1 - P(\sim A \,\&\, \sim B \,\&\, \sim C)$$

If we know that the three events are *independent*, we can use the multiplication rule to find this last probability.

$$\begin{aligned} P(A \text{ or } B \text{ or } C) &= 1 - P(\sim A \,\&\, \sim B \,\&\, \sim C) \\ &= 1 - P(\sim A)P(\sim B)P(\sim C) \end{aligned}$$

Using the complement rule again on each of the three probabilities, we get:

$$\begin{aligned} \mathrm{P(A\ or\ B\ or\ C)} &= 1 - \mathrm{P}(\sim \mathrm{A} \,\&\, \sim \mathrm{B} \,\&\, \sim \mathrm{C}) \\ &= 1 - \mathrm{P}(\sim \mathrm{A})\mathrm{P}(\sim \mathrm{B})\mathrm{P}(\sim \mathrm{C}). \\ &= 1 - (1\text{-}\mathrm{P(A)})(1\text{-}\mathrm{P(B)})(1\text{-}\mathrm{P(C)}) \\ &= 1 - 0.1 * 0.2 * 0.2 \\ &= 1 - 0.004 \\ &= 0.996 \end{aligned}$$

Thus, it is extremely likely that the document will get to New York on time.[17]

In *Bomber*, Len Deighton observed that a World War II pilot had a 2 percent chance of being shot down on each mission, and that he was "mathematically certain" to be shot down in fifty missions. But this is incorrect.[17]

The pilot will not survive if he is shot down *at least once* in the fifty missions. This phrase is a hint to use the complement rule. The event of being shot down at least once is the complement of the event of being shot down none of the times.

Let D represent the event of being shot down at least once.

17. David Freedman, Robert Pisani, and Roger Purves, Statistics (3rd ed. New York: Norton, 1997).

$$\begin{aligned} P(D) &= 1 - P(\text{never shot down}) \\ &= 1 - P(\text{not shot on 1st mission})P(\text{not shot on 2nd mission} \ldots P(\text{not shot on 50th mission}) \\ &= 1 - (0.98)50 \\ &= 1 - 0.36 \\ &= 0.64 \end{aligned}$$

There is a 64 percent chance (not 100 percent) of being shot down in fifty missions.

8.4.1. Intuitions about Disjunctive Events

Just as people tend to overestimate the probability of conjunctive events, they tend to underestimate the probability of **disjunctive** events—multipart events where success of any one stage or component makes the entire event successful, such as at least one of the three courier services getting the signature page to New York on time. This is due to the same anchoring phenomenon, since the outcome is greater than any of the component probabilities.

8.5 BAYESIAN STATISTICS

The statistical techniques discussed in the preceding three chapters are based upon the **frequentist** interpretation of probability—the idea that probabilities refer to the frequencies with which events occur in the world, over many trials. If an event has a probability of 0.5, it will occur half the time. This means that the probability assigned to an event expresses its frequency of occurrence, which can be estimated directly from experience.

As we mentioned at the start, however, there is another way of interpreting the axioms underlying probability theory. Many modern statisticians also subscribe to a **subjectivist** interpretation of probability, under which probabilities indicate the strength of belief in a proposition. If something has a probability of 0.5, it has a 50 percent chance of being true. This means that the probability you assign to an event expresses something about your beliefs. Both the frequentist and subjectivist interpretations are consistent with the axioms of probability, although they involve different perspectives about what probability means.

Frequentist statistics is concerned with $P(D|H)$ the probability of a set of data D under a hypothesis H, typically the null hypothesis H_0. A frequentist interpretation assumes that a hypothesis is either true or false, not as a random variable but as a fixed state of the world, albeit unknown. However, with a subjectivist interpretation, it is also possible to talk about P(H|D) the strength of one's belief in a hypothesis *H* after observing data *D*. Often lawyers and courts are more interested in this latter quantity—for example, the probability that a defendant is guilty based on the evidence presented—so it is worth learning to evaluate it.

Consider the following problem:

A taxicab was involved in a hit-and-run accident at night. Two cab companies, the Green and the Blue, operate in the city. You are given the following information:

1. 85 percent of the cabs in the city are Green; 15 percent are Blue.
2. A witness identified the cab as a Blue cab. The court tested her ability to identify cabs under appropriate visibility conditions. When presented with a sample of cabs (half of which were Blue and half of which were Green), the witness made correct identifications in 80 percent of the cases and erred in 20 percent of the cases.

What is the probability that the cab involved in the accident was Blue rather than Green?

Here our hypothesis *H* is that the cab was Blue; we will call it *B*. Our data *D* is the eyewitness testimony that the cab was Blue; we will call the event that she says it was Blue *SB*. Our goal is to find $P(H/D)$ in this case $P(B/SB)$ the probability that the cab was actually Blue, given that the witness said it was Blue.

First, let's go through the given information.

- The proportion of taxis in the city that are Blue is called the **base rate**; it is background information not specific to the particular event. If you had no information about the accident, the probability that the cab in the accident was Blue would be the base rate. For this reason it is also called the **prior probability** that the cab was Blue. It is your best guess for the probability that the cab was Blue **prior** to hearing the testimony. In general, the prior probability $P(H)$ is the strength of your belief in *H prior* to obtaining event-specific data. The prior probability can be determined in different ways, depending upon the situation. Sometimes it is estimated from a belief based on the investigator's experience, but typically it is taken to be the base rate. In the hit-and-run case, it is the base rate of Blue taxis, $P(B) =$ 0.15 Since this prior probability is substantially less than 50 percent, your best guess before hearing the testimony would be that the cab was Green.
- The fact that the witness says the taxi was Blue (SB), is the data, *D*.
- You have one other important additional piece of information: the probability that the witness's perception was accurate. This is the probability that the witness says the cab is Blue, given that it was actually Blue, $P(SB/B)$ In general, this is $P(D/H)$ and is called the **likelihood** of the data under

the hypothesis. It represents how likely the observed data would be if the hypothesis was true. In the example, the likelihood is $P(SB|B) = 0.8$.

8.5.1 Structuring the Taxi Problem as a Tree

As we said before, our goal is to find $P(B|SB)$, the probability that the cab was actually Blue, given that the witness said it was Blue. This probability, generically written $P(H|D)$, represents the strength of our belief in H *after* we have obtained the data D about the event. For this reason, it is called the **posterior probability** of the hypothesis. In summary, we need a way to find the posterior probability based on the information we have: the prior probability, the data, and the likelihood.

Let's represent the problem in a tree structure as shown in Figure 8.2.[18]

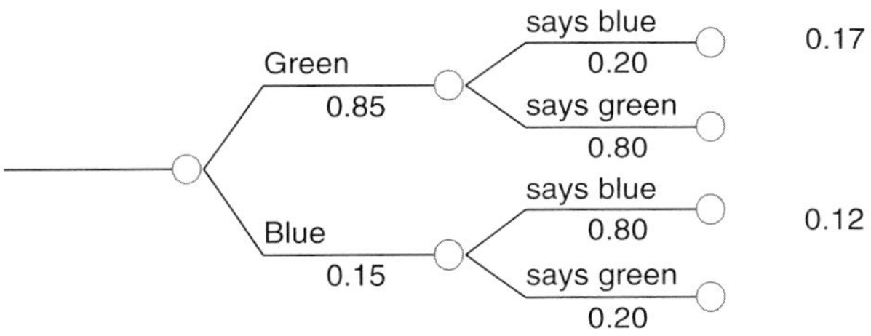

FIGURE 8.2 STRUCTURING THE TAXI PROBLEM AS A TREE.

The leftmost node represents the base rate, with 85 percent of the taxis being Green and 15 percent being Blue. The next nodes represent the likelihood, that is, the probability of the data if the given hypothesis is true. In this example, the likelihood is the probability that the witness says the taxi was a particular color, given its true color. She is accurate 80 percent of the time, so when the taxi was actually Green (upper node), she says it was Green 80 percent of the time and Blue 20 percent of the time. When the taxi was actually Blue (lower node), she says it was Blue 80 percent of the time and Green 20 percent of the time.

Now let's solve, or "fold back," the tree by using the methods of Section 8.2—that is, by multiplying the probabilities along each branch. For example, the probability that the cab *was* Blue and the witness says it was Blue is

$$P(B \,\&\, SB) = P(B)P(SB|B) = 0.15 * 0.80 = 0.12$$

or 12 percent. Similarly, if we let G represent the hypothesis that the cab was Green, the probability that it was Green and she says it was Blue is

$$P(G \,\&\, SB) = P(G)P(SB|G) = 0.85 * 0.20 = 0.17$$

18. The concept of a decision tree is described in greater detail in Section 15.2.

or 17 percent. (Since she said it was Blue, we can ignore the second and fourth branches.) The witness says the cab was Blue 17 + 12 = 29 out of 100 times and is correct 12 of those times. Dividing 12 by 29, we obtain 0.41, or 41 percent. Given her testimony that the cab was Blue, there is still only a 41 percent chance that the cab actually was Blue, so our best guess is that the cab was Green. If this answer is surprising, keep in mind the base rate: only 15 percent of cabs are Blue. As we discuss below, people tend to ignore the base rate when estimating probabilities.

8.5.2 Solving the Taxi Problem Using Bayes' Theorem

The tree structure uses **Bayes' Theorem**—developed by the Reverend Thomas Bayes, an early eighteenth-century minister and mathematician. The equation for Bayes' Theorem is:

$$P(H|D) = \frac{P(D|H)\,P(H)}{P(D)}$$

Note to Students: If you understand how to represent and analyze the taxi problem using a decision tree, you've got the gist of Bayes' Theorem. But the chapter would be incomplete without walking through how the equation actually works.

Let's replace the general formulation of Bayes' Theorem with the particulars of the taxi problem. We were given the likelihood, P(SB|B): it is 0.8. We were also given P(B), the base proportion of Blue cabs: it is 0.15. Substituting in Bayes' equation, we get:

$$P(B|SB) = \frac{P(SB|B)\,P(B)}{P(SB)} = \frac{0.8 * 0.15}{P(SB)}$$

Now we need the value of the denominator, $P(SB)$, which is the overall, or marginal, probability that the witness will say the cab was Blue. Now letting SG represent the event that the witness says the cab was Green, the probabilities of this problem are displayed in Table 8.4.

TABLE 8.4 PROBABILITY TABLE FOR THE TAXI PROBLEM

Probabilities		*Testimony*		
		SB	*SG*	Total
Truth	*B*	P(B & SB)	P(B & SG)	P(B)
	G	P(G & SB)	P(G & SG)	P(G)
	Total	P(SB)	P(SG)	1.00

There are only two ways the event SB—the witness saying it was a blue cab—can come about: either the cab is blue and she says it's blue, or the cab is green and she says it's blue. These are mutually exclusive and collectively exhaustive. Therefore,[19] P(SB)—the marginal probability of the testimony that the cab was blue—is the sum of (a) the probability that the witness says the car was Blue and it was in fact Blue, and (b) the probability that she says the car was Blue and it was in fact Green:

$$P(SB) = P(B \& SB) + P(G \& SB)$$

As with the example of finishing the brief on time (**in** Section 8.2.1 and Section 8.2.3), we calculate the two terms:

$$P(B \& SB) = P(SB|B) * P(B)$$
$$P(G \& SB) = P(SB|G) * P(G)$$

Since the witness is correct 80 percent of the time, the probability that she will say the taxi was Blue if it was Blue is 0.8, and the probability that she will say it was Blue if it was Green is 0.2. Plugging in these numbers, we get:

$$P(B \& SB) = P(SB|B) * P(B) = 0.8 * 0.15 = 0.12$$
$$P(G \& SB) = P(SB|G) * P(G) = 0.2 * 0.85 = 0.17$$
$$P(SB) = P(B \& SB) + P(G \& SB)$$
$$= 0.12 + 0.17$$
$$= 0.29$$

Above, we had the partially solved equation

$$P(B \mid SB) = \frac{0.8 * .015}{P(SB)}$$

Now that we know that P(SB) is 0.29, we can plug that into the denominator, getting:

$$P(B \mid SB) = \frac{0.8 * 0.15}{0.29} = 0.41$$

8.5.3 Diagnosticity

Recall that we can discuss uncertainty in terms of odds instead of probabilities. Here, just as we have prior and posterior probabilities of an event, we have prior

19. See Section 5.4.1.

and posterior odds, the odds of the event before and after we observe the data, respectively.

In the previous section, with the Bayes tree method, we used the likelihood to transform the prior probability—P(B) = 0.15—into the posterior probability—P(B|SB) = 0.41. To transform the prior odds into the posterior odds, we use the **likelihood ratio**.

Recall from the previous section that the likelihood is the probability of observing data given a certain hypothesis, P(D|H) In the example, the data (D) consisted of the testimony SB that the cab was Blue. The likelihood of this testimony under the hypothesis (H) that the cab was Blue is P(SB|B) = 0.8 and the likelihood under the hypothesis that the cab was Green is P(SB|G) = 0.2. The likelihood ratio, therefore is

$$\frac{P(SB\,|\,B)}{P(SB\,|\,G)} = \frac{0.8}{0.2} = 4$$

This means that the testimony that the cab was Blue is four times as likely if it actually was Blue than if it was Green. In general, the likelihood ratio is

$$\frac{P(D\,|\,H)}{P(D\,|\,{\sim}H)}$$

The numerator is the likelihood of the data given that *H* is true, and the denominator is the likelihood of the data given that *H* is false.

To transform prior odds into posterior odds, we multiply by the likelihood ratio:

$$\textit{Posterior odds} = \textit{Likelihood ratio} * \textit{Prior odds}$$

If the data are more likely when *H* is true, the likelihood ratio is greater than one, and observing the data increases the odds. If the data are more likely when *H* is false, the likelihood ratio is less than one, so observing the data decreases the odds.

The likelihood ratio is also called the **diagnosticity** because of its meaning in medical diagnostic tests.

Many diagnostic tests have significant false positive rates. If we let *D* represent a positive test result and *H* the hypothesis that a patient has the disease in question, then the true positive rate (also called the **sensitivity**) of the test is P(D|H), the probability of a positive result when the patient has the disease. The false positive rate is P(D|~H), the probability of a positive result given that the patient does not have the disease. The diagnosticity is therefore the ratio of the true positive rate to the false positive rate.

Suppose you wake up one morning with a sore throat. You have heard that, of all sore throats, 10 percent are bacterial infections and the other 90 percent are viral. In other words, for every one bacterial infection, there are nine viral infections, so you figure that your odds of having a bacterial infection—let's say strep throat—are 1:9.

You go to the doctor, and she gives you a rapid strep test. She explains that, among people with strep throat, 81 percent will get a positive test result, and among those with a virus, 1 percent will get a positive test result. In other words, the sensitivity or true positive rate is 0.81, and the false positive rate is 0.01. You calculate that the diagnosticity of the rapid strep test is 81.

The doctor calls you with the news that you tested positive. Now what are your odds of having strep?

$$\textit{Posterior odds} = \textit{Diagnosticity} * \textit{Prior odds} = 81 * 1/9 = 9/1$$

Your odds have increased dramatically from 1:9 to 9:1, because of the high diagnosticity of the test, and she writes a prescription for antibiotics.

A high diagnosticity is an indication of a good test. Whenever the diagnosticity is greater than 1, we know two things:

- Because diagnosticity is the likelihood ratio P(D|H)/P(D|~H) we know the true positive rate P(D|H) is greater than the false positive rate P(D|~H).
- Because posterior odds = Diagnosticity * Prior odds, we know that the posterior odds (after a positive test result) are greater than the prior odds. That is, a positive test result increases the odds that the patient has the disease.

FIGURE 8.3 WAY TOO GENERAL PRACTITIONER ©THE NEW YORKER COLLECTION, FEB. 14–21 2005, 120. ALL RIGHTS RESERVED. REPRINTED WITH PERMISSION.

On the other hand, if the diagnosticity of a test is 1, it does not change the odds and is not worth performing.

The rarer the disease in question, the higher a test's diagnosticity must be to give one confidence in the result. For example, in order to have better-than-even odds of having SARS, you would have to test positive on a test with very high diagnosticity, in order to make up for SARS's very low base odds. Even if your symptoms are more consistent with SARS, you might still be more likely to have the flu, just because the flu is a much more common ailment.

For an analysis of the taxi problem using the odds version of Bayes' Theorem, see the Appendix, Section 8.7.

CT scans have become a significant industry even for customers who have no particular risk of disease. Are they useful? Steven Woloshin and colleagues cite a report that people whose lung cancer is found early by such scans have a five-year survival rate of 80 percent, as opposed to 15 percent for the typical lung-cancer patient whose condition is detected later.[20] They are nonetheless skeptical about whether the scans do more good than harm.

One problem is that CT scans detect tiny tumors, but do not have a very high diagnosticity, and thus must often be followed up by biopsies, which can be painful and even dangerous. So for starters, the test can give rise to harm to people who don't have, and are not in danger of developing, lung cancer. And even when cancerous abnormalities are discovered, they may be indolent and never develop into anything dangerous. But because there's no way to know, most people who are diagnosed are treated with surgery, radiation therapy, or chemotherapy—also painful and often dangerous.

But what of the survival statistics? Here's how they are calculated: Suppose that 1000 people were diagnosed with lung cancer five years ago. If 150 are alive today, the five-year survival is 150/1000, or 15 percent; if 800 are alive today the five-year survival is 80 percent.

But Woloshin and his colleagues argue that even if CT screening raised the five-year survival rate from 15 percent to 80 percent, no one might get an extra day of life. They suggest this thought experiment. Imagine a group of people with lung cancer who will all die at age 70. If they are diagnosed when they are 67, their five-year survival rate would be zero percent. But if they were diagnosed when they were 64, their five-year survival rate would be 100 percent. Early diagnosis increases the five-year survival statistic but doesn't postpone death.

20. Steven Woloshin, Lisa Schwartz, and Gilbert Welch, *Warned, but Worse Off*, New York Times, Aug. 22, 2005.

The fact that CT scans identify small indolent tumors also inflates the survival rate. They suggest another thought experiment. Imagine a population where, after having symptoms such as a persistent cough, 1000 people are diagnosed with progressive lung cancer. Five years later,150 are alive. Suppose the entire population gets CT scans, and that 5000 are diagnosed with cancer, but the additional 4000 actually have indolent forms and are alive five years later. This would raise the five-year survival rate to 83 percent—because these healthy people would appear in both parts of the fraction: survivors/people diagnosed with cancer = (150 + 4000)/(1000 + 4000) = 4150/5000 = 83%. But what has really changed? Some people have been unnecessarily told they have cancer (and may have experienced the harms of therapy), and the same number of people (850) still died.

The phenomenon was borne out by a randomized trial of chest X-ray screening at the Mayo Clinic, where the five-year survival was higher for those who were screened, but death rates were slightly higher for those who received the screening.[21]

8.5.4 Bayes' Theorem and Intuition: Ignoring the Base Rate

When Daniel Kahneman and Amos Tversky gave the taxi problem to subjects who were not knowledgeable about Bayesian statistics, their average answer for the probability that the cab was Blue was 80 percent—they focused only on the eyewitness's testimony and completely ignored the base rates.[22] In the example of the patient with symptoms slightly more consistent with SARS than with the flu, this is analogous to the doctor diagnosing him with SARS, ignoring the flu's much higher incidence rate.

A different group of subjects was given a slight variant, in which they were told that, although the two companies are roughly equal in size, 85 percent of cab accidents in the city involve Green cabs, and 15 percent involve Blue cabs. Although the answers were highly variable, the average answer for the probability that the cab involved in the accident was Blue was 55 percent—an

21. *The New England Journal of Medicine* published the study on which the Woloshin article is based without disclosing that its principal investigator and her institution held patents related to CT scanning or that the study was funded by a cigarette manufacturer. In January 2009 the journal announced a new disclosure policy. New York Times, Jan. 9, 2009, *available at* http://www.nytimes.com/2009/01/09/us/09journal.html?_r=1&ref=health.

22. Amos Tversky and Daniel Kahneman, *Evidential Impact of Base Rates,* (1982), in Heuristics and Biases, *supra* at 153.

estimate that appears to take some account of the base rate. Kahneman and Tversky's explanation, which is supported by other experiments, is that the base rate in the variant problem provides some *causal* information: it suggests that the drivers of the Green cabs are less competent or careful drivers than the drivers of Blue cabs, and this induces people to attend to the base rates of careful and careless drivers.

Kahneman and Tversky[23] gave two groups of undergraduate students some short descriptions of individuals and asked them to judge whether the individuals were likely to be lawyers or engineers. Here is a typical description:

> Jack is a 45-year-old man. He is married and has four children. He is generally conservative, careful, and ambitious. He shows no interest in political and social issues and spends most of his free time on his many hobbies, which include home carpentry, sailing, and mathematical puzzles.

One group of students was told that the descriptions came from a sample of people of whom 70 percent were lawyers and 30 percent engineers. The other group of students was told that the descriptions came from a sample of people of whom 30 percent were lawyers and 70 percent engineers. Thus the two groups were given quite different base rates.

Most of the students judged Jack to be very likely to be an engineer. Most interestingly, their judgments were unaffected by the different base rates. In Bayesian terms, the students entirely ignored $P(H)$. Here, again, the representativeness heuristic is at work: People seem to be making decisions based upon how representative the description is of a particular profession, rather than by combining prior and likelihood information in a fashion consistent with Bayesian inference.

These and other findings suggest that humans do not combine probabilistic information in a Bayesian fashion. When told:

> Suppose . . . that you are given no information whatsoever about an individual chosen at random from the sample.

respondents correctly referred to the base rates in predicting the person's profession. But when given a diagnostically worthless description, such as:

> Dick is a 30-year-old man. He is married with no children. A man of high ability and high motivation, he promises to be quite successful in his field. He is well liked by his colleagues.

23. Amos Tversky and Daniel Kahneman, *Causal Schemas in Judgments Under Uncertainty*, (1973), in Heuristics and Biases, *supra* at 117.

Legal Problem

We have focused on people's tendency to neglect base rates. Can you think of an instruction that judges give jurors as a matter of course in criminal cases that is intended to counteract their tendency to take account of base rates?

they neglected the base rates, judging Dick to be *equally likely* to be a lawyer or an engineer regardless of the relative frequencies of these two professions in the samples.

8.6 CONFUSION OF THE INVERSE, OR THE PROSECUTOR'S FALLACY

In Section 5.6, we explained that it is easy to confuse $P(A|B)$ with $P(B|A)$, a mistake sometimes called **confusion of the inverse**. Recall the difference between P(pregnant|woman) and P(woman|pregnant).

In *People v. Collins* (introduced in Section 8.2), in addition to the error of treating events that were not independent as if they were independent when combining them, the prosecutor made the error of confusing these conditional probabilities. Based on the claim that there was only one chance in 12 million that any couple possessed all of these distinctive characteristics, the prosecutor argued that there was only one chance in 12 million that the defendants were innocent, and the jury convicted. The court caught what has since been named the **prosecutor's fallacy**. Assuming that the chances that any couple possessed all of the distinctive characteristics were 1/12,000,000, "the prosecution's figures actually imply a likelihood of over 40 percent that the Collinses could be 'duplicated' by at least one other couple who might equally have committed the San Pedro robbery."[24] The prosecutor's fallacy was confusing *P(not guilty|match)* with P(*match*|*not guilty*).

If this example of confusion of the inverse seems itself confusing, consider the following problem. Approximately 3 percent of the U.S. population has blood type AB+. The blood at the scene of the murder is AB+, the defendant's blood is AB+, and the match of blood type is the only evidence connecting him to the murder.

24. In William Fairley and Frederick Mosteller, *A Conversation About Collins, in* SELECTED PAPERS OF FREDERICK MOSTELLER (New York: Springer New York 1974), William Fairley and Frederick Mosteller show that the court's particular result—though not its fundamental critique of the prosecutor's reasoning—was in error.

Let us define *match* as the presence of the accused's *blood type*, AB+, at the scene of the crime. And let us treat the presence or absence of the accused's *actual blood* at the scene of the crime as equivalent to his being *guilty* or *not guilty*. We know that the probability of a match for a randomly selected member of the population, P(*match*) = 0.03. Applying the prosecutor's argument in *Collins* to the present case, P(*match|not guilty*) = 0.03, and therefore the prosecutor would want the jury instructed that there is a 97 percent chance that the suspect committed the murder.

But we're interested in *P(not guilty|match)*. Calculating this number requires knowing the population of people who might have committed the crime. Let's assume that the relevant population contained 1000 people, and that there is no other evidence connecting the suspect to the crime—so that if one other person in the relevant population has AB+, the suspect cannot be convicted "beyond a reasonable doubt." We can use Bayes' Theorem,

$$P(H \mid D) = \frac{P(D \mid H)\, P(H)}{P(D)}$$

to calculate *P(guilty|match)* or:

$$P(guilty \mid match) = \frac{P(match \mid guilty)\, P(guilty)}{P(match)}$$

- Since there's sure to be a match if the suspect is guilty, P*(match|guilty)* = 1.
- P(guilty), or the prior probability of the suspect's being guilty, is 1/1000 or 0.001.
- The probability of a match for a random member of the population, P(*match*), is about 0.03.

Thus, *P(guilty | match)* = 1 * 0.001/0.03 = 0.033

By the complement rule, P(*not guilty|match*) = 0.97. So instead of 97 percent chance of guilt, it is 97 percent chance of innocence.

Forensic Evidence

In addition to the hazard of confusion of the inverse, identifications based on a match of the defendant's DNA, fingerprints, etc. with traces found at the crime scene or on a victim present the simple problem of *false positives*. That is, the laboratory tests may report a match when the defendant's and the trace DNA are not the same[25]. By contrast to fingerprint matches, which courts typically treated as certain, the relative novelty of DNA evidence opened it to a probabilistic understanding, which has begun to affect more traditional forms of forensic evidence.[26]

8.6.1 Countering Faulty Intuition by Presenting Frequencies

The cognitive scientist Gerd Gigerenzer has suggested that people are less likely to fall prey to confusion of the inverse and the representativeness heuristic, and more likely to correctly integrate base rates into decisions, if the data are presented in terms of natural frequencies rather than probabilities. He posed a question along these lines to physicians:[27]

> To facilitate early detection of breast cancer, starting at a particular age, women are encouraged to participate at regular intervals in routine screening, even if they have no obvious symptoms. Imagine that you conduct such breast cancer screening using mammography in a particular region of the country. The following information is available about asymptomatic women aged 40 to 50 in such region who participate in mammography screening.

One group of physicians was given information in terms of probabilities, in essentially this form:

> The probability that a given woman in this group has breast cancer is 1 percent. If a woman has breast cancer, the probability is 80 percent that she will have a positive mammogram. If a woman does not have breast cancer, the probability is 10 percent that she will have a positive mammogram. Imagine a woman who has a positive mammogram. What is the probability that she actually has breast cancer?

Responses varied from 1 percent to 90 percent, with a median estimate of 70 percent. Only two of the twenty-four physicians in this group reasoned

25. Jonathan Koehler, *quoted in* Gigerenzer at 167, says 1 in 100 or 200. HANS ZEISEL AND DAVID H. KAYE, PROVE IT WITH FIGURES: EMPIRICAL METHODS IN LAW AND LITIGATION (New York: Springer-Verlag, 1997).

26. *See* Michael J. Saks and Jonathan J. Koehler, *The Coming Paradigm Shift in Forensic Identification Science*, 309 SCIENCE 892 (2005).

27. GERD GIGERENZER, CALCULATED RISKS: HOW TO KNOW WHEN NUMBERS DECEIVE YOU (New York: Simon & Schuster, 2002). The particular questions quoted in the text were put forth by one expert, leading to the development of a broader survey with results along the same lines.

correctly to reach the correct result of 7.5 percent. Another two were close, but their reasoning was not correct.[28]

The second group of physicians was given information in terms of natural frequencies.

> Ten out of every 1,000 women have breast cancer. Of these 10 women with breast cancer, 8 will have a positive mammogram. Of the remaining 990 women who don't have breast cancer, some 99 will still have a positive mammogram. Imagine a sample of 100 women who have positive mammogram screening. How many of these women actually have breast cancer?

Eleven of this group of twenty-four physicians gave the correct answer, and quite a few of the others were close. Gigerenzer argues that the computation based on natural frequencies is much simpler than using Bayes' Theorem—something that most readers who worked through the problems above would agree with.

We think that a tree, of the sort used in the taxi problem, provides an easy way of representing this problem, as shown in Figure 8.4.

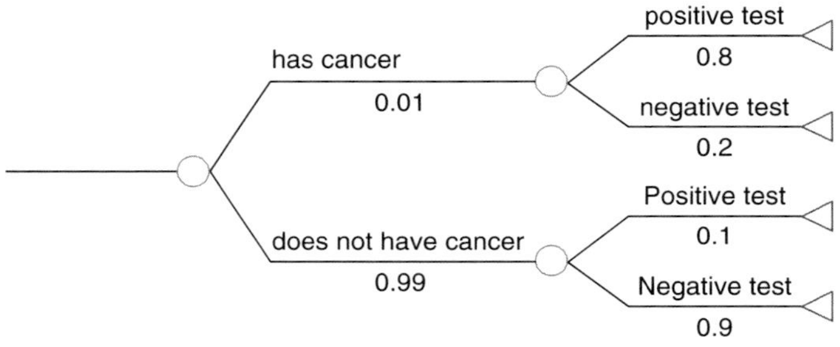

FIGURE 8.4 STRUCTURING A MEDICAL DIAGNOSIS PROBLEM AS A TREE.

Since we are only interested in cases where someone tested positive, we focus on the two branches with positive tests:

$$\textit{has cancer} * \textit{positive test} = 0.01 * 0.8 = 0.008$$

$$\textit{does not have cancer} * \textit{positive test} = 0.99 * 0.1 = 0.099$$

Adding the two products—0.008 + 0.099 = 0.107—tells us how often a woman in this population will test positive. The probability that a woman with a positive mammogram actually has cancer is the proportion of positives that are true: 0.008/0.107 = 0.075, less than 8 percent.

28. *Id.* 43. Gigerenzer states that the correct result was 8 percent, but the actual number, as derived below, is 7.476.

8.7 APPENDIX

8.7.1 Odds Version of Bayes' Theorem Applied to the Taxi Problem

The hypothesis is that the taxi was Blue, and the data set is that the witness says the taxi was Blue. The prior odds are $P(B){:}P(G) = 0.15{:}0.85 = 3{:}17$. So before hearing the testimony, based on the base rate alone, the cab is much more likely to be Green. The likelihood ratio is $P(SB|B)/P(SB|G) = 0.8/0.2 = 4$. Therefore, the testimony increases the prior odds fourfold, giving posterior odds of $(4 * 3){:}17 = 12{:}17$.

The posterior odds being less than one is equivalent to the posterior *probability* being less than 0.5. Both tell us to guess that the cab was Green. Odds of 12 to 17 mean that it is likely to occur 12 out of every 29 times. Therefore, the posterior probability $P(B|SB)$, is

$$\frac{12}{29} = 0.41$$

the same answer we obtained using each of the other two formulations of Bayes' Theorem.

If the likelihood of the data were the same whether or not H were true, the likelihood ratio would equal 1. When this is the case, the data tell us nothing, and the posterior odds equal the prior odds. In our example, this would happen if the witness were incorrect 50 percent of the time. She would have no credibility, so her testimony would not change our guess of the taxi color at all. The posterior odds would equal the prior odds of 3:17. (See Section 5.1.2a).

9. BIASES IN PERCEPTION AND MEMORY

9.1 INTRODUCTION: STAGES OF INFORMATION PROCESSING

In the introduction to Part 2, we described the application of the *lens model* to a probabilistic environment. The preceding chapters on statistics were largely concerned with what inferences can appropriately be drawn from multiple fallible indicators—in particular, what inferences can be appropriately made about an entire population when the indicators are only a sample of the population. In those chapters we generally proceed from the assumption that the empiricist was accurate in perceiving and coding the sample data, and we introduced the statistics that best allows one to make inferences. Chapter 9 focuses on errors in perceiving and interpreting the events that provide the basis for such inferences.

Cognitive psychologists have likened a person making a judgment to an "information processor" that proceeds through a number of stages from the availability of information to the generation of a response to that information. The functional components of that information processor can be represented as shown in Figure 9.1.

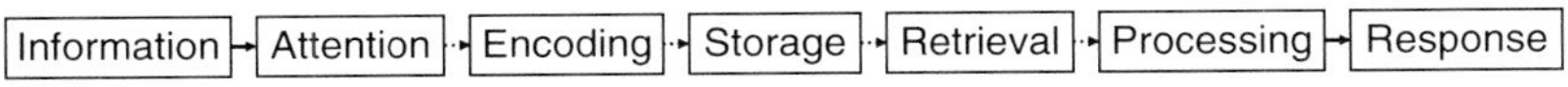

FIGURE 9.1 MODEL OF INFORMATION PROCESSING.

Let us consider those components in turn. Every moment of our lives, we are bombarded with vast amounts of *information*, of which we *attend* to only a small fraction. We *encode* the information, structuring, evaluating, and interpreting it and transforming into some sort of mental representation. You might think of *perception* (not on the chart) as overlapping attention and encoding. We *store* information in memory and, on occasion, *retrieve* it from memory (i.e., become aware of it) and *process* it with respect to particular objectives. Our *response* to processing may be a factual judgment or inference, an evaluative judgment or opinion, a choice among alternatives or decision, or a solution to a problem.[1]

This and the following chapter examine biases and distortions that can affect these stages of information processing. Although some of the psychological

1. *See* Verlin B. Hinsz, R. Scott Tindale, and David A Vollrath, *The Emerging Conceptualization of Groups as Information Processors*, 43 Psychological Bulletin 121 (1997).

phenomena considered cut across various stages, this chapter, on biases in perception and memory, centers around the first five stages, and Chapter 10, on biases in judgment, centers around the last two.

9.2 BIASES IN ACQUISITION, RETENTION, AND RETRIEVAL

We met at nine	*That carriage ride*
We met at eight.	*You walked me home.*
I was on time	*You lost a glove*
No, you were late.	*I lost a comb.*
Ah yes! I remember it well.	*Ah yes! I remember it well.*
We dined with friends	*That brilliant sky*
We dined alone.	*We had some rain.*
A tenor sang	*Those Russian songs*
A baritone.	*From sunny Spain*
Ah yes! I remember it well.	*Ah yes! I remember it well.*

 —I Remember It Well (Duet from "Gigi")

Lyrics by ALAN JAY LERNER Music by FREDERICK LOEWE
© 1957, 1958 (Copyrights Renewed) CHAPPELL & CO., INC.
All Rights Reserved
Used by Permission of ALFRED PUBLISHING CO., INC.

A large amount of any lawyer's time is focused on past events. It is the understanding and analysis of past events that give rise to legal liability—whether civil, administrative, or criminal—and that provide the basis for the predictions necessary for policy making and planning. By definition, understanding the past calls upon memory. In many contexts, however, memories tend to be highly fallible.

Our memory does not store complete representations of what was perceived, but only fragments of our *interpretations* of the relevant facts or events. Recollection requires reconstructing one's interpretation, often using (more or less) logical inferences to fill in missing details.[2] In *Eyewitness Testimony*, Elizabeth Loftus divides memory processes into three stages: *acquisition*, in which the information is entered; *retention*, the period between acquisition and the demand to "remember"; and *retrieval*, where one recollects the information.

2. ELIZABETH F. LOFTUS, MEMORY: SURPRISING NEW INSIGHTS INTO HOW WE REMEMBER AND WHY WE FORGET (Reading, MA: Addison-Wesley, 1980).

Though she focuses on visual memories, her observations apply to memories of all sorts:[3]

> Early on, in the acquisition stage, the observer must decide which aspects of the visual stimulus he should attend to. Our visual environment typically contains a vast amount of information, and the proportion of information that is actually perceived is very small. . .
>
> Once the information associated with an event has been encoded or stored in memory, some of it may remain there unchanged while some may not. Many things can happen to witnesses during this crucial retention phase. The witness may engage in conversations about the event, or overhear conversations, or read a newspaper story—all of these can bring about powerful and unexpected changes in the witness's memory.
>
> Finally, at any time after an event a witness may be asked questions about it. At this point the witness must recreate from long-term memory that portion of the event needed to answer a specific question. This recreation may be based both on information acquired during the original experience and on information acquired subsequently. In other words, both the acquisition and the retention stages are crucial to what happens during the retrieval. The answer the person gives is based on this recreation.
>
> . . . Events at any one or several of the stages can be the cause of . . . retrieval failure. The information may simply not have been perceived in the first place—a failure at the acquisition stage. The information might have been accurately perceived, but then is forgotten or interfered with during the retention stage. And finally, information may have been accurately perceived in the first place but may have become inaccessible [or distorted] during questioning—a failure at the retrieval stage.

9.3 BIASES IN THE ACQUISITION OF INFORMATION

Before turning to more complex issues involving the acquisition of information, we should note that some problems simply arise from perceptual inadequacies that are fairly universal. For example, we tend to be quite inaccurate in judging time, speed, and distance,[4] and we systematically overestimate the duration of events. More generally, Dolly Chugh and Max Bazerman describe what they call

3. ELIZABETH F. LOFTUS, EYEWITNESS TESTIMONY 21 (Cambridge, MA: Harvard University Press, 1979) [hereafter LOFTUS].

4. Participants in one experiment were told in advance that they would be asked to judge the speed of a car. The car was moving at 12 miles per hour, and their estimates ranged from 10 to 50 miles per hour. LOFTUS 29.

bounded awareness—the phenomenon where "individuals fail to see, seek, use, or share highly relevant, easily accessible, and readily perceivable information during the decision-making process."[5] Because our cognitive power is limited, we can focus only on a small part of everything that goes on around us—often only on one thing at a time.

> Mr. Hill was so engrossed in the call that he ran a red light and didn't notice Linda Doyle's small sport utility vehicle until the last second. He hit her going 45 miles per hour. She was pronounced dead shortly after. Later, a policeman asked Mr. Hill what color the light had been. "I never saw it," he answered.[6]

Much of our daily experience involves multitasking, but we aren't as good at multitasking as we would like to believe. Most of the time, we just don't notice things that are not in our mental field of vision. Sometimes this can be embarrassing—when we've lost the thread of a discussion by doing e-mail tasks at meetings or browsing the Web during class; sometimes it's dangerous—drivers cannot give full attention to the road when talking even on a hands-free phone. Eyewitness's description of crimes are notoriously unreliable, especially when their attention is riveted to the stress-inducing event. Elizabeth Loftus uses the term "weapon focus" to describe an assault victim's attention to the brandished weapon to the exclusion of other details, including features of the assailant. Chugh and Bazerman characterize the misalignment of available information of which one is unaware with the information needed for a decision as a *focusing failure*.

9.4 THE BIASING EFFECT OF SCHEMAS, EXPECTATIONS, THEORIES, AND INTERESTS

Section 1.5.2 introduced the idea that all of our perceptions are mediated by schemas or expectations: when we perceive a stimulus from our environment, our first task is to fit that information into some existing knowledge structure represented in memory. This is essential and inevitable—and a hazard for the careful empiricist. In a classic experiment, Jerome Bruner and Leo Postman briefly

5. Dolly Chugh and Max H. Bazerman, *Bounded Awareness: What You Fail to See Can Hurt You*, 6 Mind & Society 1–18 (2007).

6. Matt Richtel, Drivers and Legislators Dismiss Cellphone Risks, New York Times, July 19, 2009, http://www.nytimes.com/2009/07/19/technology/19distracted.html?hp.

showed participants five playing cards, one of which was a three of hearts colored black.[7] A vast majority of the participants engaged in "perceptual denial," confidently recalling that the card was a normal three of hearts. The phenomenon of *illusory correlation* described in Section 5.7 exemplifies the same tendency.

Elizabeth Loftus reports on an accident where hunters killed a companion: "One of the men . . . saw something moving and said to his friend, 'That's a deer, isn't it?' The friend replied that he thought so too, and the first man shot at the deer. The deer pitched forward and cried out—a sound which seemed like the cry of a wounded deer. The hunters fired more shots to bring it down." Loftus explains:[8]

> The hunters who eagerly scanned the landscape for a deer perceived the moving object as a deer. They expected to hear the cry of a deer and they heard their friend's cry that way . . . Yet a policeman testified that when he later saw a man under the same conditions he perceived the object as a man . . .[T]he policeman knew he was supposed to be looking at a man; thus, he perceived the object he saw as a man.

Consider these more complex examples:

9.4.1 They Saw a Game

A 1951 football game between Dartmouth and Princeton was unusually rough, with injuries sustained by members of both teams. Psychologists Albert Hastorf and Hadley Cantril asked students from each school—some of whom had seen the game and some a film of it—to fill out a questionnaire noting any infractions of the rules, and characterize them as "mild" or flagrant."[9]

> Nearly all *Princeton* students judged the game as "rough and dirty"—not one of them thought it "clean and fair." And almost nine-tenths of them thought the other side started the rough play. . . . When Princeton students looked at the movies of the game, they saw the Dartmouth team make over twice as many infractions as their own team made. And they saw the Dartmouth team make over twice as many infractions as were seen by Dartmouth students. When Princeton students judged these infractions as "flagrant" or "mild," the ratio was about two "flagrant" to one "mild" on the Dartmouth team, and about one "flagrant" to three "mild" on the Princeton team.
>
> As for the Dartmouth students, while the plurality of answers fell in the "rough and dirty" category, over one-tenth thought the game was "clean and

---

7. Jerome S. Bruner and Leo Postman, *On the Perception of Incongruity: A Paradigm*, 18 Journal of Personality 206 (1949).

8. Elizabeth F. Loftus and Katherine Ketcham, Witness from the Defense: The Accused, the Eyewitness, and the Expert Who Puts Memory on Trial (New York: St. Martin's Press, 1991).

9. Albert H. Hastorf and Hadley Cantril, *They Saw a Game: A Case Study*, 49 Journal of Abnormal Psychology 129 (1954).

> fair" and over a third introduced their own category of "rough and fair" to describe the action. Although a third of the Dartmouth students felt that Dartmouth was to blame for starting the rough play, the majority of Dartmouth students thought both sides were to blame . . .
>
> When Dartmouth students looked at the movie of the game, they saw both teams make about the same number of infractions. And they saw their own team make only half the number of infractions the Princeton students saw them make. The ratio of "flagrant" to "mild" infractions was about one to one when Dartmouth students judged the Dartmouth team, and about one "flagrant" to two "mild" when Dartmouth students judged infractions made by the Princeton team.

Granted that the students' perceptions of fault were biased in favor of their own schools' teams, what explains the difference in perceptions? Hastorf and Cantril answer:

> It seems clear that the "game" actually was many different games and that each version of the events that transpired was just as "real" to a particular person as other versions were to other people . . .
>
> . . . An "occurrence" on the football field or in any other social situation does not become an experiential "event" unless and until some significance is given to it. And a happening generally has significance only if it reactivates learned significances already registered in what we have called a person's assumptive form-world.

At the very least, people interpret the same ambiguous information in different ways: I see the tackle as gratuitously violent while you see it as hard-hitting but fair. At the worst, from all the events going on in the environment, we sometimes notice those that are significant from our egocentric positions, and fail to notice those that don't.

9.4.2 The Hostile Media Phenomenon

Essentially the same phenomenon surfaces in a quite different context: people who differ in their perceptions and recollections and interpretations of contentious events inevitably have very different views of what constitutes "fair" news coverage of those events. In 1985, Robert Vallone, Lee Ross, and Mark Lepper conducted an experiment in which participants who had previously identified themselves as pro-Arab, pro-Israeli, or neutral viewed extensive samples of media coverage of the massacre of Palestinians in Lebanese refugee camps by allies of Israel.[10]

---

10. Robert P. Vallone, Lee Ross, and Mark R. Lepper, *The Hostile Media Phenomenon: Biased Perception and Perceptions of Media Bias in Coverage of the Beirut Massacre*, 49 Journal of Personal and Social Psychology 577 (1985).

The pro-Arab participants saw the media as biased toward Israel; the pro-Israeli participants saw the news programs as biased against Israel. The pro-Arab participants thought that the programs applied lower standards to Israel than to other countries, that they did not focus enough on Israel's role in the massacre, and that the editors made a positive case for Israel and were biased in its favor. Pro-Israeli participants thought that the programs applied a higher standard to Israel, focused too much on Israel's role, made a negative case against Israel, and were biased against Israel. Furthermore, participants who deemed themselves more knowledgeable or more emotionally involved had stronger perceptions of bias.[11] Neutrals were about midway between the partisans. (Viewers who thought themselves knowledgeable thought the main source of bias was what was *omitted*, particularly that the media did not provide the full context.)

Just as Hastorf and Cantril believed that Dartmouth and Princeton students had seen different football games, Vallone, Ross, and Lepper concluded that "the pro-Arab and pro-Israeli participants 'saw' different news programs—that is, they disagreed about the very nature of the stimulus they had viewed." For example, the groups reported that a higher percentage of the references to Israel were, respectively, favorable or unfavorable. And each believed that the programs would lead an undecided or ambivalent viewer to favor the opposing position. The authors offer this analysis of the phenomenon:

> Our results highlight two mechanisms—one apparently evaluative or cognitive, the other apparently more perceptual in nature—that combine to produce the partisans' conviction that they have been treated unfairly. According to the first mechanism, in which opposing partisans believe, respectively, that the truth is largely "black" or largely "white," each complain about the fairness and objectivity of mediated [i.e., media] accounts that suggest that the truth might be at some particular hue of gray. According to the second mechanism, opposing partisans further disagree about the color of the account itself: One side reports it to be largely white (instead of the blackish hue that the other side thinks it should be), the other side reports it to be largely black (instead of the whitish hue that the first side thinks it should be), and both sides believe the discrepancy between the mediated account and the unmediated truth to be the intended result of hostile bias on the part of those responsible.
>
> We note that our results do not permit us to speak authoritatively about either the source or the depth of the perceptual bias we have claimed to document; nor, obviously, do they shield us from the age-old difficulties of

11. While knowledgeable neutral participants did not perceive a bias one way or the other, unknowledgeable neutrals more closely resembled the pro-Israeli than pro-Arab groups. The authors note that American public opinion tends to be pro-Israeli and that the neutrals may be more pro-Israeli than they realize.

ruling out all cognitive interpretations for an ostensibly perceptual phenomenon. Do partisans pay more attention when their side is being attacked? Do they remember such information more, perhaps because they are frustrated and annoyed by the absence of any sufficiently forceful rebuttals to such attacks? The exact mechanism remains unclear, but we believe that it is not simply a matter of differing standards or criteria in labeling particular facts, arguments, or images as pro-Israeli or anti-Israeli. Perhaps our most important, and interesting, finding in this regard is the tendency for both groups to assert that neutral viewers will turn against their side when they view the media coverage. This finding is further evidence that the specific content and overall "hue" of the report is indeed perceived differently by the partisans, even when they would wish the truth to be otherwise, for partisans surely would prefer to believe, and perhaps even expect that non-partisans would assimilate mixed information in a manner congruent with the partisans' view of the truth.

The authors suggest that their analysis may apply to perceptions of other types of mediation, including spouses' perceptions of family counselors, or labor and management's perceptions of government arbitrators.

9.4.3 Why Cases Don't Settle When They Should[12]

In many civil cases, the parties pay inordinately high litigation costs before settling or they do not settle at all. Some scholars have explained the phenomenon in terms of disputants' uncertainty about the judge or jury. An alternative explanation, put forward by Linda Babcock and her colleagues is that litigants' predictions of judicial decisions are systematically biased in a self-serving manner.

To test this hypothesis, Babcock et al. gave law and business-school students detailed testimony in a case involving a claim for damages in a motorcycle-automobile accident. The participants were informed that the same materials had been given to a judge who had decided how much, if anything, to award to the plaintiff. They were asked (1) what they thought was a fair settlement from the viewpoint of a neutral third party and (2) their best guess of the amount the judge would award. They were also instructed to negotiate a settlement: The defendant was given $10 cash (with each $1 worth $10,000 in the real world). If they could not reach a settlement in a half hour, the judge's verdict would be imposed on them.

The major experimental manipulation was that the participants in one group were assigned roles as plaintiffs or defendants *before* reading the testimony,

12. Linda Babcock, George Loewenstein, Samuel Issacharoff, and Colin Camerer, *Biased Judgments of Fairness in Bargaining*, 85 American Economic Review 1337 (1995); Linda Babcock and George Loewenstein, *Explaining Bargaining Impasse: The Role of Self-Serving Biases*, 11 Journal of Economic Perspectives 109 (1997). Abstract *available at* SSRN: http://ssrn.com/abstract=11367.

answering the questions, and negotiating, while those in the second group first read the testimony and answered the questions and were then assigned roles before they negotiated.

The assessment of what would be a fair judgment by plaintiffs and defendants who had been assigned roles *before* reading the testimony diverged by $19,756 on average; their predictions of the judicial outcome diverged by $18,555. Moreover, 28 percent of the parties in this group failed to settle. By contrast, plaintiffs and defendants in the second group did not diverge significantly in their assessments of either of fairness or the judicial outcome, and only 6 percent failed to settle. Apparently, knowing one's role in advance causes one to encode the facts in a way that is self-serving and that leads to undue optimism about the assessments likely to be made by third parties.

Not only students, but experienced litigators and negotiators are prone to this self-serving bias. Whereas purely economic analyses attribute the failure to settle to strategic behavior, the authors suggest: "Perhaps disputants are not trying to maximize their expected outcome, but only trying to achieve a fair outcome. However, what each side views as fair tends to be biased by self-interest, which reduces the prospects for settlement."

Merely informing disputants about the prevalence of self-serving bias had no effect on their bias. Is it possible to counter the bias? Babcock et al. did a follow-up experiment in which the participants, after being assigned roles and reading the testimony, were instructed:

> Disputants don't always think carefully about the weaknesses in their own case: they are therefore surprised when the judge's ruling is worse than their expectations. For plaintiffs, this means that the judge's award is often less than their expectations. For defendants, this means that the judge's award is often greater than their expectations. Therefore, please think carefully about the weaknesses in your case. In the space below, please list the weaknesses in your own case.

Being asked to assess the weaknesses of one's own case had a significant effect. When given the debiasing instruction, plaintiffs' and defendants' predictions of the judge's award differed by only $5000, and the litigants reached settlement much more quickly. The authors suggest that a debiasing procedure could be built into court-mandated pretrial settlement conferences.

9.5 DISTORTIONS IN RETENTION AND RETRIEVAL

> *It isn't so astonishing, the number of things that I can remember, as the number of things I can remember that aren't so.*
> —MARK TWAIN, A BIOGRAPHY[13]

13. Http://www.twainquotes.com/Memory.html.

For any reader who doesn't recall the phenomenon of forgetting, consider this a reminder. Of particular interest in this section are events that distort the content of what is remembered. Distorted recollections are often exacerbated by people's overconfidence in the correctness of their memories.

It is useful to treat retention and retrieval together, because *intermediate* retrievals are among the major sources of distortion of *ultimate* retrievals, including those that have legal consequences. A witness's ultimate retrieval may take place when she testifies at trial, but her recollections may be distorted by questions posed earlier by investigators or in a deposition, or by chatting with friends about the event.

One group of biases results from the phenomenon of *memory binding*, in which different components of an event, or different events, are bound together.[14] For example, a Ryder employee who observed Timothy McVeigh rent a van two days before the 1995 bombing of the Federal Building in Oklahoma City recalled there being two men. One was tall and fair, and fit McVeigh's description; the other was short, stocky, dark-haired, and had a tattoo. It turned out that a day after McVeigh rented the van (alone), two men, who matched the descriptions of McVeigh and his supposed companion, came in to rent a van. As Daniel Schacter explains: "People recall correctly a fact they learned earlier, or recognize accurately a person or object they have seen before, but misattribute the *source* of their knowledge."[15]

More broadly, experiences after an event can distort one's recollection of the event. For example, people who read an inaccurate newspaper description of an event they personally witnessed are prone to incorporate the inaccuracies into their recollections.[16] Leading or misleading questions can also distort recollection. Elizabeth Loftus and colleagues showed participants photos of a car-pedestrian accident involving a red Datsun. One group saw the car at a "stop" sign; the other saw the car at a "yield" sign. Within each group, half the participants were asked "Did another car pass the red Datsun while it was stopped at the 'stop' sign?" and half were asked "Did another car pass the red Datsun while it was stopped at the 'yield' sign?" Finally, after performing some unrelated intervening tasks designed to put temporal distance between the intermediate and ultimate retrieval, the participants were shown slides depicting the red Datsun either at a "stop" or "yield" sign and asked which comported with the original photo. Of participants who had originally seen a "stop" sign and had been asked whether the car was stopped at a "stop" sign, 75 percent responded correctly. Of participants who had been asked the misleading intermediate question—"Did another car pass the red Datsun while it was stopped at the

---

14. Daniel L. Schacter, The Seven Sins of Memory: How the Mind Forgets and Remembers 94 (New York: Houghton Mifflin, 2001) [hereafter Schacter].

15. Schacter 93.

16. Loftus 55.

'yield' sign."—only 41 percent (less than chance) responded correctly.[17] Based on this and other experiments, Loftus concludes that "casually mentioning a nonexistent object during the course of questioning can increase the likelihood that a person will later report having seen that nonexistent object."

In another study, Loftus and her colleagues showed participants a film of a traffic accident, and then asked either: "About how fast were the cars going when they *smashed into* each other?" or: "About how fast were the cars going when they *hit* each other?" The former question elicited a higher estimate. A week later, without having viewed the film again, the participants were asked, "Did you see any broken glass?" In fact, the film did not show any broken glass. However, about twice as many participants who had previously been asked the *smashed* question recalled seeing broken glass than those who had been asked the *hit* question.

Leading questions (which invite a particular answer) can distort memory. "Did you see *the* broken headlight?" elicits more inaccurate recollections that a headlight was in fact broken than "Did you see *a* broken headlight?" About a year after an El Al cargo plane crashed on take-off into an Amsterdam apartment, Dutch psychologists conducted a survey, asking "Did you see the television film of the moment the plane hit the building?" Fifty-five percent of the respondents said that they had seen the film and recalled details about the plane's speed and angle and whether it was on fire. In fact, there was no television coverage of the crash. Also, consistent with the anchoring and adjustment bias (described in Section 10.1), witnesses have different recollections when asked how *tall*, or how *short*, the suspect was.[18] Loftus concludes:

> Any time after a witness experiences a complex event, he may be exposed to new information about that event. The new information may come in the form of questions—a powerful way to introduce it—or in the form of a conversation, a newspaper story, and so on. The implication of these results for courtroom examinations, police interrogations, and accident investigations is fairly obvious: interrogators should do whatever is possible to avoid the introduction of "external" information into the witness's memory.

Indeed, it is not only external suggestions that may distort one's recollection. People who are asked to *guess* about the details of an event they witnessed are likely to turn their guess into an erroneous answer when queried later. Indeed, one's own intervening thoughts and remarks can serve as powerful anchors in subsequent recollections.[19]

Another source of distortion comes from retrieving a past event through *familiarity* rather than by *recollection*. Schacter writes: "Recollection involves

17. *Id.* 58.
18. *Id.* 95 ff.; Schacter 112, 115.
19. Loftus 83 ff.

calling to mind specific details of past experiences . . . Familiarity entails a more primitive sense of knowing that something has happened previously, without dredging up particular details . . . A strong sense of general familiarity, together with the absence of specific recollections, adds up to a lethal recipe for misattribution." Schacter reports on a study of police lineup procedures that invite such misattribution:[20]

> In standard lineup procedures, witnesses are shown a number of suspects; after seeing them all, they attempt to identify the culprit . . . [U]nder such conditions, witnesses tend to rely on relative judgments; they choose the person who, relative to the others in the lineup, looks most like the suspect. The problem is that even when the [culprit] is not in the lineup, witnesses will still tend to choose the person who looks most like him. Witnesses rely on general similarities between a face in the lineup and the actual culprit, even when they lack specific recollections.

How can one guard against such distortions? Schacter proposes some specific techniques for interviewing witnesses.[21] With respect to our own memories, he suggests cultivating a *distinctiveness heuristic*, under which we demand recollections of distinctive details of an experience before we are willing to say we remember it.[22] This would help prevent adding imagined facts to a recalled experience, which often happens when we rely only on familiarity.

9.6 THE AVAILABILITY HEURISTIC—AND A DETOUR INTO METACOGNITION

The heuristics and biases agenda, begun in the 1970s by the psychologists Amos Tversky and Daniel Kahneman, continues to inform much psychological research today, especially in social psychology and judgment and decision making (JDM). The heuristics identified by Tversky and Kahneman are based on processes that operate unconsciously and automatically in System 1, and that tend to be insufficiently corrected by the conscious analytic processes of System 2.[23] We discussed the representativeness heuristic in detail in Section 8.3. Here we consider the *availability* heuristic. While representativeness involves *categorizing*, availability involves *noticing*.

Imagine that you have been considering buying a new car for some time. After poring through *Consumer Reports* and some auto magazines, you decide that the Volvo sedan is just what you want—comfortable, safe, a good maintenance

20. SCHACTER 44, 97.
21. *Id.* 119.
22. *Id.* 103.
23. *See* on Section 1.6.1.

record; all in all, a great buy. The evening before you plan to purchase the car, you are at a dinner party where a guest describes his terrible experience with the Volvo he bought last year—a real lemon, which has spent more time in the shop than on the road.[24] How much will this one anecdote influence your decision compared to all the research you have done?

What Kahneman and Tversky call the *availability heuristic* leads people to make judgments of probability and causation based on how readily events come to mind because they are vivid, imaginable, or otherwise perceptually salient. Thus, in attributing the cause of the problems at Terra Nueva, residents will more likely be influenced by vivid stories of tenants' illnesses and media coverage of "foam insulation syndrome" elsewhere in the country than in epidemiological evidence.

In one experiment, two groups of participants were given samples of the heights of a number of individuals and asked to estimate the proportion of people over 6′ tall. Twenty percent of the individuals in both samples were over 6′ tall, but one group had several very tall outliers. The participants estimated that this sample had more individuals over 6′ tall. By the same token, participants estimated that a sample of people that included some criminals contained more criminals when some of them had committed heinous offenses than a similar sample with the same number of criminals who had only committed minor offenses.[25] What impressions do you imagine various media audiences have of the number of people with extreme versus moderate views on issues such as abortion, gun control, and gay marriage?

Consider the following problem:

> In four pages of a novel (about 2000 words), how many words would you expect to find that have the form
> _ _ _ _ _ n _ ? (five letters, then n, then another letter)
> _ _ _ _ i n g ? (four letters, then ing)

What were your estimates? In between-subjects experiments, people usually say that they expect more words of the second kind than of the first. But, of course, this cannot be true, since *ing* is a subset of *_n_*. By the same token, people estimate that there are more "dairy products" than "white foods" in a supermarket.

These are logical errors—akin to the error made in the example of Linda the (feminist) bank teller in Section 8.3. Most people understand that there cannot be more instances of a subset than of the set of which it is a part. The errors arise from people's tendency to estimate the frequency or probability of an event by how readily examples come to mind. (Consider how people would respond to the

24. Richard E. Nisbett and Lee Ross, Human Inference: Strategies and Shortcomings in Social Judgement. (Englewood Cliffs, NJ: Prentice Hall, 1980).

25. *Id.* 74–75.

question: "How many white foods are there in a supermarket?—and by the way don't forget dairy products.") It is easy to see why using availability as a proxy for frequency can be a useful strategy—if events happen more often, we tend to recall instances of such events more easily. But events can come to our attention and/or be retrieved more readily for many reasons other than the frequency of their occurrence.

9.6.1 How the Availability Heuristic Works; Metacognition

The availability heuristic can work through two different processes, reflecting the different ways that you could make estimates of these sorts. In estimating whether words that have *n* as the second-to-last letter are more or less frequent than words that end in *ing*, you might rely on the *recalled content*, i.e., on the actual number of words with each ending that come to mind. Or you might rely on the *ease or difficulty of recalling* words with each of the endings.

People often use the latter process. In one experiment, participants were asked to recall either six or twelve instances in which they had behaved assertively and then assess their own assertiveness. Those who had been asked to respond to six instances found the task relatively easy, and tended to rate themselves as being assertive. Those who had been asked to recall twelve instances managed to do so, but found the task relatively difficult, and therefore their rating of their self-assertiveness decreased even though they had twice as many examples before them.[26]

Analogously, participants who were given quite specific symptoms—e.g., muscle aches, severe headaches—of a made-up disease, believed that they were more likely to contract the disease than those given less concrete symptoms—e.g., a general sense of disorientation, a malfunctioning nervous system.[27] The specific symptoms were easier to imagine than the vague ones.[28]

These studies illustrate the phenomenon of *metacognition*—that is, cognitions about one's cognitive experience. While most theories of human judgment focus

---

26. Norbert Schwarz and Leigh Ann Vaughn, *The Availability Heuristic Revisited: Ease of Recall and Content of Recall as Distinct Sources of Information, in* Thomas Gilovich, Dale Griffin, and Daniel Kahneman, Heuristics and Biases, The Psychology of Intuitive Judgment 103 (New York: Cambridge University Press, 2002).

27. Steven J. Sherman, Robert B. Cialdini, Donna F. Schwartzman, and Kim D. Reynolds, *Imagining Can Heighten or Lower the Perceived Likelihood of Contracting a Disease: The Mediating Effect of Ease of Imagery, in* Thomas Gilovich, Dale Griffin, and Daniel Kahneman, Heuristics and Biases, The Psychology of Intuitive Judgment 98 (2002).

28. The authors of the study suggest that this has implications for preventive health, such as persuading people to have immunization shots or to take measures against hypertension: "The health profession might increase . . . compliance by making vivid presentations of the medical problems and by describing symptoms and consequences . . . in easy-to-imagine terms." Note, however, that unless this actually leads to changes in health behavior, it may just increase people's anxiety.

on how people evaluate the *content* of the information they are exposed to, theories about metacognition hinge on the fact that people also make judgments by evaluating features of the *experience of thinking*. In particular, experiencing the processing of information as easy or difficult can significantly influence our judgments of the content of that information. Of course people's prior assumptions or expectations about the ease or difficulty of a task are also relevant. For example, when the people who listed twelve examples of assertive behavior were made aware of the objective fact that listing twelve examples was not an easy task, they were less likely to attribute their experienced difficulty to lack of assertiveness.[29]

9.6.2 Other Phenomena Resulting from Evaluation of Metacognitive Experiences

The ease with which new or recalled information can be processed is often referred to as *processing fluency*. In addition to explaining some aspects of the availability heuristic, processing fluency, and metacognition generally, have been linked to judgments that extend beyond matters of probability. We take a brief detour to explore these phenomena.

9.6.2.a Fluency as a Source of Judgments of Truth and Liking Familiar information tends to be easier to process than novel information. This can lead people to infer that easy-to-process information was already seen before and then to conclude that "if it seems they heard it before, there's probably something to it."[30] (Along similar lines, people are more likely to endorse statements whose objective truth is difficult to ascertain when the statements are presented in an easy-to-read format than rather than one that is difficult to read.[31])

Ease of processing also affects people's liking for things they encounter. Psychologist Robert Zajonc coined the term *mere exposure effect*, which refers to the robust finding that people like things better simply because they have already seen them before. For example, people liked meaningless symbols better after they had been exposed to them briefly. (The use of product placements in movies assumes the effectiveness of mere exposure—though it isn't clear whether the goals is to increase liking or merely to make the product in question the mindless default option.) People need not be aware of the prior exposure: even subliminal exposure, too brief to be consciously noticeable, sufficed to enhance people's later liking of symbols and objects to which they had been exposed.[32] Indeed, subliminal exposures are protected from metacognitive correction.

---

29. Norbert Schwarz, *Metacognitive Experiences in Consumer Judgment and Decision Making*, 14 Journal of Consumer Psychology 332–348 (2004).

30. *Id.* at 340.

31. Rolf Reber, and Norbert Schwarz, *Effects of Perceptual Fluency on Judgments of Truth*, 8 Consciousness and Cognition 338–342 (1999).

32. Robert B. Zajonc, *Feeling and Thinking: Preferences Need No Inferences*, 3 American Psychologist 151–75 (1980); Sheila T. Murphy and Robert B. Zajonc, *Affect, Cognition, and Awareness: Affective Priming with Optimal and Suboptimal Stimulus Exposures*, 64 Journal of Personality and Social Psychology 723–39 (1993).

The mere exposure effect can have serious public policy consequences. Since we are constantly bombarded with facts, figures, and information, it is crucial for consumers and citizens to discern between true and false assertions. While the mere exposure effect robustly suggests that information that is frequently repeated tends to stick, experiments conducted by Norbert Schwarz and his colleagues indicate that the ability to distinguish between the truth and falsehood of that repeated information fades with time.[33] Their study also indicates that memory of context—which we use to retroactively determine whether a piece of information is true or false—declines when one is engaged in cognitively demanding tasks, while familiarity is hardly affected by such tasks.

Not only repeated false claims about an individual, product, or policy, but efforts to debunk them, can contribute to their apparent truthfulness by heightening their availability. For a vivid example of this, consider Richard Nixon's statement, "I am not a crook," in rebutting claims that he was involved in the Watergate break-in.

9.6.2.b Using Metacognitive Monitoring to Repair Judgment Biases People sometimes use metacognition to try to correct for what they perceive as biases. For example, how common is the name Kennedy? When people are asked to make such estimates, they might rely on the availability heuristic based on how easily the name comes to mind. However, people's awareness that the name of a prominent political family appears so often in the media may lead to self-correction of the heuristic. In a recent experiment, when asked to estimate the frequency of names which happened to be the names of prominent celebrities (e.g., politicians and musicians), participants estimated that the names were much *less* frequent than they actually were. In other words, they overcorrected for the bias caused by the availability heuristic.[34]

Metacognitive correction of perceived biases can have especially important implications in the domain of justice. Research done by Duane Wegener and Richard Petty[35] suggests that people can use metacognition to identify potentially biasing factors and attempt to remove bias from their perceptions and judgments. Wegener and Petty posited that when trying to prevent bias or debias initial perceptions (e.g., when on jury duty), people consult their own metacognitive beliefs about how various biasing factors might influence their perceptions.

---

33. *E.g.*, Ian Skurnik, Carolyn Yoon, Denise C. Park, and Norbert Schwarz. *How Warnings About False Claims Become Recommendations.* 31, JOURNAL OF CONSUMER RESEARCH, 713–724 (2005).

34. Daniel M. Oppenheimer, *Spontaneous Discounting of Availability in Frequency Judgment Tasks*, 15 PSYCHOLOGICAL SCIENCE 100–05 (2004).

35. *Reported in* Duane T. Wegener, and Richard E. Petty, *The Flexible Correction Model: The Role of Naïve Theories of Bias in Bias Correction, in* ADVANCES IN EXPERIMENTAL SOCIAL PSYCHOLOGY 29, (M. Zanna ed., 1997).

In one experiment, Petty and his colleagues asked college students to judge whether a person accused of the crime of rape was guilty or not. Participants in the control group were presented with ambiguous information that led them to be uncertain as to whether or not the defendant had committed the crime.[36] A second group read the same ambiguous information but also learned that the defendant had pled guilty to a prior crime of rape. A third group read the ambiguous information but also learned that the defendant had pled guilty to a prior crime of burglary.

Participants were then asked to give two judgments: their own personal opinion of the defendant's guilt, and the verdict that they would render if they were a juror. When giving their own opinions, participants were more likely to consider the defendants with prior records (rape and burglary) guilty than the defendant with no prior record. Perhaps they regarded some people as "criminal types." When acting as jurors and rendering verdicts, however, there was no difference between the defendant with the burglary and the defendant with no record. However, more participants judged the defendant with the prior rape conviction to be guilty. The researchers concluded that when trying to be good jurors, people may correct for biases due to factors they perceive as irrelevant to making an impartial judgment (prior burglary conviction for a rape suspect), but not for biases due to information they perceive as relevant (prior rape conviction for a rape suspect) even when instructed to disregard it.

People may also correct for biases that they believe resulted from stereotypes or from their mood at the time they made a judgment. But there is evidence that attempts to suppress stereotypical thinking may actually increase stereotyping, and that people sometimes *over*correct, for example, leading to a less favorable evaluation of a candidate when they are in a good mood. [37]

9.6.3 Availability, Vividness, and Inference

Richard Nisbett and Lee Ross note that "vivid information is more likely to be stored and remembered than pallid information," and thus more likely to be

---

36. Richard E. Petty, Duane T. Wegener, and Monique A. Fleming, "Flexible Correction Processes: Perceived Legitimacy Of Bias And Bias Correction," paper presented at the annual meeting of the Society for Experimental Social Psychology (Sturbridge, MA: 1996).

37. Leonard Berkowitz et al., *On the Correction of Feeling-Induced Judgmental Biases* 131, *in* FEELING AND THINKING: THE ROLE OF AFFECT IN SOCIAL JUDGMENTS (New York: Cambridge University Press, 2000); Linda M. Isbell and Robert S. Wyer, Jr., *Correcting for Mood-Induced Bias in the Evaluation of Political Candidates: The Roles of Intrinsic and Extrinsic Motivation*, 25 PERSONALITY & SOC. PSYCHOL. BULL. 237 (1999). *See also* Ehud Guttel, *Overcorrection*, 93 GEO. L.J. 241 (2004) (noting that the legal system sometimes corrects for overcorrection); C. Neil Macrae et al., *Out of Mind But Back in Sight: Stereotypes on the Rebound*, 67 J. PERSONALITY & SOC. PSYCHOL. 808 (1994).

retrieved at some later date and to affect later inference."[38] Factors that contribute to the vividness of information include:

- *Emotional interest.* Events in which we or people we know are involved have more emotional interest than those involving strangers.
- *Concreteness.* Even events involving strangers can be emotionally gripping if they are described in sufficient detail to prompt imagery. Compare "Jack was killed by a semi-trailer that rolled over his car and crushed his skull" to "Jack sustained fatal injuries in a car accident." Concrete descriptions have more information, which, even if redundant or irrelevant to the attribution of causation, is more likely to be remembered. Statistics may be the least concrete form of information.
- *Direct experience.* First-hand information has more salience than the reports of others. By the same token, a face-to-face recommendation is likely to be more effective than the same recommendation in writing.

In addition to its availability, vivid information is more likely to recruit additional information from one's memory and people are more likely to rehearse, or mull over, vivid information, making it even more memorable.

The normative problem of using vividness, and availability more generally, as criteria for inference is that they are not always strongly correlated with their evidential value. This is illustrated by a number of experiments in which vividness caused participants to generalize from obviously biased samples. For example, Ruth Hamill,Timothy Wilson and Richard Nisbett showed participants a videotape interview of a prison guard, which depicted him as either humane or brutal. Some were told that the guard was typical, some that he was highly atypical. When later asked to generalize about prison guards, both groups of participants concluded that prison guards generally tended to be like the one they had seen in the interview.[39] Vivid anecdotal evidence, can have a powerful effect on people's perceptions.

9.6.4 Vividness and the Media

> *With a summer season framed by a shark attack on a boy in Florida two days after the Fourth of July and the death of a man on Labor Day on the Outer Banks of North Carolina, the danger from sharks could easily be seen as rising dramatically.*
>
> *This is being seen as the "Summer of the Shark" as Time magazine put it in a July 30 cover story bristling with images of razor-sharp teeth . . .*

---

38. Nisbett and Ross, *supra* at 45.

39. Ruth Hammill, Timothy DeCamp Wilson, and Richard E. Nisbett, *Insensitivity to Sample Bias: Generalizing from Atypical Cases*, 39 Journal of Personality and Social Psychology 578–89 (1980).

But notwithstanding the bloody attacks . . . scientists said the new fears were overblown. There is no rampage. If anything, they say, the recent global trend in shark attacks is down, even as news media attention soars.[40]

. . . [Y]ou cannot talk sensibly about shark attacks this summer unless you talk first of the sheer number of humans who flock to the beaches in the summertime. Shark attacks will drop off precipitously now that Labor Day has come, because there will be less human flesh in the water to be bitten . . .

Twenty-eight children in the United States were killed by falling television sets between 1990 and 1997 . . . [T]hat is four times as many people as were killed by great white sharks in the 20th century. Loosely speaking, this means that "watching 'Jaws' on TV is more dangerous than swimming in the Pacific."[41]

In the aftermath of the terrorist attacks of September 11, 2001, on the World Trade Center and on the Pentagon, and the SARS epidemic in Toronto in 2003, Neal Feigenson and his colleagues studied Americans' and Canadians' perceptions of the two risks.[42]

> Canadians estimated the percentage chance that they would become seriously ill or die from SARS within the next year as 7.43%, and the percentage chance that they would suffer a similar outcome from terrorism as 6.04%, a significant difference. By contrast, Americans estimated the percentage chance that they would become seriously ill or die from SARS within the next year as 2.18%, and the percentage chance that they would suffer a similar outcome from terrorism as 8.27%, also a significant difference.

The authors estimate that the probability of a Canadian's contracting SARS was in fact less than .0008 percent and (albeit more speculatively) that the probability of an American dying from terrorism within the year was about .001 percent. They explain the different perceptions in terms of "systematically different media coverage of those risks, making those risks differently available to them":

> [A] sampling of national and local print coverage of SARS and terrorism indicates that Canadian media sources devoted about 40% more articles to SARS than American media sources did, while more than 14 times as many articles about terrorism appeared in American as opposed to Canadian print media. These threat by country interactions roughly parallel the national patterns of respondents' perceptions of SARS and terrorism risks.

---

40. William J. Broad, *Scientists Say Frenzy Over Shark Attacks Is Unwarranted*, New York Times, Sept. 5, 2001.

41. *The Statistical Shark*, New York Times, Sept. 6, 2001.

42. Neal Feigenson, Daniel Bailis, and William Klein, *Perceptions Of Terrorism And Disease Risks: A Cross-National Comparison*, 69 Mo. L. Rev. 991 (2004).

Paul Slovic and his colleagues have conducted numerous surveys of people's estimates of the frequency of causes of death. The social scientists found a strong correlation between media coverage—especially the coverage of spectacular events—and errors in estimation. "In general, rare causes of death were overestimated and common causes of death were underestimated . . . [A]ccidents were judged to cause as many deaths as diseases, whereas diseases actually take about 15 times as many lives. Homicides were incorrectly judged to be more frequent than diabetes and stomach cancer. Homicides were also judged to be about as frequent as stroke, although the latter annually claims about 11 times as many lives. Frequencies of death from botulism, tornadoes and pregnancy (including childbirth and abortion) were also greatly overestimated."[43]

Chip Heath and his colleagues studied media coverage of mad cow disease outbreaks in France to see how language frames affect the public's perception of risk.[44] Monthly beef consumption was affected more by the number of articles that referred to the disease as "mad cow" than by articles that referred to the disease by one of its scientific names, such as bovine spongiform encephalopathy (BSE.). The "mad cow" articles tended to deal less with the scientific research conducted on the disease and more with its sensational personal and social ramifications, whereas the BSE articles were more likely to include technical content and cite current studies. The authors conclude that "mad cow," which was used far more often than the scientific names, made the public more risk averse in consuming beef. (Policy makers' responses seemed more closely aligned with scientific reports in the media, suggesting a degree of deliberation independent of their constituents' fears.)

Returning to the earlier discussion of fluency as a source of judgment, research by Hyunjin Song and Norbert Schwarz suggests that people perceive objects, diseases, foods, etc. with difficult to pronounce names to be more risky or threatening than those with familiar-sounding names.[45] In particular, when people were asked to rate the dangerousness of a food additives named magnalroxate versus hnegripitrom, or roller-coaster rides named Chunta versus Vaiveahtoishi the latter, more difficult-to-pronounce additives and rides were judged to be more dangerous. The researchers conclude that easy-to-pronounce or seemingly familiar names can be processed fluently, which gives rise to the belief that one has "heard it before," and therefore to the belief that it is relatively safe.

---

43. Paul Slovic, Baruch Fischhoff, and Sarah Lichtenstein, *Rating the Risks*, *in* Paul Slovic, The Perception of Risk 105 (London: Earthscan Publications, 2000).

44. Marwan Sinaceur, Chip Heath, and Steve Cole, *Emotional and Deliberative Reactions to a Public Crisis: Mad Cow Disease in France*, American Psychological Society 247–54 (2005), http://faculty-gsb.stanford.edu/heath/documents/PsychSci-Mad%20Cow.pdf.

45. Hyunjin Song, and Norbert Schwarz, *If It's Difficult to Pronounce, It Must Be Risky*, 20 Association for Psychological Science 135–38 (2009).

9.7 EGOCENTRISM: A PARTICULAR MEMORY BIAS IN ACQUISITION AND/OR RETRIEVAL

The duet from *Gigi* quoted in Section 9.2 exemplifies how participants or observers may recall the same event differently even when there is no ostensible reason for the difference. Beyond this, people's recollections and judgments tend to be clouded by an egocentric bias. When married couples estimate their proportionate contribution to household tasks, the sum exceeds 100 percent.[46] So too of collaborators' estimates of their contributions to joint projects, such as this book. While the phenomenon may be partially explained by self-serving motives or having inflatedly positive views of oneself, it extends to negative behaviors as well. Spouses report *causing*, as well as resolving, most of the problems in their relationship,[47] and people are prone to overestimate their own errors and unattractive behaviors.[48]

One plausible explanation for the egocentric bias is that our own actions are more readily accessible to our memories than the actions of others. Furthermore, our recollection of behaviors may be guided by a theory of one's own behavior. Rather than go through the laborious process of recalling particular activities, we ask ourselves, "how often do I do this kind of thing?" and take the further shortcut of looking to our disposition by asking, "am I the sort of person who does this?" Of course, we might ask the same questions about the other person. But either because we find it "difficult or time consuming to retrieve two separate pieces of information and combine them to procedure a single judgment," or because we anchor on our own contributions and then (insufficiently) adjust for the other's, it is our own behavior that dominates.[49]

Even when an individual holds himself accountable for an outcome vis-à-vis others, the question remains open whether the outcome was due to internal factors such as skill or its absence, or to external factors, such as bad luck. In an analysis of newspaper accounts of sporting events, Richard Lau and Dan Russell found that players attributed good outcomes to their skill 75 percent of the time, but took responsibility for bad outcomes only 55 percent of the time. Sportswriters—who one might expect to have more distance—were less likely than players or coaches to attribute wins to internal factors, but even sportswriters

46. Michael Ross and Fiore Sicoly, *Egocentric Biases in Availability and Attribution*, 37 Journal of Personality and Social Psychology 322 (1979).

47. *See* Linda Babcock et al., *Biased Judgments and Fairness in Bargaining*, 85 American Economic Review 1337, 1337–38 (1995).

48. Nisbett and Ross, *supra* at 76; Justin Kruger and Thomas Gilovich, *Naive Cynicism*, in *Everyday Theories of Responsibility Assessment: On Biased Perceptions of Bias*, 76 Journal of Personality and Social Psychology 743–53 (1999).

49. Suzanne C. Thompson and Harold H. Kelley, *Judgments of Responsibility for Activities in Close Relationships*, 41 Journal of Personality and Social Psychology 469 (1981).

were more likely to provide internal attributions for their home teams' wins than for losses.[50]

Egocentrism is often correlated with self-servingness. Among people working different amounts of time in a joint enterprise, those who work more believe they should be paid more, while those who work less believe that both parties should be paid equally. People may come to self-serving results indirectly, by disproportionately valuing the particular task they contribute to the joint enterprise (e.g., washing the laundry compared to sweeping the floors). But people often believe they are entitled to a greater share than others even in the absence of joint activities. For example, in a simulation of a commons problem involving fishing associations that needed to reduce their harvests to preserve the stock of fish for long-run profits, participants believed they were entitled to a greater portion of the catch than the others.[51]

9.7.1 Debiasing Egocentrism

If egocentrism is rooted in the accessibility of one's own actions or interests, then having an individual consider other people's perspective should bring their sense of fairness more into line. And it does—though with an important and unfortunate kicker. For example, when debate team participants were just asked to allocate their contributions to a joint effort, their net allocations summed to 156 percent; when they were asked to think about others' contributions, the sum was a mere 106 percent.[52]

And now the kicker: While putting yourself in the other person's shoes often brings your perception of fairness closer to reality, it does not reduce selfish *behavior*, and in some cases may increase it—presumably because adopting the other person's perspective leads you to believe that the other person will act in an egocentric and self-interested way, which you then counter by taking more yourself. Thus in the fishing associations example, instructing participants to look at the commons problem from other associations' point of view reduced, although did not totally eliminate, egocentric assessments of what they deemed to be their fair share.[53] But that instruction actually *increased* the amount of the harvest the

---

50. Richard R. Lau and Dan Russell, *Attributions in the Sports Pages*, 39 Journal of Personality and Social Psychology 29 (1980).

51. Kimberly A. Wade-Benzoni, Ann E. Tenbrunsel, and Max H. Bazerman, *Egocentric Interpretations Of Fairness In Asymmetric, Environmental Social Dilemmas: Explaining Harvesting Behavior and the Role of Communication*, 67 Organizational Behavior and Human Decision Processes 111–26 (1996).

52. Eugene M. Caruso, Nicholas Epley, and Max H. Bazerman, *The Good, The Bad, And The Ugly Of Perspective Taking In Groups*, in E. A. Mannix, M. A. Neale, & A. E. Tenbrunsel, (series eds), Research On Managing Groups And Teams, 8 Ethics in Groups 201–224 (London: Elsevier, 2006).

53. Eugene M. Caruso, Nicholas Epley, and Max H. Bazerman. *When Perspective Taking Increases Taking: Reactive Egoism in Social Interaction*, 91 Journal of Personality and Social Psychology 972 (2006).

participants actually took in the simulation. In a sense, cynicism about the other participants resulted in *reactive egoism*.[54]

9.7.2 The Recollection of One's Own Past Beliefs, Feelings, and Events

> *Herein lies a difficulty in any autobiographical sketch which purports to deal with one's mental development. It is a story of oneself in the past, read in the light of one's present self. There is much supplementary inference—often erroneous inference—wherein "must have been" masquerades as "was so."*
> —C. Lloyd Morgan, History of Psychology in Autobiography (1930)[55]

Research suggests that emotions may not be stored directly in memory but rather "are reconstructed based on memories of the emotion-eliciting circumstances."[56] Reconstructions may go beyond emotions to involve the memories of attitudes and even actions. Michael Ross[57] argues that such memories are based on people's implicit theories of human stability and change. All things being equal, we think that attitudes are consistent over time. For this reason, when we infer past attitudes from present ones, we tend to exaggerate their consistency. For example, participants whose views changed about school busing to achieve desegregation or about the health effects of vigorous physical exercise misremembered their earlier views; university students whose attitudes toward a dating partner had changed over several months recalled their earlier impression as being more consistent with their current attitudes than was the case. Furthermore, because we tend to seek consistency in attitudes and behavior, a change in attitudes can produce inaccurate recollection of behaviors. Thus, when experimenters caused participants to believe that regularly brushing their teeth was not as important as they had thought, they recalled less brushing than they actually had done.

While a belief in personal consistency is the norm, we also have theories of change. So, for example, people who have engaged in education and self-improvement programs tend to exaggerate the difference between their past and the present knowledge or behavior. In an experiment involving a program to improve study skills, students recalled their original assessment of their study skills to be worse than they had originally reported and reported greater improvement than the facts warranted. They not only overpredicted the resulting

---

54. Kruger and Gilovich; Epley, Caruso, and Bazerman. However, selfish behavior was reduced when the group project was structured or characterized as cooperative rather than competitive.

55. *Quoted in* Michael Ross, *Relation of Implicit Theories to the Construction of Personal Histories*, 96 Psychological Review 341 (1989).

56. *Id.*

57. *Id.*

improvement in their grades, but subsequently recalled the new grades as being higher than they actually were.

9.8 CONCLUSION: NAÏVE REALISM

How narrow his vision, how cribbed and confined!
How prejudiced all of his views!
How hard is the shell of his bigoted mind!
How difficult he to excuse!

His face should be slapped and his head should be banged;
A person like that ought to die!
I want to be fair, but a man should be hanged
Who's any less liberal than I.
—Broadmindedness, in Franklin P. Adams, Something Else Again (1920)

The biases in the acquisition and recollection of information outlined above are exacerbated by three related convictions that people have about their perceptions and judgments and the perceptions and judgments of other people. These are the elements of what Lee Ross has termed *naïve realism*:[58]

1. I see actions and events as they are in reality. My perceptions and reactions are not biased: rather, they are an unmediated reflection of the "real nature" of whatever it is I am responding to.
2. Other people, to the extent that they are willing and able to see things in a similarly objective fashion, will share my perceptions and reactions.
3. When others perceive some event or react to it differently from me, they (but not I) have been influenced by something other than the objective features of the events in question. Their divergent views probably result from an unwarranted ideological rigidity or a self-serving bias that I am not influenced by. The more extreme the view is in divergence from my own, the stronger their bias probably is.

Naïve realism can be especially pernicious in the context of disagreement or conflict. It has the practical implications that:

- Partisans tend to overestimate the number of others who agree with their views—the *false consensus* effect—or at least overestimate the number who

58. Lee Ross and Donna Shestowsky, *Contemporary Psychology's Challenge to Legal Theory of Practice*, 97 Nw. U. L. Rev. 1081 (2003).

would agree with them if apprised of the "real" facts; partisans therefore assume that disinterested third parties would agree with them.

- Partisans tend to see viewpoints that differ from their own as highly revealing both of personal dispositions (for example, gullibility, aggressiveness, pessimism, or charitableness) and of various cognitive and motivational biases. In fact, differences in judgment often reflect differences in the way a given issue or object of judgment is perceived and construed rather than a difference in the perceivers' values or personality traits.
- When partisans acknowledge the influence of particular features of their experience or identity, they see it not as a bias but as a source of enlightenment, while they see the other parties unique experiences or identities as a source of bias.
- Partisans on both sides of an issue will typically perceive evenhanded media to be biased against them and to favor their adversaries. They are apt to see the same hostile bias in the efforts and decisions of evenhanded third-party mediators or arbitrators.
- Partisans will be polarized and extreme in their view of others. Once they believe a person to be biased, they tend to discount his views entirely, and will underestimate areas of agreement and underestimate the prospects of finding "common ground" through discussion or negotiation.

We have seen that being asked to articulate the weaknesses of one's own position may counter perceptual biases in some situations. A broader hope of this book is that students and readers who understanding those biases and the phenomena of naïve realism will be less likely to fall into their traps. But we should be among the first to admit that the hope does not rest on much of an empirical foundation.

10. BIASES IN PROCESSING AND JUDGING INFORMATION

The preceding chapter examined biases in empirical judgment involving the acquisition and recollection of information, while also necessarily touching on processing and analysis of information. This chapter focuses on the processing and analysis of information while necessarily touching on its recollection. The availability heuristic continues to play an important role as we examine the anchoring effect, hindsight bias, and the tendencies to seek evidence that confirms one's views and to be overconfident in one's judgment. The chapter ends by reviewing the place of intuition and analysis in empirical judgments and the role of experts.

10.1 ANCHORING, ADJUSTMENT, AND ACTIVATION

In making a numerical estimate or choice, people tend to be influenced by externally-given reference points. This is true even when the reference point is entirely arbitrary. For example, Amos Tversky and Daniel Kahneman asked people to estimate the percentage of African countries in the United Nations. Before the question was posed, a "wheel of fortune" with numbers from 1 to 100 was spun. The median estimate for participants whose wheel landed on the number 10 was 25 percent; when the wheel happened to land on the number 45, the estimate jumped to 65 percent.[1]

What Tversky and Kahneman call the *anchoring and adjustment bias* captures the fact that we intuitively anchor our judgment on the given value and then use rational processes to adjust away from it; but that our adjustments tend to be insufficient. The phenomenon would more accurately described as one involving anchoring and *insufficient adjustment.*

The participants in the United Nations quiz were not experts on geography. However, experts seem no less susceptible to the anchoring and adjustment bias. To explore how experienced auditors' estimation of fraud might be influenced by an anchor, E. E. Joyce and G. C. Biddle gave them a questionnaire with the following problem:[2]

---

1. Amos Tversky and Daniel Kahneman, *Judgment Under Uncertainty: Heuristics and Biases*. 185 SCIENCE, 1124–1130 (1974).

2. Edward J. Joyce and Gary C. Biddle, *Anchoring and Adjustment in Probabilistic Inference in Auditing*, 19 JOURNAL OF ACCOUNTING RESEARCH 120 (1981).

> It is well known that many cases of management fraud go undetected even when competent annual audits are performed . . . We are interested in obtaining an estimate from practicing auditors of the prevalence of executive-level management fraud as a first step in ascertaining the scope of the problem.
>
> 1. Based on your audit experience, is the incidence of significant executive-level management fraud more than 10 [200] in each 1000 firms (i.e., 1% [20%]) audited by Big Eight accounting firms?
> 2. What is your estimate of the number of Big Eight clients per 1000 that have significant executive-level management fraud?

For auditors given the number 10 in the first question, the mean response to the second question was 16.5 per thousand; for those given 200, the mean response was 43 per thousand.

10.1.1 Anchoring in Negotiations

In the belief that the phenomenon would affect bargaining or negotiations, Gregory Northcroft and Margaret Neale conducted an experiment involving the purchase of real estate.[3] Both amateurs and professional real estate agents were asked to appraise residential properties. They were given all of the information that would be available to real estate agents, including the owner's listing price, detailed information about the property in question, and the summary of sales in the neighborhood and city—and were also shown the property in question. The only information that differed with respect to a particular residence was the price at which the owner listed it—a variable entirely in the owner's control. Four groups of amateurs were given different listing prices for the same house; since there were fewer expert participants in the experiment, they received only two listing prices. Table 10.1 shows the listings and appraisals for a particular property.

Thus, professionals and amateurs alike adjusted their appraisal value significantly based only on the listing price. In debriefing, amateurs were aware that the listing price played a role in their judgments, while the professionals denied this—whether through a lack of self-awareness or professional pride.

Russell Korobkin and Chris Guthrie conducted an experiment in which parties engaging in settlement negotiations were offered different anchors. Plaintiffs were more likely to accept a $12,000 final offer when it followed a $2,000 opening offer than when it followed a $10,000 opening offer. The researchers hypothesize that the low anchor developed low expectations, which

---

3. Gregory B. Northcroft and Margaret A. Neale, *Experts, Amateurs, and Real Estate: An Anchoring-And-Adjustment Perspective on Property Pricing Decisions*, Organisational Behavior and Human Decision Processes 39 (1987).

TABLE 10.1 REAL ESTATE APPRAISALS

Listing Price	Amateurs' Appraised Value	Professionals' Appraised Value
$65,900	$63,571	$67,818
$71,900	$67,452	NA
$77,900	$70,423	NA
$83,900	$72,196	$76,380

made the final offer seem comparatively generous.[4] And Jeff Rachlinski, Chris Guthrie, and Andrew Wistrich presented federal judges with the facts of a personal injury case, in which the plaintiff had been hospitalized for several months and was left paraplegic and confined to a wheelchair. One group was anchored by being informed that the defendant had moved for dismissal on the ground that the case did not meet the $75,000 jurisdictional minimum for a diversity case;[5] the other group was given no such anchoring information. Though almost none of the judges granted the motion to dismiss, the average award in the anchored group was $882,000 compared to $1,249,000 in the unanchored group.[6]

Anchoring in Jury Awards. In an experiment by John Malouff and Nicola Shutte, when plaintiff's lawyer requested $100,000 damages, mock jurors awarded $90,000, and when plaintiff's lawyer requested $500,000 damages, they awarded nearly $300,000 on average.[7] While jurors assessing punitive damages often anchor on the amount of actual damages, they also anchor on the amount including punitive damages requested in the closing argument of the plaintiff's attorney. In an experiment involving a train derailment that dumped herbicide and caused serious environmental damage, plaintiff's attorney told one group of mock jurors: "So the range you may want to consider is between $15 million and about a half a year's profit, $50 million"; another group was given the range between $50 million and $150 million. The median awards by the two juries

4. Russell Korobkin and Chris Guthrie, *Opening Offers and Out-of-Court Settlements: A Little Moderation May Not Go a Long Way*, 10 Ohio State Journal on Dispute Resolution 1 (1994).

5. Federal courts can hear cases arising under state law if the amount in controversy is $75,000 or more and the plaintiff and defendant reside in different states.

6. Chris Guthrie, Jeffrey J. Rachlinski, and Andrew J. Wistrich, *Inside the Judicial Mind*, 86 Cornell L. Rev. 777 (2001).

7. John Malouff and Nicola S. Schutte, *Shaping Juror Attitudes: Effects of Requesting Different Damage Amounts in Personal Injury Trials*, 129 Journal of Social Psychology 491 (1989).

were $15 million and $50 million, respectively.[8] Experimental data also suggests that statutory caps on damages may affect settlement rates.[9]

10.1.2 Extreme and Untrustworthy Anchors

Do extreme or implausible anchors trigger the same phenomenon? Fritz Strack and Thomas Mussweiler asked participants to estimate the year that Einstein came to the United States, giving them anchors of 1215, 1905, 1939, and 1992. (The correct date is 1933.) Even the ridiculously extreme numbers had anchoring effects.[10]

What about anchors from an untrustworthy source? In 1950, in an attack on Secretary of State Dean Acheson, Senator Joseph McCarthy claimed that he had a list of fifty-seven people in the State Department who were known to be members of the American Communist Party. Even if you were highly skeptical of McCarthy's trustworthiness, how many Communists might you think he had actually identified? What might your estimate have been if he had said he had a list of five hundred Communists?

10.1.3 Cross-Modal Anchors

Studies by Danny Oppenheimer and his colleagues suggest that a nonnumeric stimulus that conveys magnitude can bias numerical estimates. When asked to guess the length of the Mississippi River, participants who had been exposed to long lines drawn across a sheet of paper produced estimates significantly longer than those produced by another group that had been exposed to shorter lines.[11]

10.1.4 Explanations for the Phenomenon

There are two fundamentally different accounts of the anchoring and adjustment phenomenon. One focuses on the *adjustment* process and asks why adjustments

---

8. Reid Hastie, David A. Schkade, and John W. Payne, *Do Plaintiffs' Requests and Plaintiffs' Identities Matter?*, *in* Cass R. Sunstein et al., Punitive Damages: How Juries Decide (Chicago: University of Chicago Press, 2002).

9. A low cap increased settlement rates while a high cap decreased them. The authors term the latter phenomenon, "motivated anchoring," in which a relatively high damage cap disproportionately anchors the plaintiff's estimate of the likely damage award. The result is a widened disparity in opposing litigants' judgments, and less settlement. Greg Pogarsky and Linda C. Babcock, "Damage Caps, Motivated Anchoring, and Bargaining Impasse" (Aug. 1, 2000), *available at* SSRN: http://ssrn.com/abstract=235296

10. Fritz Strack and Thomas Mussweiler, *Explaining the Enigmatic Anchoring Effect: Mechanisms of Selective Accessibility*, 73 Journal of Personality and Social Psychology 437 (1997).

11. Daniel M. Oppenheimer et al., *Anchors Aweigh: A Demonstration of Cross-Modality Anchoring and Magnitude Priming*, Cognition (2007). When the anchors were placed in appropriately scaled contexts—e.g., a shorter line tracing the length of the Mississippi on a small scaled map, and a longer line tracing its length on a larger scaled map—the influence of the anchoring effect diminished.

away from the initial anchor are insufficient. Under this view, we "adjust the anchor until shortly after it enters a range of plausible values for the target item. Thus, when adjusting from a high anchor, decision makers stop at the high end of plausible values, but stop at the low end when adjusting from low anchors." Adjustment is cognitively effortful, and a "lack of effort or lack of cognitive resources cause adjustment to be terminated too soon, resulting in a final response that is too close to the anchor."[12]

Alternatively, the anchor may increase the *availability* of features that the anchor and the target—e.g., the number to be determined—hold in common, selectively *activating* information about the target that is consistent with the anchor (while not activating other information).[13] Gretchen Chapman and Eric Johnson hypothesize:

> Assume a decision maker, when requested to make a judgment, can access a variety of features about the target item, either from memory or from the external environment. Some subset of this information is retrieved and used as the basis for . . . judgment. If a representative sample is retrieved, the judgment will be unbiased. However, . . . the presence of an anchor increases the activation of features that the anchor and target hold in common while reducing the availability of features of the target that differ from the anchor.
>
> For example, suppose a decision maker asked to evaluate a bus trip was presented with a low anchor [for the cost of the bus ticket]. The decision maker might contemplate a bumpy, noisy, crowded ride aboard a city-owned vehicle that spouts diesel fumes and has hard plastic seats and no air conditioning. Conversely, if a high anchor were presented, the decision maker might imagine a luxurious tour bus with reclining plush velour seats, sound system, and bar . . ..

Under either of these explanations, a person might sometimes believe that the anchor provides information relevant to the actual amount. This might be true in the fraud, real estate, and jury award examples described above (though certainly not in anchoring on the percentage of African countries in the United Nations based on the spin of a wheel.) Even so, the phenomenon is likely to result in a biased judgment.

---

12. Gretchen B. Chapman and Eric J. Johnson, *Incorporating the Irrelevant: Anchors in Judgments of Belief And Value, in* Thomas Gilovich, Dale Griffin, and Daniel Kahneman, Heuristics and Biases, The Psychology of Intuitive Judgment 127 (2002) [hereafter, Heuristics and Biases].

13. Gretchen B. Chapman and Eric J. Johnson, *Anchoring, Activation, and the Construction of Values*, 79 Organizational Behavior and Human Decision Processes 115 (1999).

10.1.5 Debiasing

The insufficient adjustment and activation theories may account for anchoring phenomena in different circumstances. In any event, the phenomenon is extraordinarily robust. Simply warning people about it does not decrease anchoring; nor does offering incentives for accurate estimates.[14]

10.2 HINDSIGHT BIAS

Baruch Fischhoff, who pioneered research in the subject, describes *hindsight bias* as follows:

> In hindsight, people consistently exaggerate what could have been anticipated in foresight. They not only tend to view what has happened as having been inevitable but also to view it as having appeared "relatively inevitable" before it happened. People believe that others should have been able to anticipate events much better than was actually the case.[15]

In a classic experiment, Fischhoff provided a description of the 1814 war between the British and the Nepalese Gurkhas and informed participants that it had four possible outcomes: British victory, Gurkha victory, military stalemate with no peace settlement, or stalemate with a peace settlement. In each of four conditions participants were told that one of the four outcomes had actually occurred and were then asked to estimate its prior probability as well as those of the three alternatives. As Fischhoff had predicted, participants' knowledge of what they believed to be the actual outcome significantly affected their estimates of the prior probability.

In an experiment examining hindsight bias in a legal context, Kim Kamin and Jeffrey Rachlinski gave two groups of participants the same facts, except that one group was asked whether to take precautions to avert a potential accident and the second was asked whether to assess liability after an accident had already occurred:

> *Foresight condition.* Participants were told that a city had constructed a drawbridge and needed to determine whether the risk of a flood warranted maintaining a bridge operator during the winter when the bridge was not in use. Hiring the operator would serve as a precaution. The operator would monitor weather conditions and raise the bridge to let debris through if the river

---

14. Gretchen B. Chapman and Eric J. Johnson, *supra*.

15. Baruch Fischhoff, *For Those Condemned to Study the Past: Heuristics and Biases in Hindsight*, *in* JUDGEMENT UNDER UNCERTAINTY: HEURISTICS AND BIASES 335, 341–42 (Daniel Kahneman, Paul Slovic, and Amos Tversky, eds. (New York: Cambridge University Press, 1982).

threatened to flood. Testimony in an administrative hearing before the city council indicated that hiring the operator would cost $100,000 annually, and that the potential damage from a flood was $1 million. The question posed to participants in the foresight condition was whether a flood was sufficiently probable that the city should appropriate funds for the operator.

Hindsight condition. Participants were asked to assume the role of jurors in a civil trial. They were told that the city had decided not to hire the operator and that during the first winter of the bridge's existence, debris lodged under it, which resulted in a flood that could have been prevented had an operator been hired. The flood damaged a neighboring bakery, whose owner then sued the city. Participants in the hindsight condition were instructed to hold the city liable if the flood was sufficiently probable that the city should have hired the operator to prevent it.

In both conditions, the participants were told to use the Learned Hand formula for tort liability, in which an actor bears the responsibility to take a precaution if the cost of taking the precaution is less than the harm it would have prevented (based on the total amount of the harm and the probability of its occurrence). In particular, with the operator costing $100,000 and flood damages predicted or stipulated to be $1 million, the city should/should have hired the operator if the probability of a flood was greater than 10 percent. Testimony in both conditions was ambiguous about whether, based on past events, the probability was greater or less than 10 percent. The results of the experiment were clear cut:

- 24 percent of the participants in the foresight condition (administrative hearing) believed the city *should take* the precaution.
- 57 percent of the participants in the hindsight condition (trial) believed that the city *should have taken* the precaution.

It can be perfectly rational to revise your earlier judgment about the probability of an event occurring based on what actually happened—if the occurrence provided information from which you could draw a valid statistical inference.[16] But it is obviously an error to believe, *after* an event has occurred, that *before* the event you would have predicted its occurrence to be more likely than you could reasonably have foreseen at that time. By the same token, it is an error to impose liability on an actor based on the erroneous notion that a reasonable person would have known in advance that the danger was as high as it now seems in hindsight.

Courts are frequently called upon to decide what a policy maker, professional, or individual "should have known" and should have done. As the drawbridge

16. *See* Mark Kelman, David Fallas and Hillary Folger, *Decomposing Hindsight Bias*, 16 Journal of Risk and Uncertainty 251 (1998).

case illustrates, this is an essential part of the negligence standard in tort liability and plays a significant role in many other legal domains, ranging from trust and estate law (did the trustee invest the beneficiary's funds prudently?) to substantive criminal law (did the defendant claiming self-defense reasonably believe that he was in danger of being killed?) and criminal procedure (did the police officer have probable cause for the arrest and search?). In all of these situations, the trier of fact is vulnerable to hindsight bias.

Summarizing the rich psychological literature since this 1975 study, Jeffrey Rachlinski[17] writes that hindsight bias

> results primarily from the natural (and useful) tendency for the brain to automatically incorporate known outcomes into existing knowledge, and make further inferences from that knowledge. For example, participants in the British-Gurkha study who were told that the British had won, probably made inferences about colonial warfare, generally. They may have concluded, for example, that the advantages that the British had over the Gurkhas (better weapons and training) were more important in such conflicts than the Gurkha advantages (better knowledge of the terrain and higher motivation). Participants informed of a Gurkha victory may have inferred the opposite. When asked to estimate the [prior] probability of a British victory, the participants relied on their new belief that better weapons and training were more important than knowledge of the terrain and higher motivation. These inferences then induced them to make high estimates for the probability of the known outcome, relative to the estimates of people who were unaware of the outcome and hence had not developed such beliefs.
>
> More generally, ignoring a known outcome is unnatural. Normally, people should integrate new information into their existing store of knowledge and use it to make future predictions. Assessing the predictability of past events requires that the outcome and the subsequent inferences that depend upon learning the outcome be ignored. Perhaps because such judgments are so uncommon and unnatural, people cannot make them accurately.

Hindsight bias is obviously related to the availability heuristic. The concreteness and vividness of the actual outcome of an event prompts us to explain it, and hindsight explanations are usually easy to provide. Moreover, we do not usually develop casual scenarios for other possible, and even more probable, outcomes that did not occur—although we could have readily explained those outcomes had they occurred. The ease of explanation, and the relative availability of explanations for occurring versus non-occurring events, becomes, in effect, a heuristic for assessing their likelihood.

---

17. Jeffrey Rachlinski, *Heuristics and Biases in the Courts: Ignorance or Adaptation?*, 69 Oregon L. Rev. 61 (2000).

Consider, for example, the many ways that another terrorist attack could be launched against the United States—explosives in air freight shipments, suicide bombers in shopping malls, dirty bombs, blowing up a chemical plant, bioterrorism, etc. Especially because we have heard warnings about all of these and many other possibilities targeted at various locations, if and when an attack does occur the causal chain will be readily available in hindsight. And, of course, people will be held accountable for having failed to take adequate precautions against the attack.[18]

10.2.1 Risk/Benefit Analysis in Hindsight

Based on an analysis of actual cases as well as a study involving mock jurors, Kip Viscusi concludes that, notwithstanding Learned Hand's seemingly reasonable formulation, jurors may actually punish a corporate defendant who explicitly used cost-benefit analysis:[19]

> . . . [J]urors chose to award punitive damages even though thorough internal risk analyses led the defendants to conclude that no additional safety improvements were warranted. This result is the opposite of what would occur if the legal system fostered better corporate risk behavior. More rational thinking about risk and a conscientious effort to achieve risk-cost balancing in line with society's valuation of safety should signal corporate responsibility rather than trigger corporate punishment.
>
> . . . Why do jurors make the mistake of punishing corporations for risk-cost balancing? A variety of conjectures are possible. People may be averse to explicitly balancing money against human lives. Money and lives might be considered incommensurable. Or, jurors might not be adequately trying to place themselves in the shoes of the corporation at the time of the tradeoff decision. At the time of the decision, the corporation sees only a small probability of an accident, not a certainty. In hindsight, a small corporate expenditure would have prevented an identifiable death, whereas ex ante the corporation would have had to make that expenditure thousands if not millions of times to decrease the risk of an abstract person's death. Comparisons involving identified victims and safety costs will overwhelm jurors' sensibilities, particularly for low-probability events with severe consequences. When corporations systematically think about risk levels yet nevertheless pursue product or environmental policies that fail to maximize safety, the juror may

---

18. For an argument that takes account of hindsight bias and nonetheless concludes that airlines and government officials should have anticipated the 9/11 attack, *see* Max H. Bazerman and Michael D. Watkins, Predictable Surprises: The Disasters You Should Have Seen Coming and How to Prevent Them (Boston: Harvard Business School, 2004).

19. W. Kip Viscusi, *Corporate Risk Analysis: A Reckless Act?*, 52 Stan. L. Rev. 547 (2000).

regard the corporate decision as "cold-blooded." This difficulty arises, in part, because of the well-documented role of hindsight bias with respect to retrospective risk judgments. What matters at the time of the corporate decision is a comparison of the costs of the safety measure with its expected benefits, which consist of the reduced probability of an accident multiplied by the value of the likely damage from an accident. But . . . jurors tend not to compare the expected benefits and costs. Rather, after the victim has been identified, they simply compare the loss to the victim against the costs to save that individual, neglecting the fact that before the accident the loss was only an abstract probability.

10.2.2 Debiasing Hindsight Bias

Because hindsight bias results from the high availability of the actual outcome, one might suppose that it can be debiased by inducing someone to think about the likelihood of other outcomes?[20] In the drawbridge litigation, Kamin and Rachlinski gave a group of jurors an instruction along these lines: "Making a fair determination of probability may be difficult. As we all know, hindsight vision is always 20/20. Therefore it is extremely important that before you determine the probability of the outcome that did occur, you fully explore all other possible alternative outcomes which could have occurred. Please take a moment to think of all the ways in which the event in question may have happened differently or not at all."

The instruction had no effect, which shouldn't be surprising in the light of the earlier discussion of metacognition. As Norbert Schwarz and Leigh Anne Vaughn note, "to the extent that attempts 'to argue against the inevitability of the outcome' are experienced as difficult, they may only succeed in convincing us, *even more*, that the outcome was, indeed, inevitable." Replicating Fischhoff's experiment with the British-Gurkha War, they asked one group of participants to give two reasons for an alternative outcome and asked another group to give ten reasons. While hindsight bias wasn't significantly attenuated in the first group, it was exacerbated in the second because the counterfactual thoughts were so difficult to imagine.

Other efforts to debias hindsight, such as paying people for accurate answers, have not been more effective.

10.2.3 The Legal System's Responses to Hindsight Bias

If hindsight bias is difficult to cure, the legal system nonetheless has ways of countering it. Rachlinski notes that "allocating the burden of production and

---

20. Norbert Schwarz and Leigh Anne Vaughn, *The Availability Heuristic Revisited: Ease of Recall and Content of Recall as Distinct Sources of Information*, *in* HEURISTICS AND BIASES 103.

setting the standard of proof . . . operate[s] against the party most likely to benefit from the hindsight bias—the plaintiff." And he goes on to describe other legal mechanisms:

> First, courts suppress evidence that would exacerbate the bias, such as subsequent remedial measures in negligence and products liability cases. Second, they rely on standards of conduct developed ex ante, when reliable standards are available. Examples include the use of custom as a defense in medical malpractice cases and the business judgment rule in corporate law. Although accurate assessments of the ex ante probabilities would be superior to these strategies, courts seem to recognize such assessments will be biased in hindsight and are therefore unattainable.

10.3 CONFIRMATION BIAS AND OTHER RESISTANCE TO MODIFYING PRIOR EXPECTATIONS AND THEORIES

> *The human understanding when it has once adopted an opinion draws all things else to support and agree with it. And though there be a greater number and weight of instances to be found on the other side, yet these it either neglects and despises, or else by some distinction sets aside and rejects, in order that by this great and pernicious predetermination the authority of its former conclusion may remain inviolate.*
> —Francis Bacon, First Book of Aphorisms (1620)

> *Faced with the choice between changing one's mind and proving that there is no need to do so, almost everyone gets busy on the proof.*
> —John Kenneth Galbraith

> *[Herbert] Spencer began, like a scientist, with observation; he proceeded, like a scientist, to make hypotheses; but then, unlike a scientist, he resorted not to experiment, nor to impartial observation, but to the selective accumulation of favorable data. He had no nose at all for "negative instances." Contrast the procedure of Darwin, who, when he came upon data unfavorable to his theory, hastily made note of them, knowing that they had a way of slipping out of the memory a little more readily than the welcome facts.*
> —Will Durant, The Story of Philosophy 296 (1926)

Recall than in the examples of Bayesian statistics in Section 8.5, $P(H)$, the *prior probability*—or the strength of our belief in the hypothesis *prior* to obtaining event-specific data—was determined by the base rate of the event in question. (In our example, the base rate was the proportion of Blue taxis in a town.) Bayes' Theorem tells us how to revise an estimate after gaining new information—say, about the eyewitness's identification of the taxi involved in the accident.

Consider, though, that at any given time we hold many beliefs that cannot readily be described in terms of base rates—for example, the belief that, as of 2003, Iraq did or did not possess weapons of mass destruction. Those beliefs are based on a variety of sources, including our own experience and the assertions of others—teachers, scientists, politicians, journalists—which we may deem more or less accurate or trustworthy. In these myriad instances, $P(H)$ does not reflect a calculable probability, but rather the subjective strength of our prior belief in H. When we are called upon to revise a prior belief in terms of new evidence, the task is not formulaic as much as intuitively combining the prior belief with the current data.

In many if not most circumstances, it is entirely rational to give considerable weight to one's prior beliefs. However, people tend to interpret conflicting evidence with a variety of *confirmation biases*, manifesting a pervasive tendency to seek evidence supporting their prior beliefs or hypotheses, and to ignore or denigrate evidence opposing them.[21] The belief by the CIA and other members of the Western Intelligence Community that Iraq had weapons of mass destruction provides a recent and dramatic example of the phenomenon. This was, in effect, the conclusion of the *Senate Select Committee on Intelligence*:[22]

> The Intelligence Community (IC) suffered from a collective presumption that Iraq had an active and growing weapons of mass destruction (WMD) program. This . . . led Intelligence Community analysts, collectors, and managers to both interpret ambiguous evidence as conclusively indicative of a WMD program as well as ignore or minimize evidence that Iraq did not have active and expanding weapons of mass destruction programs . . ..
>
> . . . [I]ntelligence analysts, in many cases based their analysis more on their expectations than on an objective evaluation of the information. Analysts expected to see evidence that Iraq had retained prohibited weapons and that Iraq would resume prohibited WMD activities once United Nations (UN) inspections ended . . ..
>
> The . . . IC had a tendency to accept information which supported the presumption that Iraq had active and expanded WMD programs more readily than information which contradicted it. . . . Information that contradicted the IC's presumption that Iraq had WMD programs, such as indications in the intelligence reporting the dual-use materials were intended for conventional or civilian programs, was often ignored . . ..
>
> The presumption that Iraq had active WMD programs affected intelligence collectors as well. None of the guidance given to human intelligence collectors

21. *See generally* Joshua Klayman, *Varieties of Confirmation Bias*, 32 The Psychology of Learning and Motivation 385 (New York: Academic Press, 1995).

22. The committee report argued that the confirmation bias was caused or reinforced by "group think."

suggested that collection be focused on determining whether Iraq had WMD. Instead . . . analysts and collectors assumed that sources who denied the existence or continuation of WMD programs and stocks were either lying or not knowledgeable about Iraq's programs, while those sources who reported ongoing WMD activities were seen as having provided valuable information.

. . . The Committee found no evidence that IC analysts, collectors, or managers made any effort to question the fundamental assumptions that Iraq had active and expanded programs, nor did they give serious consideration to other possible explanations for Iraq's failure to satisfy its WMD accounting discrepancies, other than that it was hiding and preserving WMD. . . .

The IC's failure to find unambiguous intelligence reporting of Iraqi WMD activities should have encouraged analysts to question their presumption that Iraq had WMD. Instead, analysts rationalized the lack of evidence as the result of vigorous Iraqi denial and deception efforts to hide the WMD programs that analysts were certain existed.

The Senate Select Committee on Intelligence (2004) identified another problem in the Intelligence Community's conclusion that Iraq possessed WMD: treating multiple sources of evidence that rely on each other as independent. (Recall *People v. Collins* in Section 8.2). The report asserted that "assessments were built based on previous judgments without carrying forward the uncertainties of the underlying judgments." While "building an intelligence assessment primarily using previous judgments without substantial new intelligence reporting . . . is a legitimate and often useful analytical tool in . . . understanding complex analytical problems, the process can lose its legitimacy when the cumulative uncertainties of the underlying assessments are not factored into or conveyed through the new assessments."

Confirmation biases operate in various ways:

- You might search for evidence in a way that favors your hypothesis—for example, by avoiding tests that might contradict your hypothesis.
- You might insufficiently revise your confidence in your prior hypothesis in light of new data. You might be especially prone to treat conflicting data as "exceptions that prove the rule" rather than call your hypothesis into question. Indeed, the very process of "explaining away" the exceptions may strengthen your belief in the rule.
- You might selectively evaluate and interpret the information you receive to favor your hypothesis. For example, you might take hypothesis-confirming data at face value and subject disconfirming data to critical scrutiny.

- You might have trouble generating viable new hypotheses, even when you do feel like abandoning an old one.

The opportunity to seek confirming or disconfirming evidence can take place at different phases of developing and testing hypotheses, and what is essential in one phase may be counterproductive in another. Ryan Tweney et al. write:[23]

> Success in a very difficult inference task requires that hypotheses be "good" ones in the sense that they must possess at least some correspondence to reality to be worthwhile candidates for the test. Thus, seeking confirmatory data and ignoring disconfirmatory data may be the most appropriate strategy early in the inference process, since it could then produce good hypotheses. Once such hypotheses have been found, however, deliberate attempts ought to be made to seek disconfirmatory data, as the strongest possible test of an explanation.

Most of the instances of confirmation bias examined below do not involve the development of hypotheses, but their testing.

10.3.1 Motives Underlying Confirmation Bias

Why might people be motivated to avoid disconfirming a hypothesis? Sometimes, the hypothesis may be connected to deeply held ideological or religious beliefs. If one has articulated a hypothesis in public, one may feel that abandoning it will lose the esteem of others. And there are strong internal, as well as social, pressures to be consistent.[24] Abandoning a privately held hypothesis can be costly in terms self-esteem; indeed one can feel that one is abandoning an important part of one's identity.

10.3.2 Motivated Skepticism

Even though one's long-run interests are usually served by knowing the truth, people are often motivated to be far less critical of facts and arguments that support their preferred result than an unpreferred one—a phenomenon that Peter Ditto and David Lopez term "motivated skepticism."[25] Consider whether you would be more likely to dismiss reports that caffeine consumption is harmful to your health if you love to drink six cups of coffee a day than if you don't drink coffee. Motivated skepticism seems to provide a strong explanation for persistent

---

23. Ryan D. Tweney, Michael E. Doherty, W. J. Worner, D. B. Plieske, C. R. Mynatt, K. A. Gross, and D. L. Arkkelin, *Strategies of Rule Discovery in an Inference Task*, 32 Quarterly Journal of Experimental Psychology 109 (1980).

24. *See* the discussion of the irrational escalation of commitment in Section 17.3.3.

25. Peter H. Ditto and David F. Lopez, *Motivated Skepticism: Use of Differential Decision Criteria for Preferred and Nonpreferred Conclusions*, 63 Journal of Personality and Social Psychology 568 (1992).

skepticism about the effects of climate change in the face of an increasing scientific consensus.

Ditto and Lopez conducted experiments in which two groups of participants were informed that they would be tested for the presence of the (made-up) TAA enzyme. One group was told that people who had the enzyme were ten times less likely to contract a pancreatic disease; the other that they were ten times more likely. Within each group, half the participants were asked to answer questions before receiving the test results. One set of questions was prefaced by the statement that certain factors, such as stress and lack of sleep, could affect the accuracy of the test, and participants were asked to list whether they experienced any of these factors. Other questions asked the participants to rate the seriousness of the disease and the accuracy of the test. Participants self-administered the test by putting saliva on a piece of paper, which, like litmus paper, changed color depending on the outcome. Unbeknownst to the participants, of course, the outcomes were determined and their behavior was observed.

When asked the questions *in advance*, there was no significant difference in the answers to either set of questions by participants in the groups that were told that the TAA enzyme was healthy or unhealthy. However, when asked the question *after* being told the test results, the unhealthy group recalled many more individual factors that could make the test inaccurate than the healthy group, and they rated the test as far less accurate. Participants receiving bad news engaged in frequent retesting—akin to weighing yourself again when the scale reads too high—compared to those with good news, who tended to be satisfied with a single test.

More generally, faced with preference-inconsistent information, people deny both the facts and their implications. Ditto and Lopez suggest that people faced with preference-consistent information are "less motivated to critically analyze the available data . . . Preference-consistent information is accepted 'at face value,' whereas preference-inconsistent information tends to trigger more extensive cognitive analysis."

Can motivated skepticism be debiased? A study by Claude Steele suggest that a strategy of *self-affirmation* can make people more willing to accept negative or unwelcome information by making them feel more secure about themselves.[26] People who wrote a few paragraphs about an important personal value were more

26. The underlying assumption of the self-affirmation theory is that people are ultimately motivated to see themselves as good. Claude M. Steele, *The Psychology of Self-Affirmation: Sustaining the Integrity of the Self, in* L. Berkowitz (ed.,) 21 *Advances in Experimental Social Psychology* 261 (New York: Academic Press, 1988). Most motivational biases serve that purpose—a good (or intelligent) person would not drink a lot of coffee if doing so were unhealthy, so drinking coffee must not be *that* unhealthy. Self-affirmation doesn't make people more skeptical about welcome news.

open to accepting negative health information (as well as opposing political viewpoints).

10.3.3 Biased Assimilation

Charles Lord, Lee Ross, and Mark Lepper gave participants, who had identified themselves as supporting or opposing the death penalty, two purported studies about its deterrent effect.[27] One study reported that murder rates had decreased in eleven out of fourteen states when those states adopted the death penalty. The other, which compared murder rates in ten pairs of states with different capital punishment laws, reported that in eight of those pairs the murder rate was lower in the state that did not impose the death penalty.

Most participants found the study that supported their prior view much more convincing than the other; for example, they found serious methodological flaws in the opposing study. While it makes sense to give one's hypothesis the benefit of the doubt in the face of mixed or ambiguous evidence, the participants went beyond this. Death penalty supporters and opponents alike reported that their prior views had been strengthened rather than weakened after reading the two studies with opposite results. "Such results provide strong support for the hypothesis that inconclusive or mixed data will lead to increased polarization rather to uncertainty and moderation. Moreover, the degree of polarization . . . was predicted by differences in participants' willingness to be less critical of procedures yielding supportive evidence than of procedures yielding nonsupportive evidence." The authors make these normative observations about the results:

> [T]here can be no real quarrel with a willingness to infer that studies supporting one's theory-based expectations are more probative, or methodologically superior to, studies that contradict one's expectations. When an "objective truth" is known or strongly assumed, then studies whose outcomes reflect that truth may reasonably be given greater credence than studies whose outcomes fail to reflect that truth. Hence, the physicist would be "biased," but appropriately so, if a new procedure for evaluating the speed of light were accepted if it gave the "right answer" but rejected if it gave the "wrong answer." The same bias leads most of us to be skeptical about reports of miraculous virgin births or herbal cures for cancer, and despite the risk that such theory-based and experience-based skepticism may render us unable to recognize a miraculous event when it occurs, overall we are surely well served by our bias [[28]] Our participants' willingness to impugn or defend findings as a

---

27. Charles G. Lord, Lee Ross, and Mark R. Lepper, *Biased Assimilation and Attitude Polarization: The Effects of Prior Theories on Subsequently Considered Evidence*, 37 Journal of Personality and Social Psychology 2098–2109 (1979).

28. Consider, in this respect, scientists' belief in the theory of evolution. From time to time one comes across complex functions—grist for the mill of so-called "intelligent

> function of their conformity to expectations can, in part, be similarly defended. . . .
>
> Our participants' main inferential shortcoming, in other words, did not lie in their inclination to process evidence in a biased manner. Willingness to interpret new evidence in the light of past knowledge and experience is essential for any organism to make sense of, and respond adaptively to, its environment. Rather, their sin lay in their readiness to use evidence already processed in a biased manner to bolster the very theory or belief that initially "justified" the processing bias. In so doing, participants exposed themselves to the familiar risk of making their hypotheses unfalsifiable—a serious risk in a domain where it is clear that at least one party in a dispute holds a false hypothesis—and not allowing themselves to be troubled by patterns of data that they ought to have found troubling. Through such processes laypeople and professional scientists alike find it all too easy to cling to impressions, beliefs, and theories that have ceased to be compatible with the latest and best evidence available.

Because the evidence underlying most public policy reforms is seldom unequivocal, the tendency to differentially evaluate evidence that confirms or disconfirms one's prior beliefs helps explain why policy issues sometimes seem intractable. Not only laypersons but scientists as well are prone to biased assimilation. A study by Jonathan Koehler[29] reports on an *agreement effect* in which scientists rated studies that agreed with their prior beliefs higher than those that disagreed. The phenomenon was less the result of harsh criticism of disconfirming studies than leniency in evaluating studies congruent with their prior beliefs.

10.3.4 Confirmation Bias and Positive Hypothesis Testing

Two other classic studies involve a rather different sort of confirmation bias, one not readily explainable in the same terms as people's attitudes toward the death penalty. One involves a familiar game, in which the player is given a sequence of three numbers that obeys a particular rule and is challenged to determine that rule. For help, the player can present other sequences of three numbers and will be told which of them obey the rule. It turns out that most people playing this game come up with sequences that follow the rule that they guess initially. For example, if someone is given the sequence "2 4 6" and hypothesizes that the rule is "even numbers ascending by two's," he is likely to present sequences such as "4 6 8," which follow his hypotheses. Continuing with such sequences,

---

design"—that are not readily explicable by natural selection. But the theory has proved robust in the 150 years since Darwin, and such phenomena have always ended up being accounted for.

29. Jonathan J. Koehler, *The Influence of Prior Beliefs on Scientific Judgments of Evidence Quality*, 56 Organizational Behavior and Human Decision Processes 28 (1993).

and continuing to hear the answer "yes," he will never be able to prove his hypothesis, because he will never have tested alternative hypothesis. It would be more beneficial to try sequences like "3 5 7" or "3 6 9," for which a "yes" would disprove the hypothesis.[30] Superstitious behaviors are often premised on positive hypothesis testing: if you were wearing your favorite green striped socks when you aced the exam, then you might as well wear them next time. (And if you don't do so well the next time, we've seen that there are lots of ways to explain that away.)

The second study involves a logic problem, essentially asking people to apply the rule, *if p then q*:

> Imagine four cards with the symbols *E*, *K*, 4, and 7 written on them. Each card has a number on one side and a letter on the other. I tell you: "Every card with a vowel on one side has an even number on the other," and ask you to test whether this statement is true. If you were only allowed to turn over two cards, which two cards would they be?[31]

When asked this question, most people choose the cards marked with *E* and 4.[32] In fact, this is not the best way to test whether the rule is true.

- Turning over the *E* card is a good idea, because finding an odd number on the other side would disprove the rule.
- But turning over the 4 card is not informative if the rule is false: it can only provide confirming evidence, giving us another instance in which the rule turns out to be true. Consider the two possibilities: If there is a vowel on the other side, it is consistent with the rule but cannot prove it. If there is a consonant on the other side, the card is irrelevant. since the statement tells us what to expect only for cards with a vowel on one side. Thus the 4 card cannot give us evidence against the statement.

The correct choice is *E* and 7. If there is a vowel on the other side of the 7 card, *or* an odd number on the other side of the E card, the statement is false. If there is a consonant with the 7 *and* an even number with the E, the statement is true.

It is difficult to see in these examples the motives for confirmation bias that were so apparent in the death penalty study. Rather, they seem to be instances of a more cognitive, dispassionate form of bias involving the tendency to engage in *positive hypothesis testing*, that is, testing hypotheses by looking for evidence that would support rather than disconfirm them. Participants in an experiment

---

30. Peter C. Wason, *On the Failure to Eliminate Hypotheses in a Conceptual Task*, 12 Quarterly Journal of Experimental Psychology 129–40 (1960).

31. Peter C. Wason and Phillip N. Johnson-Laird, Psychology of Reasoning: Structure and Content (Cambridge, MA: Harvard University Press, 1972).

32. *Id.*

who were asked to determine whether a person was an extrovert asked questions such as, "What would you do if you wanted to liven things up at a party?" When asked to determine whether he was an introvert, participants asked questions such as, "What makes you the most uneasy or anxious in social situations?"[33]

It turns out that people are better at hypothesis testing when solving problems that are familiar or situated in readily imaginable domains. For example, Hubert L. Dreyfus and Stuart E. Dreyfus note that that people have less difficulty with this problem than with the logically identical card-turning problem described above:[34]

> Suppose that you are a supervisor at a supermarket and have the checks received that day stacked before you—some face up and some face down. The supermarket has a rule: cashiers may only accept checks for $50 or more if approved on the back by the manager. Which checks do you need to turn over to see if the cashiers have followed the rule?[35]

As we discussed in the preceding chapters (see particularly the discussion of diagnosticity in Section 8.5.3), when testing whether a particular hypothesis is more likely than an alternative, one must consider not only the probability that the data support the hypothesis, but also the probability that the data support the alternative. This is *negative hypothesis testing*, which requires looking for data that

---

33. Mark Snyder and William B. Swann, Jr. *Behavioral Confirmation in Social Interaction: From Social Perception to Social Reality*, 14 JOURNAL OF EXPERIMENTAL SOCIAL PSYCHOLOGY 148 (1978). In a related experiment, participants read a story about a woman with an equal number of behaviors that could be characterized as introverted (e.g., spending her office coffee break by herself) or extroverted (e.g., chatting with another patient in the doctor's office). Several days later, some were asked to assess her suitability for a stereotypically introvert job (research librarian) and others for an extrovert job (real estate salesperson). Those who evaluated her for the two positions respectively recalled her introverted and extroverted behaviors and evaluated her accordingly. Mark Snyder and Nancy Cantor, *Testing Hypotheses about Other People: The Use of Historical Knowledge*, 15 JOURNAL OF EXPERIMENTAL SOCIAL PSYCHOLOGY 330 (1979).

34. HUBERT L. DREYFUS, STUART E. DREYFUS, AND TOM ANTHANASIOU, MIND OVER MACHINE: THE POWER OF HUMAN INTUITION AND EXPERTISE IN THE ERA OF THE COMPUTER 18 (New York: Free Press, 1986). *See also* Klayman, *Varieties of Confirmation Bias, supra* at 403.

35. The evolutionary psychologists Leda Cosmides and John Tooby assert that people's ability to solve this problem, or an analogous one involving a bar's checking IDs to assure that drinks are not served to minors, involves a particular "cheater-detection" capacity. JEROME H. BARKOW, LEDA COSMIDES, AND JOHN TOOBY, THE ADAPTED MIND: EVOLUTIONARY PSYCHOLOGY AND THE GENERATION OF CULTURE (New York: Oxford University Press, 1995); Leda Cosmides and John Tooby, *Neurocognitive Adaptations Designed for Social Exchange*. In EVOLUTIONARY PSYCHOLOGY HANDBOOK (DAVID M. BUSS, ed., New York: Wiley, 2005). For a critical review of this work, *see* MARK G. KELMAN, THE HEURISTICS DEBATE: ITS NATURE AND ITS IMPLICATIONS FOR LAW AND POLICY (New York: Oxford University Press, forthcoming 2010).

would *disconfirm* the hypothesis. If I observe Alex eating nothing but junk food, I could hypothesize that Alex likes to eat only junk food. Positive hypothesis testing would involve giving Alex junk food to see if he likes it. Negative hypothesis testing requires that I give Alex some healthy food to see if he might like that as well. Note that if I try giving Alex broccoli and he doesn't like it, that doesn't mean I have confirmed my hypothesis. Although broccoli is not junk food, many people who like healthy food do not like it. The strongest test of my hypothesis would be to give Alex a lot of different healthy foods and see if he likes any of them.

In many situations, though, "people rely most heavily on information about what happens when the presumed cause is present, and much less on information about what happens in its absence."[36] They have "cognitive difficulty in thinking about any information which is essentially negative in its conception."[37] This tendency is implicitly noted by the great psychologist Arthur Conan Doyle, in this dialogue from *The Adventure of Silver Blaze*:

> Inspector Gregory: "Is there any other point to which you would wish to draw my attention?"
>
> Holmes: "To the curious incident of the dog in the night-time."
>
> "The dog did nothing in the night-time."
>
> "That was the curious incident," remarked Sherlock Holmes.

Positive hypothesis testing is not necessarily an irrational strategy. It tends to uncover false positives—i.e., proffered hypotheses not supported by the data—which often are more costly than false negatives.[38] It also makes sense when you believe that the circumstances in which rules apply arise only rarely.[39]

10.3.5 Confirmation Bias as an Instance of Anchoring

Confirmation bias may be explained in terms of the anchoring-as-activation theory described above. "People tend to evaluate hypotheses by attempting to confirm them, [and] such a search generates evidence disproportionately consistent with the anchor. The absolute judgment is then biased by the evidence recruited in this confirmatory search."[40] Also related to anchoring as activation is

---

36. Klayman, *Varieties of Confirmation Bias, supra* at 389.

37. *Id.*

38. *See also* Section 5.8.

39. Mike Oaksford and Nick Chater, *Rational Explanation of the Selection Task*, 103 Psychological Review 381–91 (1996).

40. Nicholas Epley and Thomas Gilovich, *Putting Adjustment Back in the Anchoring and Adjustment Heuristic, in* Thomas Gilovich, Dale Griffin, and Daniel Kahneman, Heuristics and Biases: The Psychology of Intuitive Judgment 120 (New York: Cambridge University Press, 2002).

the idea that a hypothesis acts as a suggestion, instilling at least a transient belief in its validity.[41] This is consistent with Spinoza's view (contrary to Descartes') that *understanding* and *believing* are elided—that people at least tentatively accept or believe propositions in order to comprehend them, and only then "unbelieve" propositions that do not comport with their other beliefs.[42]

10.3.6 Belief Perseverance after Evidential Discrediting[43]

Richard Nisbett and Lee Ross make these general observations about the perseverance of beliefs, or theories (in a broad sense):[44]

1. When people already have a theory before encountering any genuinely probative evidence, exposure to such evidence (whether it supports the theory, opposes the theory, or is mixed), will tend to result in more belief in the correctness of the theory than normative dictates allow.
2. When people approach a set of evidence without a theory and then form a theory based on initial evidence, the theory will be resistant to subsequent evidence. . . .
3. When people formulate a theory based on some putatively probative evidence and later discover that the evidence is false, the theory often survives total discrediting of that evidence.

With respect to the last of these, Craig Anderson, Mark Lepper, and Lee Ross gave participants a small sample of (spurious) correlations between firefighters' indications of their risk preferences on a questionnaire and their actual performance as firefighters, and asked the participants to write down an explanation for the correlation.[45] Some participants explained what they believed to be a positive relationship and some explained a negative relationship (both plausible and explicable because one could imagine that firefighters either are more or are less risk tolerant than people at large). Even after being told that the data was completely fictitious, and that other participants had provided an explanation for the converse correlation, they held to their theories. In another experiment, Lee Ross, Mark Lepper, and Michael Hubbard[46] asked participants to distinguish between real and fake suicide notes, and randomly informed the participants

41. *See* Karen E. Jacowitz and Daniel Kahneman, *Measures of Anchoring in Estimation Tasks*, 21 PERSONALITY AND SOCIAL SCIENCES BULLETIN 1161 (1995).

42. *See* Daniel T. Gilbert, *Inferential Correction*, *in* HEURISTICS AND BIASES.

43. RICHARD E. NISBETT AND LEE ROSS, HUMAN INFERENCE: STRATEGIES AND SHORTCOMINGS IN SOCIAL JUDGEMENT 175 ff (Englewood Cliffs, NJ: Prentice Hall, 1980).

44. *Id.* 169.

45. Craig A. Anderson, Mark R. Lepper, and Lee Ross, *Perseverance of Social Theories: The Role of Explanation in the Persistence of Discredited Information*, JOURNAL OF PERSONALITY AND SOCIAL PSYCHOLOGY 39 (1980).

46. Lee Ross, Mark R. Lepper, and Michael Hubbard, *Perseverance in Self-Perception and Social Perception: Biased Attributional Processes in the Debriefing Paradigm*, 32 JOURNAL OF PERSONALITY AND SOCIAL PSYCHOLOGY 880 (1975).

that they had done well or poorly. Even after being informed that the evaluations actually had no relationship to their performance, the participants continued to believe that they were relatively good or bad, not only on the specific suicide note task but on other tasks involving social sensitivity.

Nisbett and Ross suggest several reasons why people persevere in their beliefs even after being explicitly told that they were duped: We are likely to recruit evidence from our own memory consistent with our initial beliefs ("I have always been good at guessing people's occupations") and continue to give it weight because of its availability. Moreover, we are likely to have generated a causal explanation of why the initial belief is true ("Of course I'm good at telling if suicide notes are real, I'm very empathic"), and we tend to treat the ease of explanation as evidence of its truth (ignoring how easy it is to develop explanations for almost any outcome). Not only are the recruited evidence and causal theory not discredited but, like the initial data that stimulated them, they remain available even after the data turn out to be spurious.[47]

10.3.7 The Emergence of Coherence in Making Judgments

Consider this experiment by Keith Holyoak, Dan Simon, and their colleagues: You are a judge considering a defamation action by a high-tech company against a dissatisfied shareholder who posted a negative message about the company's prospects. The company was already facing financial difficulties and, shortly after the shareholder posted the message, its stock plummeted and the company went bankrupt. A number of factors may be relevant to your decision, including: whether the defendant's message was true, whether his message caused the company's demise, whether the defendant was motivated by vindictiveness or only wanted to protect innocent shareholders, and whether the Internet site was more analogous to a newspaper (which is subject to libel law) or a telephone system (which is not). Ideally, you analyze each of these factors separately and then combine them to reach a judgment.

In fact, your judgment not only tends to evolve in favor of one or the other party as you consider the factors, but your assessment of each of these discrete factors tends to fall into line with that judgment. If you're heading in the direction of a judgment for the company, you will tend to conclude that the message was false and vindictive, contributed to the company's demise, etc. Holyoak et al.

47. In a follow-up study, an observer, who had no knowledge of the experimental manipulation, watched the actor performing the task. The actor was then debriefed in a procedure, watched by the observer, that explicitly discussed the perseverance phenomenon. Although pointed debriefing attenuated the actor's continued beliefs about her abilities, the observers' views of the actor's abilities tended to persevere. It is less clear why observers persevere in holding to their theories. Lee Ross suggests that perhaps the observers care less and do shallower processing and hence they continue to anchor on their initial impression of the actor's ability. (Personal communication.)

characterize this process as "bidirectional reasoning,"[48] capturing the idea that you not only reason from the premises to the conclusion but from the (nascent) conclusion to the premises, valuing evidence that supports the conclusion over evidence that does not. The elements of a schema or story can be related to each other in a network of connections,[49] and when particular nodes on the network (e.g., vindictiveness) are activated, they tend to activate some (e.g., causation of the harm) and deactivate others (e.g., truth of the statement). The process is akin to fitting the elements of a story together to make the "best story" not when it is over, but as you are hearing it.

The experiments by Holyoak et al. produced two other noteworthy results. First, once participants had reached a particular result, they had difficultly recalling contrary inferences they had made prior to the decision—a phenomenon related to hindsight bias. Second, the basic scenario was designed not to favor one outcome over the other and, indeed, the participants divided roughly equally in finding for the plaintiff or the defendant. Yet participants reported very high levels of confidence that they had reached the best possible decision.

10.3.8 Debiasing Strategies

Can one overcome the tendencies toward confirmation bias? Charles Lord, Mark Lepper, and Elizabeth Preston[50] found that the instruction to "be objective" had virtually no effect on people's tendency to assimilate new information in a biased manner. But instructing people to *consider the opposite*—to seriously entertain the possibility that the opposite of what they believe might actually be true—had a significant effect. This suggests that people are not necessarily *trying* to see things in a way that suits them; rather, their cognitive processes lead them to interpret new information in the light of existing beliefs.

10.4 OVERCONFIDENCE

Edward Russo and Paul Schoemaker asked 1000 American and European business managers to answer ten trivia questions calling for numerical estimates

48. Dan Simon, Lien B. Pham, Quang A. Le and Keith J. Holyoak, *Bidirectional Reasoning in Decision Making by Constraint Satisfaction*, Journal of Experimental Psychology—General 3 128 (1999); Dan Simon, Lien B. Pham, Quang A. Le, and Keith J. Holyoak, *The Emergence of Coherence over the Course of Decision Making*, 27 Journal of Experimental Psychology—Learning, Memory, and Cognition 1250 (2001).

49. *See* the discussion of connectionist networks in Section 11.3.2.

50. Charles G. Lord, Mark R. Lepper, and Elizabeth Preston, *Considering the Opposite: A Corrective Strategy For Social Judgment*. 47 Journal of Personality and Social Psychology 1231 (1984).

and to provide a "low and a high guess such that you are 90% sure the correct answer falls between the two." The questions included.[51]

- Martin Luther King's age at death.
- Length of the Nile River in miles.
- Number of books in the Old Testament.
- Diameter of the moon in miles.
- Air distance from London to Tokyo.

Most respondents got considerably more than 10 percent of their answers wrong. What is interesting about Russo and Schoemaker's experiment is not the state of the participants' substantive knowledge, but their belief that they knew more than they did. Indeed, not only amateurs answering trivia questions but professional making judgments in their own domains of expertise tend to be overconfident. Also noteworthy: although people are overconfident about particular answers, they are much more realistic in estimating their overall hit rate.[52] Unfortunately, most judgments are made one at a time.

People tend to be overconfident about nontechnical items of moderate or extreme difficulty.[53] For example, participants given the nearly impossible task of discriminating between Asian and European children's drawings or predicting fluctuations in stock prices did little if any better than chance (i.e., 50 percent correct). But their mean confidence levels were between 70 percent to 80 percent.[54] Moreover, people become more confident as they are given more information, even if the information is not diagnostic.[55] Overconfidence diminishes as the tasks become easier. Indeed, knowledgeable participants responding to easy questions tend to be *underconfident.*

Granted that people often tend to be overconfident, is there a correlation between confidence and accuracy? Alas, not. For example, in a study by Scott Plous and Philip Zimbardo, citizens were given a description of actual Soviet and American military actions, with the names of the countries removed. They were asked to identify which of the superpowers was involved and to say how

---

51. J. Edward Russo and Paul J. H. Schoemaker, Winning Decisions: Getting it Right the First Time 79–80 (New York: Doubleday, 2002).

52. Dale Griffin and Amos Tversky, *The Weighing of Evidence and the Determinants of Confidence,* in Heuristics and Biases, 411.

53. Sarah Lichtenstein, Baruch Fischhoff, and Lawrence Phillips, *Calibration of Probabilities: The State of the Art to 1980, in* Judgment Under Uncertainty: Heuristics and Biases 306 (Daniel Kahneman and Amos Tversky eds., Cambridge University Press, 1982).

54. Sarah Lichtenstein and Baruch Fischhoff, *Do Those Who Know More Also Know More About How Much They Know? The Calibration of Probability Judgements,* 3 Organizational Behavior and Human Performance 553 (1977).

55. Stuart Oskamp, *Overconfidence in Case-Study Judgments,* 29 Journal of Consulting Psychology 261 (1965).

confident they were in their answers. The respondents were correct slightly less than half the time, and their confidence ratings were almost orthogonal to the accuracy of their responses.[56]

The relationship between individuals' assessment of the probability of their beliefs being true and the actual truth is termed *calibration*. Meteorology is among the few professions—along with bookmaking on horse races—in which judgments prove to be well calibrated. By contrast, the calibration of physicians' diagnosis of pneumonia in patients examined because of a cough, and their diagnoses of skull fractures, has proven to be poor. Sarah Lichtenstein, Baruch Fischhoff, and Lawrence Phillips conjecture:

> Several factors favor the weather forecasters. First, they have been making probabilistic forecasts for years. Second, the task is repetitive; the question to be answered (Will it rain?) is always the same. In contrast, a practicing physician is hour by hour considering a wide array of possibilities (Is it a skull fracture? Does she have strep? Does he need further hospitalization?). Finally, and perhaps most important, the outcome feedback for weather forecasters is well defined and promptly received. This is not always true for physicians; patients fail to return or are referred elsewhere, or diagnoses remain uncertain.[57]

In many situations, overconfidence seems to result from the availability and anchoring and adjustment phenomena. Dale Griffin and Amos Tversky distinguish between the *strength* (extremity on the relevant predictive dimension) of evidence and its *weight* (predictive value).[58] In statistical terms, strength is analogous to the size of the effect, and weight is analogous to its significance or reliability (taking into account, for example, the size of the sample). They argue that people focus on the perceived strength of the evidence based on the degree to which available evidence is consistent with the hypothesis in question—and then adjust (insufficiently) for its weight. For example, when judging whether a coin is biased, people first focus on the proportion of heads and tails in the sample and only then (insufficiently) adjust for the number of tosses. By the same token, the fact that a suspect fails a lie detector test is treated as strong evidence of guilt notwithstanding the poor reliability of such tests.[59]

---

56. Scott L. Plous and Philip G. Zimbardo, *How Social Science Can Reduce Terrorism* (2004), Chronicle of Higher Education, Sept. 10, 2004, B9-10.

57. Sarah Lichtenstein, Baruch Fischhoff, and Lawrence D. Phillips, *Calibration of Probabilities: The State of the Art to 1980, in* Daniel Kahneman, Paul Slovic, and Amos Tversky, Judgment Under Uncertainty: Heuristics and Biases 306 (1982).

58. Dale Griffin and Amos Tversky, *The Weighing of Evidence and Determinants of Confidence, in* Heuristics and Biases, 230.

59. Lyle A. Brenner, Derek J. Koehler, and Yuval Rottenstreich, *Remarks on Support Theory: Recent Advances and Future Directions, in* Heuristics and Biases.

The tendency (discussed in Section 8.5.4) to ignore base rates and to overvalue the more immediate and available data also leads to overconfidence. For example, after interviewing individuals, participants were asked to predict whether, if given the choice, the interviewees would take a free subscription to *Playboy* or *The New York Review of Books*. Although informed that 68 percent of all the people interviewed preferred *Playboy*, participants tended to ignore this base rate and premise their predictions on their own impressions from the interviews. Participants whose predictions went contrary to the base rate were overconfident, with a mean accuracy of only about 50 percent in the face of a mean confidence of 72 percent. When they just relied on the base rate they were quite well calibrated.

Although people tend to be overconfident about their knowledge or predictions of particular items or events, they tend to be better calibrated in terms of their overall judgment about similar events. For example, entrepreneurs were overconfident about the success of their own new ventures even when they were realistic about the general failure rate for such ventures. Griffin and Tversky suggest that the entrepreneurs ignore base rates and focus on factors pertaining to the individual decision.[60] Similarly, "people often make confident predictions about individual cases on the basis of fallible data (e.g., personal interviews or projective tests) even when they know that these data have low predictive validity."[61]

Are there *individual* characteristics that correlate with calibration? While men and women were equally represented in the Plous and Zimbardo study described above, two-thirds of the highly confident respondents were male; and about twice as many of the highly confident respondents distrusted the Soviet Union and were advocates of strong defense spending than their low-confidence peers. However, in a different study of relationships between overconfidence and several personality measures—authoritarianism, conservatism, dogmatism, and intolerance of ambiguity—only authoritarianism showed a (modest) correlation with overconfidence.[62] The nature of the task seems to matter more than the individual who is performing it.[63]

As for debiasing, merely alerting participants to the difficulty of the task does not improve calibration. Nor does increasing the motivation to calibrate accurately. Paralleling a strategy for correcting self-serving biases, however,

---

60. We address overconfidence about one's future projects, or overoptimism, in Section 13.5.

61. Dale Griffin and Amos Tversky, *The Weighing of Evidence and the Determinants of Confidence*, *in* Heuristics and Biases.

62. Sarah Lichtenstein, Baruch Fischhoff, and Lawrence D. Phillips, *Calibration of Probabilities: The State of the Art to 1980*, *in* Daniel Kahneman, Paul Slovic, and Amos Tversky, Judgment Under Uncertainty: Heuristics and Biases 306 (1982).

63. *Id.*

calibration did improve when participants were asked to write down all the reasons that contradicted their answers.[64] But the most powerful strategy for improving calibration is clear and immediate feedback.

Overcoming Intuition. People's overconfidence increases to the extent their judgments rely on intuition. Could overconfidence be overcome by "forcing" the brain to think more deliberately? A 2007 finding by Adam Alter, Daniel Oppenheimer, and their colleagues indicates that intuition (and the associated overconfidence) can be overcome when faced with "metacognitive difficulty"—that is, when presented with information that makes them think harder about their intuitive assumptions and judgments. The authors postulate that cognitive disfluency (which occurs when information pertaining to a decision is difficult to process) can compel individuals to switch from System 1 cognitive processes (intuition) to System 2 cognitive processes (deliberation).[65] In other words, cognitive disfluency makes individuals "less confident" in their intuitive judgments and forces them to switch into a more deliberative thinking mode.

10.5 INTUITION, ANALYSIS, AND THE ROLE OF EXPERTS REDUX

In Chapter 1, we contrasted intuitive and analytic (or deliberative) approaches to problems. We considered their strengths and weaknesses, and their often complementary roles. The preceding chapters on statistics studied a formal analytical approach to making judgments based on probabilistic information. Chapters 9 and 10 have focused on the role of intuition, highlighting the systematic biases of the intuitive statistician.

We conclude the chapter with two questions that relate to the distinction between intuition and analysis. One concerns the relative merits of clinical and statistical methods for predicting human behavior and other events. As we will see, clinical intuitions do not fare very well. And this leads us to the second question: What good are experts anyway?

10.5.1 Clinical vs. Statistical Prediction

It's tough to make predictions, especially about the future
—Yogi Berra

64. Asher Koriat, Sarah Lichtenstein, and Baruch Fischhoff, *Reasons for Confidence*, 6 Journal of Experimental Psychology: Human Learning and Memory 107 (1980).

65. Adam L. Alter, Daniel M. Oppenheimer, Nicholas Epley, and Rebecca N. Eyre, *Overcoming Intuition: Metacognitive Difficulty Activates Analytic Reasoning*, Journal of Experimental Psychology, General 136.4 569–76 (2007).

Put yourself in the position of a Christine Lamm, who is considering law school graduates for entry-level positions in her department. Your task is to predict whether the candidate is likely to develop the requisite professionals skills (e.g., legal and policy analysis, writing) to succeed in the job. Criteria that you might employ for this task include:

- law school GPA;
- types of law school courses taken;
- extracurricular activities;
- faculty recommendations;
- LSAT score.

Which of these strike you as most predictive—and why? Suppose that you could pick and choose among the criteria and give them any weights you choose. How well could you do? Suppose that the department has ten entry-level positions and that you are considering twenty applicants. How many of the ten that you hire are likely to succeed? How many of the ten you reject would have succeeded if they had been hired (and why would you have particular difficulties in answering this question)?

How could you improve your prediction? Consider these two alternatives:

1. *Statistical*: Decide which of these criteria matter and in which direction they matter (e.g., higher GPA predicts greater success). Score them on some common scale and add up the scores.
2. *Clinical*: In addition to or instead of scoring, give considerable weight to the intangible factors that strike you from interviewing the candidate.

Both of these have elements of intuition. The first involves a rough multivariate regression analysis; it relies on your intuitions about the diagnosticity or predictive value of the relevant factors, all of which can easily be "coded." The second complements or replaces these codable criteria with noncodable intuitions.

Where clinical judgments are usually accurate—e.g., identifying a person who comes into your office as male or female—there is no need to use statistical indicators. And when the phenomena to be predicted are essentially random—e.g., daily variation in stock prices—neither clinical nor statistical methods are helpful. In most other cases, however, the statistical approach alone usually yields better predictions than the clinical approach:

- even (perhaps especially) if you only average the coded scores rather than weight them according to some regression model;
- even if you are an expert in the field;
- even if, as an expert, you have the statistical prediction in hand before making your own clinical prediction.

This is the implication of about one hundred experiments involving phenomena ranging from medical and psychiatric diagnoses, to predicting parole violations, loan defaults and bankruptcies, and the academic success of graduate students.[66] For example, while statistical prediction of parole failures based on three variables (type of offense, number of past convictions, and number of violations of prison rules) produced a (very modest) 0.22 correlation with actual parole failures, this far surpassed professional parole interviewers, whose predictions had a correlation of only 0.06.[67] In the Cook County Hospital emergency room, the use of four objective factors did a far better job than clinical diagnosis in predicting whether a patient with chest pain was in danger of suffering a heart attack.[68]

Baseball offers an interesting example of the difference between clinical and statistical decision making.[69] On the clinical side, the scout, uses his intuition to recruit players based on speed, quickness, arm strength, hitting ability, and mental toughness, and qualities such as "a live, active lower body, quick feet, agility, instinct, . . . [and] alertness." To the extent statistics play a role in evaluating a hitter's potential contribution to a team's success, they traditionally have centered around batting average, runs batted in, and home runs.

Bill James, who published the *Baseball Abstract*, found that these few statistics did not account for a player's contribution to the team's winning. He began to create new statistics that were the product of a sophisticated analysis of hundreds of games, with the ultimate measure of a hitter's success based on how many runs he creates.

Billy Beane, general manager of the Oakland Athletics, began to experiment with James's approach. He discovered that on-base percentage (the percentage of the time a batter reached base by any means) and slugging percentage (total bases divided by at-bats) were the two best predictors of success, and on-base percentage was three times as important as slugging percentage.

Beane thus selected players based upon an entirely different model than his clinically-minded competitors. Just as clinicians generally resist statistical prediction, the scouts were reluctant to yield their intuitions. In *Moneyball*, Michael Lewis recounts a paradigmatic conversation between Beane and a recruiter:

> "The guy's an athlete, Billy," the old scout says. "There's a lot of upside there."

---

66. Robyn M. Dawes, David Faust, and Paul E. Meehl, *Clinical Versus Actuarial Judgment*, *in* Heuristics and Biases; Robyn M. Dawes, House of Cards: Psychology and Psychotherapy Built on Myth (New York: The Free Press, 2002).

67. *See* Robyn Dawes, House of Cards, *supra*.

68. The studies are summarized in Malcolm Gladwell, Blink 125–36 (2005).

69. *See* Michael Lewis, Moneyball: The Art of Winning an Unfair Game (New York: Norton & Company, 2003); Cass Sunstein and Richard Thaler, *Who's on First*, New Republic (August 2003); Ehren Wassermann, Daniel R. Czech, Matthew, J. Wilson, and A. Barry Joyner, *An Examination of the Moneyball Theory: A Baseball Statistical Analysis Abstract*, 8 The Sports Journal (Winter 2005), http://www.thesportjournal.org/2005Journal/Vol8-No1/daniel_czech.asp.

> "He can't hit," says Billy.
> "He's not that bad a hitter," says the old scout.
> "Yeah, what happens when he doesn't know a fastball is coming?" says Billy.
> "He's a tools guy," says the old scout. . . .
> "But can he hit?" asks Billy.
> "He can hit," says the old scout, unconvincingly.
> [The scout] reads the player's college batting statistics. They contain a conspicuous lack of extra base hits and walks.
> "My only question is," says Billy, "if he's that good a hitter why doesn't he hit better?"

Beane's basic point was that if you want to predict future achievement, you will do better to rely on past achievements than on unrealized potential. By the same token, overachievers are more likely than underachievers to overachieve in the future. In any event, Beane was often able to acquire players who were undervalued by other teams. Consequently, the Athletics, with a much lower payroll than other teams, consistently made the playoffs after Beane began implementing his system of evaluating talent.[70]

In the large majority of the preceding examples, neither statistical nor clinical prediction does very well, but statistical prediction almost always does better. Why?

First, linear models tend to be quite robust in explaining or predicting a wide range of phenomena. It turns out that simple linear models based on averaging a number of independent variables, where increases in the independent variables predict a monotonic increase the dependent variable, tend to be pretty good approximations of empirically-derived models.[71] By contrast, people are not very good at combining or aggregating data. William Grove and Paul Meehl write.[72]

---

70. Another proponent of Beane's method of evaluating talent, Boston Red Sox General Manager Theo Epstein, saw his team win the World Series for the first time in eighty-eight years, albeit with a significantly higher payroll than Beane's As. It should be noted that the claim that statistics are more valuable than informed intuition in recruiting and deploying a baseball team has met with some vehement resistance. David Leonhardt, *To Play Is the Thing*, New York Times, Aug. 28, 2005, reviewing Buzz Bissinger, Three Nights in August (2005), and Bill Shanks, Scout's Honor (2005).

71. *See* Robyn M. Dawes and Bernhard Corrigan, *Linear Models in Decision Making*, 81 Psychology Bulletin 95 (1974). It is questionable whether one can improve on a simple linear model through the process of *bootstrapping*—of developing and implementing a regression equation based on observing an expert decision maker. *Id.*

72. William M. Grove and Paul E. Meehl, *Comparative Efficiency of Informal (Subjective, Impressionistic) and Formal (Mechanical, Algorithmic) Prediction Procedures—The Clinical Statistical Controversy*, 2 Psychology, Public Policy, and Law 293 (1996).

> The human brain is a relatively inefficient device for noticing, selecting, categorizing, recording, retaining, retrieving, and manipulating information for inferential purposes. . . . The dazzling achievements of Western post-Galilean science are not attributable to our having better brains than Aristotle or Aquinas, but to the scientific method of accumulating objective knowledge. . . . However, we need not look to science for the basic point, as it holds . . . in most areas of daily life. . . . When you check out at the supermarket, you don't eyeball the heap of purchases and say to the clerk, "Well it looks to me as if it's about $17.00 worth; what do you think?" The clerk adds it up.

Second, clinical judgments tend to be affected by extraneous factors, including most of the biases described in Chapters 9 and 10. One might analogize statistical versus clinical judgments to flying by instruments versus by flying by sight and feel. At least before the advent of modern electronic navigation, flying by instruments, though very accurate, was always subject to some error—the plane had leeway within narrow corridors—but errors tend to be regressive, clustering around the mean. Visual flying is highly accurate when conditions are good and the pilot is alert. But put even an experienced pilot in the clouds without any instruments, and his intuitions are subject to wild divergences from reality: he may, for example, believe that the plane is turning or descending when it's straight and level. Such errors are nonregressive and can, indeed, be fatally extreme. Instruments can fail, and sometimes one's intuitions can warn of their "statistical" anomalies; but more often what feels like an anomaly is actually a failure of the intuitive system.

Third, clinical judgments often manifest inconsistency. In one study, radiologists were asked to diagnose stomach cancer in one hundred patients. A week later, when they were given the same X-rays in a different order, almost a quarter of the diagnoses were different.[73] As Lewis R. Goldberg writes:[74]

> [T]he clinician . . . lacks a machine's reliability. He "has his days." Boredom, fatigue, illness, situational and interpersonal distractions, all plague him, with the result that his repeated judgments of the exact same stimulus configuration are not identical. . . . If we could remove some of this human unreliability by eliminating the random error in his judgments, we should thereby increase the validity of the resulting predictions.

These findings have been met with considerable resistance on two grounds. First, especially when making selections among candidates—for admission to

73. Paul J. Hoffman, Paul Slovic, and Leonard G. Rorer, *An Analysis-of-Variance Model for Assessment of Configural Cue Utilization in Clinical Judgment*, 69 Psychological Bulletin 338 (1968).

74. Lewis R. Goldberg, *Man Versus the Model of Man: A Rationale, Plus Some Evidence, for a Method of Improving on Clinical Inferences*, 73 Psychology Bulletin 422 (1970).

universities or for employment—the use of purely statistical methods has been criticized as cold, inhumane, or unfair. But it is hardly clear that fairness is improved by the arbitrariness of subjective impressions.

Clinical vs. Statistical Prediction in Affirmative Action Admissions Criteria

In its 1993 decisions in *Gratz v. Bollinger* and *Grutter v. Bollinger*, the Supreme Court struck down the University of Michigan's affirmative action program for undergraduate admissions because its actuarial formula for assigning weight to diversity "lacked a meaningful individualized review of applicants," but upheld the law school admissions program because it involved a "highly individualized, holistic review of each applicant's file," where race was considered among other factors but not in a mechanical way. What are the pros and cons of the Court's approach? (See William C. McGaghie and Clarence D. Kreiter, *Holistic Versus Actuarial Student Selection*, 17 TEACHING AND LEARNING IN MEDICINE 89 (2005)).

Second, the general superiority of statistical over clinical prediction raises the question—of ego as well as fact—of what use are experts? We now turn to this question.

10.5.2 The Role of Experts

No one doubts that an expert has knowledge or skills in a domain that laypersons or even students aspiring to be experts do not possess. For most of us, our ability to diagnose medical symptoms, to represent a client in a trial, or to play chess, basketball, or the cello does not compare favorably to those accomplished in those activities.

Also, because (as discussed in Section 1.5) experts often engage in schematic processing—interpreting, judging, and acting based on pattern recognition—they can often respond much more rapidly and confidently than someone who must engage in a deliberative process. Consider this example from Gary Klein's study of firefighters:[75]

75. GARY KLEIN, SOURCES OF POWER: HOW PEOPLE MAKE DECISIONS 32 (Cambridge, MA: MIT Press, 1998).

> It is a simple fire in a one-story home in a residential neighborhood. The fire is in the back, in the kitchen area. The lieutenant leads his house crew into the building, to the back, to spray water on the fire, but the fire just roars back at them.
>
> "Odd," he thinks. The water should have more of an impact. They try dousing it again, and get the same results. They retreat a few steps to regroup.
>
> Then, the lieutenant starts to feel as if something is not right. He doesn't have any clues; he just doesn't feel right about being in that house, so he orders his men out of the building—a perfectly standard building with nothing out of the ordinary.
>
> As soon as his men leave the building, the floor where they had been standing collapses. Had they still been there, they would have plunged into the fire below.

When later interviewed by Klein, the lieutenant said that he had no clue that the house had a basement, let alone that the fire was down there, but he wondered why the fire was not responding. In retrospect, the room in which the firefighters were grouped was unusually warm and, while fires are generally noisy, this one was very quiet. It was the fact that the fire didn't fit any patterns known to him that sent an unconscious alarm signal. It was the dog that did not bark in the nighttime.

Along similar lines, recall the soldier in Section 1.5.3 who sensed that a parked car was next to an improved explosive device:

> One thing did not quite fit on the morning of Sergeant Tierney's patrol in Mosul. The nine soldiers left the police station around 9 a.m., but they did not get their usual greeting. No one shot at them or fired a rocket-propelled grenade. Minutes passed, and nothing. . . . Since then, Sergeant Tierney has often run back the tape in his head, looking for the detail that tipped him off. Maybe it was the angle of the car, or the location; maybe the absence of an attack, the sleepiness in the market: perhaps the sum of all of the above. . . . "I can't point to one thing," he said. "I just had that feeling you have when you walk out of the house and know you forgot something—you got your keys, it's not that—and need a few moments to figure out what it is."[76]

Though more dramatic than most, these examples are representative of experts' intuitions. Yet there is considerable evidence that experts fall prey to many of the biases described above, and that their judgments are quite fallible on important dimensions. Here is a list of concerns and some responses to them:

---

76. Benedict Carey, *In Battle, Hunches Prove to be Valuable*, New York Times, July 28, 2009, http://www.nytimes.com/2009/07/28/health/research/28brain.html?pagewanted=2&_r=1&hp.

- *Validity*. Expert judgments in many fields are often just wrong. (Compared to what, though? Expert judgments are usually more accurate than those of laypersons.)
- *Reliability*. Given exactly the same fact situation an hour or a week later, an expert will often come to a different judgment. A review of studies of reliability found an overall correlation of 0.79 between the first judgment and a subsequent one—though meteorologists scored 0.91.[77]
- *Calibration*. Experts' certainty about their judgments tends to be poorly calibrated with their validity, with meteorologists again being an exception.[78] (On the other hand, there is some evidence that laypersons are attracted to overconfident experts.[79])
- *Under-use of available relevant information*. While one of the advantages of expertise is the ability to exclude extraneous information, experts often do not seek or use information that is relevant and diagnostic. One possible explanation, related to schematic processing, is that an expert's "feeling of knowing"—akin to the "strong sense of general familiarity" that can mislead eyewitness identification[80]—may demotivate further inquiry. When an expert "must choose either to retrieve a previously computed solution or to compute the solution anew, she may judge the likelihood that she possesses the correct answer in memory by assessing her feeling of knowing it."[81] While the expert may often be correct, overconfidence in one's initial judgment can readily lead to short-circuiting any further learning.
- *Combining indicators*. As we saw in the preceding section, experts' intuitions are not as reliable or consistent as simple linear models in combining or aggregating indicators to predict outcomes. Nonetheless, experts are an important source for determining what indicators are relevant and for discarding supposed indicators that are not. But more fundamentally, many situations that experts deal with—situations like the kitchen fire—do not have the similar, repetitive quality that allow for the application of a linear model.[82]

---

77. Robert H. Ashton, *A Review and Analysis of Research on the Test-Retest Reliability of Professional Judgment*, 13 Journal of Behavioral Decision Making 277 (2000).

78. Stuart Oskamp, *Overconfidence in Case Study Judgments*, 29 Journal of Consulting Psychology 261–65 (1965).

79. Paul C. Price and Eric R. Stone, *Intuitive Evaluation of Likelihood Judgment Producers: Evidence of a Confidence Heuristic*, 17 Journal of Behavioral Decision Making 39 (2004).

80. Daniel L. Schacter, The Seven Sins of Memory: How the Mind Forgets and Remembers (New York: Houghton Mifflin, 2001).

81. Stacy L. Wood and John G. Lynch, Jr., *Prior Knowledge and Complacency in New Product Learning*, 29 Journal of Consumer Research 416 (2002).

82. On the other hand, James Shanteau suggests that expert judgments are most reliable when dealing with relatively repetitive tasks with static stimuli. James Shanteau,

- *Expert intuitions as a safety valve.* Even if purely statistical judgments are generally more accurate than clinical judgments, statistical judgments are susceptible to at least two sorts of errors. They cannot take account of unusual individuating data, and an error in recording or transcription (e.g., the misplacement of a decimal point or the transposition of two integers in a number) can lead to a grievously wrong result.[83] On the other hand, experts probably tend to overrate their ability to identify when statistical judgments have gone off the rails.[84]

Although intuitive decision making often compares unfavorably with decision making based on actuarial models, actuarial models can sometimes be developed by observing experts making decisions to see what criteria they use and then testing the criteria in terms of their predictive accuracy. This approach, known as *bootstrapping,*[85] often does better than the experts on whose judgments it is based—in areas ranging from graduate school admission to predicting the life expectancy of cancer patients to the performance of insurance salespersons.[86]

10.6 CONCLUSION

Nisbett and Ross report that a colleague, after reading a draft of their manuscript of *Human Inference,* asked: "If we're so dumb, how come we made it to the moon?"[87] Their response is that advances in the physical and natures

Competence in Experts: The Role of Task Characteristics, 53 ORGANIZATIONAL BEHAVIOR AND HUMAN DECISION PROCESSES 252 (1992).

83. Contrasting intuitive and analytic judgment more generally, Hammond reports on an experiment in which participants estimating height of a bar with their eye were never quite right but never far out of range, while those using trigonometry were precisely right—except when they made errors in calculation, which produced absurd results. KENNETH R. HAMMOND, HUMAN JUDGMENT AND SOCIAL POLICY: IRREDUCIBLE UNCERTAINTY, INEVITABLE ERROR, UNAVOIDABLE INJUSTICE 160, 175 (New York: Oxford University Press 1996). He makes the related point that while "rigorous, analytically derived systems . . . work well . . . within the controlled circumstances for which they were constructed," intuition tends to be more robust, continuing to operate when those systems unexpectedly break down." For example, the lighthouse is infallible until it is not lit some evening.

84. *See* Dawes et al., *supra.*

85. John A. Swets, Robyn M. Dawes, and John Monahan, *Better Decisions Through Science,* SCIENTIFIC AMERICAN 82 (October 2000); Colin Camerer, *General Conditions for the Success of Bootstrapping Models,* 27 ORGANIZATIONAL BEHAVIOR AND HUMAN PERFORMANCE 411 (1981); J. EDWARD RUSSO AND PAUL J. H. SCHOEMAKER, WINNING DECISIONS: GETTING IT RIGHT THE FIRST TIME 146 (2002).

86. RUSSO AND SCHOEMAKER, 147.

87. NISBETT AND ROSS, 249.

sciences and technology are ultimately due to formal research methodology and principles of inference, and are the result of collective rather than individual learning. For example, "the individual is not usually required to detect covariation anew," but can learn from experts or through cultural transmission:

> Each culture has experts, people of unusual acumen or specialized knowledge, who detect covariations and report them to the culture at large. Thus, most (though not by any means all) cultures recognize the covariation between intercourse and pregnancy. This is a covariation detection task of enormous complexity, given the interval between the two types of events and the rarity of pregnancy relative to the frequency of intercourse, not to mention the occasional unreliability of the data ("Honest, I never did it!"). . . . [O]nce a covariation is detected and the new hypothesis seems to be confirmed by perusing available data, the entire culture is the beneficiary and may take action in accordance with the knowledge. Such a cultural transmission principle applies to almost all human affairs from farming ("Plant corn when the oak leaf is as big as a mouse's ear") to tourism ("The German restaurants in Minnesota are generally quite good") to urban survival ("The South Side is unsafe.")"[88]

Although cultures can embrace and transmit false knowledge, adaptive pressures tend to correct misinformation that has practical consequences.

88. *Id.* 111.

11. THE SOCIAL PERCEIVER
Processes and Problems in Social Cognition

11.1 INTRODUCTION

Many of the decisions that lawyers, judges, and policy professionals make involve interpreting and predicting other people's behavior. Indeed, making sense of other people figures centrally in the performance of virtually every aspect of lawyers', judges', and public officials' work. Lawyers and other "forensic professionals" functioning as investigators, or judges acting in their roles as fact-finders, for example, have to assess credibility and attribute motivation. As counselors, lawyers must understand what makes their clients "tick," win their clients' trust, and predict how their clients will feel and behave in the future. In evaluating specific cases and designing advocacy strategies, lawyers have to predict how legal decision makers, like judges, administrative officials, or jurors, will respond to specific legal or factual arguments. What arguments will they find persuasive? What narratives will they find compelling? What inferences will they draw from ambiguous evidence susceptible of varying interpretations? In negotiating an agreement or designing a process, lawyers have to structure incentives that will encourage certain behaviors and discourage others, and this requires understanding a great deal about human behavior. Policy makers have analogous tasks in dealing with constituents, legislatures, and other decision-making bodies and in regulating or otherwise influencing the behavior of individuals and entities.

Errors of judgment in any of these, and many similar contexts, can lead to bad decisions and ineffective policies. For this reason, understanding the sources of bias and error that can distort social perception and judgment, and knowing how to structure decision making so as to minimize their negative effects, will improve the quality of a lawyer or policy maker's performance in virtually every aspect of his or her professional role.

Social judgment, like judgment more generally, is influenced by systematic biases and other sources of distortion similar to those described in earlier chapters. Biases in social judgment, however, are in some ways the most insidious of all. Because social interaction constitutes so much of the grist of daily professional (and personal) life, we tend to think of ourselves as experts in understanding other people and predicting their future behavior. Our self-confidence as "common-sense" or "intuitive" psychologists often leads us to think that we understand other people better than we do.

In this chapter, we consider how people go about making sense of other people. In the process, we introduce readers to various sources of bias and distortion in social perception and judgment, describe how "intuitive" psychological theories can lead us astray in our attempts to understand and predict people's behavior, and make some suggestions as to what might be done about it.

The psychological processes we explore in this chapter, particularly those having to do with racial, gender, or other forms of stereotyping and bias, raise a number of highly controversial legal and policy issues. You have probably already been exposed to at least parts of the large and at times contentious literature engaging many of the controversies, whether you are studying law, public policy, or some other discipline. It is not our purpose in this chapter to rehearse, to weigh in on, or even to summarize, these controversies. Rather, we seek only to describe a number of the major—and for the most part, consensus—findings in empirical social and cognitive psychology about various psychological processes that can conduce to intergroup misperception and perpetuate subtle—often unintentional—forms of intergroup bias.

11.2 THE BIASING EFFECTS OF SOCIAL SCHEMAS: AN OVERVIEW

In Section 1.5.2, we introduced the role of schemas in organizing the vast amounts of data that bombard our senses every moment of the day. Schemas create expectancies, and these expectancies determine which perceptions we attend to, how we interpret them, and how we store them in memory. The schematic filters through which we make sense of incoming perceptions also influence the way we behave toward the people we perceive.

Racial, ethnic, and gender stereotypes represent one class of social schemas that we absorb from the surrounding cultural environment. But stereotypes are not unique in their ability to create subtle social expectancies. Person prototypes (i.e., "my sister, Susan") and role prototypes (i.e., "reference librarian") function in much the same way.

The content of our social schemas, and the expectancies those schemas generate, are influenced by culture and learning, by our past experiences in other contexts, and, where applicable, by our prior experiences with the person in question. But whatever an expectancy's origin, once we have schematized a person, the expectancies associated with that schema often lead us to interpret their behavior in expectancy-reinforcing ways. Our schematic expectancies, like other knowledge structures, often operate *implicitly*, outside of our attentional focus, and this makes them resistant to correction or change. Consider how difficult it is for a schoolchild whose past behavior created expectancies among his teachers and classmates to change how he is viewed, even when his behavior changes. Sometimes the only solution seems to be to switch schools.

As we will discuss later in the chapter, implicit social expectancies have serious consequences for our understanding of other people. They affect how we interpret ambiguous behavior, how we attribute causality and responsibility for it, and how we predict how people will behave in the future. Moreover, our social expectancies affect how we behave toward their targets. This, in turn, often affects how those targets behave toward us. If, for example, you apply for a job and are interviewed by someone who, because of your race, gender, or grade point average, expects you to be unqualified for the job, their attitude may leak out in subtle aspects of their behavior, such as seating distance, eye contact, and facial expressions, all of which may give you a vague sense that they don't like you. You may in turn behave in ways that project social discomfort, reticence, or self-doubt, confirming the interviewer's prior impression of you. We examine these kinds of expectancy feedback effects later in this chapter, in sections on the behavioral confirmation effect and a phenomenon known as "stereotype threat," through which a stereotyped person's fear of performing in a way that will confirm a negative stereotype about his group actually does impair his performance on a stereotype-relevant task.

For clarity's sake, much of the following discussion of the biasing effects of social expectancies centers on racial and gender stereotypes and stereotyping. Readers should bear in mind, however, that social expectancies derive from other knowledge structures as well, including individual person prototypes and role prototypes. Where possible, we will provide examples and illustrations incorporating these as well.

11.3 THE COGNITIVE MECHANICS OF SOCIAL SCHEMAS

In November 1994, in a speech to a meeting hosted by Operation PUSH in Chicago, civil rights leader Jesse Jackson made what must have been a wrenching self-observation: "There is nothing more painful for me at this stage in my life," Jackson said, "than to walk down the street and hear footsteps, and start thinking about robbery, then look around and see someone White, and feel relieved." Jackson told the story to illustrate the obstacles facing African Americans in the late twentieth century. We use it to illustrate certain basic concepts and processes in social cognition.

11.3.1 Stereotypes and Stereotyping

At its most obvious level, Jackson's anecdote reflects the operation of a stereotype, specifically, a stereotype of Black men that includes attributes of criminality and violence and that evokes fear and a spontaneous behavioral impulse toward avoidance in at least one particular situation. Many people believe that racial and other social stereotypes are the result of "prejudice"—a moral defect involving motivated hostility toward minority groups. Indeed, this was the received understanding of psychologists through at least the mid-twentieth century.[1] It is difficult to fit Jessie Jackson into this particular model of racial stereotyping.

1. John Duckitt, The Social Psychology of Prejudice (Westport, CT: Praeger Publishers, 1992); Gordon Allport, The Nature of Prejudice (New York: Perseus Books Publishing,1954).

However, Jackson's response, along with his disappointed and self-disapproving reaction to it, fits easily into the models of stereotypes and stereotyping that have emerged over the past forty years from cognitive social psychology and, more recently, social cognitive neuroscience. The last several decades of research in cognitive psychology suggest that stereotypes are just a particular instance of the schemas, categories, and other knowledge structures introduced in Section 1.5.2, which structures we necessarily adopt and apply to make sense of an otherwise impossibly complex perceptual environment.[2]

Under *social cognition theory*, stereotypes are viewed as mental structures comprising our knowledge, beliefs, affective orientation, and expectations concerning a categorized social group.[3] They contain a mixture of emotional associations,[4] abstract "knowledge" about the stereotyped group, exemplars of group members,[5] and theoretical causal theories about why members of the group "are the way they are."[6] As is the case with other types of categories, stereotypes are often organized hierarchically,[7] with higher level entities, such as "women" being divided into subtypes, such as "mothers," "old ladies," "businesswoman," and so forth.

Social stereotypes, not only of racial minorities, but of other groups, such as librarians, Muslims, personal injury lawyers, doctors, or homeless people, are culturally transmitted and then reinforced by our own experience, partially through the operation of confirmation bias. By a very early age, children have learned the stereotypes associated with the major social groups in their environment.[8] By adulthood, these stereotypes have a long history of activation and, for many people, have become "chronically accessible,"[9] meaning that they are

---

2. Susan T. Fiske and Shelley. E. Taylor, Social Cognition: From Brains to Culture (New York: McGraw-Hill, 2008); Eleanor Rosch, *Human Categorization, in* Studies in Cross-Cultural Psychology, 1, 1–2 (Neil Warren ed., 1977); Jerome Bruner, *On Perceptual Readiness*, 64 Psychological Review 123 (1957).

3. David L. Hamilton and Jeffrey W. Sherman, *Stereotypes, in* Handbook of Social Cognition 168 (Robert S. Wyer and Thomas K. Srull eds., 2d ed. Hillsdale, NJ: Erlbaum, 1994).

4. Mark P. Zanna and John K. Rempel, *Attitudes: A New Look at an Old Concept, in* The Social Psychology of Knowledge (Daniel Bar-tal and Arie W. Kruglanski eds., 1988).

5. David L. Hamilton and Jeffrey W. Sherman, *Stereotypes, supra* note 3

6. Bernd Wittenbrink, Charles M. Judd, and Bernadette Park, *Evidence for Racial Prejudice at the Implicit Level and its Relationship with Questionnaire Measures,* 72 J. Personality & Soc. Psychol. 262 (1997).

7. Renee Weber and Jennifer Crocker, *Cognitive Processes in the Revision of Stereotypic Belief,* 45 J. Personality & Soc. Psychol. 961–77 (1983).

8. Patricia G. Devine, *Stereotypes and Prejudice: Their Automatic and Controlled Components,* 56 J. Personality & Soc. Psychol. 5–18 (1989); Phyllis A. Katz, *The Acquisition of Racial Attitudes in Children, in* Towards the Elimination of Racism 125, Phyllis A. Katz ed. (New York: Pergamom Press, 1976).

9. John A. Bargh, Walter J. Lombardi, and E. Tory Higgins, *Automaticity of Person* X *Situation Effects on Impression Formation: It's Just a Matter of Time,* 55 J. Personality & Soc. Psychol. 599–605 (1988).

regularly used to classify people and then to construe, encode, recall, and predict their behavior, motivations, and character attributes.

Stereotypes often function *implicitly*, meaning that they can influence social perception and judgment outside of conscious awareness, whether or not they are believed. As social psychologist Patricia Devine has shown, even if a person has consciously rejected a particular stereotyped belief (e.g., that females, as a group, have less innate scientific aptitude than males), the stereotype may linger on as an explicit expectancy, capable of influencing a perceiver's subjective assessment of a particular male or female target's scientific aptitude or ability.[10]

Stereotypes are spontaneously activated when the stereotype-holder encounters a member of the stereotyped group. This activation is automatic, and occurs without intention or awareness, with little cost to other, ongoing mental operations. In this way, stereotypes, and other social schemas, function in much the same way as the availability, representativeness, and other heuristics described in earlier chapters. Although they can serve as useful "rules of thumb," they can also lead to poor judgment, not to mention violations of law and important social and personal ideals.

Law professor Jerry Kang illustrates the process by which stereotypes influence social perception, judgment, and behavior as shown in Figure 11.1.

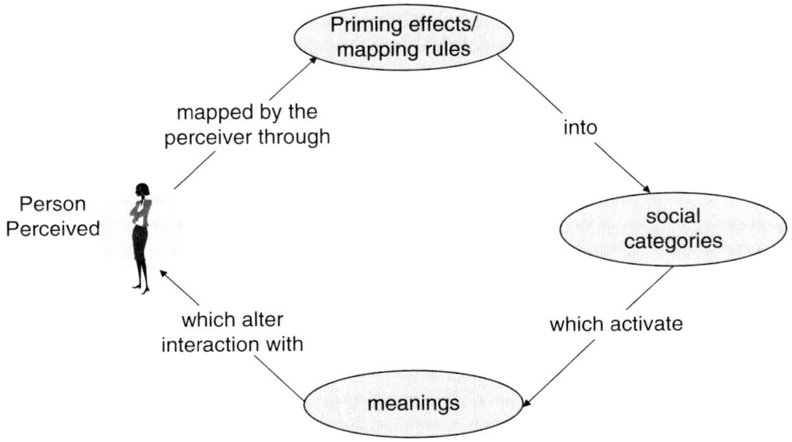

FIGURE 11.1 SOCIAL CATEGORIZATION AND PERSON PERCEPTION.

In Kang's conception, society provides the individual perceiver with a set of social categories (schemas). These social categories include "mapping rules" used to assign the person perceived to a particular social category. So, for

10. Patricia G. Devine, *Stereotypes and Prejudice: Their Automatic and Controlled Components*, *supra* n. 8.

example, a human being wearing a dress, having long, styled hair, and wearing makeup will usually be mapped as female. However, category assignment may be influenced not only by culturally provided mapping rules, but also by features of the stimulus situation, which may "prime" particular categories, increasing the likelihood that they will be used in categorizing the person perceived. So, in a drag bar, the above-mentioned human might not be spontaneously mapped as female. In either case, however, assignment of an individual to a particular category *activates* the category. The category, which comprises a network of mental associations, supplies the perceiver with a set of implicit and explicit *meanings*. These meanings, in turn, systematically influence the perceiver's judgments of and interaction with the categorized individual.

Kang's model can be thought of as a visual representation of the *schematic information processing* model of "naturalistic," or "System 1," thinking described in Section 1.6.1. Indeed, stereotyping is best understood not as something that only "prejudiced" people do, but as one type of System 1 thinking, which is automatic, rapid, associative, effortless, and process opaque.[11] Of course, this does not mean that the application of stereotypes in social judgment is inescapable. As with other types of System 1 thinking, an initial stereotype-driven impression can be revised through the application of deliberative, or System 2 thinking, which is controlled, effortful, and self-conscious.[10] We describe this correction process in Section 11.7.

11.3.2 This is Your Brain on Stereotypes: The Mental Representation of Social Knowledge

The brain comprises a vast network of individual neurons, interconnected in unimaginably complex ways at synapses, across which move electrical impulses, mediated by chemical neurotransmitters. Experience, either real (as through interaction with other people) or virtual (as through watching television), actually changes the structure of the brain, as new synaptic connections are created and strengthened through use, and as others are weakened or even eliminated from aging, damage, or lack of use.[12] But what we think of as the *mind* is larger than the sum of these myriad tiny parts.[13]

As people acquire social knowledge through direct or vicarious experience, they organize their knowledge into an interconnected web of associations,

---

11. Daniel Kahneman and Shane Frederick, *Representativeness Revisited: Attribute Substitution on Intuitive Judgment*, *in* THOMAS GILOVICH, DALE GRIFFIN, AND DANIEL KAHNEMAN, HEURISTICS AND BIASES: THE PSYCHOLOGY OF INTUITIVE JUDGMENT 49 (New York: Cambridge University Press, 2002).

12. Michael S. Gazzaniga, Richard B. Irvy, and George R. Mangun, COGNITIVE NEUROSCIENCE: THE BIOLOGY OF MIND (New York: W.W. Norton & Co., 2002).

13. STEVEN PINKER, THE BLANK SLATE: THE MODERN DENIAL OF HUMAN NATURE (New York: Penguin Books, 2002).

referred to as social "schemas"[14] or "concepts."[15] Schemas, including social schemas, contain myriad interrelated elements that represent a person's accumulated knowledge and beliefs about, experiences (both direct and vicarious) of, and affective orientations toward the schematized construct. Confronted with the task of construing a person or his behavior, we unconsciously and automatically match the incoming data against a set of plausible social schemas. An incoming bit of information that "fits" an existing schema is said to *activate* the schema. When a schema is activated, it imposes meaning on the inherently ambiguous information supplied by raw perception.[15]

To illustrate, imagine that one fall night, Jesse Jackson is walking down a street in Brooklyn, on his way to visit a former colleague. He is alone, the street is relatively deserted, and it is very dark. Hearing footsteps approaching from behind him, Jackson turns and sees walking toward him a young Black man we will call William Carter. Carter, an Amherst College sophomore and Amherst Choral Society member, is in New York City over the weekend to sing in a benefit production of Bach's B Minor Mass. Carter is walking from the subway station to a relative's house in Brooklyn following a rehearsal, and is dressed for the chilly November night in a parka, a ski cap, and the casual, oversized blue jeans he often wears when he doesn't have to dress up. Seeing Carter, Jackson feels fear, starts walking faster, and crosses the street. What happened?

Because categories such as race, age, and gender are "chronically accessible" in our society, the subcategory "young Black male" would likely have been highly accessible in Jackson's mind when he first perceived William approaching him from behind, and Jackson would have spontaneously categorized William in this way. This categorization would have "potentiated" the category's content—the web of associations comprising Jackson's schema of "young, Black, male-ness." Figure 11.2 illustrates just a tiny number of the myriad concepts that might, for Jackson or anyone else, including William himself, be associated with and in a sense constitute Jackson's "young Black male" schema.

Figure 11.2 unpacks the schema of "young Black man" into what Anthony Greenwald terms a "connectionist" model of social information processing.[16] Different nodes of the network may be activated by external stimuli and they, in turn, may activate other nodes by virtue of internal mental associations. The content of the network and the strength of the connections between its constituent parts are shaped by the surrounding culture, what one has learned from

14. Susan T. Fiske, and Shelley E. Taylor, Social Cognition, *supra* n. 2.

15. Zeva Kunda, Social Cognition: Making Sense of People (Cambridge: MIT Press, 1999).

16. Anthony G. Greenwald, Mark A. Oaks, and Hunter G. Hoffman, *Targets of Discrimination: Effects of Race on Responses to Weapon Holders*, 39 Journal of Experimental Social Psychology 399–405 (2002).

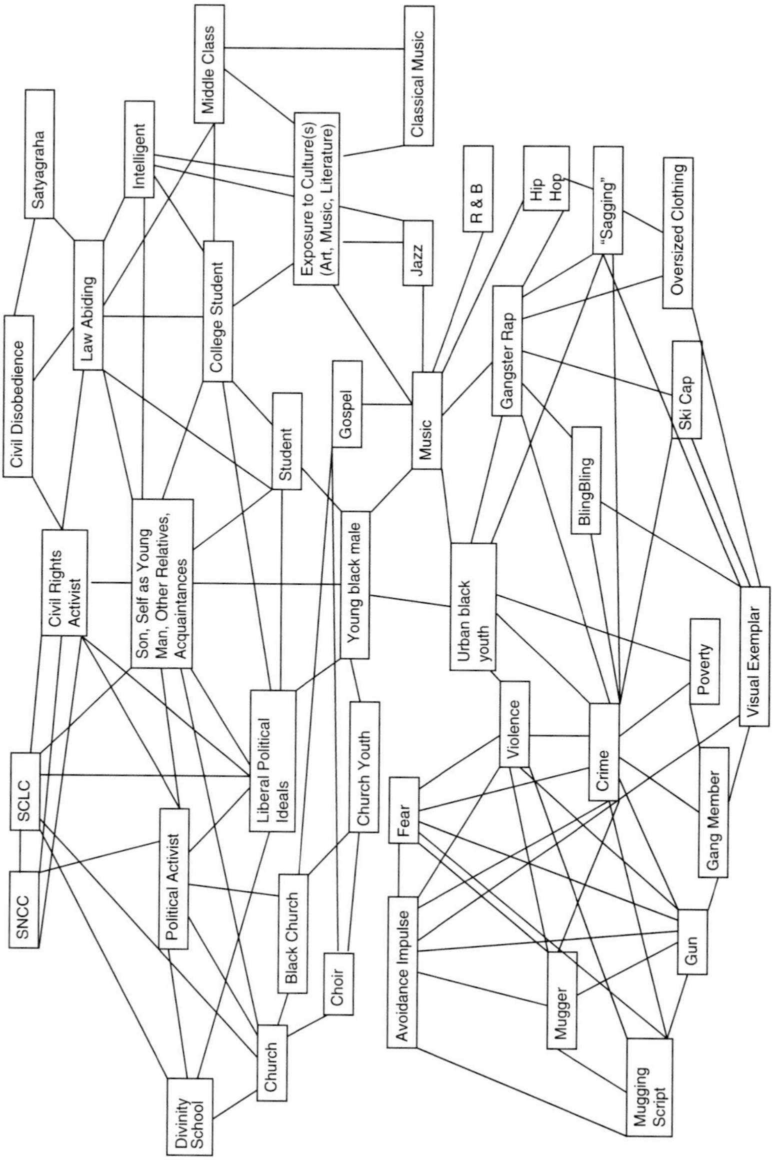

FIGURE 11.2 SCHEMATIC ASSOCIATIONS: YOUNG BLACK MALE.

parents, teachers, and friends, the media, or one's own experience and imagination. Once activated, the nodes of the network mediate subsequent social perception and judgment. Like any schema, the components of the network contain affective components (e.g., fright, pride, warmth),[17] action "scripts" (e.g., walk faster, say hello, smile), and causal theories explaining why stereotyped group members "are the way they are."[15] This is one way of understanding what it means to say that race is a "social construction." The social environment "constructs" the associative network in the brain that constitutes racial categories.

Notice in Figure 11.2 the wide variety of concepts associated with the subcategory, "young Black male." Many of these concepts, like "crime," "violence," "poverty," "gun," "gang member," and "mugging script," which are interconnected at the bottom of Figure 11.2, carry negative connotations. Taken together, they construct the schema "criminal urban Black male." But notice also that other concepts, such as "Black church," "college student," "church music," "church youth," "liberal political ideals," "exposure to culture," "self as young man," and "jazz," carry positive connotations. Grouped together, these concepts would constitute a quite different subcategory, perhaps "Black male college student."

Given all the different constructs that an encounter with William Carter might activate, how is it that, on any particular occasion, he is subcategorized and then construed—or misconstrued—in one way rather than another? Because in American culture young Black men are so frequently associated in media and other representations with urban violence, and because the dark, deserted New York street might well have primed the concept of crime in Jackson's mind, Jackson would have been predisposed, upon first seeing Carter, to categorize him as he did. Additionally, Carter's physical attributes, dress, and posture, although inherently ambiguous, would have reinforced this initial categorization, because of their association with youth gangster culture. The net effect is the activation of those elements of the Figure 11.2 associative network bolded and shaded in Figure 11.3.

What might have happened if Carter had been walking down the street singing the tenor melody from the *Gloria* section of the B Minor Mass? This new stimulus feature might have dramatically altered how Jackson classified the approaching Carter. The schematic network activated by the encounter might have looked more like Figure 11.4 than like Figure 11.3.

Presented with a William Carter singing the *Gloria* from Bach's B Minor Mass, concepts like "classical music," "sacred choral music," "church," "God," and "exposure to culture" would have been activated. These in turn would have activated other concepts, like "church youth," "choir," and "student," and from these, perhaps specific exemplars of young Black men from Jackson's own

17. Russell H. Fazio, Joni R. Jackson, Bridget C. Dunton, and Carol J. Williams, *Variability in Automatic Activation as an Unobtrusive Measure of Racial Attitudes: A Bona Fide Pipeline?*, 69 JOURNAL OF PERSONALITY AND SOCIAL PSYCHOLOGY 1013–27 (1995).

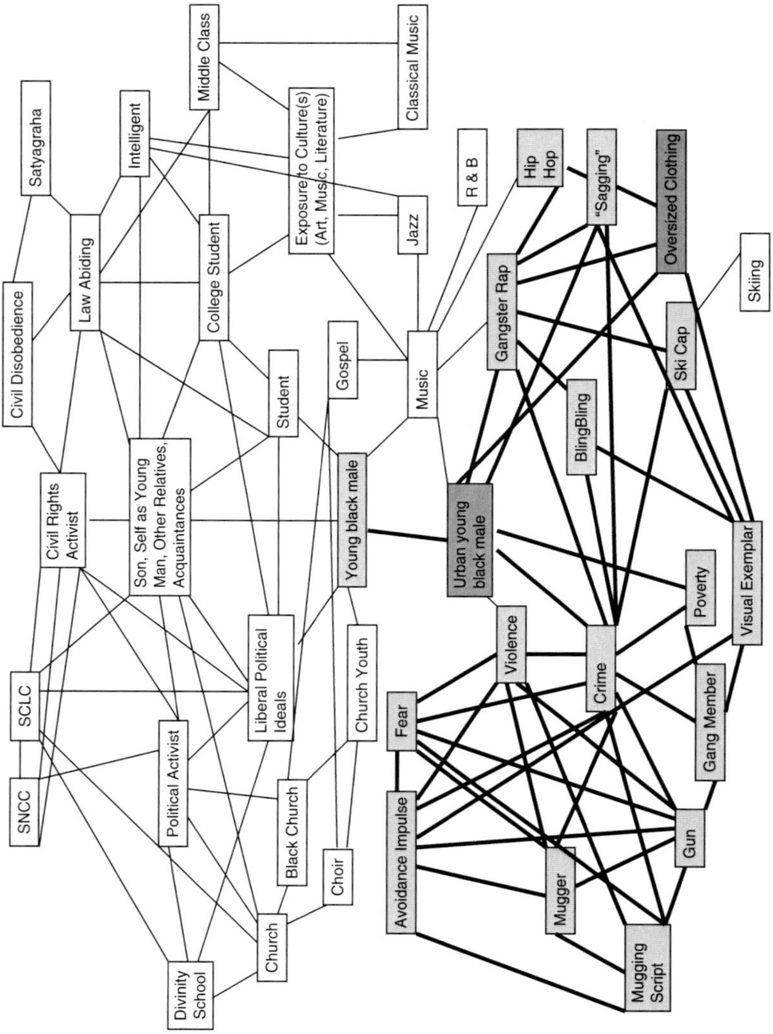

FIGURE 11.3 SCHEMATIC ASSOCIATIONS WITH NEGATIVE PRIME.

family, religious community, or even of himself as a young man. The end result would have been the instantiation of a particular subtype of "Black young man" that incorporated an interconnected network of positive associations and emotional reactions very different from those constituting the stereotype of young Black urban male criminality depicted in Figure 11.4.

Indeed, recent research suggests that the activation of certain elements of a schematic network can result not only in the activation of elements with which they are connected, but also in the *deactivation* of elements with which they are disassociated.[18] Seen in this way, the various constructs comprising our mental representations can stand in three types of relation to each other. They can be associated, in which case the activation of one will increase the probability that the other will be activated. They can be completely disassociated, in which case the activation of one will have no impact on the probability of the others' activation. Or, they can be negatively associated, or mutually inhibitory, such that the activation of one actually decreases the probability that the other will be invoked.

For example, many female executives and professionals report that, as soon as they have their first child, people at work start responding to them differently. They are given less responsible job assignments; their suggestions are taken less seriously; they are accorded less deference and respect. One explanation of this reported phenomenon is that it is very difficult for many people to associate the social role construct "mother" with the trait constructs "aggressive" or "hard-driving." The activation of "mother" not only activates a set of trait constructs, such as "nurturing," or "soft," it actually inhibits the activation of others, like "intellectually sharp" or "professionally productive."[19]

Just as it is hard for many people to think of another person simultaneously as a "new mother" and a "hard-driving executive," it is hard to think simultaneously about sacred choral musicianship and a propensity toward street violence. By singing Bach's B Minor Mass, William Carter has not only behaved in a way that will activate certain constructs in Jesse Jackson's mind, he has behaved in a way that will inhibit the activation of others. The result is a profound change in what Jackson "sees"—at least as profound as what Dartmouth and Princeton students saw in the football game recounted in Section 9.4.1.

We have presented two alternative scenarios of the external stimuli in Jackson's encounter with Carter. In our hypothetical case, whistling Bach made all the difference in terms of which schematic elements were activated. But other factors can determine which aspects of an incoming perception most influence

---

18. Paul Thagard, and Zeva Kunda, *Making Sense of People: Coherence Mechanisms, in* Connectionist Models of Social Reasoning and Social Behavior 3–26 (Stephen J. Read and Lynn C. Miller eds., Mahwah, N.J.: Erlbaum,1998).

19. Amy. J. C. Cuddy, Susan T. Fiske, and Peter Glick, *When Professionals Become Mothers, Warmth Doesn't Cut the Ice*, 60 Journal of Social Issues 701 (2004).

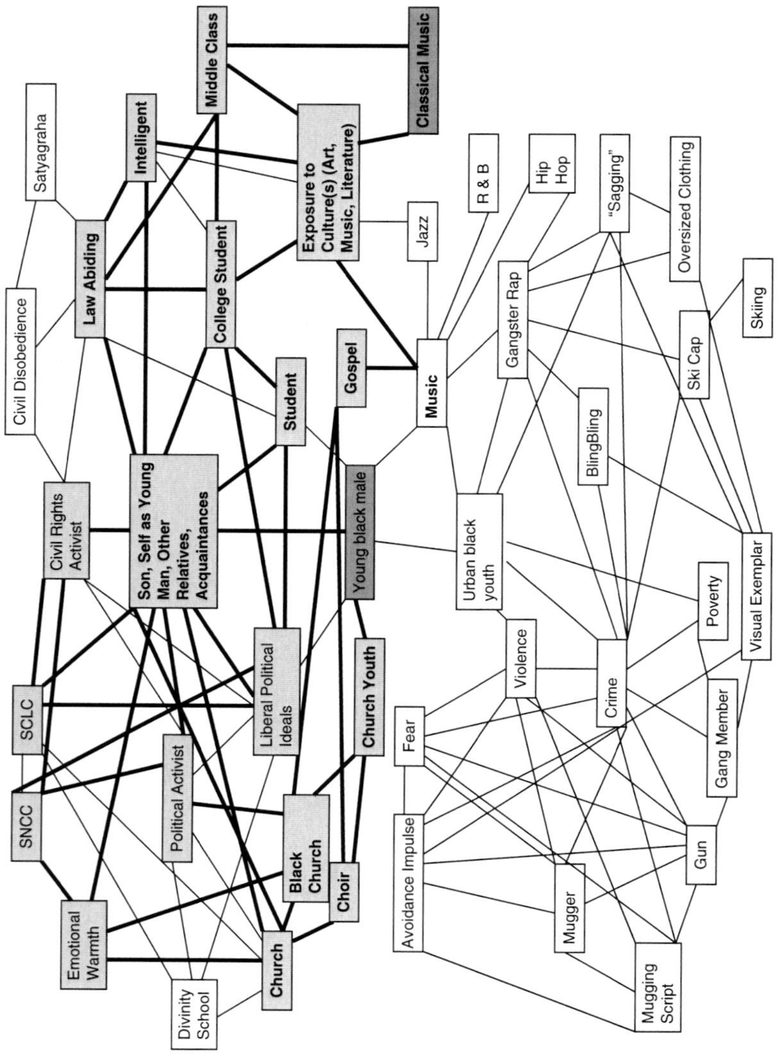

FIGURE 11.4 SCHEMATIC ASSOCIATIONS WITH POSITIVE PRIME.

schema activation. Some kinds of stimuli are more salient than others. All other things being equal: visual stimuli,[20] negative stimuli,[21] and stimuli that are unusual or unexpected (like a young person walking down a Brooklyn street singing a portion of Bach's B Minor Mass) are particularly salient.

Also, the more frequently or recently a particular schema has been activated, the more *available* it is, and thus the more likely it is to be reactivated by a stimulus that relates to it.[22] Thus, given the prominence of news stories about crimes committed by young Black men, seeing a young Black man on an empty Brooklyn street late at night is likely to activate the negative elements of a schematic network together with a "mugging" script and a fear/flight response.[23]

Priming also exerts a powerful impact on which schemas are activated by a particular stimulus. Priming refers to the notion that people's judgment, attitudes, and behavior can be influenced by incidental cues in their surroundings. Exposure to subtle situational cues, such as words, people, and even scent or physical objects, can automatically activate knowledge structures in memory such as trait concepts, stereotypes, and goals. Such automatic activation can occur without people's intention or awareness and carry over for at least a while to exert an unintended influence on judgment and behavior.

For example, John Bargh and his colleagues primed people with words related to the elderly (e.g., Florida, bingo) in what was said to be a sentence unscrambling task.[24] After completing the task, when participants believed the session had ended, the researchers measured how long it took participants to walk to the elevator on their way out of the building. Surprisingly, participants primed with words related to the elderly walked significantly more slowly than other participants who were primed with neutral words (e.g., normal, send). In another study, Bargh and his colleagues found that people primed with words related to rudeness (e.g., disturb, impolitely) were subsequently quicker to interrupt an

---

20. Susan T. Fiske and Martha G. Cox, *Person Concepts: The Effect of Target Familiarity and Descriptive Purpose on the Process of Describing Others*, 47 JOURNAL OF PERSONALITY 136–61 (1979).

21. Felicia Pratto, and John P. Oliver, Automatic vigilance: *The Attention-Grabbing Power of Negative Social Information*, JOURNAL OF PERSONALITY AND SOCIAL PSYCHOLOGY (1991).

22. Felicia Pratto, and John A. Bargh, *Stereotyping Based on Apparently Individuating Information: Trait and Global Components of Sex Stereotypes Under Attention Overload*, 27 JOURNAL OF EXPERIMENTAL SOCIAL PSYCHOLOGY 26 (1991); E. Tory Higgins, and Gilliam A. King, *Accessibility of Social Constructs: Information-Processing Consequences of Individual and Contextual Variability* (1981), *in* PERSONALITY, COGNITION, AND SOCIAL INTERACTION 69–121 (Nancy Cantor and John F. Kihlstrom eds., Hillsdale, NJ: Erlbaum, 1986); Robert S. Wyer and Thomas K. Srull, *Human Cognition in its Social Context*, PSYCHOLOGICAL REVIEW, 93, 322–59.

23. Jerry Kang, *Trojan Horses of Race*, 118 HARV. L. REV. 1489–1593 (2005).

24. John A. Bargh, Mark Chen, and Lara Burrows, *Automaticity of Social Behavior: Direct Effects of Trait Construct and Stereotype Activation on Action*, 71(2) JOURNAL OF PERSONALITY AND SOCIAL PSYCHOLOGY 230–44 (1996).

ongoing conversation between the experimenter and a third person than people primed with neutral words. These findings imply that the mental circuits used to perceive social stimuli, such as words, are closely linked to behavioral schemata and other mental representations that affect people's judgments and behavior.

Priming effects not only have consequences for simple, behavioral responses such as speed of walking, but can also affect more complex behaviors and goals.[25] One group of White participants was asked to write about a day in the life of Tyrone Walker, who most people assumed to be an African American. Other White participants were asked to write about a day in the life of Eric Walker, who they assumed to be White. Next, all participants were asked to complete a math section of the Graduate Record Examination (GRE). Participants who wrote about Tyrone Walker performed poorly compared to those who wrote about Eric Walker.

As this example illustrates, racial stereotype activation can elicit maladaptive, stereotype-consistent behavior among individuals who hold a stereotype. In other words, because the stereotype of African Americans includes an association with low academic achievement, activating the African American stereotype nonconsciously caused people to behave in a way consistent with that stereotype.

Priming can take the form of entirely unrelated stimuli occurring before the event—for example, seeing a film (not necessarily about race) that leaves the viewer with feelings of brotherly love on the one hand, or dread on the other. One can also be primed by one's own thoughts. For example, walking down a deserted Brooklyn street late at night might give rise to scary images or feelings. Such thoughts, even if subliminal and fleeting can promote, or *prime*, a negative construal of inherently incoming perception.[26]

Finally, schema activation can be influenced by the perceiver's *interaction goals*. Much of our interaction with other people is motivated toward some end. When you first meet a new coworker upon whom you must depend for the success of your own efforts, you will probably be motivated to like the person and feel confident in his or her abilities. To feel otherwise would prompt distress. Likewise, if you need surgery, you will be motivated to perceive the surgeon who will be operating on you as competent. People who are motivated to avoid prejudice tend to monitor their own reactions to members of other groups, attempting to notice and correct for the effects of stereotypes or other forms of bias. We discuss issues relating to controlling or correcting for the biasing effects of stereotype activation later in Section 11.7.

---

25. *Based on* S. Christian Wheeler, Jarvis W. Blair, and Richard E. Petty, *Think Unto Others: The Self-Destructive Impact of Negative Racial Stereotypes*, 37 Journal of Experimental Social Psychology 173–80 (2001).

26. Jerome Bruner, *On Perceptual Readiness*, 64 Psychological Review 123 (1957); Jerome Bruner, *Going Beyond the Information Given*, *in* Contemporary Approaches to Cognition, Jerome Bruner, ed., (Cambridge, MA: Harvard University Press, 1957).

11.4 THE EFFECTS OF SOCIAL SCHEMAS ON SOCIAL PERCEPTION AND JUDGMENT

To summarize, the processes by which we schematize a person encountered in our social experience are largely automatic, remarkably complex, and subject to influences that are not within our consciousness. Once activated, a social schema supplies the perceiver with a set of meanings about the person perceived. It determines what we will "see" in an individual's behavior and creates an expectation that later-perceived information about the person will match the concepts constituting the schema.

Stereotypes and other social schemas bias person perception and judgment in four broad ways, each of which is described in the material that follows. These include:

- the characterization of ambiguous behavior;
- causal attribution;
- the way experience of the schematized person is stored in and retrieved from memory; and
- the way such information is used in making judgments about the person.

Moreover, social schemas, such as stereotypes or person prototypes, influence how a social perceiver *behaves* toward the person perceived. This behavior can in turn alter how the target responds to the perceiver, often setting up a self-fulfilling prophesy effect that serves to reinforce the perceiver's stereotyped expectancies.

11.4.1 The Effects of Social Schemas on the Characterization of Ambiguous Behavior

In 1980, social psychologists H. Andrew Sagar and Janet Schofield conducted a now classic experiment examining the effects of racial stereotypes on children's characterizations of ambiguous behavior.[27] They presented elementary school students with cartoon-like drawings of two students sitting in a classroom, one behind the other, together with this verbal story: "Mark was sitting at his desk, working on his social studies assignment, when David started poking him in the back with the eraser end of his pencil. Mark just kept on working. David kept poking him for a while, and then he finally stopped." Participants were asked whether they thought David's behavior was playful, friendly, mean, or threatening. When the cartoon depicted David as Black, participants judged his behavior to be more mean and threatening and less playful and friendly. The opposite result obtained when he was White.

27. Andrew H. Sagar, and Janet W. Schofield, *Racial and Behavioral Cues in Black and White Children's Perceptions of Ambiguously Aggressive Acts*, 39 JOURNAL OF PERSONALITY AND SOCIAL PSYCHOLOGY 590–98 (1980).

Sagar and Schofield's results replicated the finding of an earlier experiment by Birt Duncan conducted in 1976. In Duncan's study, White college students watched one of four videotapes in which two males discussed alternative solutions to a problem. Participants were told they were watching a live interaction happening in another room, and that its purpose was to develop a new system for rating interpersonal behavior. While the videotape played, a buzzer rang at specified intervals, signaling participants to categorize the behavior they were then viewing in one of ten categories and to indicate its intensity on an 8-point scale.

As the videotaped discussion progressed, the dialogue became increasingly heated. Finally, one of the actors (the protagonist) shoved the other (the victim). At that point, the buzzer rang (not for the first time), and participants were asked to characterize and rate the intensity of the protagonist's behavior. As in the Sagar and Schofield study, the protagonist's race significantly affected how participants characterized the shove. If the protagonist was White, his behavior was characterized as "playing around" or "dramatizes." If he was Black, it was characterized as "aggressive" or "violent."[28]

Perhaps the most dramatic demonstration of the ways in which implicit stereotypes can influence how ambiguous behaviors are construed comes from a 1983 experiment on stereotyping and socioeconomic class by John Darley and Paget Gross. Darley and Gross had participants view one of two videotapes, each portraying a school-age child named Hannah at play. Her behavior was identical on both tapes, but one depicted Hannah playing on a stark, fenced-in, asphalt school yard in a rundown urban neighborhood. In this condition researchers told participants that Hannah's parents had only a high school education, that her father worked as a meatpacker, and that her mother was a seamstress who worked at home. The other videotape, which was shown to a second group of participants, portrayed Hannah playing in a tree-lined park in an upper middle-class neighborhood. Her school was depicted as a large, attractive, modern building, with adjacent playing fields and a shaded playground. Her father was described as an attorney and her mother as a freelance writer.

Participants were then asked to predict whether Hanna would perform academically at, above, or below grade level. Reluctantly, and often protesting being asked to base their prediction on stereotypes, most participants in both conditions predicted that Hannah would perform at grade level. In other words, they refused to express an initial prediction based on the stereotypes about academic achievement associated with high and low socioeconomic status.

28. Birt L. Duncan, *Differential Social Perception and Attribution of Intergroup Violence: Testing the Lower Limits of Stereotyping of Blacks*, 34 J. Personality & Soc. Psychol. 590–98 (1976).

Not all participants were asked to predict Hannah's achievement level right away, however. Some watched a second videotape before they were asked to predict Hannah's academic performance. This video, which was identical across both conditions, depicted Hannah responding verbally to twenty-five achievement test problems. Researchers told participants that the test included easy, moderate, and difficult problems. Hannah's performance was designed to be ambiguous. After watching the second video, participants who had seen the high socioeconomic status (SES) Hannah rated her academic ability significantly higher than did participants who saw her low SES double. Open-ended comments revealed differences in perception as well. For example, participants reported the low-income Hannah as having "difficulty accepting new information," while they frequently described high-income Hannah as demonstrating the "ability to apply what she knows to unfamiliar problems."

Darley and Gross suggested that exposure to ambiguous diagnostic information actually *promotes* social stereotyping.[29] People who do not believe it appropriate to base social predictions on stereotypes based on socioeconomic information alone, nonetheless did so in what they perceived to be a more diagnostic context—even though it was thoroughly ambiguous. From this, Darley and Gross argued that stereotypes function not so much as conscious ex ante decision rules, but as dormant expectancies that impose a hypothesis-confirming bias on the interpretation of incoming social information.

The effects of stereotypes and other schematic expectancies on social perception and judgment have been well documented across a variety of different contexts.[30] Perhaps most disturbing are recent studies showing that that a target person's race has a significant effect on whether both Black and White participants think he is holding a weapon, like a knife or a gun, as opposed to a harmless object, like a wallet or cell phone.[31]

Although most of the research on the biasing effects of social schemas has focused on race, age, and gender stereotypes, the basic idea that schemas shape how we interpret other people's behavior applies in a variety of other contexts

---

29. John M. Darley and Paget H. Gross, *A Hypothesis-Confirming Bias in Labeling Effects,* 44 J. PERSONALITY & SOC. PSYCHOL. 20–33 (1983).

30. David Dunning and David A. Sherman, *Stereotypes and Tacit Inference,* 73 J. PERSONALITY & SOC. PSYCHOL. 459–71 (1997); Zeva Kunda and Bonnie Sherman-Williams, *Stereotypes and the Construal of Individuating Information,* 19 J. PERSONALITY & SOC. PSYCHOL. 90–99 (1993).

31. Joshua Correll, Geoffrey R. Urland, and Tiffany A. Ito, *Event-Related Potentials and the Decision to Shoot: The Role of Threat Perception and Cognitive Control,* 42 JOURNAL OF EXPERIMENTAL SOCIAL PSYCHOLOGY 120–28 (2006); Joshua Correll, Bernadette Park, Charles M. Judd, and Bernd Wittenbrink, *The Police Officer's Dilemma: Using Ethnicity to Disambiguate Potentially Threatening Individuals,* 83 J. PERSONALITY & SOC. PSYCH. 1314 (2002); B. Keith. Payne, *Prejudice and Perception: The Role of Automatic and Controlled Processes in Misperceiving a Weapon,* 81 J. PERSONALITY & SOC. PSYCHOL . 181–192, 185–186 (2001).

relevant to lawyering. Consistent with naïve realism (Section 9.8), in conflict situations, for example, people tend to stereotype their adversaries as fanatical, grasping, and "out to get them" and then interpret adversaries' behavior in ways that make negotiated agreement more difficult.[32]

In any social context, once we have characterized another person in a particular way, we may misinterpret his actions or misattribute his intentions in ways that preserve our impression about him but totally miss the mark in terms of accuracy. These sorts of misapprehensions can lead to inaccurate predictions of others' future behavior and unfair attribution of blame and praise, and can also injure our relationships with constituents, clients, coworkers, business partners, witnesses, opposing counsel, and those who matter in our personal lives.

The Burden on "Tokens"

In any social situation, for any of a number of reasons, a particular person in a group may stand out. This *social salience* can derive from a number of sources. A person may be made salient, for example, by being the only woman, visibly disabled person, or member of a racial or ethnic minority in a given group. A person may become salient by behaving in an unexpected way, for example, counter-stereotypically, or by dominating the visual field by virtue of his or her physical appearance or location.[33]

Regardless of why a person becomes salient, that salience tends to affect in systematic ways how the person is perceived. So, for example, in a now classic study, Harvard psychologist Shelley Taylor and her colleagues explored the consequences of a minority group member's being a "token" or "solo" in a small group. In the first experiment in that study, participants listened to a tape recording of a discussion among six males. As each person spoke, the

32. Robert. J. Robinson and Dacher Keltner, *Defending the Status Quo: Power and Bias in Social Conflict*, 23 Personality and Social Psychology Bulletin 1066–77 (1997); Robert J. Robinson and Raymond A. Friedman, *Mistrust and Misconstrual in Union-Management Relationships: Causal Accounts in Adversarial Contexts*, 6 International Journal of Conflict Management 312–27 (1995); Roderick M. Kramer, *The Sinister Attribution Error: Paranoid Cognition and Collective Distrust in Organization*, 18 Motivation and Emotion 199–230 (1994); Dacher Keltner and Robert J. Robinson, *Imagined Ideological Differences in Conflict Escalation and Resolution*, 4 International Journal of Conflict Management 249–62 (1993).

33. Leslie Z. McArthur, What Grabs You?: The Role of Attention in Impression Formation and Causal Attribution in Social Cognition (1981); Shelley E. Taylor and Susan T. Fiske, *Salience, Attention, and Attribution: Top of the Head Phenomena, in* 11 Advances in Experimental Social Psychology 249, 264–65, Leonard Berkowitz ed. (New York: Academic Press, 1978).

experimenters projected a slide of that person's picture. By playing the same tape recording, while varying the race of the person supposedly speaking, Taylor and her colleagues compared participants' judgments of a Black person when he was the only Black person in an otherwise all White group, and when he was in a fully integrated group. In the "solo" condition, participants judged the Black person in more extreme ways and perceived him as playing a more prominent role in the discussion than Blacks were perceived in the "integrated" condition.

In a second experiment, Taylor and her colleagues found similar, even stronger effects on perceptions of solos in gender-mixed groups. Token women and minorities, in short, are rated more extremely and are viewed (for better or for worse) as playing a more prominent role in group process, than are women or minorities in integrated groups.

11.4.2 The Effects of Social Schemas on Memory

The need to reconstruct the past pervades legal problem solving and decision making in virtually every imaginable context. In describing a problematic situation to a lawyer in an initial interview, clients are almost always asked to describe "what happened?" Identifying the source of a presenting problem almost always requires piecing together information about when the problem first occurred, and what events preceded or accompanied it. Similarly, when we are called upon to make judgments of other people with whom we have had contact, we almost always search our memories for judgment-relevant events.

But social memory, like all memory, is not like looking into a filing cabinet and extracting a set of intact, relevant files. But, as discussed in Section 9.2, memory is a reconstructive process. Our recollections (or, perhaps more accurately, *re-collections*) of events are shaped by how we perceived those events as they were occurring, how we encoded them into and stored them in memory, and how we extracted them from memory and combined them with other information. Stereotypes, person prototypes, and other kinds of social expectancies operate at every stage of the memory process.

As we have already seen, stereotypes and related mental representations influence how we characterize other people's behavior. This initial understanding of what is happening in turn influences the way in which we remember what happened. This phenomenon can be attributed to a number of interrelated phenomena.

11.4.2.a Expectancies, Attention Allocation, and Encoding into Memory We are constantly bombarded with far more information than we can process, and for this reason, we selectively direct our attention to particular aspects of our physical and social environment. And as a general rule, we attend preferentially to incoming information that reinforces our prior expectancies, especially when we are stressed or emotionally agitated.[34] Increased focus on a particular event increases its memorability, which in turn increases the likelihood that it will be remembered at a later date.[35]

Expectancy-consistent events are more likely to be remembered not only because we are more likely to attend to them, but also because of the way they are encoded into memory. When we view another person's behavior, we often spontaneously assign it a trait attribution. This inferred trait itself becomes part of the stored memory of the event which triggered it.[15]

Experimental evidence supports the hypothesis that prior expectancies influence social memory at the encoding stage. One example can be found in a 1979 study by Myron Rothbart and his associates. They presented participants with identical sets of fifty behavioral descriptions of a target male individual. The items presented described actions that could be characterized as either "friendly," "unfriendly," "intelligent," "unintelligent," or unrelated to any of these four constructs. Half of the participants were led to believe that the target was intellectual and half that the target was friendly. In each group, half of the participants were given this expectancy before being presented with the behavioral descriptions and half afterward.

Rothbart found that participants recalled behaviors that confirmed their prior expectancies more readily than those which disconfirmed or were unrelated to them, but this effect was found only when the expectancy was induced *prior* to the presentation of the behaviors. Participants who viewed the behaviors before any expectancy was created were far more evenhanded in their memory for confirming and disconfirming information. From these findings, Rothbart and his colleagues inferred that selective retrieval alone could not account for the observed memorial bias in favor of expectancy-confirming events. Whatever was causing the bias operated, at least in part, much earlier in the attention/encoding/storage/recall continuum.

11.4.2.b Prior Expectancies and Retrieval from Memory Even assuming that we were to encode expectancy-confirming and expectancy-disconfirming information about other people in an evenhanded fashion, those expectancies could—and in fact do—bias memory at the point of recall. This effect is mediated by what social psychologists Joshua Klayman and Young-won Ha refer to as a "positive test strategy." (See Section 10.3.4)

To say that people use a positive test strategy means that, in evaluating the soundness of a particular proposition, people intuitively search for evidence that confirms it. This tendency applies both when searching through memory for

34. David W. Jamieson and Mark P. Zanna, *Need for Structure in Attitude Formation and Expression, in* ATTITUDE STRUCTURE AND FUNCTION 383–406 (Anthony R. Pratkanis, S. J. Breckler, and Anthony G. Greenwald eds., Hillsdale, NJ: Erlbaum, 1989).

35. Joshua Klayman and Young-Won Ha, *Confirmation, Disconfirmation, and Information in Hypothesis Testing,* 94 PSYCHOLOGICAL REVIEW 211–28 (1987).

preexisting evidence relating to a proposition,[36] and when searching the external environment for new or additional information.[35] Numerous studies have shown that expectancy-disconfirming information is also salient, but its use in a particular judgment task is often lessened through attribution to external or transient factors that leave the expectancy itself intact.[37]

To summarize what we have covered so far, once we have formed an initial impression of a person, either because we hold a stereotype relating to a social group to which they belong, or because some prior experience with them has caused us to characterize them in some way, that initial impression influences in significant ways our subsequent perceptions of and judgments about the person. Initial impressions influence subjective construal of the person's ambiguous behavior. They also influence how we will store information about the person in memory, whether and how we will retrieve it from memory, and how we will combine it with other information in making a subsequent judgment. As we will now see, our expectancies can also influence the ways in which we behave toward the target person, which in turn, may affect how they behave in response.

11.4.3 The Effects of Stereotypes on Causal Attribution and Behavioral Prediction

Stereotypes, person prototypes, and other social expectancies exert powerful effects on how we attribute people's outcomes or behaviors and on our predictions of how they will behave in the future. Specifically, when members of stereotyped groups behave in stereotype-confirming ways, we tend to attribute their behavior to stable, dispositional factors, like innate ability or character traits. However, when a stereotyped target behaves in a stereotype-inconsistent way, we tend either to explain away the discrepancy by attributing the behavior to situational factors, or to "exceptionalize" the person, rather than question the accuracy of our stereotype. Moreover, we tend to view stereotype-consistent behavior as more predictive than stereotype-inconsistent behavior. For judges, prosecutors, parole and probation officers, and social workers who make recommendations to judicial tribunals, misattribution or biased prediction of outcomes or transgressions can significantly influence, among other things, charging, sentencing, probation, parole, and child custody decisions.

The most dramatic laboratory demonstration of stereotype-driven attribution bias, and of its effects on behavior prediction and the selection of criminal penalties, appears in two experiments conducted by Galen Bodenhausen and Robert Wyer in 1985. In both experiments, participants read a case file describing a behavioral transgression by another person. In the first experiment, the case file

---

36. Mark Snyder, and Nancy Cantor, *Hypothesis Testing in Social Interaction,* 36 J. Personality & Social Psychol. 1202–12 (1979).

37. Jennifer Crocker, Darlene B. Hanna, and Renee Weber, *Person Memory and Causal Attributions,* 44 J. Personality & Social Psychol. 55 (1983).

contained only general biographic, demographic, and job-related information about the person. In the second experiment, the case file also contained information about the person's background and life circumstances at the time the transgression occurred.

After reading the case file, participants were asked to predict whether the transgression would recur and to recommend a negative sanction. In one condition, the transgression was stereotypic of the target person's ethnic group, in a second, the transgression was stereotype-inconsistent, and in a third, no stereotype was activated. When the transgression was stereotypic of the target's ethnicity, participants perceived it as more likely to recur. Participants assigned more severe punishments in that situation than when the transgression was stereotype-inconsistent or when no stereotype had been activated.[38]

Findings of this sort are not restricted to laboratory settings. In a 1998 investigation of the Washington State juvenile justice system, University of Washington sociologists George Bridges and Sara Steen demonstrated that, controlling for a large number of plausible explanatory factors, African American youth were denied probation significantly more frequently than White youth, and that this disparity could be traced to attribution bias on the part of court personnel.

Specifically, Bridges and Steen demonstrated that juvenile court officers who made probation versus incarceration recommendations to judges, tended systematically to attribute criminal behavior by African American offenders to dispositional factors, while attributing equivalent criminal behaviors by White youth to external, situational variables. These differences in the locus of attribution, in turn, influenced the officers' assessments of moral culpability and likelihood of future criminal behavior, which in turn led to racially biased recommendation relating to the probation versus incarceration decision.[39]

In short, stereotypes influence attributions. Attributions influence predictions and judgments of personal responsibility. And all three influence judgments and decisions made about the stereotyped individual.

11.5 ON THE SELF-FULFILLING NATURE OF SOCIAL STEREOTYPES

As we have seen, people tend to use social knowledge structures to fill in gaps in the information they have about another person and to predict how that person

---

38. Galen Bodenhausen and Robert Wyer, *Effects of Stereotypes in Decision Making and Information-Processing Strategies*, 48 Journal of Personality and Social Psychology 267–82 (1985).

39. George S. Bridges and Sara Steen, *Racial Disparities in Official Assessments of Juvenile Offenders: Attributional Stereotypes as Mediating Mechanisms*, 63 Am. Soc. Rev. 554 (1998).

will behave in the future.[40] Once a perceiver has formed expectancies about a target person, those expectancies can play a significant role in shaping the perceiver's behavior toward the target in subsequent interactions. This may, in turn, affect the target's behavior toward the perceiver, often in ways that confirm the perceiver's initial expectancy. This *behavioral confirmation effect* represents one way in which stereotypes can function as self-fulfilling prophesies. *Stereotype threat* represents a second process by which stereotypes become self-fulfilling. In stereotype threat situations, a person's awareness that his or her group is negatively stereotyped impairs his or her performance in a stereotype-relevant domain.

11.5.1 The Behavioral Confirmation Effect

If we think people are unimportant, or "not real bright," we may treat them dismissively. If we think they are aggressive or "chippy," we may be defensive when we interact with them, betraying our discomfort through subtle facial or verbal cues, by cutting verbal interactions short, or through our body posture. If we expect people to be talented and interesting, we are apt to be solicitous and warm in our interactions with them, drawing them out, smiling frequently, and listening attentively. Naturally, the way we behave toward other people influences how they behave toward us in response. In many cases, their responsive behavior serves to confirm our initial expectancy, providing us with further evidence of "how they are."

In one of the earliest demonstrations of this phenomenon, Robert Rosenthal and Lenore Jacobson administered an intelligence test to students in an elementary school. They randomly selected 20 percent of these students and told their teachers that their scores predicted that they would academically outperform their classmates in the near future. Eight months later, Rosenthal and his colleagues retested students at the school. They found that those randomly designated as "high performers" had in fact overperformed their peers on the subsequent test. The experimenters explained their results by suggesting that teachers formed an expectancy of the students in the randomly designated "high performer" group, and that this expectancy had influenced teachers' interactions with the students in ways that enhanced those students' performance.[41]

While Rosenthal and Jacobson's study was subsequently criticized on methodological grounds, its basic finding, that expectancies tend to create self-fulfilling prophesies, is one of the best-replicated findings in social psychology. It has been observed in connection with different types of expectancies across many different

40. James M. Olson, Neal J. Roese and Mark P. Zanna, *Expectancies, in* Social Psychology: Handbook of Basic Principles 211–38, E. Tory Higgens and Arie Kruglanski eds., (New York: Guilford, 1996).

41. Robert Rosenthal, and Lenore Jacobson, Pygmalion in the Classroom (New York: Holt, Rinehart, & Winston, 1968).

domains, including interview and therapy settings, bargaining and "get-acquainted" encounters, educational settings, and mother-infant interactions.[42]

Social psychologist Edward Jones illustrates the process components of behavioral confirmation as shown in Figure 11.5.

The first three components in this model should be familiar by now. They represent two processes discussed earlier in this chapter—the use of expectancies in interpreting ambiguous behavior and in behavioral attribution. But what evidence exists regarding step four, which Jones refers to as the *expectancy-behavior link,* and step five, the *behavior-behavior link?*

With respect to step four, there now exists a large body of evidence demonstrating that stereotypes influence subtle aspects of the stereotype-holder's behavior toward or in the presence of a stereotyped target. For example, in a now classic study conducted at Princeton in 1974, Carl Word, Mark Zanna, and Joel Cooper showed that White participants who interviewed Black and White job applicants behaved quite differently toward Black and White interviewees. (The "applicants" were actually confederates, trained to respond in uniform ways.) In interviewing Black confederate/applicants, White participants made more speech errors, maintained greater seating distances, and ended interviews sooner.[43]

In a 2001 extension of Carl Word, Mark Zanna, and Joel Cooper's findings, Allen McConnell and Jill Leibold demonstrated that participants high in implicit racial bias[44] interacted with Black as opposed to White trained experimenters with less smiling, shorter speaking times, higher rates of fidgeting, more speech errors and hesitations, and fewer extemporaneous social comments.[45]

More recently, research in social cognitive neuroscience has explored some of the physiological mechanisms mediating these expectancy-behavior links. So, for example, using functional magnetic resonance imaging (fMRI) technology

---

42. Steven L. Neuberg, *Social Motives and Expectancy-Tinged Social Interactions, in* Handbook of Motivation and Cognition, Volume 3: The Interpersonal Context, Richard M. Sorrentino and E. Tory Higgins eds., (New York: Guilford, 1996).

43. Carl O. Word, Mark P. Zanna, and Joel Cooper, *The Nonverbal Mediation of Self-Fulfilling Prophecies in Interracial Interaction,* 10 Journal of Experimental Social Psychology 109–20 (1974).

44. In this experiment, as in most recent social cognition research, implicit bias is measured through the Implicit Association Test (IAT). Using a comparative reaction time method, the IAT measures the strength of associations between group constructs (Black/White; young/old; male/female; straight/gay) and traits or global attitudes (good/bad; science/ humanities; street-smart/book-smart). Interested readers can read about and/or take a demonstration IAT by visiting the Project Implicit Web site, at http://implicit.harvard.edu/ implicit . For a discussion of the IAT, *see* Brian A. Nosek et. al., *Harvesting Implicit Group Attitudes and Beliefs from a Demonstration Web Site,* 6 Group Dynamics 101, 105 (2002).

45. Allen R. McConnell and Jill M. Leibold, *Relations Among the Implicit Association Test, Discriminatory Behavior, and Explicit Measures of Racial Attitudes,* 37 Journal of Experimental Social Psychology 435 (2001).

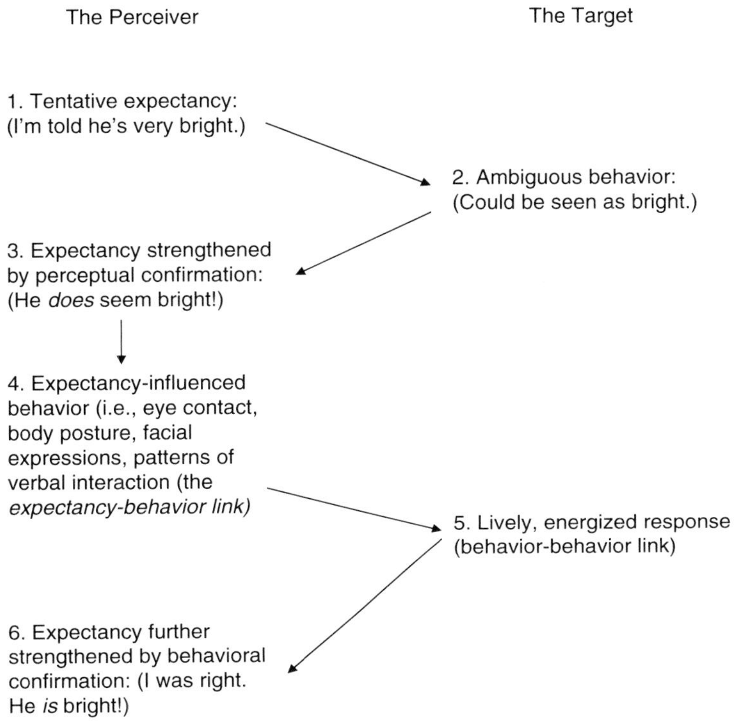
The Perceiver
The Target
1. Tentative expectancy: (I'm told he's very bright.)
2. Ambiguous behavior: (Could be seen as bright.)
3. Expectancy strengthened by perceptual confirmation: (He *does* seem bright!)
4. Expectancy-influenced behavior (i.e., eye contact, body posture, facial expressions, patterns of verbal interaction (the *expectancy-behavior link)*
5. Lively, energized response (behavior-behavior link)
6. Expectancy further strengthened by behavioral confirmation: (I was right. He *is* bright!)

FIGURE 11.5 JONES'S MODEL OF THE BEHAVIORAL CONFIRMATION PROCESS.

and facial electromyography (EMG), a technique for measuring electrical activity in facial muscles, a recent study showed that participants whose performance on the Implicit Association Test (IAT) revealed negative implicit attitudes toward Blacks exhibited both a heightened startle response (measured by EMG eyeblink potentiation) and elevated amygdala[46] activation when viewing photographs of unfamiliar Black faces.[47] A similar study showed that White participants who favored White over Black applicants in a resume review task registered more EMG activity in the muscles controlling smiling when they reviewed White applicants' resumes than when they reviewed Black applicants' resumes.

---

46. The amygdala is a small, bilateral structure located in the brain's temporal lobe. It plays a significant role in emotional learning and evaluation, and particularly in the evocation of emotional responses to fear or aggression-inducing stimuli. Ralph Adolphs, Daniel Tranel, and Antonio R. Damasio, *The Human Amygdala in Social Judgment*, 393 NATURE 470 (1998).

47. Elizabeth A. Phelps, Kevin J. O'Connor, William A. Cunningham, E. Sumie Funayama, J. Christopher Gatenby, John C. Gore, and Mahzarin R. Banaji, *Performance on Indirect Measures of Race Evaluation Predicts Amygdala Activation*, 12 J. COGNITIVE NEUROSCIENCE 729-738, 730 (2002).

Members of negatively stereotyped groups often claim that they can "just tell" when someone they are dealing with is biased against them. Given that people are exquisitely attuned to subtle facial, verbal, and other physical cues, and use these to decode others' attitudes toward them, it is certainly reasonable to believe that that subtle behavioral "leakages" from implicitly biased perceivers can be sensed by members of stereotyped groups.

Just as perceivers' behavior toward stereotyped targets is affected by the expectancies that stereotypes activate, stereotyped targets respond in kind, thus creating the *behavior-behavior* link described as step 5 of Jones's model. The earliest evidence for the behavior-behavior link comes from Rosenthal and Jacobson's 1968 study, described earlier, in which students responded to their teacher's arbitrarily created expectancies by academically outperforming their peers. Substantial additional evidence for the link has accumulated since then.

For example, in the McConnell and Leibold study described above, White confederates were trained to mimic the "friendly" and "unfriendly" interview styles that had been observed in Word, Zanna, and Cooper's 1974 experiment. In the "friendly" condition, trained interviewers sat closer to interviewees, made fewer speech errors, and extended the length of the interview. Blind raters (i.e., people who knew nothing about the nature of the experiment) coded the interviewees' behavior, and found that those interviewees who had been interviewed using the "unfriendly" style performed more poorly in the interviews than White interviewees who had been treated in the "friendly" style. Similar effects were observed in experiments manipulating perceivers' beliefs that they were speaking with either an attractive or unattractive partner[48] or to an obese or normal weight partner. More recently, Serena Chen and John Bargh demonstrated that African American targets who interacted with White participants who had been subliminally primed with pictures of African American faces were rated by condition-blind coders as behaving with more verbal hostility than African American targets who had interacted with Whites primed with Caucasian faces. The targets themselves had not been primed, and yet their behavior conformed to the stereotypic expectancies induced in their partners.[49]

In short, there is ample evidence, far more than can be reviewed here, suggesting that when subtle expectancy-consistent behaviors "leak out" of stereotype-holding perceivers, targets respond in kind, often contributing to stereotype confirmation. While these effects can be moderated by such factors as

48. Allen. R. McConnell and Jill M. Leibold, *Relations Among the Implicit Association Test, Discriminatory Behavior, and Explicit Measures of Racial Attitudes*, *supra* note 45.

49. Mark Chen, and John A. Bargh, *Nonconscious Behavioral Confirmation Processes: The Self-Fulfilling Consequences of Automatic Stereotype Activation*, 33 Journal of Experimental Social Psychology 541–60 (1997).

perceiver self-presentation goals[50] or conscious efforts by the target to behave in expectancy nonconfirming ways,[51] interrupting the cycle is difficult. We explore issues relating to this and other mechanisms for debiasing social interactions in Section 11.7.

11.5.2 Stereotype Threat

During the 1990s, Stanford psychologist Claude Steele and his colleagues conducted a series of experiments investigating the well-documented tendency of members of stigmatized groups to underperform their nonstigmatized counterparts on tests measuring academic aptitude or achievement.[52] In the first of these studies, Steele and Joshua Aronson gave a difficult verbal test to African American and European American Stanford undergraduates.[53] Half of the students (the "diagnostic" condition) were told that the test would measure their verbal ability. The other half (the "nondiagnostic" condition) were told that the purpose of the experiment was to investigate problem-solving strategies, and that performance on the test was in no way indicative of aptitude or achievement. In the diagnostic condition, African American students underperformed their White counterparts. However, when the test was presented as nondiagnostic, Black and White students performed equally well.

Steele and Aronson's basic finding has now been replicated in a variety of contexts. Rupert Brown and Robert Josephs varied the perceived diagnosticity of a difficult mathematics test for males and females with equal backgrounds in mathematics. Women underperformed when they thought the test was diagnostic, but performed equally well when they believed it was not. In another experiment, the gender effect was shown to be even stronger when the math test was described as diagnostic of *weakness* in math, as opposed to strength.[54] In other

---

50. Steven L. Neuberg, Nicole T. Judice, Lynn M. Virdin, and Mary A. Carrillo, *Perceiver Self-Presentation Goals as Moderators of Expectancy Influences: Ingratiation and the Disconfirmation of Negative Expectancies,* 64 JOURNAL OF PERSONALITY AND SOCIAL PSYCHOLOGY 409–20 (1993).

51. James L. Hilton, and John M. Darley, *Constructing Other Persons: A Limit on the Effect,* 21 JOURNAL OF EXPERIMENTAL SOCIAL PSYCHOLOGY 1–18 (1985); William B. Swann, Jr., and Robin J. Ely, *A Battle of Wills: Self-Verification Versus Behavioral Confirmation,* 46 JOURNAL OF PERSONALITY AND SOCIAL PSYCHOLOGY 1287–1302 (1984).

52. Claude M. Steele, *A Threat in the Air: How Stereotypes Shape Intellectual Identity and Performance of African Americans, 52* AMERICAN PSYCHOLOGIST 613–29 (1997).

53. Claude M. Steele and Joshua Aronson, *Stereotype Threat and the Intellectual Performance of African Americans,* JOURNAL OF PERSONALITY AND SOCIAL PSYCHOLOGY 69: 797–811 (1995).

54. Ryan P. Brown, and Robert A. Josephs, A *Burden of Proof: Stereotype Relevance and Gender Differences in Math Performance,* 76 JOURNAL OF PERSONALITY AND SOCIAL PSYCHOLOGY 246–57 (1999).

studies, stereotype threat effects have been found in Latinos and low socioeconomic status Whites.[55]

The way in which a test is framed and the conditions under which it is administered have a significant impact on whether stereotype threat occurs. For example, Steven Spencer, Claude Steele, and Diane Quinn demonstrated that the women-math stereotype threat effect could be eliminated when a test was described as being "gender fair." [56] Becca Levy found that elderly participants performed more poorly on a memory test after being primed with negative stereotypes of the elderly, but performed better when primed with positive stereotypes.[57] Stereotype threat is also affected by whether stigmatized group status is made salient before group members take a test. In one particularly fascinating study, priming Asian American women with female identity before taking a math test depressed their performance, while priming them with Asian identity enhanced it.[58]

The mechanisms underlying stereotype threat are not yet well understood. Claude Steele hypothesizes that, when members of negatively stereotyped groups know that their performance is being assessed in a stereotype-relevant domain, fear of confirming the negative stereotype impairs their performance. The effect, he suggests, occurs because this sense of self-threat raises anxiety levels and consumes cognitive resources.[59] Over time, Steele notes, the effects of stereotype threat on performance may cause promising minority and/or female students to disidentify with certain academic performance domains. Ironically, he notes, the very members of stigmatized groups who are, at the outset, *most* talented at a particular academic endeavor are also the most likely over time to suffer from stereotype threat and withdraw from academic pursuits in response to its painful effects.

---

55. Margaret Shih, Nalini Ambady, Jennifer A. Richeson, Kentaro Fujita, and Heather M. Gray, *Stereotype Performance Boosts: The Impact of Self-Relevance and the Manner of Stereotype Activation,* 83 JOURNAL OF PERSONALITY AND SOCIAL PSYCHOLOGY 638 (2002).

56. Steven J. Spencer, Claude M. Steele, and Diane M. Quinn. "*Stereotype Threat and Women's Math Performance.*" JOURNAL OF EXPERIMENTAL SOCIAL PSYCHOLOGY 35 (1999): 4–28.

57. Becca Levy, *Improving Memory in Old Age Through Implicit Self-Stereotyping,* JOURNAL OF PERSONALITY AND SOCIAL PSYCHOLOGY 71: 1092–1107 (1996).

58. *Id.*; Margaret Shih, Todd L. Pittinsky, and Nalini Ambady, *Stereotype Susceptibility: Identity Salience and Shifts in Quantitative Performance,* 10 PSYCHOLOGICAL SCIENCE 80–83 (1999).

59. Claude. M. Steele, S. J. Spencer, and Joshua Aronson, *Contending with Group Image: The Psychology of Stereotype and Social Identity Threat, in* ADVANCES IN EXPERIMENTAL SOCIAL PSYCHOLOGY (VOL. 34), 379–440 (Mark Zanna ed., New York: Academic Press, 2002).

11.6 BEYOND STEREOTYPES: DISPOSITIONISM AND SITUATIONISM IN SOCIAL ATTRIBUTION

The significance we attach to an event depends largely on the causes to which we attribute it. Without even being aware of it, we constantly ask and answer the question "why?" "Why did the head of the Terra Nueva Tenants Association cancel a meeting scheduled with Luis Trujillo?" "Why was Christine Lamm so quiet in that case strategy meeting this morning?" Human beings are prolific producers of causal theories. As we move through the social world, we are constantly attributing causation to other people's behavior and then using the resulting attributions to assign responsibility and predict how they will behave in the future.[60] Much of this happens within System 1, automatically and unconsciously.[61] Even when it is deliberate, however, we make systematic errors in attributing causation.

In attributing the causes of other people's behavior, we tend to search for explanations that are stable and informative in predicting how they will act in the future.[62] Imagine, for example, that Luis Trujillo and Christine Lamm have a meeting, which ends with a heated argument about whether Trujillo is obstructing Lamm's access to tenants at Terra Nueva by not providing her with a list of their names, addresses, and phone numbers. At one point, Trujillo explodes, "You don't think I care about the tenants? They're *my* people." Christine responds, "don't give me that crap! I'll see you in court." Lamm leaves the meeting thinking, "So this is a guy with a chip on his shoulder, always ready to play the race card." Trujillo leaves with terms like "short-fused," "paranoid," "explosive," and "loose cannon" in his mind. Each of them thinks that the other's behavior reflects character traits that will make it very difficult to cooperate going forward and starts devising strategies to deal with the other.

Like Lamm and Trujillo, most of us tend to attribute behavior to other's dispositions, character traits, or attitudes (real or imagined), and to discount situational factors—the particular social environment or context in which behavior occurs—in devising explanations for why a person behaved as he or she did on a particular occasion.

---

60. James S. Uleman, Leonard S. Newman, and Gordon B. Moskowitz, *People as Flexible Interpreters: Evidence and Issues from Spontaneous Trait Inference, in* ADVANCES IN EXPERIMENTAL SOCIAL PSYCHOLOGY (VOL. 28) 211–79 (Mark P. Zanna ed., San Diego: Academic Press, 1996).

61. Daniel T. Gilbert, *Thinking Lightly About Others: Automatic Components of the Social Inference Process, in* UNINTENDED THOUGHT 189–211 (James S. Uleman, and John A. Bargh eds., New York: Guilford Press, 1989); Yaakov Trope and Thomas Alfieri, *Effortfullness and Flexibility of Dispositional Judgment Processes*, 73 JOURNAL OF PERSONALITY AND SOCIAL PSYCHOLOGY 662–74 (1997).

62. Edward E. Jones and Keith E. Davis, *From Acts to Dispositions: The Attribution Process in Social Psychology, in* ADVANCES IN EXPERIMENTAL SOCIAL PSYCHOLOGY (VOL. 2) 219–66 (Leonard Berkowitz ed., New York: Academic Press, 1965).

This is one of the most significant findings of empirical social psychology in the latter part of the twentieth century. At least in Anglo American culture, the "intuitive psychologist" tends to overestimate the significance of dispositional factors and understate the significance of situational factors in attributing the causes of other people's behavior. Over time, this significance of this phenomenon has been judged so important that it has come to be called the "Fundamental Attribution Error."[63]

While we tend to attribute *other* people's behavior to dispositions rather than situations, when it comes to our *own* behavior, we favor situational attributions over dispositional ones—particularly when we are explaining our own personal failings.

This difference of perspective—the so-called "Actor-Observer Effect"[64]—explains interpersonal and social pathologies that can ultimately foment conflicts and make them more difficult to resolve once they emerge. Consider, for example, the dynamics leading to the breakdown of many marriages, business partnerships, and other collaborations. As difficulties are encountered and tensions mount, each party attributes her own behavior to features of the situation, and the other's to character flaws and failures. The result is an escalating cycle of blame, abdication of personal responsibility, and inattention to features of the environment (overwork, perverse incentive structures), which, if addressed, might put the conflict in a new light and assist in its resolution.

In the 1950s, Fritz Heider suggested that causal attribution plays a central role in assigning responsibility for particular outcomes and predicting people's behavior. We tend to distinguish between causes that differ on at least two dimensions. First, we distinguish between causes that are *internal* and *external* to the actor. For example, laziness or disorganization are internal explanations for tardiness, while getting stuck in a traffic jam caused by an accident is external. Second, we tend to distinguish between *stable* and *unstable* causal factors. Intelligence, for example, is stable; effort is unstable. These distinctions matter, Heider observed, because through their application we assign levels of responsibility for outcomes, and we judge how well a person's past outcomes will predict their future performance.[65]

---

63. Lee Ross, *The Intuitive Psychologist and His Shortcomings: Distortions in the Attribution Process, in* ADVANCES IN EXPERIMENTAL SOCIAL PSYCHOLOGY (VOL. 10) 173–220 (Leonard Berkowitz ed., New York: Academic Press, 1977).

64. Edward E. Jones and Robert E. Nisbett, *The Actor and the Observer: Divergent Perceptions of the Causes of the Behavior, in* ATTRIBUTION: PERCEIVING THE CAUSES OF BEHAVIOR 79–94 (Edward E. Jones, David E. Kanouse, Harold H. Kelley, Robert E. Nisbett, Stuart Valins, and Bernard Weiner eds., Morristown, NJ: General Learning Press, 1972).

65. Fritz HEIDER, THE PSYCHOLOGY OF INTERPERSONAL RELATIONS (Hoboken, NJ: John Wiley & Sons, Inc., 1958).

Bernard Weiner and his associates built on Heider's insights to construct the Heider/Weiner matrix to show how these parameters affect one's judgment and prediction of individuals' behavior. (See Table 11.1.)

TABLE 11.1 THE HEIDER/WEINER MATRIX

	Stable	Unstable
Internal Locus (dispositional)	Skill, laziness	Mood, task prioritization
	Higher predictive validity Higher moral responsibility	Lower predictive validity Higher moral responsibility
External Locus (situational)	Family resources and responsibilities, stable peer group influences, enduring commitments	Contributions of others, transient peer group influences, extenuating circumstances
	Higher predictive validity Lower moral responsibility	Lower predictive validity Lower moral responsibility

Behaviors attributed to *internal, stable* factors (i.e., skill, laziness, criminal propensity) are viewed both as highly predictive and warranting of moral judgment. Behaviors attributed to *internal, unstable* factors (e.g., moods or how one prioritizes tasks on a particular occasion) are also viewed as relevant to moral judgment, but as less predictive of future behavior. Attributions to *external, stable* factors diffuse moral responsibility, but are seen as predictive, while attributions to *external, unstable* factors do not provide a basis for either judgment or prediction.

Biases in causal attribution affect the exercise of professional judgment in lawyering, judging, policy making, and management, not to mention in our personal lives. First, our tendency to attribute our own failings or negative outcomes to situational factors (which we often overoptimistically view as transient) and to attribute others' failings or negative outcomes to internal, dispositional factors makes us vulnerable to a host of ego-enhancing biases. These biases often impair our willingness or ability to compromise with others, to be open to understanding their points of view, and to predict accurately how well or poorly we or other people will perform on future tasks.

Second, once we have formed an initial impression of another person, assigning her a set of character traits, those traits operate as prior expectancies that shape how we attribute her actions and outcomes in the future. Specifically, we tend to attribute outcomes or behaviors that confirm our impressions to stable, internal factors (the person's character), while attributing events that contradict our prior expectancies to transient or environmental causes. In this way as in others, our initial person impressions tend to be self-perpetuating.

11.7 DEBIASING SOCIAL JUDGMENT

First, the bad news. Social psychology can presently tell us far more about how social perception falls prey to the biasing effects of stereotypes and other social expectancies than about how those biases can reliably be reduced or eliminated. But there is good news as well. First, we do know *something* about bias reduction. And second, debiasing is presently a subject of intense investigation in cognitive social psychology, and it is reasonable to expect that a decade from now we will know much more than we know now about how to constrain what psychologist John Bargh calls "the cognitive monster."[66]

11.7.1 Dual Process Models of Social Cognition: High Road vs. Low Road Thinking

Much of the existing bias reduction research draws on a *dual process model* of social cognition, essentially the System 1/System 2 framework of automatic and controlled processing described in Section 1.6.1. In making sense of other people, we use two systems of information processing: a "low road" system, which is automatic, rapid, unconscious, and demanding of few cognitive resources, and a "high road" system, which is effortful, conscious, controlled, and resource-intensive.

Social attribution processes, described earlier in this chapter, fit easily into this dual process framework. Let's return to Trujillo's thoughts about his interaction with Lamm. Cognitive social psychologists[67] suggest his thought process might have gone through the following steps. First, he would automatically *categorize* Lamm's behavior as "explosive." Next, from this automatic categorization, he would spontaneously *characterize* Lamm as a "loose cannon." However, if he thought about this characterization more systematically, he might *correct* his initial, spontaneous characterization after considering the possibility that Lamm was provoked by his own behavior. If he happened to know that she was coping with the mayor's demands for immediate action, he might also consider the possibility that her behavior was attributable to tensions caused by the immediate situation.

---

66. John A. Bargh, *The Cognitive Monster: the Case against the Controllability of Automatic Stereotype Effects, in* SHELLY CHAIKEN AND YAACOV TROPE, DUAL-PROCESS THEORIES IN SOCIAL PSYCHOLOGY 361 (New York: Guilford Press, 1999).

67. James S. Uleman, Leonard S. Newman, and Gordon B. Moskowitz, *People as Flexible Interpreters: Evidence and Issues from Spontaneous Trait Inference, in* ADVANCES IN EXPERIMENTAL SOCIAL PSYCHOLOGY (VOL. 28) 211–79 (Mark P. Zanna ed., San Diego: Academic Press, 1996); Timothy D. Wilson and Nancy Brekke, *Mental Contamination and Mental Correction: Unwanted Influences on Judgments and Evaluations*, 116 PSYCHOLOGICAL BULLETIN 117 (1994); Daniel T. Gilbert, Brett W. Pelham, and Douglas S. Krull, *On Cognitive Busyness: When Person Perceivers Meet Persons Perceived*, 54 JOURNAL OF PERSONALITY AND SOCIAL PSYCHOLOGY 733–40 (1988).

Notice, however, that correction of this kind would require three things: Trujillo's *motivation* to reconsider his initial characterization; the *cognitive resources* (time, spare processing capacity) required to do so; and *information* from which a reasoned corrective judgment might be made.

There is virtual consensus among social psychologists that stereotyping includes both automatic and controlled components. If a person has learned, but then consciously rejects, the stereotypes and attitudes associated with a devalued social group, those stereotypes and attitudes do not just disappear. Indeed, techniques like the Implicit Association Test[68] show them to be present, even in many participants who rate low on measures of explicit bias or who are themselves members of the negatively stereotyped group.[69] In such situations, the older implicit attitudes and associations continue to exist alongside the newer, consciously held beliefs and commitments. The implicit attitudes function as a Type 1 or "low road" system, while the conscious beliefs function as a Type 2 or "high road" system. In fact, the neurological substrates underlying the implicit/explicit distinction can even be observed through such technologies as functional magnetic resonance imaging (fMRI).[70]

There is relative consensus within cognitive social psychology that stereotype *activation*, when it occurs, is spontaneous. But there is also a growing consensus that stereotype activation does not *necessarily* lead to stereotype expression, and that stereotype activation itself can be affected by environmental factors.

To understand the state of current thinking on these issues, consider Figure 11.6, an extension of Jerry Kang's model of social categorization portrayed earlier in Figure 11.1.

As Figure 11.6 suggests, even where a social schema (like a stereotype) is activated and generates a schema-consistent impression, that initial impression can be overridden through the application of conscious, "high road" thinking.[71]

---

68. *See* note 44, *supra*. A great deal has been written about the Implicit Association Test. For a relatively brief description of the instrument, *see* Anthony G. Greenwald & Linda Hamilton Krieger, *Implicit Bias: Scientific Foundations*, 94 CAL. L. REV. 945–967 (2006).

69. Nilanjana Dasgupta, *Implicit Ingroup Favoritism, Outgroup Favoritism, and Their Behavioral Manifestations*, 17 SOCIAL JUSTICE RESEARCH 143 (2004); Brian A. Nosek, Mahzarin R. Banaji, and Anthony G. Greenwald, *Harvesting Implicit Group Attitudes and Beliefs from a Demonstration Web Site*, 6 GROUP DYNAMICS 101 (2002).

70. William. A. Cunningham, Marcia K. Johnson, Carol L. Raye, J. Chris Gatenby, John C. Gore and Mahzarin R. Banaji, *Neural Components of Social Evaluation*, 85 JOURNAL OF PERSONALITY AND SOCIAL PSYCHOLOGY 639–49 (2003); E. A. Phelps, et al., *Performance on Indirect Measures of Race Evaluation Predicts Amygdala Activation*, *supra* note 47.

71. Margo J. Monteith and Corrine I. Voils, *Exerting Control over Prejudiced Responses*, *in* COGNITIVE SOCIAL PSYCHOLOGY: THE PRINCETON SYMPOSIUM ON THE LEGACY AND FUTURE OF SOCIAL COGNITION (Gordon B. Moskowitz ed., Mahwah, NJ: Erlbaum, 2001).

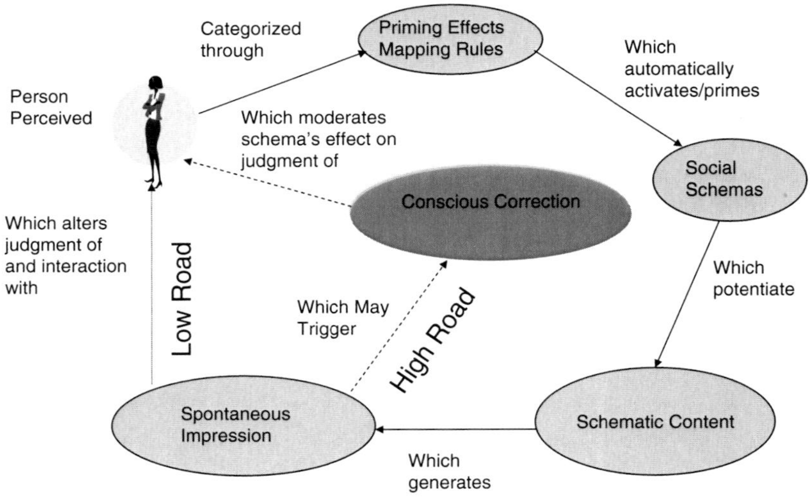

FIGURE 11.6 A DUAL-PROCESS MODEL OF SOCIAL PERCEPTION AND JUDGMENT: HIGH ROAD VS. LOW ROAD SOCIAL INFORMATION PROCESSING.

However, certain conditions must be present.[72] The perceiver must be *aware* of the possibility that his initial impression might be biased, and he must be *motivated* to correct for that bias. Of course, some behaviors, like a decision to lease an apartment to a particular tenant, are under greater conscious control than behaviors like facial expressions, speech errors, and fidgeting.[73] For correction to occur, the perceiver must also have time and attention to spare: like all System 2 processing, high road correction requires cognitive resources. In certain situations, as when a police officer has to decide whether someone is pointing a gun at her, there may be little time available, thus reducing the likelihood that correction will occur. And finally, to correct an initially biased impression, the perceiver must have available the information and analytical tools required for meaningful deliberation.

---

72. John A. Bargh, *The Cognitive Monster: The Case Against the Controllability of Automatic Stereotype Effects, in* SHELLY CHAIKEN AND YAACOV TROPE, DUAL-PROCESS THEORIES IN SOCIAL PSYCHOLOGY 361 (1999); Timothy D. Wilson and Nancy Brekke, *Mental Contamination and Mental Correction: Unwanted Influences on Judgments and Evaluations,* 116 PSYCHOLOGICAL BULLETIN 117 (1994).

73. There is some evidence indicating that, with sufficient motivation and effort on the perceiver's part, even these subtle behaviors are amenable to conscious control. *See* Steven L. Neuberg, *Expectancy-Confirmation Processes in Stereotype-Tinged Social Encounters: The Moderating Role of Social Goals, in* THE PSYCHOLOGY OF PREJUDICE: THE ONTARIO SYMPOSIUM (Vol. 7) 103–30 (Mark P. Zanna and John M. Olson eds., Hillsdale, NJ: Erlbaum, 1994).

Consider how the presence or absence of these factors might influence the degree of racial bias present in hiring decisions. If those who make hiring decisions are simply told to be "color-blind" in evaluating potential candidates, if they do not believe themselves to be race-biased, and if there are no meaningfully endorsed and enforced system of goals relating to minority hiring, conscious correction of implicitly race-biased evaluations is unlikely to occur. Under such conditions, hiring decision makers are unlikely to be aware of the possibility that implicit racial stereotypes and attitudes could be skewing their judgment, and they will have little motivation to engage in conscious correction.

In the hiring or promotion context, at least with respect to high-level jobs, ultimate decision making is often quite deliberate, with ample time available for systematic evaluation of the final competing candidates. In the formation of managers' day-to-day impressions of employee performance, however, this may not be the case. Managers often function under conditions of extreme time constraint and high cognitive load. In these situations, correction of stereotype-influenced impressions is far less likely to occur.[74]

As earlier mentioned, to correct biased impressions, decision makers also need ample decision-relevant information and access to a structured decision-making processes. Carefully spelling out the applicable evaluative criteria, providing decision makers with objective, criterion-relevant information, and requiring them to write down how the information provided relates to the relevant criteria can help reduce the biasing effect of stereotypes on evaluations.[75] Additionally, providing decision makers with systemwide information revealing broad patterns of good or bad outcomes can help them identify biases they likely would not recognize from case-by-case data.[76] Finally, as with any expectancy, "considering the opposite" can help correct expectancy-confirmation bias.

In summary, even though the implicit expectancies created by stereotypes and other social knowledge structures bias initial impression formation spontaneously, bias is, at least under certain conditions, amenable to correction. Individuals or organizations interested in maximizing the likelihood that correction will occur should implement the following strategies:

- educate decision makers that their evaluative judgments may be influenced by subtle forms of bias, no matter how sincere their conscious commitment to fairness, objectivity, and nondiscrimination;

---

74. John A. Bargh, *The Cognitive Monster: The Case Against the Controllability of Automatic Stereotype Effects*, *in* Shelly Chaiken and Yaacov Trope, Dual-Process Theories in Social Psychology 361 (New York: Guilford Press, 1999); Daniel T. Gilbert, Brett W. Pelham, and Douglas S. Krull, *On Cognitive Busyness: When Person Perceivers Meet Persons Perceived*, 54 Journal of Personality and Social Psychology 733–40 (1988).

75. Veronica F. Nieva and Barbara A. Gutek, *Sex Effects on Evaluation*, 5 Acad. of Mgmt. Rev. 267, 270–71 (1980).

76. Faye J. Crosby, Susan Clayton, Olaf Alksnis, and Kathryn Hemker, *Cognitive Biases in the Perception of Discrimination: The Importance of Format*, 14 Sex Roles 637–46 (1986).

- structure incentives and foster an organizational culture that motivates decision makers to identify and correct implicitly biased impressions or initial judgments;
- destigmatize implicit bias, so that self-examination and conscious correction are less threatening;
- monitor decisions systematically, so that broad patterns suggestive of uncorrected bias can be identified and addressed;
- reduce, where possible, decision makers' levels of cognitive busyness when making decisions;
- generate clear, objective evaluative criteria, and supply evaluators with information relevant to those criteria; and
- encourage decision makers to "consider the opposite" before acting on or attempting to justify an initial impression.

11.7.2 How Malleable Are Implicit Stereotypes?

The bias-reduction strategies discussed above all involve the conscious correction of an initial judgment that was biased by an implicit stereotype or other social expectancy. But can the implicit stereotypes we have acquired from the surrounding culture be suppressed, or better yet, replaced, through individual or organizational efforts? In other words, how malleable are implicit attitudes?

In short, we don't yet know. Indeed, these two questions now represent perhaps the hottest issues in social psychology.

In the early 1990s, few established empirical social psychologists believed that the automatic components of the stereotyping process (stereotype activation and the spontaneous formation of stereotype-consistent impressions) could be defused through individual efforts.[77] Debiasing, if it occurred at all, was thought to require motivated, effortful, subsequent correction.[78] But by the mid-1990s, a new generation of graduate students was chafing at the field's collective surrender to the inevitability of automatic stereotype activation, and these students launched a new research agenda on the malleability of implicit attitudes.

Early results emerged from Mahzarin Banaji's lab at Yale, when in 1996 graduate student Sandra Blair and Banaji reported that, under conditions of low cognitive load, participants who had rehearsed counter-stereotypic expectations

---

77. John A. Bargh, *supra* note 74, *The Cognitive Monster: The Case Against the Controllability of Automatic Stereotype Effects, in* Shelly Chaiken and Yaacov Trope, Dual-Process Theories in Social Psychology 361 (1999); Susan T. Fiske, *Examining the Role of Intent: Toward Understanding Its Role in Stereotyping and Prejudice, in* Unintended Thought, *supra* note 62, pp. 253–83.

78. *Patricia* G. Devine, *Stereotypes and Prejudice: Their Automatic and Controlled Components, supra* note 8; Susan T. Fiske, Monica Lin, and Steven L. Neuberg, *The Continuum Model: Ten Years Later, in* Dual-Process Theories in Social Psychology 231–54 (Shelly Chaiken and Yaacov Trope eds., New York: Guilford Press, 1999).

showed reduced automatic activation of implicit gender stereotypes.[79] Similar results were reported by a second research team in 2000.[80]

Subsequent experiments indicated that automatic stereotype activation could be reduced when participants were exposed to positive exemplars of a disliked group and negative exemplars of a liked group,[81] concentrated on counter-stereotypic mental images[82] or received positive feedback from a stereotyped group member.[83] Similar decreases in automatic stereotype activation resulted where participants were placed in low-status positions relative to a stereotyped target,[84] when the experiment was run by a member of the stereotyped group,[85] and when participants believed that their levels of automatic stereotyping were "out of step" with those of their peers.[86]

These studies, and others like them, provide tantalizing—if preliminary—-evidence that automatic stereotype activation can be reduced through environmental modifications and the rehearsal of counter-stereotypic reactions. But the research case should not be overstated. In the studies described above, effect sizes were relatively small, and the observed debiasing effects relatively short-lived. Moreover, in some of the studies, reduced stereotype activation was found only under conditions of low cognitive busyness, an increasingly rare luxury in a hypercharged social world.

Though debiasing research is still in its infancy, there are certainly some steps that individuals and organizations motivated to reduce their levels of implicit bias can take to achieve that end. We can control the images and other

---

79. Irene V. Blair and Mahzarin R. Banaji, *Automatic and Controlled Processes in Stereotype Priming,* 70 Journal of Personality and Social Psychology 1142–63 (1996).

80. Kerry Kawakami, John F. Dovidio, J. Moll, S. Hermsen, and A. Russin, *Just Say No (to Stereotyping): Effect of Training in the Negation of Stereotypic Associations on Stereotype Activation,* 78 Journal of Personality and Social Psychology 871–88 (2000).

81. Nilanjana Dasgupta and Anthony G. Greenwald, *On the Malleability of Automatic Attitudes: Combating Automatic Prejudice with Images of Admired and Disliked Individuals,* 81 Journal of Personality and Social Psychology 800–14 (2001).

82. Irene V. Blair, Jennifer E. Ma, and Alison P. Lenton, *Imagining Stereotypes Away: The Moderation of Implicit Stereotypes Through Mental Imagery,* 81 Journal of Personality and Social Psychology 828–41 (2001).

83. Lisa Sinclair and Zeva Kunda, *Reactions to a Black Professional: Motivated Inhibition and Activation of Conflicting Stereotypes,* 7 Journal of Personality and Social Psychology 885–904 (1999).

84. Jennifer A. Richeson and Nalini Ambady, *When Roles Reverse: Stigma, Status, and Self-Evaluation,* 31 Journal of Applied Social Psychology 1350–78 (2001).

85. Brian S. Lowery, Curtis D. Hardin, and Stacey Sinclair, *Social Influence Effects on Automatic Racial Prejudice,* 81 Journal of Personality and Social Psychology 842–55 (2001).

86. Gretchen B. Sechrist and Charles Stangor, *Perceived Consensus Influences Intergroup Behavior and Stereotype Accessibility,* 80 Journal of Personality and Social Psychology 645–54 (2001).

messages we absorb from the media, making conscious decisions to limit exposure to negatively stereotyped images of women and minorities, or making sure that we supplement those we do take in with positive, non-stereotyped portrayals as well. Organizations can take affirmative steps to ensure that members of stereotyped groups are present in leadership positions. We can change the pictures on the walls of our homes, workplaces, and schools, even on our screen savers. These situational modifications can't hurt, and in another decade, empirical research may demonstrate that, alone or in combination with other factors, they help a great deal.

PART THREE

MAKING DECISIONS

People make myriad decisions every day. Most are of little consequence: What clothes should I wear to work? What should I order for lunch? Other decisions carry more weight: What job should I take? Should I enter into this deal, and on what terms? What litigation strategy should I employ? Where should we site the wastewater treatment plant? It is the presence of options that creates both opportunities and a decision problem.

Part 1 introduced a general framework for deliberative decision making. To focus specifically on decision making (rather than problem solving in general), the framework entails:

1. Identifying and prioritizing the relevant interests and objectives.
2. Generating a range of plausible decision alternatives. (Sometimes it's a simple "yes" or "no" decision; sometimes, as in the wastewater treatment plant decision, there are numerous alternatives.)
3. Predicting the consequences of those alternatives in terms of the interests or objectives.
4. Comparing the alternatives and selecting the course of action that optimizes the interests or objectives.

We covered the first two of these in **Part 1**. The third is fundamentally an empirical undertaking, often requiring probabilistic assessments of the kinds explored in **Part 2** of the book. A decision process is good to the extent that the underlying empirical analysis follows the scientific method and that judgments of uncertain consequences adhere to the rules of probability theory.

We got a head start on the fourth step in **Chapter 4**, with the survey of various strategies for making decisions, and working through an example of a formal model of decision making—the *subjective linear model*—in which the decision making specifies the major interests involved and assigns weights to them. We continue this exploration in **Part 3**.

Chapter 12, *Choices, Consequences, and Trade-offs*, asks what people seek to achieve when they are making decisions. It introduces the concept and complexities of *utility* and the criteria for rational decision making, focusing on a widely accepted set of axioms for rational decision making—the axioms of *subjective expected utility theory*.

Chapter 13, *Complexities of Decision Making: Decision Processes; Relationships to our Future Selves*, and **Chapter 14**, *Complexities of Decision Making, Continued: The Power of Frames*, ask how one would know whether a person has made a suboptimal decision in terms of his or her (own) subjective utility, and then examine a variety of situations in which people tend to make suboptimal decisions.

Chapter 15, *Decision Making under Risk*, considers issues of decision making when risk or uncertainty about the consequences of a decision plays a major role.

And **Chapter 16**, *The Role of Affect in Risky Decisions*, continues this discussion, focusing on risk situations where emotions run high.

12. CHOICES, CONSEQUENCES, AND TRADE-OFFS

When you see a fork in the road, take it
—Yogi Berra

In Chapter 4, we surveyed a number of different strategies for choosing among alternatives and worked through an example of a formal model of decision making—the subjective linear model—in which the decision maker specifies the major interests involved and assigns weights to them. Implicit in these strategies is the idea that a decision should maximize someone's utility—one's own when making a personal decision, the client's when counseling him on a course of action, or the utility of constituents and other stakeholders when making a policy decision.

The complexities of maximizing the utility of multiple people who may have different interests are readily apparent. Different residents of Edenville—even people living in the same neighborhood—may have different views about the importance of the various factors implicated by the siting of the wastewater treatment plant. Some may care deeply about protecting the habitat in the north part of the city; others may be completely indifferent. Moreover, the decision of where to site the plant will affect the residents in different ways.

How elected or appointed officials should deal with their constituents' various interests is a contested issue of political theory and beyond the scope of this book.[1] As we will see in the next several chapters, the concept of utility turns out to be pretty complex, even in the simple case where only one person's interests are concerned. This chapter begins by unpacking this concept, and then introduces a widely accepted set of axioms for rational decision making—the axioms of subjective expected utility theory.

12.1 SUBJECTIVE UTILITY

This section is something of a grab-bag set of observations about subjective utility. It covers the following points:

- Utility is essentially a subjective matter and often includes nontangible values.
- The decision process itself affects utility, directly and through the perception or experience of outcomes

1. *See, e.g.*, HANNAH PITKIN, THE CONCEPT OF REPRESENTATION (Berkeley: University of California Press, 1967), ADAM PRZEWORSKI, SUSAN STOKES, AND BERNARD MALIN, EDS., DEMOCRACY, ACCOUNTABILITY AND REPRESENTATION (Cambridge, UK: Cambridge University Press, 1999).

- One's utility is affected by looking backward and forward in time as well as by present experience—and the relationship among these timeframes can be complex.
- More money and other goods do not necessarily affect utility linearly or even montonically. (We return to what Barry Schwartz has called the "paradox of choice"[2] in Section 14.5.)
- People tend to adapt to both good and bad life circumstances. (In the next chapter, we consider how good people are at predicting this adaptation.)

12.1.1 Sources of Utility

12.1.1.a The Arationality of Ends The goal of this book is to provide insights and tools to help you achieve your ends or assist others in achieving theirs, with the ultimate aim of maximizing your or their *utility*. The premise of our venture is captured by Mark Kelman's description of rational choice theory:

> At the most basic level, rational choice theory posits the existence of principals who articulate ends that are beyond rational reproach. Rational choice theorists view these ends as arbitrary—that is to say, the ends need no justification. Ends are also subjective; they are not things that exist in the external world that individuals apprehend, as they apprehend the natural world around them, but rather come from the subject herself. Whether an end is correct or not can be judged only by each individual subject herself, and the judgment of whether an end is correct is extremely limited. In essence, the subject can do no more than interrogate the authenticity and accuracy of the way in which he has articulated and come to understand his wishes. Ends cannot be judged from an external observer's objective viewpoint to be wrong in some transcendent and impersonal sense because they do not manifest what is most unique to human nature or interfere with a particular conception of human flourishing. Nor are ends derived by observing some external perceptible human nature. Ends are not only private and individual but, perhaps most importantly, individuating. What most clearly makes us differentiable individuals is our unique preference structure, even more so than our distinct capabilities or capacities to meet our ends. In other words, who we uniquely are is, at core, a reflection of who we want to be and what we aspire to attain, rather than what we can actually attain. . . .
>
> At the normative level, the existence of these differentiable tastes and ends is foundational for all political theories that would describe themselves as essentially liberal. A host of political theorists define liberal theory in terms of its skepticism about theories that there are good lives, rather than mere tastes for end states. Less negatively, these theorists define liberal theory in terms of

2. Barry Schwartz, The Paradox of Choice: Why More Is Less (New York: Ecco/Harper Collins Publishers, 2004).

theories that affirm that there are a multitude of good lives and that each individual is in a unique position to ascertain which of the many reasonable conceptions of the "good" best fit her circumstances and express her individuated soul.[3]

Daniel Keys and Barry Schwartz write that a complete theory of rational decision making "must consider the very broadly construed consequences of a decision. That is, it must consider short- and long-term consequences, consequences to the self and to others, consequences that are central to the decision at hand, and consequences that may be more peripheral. It must also consider consequences of decisions for the character of the decision maker, as the effects on character may have a significant impact on a host of future decisions."[4] The next several chapters suggest how difficult it is for even very thoughtful people to predict whether particular courses of action will serve their individual ends, let alone those of various stakeholders.

Gross National Happiness

The official policy of Bhutan is that "gross national happiness is more important than gross national product," because "happiness takes precedence over economic prosperity in our national development process."[5]

Bhutan's constitution assesses government programs in terms of the economy, culture, environment, and good governance. The government employs seventy-two indicators in nine different domains: psychological well-being, ecology, health, education, culture, living standards, time use, community vitality, and good governance. For example, indicators of psychological well-being include the frequencies of prayer and meditation and of feelings of selfishness, jealousy, calm, compassion, and generosity, and the absence of frustration and suicidal thoughts.[6]

People sometimes use "happiness" as a synonym for utility, but that is somewhat misleading. Many people have a conception of leading a "good" or "whole"

3. Mark G. Kelman, *Law and Behavioral Science: Conceptual Overviews*, 97 Nw. L. Rev. 1347, 1358 (2003).

4. Daniel J. Keys and Barry Schwartz, *"Leaky" Rationality: How Research on Behavioral Decision Making Challenges Normative Standards of Rationality*, 2 Perspectives on Psychological Science 162–80 (2007).

5. Orville Schell, "Frontline World, Bhutan"—The Last Place, May 2002, http://www.pbs.org/frontlineworld/stories/bhutan/gnh.html.

6. Seth Mydans, *Thimphu Journal: Recalculating Happiness in a Himalayan Kingdom*, New York Times, May 7, 2009, http://www.nytimes.com/2009/05/07/world/asia/07bhutan.html

or "balanced" life that seems trivialized by reducing it to happiness. More broadly, as Kelman has observed, "ascetics, saints, and those willing to sacrifice everything for spite all have perfectly coherent utility seeking goals."[7]

In *Because It Is There: The Challenges of Mountaineering . . . for Utility Theory*,[8] George Loewenstein examines the diaries and memoirs of individuals on serious mountain climbing explorations, "which tend to be one unrelentless misery from beginning to end." Drawing on Jeremy Bentham's categories in *The Principles of Morals and Legislation* (1789), Loewenstein discerns a number of different motivations other than the immediate experience of thrills, natural beauty, and the like.

- Mountaineers seek Bentham's "pleasure of a good name"—the desire to impress others.
- They seek the "pleasure of self recommendation" or what Loewenstein calls self-signaling—the need for self-esteem or to define oneself as having a particular set of character traits.
- They are motivated by "the almost obsessive human need to fulfill self-set goals," which may also be an aspect of self-signaling.
- They are motivated by the desire to master their environments, by the need for control.
- And they seek experiences—often near-death experiences—that will give meaning to their lives.

All of this might lead one to define utility, as does welfare economics, simply in terms of what an individual *wants*, and to specify the goal of decision making as satisfying those wants. However, people may be *mistaken* about what they want—they may "miswant."[9] But that's for the next chapter. Rather than linger on the epistemology of utility,[10] the remainder of this chapter explores some of its major dimensions.

---

7. Kelman, *supra* at 1364 n.31.

8. George Loewenstein, *Because It is There: The Challenges of Mountaineering . . . for Utility Theory*, 52 KYKLOS 315 (1999).

9. *See* Daniel T. Gilbert and Timothy D. Wilson, *Miswanting: Some Problems in the Forecasting of Future Affective States, in* FEELING AND THINKING: THE ROLE OF AFFECT IN SOCIAL COGNITION, (Joseph Forgas ed., New York: Cambridge University Press, 2001).

10. Mark G. Kelman, *Hedonic Psychology and the Ambiguities of "Welfare,"* 33 PHILOSOPHY & PUBLIC AFFAIRS 413 (2005).

Patrick has a serious phobia about flying. The very anticipation of flight creates an almost physical sense of dread. As a result, he avoids business and pleasure trips that require flying, and he drives extraordinarily long distances, all at tremendous professional and personal costs. Patrick believes that statistics show that flying is safe compared to driving and, indeed, to many other activities he engages in. He acknowledges that the phobia is irrational. Is it irrational for him to take account of his fear of flying in making travel decisions?

The following sections note some other sources of utility that do not seem reducible to purely material ends.

12.1.1.b Existence and Option Value Considerable research has gone into measuring the material benefits of ecosystems—for example, as sources of pure drinking water. But some environmental legislation, such as the Endangered Species Act, treats species, habitats, and natural landscapes as having an *existence value* independent of any human uses—for example, the value attributed to the protection of an endangered species in a remote part of the world that most people will never encounter. A cousin of existence value is the *option value* of a natural resource—the value one assigns to the possibility of using it sometime in the future. For example, you may have no plans to visit a wilderness area but nonetheless place some value on the possibility of visiting it in the future. We'll say more about how economists assess these values in the discussion of cost-benefit analysis in Section 12.3.

12.1.1.c Affection In a charming mind experiment, Christopher Hsee and Howard Kunreuther demonstrate what they call the *affection effect*.[11]

> On a visit to Europe, Helen and Laura each bought a painting for $100 and shipped it back to the United States, each purchasing a $100 shipping insurance policy. The paintings were damaged beyond repair, but claiming the insurance will require a time-consuming trip to the shipping company. Helen loved her painting a great deal. Laura thought hers was just OK. Who is more likely to spend the time collecting the insurance compensation?

From a purely economic point of view, there is no difference between the choices facing Helen and Laura: $100 is $100, whatever its source and rationale. However, Helen, who has great affection for the painting, is more likely to take

11. Christopher K. Hsee and Howard C. Kunreuther, *The Affection Effect in Insurance Decisions*, 20 Journal of Risk and Uncertainty 141 (2000). We have simplified the scenarios.

the time to collect the insurance compensation than Laura. Hsee and Kunreuther explain the difference in terms of what they call the "consolation hypothesis":

> Compensation has symbolic value. It is redemption for the lost object; it is a token of consolation for the pain caused by the loss. The utility of a given amount of compensation has two components: (a) the utility of that particular amount of money, and (b) the utility of its symbolic consolation value. . . . The consolation value, in turn, depends on one's level of affection for the object. The more affection one has, the more pain one experiences, and the more one needs the consolation.

The main focus of this chapter is on decisions made in advance of knowing just what the consequences will be—for example, whether one will suffer a loss. But just as individuals anticipate the experience of regret, they can anticipate the need for consolation. In another part of the experiment, Hsee and Kunreuther in effect asked Laura and Helen how much they would pay (in advance) for insurance to ship their paintings. Not surprisingly, Helen, who has strong affection for her work of art, would pay significantly more than Laura—almost twice as much. By the same token, people would be more willing to buy a warranty for a beautiful used convertible than for a utilitarian used station wagon even if the expected repair expenses and the cost of the warranty were identical.[12]

> Suppose that your dog is dying of either Virus A or Virus B. They are equally likely, but which one it is cannot be known. There are different medicines for Virus A and Virus B, each equally effective for its intended target, that cost $1 and $20 respectively. They interact in a way that they cannot be given together. Which one would you choose?
>
> When the dog was described as friendly or faithful, 43 percent of respondents would have opted for the $20 medicine and said that they would have felt better paying more. The effects were significantly diminished when the dog was described as unfriendly or unfaithful.
>
> Christopher Hsee and Howard Kunreuther, *The Affection Effect in Insurance Decisions*, 20 JOURNAL OF RISK AND UNCERTAINTY 141 (2000).

12.1.1.d The Allure of the Free Suppose you were offered the choice between buying a Hershey's Kiss for 1 cent and buying a delicious Swiss truffle, made by Lindt, for 15 cents; which would you choose? Now imagine that instead of

12. CHRISTOPHER K. HSEE, AND GEETA MENON, AFFECTION EFFECT IN CONSUMER CHOICES, unpublished data (University of Chicago, 1999).

costing 1 cent, the Hershey's Kiss were free and the Lindt truffle cost 14 cents. Would your preference be different? Research by Dan Ariely and his colleagues[13] suggests that it would. When they sold Hershey's Kisses and Lindt truffles to the public for 1 cent and 15 cents respectively, 73 percent of their "customers" went for the Lindt truffle, which, considering their usual retail prices, is a much better deal. However, when they dropped the price of each chocolate by a penny, so the Kiss was free and the truffle cost 14 cents, only 31 percent opted for the truffle. The rest—a large majority—now chose the Kiss.

The relative value of the two chocolates had not changed, and nor had the price difference. So why did people's choices change? Ariely and his colleagues suggest that we enjoy a benefit when it is untainted by costs, which take an affective toll that compromises our enjoyment of the benefit. (By the same token, we may enjoy a vacation more if we de-couple the experience from its cost by paying in advance.)

12.1.2 The (Dis)utility of the Decision Process—And "Leaky" Decisions

Regardless of whether utility can be reduced to happiness, or is more complex and nuanced, most discussions of utility focus on the utility of the *outcome*. The decision process is thus evaluated solely on its contribution to the outcome.

However, the process of decision making is often itself a cost—and one that must be weighed against the likelihood of its contributing to a better outcome. (While Christine Lamm's use of the subjective linear model was helpful in deciding where to site a wastewater treatment plant, imagine her employing that approach in selecting a restaurant, let alone in choosing from a menu. In addition to the time and money involved, some decision processes carry emotional costs, such as the stress of making difficult trade-offs.

Beyond these obvious points, though, the decision process may itself be a source of utility or disutility. To use Daniel Keys and Barry Schwartz's evocative phrase, the process may "leak" into the outcome.[14]

12.1.2.a Fairness People attribute value to the *fairness* of a decision process. Litigants are more willing to accept and abide by an adverse judgment if they believe that the process was fair, and this may be true for citizens who must live with the outcomes of policy decisions, such as siting a wastewater

---

13. Kristina Shampanier, Nina Mazar, and Dan Ariely, *Zero as a Special Price: The True Value of Free Products*, 26 Marketing Science 742–57 (2007); Dan Ariely, Predictably Irrational: The Hidden Forces That Shape Our Decisions (New York: HarperCollins 2008).

14. Daniel J. Keys and Barry Schwartz, *"Leaky Rationality: How Research on Behavioral Decision Making Challenges Normative Standards of Rationality*, 2 Perspectives on Psychological Science 162–80 (2007). The authors acknowledge Deborah Frisch's article, *Reasons for Framing Effects*, 54 Organizational Behavior and Human Decision Processes 399–429 (1993), for the concept of what they term "leakage."

treatment plant.[15] In a summary of the research, Donna Shestowsky suggests that people define fairness in terms of how much control they retain over the development of information that will be used to resolve an issue, and how respectfully the decision maker treats them.[16]

People's behavior in the so-called "ultimatum game" provides a dramatic example of the role of fairness in decision making. In this game, two players are given a sum of money to split between them. The "proposer" suggests a way to split the sum. The "responder" can then either accept or reject this offer. If the responder accepts the offer, the sum is distributed to both players as offered. If the responder rejects the offer, neither player receives any of the money.

If the responder's only utility consisted of the money gained, he would accept a penny regardless of how small a percentage it was of the total sum; if the proposer believed that the responder would act in this way or if the proposer's only utility was in money gained, she would offer only a penny. In fact, proposers usually offer 30 to 40 percent, and responders usually reject offers of less than 20 percent.[17] The results seem to be the same when one hundred dollars are at stake as for ten dollars.[18] Cross-cultural comparisons of ultimatum game experiments suggest that people from Ljubljana, Pittsburgh, and Tokyo play the game with similar results, although people may play differently in traditional societies.[19]

The "dictator" game controls for the proposer's anticipation of the respondent's response. The dictator divides a fixed amount of money between herself and the "recipient," who cannot respond. When the game is played anonymously with participants knowing nothing about the other player, most dictators keep the entire sum or allot a paltry amount to the recipient.[20] However, when dictators are provided information about recipients—pictures or surnames, for example—they

15. Jonathan D. Casper, Tom Tyler, and Bonnie Fisher, *Procedural Justice in Felony Cases*, 22 LAW AND SOCIETY REVIEW 483–508 (1988).

16. Donna Shestowsky, *Misjudging: Implications for Dispute Resolution*, 7 NEV. L.J. 487, 493 (2007).

17. Colin Camerer and Richard H. Thaler, *Anomalies: Ultimatums, Dictators and Manners*, 9 THE JOURNAL OF ECONOMIC PERSPECTIVES 210 (1995).

18. Elizabeth Hoffman, Kevin A. McCabe, and Vernon L. Smith, *On Expectations and the Monetary Stakes in Ultimatum Games*, 25 INTERNATIONAL JOURNAL OF GAME THEORY 289–301 (1996).

19. Alvin E. Roth, Vesna Prasnikar, Masahiro Okuno-Fujiwara, and Shmuel Zamir, *Bargaining and Market Behavior in Jerusalem, Ljubljana, Pittsburgh, and Tokyo: An Experimental Study*, 81 AMERICAN ECONOMIC REVIEW 1068–95 (1991).

20. Elizabeth Hoffman, Kevin McCabe, Keith Shachat, and Vernon Smith, *Preferences, Property Rights, and Anonymity in Bargaining Games*, 7 GAMES AND ECONOMIC BEHAVIOR 346–80 (1994); Elizabeth Hoffman, Kevin McCabe, and Vernon Smith, *Social Distance and Other-Regarding Behavior in Dictator Games*, 86 AMERICAN ECONOMIC REVIEW 653–60 (1996).

increase their giving.[21] The dictator's behavior is also affected if she adverts to being observed. In an experiment where players conducted the game on computers to ensure anonymity, dictators gave more when the background of the computer screen featured a robot with human eyes.[22] Commenting on the ultimatum game, Martin Nowak suggests that objecting to unfairness is a way of asserting one's reputation: "Rejecting low offers is costly, but the cost is offset by gaining the reputation of being somebody who insists on a fair offer."[23] In the dictator game, perhaps the image of the observer reminds the dictator of her reputational interests.

12.1.2.b Transaction Utility Richard Thaler's idea of *transaction utility* stems at least partly from a sense of fairness as well. Thaler gives this example:

> You are lying on the beach on a hot day. For the last hour you have been thinking about much you would enjoy a nice cold bottle of your favorite brand of beer. A companion gets up to go make a phone call and offers to bring back a beer from the only nearby place where beer is sold [a fancy resort hotel/a small run-down grocery store]. He says that the beer might be expensive and so asks how much you are willing to pay for it. He says he will buy the beer if it costs as much or less than the price you state. What price do you tell him?

When the beer would be purchased from the resort, participants were, on average, willing to pay $2.65. When it would be purchased from the grocery store, they were only willing to pay $1.50. Thaler suggests that while the consumption utility is the same in both cases, they have different "transaction" utilities. Just as we get special pleasure from a "good deal"—sometimes even if we really didn't want the item all that much and end up not using it—we get negative transaction utility from a bad one. We expect the resort to charge a premium, but feel we're being taken if the grocery store charges too much.

12.1.2.c The Effect of Expectations on Experienced Utility One's expectations about an experience can affect the experience itself, and expectations can

21. Terrence C. Burnham, *Engineering Altruism: A Theoretical and Experimental Investigation of Anonymity and Gift Giving*, 50 Journal of Economic Behavior and Organization 133–144 (2003); Gary Charness and Uri Gneezy, *What's in a Name? Reducing the Social Distance in Dictator and Ultimatum Games*, 68 Journal of Economic Behavior and Organization 29–35 (2008).

22. Terrence C. Burnham and Brian Hare, *Engineering Human Cooperation: Does Involuntary Neural Activation Increase Public Goods Contributions?*, 18 Human Nature 88–108 (2007).

23. Martin A. Nowak, Karen M. Page, and Karl Sigmund, *Fairness versus Reason in the Ultimatum Game*, 289 Science 1774 (2000).

be affected by framing the same item in different terms.[24] People given a yogurt described as having "only 5% fat" found it richer tasting than the same food described as "95% fat-free." They thought that 7UP in a yellow bottle tasted more like lemon than the same drink in a green bottle.

Deborah Frisch asserts that "framing has an effect on decisions because it has an effect on experience."[25] But does framing actually *change* people's experiences or just provide independent information about the utility of a product or experience? That is, do people think 7UP in a yellow bottle tastes more like lemon because the color of the bottle changes the way the drink tastes to them, or does the bottle's color provide them with independent information about how lemony the drink is? Leonard Lee, Shane Frederick, and Dan Ariely probed this question with a series of clever experiments involving beer.[26] They approached patrons of a pub on MIT's campus and offered them two small free samples of beer. One was ordinary Budweiser or Samuel Adams and the other was called "MIT Brew," which was prepared by adding a few drops of balsamic vinegar to ordinary beer.

Participants all drank the two small samples of beer and then were offered a full glass of the beer of their choice. In the *blind* condition, participants tasted the two samples and choose their free beer without knowing MIT Brew's secret ingredient. In the *before* condition, participants were told the ingredients in both samples before tasting them, and in the *after* condition, they were told the ingredients after they had tasted the samples but before they chose their free beer.

Although beer mixed with vinegar may sound unappealing, the majority of participants in the *blind* condition preferred the MIT Brew to the unadulterated beer. The majority of participants in the *before* condition, turned off by the prospect of vinegar-laced beer, preferred the unadulterated beer to the MIT Brew.

What did people choose in the *after* condition? If our expectations (about the taste of vinegar) provide independent *information* that influences our ratings of utility, then it should not matter whether this information comes before or after tasting the samples. The information should simply be combined with the taste information to reach a conclusion about preference. If, on the other hand, our expectations affect the *experience* of tasting the beer, then they should have a stronger effect when independent information is presented before tasting than after, when it is too late to affect the tasting experience. As it turned out, when participants were told about the vinegar in the MIT Brew after tasting the samples, they still liked it as much as those in the *blind* condition and significantly more than those in the *before* condition. Thus participants' expectations actually influenced their experience of the beer.

---

24. The examples are taken from *Leaky Rationality, supra.*

25. Frisch (2003) *quoted in Leaky Rationality, supra.*

26. Leonard Lee, Shane Frederick, and Dan Ariely, *Try It, You'll Like It: The Influence of Expectations, Consumption, and Revelation on Preferences for Beer,* 17 Psychological Science 1054–58 (2006).

Lee and colleagues speculate that expectations may have affected people's experiences by biasing them to focus on the negative aspects of the complex experience of tasting beer. People may then have erroneously attributed those negative aspects of the experience to the presence of vinegar. (This is not unlike the process involved in confirmation bias, discussed in Section 10.3.) When people expected the beer to taste bad, they may have searched for evidence in the tasting experience to confirm that expectation, ignoring evidence to the contrary.[27]

Another set of experiments, by Baba Shiv, Ziv Carmon, and Dan Ariely, indicates that the price we pay for a product can affect the utility we get from it.[28] In a series of three studies, participants were given a number of difficult anagrams to solve (for example, participants were given the letters TUPPIL and asked to rearrange them to form a word—in this case PULPIT). Before doing the anagram, participants were given a bottle of SoBe Adrenaline Rush (an iced tea drink that claims on its package to improve mental functioning). Some of them were asked to pay the full retail price for their bottle of iced tea ($1.89) while others were given a heavily discounted price (89). The price participants paid affected their subsequent performance on the anagram task. Those who paid less for the iced tea consistently performed worse than those who paid full price. They had lower expectations about how much of a boost they would get than those who paid full price, and this led them to perform less well on the anagram task.

In another study, Shiv and colleagues also found that inflating expectations about the effectiveness of the drink led to a significant increase in performance on the anagram task. Some participants were told that numerous studies had established that SoBe produced a "significant" boost in mental acuity, while others were told that it only produces a "slight" boost. People experienced what they were led to expect: those who were led to expect a "significant" boost experienced just that, and those who were led to expect a "slight" boost had a slightly deflated performance. Price, meanwhile, continued to play its role: those who believed that SoBe produced a "significant" boost and paid full price did best on the anagram task. Those who paid a discounted price did and believed that SoBe only produced a "slight" boost to begin with did worse.

In a related experiment, participants were exposed to a series of painful electric shocks after being given a placebo pill that they were told was a new type of painkiller.[29] Some were told the painkiller's retail price would be $2.50 per dose while others were told it had been discounted from $2.50 to 10 cents. As you

---

27. *See also* Stephen J. Hoch and Young-Won Ha, *Consumer Learning: Advertising and the Ambiguity of Product Experience*, 13 JOURNAL OF CONSUMER RESEARCH 221–33 (1986).

28. Baba Shiv, Ziv Carmon, and Dan Ariely, *Placebo Effects of Marketing Actions: Consumers May Get What They Pay For*, 42 JOURNAL OF MARKETING RESEARCH 383–93 (2005).

29. Rebecca Waber, Baba Shiv, Ziv Carmon, and Dan Ariely, "Paying More for Less Pain," working paper, MIT (2007).

might expect by now, participants who were told the pill was expensive reported that they experienced significantly less pain than those who were told it was inexpensive. This effect may depend on people not adverting to the inference they are making based on price. In one of the iced tea studies, when participants were asked how effective they thought the SoBe would be at boosting their performance *given the price they had paid for it*, the effect of price on performance was completely erased. (Recall the discussion of *metacognition*, in Section 9.6.2.)

Later in this chapter and in the next, we discuss other situations in which the decision process may affect satisfaction with the outcome. Perhaps the most pervasive of these involve the phenomenon of *regret*, closely followed by the effects of *choice overload*—of being faced with a decision that involves too many choices.

Disconnecting the decision process from the experience falls into what Daniel Gilbert and Jane Ebert (2002) have called the "illusion of intrinsic satisfaction"—people's belief that "hedonic experiences [are] due entirely to the enduring intrinsic properties of their outcomes, as though the wonderfulness or awfulness they are experiencing was always there 'in the outcome' waiting to be experienced, and none of these properties were altered or induced by the mere act of making the outcome their own."[30] Daniel Kahneman similarly writes that "a theory of choice that completely ignores feelings such as the pain of losses and the regret of mistakes is not just descriptively unrealistic. It also leads to prescriptions that do not maximize the utility of outcomes as they are actually experienced."[31]

12.1.3 The Effects of Looking Forward and Backward

12.1.3.a Utility from Current Experience, Memory, and Anticipation When Christine Lamm eats at a restaurant, visits her parents, runs a marathon, or visits the dentist, she experiences immediate pleasure or pain. She may also experience pleasure or pain in the anticipation or recollection of these events.

Jon Elster and George Loewenstein make a number of interesting observations about utility from memory and anticipation.[32] The authors define *primary emotions* as those that arise in one's immediate encounters with the external world—the pleasure of riding a bicycle or the pain of falling off it. One can have *nonprimary emotions* through the *backward effect* of contemplating past

30. Daniel T. Gilbert and Jane E. J. Ebert, *Decisions and Revisions: The Effective Forecasting of Changeable Outcomes*, 82.4 Journal of Personality and Social Psychology 503–14 (2002).

31. Daniel Kahneman, *A Perspective on Judgement and Choice*, 58.9 American Psychologist 697–720 (2003).

32. *See* Jon Elster and George Loewenstein, *Utility from Memory and Anticipation, in* Choice Over Time (George Loewenstein and Jon Elster eds., New York: Russell Sage Foundation 1992).

experience and the *forward effect* of contemplating the future. Whether through memory or anticipation, the nonprimary emotions can result from:

- *the consumption effect,* where present positive or negative emotions are based on reliving positive or negative experiences from the past or anticipating them in the future (e.g., remembering a lovely concert or dreading a trip to the dentist), or
- *the contrast effect,* where one's present emotions are affected by the contrast of one's present primary experience with one's recalled or anticipated experience in the past or future (e.g., remembering what it was like to have a well-paying job when currently unemployed).

"While each of the Wosileskis had experienced their rare moments of happiness, John thought that they might have been better off had they not; that the moments of happiness served only to accentuate despair. Had John . . . never known those excruciatingly beautiful seconds with Valentine Kessler, had Mrs. Wosileksi, twenty-four years ago, not walked down the aisle as a grateful bride and hopeful mother-to-be, had Mr. Wosileski not, those same twenty-four years ago minus a few months, known a surge of pride and love at the sight of his newborn, had he not twice—twice!—bowled a perfect game, then the Wosileskis might not have understood that they were unhappy now. With nothing to compare it to, a dreary life would've been a flatline, which is something like a contented one. But they did know rapture and so the loss of it, the fleetingness of it, rendered the sadness that much more acute."
—Binnie Kirshenbaum, An Almost Perfect Moment 180 (2004).

Under the consumption effect, the secondary emotion—empathy, recollection, or anticipation—has the same hedonic sign (pleasant or painful) as the primary experience; also, the pleasure or pain of looking forward or backwards tends not to depend critically on one's present level of well being. Under the contrast effect, the relationship is inverse: "The more perfect was the past, the more deficient appears the present; the grander our neighbor's house, the more inadequate seems our own."

Elster and Loewenstein discuss these and related phenomena in a highly nuanced way. For example, they note that we may experience present (consumption) pleasure from a miserable past experience (e.g., the successful culmination of an arduous mountain ascent); or present (consumption) pain in recalling a pleasurable past experience (e.g., a lovely evening with the lover who jilted you). They write that "the consumption effect swamps the contrast effect when the future is inferior to the present," and conclude that this creates "a strong incentive to build improvement over time into one's plans." Quoting the narrator's desire to defer a goodnight kiss in Marcel Proust's *Swann's Way*—"So much did

I love that goodnight kiss that I reached the stage of hoping it would come as late as possible, so as to prolong the time of respite during which Mamma would not have appeared." As Elster and Loewenstein say: "On the one hand, the narrator wants to be able to look forward to the goodnight kiss (a forward consumption effect). On the other hand, he doesn't want to be in a position in which the kiss has already occurred (a backward contrast effect)."

Proust's desire to postpone his mother's kiss, and thus savor its prospect, deviates from people's general tendency to be *impatient* (captured in the typical model of discounting discussed in Section 13.6)—the preference to enjoy a good experience sooner rather than later. On the negative side, people sometimes prefer to hasten experiencing a bad event rather than dread its prospect over a period of time. In an experiment by Gregory Berns and his colleagues,[33] participants chose to receive an electric shock sooner rather than later, and some preferred to receive a more severe shock now rather than delay a smaller one. As with the instances of deferring enjoyment, the authors suggest that "waiting enters the utility function separately from the outcome." Hastening even an unpleasant outcome affords relief from dread.[34]

12.1.3.b The Uncertain Relationship Between Momentary and Recollected Experience (1) We experience events at the *moment* they occur, (2) we remember events in *retrospect*, and (3) we *predict* how we are likely to feel about similar events in the future. There can be significant differences between momentary and recalled experience. For example, a study of students' spring-break vacations indicated that their recollections were more positive than their experience at the time. The students' prediction of future experiences was based largely on the remembered experience.[35] As Dave Barry notes, "The human race is far too stupid to be deterred from tourism by a mere several million years of bad experiences."[36]

Daniel Kahneman and Jason Riis write:[37]

> When we are asked "how good was the vacation," it is not an experiencing self that answers, but a remembering and evaluating self, the self that keeps score

---

33. Gregory S. Berns et al., *Neurobiological Substrates of Dread*, 312 Science 754–58 (2006).

34. *Id.* 754, 757.

35. Derrick Wirtz, Justin Kruger, Christie Napa Scollon and Ed Diener, *What to Do on Spring Break? The Role of Predicted, On-line, and Remembered Experience in Future Choice*, 14 Psychological Science 520 (2003). Interestingly the students recollected more negative as well as positive moments than they experienced at the time, and overestimated the intensity of the recalled experience. The authors speculate that one tends not to remember the (many) moments of relatively neutral affect.

36. Dave Barry's Only Travel Guide You'll Ever Need (New York: Ballantine 1991).

37. Daniel Kahneman and Jason Riis, *Living and Thinking About It: Two Perspectives on Life*, *in* The Science of Well Being (Felicia A. Huppert, Nick Baylis, and Barry Keverne eds., Oxford: Oxford University Press 2005).

> and maintains records. Unlike the experiencing self, the remembering self is relatively stable and permanent. It is a basic fact of the human condition that memories are what we get to keep from our experience, and the only perspective that we can adopt as we think about our lives is therefore that of the remembering self. For an example of the biases that result from the dominance of the remembering self, consider a music lover who listens raptly to a long symphony on a disk that is scratched near the end, producing a shocking sound. Such incidents are often described by the statement that the bad ending "ruined the whole experience." But in fact the [momentary] experience was not ruined, only the memory of it.

The recollection of painful experiences appears to follow a quite robust rule, called the *peak-end phenomenon*. Figure 12.1 shows the pain of two patients, as reported every ten minutes, while they were undergoing colonoscopies (before the use of the most recent sedatives). Patient A's procedure lasted less than ten minutes, and included one period when he reported a pain level of 7, and one with an ending pain level of 8 on a 10-point scale. Patient B's procedure lasted twenty-five minutes, with one period at a pain level of 8 and several with pain levels ranging from 4 to 6,and with the last few minutes being relatively painless. Taking the amount of the pain and its duration into account, it seems apparent that Patient B had a more painful experience than Patient A. Yet, when asked about the experience retrospectively, Patient B reports having had a less painful procedure.

In this and similar experiments—e.g., immersing one's hand in freezing water—people's retrospective evaluation follows the peak-end rule: they report the painfulness of the event as the arithmetic mean of the most painful moment and the last moments of the experience.[38]

It is not surprising that retrospective assessments of past affective experiences differ from affect at the moment of the experience. Like other memories, retrospective assessments are not simply "remembered"; they are constructed. What is so striking about the peak-end phenomenon is its apparent *duration neglect*, which violates the assumption of *temporal monotonicity*—that adding moments of negative affect should make the experience worse.

The most obvious explanation for the peak-end phenomenon is that the peak and end of an experience may be the two events most *available* to one's memory. Barbara Fredrickson also suggests that, like the representative heuristic, it is an example of judgment by prototype, where a "global evaluation of a set is dominated by the evaluation of its prototypical element or exemplar." Analogous to ignoring base rates in identifying Jack's occupation (Section 8.5.4), people

38. *See generally* Barbara L. Fredrickson, *Extracting Meaning from Past Affective Experience: The Importance of Peaks, Ends, and Specific Emotions*, 14 COGNITION AND EMOTION 577 (2000). The phenomenon manifests itself in rats as well as humans.

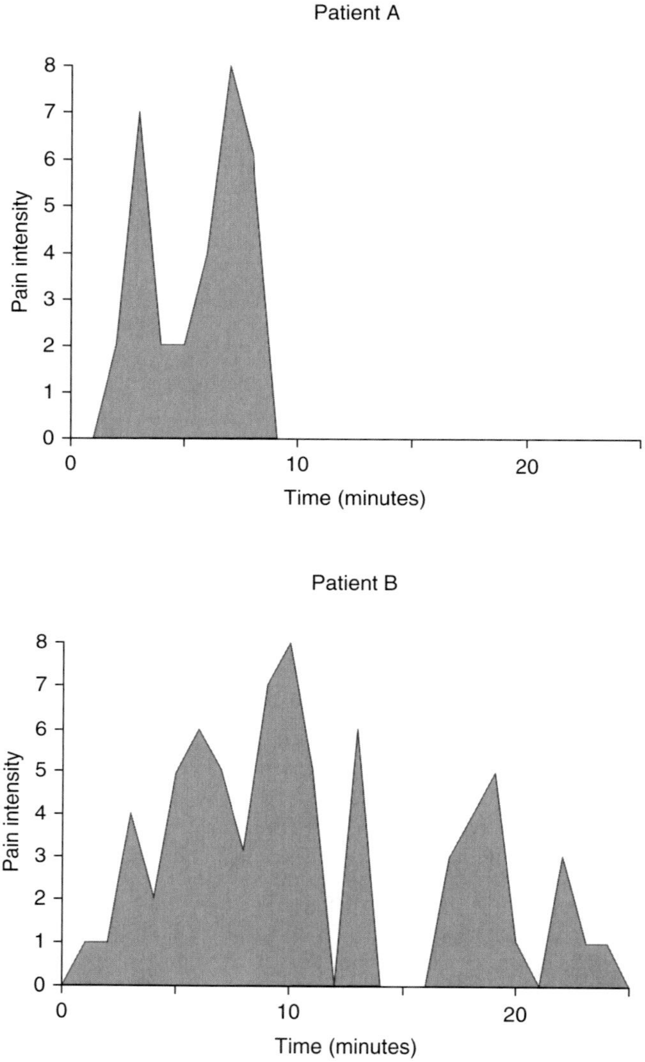

FIGURE 12.1 THE PEAK-END PHENOMENON. FROM DANIEL KAHNEMAN AND SHANE FREDERICK, *Representativeness Revisited: Attribute Substitution in Intuitive Judgment, in* GILOVICH, GRIFFIN, KAHMENAN, HEURISTICS AND BIASES: THE PSYCHOLOGY OF INTUITIVE JUDGMENT 49 (CAMBRIDGE UNIVERSITY PRESS, NEW YORK, USA (2002).

ignore the duration of the event and focus on the prototypical moments of peak and end.

Fredrickson proposes the alternative (but not inconsistent) explanation that peaks and ends are particularly meaningful aspects of experience. Peak discomfort informs a person of the "personal capacity necessary for achieving, enduring, or coping with that episode. . . . [J]ust as you need to know the maximum height of the sailing boat you are towing before you drive under a low bridge, peak affect is worth knowing to decide whether you can handle experiencing a particular affective episode again." And endings "signal that episodes are completed, safely in the past, and therefore knowable. . . . [They] also carry residual meaning about personal capacity. After all, by definition, if you have encountered the end of an episode, you have survived it—you lived to tell the story."[39]

Kahneman and his colleagues suggest that the momentary experience is real, while the remembered experience is an illusion. As the earlier excerpt from Kahneman and Riis concludes: "The experience of the symphony was almost entirely good, and the bad end did not undo the pleasure of the preceding half hour. The confusion of experience with memory that makes us believe a past experience can be ruined is a compelling cognitive illusion. The remembering self is sometimes simply wrong."

Putting to one side these epistemological issues,[40] the divergence between momentary and remembered experience has interesting practical consequences. Suppose that you are considering whether to repeat the event—a similar vacation, a colonoscopy, putting your hands in freezing water. Your prediction is likely to be based on remembered experience (though in the case of the vacation you might have a diary, or letters, or a friend who reminds you how miserable you thought it was at the time). And this means that you may have a miserable time again.[41] Later on, however, you may have a positive recollection of the second miserable time, and perhaps those good memories will prove to be longer and stronger than the experience itself. We will return below to the so-called *psychological immune system*, which tends to mitigate regret. Meanwhile, consider what, if any, implications the peak-end phenomenon has for reducing recidivism after a prisoner is released after spending time in prison,

12.1.3.c The Dubious Relationship Between Daily Experiences and One's General Sense of Well-Being Other work by Daniel Kahneman and colleagues examines an analogue to momentary and retroactive assessment of pain—the relationship between people's (positive and negative) affective experiences during the day and their overall, or global, assessment of their well-being. The relationship often is quite weak. For example, parents whose daily interactions with their children are fraught with negativity are, on the whole, quite satisfied with their children. Kahneman et al. comment: "The contrasting results reflect

---

39. Frederickson, *supra*.

40. *See* Mark Kelman, *Hedonic Psychology and the Ambiguities of "Welfare,"* 13 Philosophy & Public Affairs 413 (2005).

41. Of course, this may ultimately conduce to the health of patients who undergo colonoscopies or similarly uncomfortable medical procedures.

the difference between belief-based generic judgments ('I enjoy my kids') and specific episodic reports ('But they were a pain last night')."[42]

12.1.4 How Much Better Is More?

12.1.4.a Absolute vs. Relative Wealth and Happiness The so-called *Easterlin paradox* observes that while rich people tend to be happier than poor people within a society, rich societies as a whole are not much happier than poor societies and, therefore, economic growth does not increase happiness. This has been variously explained in terms of a "hedonic treadmill," where people adapt to a particular level of well-being, and to assessing their own well-being by comparison to others'. In *Economic Growth and Subjective Well-Being: Reassessing the Easterlin Paradox,* Betsey Stevenson and Justin Wolfers examine subsequent comparisons across countries and argue that the factual assumptions of the Easterlin paradox do not hold and that economic growth is in fact associated with rising happiness.[43]

12.1.4.b Declining Marginal Utility

Money brings some happiness. But after a certain point, it just brings more money.
—Neil Simon

Although one can think of cases where too much money leads an individual to make decisions not in his best interests, all things being equal, more is better. But how much better?

The eighteenth-century scientist Daniel Bernoulli observed that for most people, the marginal value of money declines as the amount increases. For example, the subjective value of increasing one's wealth from $100 to $200 is greater than the subjective value of increasing one's wealth from $100,100 to $100,200. This is a *psychological* observation, rather than a logical one. But it does appear to hold broadly across a wide variety of people in a wide variety of situations. A graph of this "utility function" would be concave downward, as shown in Figure 12.2.

Before she took her current job, Christine Lamm was considering two government positions, which offered salaries of $90,000 and $100,000, respectively; and two jobs in the private sector, respectively offering $190,000 and $200,000. The idea of declining marginal utility suggests that the $10,000 difference

42. Daniel Kahneman, Alan B. Krueger, David Schkade, Norbert Schwarz, and Arthur A. Stone, *A Survey Method for Characterizing Daily Life Experience: The Day Reconstruction Method (DRM)*, 306 SCIENCE 1776–80 (2004).

43. Betsey Stevenson and Justin Wolfers, "Economic Growth and Subjective Wellbeing: Reassessing the Easterlin Paradox," Institute For the Study of Labor Discussion Paper No. 3654 1–80 (August 2008).

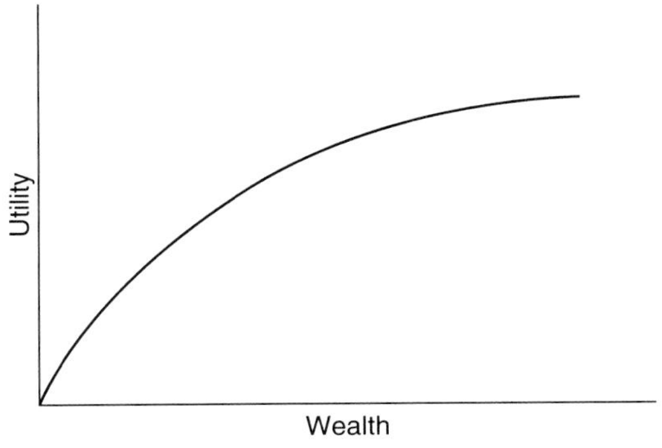

FIGURE 12.2 BERNOULLI'S CURVE FOR WEALTH AND UTILITY.

between the two government positions may be more important to her than the $10,000 difference between the two higher paying positions.

We'll return to these concepts below, but definitionally, the *expected value* (EV) of Christine's choice is her expected net salary. You could compute it just using a calculator and without knowing anything about her individual preferences. Her subjective satisfaction is the *expected utility* (EU) of the choice. The declining marginal utility of money (and some other goods as well) is an important category in which EU deviates from EV.

12.1.4.c Psychophysical Numbing

One death is a tragedy; a million is a statistic.
—Joseph Stalin

I am deeply moved if I see one man suffering and would risk my life for him. Then I talk impersonally about the possible pulverization of our big cities, with a hundred million dead. I am unable to multiply one man's suffering by a hundred million.
—Albert Szent-Gyorgi

Participants in a study were given a scenario in which a foundation was prepared to make a $10 million grant to a medical institution to implement a new treatment to reduce deaths from disease. They were told about three institutions concerned with three different diseases with respective annual fatalities of 15,000, 160,000, and 290,000, and asked the minimum number of lives the institution must save to merit the grant. Two-thirds of the respondents required that more lives be saved as the size of the at-risk population increased, requiring that the institution dealing with the largest disease group save eleven times more people than the institution addressing the smallest disease group.[44]

44. *Quoted in* David Fetherstonhaugh, Paul Slovic, Stephen Johnson, and James Friedrich, *Insensitivity to the Value of Human Life: A Study in Psychophysical Numbing*, 14 Journal of Risk and Uncertainty 28 (1997).

David Featherstonehaugh and his colleagues relate this phenomenon to *Weber's law*,[45] a psychophysical phenomenon that holds across a variety of stimuli. Suppose that you are hearing a soft noise or seeing a dim light, and the sound or brightness diminishes just enough for you to notice the change. Now suppose that you are hearing a loud noise or seeing a bright light, and the sound or brightness diminishes by the same absolute amount as before. You would not notice the change. To be noticed, the change must bear some proportional relationship to the intensity of the background stimulus. The difference is described by a logarithmic rather than a linear function. Featherstonehaugh et al. write:

> Just as a fixed decrease in brightness seems greater when the original intensity is small than when it is large, an intervention saving a fixed number of lives seems more valuable when fewer lives are at risk to begin with—when the lives saved constitute a larger proportion of the number at risk. When such psychophysical numbing occurs, the value of a life-saving intervention is inversely proportional to the magnitude of the threat rather than being determined by the absolute number of lives the intervention can save.[46]

---

45. Articulated by the nineteenth-century psychologists Ernst H. Weber and Gustav Fechner.

46. Although proportion dominance is strong, a substantial minority of respondents base their life-saving decisions on numbers alone. James Friedrich and his colleagues suggest that there may be individual differences between members of the two groups. Those in the former category tended to value saving lives more highly (i.e., requiring fewer lives saved to justify intervention) than those in the latter, and to eschew cost-benefit analysis. Friedrich and his colleague speculate that the phenomenon may result from applying percentage discount heuristics used in making consumer choices. James Friedrich, Paul Barnes, Kathryn Chapin, Ian Dawson, Valerie Garst, and David Kerr, *Psychophysical Numbing: When Lives are Valued Less as the Lives at Risk Increase*, 8 J. CONSUMER PSYCH. 277 (1999).

The presentation of the decision can affect how one approaches the decision. In a variation on the medical institution problem, respondents were asked to rank order three institutions based on whether they should receive the $10 million grant. They were told that:

- Institution X would reduce annual deaths from disease A from 15,000 to 5,000.
- Institution Y would reduce annual deaths from disease B from 160,000 to 145,000.
- Institution Z would reduce annual deaths from disease C from 290,000 to 270,000.

Notice that there is an inverse relationship between the *number* of lives saved and the *proportion* of lives saved. Interestingly, 60 percent of the respondents preferred Institution Z, thus maximizing the number of lives saved, with only 16 percent choosing Institution X. Featherstonehaugh et al. explain that the information highlighted the magnitude of each intervention's life-saving potential and that the ease of comparability—evaluability—may also have been a factor. Nonetheless, they conclude that "psychophysical numbing is a robust phenomenon—ingrained in the workings of our cognitive and perceptual systems."

12.1.4.d When More Is Less: Idiosyncratic Matching The phenomenon of declining marginal utility suggests that more of a good thing is better—just not as much better as the last increment. But there are some situations in which more of a good thing is actually worse: You begin a meal with each bite having a high utility, but the utility of bites decreases as the meal progresses and eventually declines. If you continue eating after you're stuffed, the utility curve reverses direction.

Are there situations where you would pay not to have more of something that you are *indifferent* to? For example, suppose that you are a fan of first-run movies and receive an offer of a new channel, "Best Newly Released Movies," from your cable TV company. How much would you pay for the subscription? Now suppose that this movie channel comes a part of a package of three channels, including two in which you have absolutely no interest—say, one has only infomercials and the other is in Urdu. How much would you pay for the package?

Many people would pay less for the three-channel package that included the movie channel than for the movie channel alone; indeed, they would pay to have the unwanted channels removed from the package—not because they are repulsed by the additional channels, or because of the burden of flipping through them, but because the three channels do not match their tastes as closely as the single one.[47] Perhaps this apparent violation of dominance (see Section 12.2.2.a) in particular choices reflects the application of a heuristic that is for the most part useful—for example, that a package deal signals the inferiority of the components of the package. Buying something that closely fits your tastes feels like a relatively "good deal." Perhaps it is also an application of the representativeness heuristic.

Varda Liberman and Lee Ross, who conducted the cable TV studies, did a variation that inquired whether the value that viewers place on a channel they desired would be affected by others' tastes for the same channel. It turned out that participants were willing to pay more for the channel when it matched their idiosyncratic tastes than when many others shared their tastes. On the one hand, people often seek validation of their own tastes by looking to others. On the other hand, in addition to the sense of a bargain for a unique match, something that fits your own idiosyncrasies may also affirm your distinct identity or special status.

---

47. *See* Varda Liberman and Lee Ross, *Idiosyncratic Matching and Choice: When Less Is More*, 101 ORGANIZATIONAL BEHAVIOR & HUMAN DECISION PROCESSES (2006); Itamar Simonson, Ziv Carmon, and Suzanne O'Curry, *Experimental Evidence on the Negative Effect of Product Features and Sales Promotion on Brand Choices*, 13 MARKETING SCIENCE 23 (1994); Ran Kivetz and Itamar Simonson, *Earning the Right to Indulge: Effort as a Determinant of Customer Preferences Toward Frequency Reward Programs*, 39 JOURNAL OF MARKETING RESEARCH 155 (2002); Ran Kivetz and Itamar Simonson, *The Role of Effort Advantage in Consumer Response to Loyalty Programs*, 40 JOURNAL OF MARKETING RESEARCH 454 (2003).

12.1.5 Hedonic Adaptation

> *[With] never-failing certainty . . . all men, sooner or later, accommodate themselves to whatever becomes their permanent situation . . . [I]n every permanent situation, where there is no expectation of change, the mind of every man, in a longer or shorter time, returns to its natural and usual state of tranquility. In prosperity, after a certain time, it falls back to that state; in adversity, after a certain time, it rises up to it."*[48]
>
> —Adam Smith
>
> *Imagine that one morning your telephone rings and you find yourself speaking with the King of Sweden, who informs you in surprisingly good English that you have been selected as this year's recipient of a Nobel prize. How would you feel, and how long would you feel that way? . . . Now imagine that the telephone call is from your college president, who regrets to inform you that the Board of Regents has dissolved your department, revoked your appointment, and stored your books in little cardboard boxes in the hallway. How would you feel, and how long would you feel that way?*[49]
>
> —Daniel Gilbert

Humans adapt to both good and bad events.[50] Such "hedonic adaptation" may occur through a number of mechanisms, including ones that parallel our adaptation to changes in sound, light, and other physical phenomena.[51] In Chapter 1 we discussed people's strong need to have a coherent view of the world—to see patterns, causes, and explanations. Daniel Gilbert and Timothy Wilson describe four aspects of this need that may play a special role in making our emotional reactions to events more evanescent than we generally imagine:[52]

1. People orient to unexpected but relevant information in their environment.
2. People have more intense emotional reactions to unexpected information than to other events.

---

48. Adam Smith, Theory of Moral Sentiments (1759).

49. Daniel T. Gilbert, Elizabeth C. Pinel, Timothy D. Wilson, Stephen J. Blumberg, and Thalia P. Wheatley, *Immune Neglect: A Source of Durability Bias in Affective Forecasting,* 75 Journal of Personality & Social Psychology 617 (1998).

50. *See* Shane Frederick and George Loewenstein, *Hedonic Adaptation, in* Daniel Kahneman, Ed Diener, and Norbert Schwarz, Well-Being: The Foundations of Hedonic Psychology 302 (1999).

51. Although the phenomena are contested, some commentators have suggested that people whose life circumstances improve may be on a "hedonic treadmill," where they became accustomed to the improvements, or on an "aspiration treadmill," with increased expectations or standards for what it takes to be satisfied.

52. Daniel T. Gilbert and Timothy D. Wilson, *Affective Forecasting, in* 35 Advances in Experimental Social Psychology 345–411 (Mark P. Zanna ed., 2003).

3. Once an unexpected event occurs and people have a relatively intense emotional reaction, they tend to make sense of the event, quickly and automatically.
4. When people make sense of an event, it no longer seems surprising or unexpected, and as a result they think about it less and it produces a less intense emotional reaction. The process of sensemaking "ordinizes" events in a way that robs them of their emotional power.

The easier is it for people to make sense of an experience, the more quickly they return to the baseline. With respect to negative events in particular, psychologists have posited a *psychological immune system* that protects individuals from an overdose of gloom[53]— analogous to the well-documented processes of physical homeostasis that cause most life forms and complex systems to maintain their internal equilibrium. In addition to other adaptive mechanisms, *rationalization* can often play an important role. The easier it is to rationalize a bad experience (breaking up with a romantic partner, not getting a job), the easier it is to recover.

We tend to mitigate regret over an outcome by reconstruing our responsibility for its cause. As between blaming oneself for missing a plane by a few minutes ("if only I had left the house earlier") and tending to cast the blame on others ("if only they hadn't shut the doors sooner than the departure time"), most people opt for the latter.[54] We also reconstrue our intentions and desires, for example, responding to a job rejection by thinking "that wouldn't have been a good firm to work for anyway." Indeed, the anticipation of regret may lead to anticipatory reconstrual: "I don't know how well my interview went from their point of view, but I've got to say that I wasn't particularly impressed with them."[55]

---

53. Gilbert et al., *supra*.

54. Daniel T. Gilbert, Carey K. Morewedge, Jane L. Risen, and Timothy D. Wilson, *Looking Forward to Looking Backward: The Misprediction of Regret*, 15 Psychological Science 346 (2004).

55. Anticipatory reconstrual can backfire, however: The applicant who downgrades the employer may appear lackluster in an interview, thus creating a self-fulfilling prophecy; or, if she gets the job she may not be as satisfied as she would have been if she had not downgraded it in the first place. Timothy D. Wilson, Thalia P. Wheatley, Jamie L. Kurtz, Elizabeth W. Dunn, and Daniel T. Gilbert, *When to Fire: Anticipatory versus Postevent Reconstrual of Uncontrollable Events*, 30 Personality and Social Psychology Bulletin 340 (2004).

Cognitive Dissonance Theory

Cognitive dissonance[57] theory proposes that we reduce inconsistencies in our beliefs (cognitions) and behavior through one of three strategies: (1) reduce the importance of dissonant cognitions, (2) increase the importance of consonant cognitions so as to outweigh the dissonant ones, or (3) change cognitions or behavior. To cite an example used by Leon Festinger, who developed the theory, a smoker who learns that smoking is harmful to his health can (1) discount the risks of smoking ("It adds little risk to inhaling air in the city every day"); (2) think about the benefits ("It keeps my weight under control"); or (3) stop smoking. Although the theory has undergone revisions and been challenged by alternatives since it was introduced in 1957, the essential ideas remain quite robust.

Cultural differences. Most of the participants in research experiments on judgment and decision making have been middle-class members of Western cultures (broadly speaking). Research by Hazel Markus and her colleagues indicates that there may be systematic cultural differences with respect to well-being and the values of autonomous choice.[57] It remains to be learned to what extent the phenomena described in this and the following two chapters are applicable in quite different cultural settings.

12.2 CRITERIA FOR RATIONAL DECISION MAKING: THE FOCUS ON CONSEQUENCES AND TRADE-OFFS

People are in principle capable of pursuing their ends—whatever they may be—in a rational manner. We will tentatively define a *rational* decision-making process as one that *tends* to achieve the decision maker's objectives—that is, the quality of the process is ultimately measured in terms of its *consequences*.[58] A good process is one that works (most of the time). This seemingly tautological premise is more complicated that it appears.

First, even the best possible decision-making processes do not always lead to the desired consequences. For example, a decision maker may lack the

56. *See generally* Eddie Harmon-Jones and Judson Mills, eds., Cognitive Dissonance: Progress on a Pivotal Theory in Social Psychology (American Psychological Association (APA), 1999).

57. The literature is summarized on Hazel Markus's home page, http://www-psych.stanford.edu/~hmarkus/

58. Deborah Frisch and Robert T. Clemen, *Beyond Expected Utility: Rethinking Behavioral Decision Research*, 116 Psychological Bulletin 46 (1994).

information necessary to accurately predict the consequences, or the decision may be based on an accurate assessment of the probability of events conducive to a desired consequence but—probabilities being what they are—the events may or may not occur.

Second, as mentioned above, the decision maker may be concerned about the *process* of decision making as well as the consequences. The most obvious and often acknowledged concern about process is with the costs of making the decision, which must be weighed against the benefits of an optimal outcome. In addition to the tangible costs of time and money, some decision processes carry emotional costs, such as the stress of making difficult trade-offs. They may have emotional benefits as well: We know people who positively enjoy the process of shopping for the best deal, no matter how long it takes. A decision maker might also take pleasure in a procedure, such as referring to a horoscope, that has a dubious relationship to outcomes.

Third, real-life decision makers sometimes subordinate the consequences of a decision to other values. For example, an outcome-oriented decision is necessarily based on the decision maker's current assets,[59] not assets once possessed but already spent. Yet who has not been tempted by, if not succumbed to, the "sunk cost fallacy"? (See Section 14.3) Although we will generally assume that deviations from outcome-oriented strategies are errors, their pervasiveness suggests that decision makers sometimes may be pursuing interests other than their apparent or stated outcomes—or that people's interests can be more complex than they appear to be. We are not referring to situations where deontological principles—promises, duties to family, country, God, and the like—trump utilitarian ones, but rather to mundane decisions such as the purchase of consumer products, where, for example, ignoring sunk costs may make one appear foolishly wasteful in one's own or others' eyes. We return to this question in the next chapter.

Finally, especially because much of this chapter focuses on deliberative decision making, it is worth emphasizing that there is no a priori reason to believe that deliberative decision processes inevitably (or even usually) produce better decisions than naturalistic or intuitive processes. According to Paul Slovic and his colleagues: [60]

> Images, marked by positive and negative affective feelings, guide judgment and decision making. Specifically, . . . people use an *affect heuristic* to make judgments. That is, representations of objects and events in people's minds

59. These include money, tangible goods, physiological and psychological capacities, social relationships. *See* REID HASTIE AND ROBYN M. DAWES, RATIONAL CHOICE IN AN UNCERTAIN WORLD 18 (Thousand Oaks, CA: Sage Publications, 2001).

60. Paul Slovic, Melissa L. Finucane, Ellen Peters, and Donald G. MacGregor, *Rational Actors or Rational Fools? Implications of the Affect Heuristic for Behavioral Economics* 31 JOURNAL OF SOCIO-ECONOMICS, 329–42 (2002).

> are tagged to varying degrees with affect. In the process of making a judgment or decision, people consult or refer to an "affect pool" containing all the positive and negative tags consciously or unconsciously associated with the representations. Just as imaginability, memorability, and similarity serve as cues for probability judgments (e.g., the availability and representativeness heuristics), affect may serve as a cue for many important judgments. Using an overall, readily available affective impression can be far easier—more efficient—than weighing the pros and cons or retrieving from memory many relevant examples, especially when the required judgment or decision is complex or mental resources are limited. This characterization of a mental short-cut leads to labeling the use of affect a "heuristic." . . .

Like other heuristics, the *affect heuristic* can conduce to good decision making, but it also has the potential to distort the process. Whether intuition and affect play a constructive role in decision making depends on the nature and context of the decision at hand.[61]

12.2.1 Two Concepts of Rational Decision Making

As the preceding discussion suggests, people's objectives are multifaceted and conflicting, and even an excellent decision process will not always produce the desired outcomes. There are at least two definitions of rational decision making.[62]

12.2.1.a Consequential Rationality If the quality of a process ultimately depends on the results it produces, then the ideal way of assessing its rationality is in terms of its consequences. An intuitive decision-making process that is opaque even to the decision maker herself—for example, "I just follow my gut instinct"—is rational in this sense if it regularly produces the desired outcomes.

Evaluating a decision process in terms of its ability to produce desired outcomes is a difficult task, however. It requires specifying the desired outcome and then examining a large number of virtually identical decisions to assess the strength of the correlation between the decision and outcome. This is feasible with respect to repetitive decisions within an organization (for example, a bank's criteria for making loans). But a process that is effective in one environment (e.g., making investment decisions) may not be effective in another (deciding which job to take).

12.2.1.b Procedural Rationality: Subjective Expected Utility Theory Consequential rationality is concerned with the decision procedure's

---

61. *See* Kenneth R. Hammond, Human Judgment and Social Policy: Irreducible Uncertainty, Inevitable Error, Unavoidable Injustice 60 (New York: Oxford University Press 1996).

62. These roughly map on to the correspondence and coherence theories of truth in philosophy. *See, e.g.*, "The Stanford Encyclopedia of Philosophy," http://plato.stanford.edu/entries/truth-coherence/.

correspondence to desired outcomes. By contrast, *subjective expected utility theory* (SEU) sets out a theory of decision making that defines a rational procedure in terms of its adherence to a set of *axioms*, or norms. (The word *subjective* emphasizes its concern with the decision maker's own utility rather than some external measure.) SEU is not indifferent to outcomes. On the contrary, it claims that violation of its axioms will produce inferior outcomes.

To a large extent, the test of the axioms is intuitive. But the theory makes stronger claims to validity. For example, in a game theory scenario a player of a multiround game could bankrupt an opponent who systematically violated at least some of the axioms.[63] In the belief that SEU provides a pretty good benchmark for assessing analytic decision-making processes, we now describe its essential axioms.

12.2.2 The Axioms of Subjective Expected Utility Theory

Rather than describe the axioms all at once, in this chapter we present those that underlie decision making where risk is not an issue. In Chapter 15, we revisit some of these in conditions of risk and set out several new axioms as well.

12.2.2.a Completeness, Dominance, and Trade-offs The *completeness* axiom holds that, faced with a choice between alternatives A and B, you must prefer A to B, or prefer B to A, or be indifferent between A and B. This is obviously true when the alternatives have only one attribute, e.g., the choice between a chocolate and vanilla ice-cream cone. However, is also true when the alternatives have multiple attributes that require making trade-offs, as in the decision of siting the wastewater treatment plant. Suppose that firm A offers you a higher salary, but does not offer as good support and mentorship as firm B. Just as in making a choice involving a single characteristic, the axioms of rational decision making posit that ultimately you must either prefer firm A to firm B, or B to A, or be indifferent between them—in which case you'd flip a coin.

A *dominates* B if A is preferable to B in at least one respect and is at least as desirable as B in all other respects. If so, you should choose A and reject B. Referring to the siting the wastewater treatment plant: if one potential site were inferior to the others in every respect, it would be dominated by the others and could be eliminated from the rankings.

But dominance seldom eliminates all but a single choice, and trade-offs are often neither obvious nor easy. Even personal decisions often require making trade-offs among more or less incommensurable wants. Many decisions involving public policy require making trade-offs that have deep and contested ethical dimensions, for example between money on the one hand, and health, safety, or the environment on the other.

---

63. *See* the discussion of transitivity, Section 12.2.2.d.

The problem goes beyond the cognitive incommensurability of the values and involves what Philip Tetlock and his colleagues call *constitutive incommensurability*—based on cultural values and norms:[64]

> The guiding idea is that our commitments to other people forbid certain comparisons. To transgress these normative boundaries, to attach a monetary value to one's friendships or one's children or one's loyalty to one's country is to disqualify oneself from certain social roles, to demonstrate that one "just doesn't get it"—that one does not understand what it means to be a true friend or parent or citizen. We run into constitutive incommensurability whenever treating values as commensurable subverts one or both of the values in the trade-off calculus. To compare is to destroy. Even to think about certain trade-offs (less still to make them) is to corrupt and degrade one's standing as a moral being in the community.

For these among other reasons, the use of cost-benefit analysis to guide public or corporate policy making has sometimes been criticized for requiring "immoral commodification"[65] by placing a dollar value on life's unquantifiables—such as human life, health, or the existence of a wilderness area.[66] In *Retaking Rationality*, Richard Revesz offers a rebuttal to this criticism:

> "This criticism confuses pricing with commodification. Pricing, a mechanism used to allocate society's resources, is the most effective way to aggregate information and allocate scarce resources to produce the most benefit . . . Commodification has to do with the social significance of pricing—the fear that assigning a price to the good things in life obscures their inherent worth."[67]

To be sure, some decisions call for existential choices—for example, trade-offs between peace and justice—that far transcend the capacity of cost-benefit analysis.[68] But as Robert Frank notes:

---

64. Philip E. Tetlock, *Coping with Trade-offs: Psychological Constraints and Political Implications, in* POLITICAL REASONING AND CHOICE ELEMENTS OF REASON: COGNITION, CHOICE, AND THE BOUNDS OF RATIONALITY (Arthur Lupia, Matthew D. McCubbins, and Samuel L. Popkin eds., Berkeley: University of California Press; Cambridge, UK: Cambridge University Press, 2001); Alan P. Fiske and Philip E. Tetlock, *Taboo Tradeoffs: Constitutive Prerequisites for Political and Social Life, in* POLITICAL PSYCHOLOGY: CULTURAL AND CROSS CULTURAL FOUNDATIONS (Stanley A. Renshon and John Duckitt eds., New York: NYU Press 2000).

65. RICHARD L. REVESZ AND MICHAEL A. LIVERMORE, RETAKING RATIONALITY: HOW COST-BENEFIT ANALYSIS CAN BETTER PROTECT THE ENVIRONMENT AND OUR HEALTH 78–79 (New York, Oxford University Press 2008) [hereafter, RETAKING RATIONALITY].

66. For a sustained critique, arguing that cost-benefit analysis is fundamentally flawed, *see* FRANK ACKERMAN AND LISA HEINZERLING, PRICELESS: ON KNOWING THE PRICE OF EVERYTHING AND THE VALUE OF NOTHING (New York: The New Press, 2004); *See also* Steven Kelman, *Cost-Benefit Analysis: An Ethical Critique,* 5 J. GOV'T & SOC. REG. 33 (1981).

67. RETAKING RATIONALITY 13.

68. On the national and international level, the issue arises with respect to whether to subject the perpetrators of massive crimes against citizens to criminal punishment or to

> Scarcity is a simple fact of the human condition. To have more of one good thing, we must settle for less of another. Claiming that different values are incommensurable simply hinders clear thinking about difficult tradeoffs.
>
> Notwithstanding their public pronouncements about incommensurability, even the fiercest critics of cost-benefit analysis cannot escape such tradeoffs. For example, they do not . . . get their brakes checked every morning. The reason, presumably, is not that . . . auto safety does not matter, but that they have more pressing uses of their time. Like the rest of us, they are forced to make the best accommodations they can between competing values.[69]

Policy makers (and others) use various strategies to avoid explicit trade-offs between constitutively incommensurable values.[70] When they cannot avoid a conscious or public trade-off, they engage in buck-passing, procrastination, and obfuscation.[71] And when responsibility for a decision cannot be avoided, they tend to "spread the alternatives," "playing down the strengths of the to-be-slighted value and playing up the strengths of the to-be selected value."[72]

Jurors' Aversion to Corporate Cost-Benefit Analysis Involving Human Safety

Recall Kip Viscusi's discussion, in Section 10.2.1, of jurors' imposing punitive damages on corporate defendants who engaged in cost-benefit analysis. In addition to explaining the phenomenon in terms of hindsight bias, he speculates that "[p]eople may be averse to explicitly balancing money against human lives. Money and lives might be considered incommensurable. . . . When corporations systematically think about risk levels yet nevertheless pursue product or environmental policies that fail to maximize safety, the juror may regard the corporate decision as 'cold-blooded.'"

---

the processes of "truth and reconciliation" commisions, as well as in negotiations between warring nations. The Israeli philosopher, Avram Margalit, has argued that when peace brings an end to cruelty and humiliation, "peace can be justified by being just a peace without being a just peace." (Stanford University Tanner Lectures on Human Values, May 4, 2004, *Stanford Report*, May 10, 2004).

69. Robert Frank, *Why Is Cost-Benefit Analysis so Controversial?*, 29 Journal of Legal Studies 913, 914 (2000).

70. *See* Jonathan Baron, and Mark Spranca *Protected Values*, 70 Organizational Behavior and Human Decision Processes 1–16 (1997).

71. Philip E. Tetlock and Richard Boettger, *Accountability Amplifies the Status Quo Effect When Change Creates Victims*, 7 Journal of Behavioral Decision Making 1–23 (1994).

72. Philip E. Tetlock, *Coping with Trade-offs: Psychological Constraints and Political Implications, supra*.

12.2.2.b Invariance The order or manner in which choices are presented should not affect the outcome of your decision. Thus, Christine Lamm's choices among the potential sites for the wastewater treatment plant should not depend on which one she considers first. (Does Paul's strategy of buying the first suit he sees in a store that fits necessarily violate the axiom of invariance? Is it rational?)

12.2.2.c Independence from Irrelevant Alternatives The relative ranking of a particular set of options should not vary with the addition or deletion of other options. If Lamm is deciding between sites A and C, the fact that she learns about a possible new site, E, in a completely different location from any of the ones she has considered, should not affect her ranking of A and C (unless it somehow provides new information relevant to them).

12.2.2.d Transitivity The Transitivity axiom entails that if you prefer A to B, and prefer B to C, then you must prefer A to C.

The rationality of transitivity is illustrated by considering the plight of a person who is systematically intransitive. She could be used as a "money pump" in the following way. Suppose that Lamm has chosen a model of car to buy and is considering three colors, and suppose that (intransitively) she

- prefers blue to green,
- prefers green to white,
- prefers white to blue.

Lamm buys the blue car. You then offer to trade her the white car for the blue car if she gives you $1; she accepts the trade, because she prefers white to blue. Now that she has the white car, you offer to trade the green car for it if she gives you $1, which she accepts, because she prefers the green to the white. Now, you offer to trade her the blue car for the green if she gives you $1, which she accepts, because she prefers the blue to the green. And we start the process again—until she runs out of money. Later in the book, we will show circumstances under which people—perhaps yourself included—act in an intransitive manner.

Parsimoniousness, Completeness, Decomposability

Albert Einstein suggested: "Make everything as simple as possible, but not simpler." Thus, a decision maker should consider all those but only those factors that could significantly affect her objectives or interests. In identifying the criteria relevant to siting the wastewater treatment plant, Christine Lamm has tried to be complete. Sometimes, however, she may lump a number of criteria together. For example, environmental impact comprises a number of factors, but it may not be worth her time and energy to consider each one separately, rather than make an overall assessment.

* * *

This concludes our first look at the axioms of subjective expected utility theory. We consider some axioms relevant to decision making under risk in Section 15.1. Before moving on, we note two points about SEU.

First, SEU provides a generalized framework for rational choice. But evolutionary psychologists such as Leda Cosmides, John Tooby, and Gerd Gigerenzer have argued that much individual decision making is not based on general principles of rationality, but is modularized to address specific problems in particular domains. They use the term *ecological rationality* to refer to the success of a process in producing outcomes in a particular environment or context.[73] Granted that individuals often depart from the norms of SEU, however, there is considerable doubt whether decision making is as highly contextual as these social scientists claim, let alone to what extent modularized decision making leads to successful outcomes.[74] In any event, lawyers and policy makers are often called upon to make decisions that cut across many domains.

Second, most applications of expected utility theory focus on *outcomes*. But earlier in the chapter we considered how the very *process* of choosing can produce gains or losses of utility for the decision maker. This phenomenon can confound decision makers, or at least confound understanding whether particular choices are rational from the decision maker's point of view. We will return to this matter in the next several chapters.

12.3 FROM EXPECTED UTILITY TO EXPECTED RETURN: COST-BENEFIT ANALYSIS

Under the concept of dominance in expected utility theory, if alternatives can be converted to a common metric—typically dollars—it is rational to choose the alternative that is worth the most. This is the idea behind cost-benefit analysis (CBA), under which an activity or program is justified only if its benefits outweigh its costs. Cost-benefit analysis builds on program evaluations of the sort described in Chapter 7, essentially translating the importance and size of effects into dollar values. Governments frequently require that regulatory decisions be subject to cost-benefit analysis. For example, Executive Order 12866,[75] signed by

---

73. *See* Leda Cosmides and John Tooby, *Origins of Domain Specificity: The Evolution of Functional Organization*, *in* MAPPING THE MIND: DOMAIN SPECIFICITY IN COGNITION AND CULTURE 85, 89–90 (Lawrence A. Hirschfeld and Susan A. Gelman eds., Cambridge, UK: Cambridge University Press, 1994); GERD GIGERENZER, PETER M. TODD AND ABC Research Group, SIMPLE HEURISTICS THAT MAKE US SMART (New York: Oxford University Press, 1999).

74. JERRY FODOR, THE MIND DOESN'T WORK THAT WAY: THE SCOPE AND LIMITS OF COMPUTATIONAL PSYCHOLOGY 58–61 (Cambridge, MA: The MIT Press, 2000); MARK G. KELMAN, THE HEURISTICS DEBATE: ITS NATURE AND ITS IMPLICATIONS FOR LAW AND POLICY (Oxford University Press, forthcoming 2010).

75. *See* Office of Management and Budget (OMB), "Economic Analysis of Federal Regulations Under Executive Order 12866," Jan. 11, 1996, http://www.whitehouse.gov/

President Bill Clinton in 1993, requires federal agencies to "assess all costs and benefits of available regulatory alternatives, including the alternative of not regulating."

The most difficult and contested applications of CBA involve risk, a matter that we discuss in Chapter 15. Even when risk is not a major factor, however, CBA can present difficulties in monetizing benefits and in making distributional decisions (for example, where the benefits flow partly to an individual beneficiary of a program and partly to taxpayers). And even when the calculation is reasonably clear, there may be reasons not to follow the logic of CBA: For better or worse, politics, ideology, and issues of fairness and rights may trump CBA. But CBA almost always provides a useful norm or reference point for decision making.

The longitudinal analysis of the Perry Preschool program in Michigan provide a classic example of CBA. This precursor of Head Start had low student-teacher ratios; all the teachers were certified in both early childhood and special education, and they made weekly visits to every family.[76] The program produced long-term gains in school attendance, academic achievement, graduation rates, and earnings.

> In constant discounted dollars, the economic return to society of the program was more than $17 per dollar invested ($258,888 on an investment of $15,166 per student). Seventy-five percent of that return accrued to the general public ($12.90 per dollar invested), and 25 percent to each participant ($4.17 per dollar invested). While net benefits derive from many sources, such as increased earnings and taxes paid, with Perry Preschool students having significantly fewer lifetime arrests and fewer arrests for violent crimes than students not in the program, a significant share of the public benefits come from the avoidance of these significant costs to society.[77]

Thus, even when limiting the benefits to those returned to taxpayers, the program had a benefit-cost ratio of almost 13 to 1. Economists at the Federal Reserve Bank in Minneapolis estimated that the Perry Preschool program generated a 16 percent rate of return on investment, of which 12 percent was a public return.[78]

---

omb/inforeg/riaguide.html; Environmental Protection Agency, "Executive Order 12866 Regulatory Planning and Review," Sept. 30, 1993, http://www.epa.gov/fedrgstr/eo/eo12866.html.

76. Jonathan Crane and Mallory Barg, "Do Early Childhood Intervention Programs Really Work," Coalition for Evidence-Based Policy, April 2003, 10.

77. Michael A. Stegman, The Power of Measuring Social Benefits, The John D. and Catherine T. MacArthur Foundation (2009 unpublished).

78. Art Rolnick and Rob Grunewald, *Early Childhood Development: Economic Development with a High Public Return*, FedGazette, March 2003. http://www.minneapolisfed.org/pubs/fedgaz/03-03/earlychild.cfm.

12.3.1 An Example: A CBA Analysis of a Workforce Development Program

Not only governments, but nonprofit organizations and their funders, evaluate social programs in terms of costs and benefits. For example, the New York–based Robin Hood Foundation examines the benefit-cost ratio of the workforce development programs it supports so it can compare them not only to similar programs, but also to its grants in education, health, and other areas.[79]

Robin Hood measures impact in terms of the personal benefits that accrue to its grantee organizations' poor clients and their families. For example, in a job training program for ex-offenders, the foundation estimates the impact of job placements on trainees' recidivism and on their future earnings. In supporting early childhood programs, it estimates the impact of reading readiness on high school graduation rates and on the children's projected earnings as adults. Although Robin Hood does not make information about particular grantees publicly available, it demonstrates its approach through a fictional example: Bob's Jobs, a workforce training program for women to become construction workers that is based on Robin Hood's actual programs.

Calculating benefits. One hundred fifty women enrolled in Bob's Jobs and seventy-two completed the training. Of these seventy-two newly minted construction workers, forty-one held on to their jobs for only three months. The remaining thirty-one still had jobs at the end of one year.

How much does Bob's Jobs benefit trainees? Robin Hood compares the salary of each participant before she entered the program and after she graduated. The forty-one women with short-term employment enjoyed an average salary increase of about $2900, or $120,000 in total. The average annual salary increase for the thirty-one women who held jobs for at least a year was approximately $12,000, or $372,000 in total. To compute the value of the program for these thirty-one women, Robin Hood makes the following assumptions:

1. They will continue to be employed for thirty years.
2. Their annual salaries will increase by 1.5 percent above inflation.
3. They have an average of 1.8 children each; given research findings on the effects of parents' employment, each family will realize an intergenerational income boost of $56,000.
4. The discount rate—that is, the number used to calculate how much an amount of future money is worth today—is 3.5 percent.[80]

On the basis of these assumptions, Robin Hood estimates that the net present value of the benefits to the thirty-one long-term workers is $9.1 million. Adding the onetime salary boost for the forty-one short-term workers, the total benefit of the program is $9.2 million. Robin Hood does not further discount the

79. See Paul Brest, Hal Harvey, & Kelvin Low, *Calculated Impact*, STANFORD SOCIAL INNOVATION REVIEW, Winter 2009.

80. For more on discount rates, *see* Section 13.6.1.

value of the benefits based on the probability of success; it discounts its own role in generating these benefits by 50 percent to account for the fact that other donors, both private and public, support Bob's Jobs. Thus, Robin Hood attributes $4.6 million of the program's benefits to its philanthropic investment.

Calculating costs. What about the costs? The grant to Bob's Jobs was $200,000.[81] Dividing $4.6 million by $200,000 results in a net benefit of $23 per $1 invested. That is, for each dollar that Robin Hood spends on Bob's Jobs, trainees and their families gain $23—a pretty good return on investment.

Robin Hood has made similar calculations for its other poverty programs, including a program to help people manage budgets, bank accounts, and loans (net benefit = $1.90) and a clinic that deals with asthma, hepatitis, and cancer (net benefit = $12).

Although Robin Hood considers cost-benefit analysis in its grant-making, it does not rely on this measure exclusively. The foundation recognizes that the metrics are imprecise, with each CBA calculation depending on complex and uncertain empirical assumptions. Thus Robin Hood continues to test its metrics against the informed intuitions of program officers and experts in the field. At the same time, the foundation presses its staff to justify their intuitions against the numbers generated by analysis.

12.3.2 Cost-Effective Analysis (CEA)

Since CBA monetizes benefits, it can be used (at least in principle) to compare benefits across different domains, for example, workforce development, early childhood, and health programs. When comparing specific benefits within a particular domain, one can use *cost-effective analysis (CEA)*, which attempts to determine which policy option will maximize specific benefit at the least cost. CEA does this by computing the ratio of cost to the nonmonetary benefit for each option. For example, CEA allows one to compare two similar education programs in terms, say, of the cost per child graduating from high school. While CBA's monetization seeks to compare apples to oranges, CEA compares apples to apples. CEA analyses of health often measure benefits using the metric of QALYs (Quality-Adjusted Life Years), which we will discuss below.

12.3.3 Quantifying Reduced Risks in Mortality

Some of the most divisive debates surrounding CBA concern the valuation of human life—an issue that arises in government regulatory efforts to reduce workplace, toxic, and other risks. (We'll defer discussing another divisive issue, evaluating public environmental goods such as wilderness areas, to Section 14.6.)

---

81. Robin Hood does not include the administrative costs of making the grant, both because these costs are not large and because they do not differ significantly from those of the other poverty-fighting programs to which it will compare Bob's Jobs.

Suppose that 2.5 million people are exposed to an environmental pollutant that causes cancer in every one of 10,000 people exposed, and thus is expected to cause 250 cases of cancer. Regulations designed to reduce or obviate the risk are likely to impose costs on governments, businesses, consumers, and their intended beneficiaries (for example, employees whose compensation or even job opportunities may be diminished by a regulation prohibiting exposure to toxic chemicals). When conducting a cost-effectiveness analysis, how can one quantify the value of each life saved?

Currently, there exist three main methods for the assessment of human life: VSL (Value of a Statistical Life),VSLY (Value of Statistical Life Years), and QALYs (Quality-Adjusted Life Years). QALYs are also often used to compare health procedures in cost-effective analysis (CEA), which compares benefits and costs that occur within the same domain without necessarily assigning monetary valuations.

12.2.3a Value of a Statistical Life (VSL) Perhaps the most widely used method, VSL assigns a fixed monetary value to every human life in a certain population. It does not seek to estimate the *intrinsic* value of an individual human life, but is based on people's willingness to pay (WTP) to avoid an aggregation of many small health and safety risks in their lives. As Richard Revesz summarizes, "the value of a statistical life might be more accurately called '10,000 times the value of eliminating a 1 in 10,000 risk.'"[82]

VSL can be determined through WTP by using:

(1) people's *stated preferences* for how much they would pay to eliminate risks, or
(2) people's *revealed preferences*, analyzing decisions that people have already made about risk trade-offs for goods and/or workplace risk reductions.

Utilizing both these techniques, the Environmental Protection Agency reviewed twenty-six peer-reviewed value-of-life studies from academic literature to arrive at a single VSL of $6.3 million for the United States (in year 2000 dollars). Subsequently, however, an Environmental Protection Agency work group asserted that, since VSL values vary widely by social and economic status, race, population, and country, there "does not appear to be a universal VSL value that is applicable to all specific subpopulations." Furthermore, the work group recommended that VSL studies using stated and revealed preferences be analyzed separately, since they sometimes lead to significantly different estimates.

Citizens of a developing country, such as India, have a lower WTP and thus a lower VSL than an economically developed country, such as the United States. In fact, VSL evaluations conducted around the world range from $70,000 to

82. Retaking Rationality 45.

$16.3 million.[83] Nonetheless, some scholars advocate, on moral grounds, the use of a universal VSL for all peoples, regardless of their economic status or willingness to pay. On the other hand, others, including Cass Sunstein, assert that policy makers should establish specific, local VSLs for communities and countries. Sunstein argues that VSLs should be assessed within the population where regulations force the beneficiaries to bear the costs. If an inflated VSL is used, poorer citizens may be forced to "spend" their money to reduce a workplace risk when they would prefer to put that money to other uses.[84]

12.3.3b Value of Statistical Life Years (VSLY) VSL treats the lives of the very young and very old as equally valuable. Under the VSLY approach, benefits to individuals are assessed based on their estimated remaining years of life. VSLY values are derived from VSLs drawn from age-specific populations.[85] Michael J. Moore and W. Kip Viscusi, proponents of this approach, note that "in the case of fatalities, a young person loses a much greater amount of lifetime utility than does an older person," and thus assert that it doesn't make sense to use the same value for an elderly person with a remaining five-year life expectancy as for a 25-year-old.[86] Critics of VSLY term it the "senior death discount."

Revesz uses ozone emission standards to demonstrate the difference between the VSL and VLSY approaches.[87] Assume for the sake of argument that elderly individuals with existing respiratory problems would be the most likely to benefit from stricter ozone regulations, and that these individuals have an average life expectancy of five years. Under a VSLY calculation, the benefit of a stricter regulation, using a $180,000 life-year value, would be $900,000. By assessing benefits at $900,000 per individual instead of at the $6.3 million VSL, the total estimated regulatory benefit is reduced by 85 percent.

The VSLY approach assumes a decreasing relationship between willingness to pay and age that is proportional to remaining life expectancy. This empirical assumption remains contested despite considerable research.[88] Some studies

---

83. *Id.*135.

84. Cass R. Sunstein, Laws of Fear: Beyond the Precautionary Principle 170 (New York: Cambridge University Press 2005). This distributional problem is further confounded when the costs for this population are subsidized or covered by a grant: in this case, people "will be helped even if risk reduction is based on an excessive VSL."

85. *See* Joseph E. Aldy and W. Kip Viscusi, *Adjusting the Value of Statistical Life for Age and Cohort Effects*, April 2006, RFF DP 06–19.

86. Michael J. Moore and W. Kip Viscusi, *The Quantity-Adjusted Value of Life*, 26 Econ. Inquiry 269 (1988).

87. Retaking Rationality 78–79.

88. *Id.* 81–82.

suggest that WTP peaks around age fifty;[89] but elderly citizens may be willing to pay enormously for risk reductions that prolong life. Because both VSL and VSLY "may change with age, life expectancy, anticipated future health, income, and other factors,"[90] the U.S. Office of Management and Budget has encouraged federal agencies to conduct analysis using both approaches.[91]

12.2.2 c Quality-Adjusted Life Years (QALYs) QALYs incorporate a coefficient that measures "quality of life" and can be used to assess the efficiency of health care policies and procedures. Consider an example by Dr. Fritz Allhoff:

> "If treating a patient would lead to a life expectancy of 20 years with a high quality of life (e.g., hypertension, which only requires daily pills and rarely manifests negative symptoms), coverage for this patient's treatment should presumably have priority over treatment for a patient who would have a life expectancy of 20 years with a comparatively low quality of life (e.g., diabetes, which requires daily injections and often manifests symptoms such as neuropathy, blindness, etc)."[92]

This "quality of life" coefficient ranges from 0 to1,valuing a healthy year of life at 1 and a year where one suffers under a disease or disability at some fraction of 1. The QALYs assigned to a particular reduction in mortality, then, are based on the expected number of years of life gained adjusted by their perceived quality of life. Proponents of this method argue that this system distributes finite resources as efficiently and fairly as possible.

The perceived quality-of-life coefficient, which has a large impact on the final assigned value, is typically determined through contingent valuation, asking "healthy people, ex ante, to evaluate various health states."[93] But healthy individuals may fail to take *adaptation* into account and thus underestimate the quality of life of disabled persons, leading to disproportionately low QALY values. Additionally, as Revesz notes, the "empirical work comparing how willingness to pay relates to QALYs confirms there is no simple dollar-per-QALY

89. Thomas J. Kniesner, W. Kip Viscusi, and James P. Ziliak, *Like-Cycle Consumption and the Age-Adjusted Value of Life*, 5 Contributions, Economic Analysis and Policy 1524 (2006).

90. James K. Hammitt, *Risk in Perspective: Valuing "Lives Saved" vs. "Life-Years Saved*, Harvard Center for Risk Analysis, March 2008, Volume 16, Issue 1.

91. *Id.*

92. Fritz Allhoff, *The Oregon Plan and QALY's*, Virtual Mentor, Policy Forum, February 2005, Volume 7, Number 2.

93. Retaking Rationality 90.

conversion rate."[94] Although valuations of about $50,000 are often used,[95] a study by the Harvard Center for Risks Analysis reveals that willingness to pay per QALY fluctuates depending on "both the severity and duration of the illness."[96]

The State of Oregon was a leader in using QALYs to prioritize treatments after deciding to make fewer Medicaid-funded services available to a larger number of people. In 1989, a commission determined "quality-of-life" coefficients based on numerous community meetings and phone surveys.[97] The commission assigned QALYs to 709 procedures, providing coverage only for those ranked higher than 587. More specifically, "treatments that prevented death with a full chance of recovery were ranked first, maternity care was ranked second, treatments that prevented death but did not guarantee full recovery were ranked third, and treatments that led to minimal or no improvements in quality of life were ranked last. For example, "Diagnosis: severe or moderate head injury, hematoma or edema with loss of consciousness; Treatment: medical and surgical treatment' was ranked at the top of the list and 'Diagnosis: mental disorders with no effective treatment' . . . was ranked near the bottom."[98]

Inevitably, the rankings produced some seemingly arbitrary and politically vulnerable choices. For example, "acute headaches" were ranked higher than some treatments for AIDS or cystic fibrosis.[99] The plan was originally rejected by Health and Human Services, but approved in 1993 under the Clinton administration after some changes in methodologies and safeguards against discrimination.[100]

Britain's National Health Service, which provides 95 percent of the nation's care, also uses QALYs to ration health care. The National Institute for Health

---

94. The results of several studies are summarized in James K. Hammit, "Methodological Review of WTP and QALY Frameworks for Valuing Environmental Health Risks to Children" (paper presented at OECD VERHI-Children Advisory Group Meeting, Sept. 2006).

95. Richard A. Hirth, Michael E. Chernew, Edward Miller, A. Mark Fendrick, and William G. Weissert, *Willingness to Pay for a Quality-Adjusted Life Year: In Search of a Standard*, 20 Med. Decis. Making 332–42 (2000).

96. *See* Kevin Haninger and James K. Hammitt, Willingness to Pay for Quality-Adjusted Life Years: Empirical Inconsistency Between Cost-Effectiveness Analysis and Economic Welfare Theory (2006).

97. *See* Gina Kolata, *Ethicists Struggle to Judge the "Value" of Life*, New York Times, Nov. 24, 1992.

98. Fritz Allhoff, "*The Oregon Plan and QALYs*—a controversial oregon plan used quality-of-life assessments to provide fewer health care services to a larger pool of medicaid patients," virtual mentor, February 2005, volume 7, number 2, http://virtualmentor.ama-assn.org/2005/02/pfor2-0502.html.

99. Virginia Morell, *Oregon Puts Bold Health Plan on Ice*, 249 Science, 468, 469–71.

100. *See* Timothy Egan, *Oregon Health Plan Stalled by Politics*, New York Times, March 17, 1993,http://www.nytimes.com/1993/03/17/us/oregon-health-plan-stalled-by-politics.html?sec=&spon=&partner=permalink&exprod=permalink.

and Clinical Excellence (NIHCE), which approves treatments and drugs for the Health Service, determined that, in effect, six months of good quality life is worth about $22,750. It automatically approves drugs that provide six months of good quality life for $15,150 or less.[101] Dr. Andreas Seiter, a senior health specialist at the World Bank, notes that "all the middle-income countries—in Eastern Europe, Central and South America, the Middle East and all over Asia—are aware of NIHCE and are thinking about setting up something similar."[102]

Quantifying Effects on Psychological Health

In *Metropolitan Edison Co. v. People Against Nuclear Energy*, 460 U.S. 766 (1983), involving the operation of a nuclear power plant near a residential area the Nuclear Regulatory Commission, the Court was asked to review the Commission's assessment of adverse psychological affects under the National Environmental Policy Act. Justice William Rehnquist noted that "any effect on psychological health is an effect on health," but he wondered how one could distinguish between "genuine" adverse psychological effects that are caused directly by a policy from claims that are rooted in discontent.

12.3.4 Difficult-to-Measure Benefits

Many regulations and programs aim to improve quality of life in ways that are not readily measurable by an increase in wage earnings or life years. (The Office of Management and Budget (OMB) asserts that "a complete regulatory analysis includes a discussion of non-quantified as well as quantified benefits and costs."[103]) For example, the benefits of the Perry Preschool program were measured by long-term gains in school attendance, academic achievement, graduation rates, and earnings, all of which were converted to monetary values. However, as Lynn Karoly asserts, there still exists a subset of social benefits that

101. Michael D. Rawlins and Anthony J. Culyer, *National Institute for Clinical Excellence and Its Value Judgments*, BMJ 2004 Jul 24; 329 (7459):227–9. This has "led many companies to offer the British discounts unavailable almost anywhere else." Gardiner Harris, *The Evidence Gap: British Balance Benefit vs. Cost of Latest Drugs*, NEW YORK TIMES, Dec. 2, 2008.

102. *See id.*

103. OMB, Circular A-4, "Regulatory Analysis: Memorandum to the Heads of Executive Agencies and Establishments" 3 (Sept. 17, 2003).

are often not assigned valuations (or "shadow prices").[104] She offers these categories with respect to social programs targeting youth:

- *Outcomes rarely or never monetized*: child/youth behavioral/emotional outcomes (e.g., behavior problems, school suspensions/expulsions, mental health outcomes), child/youth cognitive outcomes (e.g., IQ scores), K–12 grades, school attendance, school engagement, general health status of children/youth, contraceptive use, adult parenting measures, marriage and divorce, adult mental health, adult reproductive health, employment, income, and poverty status.
- *Outcomes without clear consensus on monetization*: achievement test scores, high school graduation, college attendance, teen pregnancy, tobacco use, alcohol abuse, illicit drug use, crime and delinquency, and child abuse and neglect.
- *Outcomes with more-established methodology for monetization*: special education use, grade retention, transfer payments, and other means-tested programs

Even if one can assign values to such benefits, questions of judgment remain about which to include in CBA. These are appropriately questions not for economic experts, but for policy makers.[105]

12.3.5 Ancillary Costs and Benefits

Government regulations and policies can give rise to both foreseen and unforeseen harms and benefits. Direct-risk trade-offs occur when diminishing one risk of harm creates a countervailing risk: for example, reducing chlorine levels in water may decrease the risk of cancer but increase microbial disease.[106] A substitution effect occurs when a regulation (for example making flying more onerous) causes a shift in behavior toward taking other risks (driving accidents).

However, regulations can also produce ancillary benefits. To comply with the Clean Air Act, "municipalities have constructed wetlands as an alternative to conventional wastewater treatment facilities," thereby generating "habitat creation and preservation, carbon sequestration, erosion control, and recreational and research opportunities"[107]

---

104. Lynn A. Karoly, "Valuing Benefits in Benefit-Cost Studies of Social Programs," RAND: Labor and Population, pg. 78, chart 4.1, http://www.rand.org/pubs/technical_reports/TR643/.

105. Jeffrey L. Harrison, Thomas D. Morgan, and Paul R. Verkuil, Regulation and Deregulation: Cases and Materials, American Casebook Series 424 (2d ed. St. Paul: West Publishing Co., 1997).

106. *See* John D. Graham and Jonathan Baert Wiener, *Confronting Risk Tradeoffs, in* Risk Versus Risk: Tradeoffs in Protecting Health and the Environment (Cambridge, MA: Harvard University Press, 1995).

107. *See* Steven Piper and Jonathan Platt, *Benefits From Including Wetland Component in Water Supply Projects*, 124 J. Water Resources Planning & Mgmt. 230 (1998) and EPA,

One study indicated that the regulation of carbon monoxide emissions from motor vehicles to improve air quality had an enormous ancillary benefit of reducing cancer risks, thus saving an average of 25,000 lives per year—whereas other health benefits had been estimated only at 212 to 515 lives annually.[108] And health or safety regulations may have what Revesz calls an "attentiveness effect," inducing people to become more conscious of safety issues beyond what is mandated.[109]

Policy makers often only consider unintended costs. However, the OMB recommends that agencies account for ancillary benefits of regulations as well,[110] and Revesz argues that a complete cost-benefit analysis requires as much.[111] In a 2007 decision, the U.S. Court of Appeals for the Ninth Circuit invalidated the National Highway Traffic Safety Administration (NHTSA)'s fuel economy standards for light trucks, noting that while NHTSA had accounted for the negative consequences of the policy on employment and automobile sales, it failed to include the ancillary beneficial effects on climate change. The court said that "NHTSA could not put a thumb on the scale by undervaluing the benefits."[112]

12.3.6 The Value and Limits of Cost-Benefit Analysis

Cost-benefit analysis depends on determining people's WTP for certain benefits. Yet individuals' WTP is essentially irrelevant to many important policy decisions, such as discrimination and abortion; as Cass Sunstein notes, these are appropriately resolved by citizens' preferences and values.[113] At least with respect to environmental decisions, Frank Ackerman, Lisa Heinzerling, and Mark Sagoff argue that CBA is a "crude tool . . . that buries indefensible judgments of morality and politics"[114]

But environmental policies often do impose costs in return for benefits, and it seems equally indefensible for policy makers to blind themselves to these. Following Sunstein, our own view is that if one is explicit about its inaccuracies, biases, and limitations, CBA can provide a "concrete sense of what actually is

---

Office of Water, Constructed Wetlands for Wastewater Treatment and Wildlife Habitat (91993), EPA 832-R-93-005, *available at* http://www.epa.gov/owow/wetlands/construc/.

108. *See* M. Shelef, *Unanticipated Benefits of Automotive Emission Control: Reduction in Fatalities by Motor Vehicle Exhaust Gas*, 146/147 Sci. Total Envtl. 93 (1994).

109. Retaking Rationality 175.

110. OMB, Circular A-4, "Regulatory Analysis: Memorandum to the Heads of Executive Agencies and Establishments" 3 (Sept. 17, 2003).

111. Retaking Rationality 145.

112. Center for Biological Diversity v. National Highway Traffic Safety Administration (NHTSA), No. 06-71891, 13,871 (9th Cir. Nov. 15, 2007).

113. Cass R. Sunstein, Laws of Fear: Beyond the Precautionary Principle, *supra*.

114. Frank Ackerman and Lisa Heinzerling, *supra*. *See also* Mark Sagoff, The Economy of the Earth: Philosophy, Law, and the Environment (Cambridge Studies in Performance Practice).

at stake."[115] Consider James Hammit's March 2003 letter to the editor of the *New York Times*:[116]

> The Office of Management and Budget's interest in applying cost-benefit analysis to homeland security measures is laudable. Even if precise quantification of the benefits to security and harms to civil liberties is impossible, analytic consideration of the trade-offs is wise.
>
> As John Graham, director of regulatory affairs at O.M.B., says, "Simply identifying some of these costs will help understand them and get people to think about alternatives that might reduce those costs."
>
> Cost-benefit analysis should also have been used to evaluate the potential war in Iraq. The benefits of ousting Saddam Hussein should be measured against the costs of casualties, waging war, reconstruction, retaliatory terrorism and increased anti-Americanism. Such analysis would prompt us "to think about alternatives that might reduce those costs."

---

115. Cass R. Sunstein, Laws of Fear: Beyond the Precautionary Principle, *supra* at 174.

116. James K. Hammitt, *Security, at a Price: Letter to the Editor*, New York Times, March 14, 2003, http://query.nytimes.com/gst/fullpage.html?res=9F02E4DC103EF937A25750C0A9659C8B63.

13. COMPLEXITIES OF DECISION MAKING
Decision Processes; Relationships to our Future Selves

Neoclassical economics and the axioms of expected utility theory posit a model of the individual as *homo economicus*. In Gary Becker's words, all human behavior can be viewed as involving participants who maximize their utility from a stable set of preferences and accumulate an optimal amount of information and other inputs in a variety of markets.[1]

The next several chapters inquire whether and when decision makers deviate from this model. This chapter begins with a compilation of characteristics of a decision that may lead to suboptimal outcomes, and then discusses how the choice of decision-making strategies can affect outcomes. The bulk of the chapter focuses on people's relationships with their own future selves—their beliefs about how today's decisions will affect their futures, and limits on their capacity to plan and implement plans to improve their future well-being. Chapter 14 considers how the outcomes of decisions can be affected by the ways that choices are framed. Chapter 15 considers the effects of framing and other matters when decisions are made in conditions of risk or uncertainty. Chapter 16 continues the discussion of risk in situations of high affect.

13.1 HOW WOULD ONE KNOW IF A PERSON MADE A SUBOPTIMAL DECISION?

Since introducing the concept of bounded rationality in Section 1.6.2, we have referred to the fact that human beings have neither infinite computational power nor infinite time to make decisions. Because gathering and comparing the information that bears on a decision can be a time-intensive, costly, and mentally effortful process, we usually *satisfice* rather than try to maximize expected utility. We implicitly take into account the time, money, and psychological impact of making the decision by using shortcuts or heuristics, including noncompensatory strategies of the sort described in Section 4.3.

Doubtless, many particular decisions that seem suboptimal make perfect sense—indeed become optimal—when one takes these decision costs into account. Our goal for the chapter is not to assess particular decisions, however, but to see whether there are *systematic* ways in which people make

1. Gary S. Becker, The Economic Approach to Human Behavior 14 (Chicago: University of Chicago Press, 1976).

suboptimal decisions. This raises the preliminary question of how one would know whether a decision maker had made a suboptimal decision. The following characteristics do not necessarily lead to poor decisions, but they all reflect potential hazards for optimal decision making:

1. The decision is based on incorrect data or the incorrect analysis of data—whether the result of biases (e.g., the availability or representativeness heuristic), poor predictions of one's own future desires or what it will take to achieve them, or simple miscalculation.
2. The decision violates one of the axioms of expected utility, or rational choice. (See Section 12.2.2). For example, it violates the principle of dominance or transitivity.
3. The decision maker poorly integrates utilities from the decision-making process with utilities from the outcome of the process—for example, giving excessive weight to the utility of avoiding confronting a stressful choice compared to the enduring consequences of making a poor choice.
4. The decision is sensitive to the way the issue is framed and is made in a context where the framing is highly variable or manipulable. (See Chapter 14.)
5. The decision is sensitive to affect (i.e., emotion) and is made in a context where affect is highly variable or manipulable, or where present affect is likely to be very different from affect when experiencing the consequences of the decision. (See Chapter 16.)
6. The decision maker was subjected to undue social influence. (We postpone consideration of this subject to Chapter 17.)

We will examine some of these phenomena and other factors that can affect the decision-making process, often for the worse.

13.2 THE CHOICE OF DECISION-MAKING STRATEGIES

13.2.1 Overview of the Decision-Making Process: Decision-Making Bricolage and the Ad Hoc Construction of Preferences[2]

Christine Lamm approached the problem of siting the wastewater treatment plant knowing in advance that she would employ a particular decision-making strategy—the subjective linear model. And even though quantifying the relative

---

2. The French word *bricolage* means "doing odd jobs." Borrowing from Claude Levi-Strauss's use of the term, a *bricoleur* is someone who improvises and uses any means or materials that happen to be lying around in order to tackle a task. CLAUDE LEVI-STRAUSS, THE SAVAGE MIND 19 (Chicago: The University of Chicago Press, 1966).

values of the factors, or attributes, involved had an inevitable degree of arbitrariness, she was reasonably clear about the city's interests and objectives.

In actuality, though, people often do not decide on a particular decision-making strategy in advance. Rather they begin with whatever process consciously or unconsciously suggests itself as appropriate for the issue, and often switch strategies as the process develops. Also, as we observed in Chapter 2, "human beings have unstable, inconsistent, incompletely evoked, and imprecise goals."[3] For these reasons, preferences are often constructed during the decision-making process.[4] Much of this chapter is concerned with the malleability or lability of preferences. But first a few notes about the processes of decision making.

Most important decisions require making trade-offs among a number of attributes. The values of different attributes may be unclear; the time horizons of the benefits and costs of particular outcomes may differ; and some trade-offs can cause emotional conflict. Ola Svenson has described decision making as "a kind of conflict resolution in which contradictory goals have to be negotiated and reconciled."[5] A decision maker's strategy may thus depend on the cognitive and emotional difficulties of making the decision. The choice of strategy may itself reflect a trade-off between accuracy on the one hand, and minimizing cognitive effort and negative affect on the other.

For example, as the cognitive or emotional costs increase, people tend to employ simplified noncompensatory strategies described in Section 4.3, such as elimination by aspects (EBA). Some decisions demand making "taboo trade-offs"[6] between commodifiable and a noncommodifiable attributes, such as cost versus safety. Merely considering such trade-offs elicits personal moral discomfort, and may subject the decision maker to moral censure. For example, participants in one study expressed outrage when they read about a hospital administrator who considered spending $100,000 on improving the hospital rather than on saving the life of one child—even when the administrator ultimately chose to save the child. By contrast, an administrator who chose to save the child without considering the trade-off elicited little outrage.[7] No wonder,

---

3. James G. March, *Bounded Rationality, Ambiguity, and the Engineering of Choice*, 9 Bell Journal of Economics 587 (1978).

4. Sarah Lichtenstein and Paul Slovic, Construction of Preferences (New York: Cambridge University Press, 2006)

5. Ola Svenson, *Decision Making and the Search for Fundamental Psychological Regularities: What Can Be Learned from a Process Perspective?*, 65 Organizational Behavior and Human Decision Processes 252 (1996).

6. Philip E. Tetlock, *The Impact of Accountability on Judgment and Choice: Toward a Social Contingency Model*, in M. Zanna (ed.), 25 Advances in Experimental Social Psychology 331–376 (New York: Academic Press, 1992).

7. Philip E. Tetlock, Orie V. Kristel, S. Beth Elson, Melanie C. Green, and Jennifer S. Lerner, *The Psychology of the Unthinkable: Taboo Trade-offs, Forbidden Base Rates, and Heretical Counterfactuals*, 78 Journal of Personality and Social Psychology 853 (2000).

then, that decision makers faced with taboo trade-offs often use choice-avoidance strategies like putting off the decision indefinitely or delegating the responsibility of deciding to someone else.[8] The emotional difficulties of making taboo trade-offs—as well as the risk that others will condemn the person who considers them—can thus shape the strategy that decision makers select.

13.3 VALUE-BASED AND REASON-BASED DECISION-MAKING STRATEGIES

In Section 4.4, we examined two kinds of systematic decision-making strategies: value-based and reason-based. Recall Christine Lamm's use of a subjective linear decision-making model in deciding where to site the wastewater treatment plant and Charles Darwin's approaches to marriage. Christine's procedure was *value-based*: She assigned a (subjective) value to the attributes she deemed important, summed the values for each alternative, and chose the alternative that maximized the total value. Darwin followed a *reason-based* approach, giving reasons for and against the alternatives under consideration. Each approach has its pros and cons.

13.3.1 Value-Based Decision-Making Strategies: Difficulties in Evaluating Certain Aspects of the Alternatives Being Considered

We return briefly to a cost-benefit analysis issue raised in Section 12.3: difficulties in evaluating certain aspects of the alternatives being considered.

While making trade-offs among different values can be exceedingly difficult, expected utility theory depends fundamentally on a decision maker's ability to evaluate the attributes of a particular decision. Christine finds the attributes relevant to siting the wastewater treatment plant evaluable—for example, she has very good criteria for determining cost, and reasonably good criteria for evaluating environmental and traffic impacts and the other factors.

But evaluating even quantifiable information can sometimes be difficult. *Evaluability* refers to the ease or difficulty of evaluating an attribute of the alternative choices you are considering. Experiments suggest that when options or alternatives "involve a trade-off between a hard-to-evaluate attribute and an easy-to-evaluate attribute, the hard-to-evaluate attribute has a lesser impact in separate evaluation than in joint evaluation, and the easy-to-evaluate attribute has a greater impact."[9]

---

8. Tetlock, *The Impact of Accountability on Judgment and Choice, supra.*

9. Christopher Hsee, *The Evaluability Hypothesis: An Explanation for Preference Reversals between Joint and Separate Evaluations of Alternatives*, 67 ORGANIZATIONAL BEHAVIOR AND HUMAN DECISION PROCESSES 247–57 (1996).

For example, participants in a study were asked to assume that they were music majors purchasing a music dictionary in a used book store. In the joint-evaluation condition, they were told that there were two music dictionaries for sale:

- one dictionary was "like new" and had 10,000 entries;
- the other had a torn cover and had 20,000 entries.

On average, the participants were willing to pay $19 for the first and $27 for the second. But when participants were told that there was only one music dictionary in the store, those presented with only the first dictionary were willing to pay $24 and those presented with only the second were willing to pay $20: a torn cover is easy to evaluate without comparison, while the number of entries is difficult to evaluate. This phenomenon of preference reversals seems robust in a variety of different contexts. Table 13.1 provides some examples where people's preferences were reversed in separate and joint evaluations.

TABLE 13.1 EASY AND HARD TO EVALUATE ATTRIBUTES

Options	Easy-to-evaluate	Hard-to-evaluate
Computer programmer job applicants[10]	4.9 GPA vs. 3.0 GPA	Number of computer programs written in past 2 years: 10 vs. 70
Eye surgeons for laser surgery[11]	Harvard MD Degree vs. Iowa MD Degree	Number of similar successful procedures: 80 vs. 300

Especially when the values of attributes are not readily monetizable, people are often influenced more by proportions than absolute values. For example, Paul Slovic and his colleagues found that, in separate evaluations, people supported an airport-safety measure expected to save 98 percent of 150 lives at risk more strongly than a measure expected to save 150 lives (period).[12] They explain: "Saving 150 lives is diffusely good, hence only weakly evaluable, whereas saving 98% of something is clearly very good because it is so close to the upper bound on the percentage scale, and hence is readily evaluable and highly weighted in the support judgment." They report that "subsequent reduction of the

10. *Id.*

11. Brian J. Zikmund-Fisher, Angela Fagerlin, and Peter A. Ubel, *Is 28% Good or Bad? Evaluability and Preference Reversals in Health Care Decisions*, 24 Medical Decis. Making 142 (2004). Evaluation was on a scale of 0 (extremely bad choice) to 10 (extremely good choice) rather than WTP.

12. Paul Slovic, Melissa Finucane, Ellen Peters, and Donald G. MacGregor, *Rational Actors Or Rational Fools: Implications Of The Affect Heuristic For Behavioral Economics*, 31 Journal of Socio-Economics 329 (2002).

percentage of 150 lives that would be saved to 95%, 90%, and 85% led to reduced support for the safety measure but each of these percentage conditions still garnered a higher mean level of support than did the save 150 lives condition."

Suppose that, in the 1990s, there were two camps for Rwandan refugees in neighboring Zaire. One camp holds 250,000 refugees and the other 11,000. Cholera is rampant in both camps. A nongovernmental organization can provide enough clean water to save the lives of a total of 4,500 refugees suffering from cholera in one or the other camp. Which one would you chose? From a moral or policy point of view, the number of refugees in the camps makes no difference,[13] and 42 percent of the participants in a study said so. However, 44 percent would have directed the resources to the smaller camp, where a larger proportion of lives would have been saved.[14] Slovic observes that number of lives saved, standing alone, appears to be poorly evaluable, but becomes clearly evaluable and important in side-by-side comparisons.

13.3.2 Reason-Based Decision-Making Strategies[15]

We often think and talk about choices in terms of reasons—especially when faced with conflicts among choices. The rule of law depends on lawyers, judges, and policy makers explaining the reasons for their decisions; and it is difficult to imagine a lawyer effectively counseling a client without the two engaging in reasoned discourse. Especially in making personal decisions, reasons may include considerations, such as anticipating regret for a bad choice, that are not readily captured by a value-based approach. A reason-based approach can also obviate the seeming false precision required by assigning numbers to intangible values.

However, reasons often suffer from the opposite problem—of being vague, or of the decision maker's omitting potentially salient reasons pro or con. Moreover, people may be unaware of what actually motivated their choice.

13.3.2.a The Effect of Giving Reasons on Decision Strategies and Outcomes Consider the position of Adele, in charge of entry-level hiring at a law firm or government agency. If she were going to use a subjective linear model to decide which, among many applicants, to invite to spend a day interviewing, she would initially determine a set of attributes—e.g., GPA, quality of the school—and rank each candidate in terms of them.

---

13. Actually, one could imagine variables, such as preventing riots or contagion, that would affect the policy choice. But such factors did not play a role in the participants' decisions.

14. In another set of questions focusing on only one camp, one group of participants was told that prior aid had met 5 percent of the camp's water needs, and that the new aid would bring the total to 7 percent; another group was told that prior aid met 95 perecnt of the needs and the new aid would bring the total to 97 percent. Most participants would have directed aid to the latter.

15. This section draws heavily on Eldar Shafir, Itamar Simonson, and Amos Tversky, *Reason-based Choice*, 49 COGNITION 11 (1993).

Now suppose that Adele delegates the decision to Barbara, who, rather than using a subjective linear model, looks at the files one by one, intuitively sorting them in "yes" or "no" piles. Do you think she will reach the same result as Adele did? Consider the role of the *availability* heuristic, discussed in Section 9.6.

Suppose that Adele gives the identical files to Clara and David and asks Clara to produce a list of the names of candidates to invite to *interview* and David to produce a list of those who should be sent a *rejection letter*. Who is likely to have more candidates in the running? Experiments suggest that David will leave more candidates in the running than Clara. Resumes and application letters tend to favor a candidate's strong points rather than weaknesses. Clara will only select candidates who stand out among the rest, while David will find fewer negative characteristics on which to reject the candidates.[16]

Along these lines, Eldar Shafir and his colleagues conducted an experiment in which participants were given the following scenario: Imagine that you serve on the jury of an only-child sole-custody case following a relatively messy divorce. The facts of the case are complicated by ambiguous economic, social, and emotion considerations, and you decide to base your decision entirely on the characteristics shown in Table 13.2.

TABLE 13.2 PARENTS' QUALITIES IN A CHILD-CUSTODY DISPUTE

Parent A	Parent B
Average income	Above-average income
Average health	Minor health problems
Average working hours	Lots of work-related travel
Reasonable rapport with the child	Very close relationship with the child
Relatively stable social life	Extremely active social life

Notice that Parent A is average in all respects, while Parent B has some strong and weak points.

When asked to whom they would *award* sole custody, the majority of participants (64 percent) chose Parent B to receive custody. Yet when a different group of participants was asked to whom they would *deny* sole custody, the majority (55 percent) chose the opposite outcome and *denied* custody to Parent B.

Based on this and similar experiments, the researchers conclude that when people are basing decisions on reasons, "the positive features of options (their pros) will loom larger when choosing, whereas the negative features

16. Vandra L. Huber, Margaret A. Neale, and Gregory B. Northcraft, *Decision Bias and Personnel Selection Strategies*, 40 Organizational Behavior and Human Decision Processes 137 (1987).

of options (their cons) will be weighted more heavily when rejecting."[17] But this phenomenon violates the axiom of *invariance* (Section 12.2.2.b): the way in which the question is framed should not, by itself, affect the outcome.

13.3.2.b Preference Reversals Between Prices and Choices Suppose you are presented with two gambles:

- Gamble A: 0.9 chance to win $8
- Gamble B: 0.2 chance to win $30

Suppose that you are asked to *choose* between the two gambles? Now suppose you are asked to *price* each gamble—e.g., suppose that you own tickets entitling you to each, at what price would you would be willing to *sell* the tickets? On average, people asked to choose select gamble A, which has a much higher probability of winning. But when asked to *price* each gamble, they demand more for B.[18]

There are two explanations for this violation of invariance: the compatibility effect and the prominence effect.[19] Under the compatibility effect, when subjects are thinking in terms of dollars, as they do when asked to set a price, they are more likely to evaluate their response in terms of dollars. Under the prominence effect, choice invokes *reasoning* in a way that pricing doesn't—people feel a need to explain the choice at least to themselves—and the gamble with the higher probability is easier to explain.

Such preference reversals have been manifested in other situations, including people's valuations of reducing the risks from chemical products, improvements in consumer goods, and improvements in the environment.[20] We will say a word more about this in a discussion of contingent valuation in Section 14.6.

13.3.2.c The Effect of Giving Reasons on the Quality of Choices and Satisfaction with Them Using reasons as a strategy can make decision making easier and more transparent. However, excessive reliance on reasons and deliberation has its own drawbacks. A number of experiments by Timothy Wilson and his colleagues suggest that giving reasons for one's preferences

17. Eldar Shafir, *Choosing versus Rejecting: Why Some Options Are Both Better and Worse than Others*, 21 Memory & Cognition 546–56 (1993).

18. Amos Tversky and Richard H. Thaler, *Anomalies: Preference Reversals*, 4 Journal of Economic Perspectives 193–205 (1990).

19. Paul Slovic, Dale Griffin, and Amos Tversky, Compatibility Effects in Judgment and Choice, in Insights in Decision Making: A Tribute to Hillel J. Einhorn 5–27 (Robin M. Hogarth ed., Chicago, IL: University of Chicago Press, 1991); Amos Tversky, Schmuel Sattath, and Paul Slovic, *Contingent Weighting in Judgment and Choice*, 85 Psychological Review 371–84 (1988).

20. Julie R. Irwin, Paul Slovic, Sarah Lichtenstein, and Gary H. McClelland, *Preference Reversals and the Measurement of Environmental Values*, 6 Journal of Risk and Uncertainly 5–18 (1993).

before making a choice sometimes leads to suboptimal decisions and to less satisfaction with the choice.[21] For example, students were asked to evaluate five posters—two of paintings by Monet and Van Gogh and three contemporary humorous cartoons or photos. Members of the control group, who were not asked to consider their reasons for liking or disliking the posters, tended to prefer the paintings. By contrast, students who were asked to consider the reasons underlying their preferences tended to prefer the humorous posters.

The students in both groups were then given the posters of their choice. At the end of the semester, they were asked about their satisfaction with the poster, including whether it was hanging on their wall. Members of the control group were significantly more satisfied with their choices than those who had been ask to introspect. "Apparently the qualities of the art posters that made them appealing to our subject population were relatively difficult to verbalize, whereas positive features of the humorous posters were easy to verbalize, producing a biased sample of reasons" While "verbalizing these reasons caused participants to adopt the attitude they implied," over time the student returned to their initial, unreflective evaluations.

A centipede was happy quite, until a toad in fun
Said, "Pray, which leg comes after which?"
This raised his doubts to such a pitch
He fell distracted in the ditch
Not knowing how to run
—Old rhyme

Similar experiments have been conducted with respect to the choice of jams, college courses, and other items—with similar results. With respect to the effects of reason giving, Timothy Wilson and Jonathan Schooler write:[22]

> Forming preferences is akin to riding a bicycle; we can do it easily but cannot easily explain how. Just as automatic behaviors can be disrupted when people analyze and decompose them, so can preferences and decisions be disrupted when people reflect about the reasons for their feelings. We suggest that this

21. *See* Timothy D. Wilson and Jonathan W. Schooler, *Thinking Too Much: Introspection Can Reduce the Quality of Preferences and Decisions*, Journal of Personality and Social Psychology 181 (1991); Timothy D. Wilson et al., *Introspecting About Reasons Can Reduce Post-Choice Satisfaction*, 19 Personality and Social Psychology Bulletin 331 (1993).

22. Timothy Wilson and Jonathan Schooler, *Thinking Too Much: Introspection Can Reduce the Quality of Preferences and Decisions*, 60 J Pers. Soc. Psychol. 181–192 (1991).

> can occur as follows. First, people are often unaware of exactly why they feel the way they do about an attitude or an object. When they reflect about their reasons, they thus focus on explanations that are salient and plausible. The problem is that what seems like a plausible cause and what actually determines people's reactions are not always the same thing. As a result, when asked why they feel the way they do, people focus on attributes that seem like plausible reasons for liking or disliking the stimulus, even if these attributes have no actual effect on their evaluations.
>
> . . . [U]nder some circumstances . . . people will focus on reasons that imply a different attitude than they held before and will adopt the attitude implied by these reasons. . . . [P]eople often do not have a well-articulated, accessible attitude and thus do not start out with the bias to find only those reasons that are consistent with an initial reaction. They conduct a broader search for reasons, focusing on factors that are plausible and easy to verbalize even if they conflict with how they felt originally.
>
> [W]e suggest that reflecting about reasons will change people's attitudes when their initial attitude is relatively inaccessible and the reasons that are salient and plausible happen to have a different valence than people's initial attitude.

In short, because what you can readily articulate doesn't necessarily reflect what you deem most important, articulating reasons for your preferences can lead to choices inconsistent with your actual preferences. Does articulating reasons interfere with judgments more generally? Research by John McMakin and Paul Slovic suggests that it depends on the kind of judgment being made. In one study, McMakin and Slovic asked participants to estimate how their peers would react to a series of advertisements. As with judging one's own preference for posters, this task requires a holistic, intuitive approach. As in Wilson and Schooler's study, participants who were asked to articulate reasons for their estimate provided less accurate estimates than those not asked to articulate reasons. In a second study, however, McMakin and Slovic had participants make judgments that required analytic rather than intuitive thinking, such as estimating the length of the Amazon river. For this task, generating reasons *increased* the accuracy of estimates.

Why would the first judgment task have been better suited for intuitive thinking, while the second demand more analytic thinking? The complexity and ambiguity of the task may provide part of the answer. Posters and advertisements vary in countless ways that affect preferences; identifying the relevant dimensions and keeping all in mind simultaneously is a complex task with ambiguous criteria. By contrast, estimating the length of the Amazon is a problem that, while difficult, does not involve multiple, ambiguous dimensions.

Is it possible that holistic, intuitive thinking may lead to better judgments for more complex tasks while analytic, reasons-based thinking may work better for less complex tasks? Some evidence for this proposition comes from work by Ap Dijksterhuis and his colleagues.[23] In one study, participants tried to choose the best car from a selection of descriptions that varied on either twelve dimensions (a relatively complex task) or on only four dimensions (a relatively simple task). The descriptions were crafted so that, in each condition, one car was objectively superior to the others. The researchers instructed half of the participants to spend four minutes thinking carefully about their judgment, and the other half to spend four minutes doing a task that distracted them from thinking about the matter. Results showed that participants told to think carefully made more accurate judgments about the cars when the task was simple than when it was complex. By contrast, participants who were distracted from generating reasons for their judgment were more accurate when the task was complex than when it was simple.

It would be a mistake to conclude that one should always eschew reasoned analysis of complex decisions in favor of intuition. First, one might question the generalizability of these findings to the sorts of consequential decisions facing policy makers, who often have longer to deliberate than the participants in these studies. More fundamentally, as we see throughout this book, "gut feelings" can be biased by emotions unrelated to the decision at hand, or by prejudices and stereotypes that can only be mitigated by deliberate reflection.

Still, the research reviewed in this section indicates that reason-based decision making does not always lead to optimal judgments. As Eldar Shafir's study about custody awards demonstrates, the way a question is framed can affect the kinds of reasons that one generates. Additionally, when we grapple with complex problems, the reasons we generate may indicate more about what is easy to articulate than about what is most relevant to the judgment at hand. Without ignoring the ability of reasoned analysis to enhance judgment, then, we should exercise caution in over-relying on those reasons that come most easily to mind.

13.4 PREDICTING OUR FUTURE WELL-BEING

There are two tragedies in life. One is not to get your heart's desire; the other is to get it.
—George Bernard Shaw

Vronsky meanwhile, although what he had so long desired had come to pass, was not altogether happy. He soon felt the fulfillment of his desires gave him only one grain of the mountain of happiness he had expected. This fulfillment showed him the eternal error men make in imagining that their happiness depends on the realization of their desires.
—Leo Tolstoy, Anna Karenina (1887)

23. Ap Dijksterhuis, Maarten W. Bos, Loran F. Nordgren, and Rick B. van Baaren, *On Making the Right Choice: The Deliberation-Without-Attention Effect*, 311 SCIENCE 1005 (2006).

It seems that the linear model used by Christine Lamm in the wastewater treatment plant problem might be able to overcome some of the shortcomings of the reason-based choice strategy we have just reviewed. However, decision makers almost never have perfect information relating to a decision—especially in conditions of risk and uncertainty. In Chapter 15, we will discuss how to deal with uncertainties about *objective* matters—for example the weather or, in Lamm's case, problems involving acquiring the site near Edenville's airport.

Even more difficult to determine are uncertainties about *subjective* matters—for example, how the residents of north Edenville will actually experience having the wastewater treatment plant in their neighborhood.

The following sections explore ways that people may make systematic errors—akin to the cognitive biases discussed in earlier chapters—in predicting how they will feel about things in the future. In addition to considering their relevance to individual decision making, it will be interesting to ask how a policy maker should take them into account.

Your actual experience of the consequences of the decision is termed the *experienced utility* of a decision. At the time you make a decision, however, you can only predict the decision's effect on experienced utility. Ideally, your *predicted utility* is perfectly congruent with experienced utility. Unfortunately, as we all know from personal experience, they can diverge. The giant-size box of popcorn you bought when entering the movie theater no longer seems so appealing when you've eaten half of it. The dress that seemed to make a daring fashion statement in the store sits in your closet after being worn only once. While "the ability to predict the intensity of one's future likes and dislikes appears to be an essential element of rational decision making," the task of predicting one's future feelings and tastes "turns out to be surprisingly difficult."[24]

We separate these issues into two related parts. The first concerns what Daniel Gilbert and Timothy Wilson have termed *impact bias*—mispredictions of how you will feel in the future about a current occurrence or event, assuming that your basic preferences have not changed in the interim.[25] The second involves what George Loewenstein and his colleagues have termed *projection bias*—mispredictions of your future preferences.[26]

---

24. Daniel Kahneman and Jackie Snell, *Predicting a Changing Taste: Do People Know What They Will Like*, 5 Journal of Behavioral Decision Making 187 (1992).

25. Daniel T. Gilbert, Elizabeth C. Pinel, Timothy D. Wilson, Stephen J. Blumberg, and Thalia P. Wheatley, *Immune Neglect: A Source of Durability Bias in Affective Forecasting*, 75 Journal of Personality and Social Psychology 617–38 (1998).

26. *See* George Loewenstein and Erick Angner, *Predicting and Indulging Changing Preferences*, *in* George Loewenstein, Daniel Read, and Roy Baumeister eds., Time and

Legal Note

Your client, a historian, enraged by claims that a critic has made that portions of the book were plagiarized, wants to sue the critic for defamation. Your tell your client that he has a fairly good chance of ultimately winning a small judgment but that, in addition to financial costs, litigants tend to incur heavy emotional costs during the process, which often outweigh the satisfactions of victory. However, your client is focused on vindication.

See Jeremy Blumenthal, *Law and the Emotions: The Problems of Affective Forecasting*, 80 IND. L.J. 155 (2005).

13.4.1 Impact Bias: Mispredicting Emotional Reactions to Future Events

A personal decision implicitly requires predicting your future feelings about people (a spouse or partner), objects (a new car), or changed life circumstances (aging). Most people make pretty good predictions much of the time. But here are some examples of situations where predictions tend to be exaggerated:[27]

- People who had won the lottery predicted that they would be significantly happier a year later than they turned out to be, and people who had suffered an accident that left them paraplegic did not report themselves as greatly less happy than a control group—though we have little doubt that they would have paid a great deal to restore their mobility.
- Asked about how environmental and personal changes (e.g., air quality, income, and body weight) had affected their well-being and would affect it in the future, people predicted that future changes would have a much greater effect than they reported from past changes of the same nature. Though predicting that the difference in climates would make a big difference, students at California and Midwestern universities reported the same level of well-being.
- People residing near a newly opened highway underestimated how much they would adapt to the noise.

DECISION: ECONOMIC AND PSYCHOLOGICAL PERSPECTIVES ON INTERTEMPORAL CHOICE 351 (New York: Russell Sage Foundation, 2003) [hereafter TIME AND DECISION].

27. This section draws heavily on the excellent review essay, George Loewenstein and David Schkade, *Wouldn't It Be Nice*, *in* DANIEL KAHNEMAN, ED DIENER, AND NORBERT SCHWARZ eds., WELL-BEING: THE FOUNDATIONS OF HEDONIC PSYCHOLOGY 95 (New York: Russell Sage Foundation, 1999).

- Assistant professors predicted that they would be less happy during the first five years after being turned down for tenure, and happier during the first five years after gaining tenure, than they actually were.
- Dental patients, and especially those who were anxious about their appointments, overpredicted the amount of pain they would experience.
- People being tested for HIV or for (unwanted) pregnancy overpredicted misery from a positive result and elation from a negative result.
- People overpredict their happiness if their favored teams or political candidates wins and their unhappiness if they lose.

Most of these predictions involve errors in what Gilbert, Wilson, and their colleagues have termed *affective forecasting*. Predictions can err in several respects.

Although we are usually correct in predicting whether an emotion will have positive or negative valence, we may oversimplify situations that evoke complex emotions by focusing on only positive or negative affect—e.g., students looking forward to graduation with joy and pride, overlooking sadness about leaving friends and apprehension about their futures.[28] We also sometimes mispredict the specific positive or negative emotions we will experience—e.g., women who predicted that they would respond with anger to sexually harassing questions in a job interview tended instead to respond with fear.[29]

More generally, as illustrated by Figure 13.1,[30] we often mispredict the intensity and duration of emotional experiences. The remainder of this subsection explores the possible causes of problems in *impact bias*—"the tendency to overestimate the enduring impact that future events will have on our emotional reactions."[31]

13.4.1.a Focalism One reason that we fall prey to the impact bias is that our affective forecasts tend to place disproportionate emphasis on whatever our attention is focused on at the moment. Such *focalism* can lead to systematic errors in affective forecasting because features that are particularly salient when *predicting* an event may be joined and even swamped by a host of other factors when *experiencing* the event. This phenomenon is reinforced by the fact that "predictions of future feelings inevitably involve some type of stylized representation of future events. Mental images of future vacations and holidays, for example, typically do not include features such as rain, mosquitoes, and rude

---

28. Jeff T. Larsen, A. Peter McGraw, and John T. Cacioppo, *Can People Feel Happy and Sad at the Same Time?*, 81 Journal of Personality and Social Psychology 684–96 (2001).

29. Julie A. Woodzicka and Marianne LaFrance, *Real versus Imagined Reactions to Sexual Harassment*, 57 Journal of Social Issues, 15–30 (2001).

30. Timothy D. Wilson and Daniel T. Gilbert, *Affective Forecasting*, *in* Advances in Experimental Social Psychology, Vol. 35 345–411 (Mark P. Zanna ed., San Diego, CA: Academic Press, 2003).

31. *Id.* Much of the following discussion is drawn from Wilson and Gilbert's excellent review essay.

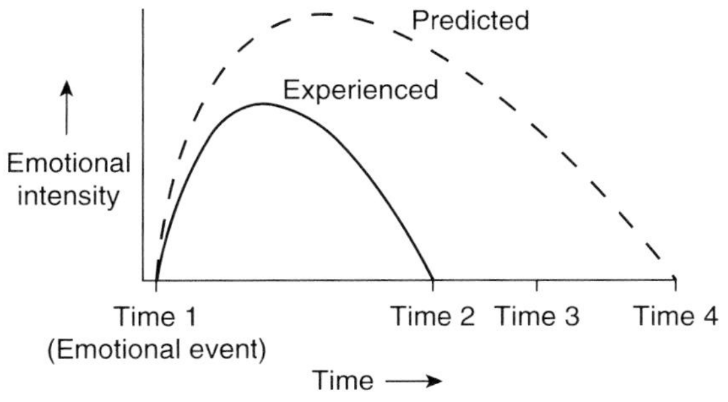

FIGURE 13.1 INTENSITY AND TIME COURSE OF PREDICTED VERSUS EXPERIENCED EMOTION.

Source: From Timothy Wilson and Daniel Gilbert, Affective Forecasting 35 Advances in Exterimental Social Psychology (2003). Copyright © 2003 Elsevier Science (USA). Reprinted with permission.

service people . . ."[32] People may overpredict the benefits of moving to a location with nicer weather, not realizing that weather is just one of many factors affecting their happiness—and that the weather is not always nice. When asked to predict two months in advance how happy they would feel after a game if their team won, football fans predicted a strong impact lasting a number of days.[33] In fact, although their happiness rose right after the Saturday game, it declined to their normal baseline by the following Monday. In a parallel study that both demonstrates the mechanics of focalism and suggests corrective action, participants made more realistic predictions about their happiness when they were asked to write a "prospective diary" describing what particular activities they would engage in on the Monday following the game.

Focalism also biases our affective forecasts when we focus our attention on the immediate consequences of an event rather than on its effects in the longer term. As Daniel Kahneman writes, we evaluate "an entire extended outcome by evaluating the transition to it. For example, errors in predicting the well-being of paraplegics may reflect people's treating the tragic event of *becoming* a paraplegic as a proxy in evaluating the long-term state of *being* a paraplegic."[34] And paraplegics spend much of their time in activities that are not compromised by their disability.

Focalism is also encouraged by some decision-making processes, such as elimination by aspects (See Section 4.3), that cancel out attributes that are shared across alternatives and focus on those attributes that differ. Elizabeth Dunn and

32. Loewenstein and Schkade, *supra*.

33. Timothy D. Wilson, Thalia Wheatley, Jonathan M. Meyers, Daniel T. Gilbert, and Danny Axsom, *Focalism: A Source of Durability Bias in Affective Forecasting*, 78 JOURNAL OF PERSONALITY AND PSYCHOLOGY 821 (2000).

34. Daniel Kahneman, Peter P. Wakker, and Rakesh Sarin, *Back to Bentham? Explorations of Experienced Utility*, 112 QUARTERLY JOURNAL OF ECONOMICS 375 (1997).

her colleagues asked students to predict their happiness in living in various dormitories, whose physical features differed considerably more than the social aspects of dorm life.[35] The students predicted their happiness or unhappiness based solely on the former; yet, a year later, it turned out that their happiness was not at all correlated with physical features, but was significantly correlated with social life. When forecasting which of several options will make them happiest, people tend to ignore the features that the options share (all dorms have active social lives), while giving undue weight to features that make each option unique (all dorms had different architecture).

Following Kahneman and Tversky,[36] Dunn and colleagues called this special case of focalism the *isolation effect*, because decision makers isolate the unique features of each option. Focusing on the differences among competing alternatives is not a poor decision strategy as such, as long as one takes account of this phenomenon: "It would be quite reasonable to focus on location when choosing between [college] houses that varied a great deal on this dimension but not on others. When imagining a life in a specific house with a terrible location, however, it would be unwise to expect lasting misery while neglecting the happiness derived from living with one's wonderful roommates."

13.4.1.b Adaptation and "Ordinization" Neglect A second reason why the impact bias occurs is that people tend not to consider the psychological processes that keep our feelings and moods close to an emotional set-point. Processes of hedonic adaptation blunt the effects of both good and bad events. (See Section 12.1.5) Affective reactions are generally most intense at the onset and diminish over time. After experiencing setbacks, people usually get on with life, sometimes with reduced aspirations. Indeed, intensely disappointing experiences tend to trigger proportionally stronger psychological coping mechanisms—such as rationalizing and blaming others for one's errors—than moderately disappointing ones. Gilbert and Wilson call this the "psychological immune system." They term people's tendency to underpredict these homeostatic tendencies *ordinization neglect*.[37]

Predicting our emotional response to future events is no simple task. Yet, given that we all accumulate years of experience forecasting and experiencing emotional events, why do we continue to make forecasting errors without learning from our past mistakes? Gilbert and Wilson identify three reasons: (1) it is

35. Elizabeth W. Dunn, Timothy D. Wilson, and Daniel T. Gilbert, *Location, Location, Location: The Misprediction of Satisfaction in Housing Lotteries*, 29 Personality and Social Psychology Bulletin 1421 (2003).

36. Daniel Kahneman and Amos Tversky, *Prospect Theory: An Analysis of Decision Under Risk*, 47 Econometrica 263–91 (1979).

37. Daniel T. Gilbert, Matthew D. Lieberman, Carey K. Morewedge, and Timothy D. Wilson, *The Peculiar Longevity of Things Not So Bad*, 15 Psychological Science 14 (2004).

difficult to remember emotional experiences accurately; (2) we commit hindsight bias,[38] recalling our predictions as more accurate than they really were; and (3) the processes of adaptation that make our experiences less emotionally potent and enduring than we predict function outside of our awareness.

13.4.2 Projection Bias: Mispredicting Future Preferences

Just as we make systematic errors in predicting the intensity and duration of our emotional responses, we err when predicting our future preferences for goods and experiences.

> **Legal Note**
>
> A healthy client asks you to prepare an advance health directive, specifying that life-sustaining measures be withheld or withdrawn if she has an illness that is so severe that there is no reasonable prospect that she will recover and be able to live without continuing life-sustaining measures. What concerns would you raise with her?
>
> See Jeremy Blumenthal, *Law and the Emotions: The Problems of Affective Forecasting*, 80 IND. L.J. 155 (2005).

Projection bias refers to people's tendency to "behave as if their future preferences will be more like their current preferences than they actually will be—as if they project their current preferences onto their future selves."[39] Our predictions tend to be regressive—that is, they are anchored by our current preferences. To a large extent this results from the difficulty of imagining oneself having different preferences than one currently has. After all, one's individual identify consists in large part of preferences, and predicting a significant change of one's preferences is tantamount to predicting being a different person.

- Most healthy people say they would not want heroic measures to be taken if they were terminally ill. However, a majority of terminally ill patients want treatment even if it would extend their lives by only a week. George Loewenstein and David Schkade suggest that healthy people tend to underestimate the quality of life of sick people. (It is also possible that younger, healthy people are making a normative judgment at time-1 about the

---

38. *See* Section 10.2.

39. Loewenstein and Angner, *Predicting and Indulging Changing Preferences, in* TIME AND DECISION.

allocation of resources to their older, sick future selves at time-2, which they then resist at time-2.)

- When people are in a "cold" state, they tend to overestimate the strength of their own willpower in a "hot" state. People shopping for food on an empty stomach purchase more than they planned to. People who plan to refrain from sex on a date, or who plan to use a contraceptive device, often do not behave as they planned.
- People are systematically overconfident about the likelihood that they can experiment with drugs or cigarettes without becoming addicted. People purchasing credit cards tend, unrealistically, to believe that they will maintain a zero balance.
- With respect to the endowment effect (Section 14.1) people who do not already possess an object or entitlement do not predict that their willing to accept (WTA) to abandon the object is greater than their willingness to pay (WTP) to acquire it.

> Students were given a choice among six snacks, one of which would be eaten in each of three successive class sessions. Some were required to choose their snacks for all three days on the first day of the study. Others could choose the snack on the day it was to be eaten. Those making all three choices in advance chose a substantially more varied group of snacks than those making choices day by day.[40]

These are all examples of how people mispredict changes of their tastes, preferences, or behaviors over time or under different circumstances. George Loewenstein and Eric Angner describe a variety of processes in which preferences can change:

- *Habit formation*, where consuming a substance or having an experience increases one's preference for it.
- *Satiation*, where consuming a substance or having an experience decreases its marginal utility. (Satiation is not necessarily a continuous function; you may suddenly stop enjoying an experience or commodity one day.)
- *Refinement*, where people sometimes expose themselves to experiences in art, literature, or music to improve their appreciation of them.

40. Itamar Simonson, *The Effect of Purchase Quantity and Timing on Variety Seeking Behavior*, 27 Journal of Marketing Research 150–62 (May 1990).

- *Conditioning*, where preference changes are induced by rewards or punishments.
- *Maturation*, where one's preferences change as one ages.
- *Social influence*, where one looks to others for cues about valid preferences or just seeks their approval. (See Chapter 17.)
- *Dissonance reduction*, where preferences are realigned to fit circumstances or behaviors.

Visceral states produce a special lack of imagination, which Loewenstein and his colleagues have termed the *hot/cold empathy gap*. Strong positive or negative emotions at the time of making a decision can bias one's affective forecasting. Consider someone with a bad cold who has just received an invitation to a party a month hence, trying to imagine how she will feel then. In its strongest manifestation, people in a "hot" state—with respect to basic needs, such as hunger, thirst, and sex—have difficulty imagining how they would feel in a "cold" state, and vice versa. The effects of shopping without a list when hungry, or satiated, is a milder example. The feelings need not be somatic: Loewenstein and Adler gave participants a trivia quiz and offered them, as compensation, a choice between a candy bar and learning the right answers to the quiz. Most participants in a cold state—-i.e., who made the choice before their interest had been piqued by answering the questions chose the candy bar—predicted that they would choose a candy bar afterwards. In fact, a majority of those who made the choice after taking the quiz—a relatively hot state because of curiosity—chose instead to learn the answers.[41]

13.4.2.a Attitudes Toward Our Long-Run Preferences Do people sometimes try to resist changes in long-run preferences? Loewenstein and Angner point to concerns about one's becoming *corrupted*—of one's preferences changing in ways that our present selves think undesirable.[42] Daniel Boone is said to have fled civilization to avoid its corrupting influence.[43] For students reading this book, the concern may be whether taking a high-paying job after graduation will stamp out their idealism.

13.4.3 The Consequences of the Impact and Projection Biases and the Possibility of Becoming More Accurate

The point of the preceding discussion is not that we usually mispredict our own future feelings and preferences, but that we may do so in some situations that have important consequences. These errors are not inevitably dysfunctional.

41. George Loewenstein and Daniel Adler, *A Bias in the Prediction of Tastes*, 105 Economic Journal 929–37 (July 1995).

42. Loewenstein and Angner, *Predicting and Indulging Changing Preferences*, in Time and Decision.

43. John Mack Frargher, Daniel Boone: The Life and Legend of an American Pioneer (Holt Paperbacks Press, 1993).

People may overestimate the duration of positive or negative events to motivate themselves to action ("If I pass the exam tomorrow, my career will be vastly enhanced; if I flunk it my life will be ruined forever") or to protect themselves against disappointment. But there are significant downsides as well. Short-term fluctuations in visceral states coupled with poor affective forecasting may lead to long-term commitments to marry, have children, and (very long-term) to commit suicide.[44] In making "advanced directives" or "living wills," healthy individuals may seriously mispredict their desires when they are in extremely poor health.[45]

Loewenstein and Schkade are fairly skeptical about our general ability to improve affective predictions. In addition to the reasons discussed above, the memories of experiences from which one might learn may themselves be biased, and learning from experience typically requires repeated observations of the same error.[46] But there may be ways to improve affective forecasting in particular contexts—for example, improving informed consent to medical procedures by focusing the patient's attention on future scenarios. Loewenstein and Schkade suggest that an "educational approach would seem to be least promising for errors that result from hot/cold empathy gaps, whose very existence suggests a resistance to cognitive interventions." In such cases, governments or other third parties may find it prudent to intervene to prevent any negative consequences of forecasting error, such as by mandating a "cooling off" period before an individual signs a contract.[47]

13.5 POSITIVE ILLUSIONS: I'M ABOVE AVERAGE, AND MY FUTURE LOOKS ROSY

We base important decisions not only on our forecasts of how various outcomes would make us feel, but also on our judgments about how likely these outcomes are to occur, as well our likelihood of contributing to bringing them about. For example, an undergraduate might decide whether or not to apply to a competitive law school based on her assessment of her academic skills, as well as her intuitions about her likelihood of acceptance. Yet these judgments tend to be

44. Loewenstein, O'Donoghue, and Rabin, *Projection Bias in Predicting Future Utility*, QUARTERLY JOURNAL OF ECONOMICS 1209 (2003).

45. *Id.* The authors report on a study in which only 10 percent of healthy respondents predict that they would accept a grueling course of chemotherapy to extend their lives by three months, compared to 42 percent of current cancer patients.

46. George Loewenstein and David Schkade, *Wouldn't It Be Nice?: Predicting Future Feelings*, *in* HEDONIC PSYCHOLOGY: SCIENTIFIC APPROACHES TO ENJOYMENT, SUFFERING, AND WELL-BEING (New York: Russell Sage Press, 1998).

47. *See* Jeremy A. Blumenthal, *Emotional Paternalism*, 35 FLA. ST. U. L. REV. 1 (2007).

systematically biased in ways that create *positive illusions* about oneself.[48] In particular, people tend to be overly optimistic about their futures, and overestimate their skills in a variety of domains. We consider each of these observations in turn.

13.5.1 Overoptimism

In *When Every Relationship Is Above Average: Perceptions and Expectations of Divorce at the Time of Marriage*,[49] Lynn Baker and Robert Emery asked couples applying for marriage licenses to estimate the percent of couples in the United States who marry today who will get divorced at some time in their lives. The average estimate was 50 percent—a fairly accurate prediction based on current statistics. When asked about the likelihood that *they* would ever be divorced, virtually no one thought so. Earlier, we mentioned a study that showed that entrepreneurs who were realistic about the general failure rate for new ventures were overconfident about the success of their own ventures. By the same token, "most people expect that they will have a better-than-average chance of living long, healthy lives; being successfully employed and happily married; and avoiding a variety of unwanted experiences such as being robbed or assaulted, injured in an automobile accident, or experiencing health problems."[50]

In an article on what they term the *planning fallacy*, Roger Buehler, Dale Griffin, and Michael Ross describe some mega-projects that have taken much more time and money to complete than originally projected—such as the Denver International Airport, Boston's Central Artery/Tunnel project (the "Big Dig")—and many more quotidian ventures, such as term papers, honors theses, and finishing shopping for Christmas presents. The authors wonder at the ability of people "to hold two seemingly contradictory beliefs: Although aware that most of their previous predictions were overly optimistic, they believe that their current forecasts are realistic."[51] Does this describe the reader's personal experience?

Although overoptimism often involves predictions of one's own future, a study of physicians' predictions of the life expectancy of terminally ill patients indicated a strong bias toward overoptimism, with only 20 percent being accurate (within 33 percent of actual survival), 17 percent being overly pessimistic,

---

48. Shelley E. Taylor, Positive Illusions: Creative Self-Deception and the Healthy Mind (New York: US Basic Books, 1989).

49. Lynn A. Baker and Reobert E. Emery, *When Every Relationship Is Above Average. Perceptions and Expectations of Divorce at the Time of Marriage*, 17 Law and Human Behavior 439 (1993).

50. David A. Armor and Shelley E. Taylor, *When Predictions Fail: The Dilemma of Unrealistic Optimism*, *in* Thomas Gilovich, Dale Griffin, and Daniel Kahneman eds., Heuristics and Biases, The Psychology of Intuitive Judgment 334 (New York: Cambridge University Press, 2002) [hereafter, Heuristics and Biases].

51. Roger Buehler, Dale Griffin, and Michael Ross, *Inside the Planning Fallacy: The Causes and Consequences of Optimistic Time Predictions*, *in* Heuristics and Biases.

and 63 percent greatly overestimating survival.[52] Interestingly, the better the doctor knew the patient, the more likely his overoptimism.

People are not indiscriminately overoptimistic, however, and even when overoptimistic, "correlations between predictions and outcomes are positive and often substantial."[53]

What conduces to overoptimism in planning? Buehler, Griffin, and Ross suggest that when developing their own plans and predictions, people assume an internal view, considering unique features of the task at hand and constructing a scenario for how the project will unfold, in contradistinction to an external view that places the task in a broader context. Focusing on a particular scenario for the successful completion of the project diverts attention from the many ways in which the future might unfold, including events—whether our own conduct or external forces—that would compromise success. We don't take adequate account of our own past experiences, or personal base rates, because the scenario necessarily focuses on the future, because we may perceive each new plan as unique, and because we tend to "explain away" past failures. In addition (as we saw in Section 8.2.3), people tend to underestimate the total probability of a chain of independent conjunctive events.[54] Overoptimism bears a strong resemblance to the anchoring bias—we anchor on the successful scenario and fail to adjust adequately for alternative possibilities and (less vivid) base rates. Not surprisingly, the planning fallacy diminishes or disappears when we forecast the success of *other people's* plans.

Overoptimism may also be fostered by temporal distortions: "Distant tasks (in time) are analyzed at a higher level of abstraction than are tasks close at hand. . . . In general, a more detailed and low-level construal of the task highlights difficulties, and so predictions made at a more distant time should tend to be more optimistic."[55]

Overoptimism can be caused by the schematic and self-serving processing of experiences. In an experiment similar to one described in Section 9.4.3, participants were assigned the roles of plaintiffs or defendants in advance of a negotiation, then given the facts and asked to negotiate. When subsequently asked to write down facts about the case that favored or disfavored their position, they recalled significantly more facts favoring their own position than the other's.[56]

---

52. Nicholas A. Christakis and Elizabeth B. Lamont, *Extent and Determinant of Error in Doctors' Prognoses in Terminally Ill Patients: Prospective Cohort Study*, 320 British Medical Journal 469 (2000).

53. Armor and Taylor, *supra*.

54. *See* Section 8.2.3.

55. Armor and Taylor, *supra*.

56. George Loewenstein, Samuel Issacharoff, Colin Camerer, and Linda Babcock, *Self-Serving Assessments of Fairness and Pretrial Bargaining*, 22 Journal of Legal Studies 135 (1993); Leigh Thompson and George Loewenstein, *Egocentric Interpretations of Fairness*

Russell Korobkin invokes his own experience as a mediator to illustrate the effects on negotiation when parties differentially focus their attention on their strongest issues and underappreciate the issues on which their position is weaker.[57]

> The plaintiff alleged a variety of breaches of contract and tort claims. The defendant's attorney believed that the suit was duplicative of an earlier lawsuit brought by the same plaintiff in which the defendant had prevailed. She believed that her client would prevail in a motion to dismiss on the ground of res judicata[58] and was even more confident in her ability to prevail at trial on the merits even if she lost the motion. The plaintiff, for his part, was convinced that the claims, while involving the same two parties, were completely distinct, and that a judge would so conclude. Although I believed that the defendant was likely to prevail on the substantive merits of the dispute, I agreed with the plaintiff that his claims were not duplicative of earlier litigation and were, therefore, likely to survive the defendant's motion to dismiss. Because of the defendant's confidence in and focus on the merits of his case, the defendant, in my opinion, undervalued the expected transaction costs of continuing with litigation. . . . Consequently, the defendant was unwilling to offer more than a token amount to settle the dispute. On the other hand, the plaintiff's confidence in his ability to survive the motion . . . caused him to focus too much attention on the motion and pay too little attention to the proof problems he faced on the merits of the dispute. The result was an overall level of confidence in ultimate success that was . . . unjustified, and translated into a high reservation price for settlement.

We have various ways to avoid learning from errors caused by overoptimism. We put a positive spin on bad outcomes, conveniently forget what we predicted, explain away failure, or adapt to disappointment through the workings of the psychological immune system.

Can overoptimism nonetheless be debiased? With respect to health risks, informing people about risk factors, asking them to describe how the factors fit their own profiles, and encouraging them to compare themselves to low-risk individuals who nonetheless succumbed to the risk had no effect—and were in some instances counterproductive.[59] Providing incentives for timely completion of projects is not likely to work, since the incentives tend to focus people's minds on

---

and Interpersonal Conflict, 51 Organizational Behavior and Human Decision Processes 176 (1992).

57. Russell Korobkin, *Psychological Impediments to Mediation Success: Theory and Practice*, 21 Ohio St. J. on Disp. Resol. 281, 281 (2006).

58. For nonlawyers, this is roughly the civil analog to double jeopardy.

59. Neil D. Weinstein and William M. Klein, *Resistance of Personal Risk Perceptions to Debiasing Interventions*, *in* Heuristics and Biases.

optimistic scenarios. Having people think about alternative scenarios is not successful in countering overoptimism. The favored scenario provides too strong an anchor. Although there is not much experimental evidence, Buehler, Griffin, and Ross suggest that the most promising strategy with respect to personal projects may be to draw people's attentions to their past experiences in completing similar projects, in effect tempering optimistic scenarios with actual personal base rates.

13.5.2 The Above-Average Effect

Closely related to overoptimism, people tend to believe that their own skills and personality traits are above average in areas ranging from driving and athletics to leadership and sensitivity. Most drivers believe that they are better and safer drivers than average. Most college professors think they are better teachers than average.[60] David Dunning, Judith Meyerowitz, and Amy Holzberg did a series of experiments that suggest that this tendency arises in situations in which the skills or traits are not precisely defined. Given ambiguity in the characteristics, people select those that place them in the most positive light.[61] Rather than having hopelessly distorted self-assessments, the participants may have provided rankings that were accurate given their own idiosyncratic definitions. Yet there are examples of the phenomenon in relatively unambiguous circumstances. For example, in a survey of magistrate judges, 56 percent believed that their rate of reversal on appeal was in the lowest quartile, and 88 percent believed that at least half of their peers had a higher rate of reversal than they did.[62]

The above-average effect may have motivational causes, such as maintaining people's self-esteem, but it may also be a consequence of the availability heuristic, in which ones own best traits are the ones most readily brought to mind.

13.5.3 Are Positive Illusions Always Detrimental?

> *"Each of us has his own way of deceiving himself. The important thing is to believe in one's own importance.*
>
> —Andre Gide"[63]

Psychologist Shelley Taylor argues that overoptimism, the above-average effect, and the illusion of control (see Section 5.7.2) have important benefits as

---

60. The studies are summarized in Russell Korobkin, *Psychological Impediments to Mediation Success: Theory and Practice*, 21 Ohio Journal on Dispute Resolution 281 (2006).

61. David Dunning, Judith A. Meyerowitz, and Amy D. Holzberg, *Ambiguity and Self-Evaluation: The Role of Idiosyncratic Trait Definitions in Self-Serving Assessments of Ability, in* Heuristics and Biases 324.

62. Chris Guthrie, Jeffrey J. Rachlinski, and Andrew J. Wistrich, *Inside the Judicial Mind*, 86 Cornell Law Review 777 (2001).

63. Andre Gide, Journals of Andre Gide Vol. 1, 1889–1927 (J. O'Brien trans., 1987).

well as downsides.[64] She writes that overoptimism usually "is not a Panglossian whitewash that paints all positive events as equally and commonly likely and all negative events as equally and uncommonly unlikely. Rather, unrealistic optimism shows a patterning that corresponds quite well to the objective likelihood of events, to relevant personal experiences with events, and to the degree to which one can actively contribute to bringing events about. Positive events are simply regarded as somewhat more likely and negative events as somewhat less likely to occur than is actually the case." More broadly, Taylor argues that these moderate illusions create self-confidence that motivates people to persevere in tasks that they might not otherwise attempt:

> [P]eople who hold positive illusions about themselves, the world, and the future may be better able to develop the skills and organization necessary to make their creative ideas and high level of motivation work effectively for them. They seem more able to engage in constructive thinking. They can tie their illusions concretely to the project at hand, developing a task-oriented optimism and sense of control that enable them to accomplish more ambitious goals. They are more likely to take certain risks that may enable them to bring their ventures to fruition. And they seem better able to choose appropriate tasks, gauge the effort involved, and make realistic estimates of their need to persevere. Moreover, by developing the ability to postpone gratification, they are able to commit themselves to a longer term task that may involve sacrifices and delayed rewards along the way."

Andy Grove (Former Intel CEO) on the Value of Self-Deception

"Well, part of [success] is self-discipline and part of it is deception. And the deception becomes reality—deception in the sense that you pump yourself up and put a better face on things than you start off feeling. After a while, if you act confident, you become more confident. So the deception becomes less of a deception. But I think it is very important for you to do two things: act on your temporary conviction as if it was a real conviction; and when you realize that you are wrong, correct course very quickly."

Quoted in JEFFREY PFEFFER AND ROBERT I. SUTTON, HARD FACTS, DANGEROUS HALF-TRUTHS AND TOTAL NONSENSE: PROFITING FROM EVIDENCE-BASED MANAGEMENT (Cambridge, MA: Harvard Business Press, 2006) 201.

In sum, overoptimism is not inevitably harmful and may sometimes conduce to improvements in performance and health, and to adaptation to life's inevitable

64. SHELLEY E. TAYLOR, POSITIVE ILLUSIONS: Creative Self-Deception and the Healthy Mind (New York: Basic Books, 1989).

difficulties. Indeed, people sometimes counsel others to be overoptimistic rather than pessimistic or even accurate about the future.[65] All things considered, though, you might prefer to keep your optimism within bounds; and to be realistic in assessing whether plans are unfolding as anticipated, so that you can make corrections if they are not.

Notwithstanding the costs and benefits of overoptimism to the individual, the phenomenon may be beneficial to the broader society. Given the likelihood of success, how many people would start restaurants? Given an accurate appraisal of the likelihood of being an acclaimed performer, how many musicians or actors would undertake years of rigor and tedium of study and practice?

13.6 INTERTEMPORAL CHOICE

13.6.1 Discount Rates

People generally prefer to have a good thing today rather than at some future time. Suppose that a firm offers you a $7500 signing bonus under alternative plans. You can choose to receive the $7500 on your first day of work. Alternatively, the firm will put the $7500 in an escrow account to be paid one year after you start working for the firm, and this amount is absolutely guaranteed—even if you are fired for cause before the year is up. Which plan would you prefer?

All things considered, you would prefer the $7500 today because having it now gives you a choice that you wouldn't otherwise have. Moreover, you could put it in a savings account or a one-year certificate of deposit and almost surely end up with more than $7500 a year from now.

Suppose the firm gives you a choice between a signing bonus of $7500 today or $8000 a year from now? To decide between the alternatives, you must know how much $8000 a year from now is worth to you today. This is the idea *net present value,* or *present discounted value.* If you were planning to put the funds in a one-year certificate of deposit at your bank, then your decision would depend on how much interest the bank would pay you on your deposit. The graph in Figure 13.2 shows that you would be indifferent between $7500 today or $8000 a year from now if the interest rate were 6.667 percent. At a lower interest rate you would prefer to wait a year for the $8000 bonus; and the higher interest rate you would take the $7500 today.

Net present value reflects how much a given amount of money in the future is worth today. The formula is:

$$NPV = X/(1-r)^n$$

65. David A. Armor, Cade Massey, and Aaron M. Sacket, *Prescribed Optimism: Is It Right to Be Wrong About the Future?*, 19 Psychological Science 329–31 (2008).

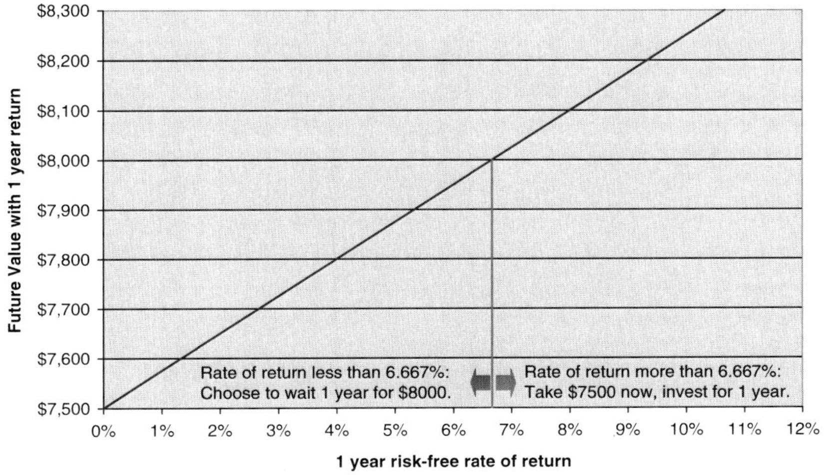

FIGURE 13.2 DO YOU PREFER $7500 NOW OR $8000 IN ONE YEAR?

where X is the amount of the future payment, r is the annual rate of return, and n how many years in the future you will receive the payment. To say that a discount rate is *high* means that you anticipate a high rate of return if you have the funds today and are able to invest them.

13.6.2 Discounted Utility, Dynamically Inconsistent Preferences, and the Pervasive Devaluation of the Future

> *To secure a maximum of benefit in life, all future events, all future pleasures and pains, should act upon us with the same force as if they were present, allowance being made for their uncertainty. The factor expressing the effect of remoteness should, in short, always be unity, so that time should have no influence. But no human mind is constituted in this perfect way; a future feeling is always less influential than a present one.*
>
> —W. S. Jevons, The Theory of Political Economy (1871)

> *People distribute their resources between the present, the near future and the remote future on the basis of a wholly irrational preference. When they have a choice between two satisfactions, they will not necessarily chose the larger of the two but will often devote themselves to producing or obtaining a small one now in preference to a much larger one some years hence.*
>
> —A. C. Pigou, The Economics of Welfare (1920)

> *Hard work often pays off after time, but laziness always pays off now.*
>
> —Author unknown

If choosing the alternative with the greater net present value usually seems the sensible strategy, there are obvious exceptions. For example, suppose that the interest rate is 6.7 percent, and

- the choice is between: $7400 today and $8000 a year from now. Even though the $8000 is a great deal, taking the smaller amount now would allow you to purchase a $7400 painting that you covet, which will not be available in a year;

or

- the choice is between $8000 today and $8000 a year from now. You are a compulsive gambler and know you'll blow any money you now have in Las Vegas, but you're about to enroll in a 12-step program.

These examples suggest that intertemporal preferences cannot be subject to global criteria of rationality (like those of the axioms of subjective expected utility theory), but rather depend on an individuals' own tastes and plans. That said, when people deviate significantly from the standard model or act as if the discount rate were extraordinarily high, it raises a warning flag that they may not be acting in their own best interests.

The standard model of discounted utility, first proposed by Paul Samuelson in 1937, assumes that people discount at a constant rate over time, with the difference in utility between receiving $100 today and $200 a year from now being proportional to the difference in utility between receiving $100 in ten years and $200 eleven years from now. As shown in the solid line in Figure 13.3, this is an exponential function.

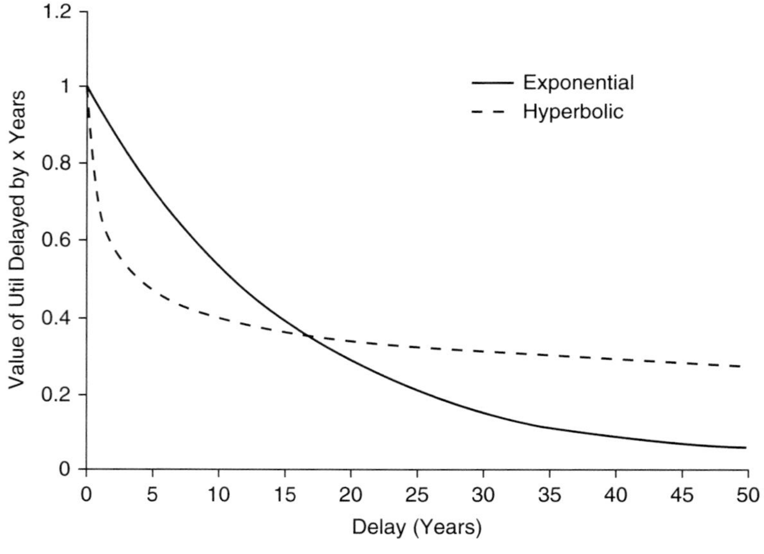

FIGURE 13.3 PRESENT BIAS.

From George-Marios Angeletos, David Laibson, Andrea Repetto, Jeremy Tobacman, and Stephen Weinberg. Figure 18.1 "Discount Functions." In *Time and Decision.* © 2003 Russell Sage Foundation, 112 East 64th Street, New York, NY 10021. Reprinted with permission.

In fact, people often manifest a strong *present bias*, or *excessive impatience*. They accord near-term gratification considerably greater value than deferred gratification, and do not distinguish much among deferred gratifications with different maturity dates—that is, between gains that are a few years away and those that lie many years in the future. Rather than being time-consistent, our preferences are dynamically inconsistent over time, and seem to follow a pattern of hyperbolic rather than exponential discounting, as shown by the dashed line in Figure 13.3.[66] (fMRI studies indicate that immediate and future rewards activate different regions of the brain.[67])

- In a dramatic example of the pervasive devaluation of the future, Howard Kunreuther, Ayse Onculer, and Paul Slovic[68] asked people to indicate the maximum they would be willing to pay for measures that would protect them from burglary (a dead-bolt lock) or earthquake damage (bracing the foundation of one's house) over time periods ranging between one and ten years. Most respondents were willing to pay the same amounts for short-term and long-term protection.
- A study of actual air conditioner purchases showed that in trading off higher operating costs for a lower purchase price, consumers acted as though the annual rate of return was an incredible 89 percent.[69]
- In another study, participants were asked to choose between receiving a prize of a certified check for $1000 that could be cashed next week and a $2000 certified check that could be cashed only after some delay, and were asked to name the length of the delay at which they would be indifferent between the two checks. On average, people would wait less than forty days for the larger check, implying a staggering rate of return.[70]
- The British sociologist, Anthony Giddens, observes that changes in individual behavior necessary to reduce obesity, high blood pressure, diabetes,

66. Some recent experimental evidence suggests that this may not be due to the difference between the present and future as such, but to the fact that people tend to have a greater discount rate for periods of shorter duration whenever they occur. *See* Daniel Read, *Subadditive Intertemporal Choice*, *in* Time and Decision 301.

67. Samuel M. McClure, David I. Laibson, George Loewenstein, and Jonathan D. Cohen, *Separate Neural Systems Value Immediate and Delayed Monetary Rewards*, 306 Science 503–07 (Oct 15, 2004).

68. Howard Kunreuther, Ayse Onculer, and Paul Slovic, *Time Insensitivity for Protective Investments*, 16 Journal of Risk and Uncertainty 279 (1998).

69. George Ainslee and Nick Haslam, *Hyperbolic Discounting*, *in* Choice Over Time 61 (George Loewenstein and Jon Elster eds., New York: Russel Sage Foundation, 1992).

70. George Ainslie and Vardim Haendel, *The Motives of Will*, in E. Gottheil, K. Druley, T. Skolda and H. Waxman (eds.), Etiologic Aspects of Alcohol and Drug Abuse 61 (Springfield, IL: Charles C. Thomas, 1983).

heart disease and cancer, excessive drinking, and drug dependence are impeded by hyperbolic discounting.[71]

- Giddens also argues that "hyperbolic discounting is one of the main factors explaining the lazy attitude most people have towards the threats posed by global warming. Surveys show that the majority now accept both that climate change is real and dangerous and that it is created by our own behaviour. However, the proportion that has made any significant behaviour change is very low. The implications are disturbing. Consciousness-raising and green taxes, even if carefully thought out and organised, may have only marginal effects—and they might be widely resisted even then."[72]

In short, we "tend to grab immediate rewards and avoid immediate costs that our 'long-run selves' do not appreciate."[73] Procrastination, in which postponing inevitable costs often leads to increased costs (the paper poorly done at the last minute, or the brief filed a day after the deadline) is a common example. Addictions are another example. George Loewenstein notes that "visceral factors, such as the cravings associated with drug addiction, drive states (e.g., hunger, thirst, and sexual desire), moods and emotions, and physical pain . . . [can] cause people to behave contrary to their own long-term self-interest, often with full awareness that they are doing so."[74]

There is evidence that children's ability to defer gratification predicts their success later in life. Walter Mischel conducted an experiment in which four-year-olds had a marshmallow placed in front of them, and were given a choice between eating it immediately or waiting a few minutes and getting

Personal Note

You are a very busy associate at a law firm. The firm's pro bono coordinator asks if you could commit to doing some work on a project that will require about five hours a week for a number of weeks. You reply that this isn't a good time, but volunteer to do the work in several months—even though you'll be at least as busy then as you are now.

---

71. Anthony Giddens, *This Time It's Personal*, The Guardian, Jan. 2, 2008, http://www.guardian.co.uk/commentisfree/2008/jan/02/thistimeitspersonal.

72. *Id.*

73. Ted O'Donoghue and Matthew Rabin, *Doing It Now or Later*, 89 American Economic Review 103 (1999).

74. George Loewenstein, *Out of Control: Visceral Influences on Behavior*, 65 Organizational Behavior and Human Decision Processes 272 (1996).

a second marshmallow. In a follow-up study fourteen years later, those who deferred on the whole were more highly rated in terms of coping skills, self-esteem, and other social skills, and scored significantly higher on their SATs.[75]

Ainslie and Haslam note that "short-term interests are not aberrant phenomena. . . . [T]hey cannot be 'cured' be any means, or controlled just by insight into what one's longest range interests are,"[76] but rather require the intentional adoption of behavioral strategies along the following lines.[77]

13.6.2.a Repression We can avoid thoughts and behavior that might lead to impulses. In Walter Mischel's experiments, the children who managed not to eat

> "The belief that a person should weight all utility the same, regardless of its temporal position, implicitly assumes that all parts of one's future are *equally* parts of oneself; that there is a single, enduring, irreducible entity to whom all future utility can be ascribed. However, some philosophers—most notably, Derek Parfitt—deny this assumption. They argue that a person is nothing more than succession of overlapping selves related to varying degrees by physical continuities, memories, and similarities of character and interests. On this view, the separation between selves may be just as significant as the separation between persons, and discounting one's 'own' future utility may be no more irrational than discounting the utility of someone else."
> —Shane Frederick, *Time Preference and Personal Identity*, *in* TIME AND DECISION 89

the marshmallows used various strategies of this sort. An observer of video footage reports: "Some cover their eyes with their hands or turn around so that they can't see the tray. Others start kicking the desk, or tug on their pigtails, or stroke the marshmallow as if it were a tiny stuffed animal.[78]

13.6.2.b Self-Control, Habits, and Routines We can develop personal rules, such as "no desserts" or "twenty minutes on the treadmill every morning." Self-control strategies often rely on creating a feeling of fear or guilt when faced with the temptation to be avoided. In George Loewenstein's and Ted O'Donoghue's words they "*immediatize* the delayed costs in the form of immediate [negative] emotions." However, using dieting as an example, Loewenstein and O'Donoghue

---

75. Yuichi Shoda, Walter Mischel, and Philip K. Peake, *Predicting Adolescent Cognitive and Self-Regulatory Competencies from Preschool Delay of Gratification: Identifying Diagnostic Conditions*, 26 DEVELOPMENTAL PSYCHOLOGY 978–86 (1990).

76. George Ainslee and Nick Halsam, *Self Control*, in CHOICE OVER TIME, *supra*.

77. We have given different names to some of the strategies.

78. Jonah Lehrer, *Don't!: The Secret of Self Control*, THE NEW YORKER, May 18, 2009.

observe that the immediate costs are only justifiable in terms of the long-term benefits, which (realistically) are often not achieved.[79]

Perhaps a more promising strategy than pure self-control is to develop habits or *routines* that guard against self-defeating behavior. Although habits must be learned over time through repetition, a program of research by Peter Gollwitzer suggests that people can often obtain the benefits of good habits immediately by engaging in a very simple cognitive exercise.[80] In a series of studies, Gollwitzer and his collaborators asked people with specific goals (such as writing a school paper over their holiday break or performing a breast self-examination in the subsequent month) to come up with a specific plan for the implementation of those goals. Such "implementation intentions" involved specifying when, where and how participants intended to pursue their goals. By creating "instant habits" and making goal pursuit automatic when the right circumstances present themselves implementation intentions increase the likelihood that people will accomplish their goals. For example, if your implementation intention is to "order fruit" for dessert at a restaurant, you are more likely to automatically order fruit when the waiter hands you the dessert menu.

The motivations to exercise self-control are complex. As Drazen Prelec and Rodnit Bodner note, "the gap between a single act of dietary self-sacrifice and its benefits—slimness, leading to beauty, health, and virtue—is not only temporal but also *causal*. A single low-calorie salad does not cause slimness. . . . Rather, the benefits or costs are properties of a long-run policy or lifestyle, and an integral policy or lifestyle cannot be obtained with a single decision. . . ."[81] The authors posit that postponing gratification produces a *diagnostic* reward—the pleasure of learning something about yourself, in this case, about your willpower. These inferences about a person's own character and prospects are "a source of *immediate* pleasure and pain, which contributes to his/her ability to exercise self-control."[82] More broadly, we tend to see our lives in terms of narratives, where deferring gratification today leads to better outcomes over time.

13.6.2.c Extrapsychic Mechanisms We can make decisions now that substitute for, or significantly aid, the exercise self-control in the future. The classic

79. George Loewenstein and Ted O'Donoghue, *We Can Do This the Easy Way or the Hard Way: Negative Emotions, Self-Regulation, and the Law*, 73 Chicago Law Review 183 (2006).

80. Peter M. Gollwitzer, *Implementation Intentions: Strong Effects of Simple Plans*, 54 American Psychologist 493–503 (1999).

81. Drazen Prelec and Ronit Bodner, *Self-Signaling and Self-Control, in* Time and Decision 277.

82. Baumeister and Kathleen D. Voss analogize the exercise of willpower to physical endurance, which is subject to exhaustion. Emotional distress undermines self-regulation by changing people's priorities to focus on feeling good in the immediate present. Roy Baumeister and Kathleen D. Voss, *Willpower, Choice, and Self-Control, in* Time and Decision 201. In any event, the resources that contribute to self-control are limited.

example is Ulysses having his sailors tie him to the mast so he could not respond to the Sirens' temptations. Keeping the refrigerator free of caloric snacks, or leaving one's credit card at home, are more mundane examples. Thomas Shelling describes a drug addiction clinic in which patients subject themselves to self-extortion: Patients write a self-incriminating letter confessing their drug addiction, which will be mailed to an appropriate person (e.g., a physician's letter is addressed to the state board of medical examiners) if he or she is caught taking drugs.[83] The Web site, http://www.stickk.com/ invites people to make "Commitment Contracts" for health and other personal goals, contracting to pay charities (including causes they abhor) if they don't meet milestones in achieving their goals.

Studies by Dan Ariely and Klaus Wertenbroch show how students use extra-psychic mechanisms to counter the temptation to procrastinate. Students in three sections of a marketing class at MIT were assigned three short papers to be written during the semester. In one section, students were told that they could hand in the papers anytime they wanted as long as all three papers were in by the last day of class. In the second section, the professor imposed fixed, evenly-spaced deadlines such that students had to complete one paper by the end of each third of the course, and would be penalized for handing a paper in late. In the third section, students were given the opportunity to set their own deadlines for the papers. They could choose any deadlines they wanted as long as all three papers were in by the end of the quarter, but once they had chosen their deadlines, they had to stick to them or they, too, would be penalized.

When given the opportunity to set their own deadlines, most students did *not* choose the schedule that would have given them the most flexibility: setting the deadlines for all three papers as late as possible. From a purely economic perspective, this would have been the schedule with the greatest utility, since you can always complete the papers earlier than the deadline. So why give up flexibility, and risk being penalized for a late paper? The students were self-aware enough to realize that if they weren't forced to complete at least one of the papers early in the semester, they were likely to procrastinate and be stuck trying to write all three of them at the last minute.

It turned out that students who chose their own deadlines received higher grades, on average, than students who were given no deadlines at all. However, students whose professors imposed evenly-spaced deadlines did even better.

83. T. C. Shelling, *Self-Command: A New Discipline, in* CHOICE OVER TIME.

Discounting and Future Generations

Forestalling climate change is one of a number situations where the benefits from costs paid today may redound to the benefit of future generations. If people often discount in planning for their own lives, should they do so for the lives of future generations? Noting that you would almost certainly prefer $1000 now to $1000 in twenty years, Cass Sunstein asks: "Is a life twenty years hence worth a fraction of a life today?"[84]

The Office of Management and Budget (OMB) suggests that policy makers "consider generational discounting in the same way as individual discounting, but with an explicit discussion of the intergenerational concerns."[85] Alternatively, OMB suggests "discounting for future generations at a slightly lower rate."[86] But some scholars argue that generational discounting is radically different from individual discounting, and that it is morally objectionable because it does not give equal consideration to those living in the future.[87] They argue for a zero rate of discounting for intergenerational decisions.[88] While we flag this complex and controversial issue, it is beyond the scope of the book.

84. Cass R. Sunstein, Worst-Case Scenarios 11 (Cambridge, Massachusetts, Harvard University Press, 2007).

85. OMB, Circular A-4, "Regulatory Analysis: Memorandum to the Heads of Executive Agencies and Establishments" (Sept. 17, 2003).

86. *Id.*

87. Richard L. Revesz and Michael A. Livermore, Retaking Rationality: How Cost-Benefit Analysis Can Better Protect The Environment and Our Health 111 (New York: Oxford University Press, 2008).

88. Tyler Cowen and Derek Parfit, *Against the Social Discount Rate, in* Justice Across the Generations: Philosophy, Politics, and Society 144–61 (James S. Fishkin and Peter Laslett eds., New Haven, CT: Yale University Press, 1992). Robert M. Solow, *The Economics of Resources or the Resources of Economics,* 64 American Economic Review 1–14 (May 1974).

14. COMPLEXITIES OF DECISION MAKING CONTINUED

The Power of Frames

In Chapter 2 we considered how the metaphors that we use to frame problems can affect our solutions to them. Here we consider frames of a quite different sort: how decisions can be affected by ways that choices are presented to us—for example, as gains or losses, or in comparison with various alternatives.

14.1 PROSPECT THEORY, THE ENDOWMENT EFFECT, AND STATUS QUO BIAS[1]

Neoclassical economics and its cousin, expected utility theory, posit that rational choices maximize one's overall wealth or, more generally, one's overall utility. Subject to Bernoulli's observation (in Section 12.1.4) that people often display a diminishing marginal utility of additional wealth, neoclassical economics, and expected utility theory posit that a penny gained has as much positive value as a penny lost has negative value. In fact, however, people systematically violate this norm when evaluating changes from the status quo. Amos Tversky and Daniel Kahneman formalized this aspect of the psychology of decision making in *prospect theory*, which is illustrated by the S-shaped curve in Figure 14.1.

In this chapter, we discuss prospect theory in circumstances where risk or uncertainty is not a significant factor. The value function described by prospect theory has three important characteristics.

1. Individuals do not think of the outcomes of decisions in terms of their overall wealth (as neoclassical economics holds). Rather, they consider outcomes in terms of gains and losses from some *reference point*.
2. Individuals are *loss averse*. The slope of the of the curve for losses is steeper than the slope for gains. This means that people experience losses from the reference point as greater than equivalent gains. Loss aversion is captured by the phrase that "losses loom larger than gains."

1. This section draws heavily on Daniel Kahneman, Jack L. Knetsch, and Richard H. Thaler, *The Endowment Effect, Loss Aversion, and Status Quo Bias, in* Choices, Values, and Frames (Daniel Kahneman and Amos Tversky, eds., Cambridge, UK: Cambridge University Press, 2000) 159. (2000), and Russell Korobkin, *The Endowment Effect and Legal Analysis*, 97 Northwester University Law Review 1227 (2003).

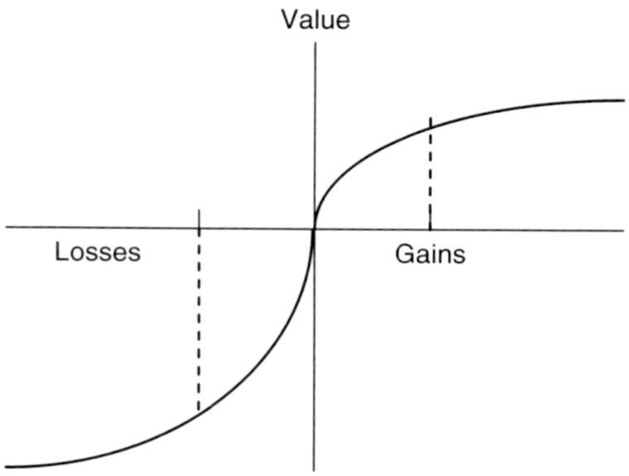

FIGURE 14.1 THE PROSPECT THEORY VALUE FUNCTION.

3. Both the gain and loss functions display *diminishing sensitivity*. They are not straight lines. Rather, the gain function is concave downward and the loss function is concave upward.

Two behavioral economists' explanation of the so-called *equity premium puzzle* provides a nice example of loss aversion. The puzzle is why people are overinvested in low-yield treasury bills compared to equities. A dollar in stocks in 1926 would have been worth over $1800 at the close of the twentieth century, while a dollar invested in treasury bills would have been worth only about $15. Ordinary degrees of risk aversion do not account for so large a disparity. Shlomo Benartzi and Richard Thaler explain the puzzle in terms of what they call *myopic loss aversion*: Many investors examine their portfolios' performance on a daily, if not more frequent, basis, and tend to reset their reference point each time they look. If losses loom larger than gains, the pain of a dollar's loss is greater than the pleasure of a dollar's gain. Thus the excessive risk aversion caused by frequent evaluation of their portfolios prevents investors "from adopting a strategy that would be preferred over an appropriately long time horizon."[2]

As this example suggests, there is no objectively correct reference point. An individual's conscious or unconscious choice of a reference point in a particular situation is subjective, context-sensitive, and labile. Two people—for example, two parties negotiating a contract—may have different references points for exactly the same situation or transaction. Whatever reference point one chooses, though, a potential loss is more unattractive than an equivalent potential gain is attractive.

2. Shlomo Benartzi and Richard H. Thaler, "Myopic Loss Aversion and the Equity Premium Puzzle," NBER Working Paper No. W4369. May 1993, *available at* SSRN: http://ssrn.com/abstract=227015.

The example also illustrates that people often choose the status quo as a reference point from which to evaluate change. As a consequence of loss aversion, all things considered, people like things the way they are more than they like change. This general phenomenon is called the *status quo* bias. We begin by describing an important subset of status quo bias, the *endowment effect*, which captures the fact that people often demand more to give up a good or entitlement than they would be willing to pay to acquire it. The endowment effect arises in many contexts and often confounds policy making.

For example, *contingent valuation* (discussed in Section 14.6) is a common method, used in cost-benefit analysis and the assessment of damages, for placing a value on environmental goods or harms: affected individuals are surveyed to determine how much they would be willing to pay (WTP) to gain an environmental good or how much they would be willing to accept (WTA) to suffer the loss of that good. Contingent valuation is premised on the assumption that an individual's WTP and WTA for a good are identical. But it turns out that WTP and WTA often differ by large amounts. Russell Korobkin reports:

> In one notable study, 2000 duck hunters were surveyed about the value they would place on protecting a wetland from development. Hunters were willing to pay $247 per person per season, on average, for the right to prevent development to make hunting viable, while they would demand, on average, $1044 dollars each to give up an entitlement to hunt there. . . . [Another] survey found that a sample of residents of a region of the southwest would pay $4.75 per month, on average, to maintain 75 miles of air visibility in the face of potential pollution that would reduce visibility to 50 miles. In contrast, however, people drawn from the same pool and told that they collectively enjoyed the right to prohibit the pollution, reported that they would demand $24.47 per month before being willing to permit the pollution.[3]

In a classic demonstration of the endowment effect,[4] half the students in a classroom—the sellers—were handed decorated university mugs (costing $5 at the university bookstore) and given a questionnaire that stated: "You now own the object in your possession. You have the option of selling it if a price, which will be determined later, is acceptable to you. For each of the possible prices below, indicate whether you wish to sell your object and receive this price; or keep your object and take it home with you." The participants indicated their decision for prices ranging from $0.50 to $9.50 in increments of 50 cents. Students who had not received a mug—the buyers—received a similar questionnaire, informing them that they would have the option of receiving either a mug

---

3. Russell Korobkin, *supra*.

4. Daniel Kahneman, Jack L. Knetsch, and Richard H. Thaler, *Experimental Tests of the Endowment Effect and the Coase Theorem*, 98 Journal of Political Economy 1325–48 (December 1990).

or a sum of money to be determined later. They indicated their preferences between a mug and sums of money ranging from $0.50 to $9.50.

The median price that buyers were willing to pay (WTP) for the mug was $3.31, while the sellers' median willingness to accept (WTA) was $7.06. Amos Tversky and Daniel Kahneman explain that the buyers and the sellers face precisely the same decision problem, but from different reference states. The buyers face the positive choice of receiving either the mug or cash. The sellers must choose between keeping the mug (retaining the status quo) or giving it up in exchange for money. "Thus, the mug is evaluated as a gain by the [buyers], and as a loss by the sellers. Loss aversion entails that the rate of exchange of the mug for money will be different in the two cases."[5]

Why doesn't the buyer feel a similar loss aversion with respect to the money given up? Although the endowment effect is not limited to unique items, it is attenuated for ordinary market goods that have close substitutes, and it disappears for items, such as money, that have only an exchange value.[6] Moreover:

> Selling an item, even a minor one, may be thought to involve a choice in a deeper or more vivid sense than buying; after all, selling is a far rarer activity for the average individual, so that the choice to sell or not may seem rather weighty. In contrast, the decision whether to buy or not is made by individuals nearly constantly, in a wide variety of highly impersonal settings. Another way of seeing this point is that the act of selling seems more permanent than that of not-buying, so that one is more reluctant to sell than not to buy.[7]

The endowment effect has been replicated in many studies. In one experiment, participants were given either a lottery ticket that costs $2 or $2 cash, and then offered the opportunity to trade the lottery ticket for cash or vice versa.

---

5. Amos Tversky and Daniel Kahneman, *Loss Aversion in Riskless Choice: A Reference-Dependent Model*, 106 QUARTERLY JOURNAL OF ECONOMICS 1039 (1991). In another experiment, half the participants were given pens, and half were given a token redeemable for an unspecified gift. Then, all of the participants were given a choice between the pen and two chocolate bars. Fifty-six percent of those who already had the pen preferred the pen, compared to 24 percent of the others. In a separate part of the experiment, when asked to rank the attractiveness of a number of items, including the pens and chocolate bars, the participants rated the chocolate bars as at least as attractive. "This suggests that the main effect of endowment is not to enhance the appeal of the good one owns, only the pain of giving it up." Kahneman, Knetsch, and Thaler, *supra.* In yet another experiment involving mugs and chocolate, participants were randomly given either a coffee mug or a large Swiss chocolate bar and offered the opportunity to trade. Only 11 percent and 10 percent of the participants, respectively, were willing to trade.

6. Jennifer Arlen, Matthew Spitzer, and Eric Talley, *Endowment Effects within Corporate Agency Relationships*, 31 JOURNAL OF LEGAL STUDIES 1 (2002).

7. Edward McCaffrey, Daniel Kahneman, and Matthew Spitzer, *Framing the Jury: Cognitive Perspectives on Pain and Suffering Awards*, 81 VIRGINIA LAW REVIEW 1341 (1995).

Very few switch.[8] As a real-world analogue, consider the large number of individual investors who will hold on to shares of stock when they would not purchase the same stock at the same or even a lower market price. Consider whether the various legal doctrines that reflect the saying that "possession is nine points of the law," or doctrines that give greater due process rights to someone already holding a government job or benefit than one seeking it, may reflect the endowment effect.

People may gain "psychological ownership" merely by having an item in their physical possession. In a recent variation on the mug experiment, students were asked to physically examine the mugs for different periods of time before bidding on them in an auction. Those who held the mugs for longer period of time bid more.[9]

As we mentioned, the endowment effect is a subset of the *status quo bias*—the general phenomenon whereby people attach a value to the present state of the world compared to alternative states, even when no property right or legal entitlement is involved. For example, as of the 1990s, the standard auto insurance policy in New Jersey did not provide a right to recover for pain and suffering for minor injuries, though one could obtain that right by purchasing a higher priced policy. In Pennsylvania, the standard policy *did* provide the right to recover, but one could purchase a cheaper policy that relinquished the right. In a survey of residents of the two states, only 20 percent of New Jersey respondents and 25 percent of Pennsylvanians indicated they would switch from their state's default policy.[10]

Also, as we noted above, what one treats as a reference point is essentially a subjective matter. Russell Korobkin conducted an experiment to explore whether the parties negotiating a contract would treat a default contract term as the status quo.[11] Students played the role of lawyer negotiating a shipping contract on behalf on an overnight delivery company. In one scenario, they were told that there were two possible terms that could be used to deal with consequential damages for loss or delay of packages: (A) the delivery company would be liable only for reasonably foreseeable damages, or (B) the delivery company would be liable for all consequential damages, whether or not foreseeable. In another scenario they were told that there were two possible terms for dealing with unforeseen circumstances that make delivery commercially impracticable: (A) the delivery company would be excused from its obligation to deliver, or (B) the delivery

8. Tversky and Kahneman, *Loss Aversion in Riskless Choice, supra.*

9. James R. Wolf, Hal R. Arkes, and Waleed A. Muhanna, *The Power of Touch: An Examination of the Effect of Duration of Physical Contact on the Valuation of Objects,* Judgment and Decision Making 476–82 (August 2008).

10. Eric J. Johnson, John Hershey, Jacqueline Meszaros, Hershey, and Howard Kunreuther, *Framing, Probability Distortions, and Insurance Decisions,* 7 Journal of Risk and Uncertainty 35 (1993).

11. Russell Korobkin, *The Status Quo Bias and Contract Default Rules,* 83 Cornell Law Review 608 (1998).

company would be liable for damages. Participants were then given estimates of the differential costs to their client (on a per-package basis) of performing its obligations if the contract contained term B rather than A, and were then asked to value term A relative to term B.

One-half of the participants were told that term A was the default rule and were asked to provide their WTA price (how much their clients would need to be paid per package) to agree to insert term B into the agreement to contract around the default rule. The other half of the participants were told that term B was the default rule and were thus asked to provide their WTP for inserting term A into the contract in order to contract around the default rule. In both scenarios, WTA significantly exceeding WTP; in other words, the strength of the participants' preferences for the term that benefited their client was biased in favor of whichever term was identified as the default.

In Korobkin's experiment, the contracting parties were induced to treat the legal default rule as the status quo. However, Marcel Kahan and Michael Klausner hypothesized that contracting parties might treat the terms embodied in a standard form contract as the reference point. "Although these parties have no formal property (or other) rights in a standard term, the standard sets terms for an expectational baseline . . ."[12] Korobkin subsequently tested this hypothesis by redesigning his experiments to inform the participants negotiating a contract term about both the legal default rule and the term in the standard form contract. They were told that the form term was the opposite of the legal default rule, so that if they contracted around the form term, they would reestablish the default term that the standard form circumvented. The participants' preferences turned out to be biased in favor of the form term rather than the default rule. Korobkin concludes:

> These results suggest that contract terms will be biased in favor of the status quo, but that the reference point that identifies the status quo for contracting parties is extremely dependent on context. The implication for legal policy is that the content of contract law probably substantively affects the content of contracts, but not all the time. The effect of contract law can be swamped by other reference points, depending on the circumstances. The prescriptive implications for contract lawyers seems more clear: "negotiators who are able to define the status quo position, against which all proposed terms are judged, are likely to enjoy an important bargaining advantage."[13]

---

12. Marcel Kahan and Michael Klausner, *Path Dependence in Corporate Contracting: Increasing Returns, Herd Behavior and Cognitive Biases*, 74 Washington University Law Quarterly 347, 361 (1996).

13. Russell B. Korobkin, *The Status Quo Bias and Contract Default Rules*, 83 Cornell Law Review (1998).

In a torts suit, the instructions to a jury assessing damages could be framed from either of two perspectives. The jury might be asked

1. to imagine being the plaintiff before the injury and ask how much you would demand to suffer the injury, or
2. to imagine being the plaintiff after the injury and ask how much is needed to "make you whole."

The former perspective frames the issue as a loss—from the plaintiff's being healthy to being injured—while the latter frames it as a gain, and prospect theory predicts that the loss will be perceived as greater than an equivalent gain. A series of experiments by Edward McCaffrey, Daniel Kahneman, and Matthew Spitzer demonstrated just this result with respect to awards for pain and suffering: participants playing the role of jurors awarded twice as much in the loss frame than in the gain frame.[14] The authors suggest that, in addition to providing a "healthy" reference point, the ex ante perspective captures the value of the plaintiff's exercising the free choice of whether or not to incur the injury. (The authors argue that the make-whole instruction is normatively preferable to the ex ante instruction: because of the phenomenon of impact bias (Section 13.4.1), someone anticipating the effect of injury is likely to underestimate the plaintiff's resiliency and adaptability and therefore overestimate the disutility of the injury.)

In discussing the concept of external validity in Section 7.6.2, we described some skepticism about whether the endowment effect actually exists. The leading critique is by Charles R. Plott and Kathryn Zeiler,[15] who assert that gaps between WTP and WTA may be explained by participants' misconceptions about the parameters in the experimental auctions. They suggest that the WTP-WTA gap may be explained by factors including the role of anonymity in the experiment for both the buyers and the sellers, the elicitation mechanisms used, and whether or not the auction participants have a thorough understanding of the auction's rules. Plott and Zeiler conducted a series of experimental auctions designed specifically to control these factors and concluded that there was no evidence of an endowment effect. While their criticism is far from conclusive, their results suggest that the precise conditions under which a WTP-WTA gap does and does not occur must be sorted out to more fully understand the nature and scope of the endowment effect.

* * *

14. Edward McCaffrey, Daniel Kahneman, and Matthew Spitzer, *Framing the Jury: Cognitive Perspectives on Pain and Suffering Awards*, 81 Virginia Law Review 1341 (1995).

15. Charles R. Plott and Kathryn Zeiler, *The Willingness to Pay/Willingness to Accept Gap, The "Endowment Effect," Subject Misconceptions and Experimental Procedures for Eliciting Valuations*, 95 American Economic Review 530–45 (2004).

At the beginning of this section, we attributed the endowment effect and status quo bias to loss aversion. But what causes or explains loss aversion? In some, but not most, circumstances, the phenomenon can be attributed to the individual's emotional attachment to an object or the status quo. Indeed, people exhibit more attachment to items that they have earned rather than gained by chance.[16] In some (but not all) circumstances it may also reflect people's discomfort in participating in market transactions, especially with respect to goods that are difficult to value. It is interesting that the effect may be diminished when someone holds an asset for the purpose of making a deal to exchange it rather than for its use value—as when the holder is a broker or agent acting on behalf of a principal rather than the principal herself, or when the decision maker is a corporation rather than an individual.[17]

In other situations, people may value the default because it reflects what most (informed) people do, which is often a plausible basis for one's own choice in the absence of other information. Cass Sunstein thus writes of 401(k) savings plans:[18]

> Most 401(k) plans use an opt-in design. When employees first become eligible to participate in the 401(k) plan, they receive some plan information and an enrollment form that must be completed in order to join. Under the alternative of automatic enrollment, employees receive the same information but are told that unless they opt out, they will be enrolled in the plan (with default options for savings rates and asset allocation). In companies that offer a "match" (the employer matches the employee's contributions according to some formula, often a 50 percent match up to some cap), most employees eventually do join the plan, but enrollments occur much sooner under automatic enrollment. . . .
>
> In many settings, any starting point will carry some informational content and will thus affect choices. When a default rule affects behavior, it might well be because it is taken to carry information about how sensible people usually organize their affairs. . . . Some workers might think, for example, that they should not enroll in a 401(k) plan and have a preference not to do so;

16. Arlen, Spitzer, and Talley, *supra*.

17. Arlen, Spitzer, and Talley, *supra*.

18. CASS R. SUNSTEIN, LAWS OF FEAR: BEYOND THE PRECAUTIONARY PRINCIPLE 132, 138 (New York: Cambridge University Press, 2005). *See* James J. Choi, David Laibson, Brigitte C. Madrian, and Andrew Metrick, *Defined Contribution Pensions: Plan Rules, Participant Choices, and the Path of Least Resistance, in* TAX POLICY AND THE ECONOMY 67, 70 (James M. Poterba, ed., Cambridge, MA: MIT Press, 2002); Brigitte C. Madrian and Dennis F. Shea, *The Power of Suggestion: Inertia in 401(k) Participation and Savings Behavior*, 116 QUARTERLY JOURNAL OF ECONOMICS 1149, 1149–50 (2001); *See* Richard H. Thaler and Shlomo Benartzi, *Save More Tomorrow: Using Behavioral Economics to Increase Employee Saving*, 112 JOURNAL OF POLITICAL ECONOMY, 2004, S164 (2004).

> but the thought and the preference might shift with evidence that the employer has made enrollment automatic. With respect to savings, the designated default plan apparently carries a certain legitimacy for many employees, perhaps because it seems to have resulted from some conscious thought about what makes most sense for most people. This interpretation is supported by the finding that the largest effects from the new default rule are shown by women and African-Americans. We might speculate that members of such groups tend to be less confident in their judgments in this domain and may have less experience in assessing different savings plans.

But there are many situations where the status quo or the fact that one is endowed with an object provides no informational content.

The endowment effect may be affected by the phenomenon of *projection bias* described in Section 13.4.2, which may lead to exaggerated predictions of feelings of loss.[19] On the other hand, a failure of empathy may lead buyers to *underestimate* the strength of the endowment effect on owners and thus cause distortions in negotiations "because buyers will tend to underestimate owners' reservation prices. By the same token, owners will tend to overestimate buyers' reservation prices."[20]

Another explanation for the endowment effect and status quo bias is the desire to *avoid regret*—"the painful feeling a person experiences upon determining she could have obtained a better outcome if she had decided or behaved differently."[21] Of course, people also rejoice when the actual outcome is superior to what might have happened. But, consistent with loss aversion, the negative emotion of regret tends to be stronger.

Consistent with a "regret avoidance" account of the endowment effect, Ziv Carmon and Dan Ariely have shown that, when contemplating a sale, both buyers and sellers tend to focus on what the sale would cause them to forgo in determining what they think the price should be. Since buyers and sellers forgo different things in a sale (sellers forgo the item that is being sold and buyers forgo the money they spend in the sale), buyers' WTP and sellers' WTA are likely to diverge. Carmon and Ariely asked students at Duke University to contemplate a sale of tickets to a basketball game. They found that buyers' WTP was mainly

19. George Loewenstein, Ted O'Donoghue, and Matthew Rabin, *Projection Bias in Predicting Future Utility*, Quarterly Journal of Economics 1209 (2003).

20. *Id.* Leaf Van Boven, David Dunning, and George Loewenstein conducted an experiment in which sellers endowed with coffee mugs were asked to estimate how much buyers would pay, and buyers were asked to estimate how much sellers would charge. Sellers predicted that buyers would pay $3.93, compared to buyers' WTP of $1.85; buyers predicted that sellers would demand $4.39, compared to sellers WTA of $6.37. *Egocentric Empathy Gaps Between Owners and Buyers: Misperceptions of the Endowment Effect*, 79 Journal of Personality and Social Psychology 66 (2000).

21. Chris Guthrie, *Better Settle Than Sorry: The Regret Aversion Theory of Litigation Behavior*, 1999 U. Ill. L. Rev. 43.

influenced by monetary considerations such as the base price of the tickets and how heavily they were discounted. Meanwhile, sellers' WTA was more heavily affected by factors related to the experience of the game, including the atmosphere of the stadium and the importance of the game.[22]

14.2 REGRET AVERSION

If there is something to desire,
there will be something to regret.
If there is something to regret,
there will be something to recall.
If there is something to recall,
there was nothing to regret.
If there was nothing to regret,
there was nothing to desire.

—Vera Pavlova, Four Poems. From IF THERE IS SOMETHING TO DESIRE: ONE HUNDRED POEMS by Vera Pavlova, translated by Steven Seymour, translation copyright © 2010 by Steven Seymour. Used by permission of Alfred A. Knopf, a division of Random House, Inc.

In Section 13.1, we listed characteristics of the decision process that predicted suboptimal outcomes. One ex-post indicator of a poor outcome is that the decision maker subsequently *regrets* the decision she made. Regretting a large purchase or feeling bloated after eating too much are common examples. Subject to several provisos, ex-post regret is a plausible indication that the decision was not a good one:

- First, the decision maker's values must be essentially the same when she made the decision and when she regrets it; if her values have changed significantly in the interim, regret does not indicate a poor decision.
- Second, people may regret that an advertently risky decision turned out badly, but, again, this does not mean the decision was a poor one.[23]
- Third, people are quite adept at rationalizing bad outcomes, and may have different regrets immediately after making a decision and in the long run.

---

22. Ziv Carmon and Dan Ariely, *Focusing on the Forgone: How Value Can Appear So Different to Buyers and Sellers*, 27 JOURNAL OF CONSUMER RESEARCH 360–70 (2000).

23. Although a decision maker cannot undo the behavior that she now regrets, a decision maker may learn from her own experience and avoid the regret-causing behavior in the future. Moreover, there may be categories of cases where regret is so ubiquitous that a counselor to the decision maker would predict the consequences.

> This makes it difficult to use regret to establish a neutral vantage point from which to assess the quality of the decision.

Because regret is a *dis*utility, decision makers often try to make decisions in a way that avoids regret. Minimizing regret plays a role in decisions by consumers, investors, professionals, and policy makers. Indeed, even in situations where decision makers are risk-averse, regret-aversion may trump risk aversion.[24]

14.2.1 Imagining the Counterfactual Outcome

We only regret a decision if its outcome is worse than the outcome of a different choice would have been. We can learn of the counterfactual outcome through actual feedback or by imagining it. The easier it is to imagine the better outcome—the more "mutable" the event is—the more likely we are to regret actions that had bad consequences.

Mutability explains why regret is enhanced when the good outcome *almost* happened. For example, Daniel Kahneman and Dale Miller posed this problem:

> Mr. C and Mr. D were scheduled to leave the airport on different flights at the same time. They traveled from town in the same limousine, were caught in a traffic jam, and arrived at the airport 30 minutes after the scheduled departure time of their flights. Mr. D is told that his flight left on time. Mr. C is told that his flight was delayed, and only left 5 minutes ago.

Ninety-six percent of respondents thought that Mr. C would be more upset than Mr. D.[25]

In many cases, the outcome that might have occurred is clearly superior or inferior to what actually occurred. But sometimes this may be a matter of framing. Who is likely to be unhappier after an Olympic event, someone who won a silver medal or someone who won a bronze? Victoria Medvec and her colleagues studied contestants' reactions immediately after the event, and concluded that the former, though objectively better off, were actually less happy:[26]

---

24. Marcel Zeelenberg, Jane Beattie, Joop van der Pligt, and Nanne K. de Vries, *Consequences of Regret Aversion*, 65 Organizational Behavior and Human Decision Processes 148 (1996).

25. By the same token, we especially regret bad outcomes from exceptions to our routines: "Mr. Adams was involved in an accident when driving home after work on his regular route. Mr. White was involved in a similar accident when driving on a route that he only takes when he wants a change of scenery." Eighty-two percent thought that Mr. White would be more upset than Mr. Adams. Daniel Kahneman and Dale T. Miller, *Norm Theory: Comparing Reality to Its Alternatives* 93 Psychological Review 136–53 (1986).

26. Victoria H. Medvec, Scott F. Madley, and Thomas Gilovich, *Where Less Is More: Counterfactual Thinking and Satisfaction Among Olympic Medalists*, Journal of Personality and Social Psychology 625 (1995).

> Consider the counterfactual thoughts of bronze and silver medalists. . . . One would certainly expect the silver medalist to focus on almost winning the gold because there is a qualitative difference between coming in first and any other outcome. . . . Moreover, for the silver medalist, this exalted status was only one step away. . . . In contrast, bronze medalists are likely to focus their counterfactual thoughts downward. . . . [T]here is a categorical difference between finishing third and finishing fourth.

The researchers did not study how long the disappointment lasted, but they cite some anecdotal evidence of contestants in a spelling bee and an Olympic race being plagued by the results later in their lifetimes.

14.2.2 Action vs. Inaction

At least in the short run, people tend to regret an *action* that turned out badly (e.g., choosing to enter into a transaction that changes the status quo) more than a *failure to act* that has unfortunate consequences.[27] Thus, giving up an entitlement is more likely to cause future regret than not gaining it in the first place. Consider this question posed to participants by Kahneman and Tversky:[28]

> Mr. Paul owns shares in Company A. During the past year, he considered switching to stock in Company B, but decided against it. He now finds out that he would have been better off by $1,200 if he had switched to the stock of Company B. Mr. George owned shares in Company B. During the past year he switched to stock in Company A. He now finds that he would have been better off by $1,200 if he had kept his stock in Company B. Who feels greater regret?

A striking 92 percent of the respondents thought that Mr. George would experience more regret.

Actions are often more salient and may involve a greater sense of personal agency. Dale Miller and Brian Taylor suggest that some practices or superstitions that counsel inaction are designed to anticipatorily avoid regret.[29] For example, contrary to an optimal strategy, most blackjack players will stand rather than take another card when their cards total 16. And some people superstitiously believe that switching lines in a supermarket risks that the former line

---

27. This may also be due to the availability heuristic: taking actions is often more vivid and memorable than doing nothing.

28. Daniel Kahneman and Amos Tversky, *The Psychology of Preferences*, 246 SCIENTIFIC AMERICAN 246 (1982). See also Daniel Kahneman and Dale Miller, *Norm Theory: Comparing Reality to Its Alternatives, in* HEURISTICS AND BIASES: THE PSYCHOLOGY OF INTUITIVE JUDGMENT 397, 348 (THOMAS GILOVICH, DALE GRIFFIN, AND DANIEL KAHNEMAN eds., New York: Cambridge University Press, 2002) [hereafter HEURISTICS AND BIASES].

29. Dale Miller and Brian Taylor, *Counterfactual Thought, Regret, and Superstition: How to Avoid Kicking Yourself, in* HEURISTICS AND BIASES, at 367.

will speed up and the new one will slow down. "To undertake a risky action one easily imagines otherwise . . . is to tempt fate. . . . One is just 'asking for it' if one takes an action he or she knows, in retrospect, will be easy to imagine otherwise.[30] Daniel Keys and Barry Schwartz note the superstition that bullfighters should not substitute for other matadors at the last minute as an example of how regret in the decision process can "leak" into outcomes (See Section 12.1.2). "This superstition may be rational, as the negative consequences of a matador being gored include not just the physical damage to the matador but also the regret, doubt, and other emotional suffering that can spread throughout the bullfighting community after a goring. A last-minute matador switch is a salient event that tends to induce counterfactual thinking and increase susceptibility to regret."[31]

Actions can cause regret directly when they end in negative outcomes—as when the decision to take a card makes a blackjack player "bust." And actions can also cause regret indirectly by changing the way one thinks about one's past behavior. Consider this example: Artie is about to take his first trip on Global Airlines and is invited to join its frequent flier program. Ben is in the same position, but Ben took a long trip on Global Airlines last month and didn't take the trouble to enroll in the frequent flier program then. Who is more likely to enroll on this trip?

Research by Orit Tykocinski and Thane Pittman suggests that Artie is more likely to enroll in the frequent flyer program than Ben.[32] If he joined the frequent flier program *now*, Ben would have to admit that his failure to join earlier had been a mistake. His current action would make him regret his past inaction. As the authors put it, "by quickly turning down the subsequent action opportunity . . . one can avoid thinking about the inferior current opportunity that triggers the perception of loss." Unlike the blackjack players, who do not know whether the next card will make them win or bust, Ben knows in advance that joining the frequent flier program will have beneficial results. Yet they still avoid taking these actions because doing so would make them regret their previous procrastination.

In some circumstances, *inaction* is more likely to cause more regret than action—even in the short run. Consider the dilemma of the soccer goalie as his opponent swings his foot back for a penalty kick. Should the goalie move left, right, or stay put? Although goalies are more than twice as likely to make a save

---

30. Miller and Taylor, *supra*.

31. Daniel J. Keys and Barry Schwartz, *"Leaky" Rationality: How Research on Behavioral Decision Making Challenges Normative Standards of Rationality*, 2 Perspectives on Psychological Science 162–80 (2007).

32. Orit E. Tykocinski and Thane S. Pittman, *The Consequences of Doing Nothing: Inaction Inertia as Avoidance of Anticipated Counterfactual Regret*, 75 Journal of Personality and Social Psychology 607 (1998).

if they stay in the center of the goal, it turns out that they only rarely stay put. The anticipation of regret may help explain these findings: professional goalkeepers indicated that they would feel more regret if they let a penalty kick go by without moving than if they had taken an ineffective action. Why would inaction cause more regret in this case than action? The answer may relate again to the ease of generating counterfactuals. Because goalkeepers are expected to act, action may be less mutable than inaction. In other words, it may be easier to generate the counterfactual "if only I'd jumped for the ball" than it is to think, "if only I'd stayed put."[33] Perhaps action *is* the status quo for many athletes.

Whether actions or inactions beget more regret also seems to depend on the time horizon. While in the short run people most regret actions, in the long run they most regret failures to act.[34] Research by Thomas Gilovich and Victoria Medvec found that people's most lasting regrets involved not failures to take discrete actions, such as failing to sign up for the discounted Tuscany tour, but rather *patterns* of inaction, such as not investing sufficiently in educational opportunities or spending enough time with friends. Still, some discrete inactions, such as failure to seize a romantic or business opportunity, can have lasting consequences. A popular web comic humorously illustrates this point with a bar graph entitled "Number of Google Results For I ______ Have Kissed Her (Or Him)." (See Figure 14.2.) The bar that fills in the blank with "should" reveals almost nine times more hits than the bar for "shouldn't." [35]

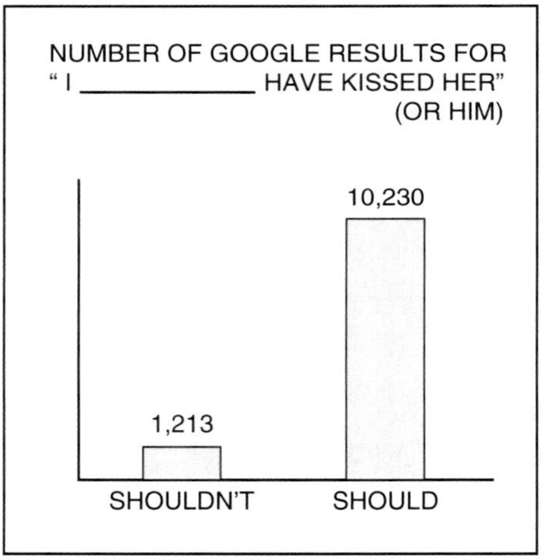

FIGURE 14.2 NUMBER OF GOOGLE RESULTS FOR "I____ HAVE KISSED HER (OR HIM). http://xkcd.com/458/. reprinted by permission of xkcd.

33. Patricia Cohen, *The Art of the Save, for Goalie and Investor*, NEW YORK TIMES, March 1, 2008, Business Section, online edition.

34. Thomas Gilovich and Victoria H. Medvec, *The Experience of Regret: What, When, and Why*, 102 PSYCHOLOGY REVIEW 379 (1995).

35. XKCD webcomic, http://xkcd.com/458/.

Gilovich and Medvec identify a number of factors that may diminish regret about actions and increase regret about inactions over time:

- Elements that reduce the pain of regrettable actions so that the initial pain of the regrettable action diminishes over time:
  - Ameliorating the action. The pain of regrettable action is felt more quickly and the action can often be ameliorated. (If you marry Mr. Wrong, you can get divorced; if you fail to marry Mr. Right, he may no longer be available.)
  - Reducing dissonance, for example, by identifying silver linings ("At least we had wonderful children"; "I learned a lot from making that bad investment.")
- Elements that bolster the pain of regrettable inactions.
  - The passage of time makes one more confident that one could have succeeded in the forgone action, thus making it easy to mentally "undo" the inaction. ("We thought religious differences would get in the way of our marriage, but we could have worked them out.")
  - While regrets about actions focus on bad things that actually happened, regrets about inactions concern good things that *might* have happened—an open-ended category that can grow in scope and importance with the passage of time.
- Elements that differentially affect cognitive availability. Many regrets about inaction involved unrealized ambitions and unfulfilled intentions that are more available to our minds than goals that have been fulfilled.

14.2.3 The Effects of Anticipating Feedback about What Would Actually Have Happened

Are people's decisions affected by the knowledge that they will learn about the consequences of the foregone option and that this might induce regret? An experiment by two business school professors, Richard Larrick and Terry Boles, found that negotiators were more prone to reach agreement when doing so would shield them from knowing their opponents' BATNA (best alternative to a negotiated agreement) than when they knew they would learn their opponents' BATNA and then possibly regret having made the deal.[36]

Against the background of this and similar studies, Chris Guthrie conducted an experiment to shed light on litigants' settlement behavior. Participants were given the facts of two cases—one involving an employee's claim for overtime, the other a "slip and fall" injury—and told that they might be litigated in either of two jurisdictions. In the traditional jurisdiction, if the parties settle, they

36. Richard P. Larrick and Terry L. Boles, *Avoiding Regret in Decisions with Feedback: A Negotiation Example*, 63 Organizational Behavior and Human Decision Processes 87–97 (1995).

will have no idea what the judge would have awarded had the case gone to trial. In the "regret" jurisdiction, the judge informs the parties what he would have awarded. By a large margin, the participants predicted that the parties—-defendants as well as plaintiffs—would be more prone to settle in the traditional jurisdiction, where they would be shielded from knowledge of the foregone outcome and thus shielded from regret.[37] Whether to encourage settlement or just to avoid the costs of unnecessary adjudication, most real-world procedures shield parties negotiating a settlement from learning what the specific foregone outcome might have been.

14.2.4 Regret and Suboptimal Learning Processes

Faced with the prospect of learning about the foregone outcome and experiencing regret, a decision maker has three options: (1) make the decision that reduces anticipated regret, (2) avoid feedback about the foregone outcome, or (3) just ignore the anticipated regret. As we have seen, the problem with the first is that people are often not good at forecasting future affective states, and especially tend to ignore the anodyne workings of the psychological immune system.[38] Although the second may be a useful self-protective device for one-time decisions, feedback is the only way to improve one's performance in repeated decisions. Such "myopic regret aversion"[39] is especially counterproductive for professionals, whether in law, policy, business, or medicine. The third option is often the best, but it is not costless. Even if regret dissipates over time, it can be a strong negative emotion and thus a real hedonic loss while it lasts—and who knows how long that may be?

14.3 SUNK COSTS[40]

Suppose that you are watching a movie and you find it to be boring and unlikely to get any better. Do you nonetheless keep watching the movie? Suppose that you paid $10 to see the movie. Does that affect your decision? In a study by

37. Guthrie, *Regret Aversion Theory, supra.*

38. Section 12.1.5.

39. Jochen Reb and Terry Connolly, "Myopic Regret Aversion and Feedback Avoidance in Repeated Decisions" (working paper 2005), http://www.sie.arizona.edu/MURI/cd/content/Reb%20Connolly%20Myopic%20reg%20av%20and%20reason%20based%20choice%20Thrust%20A.doc.

40. *See generally* Daniel Friedman, Kai Pommerenke, Rajan Lukose, Garret Milam, and Bernardo A. Huberman, Experimental 0407008, Economics Working Paper Archive EconWPA (2004), http://ideas.repec.org/p/wpa/wuwpex/0407007.html.

Deborah Frisch, 57 percent of people who said they would stop watching a free movie said they would keep watching it if they had paid $10.[41]

This phenomenon of valuing sunk costs was replicated in an experiment involving a campus theater company at the University of Ohio. Theatergoers who were about to buy season tickets were randomly placed into groups that either paid full price or received a discount. During the first half of the season, those who paid full price attended many more plays than those who had received the discount—though the rates of attendance converged for the second half of the season.[42]

Economic theory holds that the price they paid for the ticket should not affect ticket-holders' decision whether to attend. Whether they paid full price or received a discount, the cost of the ticket is "sunk" and can have no effect on the utility of attending—as compared to whether or not it is snowing that evening, or the ticket holder has a paper due the next day, or is or just isn't in a theater-going mood. But for those who paid full price, the loss of the money was more salient than for those who got the discount.

The phenomenon of honoring sunk costs manifests itself in many personal, government, and business decisions. For example:[43]

- Members of a health club with semi-annual dues made greater of use of the facility in the month after they paid dues; use declined over the next five months, until the cycle repeated itself.[44]
- A soldier on the first day of the Gulf War in 1991: "Finally, the day has finally come. You've got to think logically and realistically. Too much money's been spent, too many troops are over here, too many people had too many hard times not to kick somebody's ass."
- The parents of American troops killed in Iraq:[45] "To say the war right now is worthless or that it is without cause or unjust, would be saying that my son, for all he had in him to go over there to preserve the freedom of his country, would have died in vain." "Don't take our soldiers out of Iraq. If you do, it means our loved ones will have died for nothing." (This is not the universal view.

41. Deborah Frisch, *Reasons for Framing Effects, Organizational Behavior and Human Decision Processes*, 54, 399–429 (1993), *cited in* Daniel J. Keys and Barry Schwartz, *"Leaky" Rationality: How Research on Behavioral Decision Making Challenges Normative Standards of Rationality*, 2 Perspectives on Psychological Science, 162–80 (2007) [hereafter *Leaky Rationality*].

42. Hal R. Arkes and Catherine Blumer, *The Psychology of Sunk Cost*, 35 Organizational Behavior 124 (1985).

43. Many of the quotations come from Reid Hastie and Robyn Dawes, Rational Choice in an Uncertain World: The Psychology of Judgment and Decision Making (Sage Publications: Thousand Oaks, CA, 2001) 32.

44. John T. Gourville and Dilip Soman, *Payment Depreciation: The Effects Of Temporally Separating Payments from Consumption*, 25 Journal of Consumer Research 160 (1998).

45. New York Times, Sept. 9, 2004.

The mother of a soldier who died in Iraq said: "It pains me to hear that more people should die because those people have died. That makes no sense. We can honor them by having an intelligent, honest policy."[46])

- Senator Jim Sasser arguing for further investment in a project that would be worth less than the amount of money necessary to finish it: "Completing Tennessee-Tombigbee is not a waste of taxpayers' dollars. Terminating the project at this late stage of development would, however, represent a serious waste of funds already invested."
- A businessman: "I've already invested so much in the Concorde airliner . . . that I cannot afford to scrap it now."
- Members of Congress arguing for the dollars and lives already spent on NASA's space shuttle program as a reason for continuing it.[47]
- The more people pay for advice from consultants or other experts with respect to business or personal decisions, the more likely they are to follow the advice.[48]

If taking account of sunk costs doesn't make economic sense, is it therefore always irrational? Consider:

- *Avoiding regret.* If the $500 treadmill you bought several months ago is sitting idly in your family room, you may mentally kick yourself each time you look at it and regret the purchase decision. Like all feelings, the sense of regret is *a*rational. Whether it leads to behaviors that are in your long-term self-interest is a matter of chance. While anticipatory regret about the idle treadmill may lead you to exercise more often, anticipatory regret about wasting the nonrefundable airline ticket to a country that has had an upsurge in terrorism may lead you to take a dangerous and anxiety-laden trip.
- *Reputation.* Individuals and organizations may rationally value their reputations for not making poor decisions, for adhering to commitments, and for not being wasteful. Thus, even if a policy maker recognizes that it is suboptimal to continue a project or activity, she may decide that it is in her or the agency's interest to obscure a poor decision by sticking with it[49]—or not to be seen as a "flip-flopper." We imagine that circumstances of this sort often give rise to conflicts of interest between agents and principals—for example, between the interests of a decision maker and the clients or constituents she represents (who bear the costs of continuing a bad project).

---

46. New York Times, Aug. 23, 2005.

47. *See The Space Shuttle: Old, Unsafe, and Costly*, The Economist, Aug. 28, 2003, 77.

48. Francesca Gino, "Getting Advice from the Same Source but at a Different Cost: Do We Overweigh Information Just Because We Paid for It?" Harvard Business School Working Paper, No. 05-017, 2004.

49. *See* Douglas Walton, *"The Sunk Cost Fallacy or Argument from Waste,"* 16 Argumentation 473 (2002).

- *Sense of self, and self-education.* "Reputation" refers to how other people think of you. But you may also have a sense of yourself—a *self-reputation*—as a person who is not wasteful and who follows through with plans and commitments. Moreover, you may want to discipline yourself to be that kind of a person. Keeping commitments that you wish you had not made may teach you to be more cautious in the first place.[50]
- *Precommitment.* In Section 13.6.2 we discussed strategies through which individuals could commit themselves to long-run valued behaviors in the face of short-run temptations. Unlike Ulysses tying himself to the mast, most of our precommitments are open to subsequent reneging. Giving weight to sunk costs—e.g., the $500 treadmill sitting in your family room—can be a psychic incentive for maintaining those commitments.[51]
- *Respect for prior decisions and finality.* Like judges' respect for precedent, sticking with earlier decisions even when they seem questionable may reflect a combination of respect for their predecessors and the costs of constantly revisiting earlier judgments. Even for personal decisions, individuals may believe that they do not have a better vantage point now than when they initially made the decision.
- *Meaning.* The parents' comments about loss of their children in Iraq suggest that attending to sunk costs may give meaning to terrible events in our lives—though sometimes at the cost of creating more terrible events.

Whether or not taking account of sunk costs sometimes makes sense for individuals, we are skeptical about its value to governments and private organizations. In any event, it is important to understand that a decision that takes account of sunk costs inevitably compromises the pursuit of other goals by diverting resources that might be used more productively or, occasionally, by continuing to endanger people's welfare and lives. We will return to the issue of sunk costs when we discuss the escalation of commitment in Section 17.3.3.

14.4 MENTAL ACCOUNTING[52]

Under classic economic theory, a decision maker views the money or other assets she spends on, or gains from, a transaction in terms of their effect her overall

---

50. *See* RICHARD EPSTEIN, SKEPTICISM AND FREEDOM: A MODERN CASE FOR CLASSICAL LIBERALISM, ch. 8 (Chicago, IL: University of Chicago Press, 2003); Walton, *supra.*

51. Consider, though, whether taking account of the sunk costs to goad you into exercising is best characterized as a "rational" decision, or whether it would be more accurate to say that the overall strategy is (rationally) based on the prediction that you will (irrationally) take account of sunk costs.

52. This section relies heavily on Richard H. Thaler, *Mental Accounting Matters, in* CHOICES, VALUES, AND FRAMES (DANIEL KAHNEMAN AND AMOS TVERSKY, eds., Cambridge, UK: Cambridge University Press, 2000) 241 [hereafter, *Mental Accounting Matters*]. *See also* Richard H. Thaler, *Mental Accounting and Consumer Choice,* 4 MARKETING SCIENCE 199 (1995).

wealth or well-being. In fact, however, people tend not to consider decisions in such comprehensive terms, but rather frame them in terms of separate *accounts* that are not necessarily fungible. In a pathbreaking article, Richard Thaler examines a variety of such "mental accounting" phenomena. Starting from the presumption that people employ decision-making criteria that are intended to make them as happy as possible, he derives the following principles of *hedonic framing* from prospect theory.

1. *Segregate gains* (because the gain function is concave downward[53]). That is, three separate gains of *n* are experienced as more pleasurable than one gain of *3n*. For example, when asked whether one would be happier winning two lotteries that pay $50 and $25 respectively, or winning one lottery that pays $75, most respondents choose the two lotteries.
2. *Integrate losses* (because the loss function is concave upward). That is, one loss of *3n* is experienced as less painful than three separate losses of *n*. For example, an employer planning to require employees to pay a larger share of their health insurance premiums may cause less unhappiness by moving to the target all at once rather than spreading it out over a number of years. Consider credit cards, or debt consolidation loans, which pool many small losses into one large one, or buying a few optional features when purchasing a car. Lee Ross has termed such integrations, which avoid resetting the reference point with each cost incurred, "hedonic laundering."
3. *Integrate smaller losses with larger gains* (to offset loss aversion). Thaler gives the example of vacationing in Switzerland with his wife where he gave a lecture for a fee. The Swiss franc was very high and everything seemed expensive. They mentally "deducted" the meals from his speaking fee, which they were mentally "allowed" to do because it was in the same account.
4. *Segregate small gains (silver linings) from larger losses.* Because the gain function is steepest at its origin, the utility of a small gain can exceed the utility of slightly reducing a large loss. Consider, for example, car dealers who offer a "rebate" rather than the equivalent reduction in the price of the car.

> "Injuries, therefore, should be inflicted all at once, that their ill savor being less lasting may the less offend; whereas, benefits should be conferred little by little, that so they may be more fully relished."
>
> —MACHIAVELLI, THE PRINCE

53. *See* Figure 14.1.

14.4.1 Decoupling Decisions and Consequences: The Value of Feedback

Would you rather pay a flat rate for phone service or pay for each phone call? Many people opt for the former, even when the latter is less expensive. "Prepayment separates or 'decouples' the purchase from the consumption and in so doing seems to reduce the perceived cost of the activity."[54] Similarly, many people prefer to prepay for a vacation, so as not to have the pleasurable experienced compromised by the thought of having to pay for it later.[55] At Club Med resorts, the room cost includes meals, bars, and entertainment.

Using credit cards to defer the payment of purchases also has this decoupling effect. But by mitigating the pain of paying for a purchase, a credit card encourages overpurchasing. And, as Loewenstein and O'Donoghue note, "when the credit-card bill comes, people still experience the pain of paying, and in fact, because payments aren't clearly linked to specific purchases, consumers seem to find it especially painful to pay off credit-card debt."[56]

The following are some examples of mental accounting.

14.4.2 Budgeting

Kahneman and Tversky posed essentially these questions to two randomly selected groups in 1984.

- Imagine that you have decided to see a play presented by a campus theater company and paid the admission price of $10 per ticket. As you enter the theater, you discover that you have lost the ticket. Seats were not assigned, and the ticket cannot be recovered. Would you pay $10 for another ticket?
- Now imagine the same scenario, except that you haven't yet purchased the ticket. As you enter the theater, you discover that you have lost a $10 bill. Would you still pay $10 for a ticket to the play?

Only 46 percent of those who lost the ticket would purchase a new ticket, while 88 percent of those who lost the $10 bill would purchase another one. Why would this be? Kahneman and Tversky explain: "Going to theater is normally viewed as a transaction in which the cost of the ticket is exchanged for the experience of seeing the play. Buying a second ticket increases the cost of seeing the play to a level that many respondents apparently find unacceptable. In contrast, the loss of the cash is not posted to the account of the play, and it affects the

---

54. *Mental Accounting Matters* at 252.

55. Drazen Prelec and George Loewenstein, *Beyond Time Discounting*, 8 MARKETING LETTERS 97 (1997).

56. George Loewenstein and Ted O'Donoghue, *We Can Do This the Easy Way or the Hard Way: Negative Emotions, Self-Regulation, and the Law*, 73 CHICAGO LAW REVIEW 183 (2006).

purchase price of a ticket only by making the individual feel slightly less affluent."[57]

In another study, participants in one group were told that they had spent $50 for a ticket to a basketball game earlier in the week and asked if they would be willing to buy a theater ticket. Participants in the second group were told that they had paid $50 for a parking violation and asked if they would purchase the theater ticket. Because the theater ticket was drawn from the "entertainment" budget, people who had spent the $50 for a baseball ticket were less likely to buy the theater ticket than those who paid $50 for the parking fine.

Dividing spending into budget categories serves two purposes. It can make the trade-offs between competing uses of funds transparent and, to the extent that certain accounts are "off limits," it can assist in self-control. When budgets are not treated as fungible, however, the existence of separate accounts can have distorting economic effects.

14.4.3 Self-Control, Gift-Giving, and Income Accounting

From a purely economic point of view, a gift of cash is ideal because it is completely fungible; next best is the gift of an item that the recipient would have purchased anyway. But a luxurious present may have great value for a recipient who maintains budget limits for reasons of self-control or a sense of appropriateness. Richard Thaler notes that the National Football League had difficulty in getting superstar players to attend the Pro Bowl by offering money, but succeeded when they offered the players two first-class tickets and luxury accommodations in Hawaii.

People tend to match the source of funds with their use, so that money from the windfall of winning an office football pool will be spent at a fancy restaurant, while the same amount in a tax refund will be used to pay the bills.

Funds from the same source can be framed in different ways with different consequences. Consider whether government should frame a tax give-back as a "rebate" or a "bonus." When, in 2001, the federal government gave tax "rebates" in order to stimulate consumer spending, only 28 percent of people surveyed said that they spent the money immediately.[58] Because the "rebate" was simply their money being returned to them, they were most likely to save it. Experiments suggest that framing the same scheme as a bonus, implying a windfall, would have led to more spending.[59]

---

57. Daniel Kahneman and Amos Tversky, *Choices, Values, and Frames*, 39 AMERICAN PSYCHOLOGIST 341 (1984).

58. Matthew D. Shapiro and Joel Slemrod, "Consumer Response to Tax Rebates," working paper, University of Michigan and NBER (2001).

59. Nicholas Epley, *Rebate Psychology*, NEW YORK TIMES, Op-Ed section, Jan. 1, 2008.

14.4.4 Budgeting Time

As you are about to purchase a clock radio for $50 at a consumer electronics store, a reliable friend informs you that the identical radio is on sale for $40 at a discount store fifteen minutes away. Do you make the trip? Now you are about to purchase a television set for $500 at a consumer electronics store, when the reliable friend informs you that the identical TV set is on sale for $490 at a discount store fifteen minutes away. Do you make the trip?

If you are like most people, you are more likely to take fifteen additional minutes to buy the clock radio than the television set at the discount store.[60] Similarly, when asked how much they would be willing to pay to avoid waiting in a ticket line, people were willing to pay twice as much to avoid the wait for a $45 ticket than for a $15 ticket.[61]

This does not make economic sense. "A rational person should allocate time optimally," and "the marginal value of an extra minute devoted to any activity should be equal."[62] At the end of the day, if you purchased the clock radio for $40 your bank balance is $10 better off, and so too if you purchased the television set for $490. However, our mental accounting considers the time taken in doing a transaction in terms of the dollar value of the transaction. Recall, also, the discussion of the evaluability of proportions in Section 13.3.1.

14.4.5 Conclusion: So What?

The endowment effect, the status quo bias, and other mental accounting phenomena conflict with rational choice theory. Do they also result in suboptimal individual decision making?

Looking at the indicators of suboptimal decisions mentioned in Section 13.1, the phenomena render at least some decisions sensitive to the way the issue is framed, and may subject the decision maker to manipulation by others. Consider, for example, the framing of "status quo" contract provisions in terms of the legal defaults or form contracts. On the other hand, the phenomenon of regret-avoidance implies that decisions based on loss avoidance minimize the decision maker's subsequent regret. Moreover, to say that mental accounting violates the precepts of rational economic choice is not to say that it is necessarily bad for us. Thaler suggests:[63]

---

60. Amos Tversky and Daniel Kahneman, *The Framing of Decisions and the Psychology of Choice*, 211 SCIENCE 453 (1981); Richard H. Thaler, *Toward a Positive Theory of Consumer Choice*, *in* CHOICES, VALUES, AND FRAMES 269 (New York: Cambridge University Press, 2000).

61. France LeClerc, Bernd H. Schmidt, and Laurette Dube, *Decision Making and Waiting Time: Is Time Like Money?*, 22 JOURNAL OF CONSUMER RESEARCH 256 (1995).

62. *Mental Accounting Matters* 256.

63. *Mental Accounting Matters* 267.

> Mental accounting procedures have evolved to economize on time and thinking costs and also to deal with self-control problems. As is to be expected, the procedures do not work perfectly. People pay attention to sunk costs. They buy things they don't need because the deal is too good to pass up. . . . They put their retirement money in a money market account.
>
> It is not possible to say that the system is flawed without knowing how to fix it. Given that optimization is not feasible (too costly), repairing one problem may create another. For example, if we teach people to ignore sunk costs, do they stop abiding by the principle, "waste now, want not?" If we stop being lured by good deals, do we stop paying attention to price altogether?

This sounds right for many ordinary personal decisions. However, lawyers and policy makers are agents, who counsel clients and make public decisions in which the dollars and human welfare at stake can be momentous. Thaler tells of the congressional investigation of the disaster that ensued when Teton Dam in southern Idaho broke in June 1976. The investigation focused, among other things, on "the inclination on the part of the Bureau of Reclamation to continue dam construction, once commenced, despite hazards which might emerge during the course of construction." A witness for the Bureau could not think of a single example in which dam construction, once begun, had been even temporarily interrupted because of such concerns.

14.5 THE DOWNSIDES OF CHOICES OR OPTIONS

14.5.1 Choice Overload

> *No idea is more fundamental to Americans' sense of themselves as individuals and as a culture than choice. The United States has come to epitomize the "republic of choice."*
> —Sheena S. Iyengar and Mark R. Lepper, Choice and Its Consequences: On the Costs and Benefits of Self-Determination[64]

> *Look at this peanut butter! There must be three sizes of four brands of four consistencies! Who demands this much choice? I know! I'll quit my job and devote my life to choosing peanut butter! Is "chunky" chunky enough or do I need extra chunky? I'll compare ingredients! I'll compare brands! I'll compare sizes and prices! Maybe I'll drive around and see what other stores have! So much selection and so little time!*
> —Bill Watterson, It's A Magical World (1996) (Calvin & Hobbes)

64. Sheena S. Iyengar and Mark R. Lepper, *Choice and Its Consequences: On the Costs and Benefits of Self-Determination* (2002), *in* ABRAHAM TESSLER, DIEDERIK A. STAPEL, AND JOANNE V. WOOD (EDS), SELF AND MOTIVATION: EMERGING PSYCHOLOGICAL PERSPECTIVES) (Washington, DC, American Psychological Association, 2002) 71, citing LAWRENCE M. FRIEDMAN, The Republic of Choice (Cambridge: Harvard University Press, 1990).

All things being equal, we think it is good to have options—the more that are available, the more likely we'll find one that's a good fit with our interests, needs, or objectives. But choices carry costs as well. As the number of choices increase, decision making becomes more difficult, time consuming, and even stressful.

People faced with many options tend to employ simplifying decision strategies.[65] For example, in studies of how people evaluate home housing purchases, participants used compensatory procedures when choosing among three options, but switched to a noncompensatory procedure when choosing among a dozen.[66] As the number of housing options increased, the percentage of choices that reflected the participants' real preferences (as elicited in a separate process) declined from 70 percent when considering five houses to 37 percent when considering twenty-five.[67] A study of professional health care purchasers for large corporations showed that the large majority used noncompensatory strategies in choosing among health plans that had many different attributes.[68]

The remainder of this section considers another set of problems caused by options, most of which involve (1) violation of the axiom of *independence from irrelevant alternatives*, which holds that the relative ranking of a particular set of options should not vary with the addition or deletion of other options, or (2) violation of the axiom of *invariance*, which holds that the order in which choices are presented (or the way they are described) should not affect the outcome of the decision. (See Section 12.2.2)

14.5.2 Option Devaluation

Chris Guthrie presents this problem:[69] Suppose that you are considering which law school to attend. In one scenario, you have been admitted only to Harvard Law School; in the second, you have been admitted to both Harvard and Stanford. Will your assessment of the quality of Harvard differ in the two scenarios?

---

65. *See generally* John W. Payne, James R. Bettman, and Eric J. Johnson, The Adaptive Decision Maker (New York: Cambridge University Press, 1993).

66. See Chapter 4 for the distinction between these procedures.

67. Richard W. Olshavsky, *Task Complexity and Contingent Processing in Decision Making: A Replication and Extension*, 24 Organizational Behavior and Human Performance 300 (1979); Naresh K. Malhorta, *Information Load and Consumer Decision Making*, 8 J. Consumer Res. 419 (1982)—both summarized in Chris Guthrie, *Panacea or Pandora's Box? The Costs of Options in Negotiations*, 88 Iowa Law Review 601, 632–33 (2003) [hereafter, Guthrie, *Options*].

68. Judith H. Hibbard, Jacquelyn J. Jewett, Mark W. Legnini, and Martin Tusler, *Choosing a Health Plan: Do Large Employers Use the Data?*, Health Affairs 172 (Nov.–Dec. 1997). Also summarized in Guthrie, *Options*.

69. Guthrie, *Options*.

Although there is no good reason why it should—after all, your admission to Stanford has given you no new information about Harvard—the phenomenon of *comparative loss aversion* suggests that the attractiveness of Harvard will be at least somewhat diminished. Comparing the two schools brings to mind the advantages and disadvantages of each one—in terms of climate, size, prestige, or whatever other factors matter to the applicant. However, as prospect theory suggests, losses loom larger than gains; thus, the disadvantages of each school will make it more unattractive than the advantages make it attractive. So, wherever you end up going, you will view the prospect less favorably than had you been admitted to only one of the schools.

Lyle Brenner, Yuval Rottenstreich, and Sanjay Sood demonstrated comparative loss aversion in several experiments. For example, three groups of participants were asked how much they would pay for subscriptions to one or all of the magazines: *People*, *Time*, *Business Week*, and *The New Yorker*.

- members of the *isolated group* were asked what was the maximum they would pay for one of these magazine without comparing it to the others;
- members of the *accompanied group* were asked what they would pay for subscriptions to each of the four magazines; and
- members of the *ranked group* were asked to rank the magazines and then state how much they would pay.

On average, participants in the *isolated group* were willing to pay $21.42 for *People*; those in *accompanied* and *ranked groups* were willing to pay $15.96 and $15.09, respectively. The phenomenon of participants' willingness to pay more for the isolated item than when it was accompanied by other options or ranked was robust across the magazines and across other items, including videotapes and airplane roundtrips to various locations.[70] The mere presence of options engendered some comparisons, and the ranking exercise forced the participants to make explicit comparisons.

Guthrie replicated the experiment in the context of a car purchase. In the one-car group, participants on average said they would pay a maximum of $13,125 for a Toyota Corolla. After being asked to rank the Toyota with a Honda Civic and Mazda Prestige, the average willingness to pay dropped 13 percent to $11,447.

The effects of grouping. In the example of choosing an apartment in Section 4.3, we noted that using the common decision-making procedure, elimination by aspects (EBA), can alter the probability of achieving a particular outcome in a way that is, at best, orthogonal to the decision maker's interests. This is especially likely when, rather than considering the criteria (cost, size, etc.) in their order of *importance*, they make the *easiest* comparisons first. Amos Tversky gives

---

70. Lyle Brenner, Yuval Rottenstreich, and Sanjay Sood, *Comparison, Grouping, and Preference*, 10 Psychology of Science 225 (1999).

this example:[71] Suppose that you are offered a choice between a recording of a Beethoven symphony and Debussy piano works. You like the composers about the same, so the probability of choosing one or the other is about 0.5. Now suppose you are offered a choice among three recordings—the Debussy and two versions of the Beethoven symphony. Is the probability of each choice now 0.33? Regardless of the comparative excellence of the recordings, it's closer to 0.25 for each of the Beethoven's and 0.50 for the Debussy. Most likely, you first consider attributes that make you favor the Beethoven or Debussy recording at this time—you're in a German or French mood, or the sound of a symphony or of a piano seems more appealing—and then, only if you choose Beethoven, do you compare the two Beethoven discs.

Brenner et al. did some further experiments to see how grouping affected people's choices among options. Participants were asked to choose among four items—for example four kinds of restaurants, four videotapes, or four gifts. In each case, three of the items were grouped together and one was alone, and the participants were asked to indicate their preference either for the solo option or their choice of one of the three grouped options. For example, participants were asked whether they would prefer to eat at (1) a seafood restaurant, or (2) their choice of a Mexican, Italian, or Thai restaurant. Participants consistently devalued options in the group of three restaurants compared to the solo item. Apparently participants first compared the members of the group with each other to choose a favorite, which they then compared to the option that stood alone. "Comparative loss aversion implies that the greater degree of within-group comparisons will sharply reduce the attractiveness of each of the grouped options. However, because of the lesser degree of between-group comparisons, the attractiveness of the lone option will not decrease as much." The authors observe that advertisers or salespersons can employ the grouping phenomenon to manipulate consumers' choices:

> Consider choosing between three cars. One is a Japanese sedan, the second a Japanese sports car, and the third is an American sports car. Our findings suggest that the American car is more likely to be chosen when the cars are grouped by country of origin (because it is the only American option) and less likely to be chosen when the cars are grouped by body style (because it is in the sports-car group). Similarly, the Japanese sedan is more likely to be chosen when the cars are grouped by body style and less likely to be chosen when the cars are grouped by country of origin. . . . [S]alespeople have been known to emphasize the relative merits of Japanese and American cars, or the virtues of sedans and sports cars, in an attempt to guide the consumer toward a particular purchase.

71. Amos Tversky, *Elimination by Aspects: A Theory of Choice*, 79 Psychological Review 281 (1972).

Along similar lines, Donald A. Redelmeier and Eldar Shafir asked physicians to decide whether, after unsuccessfully trying a number of anti-inflammatory medicines on a patient with osteoarthritis in his hip, to refer the patient for hip-replacement surgery or try different medication. Physicians given the option to prescribe one of several drugs that had not previously been tried on the patient were more likely to choose surgery than those told that there was only one untried drug.[72]

14.5.2.a The Downside of Having Too Many Choices Sheena Iyengar and Mark Lepper have studied how consumers dealt with different numbers of choices of food products.[73] For example, customers entering an upscale food market on different days encountered a display inviting them to taste either six (limited choice) or twenty-four (extensive choice) different Wilkin & Sons preserves. Anyone who approached the display received a $1 certificate toward the subsequent purchase of a Wilkin & Sons preserve from the store's regular shelves. Both groups of customers actually tasted about the same number of samples, but those who were offered the limited choice were much more likely to purchase the product. A similar experiment, involving Godiva chocolates, indicated that although participants enjoyed choosing from the extensive choice options, those given the limited choice liked their chocolate better than those who chose from the large sample. Those in the extensive choice group felt more responsible for their choices, more dissatisfaction, and more regret about their choices. Iyengar and Lepper speculate that they were relatively unsure about the choice and "burdened by the responsibility of distinguishing good from bad decisions."

There is reason to believe that this phenomenon extends to more important decisions than the choice of gourmet foods. Many employers offer 401(k) retirement savings plans, some of which allow the employee to invest in just a few funds, some in many. A large-scale survey across many industries indicated that 75 percent of employees participated in retirement savings plans that offered two funds, while only 60 percent participated in plans with fifty-nine funds.[74]

72. Donald A. Redelmeier and Eldar Shafir, *Medical Decision Making in Situations that Offer Multiple Alternatives*, 274 Journal of the American Medical Association 302 (1995).

73. Sheena S. Iyengar and Mark R. Lepper, *When Choice Is Demotivating: Can One Desire Too Much of a Good Thing?*, 76 Journal of Personality and Social Psychology 995–1006 (2000).

74. *How Much Choice Is Too Much: Determinants of Individual Contributions in 401K Retirement Plans, in* Developments in Decision-Making Under Uncertainty: Implications for Retirement Plan Design and Plan Sponsors (O. S. Mitchell and S. P. Utkus eds., Oxford: Oxford University Press, 2004).

Are There Social or Cultural Differences in the Value of Choice?

Barry Schwartz, Hazel Markus, Alana Connor Snibbe, and Nicole Stephens describe a series of experiments concerning whether people of different socio-economic status placed different values on choice.[75] Among their conclusions:

- For middle-class respondents, "choice" meant "freedom," "action," and "control"; for working-class respondents, choice was connected with "fear," "doubt," and "difficulty."
- While middle-class respondents preferred items that they had chosen themselves, working-class respondents were more satisfied with choices that others made for them.
- When a neighbor bought the same car they owned, middle-class respondents were upset because it undercut the uniqueness of their choice, while lower-class respondents were pleased that it affirmed that they had made a good choice.

Iyengar and Lepper refer to a body of research that suggests:

> Both preferences for, and the benefits of, choice might well vary across different cultural contexts. . . . [W]hereas individual agency is an essential element of the self-constructs of American individualists, it may be considerably less relevant to the self-constructs of members of more collectivistic cultures, characteristic of Asia and elsewhere.
>
> Westerners . . . [may] possess a model of the self as fundamentally independent. Such individuals strive for personal independence, desire a sense of autonomy, and seek to express their internal attributes in order to establish their uniqueness from others within their environments. . . .
>
> By contrast, members of non-Western cultures . . . [may] possess an interdependent model of the self and to strive for the super-ordinate goal of a sense of interconnectedness and belongingness with one's social in-group. . . . Indeed, in some situations, the exercise of personal choice might even pose a threat to individuals whose personal preferences could prove at variance with of their reference group. Interdependent selves, therefore, might actually prefer to have choices made for them, especially if the situation enables them

75. *See* Barry Schwartz, Hazel K. Markus, and Alana Connor Snibbe, *Is Freedom Just Another Word for Many Things to Buy*, New York Times, Feb. 26, 2006. The SES-related variable in the various studies included parents' educational attainment and whether the participants were in white- or blue-collar jobs.

to be both relieved of the "burden" associated with identifying the socially sanctioned option and, at the same time, to fulfill the super-ordinate cultural goal of belongingness. Consequently, for members of interdependent cultures, it is not the exercise of choice that is necessary for intrinsic motivation, but the perception of themselves as having fulfilled their duties and obligations toward their reference groups.[76]

14.5.2.b The Downsides of Keeping Your Options Open after a Decision In Chapter 3 we suggested that when you lack the information to make a well-informed choice, a useful decision strategy may be to keep your options open. However, there is evidence that, largely as a result of loss-aversion, "decision makers overvalue their options and are willing to overinvest to keep those options from disappearing."[77]

Moreover, in some circumstances, keeping one's options open after making a decision can exact a psychological cost. An obvious example is someone who chooses a romantic partner but keeps an eye out for someone better. The lack of a whole-hearted commitment is likely to detract from his or her satisfaction with the relationship. Even if the partner is not ideal in every respect—and who is?—the phenomenon of adaptation (described in Section 12.1.5) tends to lead to satisfaction over time.

The same phenomenon applies to consumer choices. For example, students who were offered a gift of either of two art posters and were told that they could exchange it any time in the next month were less satisfied—even minutes later—than those who were told that it was not exchangeable. In similar studies, the satisfaction of those stuck with their choice stabilized over time while the dissatisfaction of the former group lingered. (However, most people mispredict that they would be happier having the option to change their minds.[78])

14.5.2.c The Effect of Options on Whether to Decide Now or Defer Suppose you are considering buying a CD player and have not yet decided what model

76. Iyengar and Lepper, *supra*, citing Hazel Markus and Shinobu Kitayama, *Culture and the Self: Implications for Cognition, Emotion, and Motivation*, 98 Psychological Review 224–53 (1991).

77. Jiwoong Shin and Dan Ariely, *Keeping Doors Open: The Effect of Unavailability on Incentives to Keep Options Viable*, 50 Mgmt. Sci. 575, 575 (2004).

78. Daniel T. Gilbert and Jane E. J. Ebert, *Decisions and Revisions: The Affective Forecasting of Changeable Options*, 82 Journal of Personality and Social Psychology 503 (2002).

to buy. You pass by a store that is having a one-day clearance sale. Consider these scenarios and the percentage of responses:[79]

Low conflict: The store offers a popular Sony player for $99—well below the list price. Do you:

Buy the Sony player ($99) 66%
Wait until you learn more about the model 34%

High conflict: The store offers a popular Sony player for $99 and a top-of-the-line AIWA player for $169—both well below the list price. Do you:

Buy the AIWA player ($169) 27%
Buy the Sony player ($99) 27%
Wait until you learn more about the models 46%

While the first decision seems easy, the second creates a mental conflict, which can be avoided by deferring. But choosing in one case and deferring in the other does not make sense in terms of a value-maximizing approach to decision making, for the decision maker has precisely the same information about the Sony player in both cases. But the phenomenon is easy to understand in terms of reason-based decision making. While there are compelling arguments for choosing the Sony when it is the only attractive product one is considering, "choosing one out of two competing alternatives can be difficult: the mere fact that an alternative is attractive may not in itself provide a compelling reason for its selection, because the other option may be equally attractive. The addition of an alternative may thus make the decision harder to justify, and increase the tendency to defer the decision."[80]

The phenomenon applies to public policy as well as personal decisions. In a study, legislators were asked to recommend whether to close a hospital. Hospital A was a 100-bed community hospital providing 200 jobs in a small urban area which was also served by two other hospitals, which had a higher quality of care and lower costs. Hospital B was a 250-bed teaching hospital providing 500 jobs in a large urban area served by three other hospitals, which also had a higher quality of care and lower costs. In both cases, the legislators were told that they could also make "no recommendation." When asked only whether to close Hospital A, only 26 percent declined to make a recommendation. When asked whether to close either Hospital A or Hospital B were options, 64 percent declined to make a recommendation.[81]

The obvious solution to avoiding these odd changes of preferences is to compare all three options (including the status quo of doing nothing) using a value-based approach like the subjective linear model.

---

79. Amos Tversky and Eldar Shafir, *Choice under Conflict: The Dynamics of Deferred Decision*, 3 Psychological Science 358–61 (1992).

80. *Ibid.*

81. Donald A. Redelmeier and Eldar Shafir, *Medical Decision Making in Situations that Offer Multiple Alternatives*, 274 Journal of the American Medical Association 302 (1995).

14.5.3 Context Dependence

14.5.3.a Trade-off Contrast, or Asymmetrical Dominance Suppose that a store offers a popular Sony player for $99—well below list price—and an obviously inferior Panasonic player for the regular list price of $105. Do you:

Buy the Panasonic player 3%
Buy the Sony player 73%
Wait until you learn more about the various models 24%

Here, rather than detracting from the reasons for buying the premium Sony player, the existence of the inferior alternative highlights the reasons for buying the Sony rather than deferring the purchase to learn more. The trade-off between the cost and quality of the Panasonic and Sony is so great that it make the Sony look all the more attractive.

The phenomenon where the same option is evaluated more favorably in the presence of similar inferior options than in their absence is called *trade-off contrast* or *asymmetrical dominance,* reflecting the fact that the chosen option dominates (or in other examples, nearly dominates) the similar option that is not chosen. Itamar Simonson and Amos Tversky liken the phenomenon to perceptual contrast effects: "The same circle appears large when surrounded by small circles and small when surrounded by large ones. Similarly, the same product may appear attractive on the background of less attractive alternatives and unattractive on the background of more attractive alternatives."[82] In a classic study, they asked participants randomly assigned to the two-option group to choose between $6 and a Cross pen, and asked participants in the three-option group to choose among $6, the Cross pen, and an obviously inferior pen. While only 36 percent of participants in the two-option group chose the Cross pen, this rose to 46 percent in the three-option group.[83]

Of course, the presence of options sometimes provides information that contributes to value-maximizing decision making. Mark Kelman et al. suggest that if you are ordering from a restaurant menu and you prefer chicken over pasta, the presence of fish on the menu should not alter your preference, but that you might reverse your preference upon learning that the restaurant also serves veal parmesan, since this may suggest that the restaurant specializes in Italian food.[84] But in the examples in this subsection, it is difficult to discern the informational value of the added options. In these cases, trade-off contrast is inconsistent with principles of rational decision making.

---

82. Itmar Simonson and Amos Tversky, *Choice in Contrast: Tradeoff Contrast and Extremeness Aversion,* 29 Journal of Marketing Research 281 (1992).

83. Simonson and Tversky. Only 2 percent of participants chose the inferior pen, thus confirming its inferiority.

84. Mark Kelman, Yuval Rottenstreich, and Amos Tversky, *Context-Dependence in Legal Decision Making,* 25 Journal of Legal Studies 287 (1996).

Kelman and his colleagues conducted a number of experiments applying the contrast effect to legal settlements.[85] In one, participants were placed in the role of a lawyer representing a woman faculty member in the Economics Department who was not promoted to tenure, and claims sex discrimination. The client is interested in being compensated for the injury and in having the university publicly admit guilt in her case. She is also interested in pressing for affirmative action for women in the Economics Department. The university's lawyer has offered the plaintiff a choice of settlement packages.

One group of participants faced an alternative between two settlement offers. The percentage of those who accepted each is shown:

- Affirmative action plan; no damages 50%
- Public admission plus $45,000 damages 50%

Another group was given a choice between these two plus a third, which was similar to the second choice, but obviously inferior to it:

- Affirmative action plan; no damages 20%
- Public admission plus $45,000 damages 74%
- Public admission plus $35,000 gift to charity of client's choice 6%

The change of preferences exemplifies the contrast effect—that an option is seen as more valuable in the presence of a clearly inferior alternative.

14.5.3.b Extremeness Aversion, or the Compromise Effect People often evaluate the same option more favorably when it is seen as intermediate in the set of options under consideration than when it is extreme. For example, when Simonson and Tversky asked one group to evaluate the attractiveness of a mid-level Minolta camera and a low-end camera in terms of their features and price, 50 percent chose each camera. When a third, high-end camera was added to the options, the number choosing the mid-level Minolta camera rose to 72 percent. Introduction of the high-extreme option reduced the "market share" of the low extreme option, but not of the intermediate option.

The phenomenon can be explained in terms of loss aversion: if the disadvantages of the two extremes—high cost in one case, low quality in the other—loom larger than their advantages, this tends to favor the intermediate option, which has only small disadvantages compared to either one.[86] It is also a feature of reason-based decision making, where a "compromise" often seems easier to justify than either extreme.

Kelman et al. tested the compromise effect in decisions involving the grading of homicides. In one scenario, the defendant admitted poisoning her husband, causing a protracted and painful death. She did this after she overheard her

85. *Id.*
86. Simonson and Tversky.

seventeen-year-old daughter from her first marriage say that the deceased had, once again, tried to sexually molest her. The evidence also showed that the defendant stood to inherit a large amount of money from her husband and that she had been involved with another man for the last half year. One group of participants was given the choice (that jurors would have had in the District of Columbia) between convicting her of manslaughter (homicide under extreme emotional disturbance) or murder. The results:

- Manslaughter (extreme emotional disturbance) 47%
- Murder 53%

A second group was given the choice (that jurors would have had in California) among convicting her of manslaughter, murder, or special circumstances murder (committed for financial gain, or in an exceptionally heinous fashion, or by the administration of poison). The results:

- Manslaughter (extreme emotional disturbance) 19%
- Murder 39%
- Special circumstances (financial gain, heinous, poison) 42%

But if the defendant was acting under emotional distress, she didn't commit murder at all, with or without special circumstances. As the authors note, the choice between manslaughter on the one hand, and the murder verdicts on the other, should not be sensitive to whether, if the defendant were acting deliberately, she killed for financial gain, etc.

Another scenario involved the intentional killing of an off-duty police officer working as a security guard at a shopping mall by an African American man he suspected of burglary. When the defendant refused to be patted down, the guard grabbed him, the guard shouted a racist epithet, and the defendant shot him. Participants were informed that there were four possible verdicts:

- special circumstances murder—for the killing of a police officer acting in the line of duty;
- murder;
- voluntary manslaughter—if the defendant was provoked or acting under extreme emotional disturbance; or
- involuntary manslaughter—if the defendant subjectively, but unreasonably, believed he was entitled to defend himself.

Participants in one group were told that the judge had ruled, as a matter of law, that there was no evidence that the defendant believed he was acting in self-defense, so that they could not treat the homicide as involuntary manslaughter. The results were:

- Special circumstances murder 12%
- Murder 57%

- Voluntary manslaughter 31%
- ~~Involuntary manslaughter~~

Participants in another group were told that the judge had ruled, as a matter of law, that a police officer working as a security guard is not acting in the line of duty, so that they could not treat the homicide as special circumstances murder. The results:

- ~~Special circumstances murder~~
- Murder 39%
- Voluntary manslaughter 55%
- Involuntary manslaughter 6%

In analyzing this case, the authors explain:

> It seems reasonable to assume . . . that the options are naturally ordered in terms of their "severity." (Special circumstances murder is more severe than murder, which is more severe than voluntary manslaughter, which is more severe than involuntary manslaughter.) Consider any subset consisting of three of the options. Preferences satisfy *betweenness* if someone who prefers one of the extreme options in the subset over the intermediate option in the subset is more likely to prefer the intermediate option over the other extreme option than someone who does not. In the [shopping-mall guard] case, betweenness is natural: someone preferring special circumstances murder to murder would almost surely prefer murder to voluntary manslaughter. Someone preferring murder to voluntary manslaughter would almost surely prefer voluntary manslaughter to involuntary manslaughter.
>
> Given betweenness, context-independence requires that the ratio of murder verdicts to voluntary manslaughter verdicts be higher in the second group than the first. To see why, take choices in the first group as given and consider how these choices should be translated into the second group. Anyone choosing special circumstances murder in the first group should select murder. Any movement to involuntary manslaughter should come from voluntary manslaughter. Thus, as we move from the first to the second group, the number of murder verdicts should rise, and the number of manslaughter verdicts should decline.

14.5.3.c Do Context-Dependent Decisions Result in Suboptimal Decisions? Do context-dependent decisions cause harm or result in suboptimal decisions? In the case of grading homicides, it seems to conflict with the public policy underlying the grading scheme. Kelman et al. write:

> Once we declare, for instance, that the purpose of differentiating murder from manslaughter is (for instance) to show a certain level of mercy to those acting in atypically stressful circumstances, then we have failed to meet that stated goal if we differentiate defendants on some other basis (for example,

> the presence of an option in which we condemn murderers of policemen more than ordinary murderers). . . .

What about individual decision making? Consider that marketers frequently use the phenomenon of context-dependent decisions to their advantage—for example by showing the customer an item that is obviously inferior to the one they hope he or she will buy. The social psychologist Robert Cialdini writes:[87]

> I accompanied a salesman [Phil] on a weekend of showing houses to prospective home buyers. . . . One thing I quickly noticed was that whenever Phil began showing a new set of customers potential buys, he would start with a couple of undesirable houses. I asked him about it, and he laughed. They were what he called "setup" properties. The company maintained a run-down house or two on its list at inflated prices. These houses were not intended to be sold to customers but only to be shown to them, so that the genuine properties in the company's inventory would benefit from the comparison. . . . He said he like to watch prospects' "eyes light up" when he showed the places he really wanted to sell them after they had seen the rundown houses. "The house I got them spotted for looks really great after they've first looked at a couple of dumps."

Williams-Sonoma used to offer one bread-baking appliance for $275. Subsequently, the store added a larger appliance, similar to the first, but costing $429. There were few sales of the more expensive item, but sales of the original appliance doubled.[88]

With respect to personal decisions, Kelman et al. write:

> Because consumers do not have explicit policies or goals, it is less clear in what sense differential evaluation of options on the basis of context hinders consumers' interests. The notion that the consumer harms herself by breaches of context-independence is grounded in two observations. First, we suspect that the consumer herself would be prone to reevaluate (if not alter) her decision if she became aware of the fact that she made it on the basis of nonprobative facts. . . . Second, to the extent that people do not have a stable, context-independent preference order, their choices can be manipulated by the composition of the set of options under consideration. As we have noted,

87. Robert B. Cialdini, Influence: Science and Practice 14–16 (Needham Heights, MA: Allyn and Bacon, 4th ed. 2001).

88. Steven Pearlstein, *The Compromise Effect,* Washington Post, Jan. 27, 2002. *Quoted in* Guthrie, *Options.*

> such manipulations are common in the marketplace. They suggest that harm befalls context-dependent consumers since someone manipulated into choosing the option favored by another party, with her own set of interests, is less likely to maximize his own well-being.

Although there is reason for skepticism whether people can be educated to avoid context-dependent decisions, it seems plausible that eliminating explicit irrelevant options will reduce context-dependent decisions. How and when that can be done depends on, well, the context.

14.6 COST-BENEFIT ANALYSIS (CONTINUED): VALUING ENVIRONMENTAL AND OTHER PUBLIC GOODS

In Section 12.3, we introduced cost-benefit analysis as an application of expected utility theory. We deferred the problem of how to value the existence and option values of environmental goods until we could cover some additional material, which we have now done.

One valuation technique involves *revealed preference* technique, in which consumers' preferences and valuations of certain goods can be ascertained by an analysis of consumption behavior in the face of multiple purchasing choices. To use revealed preferences to determine how much people value a residence in the San Francisco Bay Area with a view of the bay, one would look the real estate prices properties of this sort (controlling for other important variables, such as lot size).

Policy makers have sometimes used this technique to determine how much consumers and employees are willing to pay for product and workplace safety. Could you use a similar technique to assessing the public's valuation of, say, Yosemite National Park? Perhaps you could use visitors' traveling costs as their revealed willingness to pay (WTP) for the National Park (controlling for variables such as the distance traveled). But the assumption that a decision not to "consume" (i.e., visit the park) implies zero value is hardly obvious. What other weaknesses do you see in this approach?

Perhaps because of the difficulty of measuring revealed preferences for public goods, policy makers often use *contingent valuation*, which relies on people's *expressed preferences* for how much they would be willing to pay for, say, the preservation of a natural resource. Contingent valuation often produces very different results than revealed preference methods, and it is subject to a number of criticisms. Because respondents are not "playing with real money"[89] they may overestimate their WTP for a particular outcome. Respondents also may enter

89. Richard Revesz and Michael Livermore, Retaking Rationality: How Cost Benefit Analysis Can Better Protect the Environment and Our Health, 127 (New York, Oxford University Press, 2008).

very large or small "protest values" to indicate their opposition to a certain policy.[90] Some other weaknesses of contingent valuation include:

- When asked about their WTP to protect against injuries, healthy respondents may underestimate the extent that people adapt to disabling events.
- As prospect theory suggestions, people's valuation of things—whether tangible items, or health or environmental goods such as clean air—may be quite different depending on whether they already possess the benefit or just hope to acquire it.
- Contingent valuation surveys ask respondents to price rather than choose things. But we have seen that people make different assessments when values are elicited by one means or the other. (See Section 13.3.2.b) In an experiment by Julie Irwin, Paul Slovic, and their colleagues, an improvement in air quality was valued more highly in 86 percent of direct choices but only in 40 percent of choices inferred from respondents' WTP,[91] raising the question of which method elicited the "correct" value.
- Related to the phenomenon of psychophysical numbing described in Section 12.1.4.c, WTP values often do not account for the scope of the issue: for example, in one study, respondents were not willing to pay substantially more "to save 200,000 birds rather than 2,000 birds" from an oil spill.[92] WTP may be strongly influenced by their affective response to the image of a bird dying, without regard to the numbers involved.[93]
- People are not good at distinguishing between, say, a 1/100,000 probability and a 1/1 million chance of a bad event occurrig.

---

90. *Id.*

91. Irwin et al., *supra.*

92. Daniel Kahneman and Shane Frederick, *A Model of Heuristic Judgment*, in KEITH HOLYOAK AND ROBERT MORRISON eds., CAMBRIDGE HANDBOOK OF HEURISTIC REASONING (New York: Cambridge University Press, 2005).

93. *See* Daniel Kahneman, Ilana Ritov, and David Schkade, *Economic Preferences or Attitude Expressions? An Analysis of Dollar Responses to Public Issues, in* CHOICES, VALUES, AND FRAMES 642–672 (D. KAHNEMAN AND A. TVERSKY eds., New York: Cambridge University Press, 2000); Christopher K. Hsee and Yuval Rottenstreich, *Music, Pandas, and Muggers: On the Affective Psychology of Value*, 133 J. EXPERIMENTAL PSYCHOL.: GEN. 23, 23–24 (2004).

In 1995, a panel of economists, headed by Kenneth Arrow and Robert Solow under the auspices of the National Oceanic and Atmospheric Administration (NOAA), recommended methods for improving the accuracy of this inherently imprecise survey technique. Among other things, the panel recommended that respondents be asked to vote for or against a specific tax to protect a particular resource, and that they be given detailed information about its ecological importance, the threats to which it was vulnerable, and possible outcomes of measures to protect it.[94]

Even with the procedural reforms recommend by the Arrow-Solow panel, contingent valuation is very inaccurate and vulnerable to biases. Nonetheless, it is widely used for valuing natural resources and other benefits that are poorly reflected in markets.[95]

---

94. http://en.wikipedia.org/wiki/Contingent_valuation.

95. For a discussion of alternative procedures for assessing people's values for non-market goods, *see* Jonathan Baron, Thinking and Deciding (4th ed. Cambridge, UK: Cambridge University Press, 2000).

15. DECISION MAKING UNDER RISK

In this chapter, we examine decision making where risk or uncertainty is a major factor. The goal here, as earlier, is to maximize the decision maker's own goals or values, or those of her clients or constituents, recognizing that individuals may have very different goals or values and that they also may have different attitudes about taking risks. Paralleling Chapters 4 and 12, we begin by laying out a model of rational decision making under risk; then (as in the immediately preceding chapters), we examine factors that conduce to departures from rationality.

For most of the chapter we will use the terms *risk* to refer to decisions where the outcome is less than certain and where the probability of its occurring can be specified or at least approximated as a value greater than 0 and less than 1. Later we will discuss situations where, for all practical purposes, the decision maker has no idea what the probability is—situations that economists term *uncertainty* and some psychologists term *ambiguity*.

15.1 EXPECTED UTILITY IN DECISION MAKING UNDER RISK

Section 12.2.2 introduced the concept of expected utility theory in situations where risk was not a major issue. Where risk *is* an issue, expected utility is described by the equation:

$$\boldsymbol{EU}_{(E)} = \boldsymbol{U}_{(E)} \times \boldsymbol{P}_{(E)}$$

$\boldsymbol{EU}_{(E)}$ is the expected utility of event E. $\boldsymbol{U}_{(E)}$ is the subjective utility of the event. $\boldsymbol{P}_{(E)}$ is the probability of the event's occurrence.

We begin with the simplifying assumption that the decision maker is *risk neutral*. This means that the decision maker is indifferent between a payoff with certainty and a gamble with the same expected payoff, for example, between

- a 100 percent chance to get $100, or
- a 50 percent chance to get $200 and a 50 percent chance to get nothing.

If a decision maker is risk neutral, then the *expected utility* ($\boldsymbol{U}_{(E)}$) of an event is exactly the same as the *expected value* ($\boldsymbol{V}_{(E)}$) of the event—that is, its monetary (or monetizable) value. Later, we address the fact that decision makers are often not risk neutral, but may have different preferences or tolerances for risks in different circumstances. Under these circumstances, expected utility and expected value will diverge.

The axioms of rational decision making set out in Section 12.2.2 apply here as well. We shall discuss their application to decision making in conditions of risk and introduce some new axioms that bear on particular issues presented in this chapter.

Expected utility under the probability axiom. Underlying all the problems in this chapter is the assumption—actually, another axiom of rational decision making—that one can assign a probability to every possible outcome. In this context, a probability is simply a degree of belief that the outcome will occur. (See Section 5.1.2b) Sometimes the decision maker may arrive at the probability through the statistical analysis of a large sample. More often, however, she must use a subjectivist, Bayesian approach and, particularly in the case of one-time decisions, she can only hazard a guess about the probability. Be that as it may, every outcome, in principle, has a probability somewhere between 0.0 and 1.0.

With the *probability axiom* as background, the essential assumptions about *completeness, dominance,* and *trade-offs* that we discussed in Section 12.2.2 apply to decisions under risk. To evaluate alternatives, you multiply the utility of each possible outcome by the probability of its occurring to determine the expected utility of that alternative. If the expected utility of alternative number 1 is greater than that of alternative number 2, then the former dominates the other. Let's look at some decision tools that help guide decisions under risk.

15.2 DEPENDENCY DIAGRAMS AND DECISION TREES

Many decisions under conditions of risk involve causal chains that are not readily modeled by a matrix of the sort that Christine Lamm used for the wastewater treatment plant decision in Section 4.5. Two conventional means of modeling them are dependency diagrams and decision trees. These tools actually serve two purposes. First, quite apart from any quantitative analysis, they can assist in *structuring* a decision—in laying out the sequence of the decision, identifying uncertainties, specifying relationships between issues, and describing the outcomes associated with different scenarios. Second, if one attaches probabilities and values to the various nodes, they can compute expected value.

We begin this section with very simple examples showing how a dependency diagram (also called an *influence diagram*) can help structure a decision and how a decision tree can be used to compute expected value. (Actually, the dependency diagram is an even more powerful computational tool than the decision tree, but the computations are less transparent to the user.) A dependency diagram shows causal links where an event or decision affects another event, decision, or outcome.

15.2.1 Dependency Diagrams

Figure 15.1 shows every variable relevant to your decision whether or not to carry an umbrella on a day when it might rain. For purposes of this example, we treat (1) rain and (2) not-rain (or sun, or shine) like two sides of a coin, as mutually exclusive and collectively exhaustive (MECE).

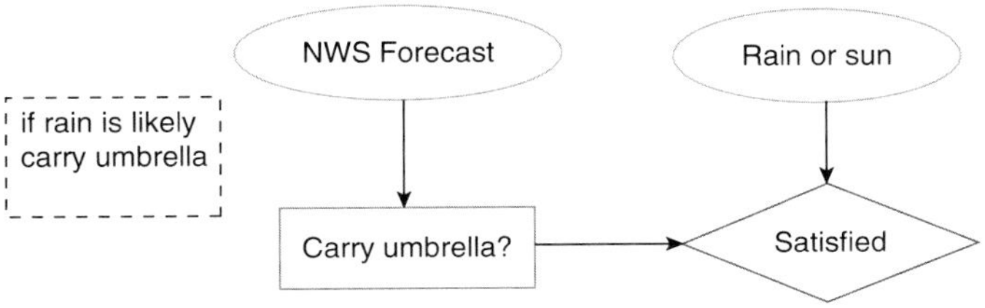

FIGURE 15.1 DEPENDENCY DIAGRAM FOR CARRYING AN UMBRELLA BASED ON NWS FORECAST.

The differently shaped objects are called *nodes*. Your satisfaction or utility (diamond-shaped node) depends on the relationship of two variables: your decision to carry (or not carry) an umbrella (rectangular node) and whether it rains (oval node). You will be

- very dissatisfied if it rains and you do not have an umbrella, and
- mildly dissatisfied if you carry the umbrella around unnecessarily.

Your decision whether to carry an umbrella is based on the National Weather Service (NWS) forecast.

The arcs, or lines, of the dependency diagram show the relations among these elements. The presence of an arc indicates that there is *some* possibility that the node pointed to is dependent on the node from which the arc originates. The absence of an arc is, if anything, more informative than its presence: its absence asserts that the nodes that are not connected are, in fact, independent. There is no arc between the forecast and your satisfaction, for the only role of the forecast is to inform your decision whether to carry an umbrella (which will affect your satisfaction).

Were you to make the decision based on a combination of the NWS forecast and your own forecast, the dependency diagram might look like Figure 15.2.

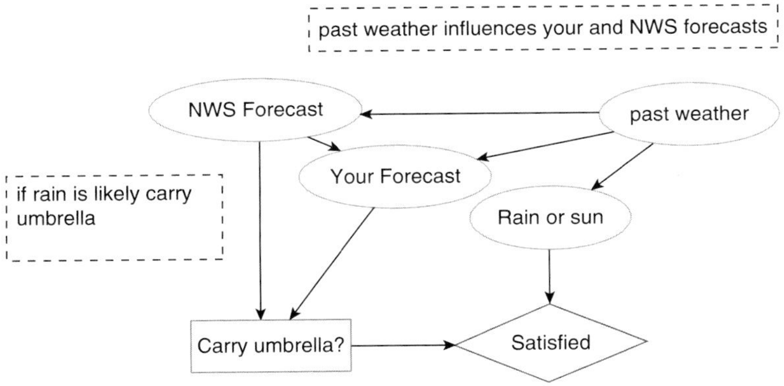

FIGURE 15.2 DEPENDENCY DIAGRAM FOR CARRYING AN UMBRELLA BASED ON NWS AND YOUR OWN FORECAST.

This shows that both the NWS weather forecast and your own forecast rely on what the weather has been in the past. It shows that you take account of the NWS forecast, but that NWS doesn't take account of yours. Since today's actual weather (rain or sun) also depends on past weather, we draw those arcs as well.

Even without using a dependency diagram quantitatively, it has value as a checklist of all the factors that should affect your decision—and equally important it identifies factors present on the landscape that do not affect your decision.

15.2.2 Decision Trees

A decision tree represents the decision and its consequences, and makes the choice and outcome alternatives explicit. The square node in the tree in Figure 15.3 indicates your choices. The circular nodes indicate the uncertainties that attend each choice.

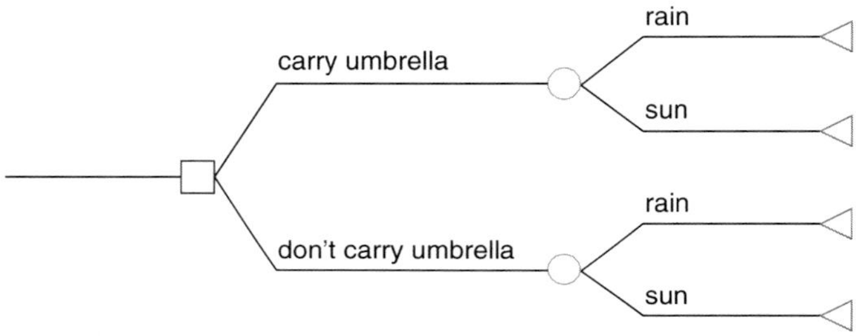

FIGURE 15.3 THE STRUCTURE OF A DECISION TREE.

Both the decision nodes and the outcome nodes of a decision tree are *mutually exclusive and collectively exhaustive* (MECE). For example, we have posited that there are only two possible outcomes—rain or sun—and if one occurs the other cannot. But in fact, there are many other possible states of the weather, ranging from snow, sleet, and hail to partly cloudy with occasional showers, and we could represent all of them in the decision tree. A decision tree can have as many outcomes as you wish—as many as may be relevant to the decision at hand—but in aggregate they are MECE.

In a simple case like this one, the bare tree does not advance your understanding of the decision. The tree's power becomes more evident, however, when we take a further step and add two sorts of numbers to the tree.

One set of numbers is the probability that it will (or will not) rain. Let us suppose that the weather forecaster says there's a 40 percent chance of rain, which (following the conventions described in Chapter 5) we'll write as 0.4. Because rain and sun are MECE, the probability of sun is 0.6.

The second set of numbers indicates how satisfied or dissatisfied you will be with the outcome. Let's use a 100 point scale, and (since we're talking mainly about dissatisfaction) we'll treat 0 as your being perfectly happy if the sun shines and you don't have an umbrella, and –100 as being miserable if it rains and you don't have an umbrella. You don't like either rain or carrying umbrellas. Each independently gives you a (dis)utility of -30. So if you are carrying the umbrella and it's a sunny day, your utility is down -30, and if it rains it's down -60. (See Figure 15.4.)

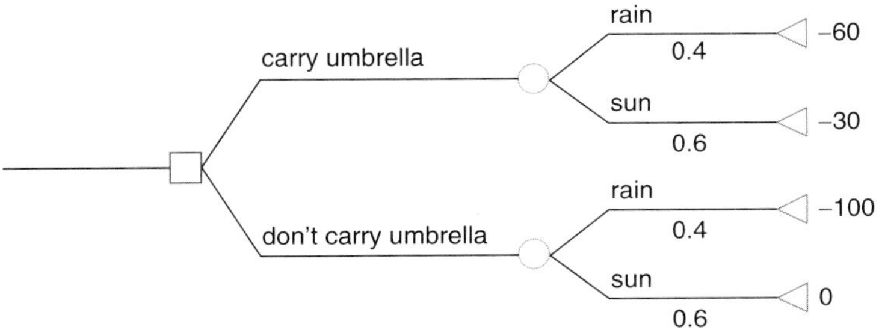

FIGURE 15.4 THE DECISION TREE WITH UTILITIES AND PROBABILITIES.

For each branch of the tree, you calculate the expected utility by multiplying the probability of rain (or shine) by the satisfaction of the outcome, and sum the products as shown in Table 15.1.

TABLE 15.1 SOLVING THE DECISION TREE

		Probability	Outcome	EU
Umbrella	Rain	0.4	−60	−24
	Sun	0.6	−30	−18
				−42
No umbrella	Rain	0.4	−100	−40
	Sun	0.6	0	0
				−40

The total expected utility of carrying an umbrella is -42, while the utility of not carrying the umbrella is -40. What does the imply if you are risk neutral? Would you in fact follow its implications?

15.2.3 A Problem: Newport Records

Let's use a dependency diagram and decision tree to analyze a more realistic problem than whether to carry an umbrella. Recall the case in Chapter 1, in which Clyde Evers has sued Newport Records, a small recording company that refuses to pay $600,000 due for accounting software that Evers customized and installed. Newport Records says the software does not do what Evers said it would do. After deciding not to seek summary judgment, Evers' lawyers, Luis Trujillo and his associate Anna Wilkins, are simultaneously considering settlement and working through the scenario of a trial. After all, while Evers needs the money, the amount for which he would settle—his "reservation price"—will be influenced by what he could gain (or lose) by litigating the case.

In predicting the outcome of the trial, these factors seem relevant:

- If the case goes to trial, Evers' costs of litigation will be $100,000.
- Evers made extravagant oral representations about how the software would perform, and he acknowledges to the lawyers that its performance is not entirely what he said it would be.
- The contract disclaims all warranties of performance. It also has a so-called "integration clause," which says that the written contract is the sole agreement between the parties, notwithstanding any oral representations.
- The law requires that warranty disclaimers be in a particular typeface, somewhat different from the disclaimer in the contract with Newport Records. The judge might or might not regard the difference as immaterial.
- If the judge finds that the disclaimer's typeface deviates materially from the statutory requirements, he will instruct the jury to find the disclaimer effective only if the president of Newport Records actually read and understood it.
- If the disclaimer is ineffective, and notwithstanding the integration clause, the judge may permit the jury—as part of its determination of whether the software performed "as promised"— to hear about Evers' oral representations, in order to resolve an alleged ambiguity in the contractual description of the software's function.

Trujillo suggests that it would be helpful to model these factors in a dependency diagram, to be sure to understand how they combine to affect the outcome of the trial, as shown in Figure 15.5.

With the dependencies thus clear, the lawyers construct the skeleton of a decision tree. Although they may refine this analysis later, the applicable contract law indicates that Evers will either obtain a judgment for the $600,000 due under the contract, or get nothing. This is shown by the outcome values on the right side (see Figure 15.6). (Once we solve for the case on its merits, we will take into account the $100,000 costs of litigating the case.)

Trujillo and Wilkins then discuss how to determine the likelihood of Evers' prevailing (or losing). Rather than leap immediately to guessing probabilities, they ask what reasons would lead the judge or jury to decide for or against Evers on each issue. For example, whether the written disclaimer meets the statutory requirements is a question of law to be decided by the judge, and they consider the reasons why the judge might decide one way or the other, as shown in Table 15.2.

If the judge determines that the disclaimer did not meet the statutory requirements because it was in the wrong typeface, the jury would determine whether the president of Newport Records nonetheless understood that any warranty was being disclaimed, as shown in Table 15.3.

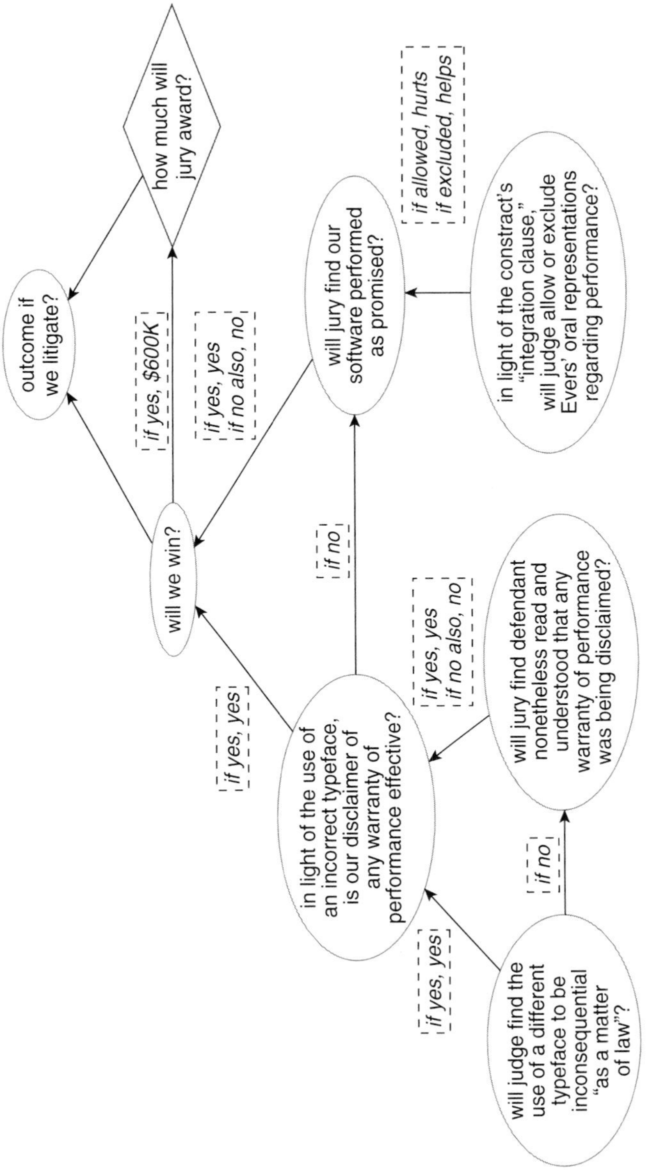

FIGURE 15.5 DEPENDENCY DIAGRAM FOR NEWPORT RECORDS.

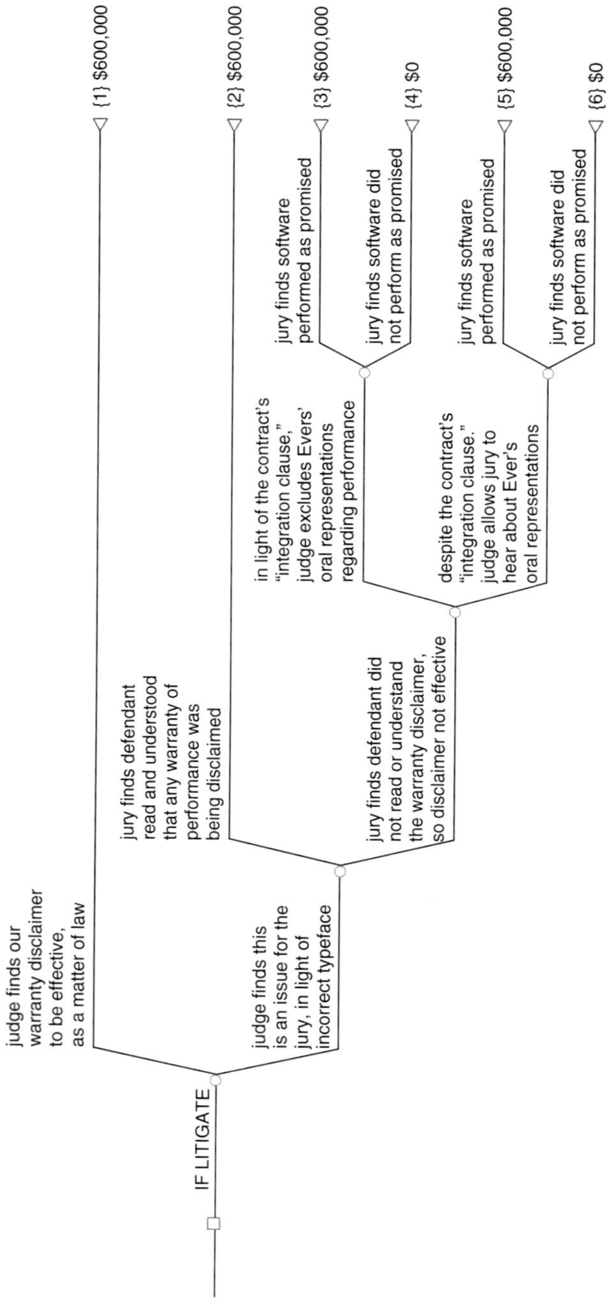

FIGURE 15.6 DECISION TREE FOR NEWPORT RECORDS.

TABLE 15.2 IS THE WRITTEN DISCLAIMER BINDING?

Reasons why the judge would find the written disclaimer *does not meet* the statutory requirements	Reasons why the judge would find the written disclaimer *meets* the statutory requirements
• The statute is unequivocal about the required typeface. • In the only litigated cases in the state, courts have held the seller to strict standards. • Although not legally relevant, the judge may be moved by knowledge of Evers' extravagant oral representations about the software.	• The typeface used stands out as much as that required by the statute. • The litigated cases all involved consumers rather than commercial purchasers. The buyer is a business and does not need same degree of protection as an ordinary consumer. • The whole point of a written disclaimer and an integration clause is to avoid litigating over alleged representations.

After listing the pros and cons on the remaining issues, Trujillo and Wilkins now begin to think hard about probabilities.[1] They begin with qualitative judgments, such as "likely" or "very likely," but eventually realize they need to translate these into numbers.

15.2.3.a Estimating probabilities. It is easy to estimate the probability of an event's occurring when there are sufficient instances that you can apply frequentist statistics along the lines introduced in Chapters 5 and 6. But many decisions faced by lawyers and policy makers are one-time events, susceptible only to a subjective estimate. Trujillo's and Wilkins's strategy of articulating the reasons why a particular outcome might or might not occur is often helpful background. Here are some techniques—by no means mutually exclusive—for use in various circumstances:[2]

1. *See* Marc B. Victor et al., *Evaluating Legal Risks and Costs with Decision Tree Analysis in* SUCCESSFUL PARTNERING BETWEEN INSIDE AND OUTSIDE COUNSEL ch. 12 (West Group & ACCA 2000–2007).

2. *See* Douglas A. Wiegmann, "Developing a Methodology for Eliciting Subjective Probability Estimates During Expert Evaluations of Safety Interventions: Application for Bayesian Belief Networks," final technical report, AHFD-05-13/NASA-05-4 (October 2005) 9 (Aviation Human Factors Division Institute of Aviation, University of Illinois at Urbana-Champaign), http://www.humanfactors.uiuc.edu/Reports&PapersPDFs/TechReport/05-13.pdf#search=%22probability%20wheel%22.

TABLE 15.3 DID THE PLAINTIFF UNDERSTAND THE WRITTEN DISCLAIMER?

Reasons why the jury would find that Newport *did not understand* the disclaimer	Reasons why the jury would find that Newport *understood* the disclaimer
• The disclaimer is written in legal jargon. • Newport's president negotiated the agreement himself, without a lawyer. • The disclaimer appears near the end of a 30-page contract, which most people would not have the patience to wade through.	• The language of the disclaimer is standard, and found in many contracts. • The typeface used stands out as much as that required by the statute. • Newport's president is highly educated, with a graduate degree, and will come across to the jury as such. • Newport's president initialed every page.

- Ask how many times out of one hundred you would expect an event to occur.
- Choose between a certain payoff (e.g., a settlement) or a gamble (litigate) where the payoff depends on the probability in question, and adjust the amount of the certain payoff until you are indifferent between the two choices.

Of course, these elicitation methods depend on your actually having a (reasonably good) estimate of the probability in your head. And they are subject to the cognitive biases discussed in earlier chapters.

Trujillo and Wilkins are aware of the hazards of overoptimism and confirmation bias (discussed earlier in the book). While they believe that their professional distance creates a degree of immunity from these biases, Wilkins suggests that they err on the side of conservatism. But Trujillo responds that they would do best just to be as realistic as possible—to avoid undervaluing Evers' lawsuit. (If Evers wants to be conservative, he can adjust his settlement position accordingly.) The lawyers end up filling in the probabilities, as shown in Figure 15.7.

Finally, they roll back, or solve, the tree. The process involves multiplying the outcome of each branch of the tree by the probabilities of achieving it, and adding up the results. Go from top to bottom and right to left in Table 15.4.

Rather than do this manually, or even using Microsoft Excel, they use dedicated software—in this case, a program called TreeAge, which happily performs just as warranted. (See Figure 15.8.)

Based on their best estimates of the probability of winning on each issue, the expected value of the case is $420,000. But it will cost $100,000 to litigate, so the net value is reduced to $320,000.

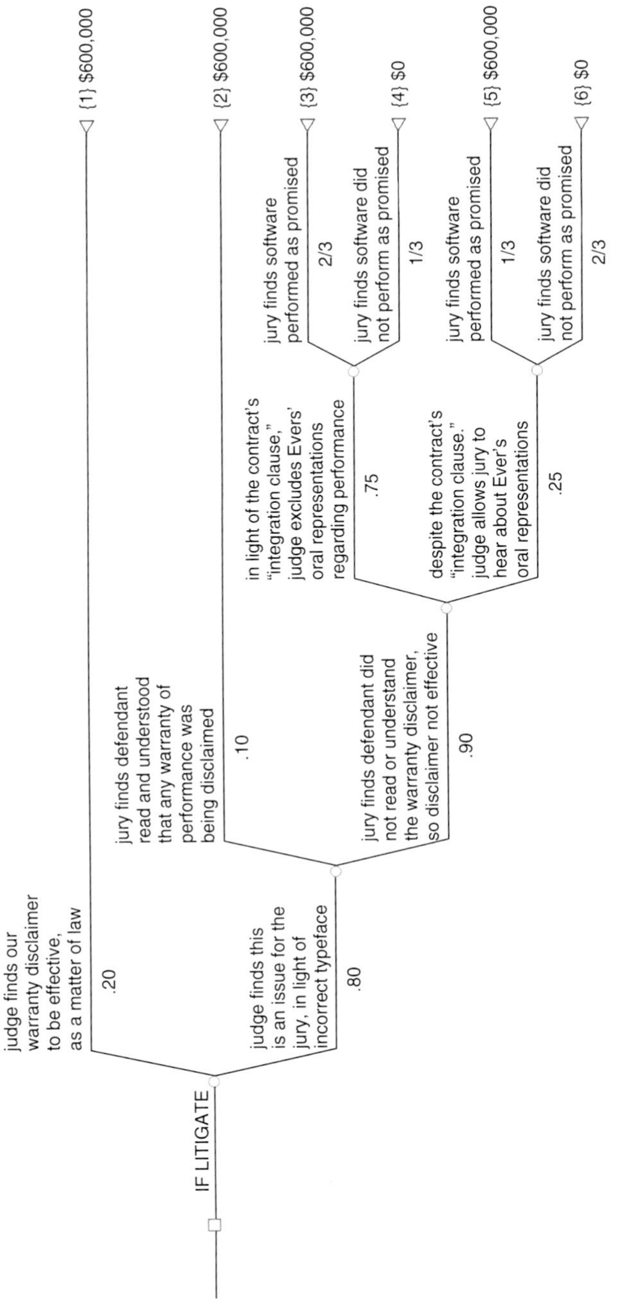

FIGURE 15.7 NEWPORT RECORDS DECISION TREE WITH PROBABILITIES.

TABLE 15.4 SOLVING THE NEWPORT RECORDS DECISION TREE BY HAND

(1)	0.20							=	**0.20**	x	$600,000	=	$120,000
(2)	0.10	x	0.80					=	**0.08**	x	$600,000	=	$48,000
(3)	0.67	x	0.75	x	0.90	x	0.80	=	**0.36**	x	$600,000	=	$216,000
(4)	0.33	x	0.75	x	0.90	x	0.80	=	**0.18**	x	$0	=	$0
(5)	0.33	x	0.25	x	0.90	x	0.80	=	**0.06**	x	$600,000	=	$36,000
(6)	0.67	x	0.25	x	0.90	x	0.80	=	**0.12**	x	$0	=	$0
													$420,000

What size settlement should Evers be willing to accept? Assuming for the moment that he is risk neutral (more about that later), he might take into account these considerations:

- If the case goes to trial, it is not likely to be resolved for a couple of years. But Evers is eager to have funds to start a new business.
- Also, any sum received today is worth more than the same amount received a couple of years in the future.[3] (See Section 13.6.1).
- Evers' lawyers estimate that their fee for their engaging in settlement negotiations will be $5,000.
- And, of course, it's possible that Newport Records will not agree to settle for anything that Evers deems acceptable.

All things considered, Evers and his lawyers conclude that a settlement of about $300,000 would be acceptable.

15.2.3.b Sensitivity analysis. If the disclaimer fails to meet the statutory requirements, the evidence bearing on whether the president of Newport Records read and understood the warranty disclaimer will be based on his deposition and testimony at trial. Other than being shrewd cross-examiners, there is not much that Evers' lawyers can do to affect that.

But they may be able to affect the jury's judgment about whether the software performed as promised. Perhaps, if understood in the context of the reasonable needs of a small business and prevailing standards for accounting systems, Evers may not have egregiously overstated the capabilities of his product. But establishing the prevailing norms will require expert testimony. Based on preliminary conversations, the expert they have in mind (a business school professor) would likely conclude that under the prevailing standards the software materially met the specifications. But she will charge $20,000 to do the analysis to establish this and then testify.

Is it worth hiring the expert witness? That depends on how her testimony will affect the value of the case. And that, in turn, depends on how much her

3. We put aside the possibilities and complications of prejudgment interest.

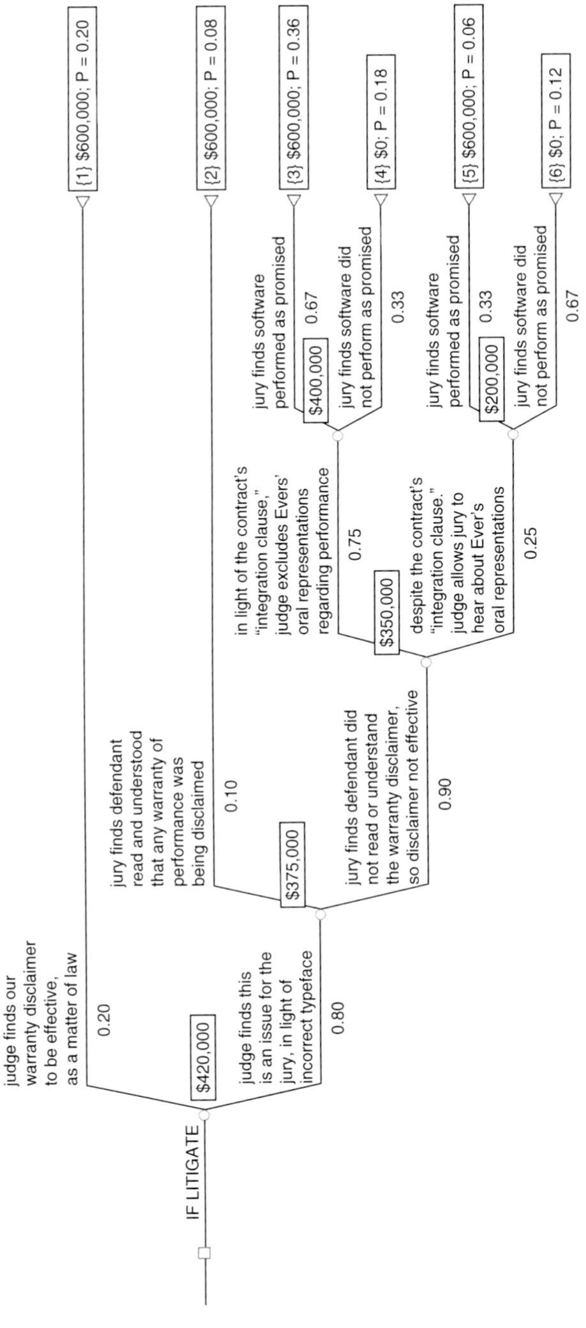

FIGURE 15.8 SOLVING THE DECISION TREE IN NEWPORT RECORDS WITH A TREE PROGRAM.

testimony will increase the likelihood of persuading the jury on that issue. Right now, the lawyers estimate this likelihood as being 0.67 if the judge excludes Evers' oral representations, and 0.33 if he allows them into evidence. The lawyers believe that the expert's testimony would increase the likelihood in the former case to 0.80, and in the latter case to 0.20.

The decision tree makes it easy to determine whether it is worth the cost of the expert witness. Solving the tree with these increased probabilities produces an expected value of $470,400. Since this is an increase in case value of over $50,000 for a cost of only $20,000, the investment in the expert witness would be well worth her cost.

15.2.3.c The probability of different jury awards. We simplified the problem by assuming that the jury would either award $600,000 or nothing. But it is easy to imagine reasons that the jury would award Evers some amount in between. For example, although he claimed that the software would do more than it did, it performed reasonably well, and Newport Records was not justified in refusing to pay anything—especially if it actually continued using the software. At this point, you have the concepts and tools for factoring this in as well.

15.2.4 Of Garbage, Anchoring, and Decision Costs

A decision tree can be helpful in structuring and analyzing a problem, and may help inform your intuitions about the likelihood of achieving objectives, even if you don't plug any numbers into it. However, the true usefulness of a decision tree is its ability to calculate expected value—and with this come several cautions.

First, the expected value calculation is only as good as the data and judgments on which it relies. In some cases, such as weather forecasts, one can assign probabilities with reasonable confidence. This is even true for some aspects of litigation; for example, there are databases that collect the size of jury verdicts in certain types of tort cases in particular jurisdictions. However, one-time guesses, like those in the Newport Records case, are more problematic. "Garbage in, garbage out" applies not only to estimates of probabilities but to estimates of the values of outcomes and the costs of pursuing them: simply put, you cannot create a trustworthy decision tree without accurate estimates of probabilities and of expected costs and benefits.

Second, the danger of treating garbage like a gourmet dish is enhanced by the *anchoring* bias—our tendency to anchor on a number and insufficiently adjust away from it. (See Section 10.1) We have seen that just being aware of the phenomenon does not avoid being caught in its snare. This does not mean that you should not use decision trees even when you do not have great confidence in the numbers. But it does counsel caution.

Finally, we should note that constructing a decision tree requires great cognitive effort. A decision tree is just a procedure for determining expected utility.

And as Gerd Gigerenzer notes, referring to Darwin's decision process involving whether to marry (Section 4.4.1):[4]

> Imagine that Darwin had attempted to resolve his Question by maximizing his subjective expected utility. To compare his personal expected utility for marrying, he would have had to determine *all* of the possible consequences that marriage could bring (e.g., children, constant companion, and an endless stream of further possibilities not included in his short list), attach quantitative probabilities to each of these consequences, estimate the subjective utility of each consequence, multiply each utility by its associated probability, and finally add all these numbers up. The same procedure would have to have been repeated for the alterative "not marry." Finally, he would have had to chose the alternative with the higher total expected utility. To acquire reliable information about the consequences and their probabilities, Darwin might have had to invest years of research—time he could have spent studying barnacles or writing *Origin of Species.*

FIGURE 15.9 THE LAST WORD ON EXPECTED VALUE ANALYSIS. DILBERT © SCOTT ADAMS/DIST. BY UNITED FEATURE SYNDICATE, INC. REPRINTED BY PERMISSION.

15.3 RISK TOLERANCE AND UTILITY FUNCTIONS

So far, we have assumed that Evers is risk neutral in approaching his decision whether to litigate or settle the case against Newport Records. But this needn't be the case. Evers may prefer to accept a settlement lower than the expected value of the litigation, either because he wants funds now to start his new venture or just as a matter of personal preference. Or he might wish to take a gamble on the litigation even if the expected value happens to be less than that of a settlement.

There are essentially three conditions of *risk tolerance* (or *risk attitude,* or *risk preference*). We'll illustrate these with a simple example.

---

4. Gerd Gigerenzer, Peter M. Todd, and the ABC Research Group, Simple Heuristics That Make Us Smart 9 (New York: Oxford University Press, 1999).

Suppose you are offered the choice between a certain $100 and a 0.5 chance of winning $200 and a 0.5 chance of winning nothing. (This kind of choice, referred to as a "gamble" or "lottery," is used to determine a variety of individual preferences involving risk.)

- If you are indifferent between the choices, you are *risk neutral.*
- If you would demand more than a $200 payoff, or a greater than 0.5 chance of winning, before you accepted the gamble, you are *risk averse.* The additional amount of payoff you would demand is the *risk premium.*
- If you would take the gamble for less than a $200 payoff, or a smaller than a 0.5 chance of winning, you are *risk seeking.*

If you are risk neutral in this situation, your (subjective) expected utility of the certain $100 or the .05 chance of winning $200 is identical to the (objective) expected value. But if you are risk averse or risk seeking, your expected utility will diverge from expected value. Let's consider your utility function if you are risk averse.

Recall Bernoulli's observation about the declining (subjective) marginal value of money (Section 12.1.4.b). The subjective value of increasing your wealth from $100 to $200 is greater than the subjective value of increasing your wealth from $1100 to $1200. A graph of this "utility function" would be downwardly concave.

Bernoulli's curve describes risk aversion as well as the declining marginal utility of money: If you prefer a sure gain of $100 (lower on the curve) over a 0.5 chance of $200 (higher on the curve), then you are willing to pay a bit more (and sacrifice some expected value) for the certainty. The extra amount you are willing to pay is the risk premium. Risk aversion and the declining marginal utility of money are two sides of the same coin. When we describe the declining marginal utility of money, we say that increments to an already large amount bring less utility than the equivalent increments to a small amount. When we describe risk aversion, we say that a bird in the hand is worth two in the bush.

The same person may have a different risk preference in different situations (e.g., finance, health and safety, social situations, and recreation).[5] "Individuals who exhibit high levels of risk-taking behavior in one content area (e.g., bungee jumpers taking recreational risks) can be risk averse in other domains (e.g., financial)."[6]

And different people may have different risk preferences in the same situation. If Alex and Andrea exhibit different risk preferences for flying on airlines with poor safety records, it could be because they have different perceptions of the risk

5. Ann-Renee Blais and Elke U. Weber, *A Domain Specific Risk-Taking (DOSPERT) Scale for Adult Populations,* 1 JUDGMENT AND DECISION-MAKING 33 (2006).

6. Hanoch, Joseph Johnson, and Andreas Wilke, *Domain Specificity in Experimental Measures and Participant Recruitment, An Application to Risk-Taking Behavior,* 17 PSYCHOLOGICAL SCIENCE 300 (2006).

or of the benefits from taking the risk, or differences in their willingness to take on a (perceived) risk.[7] While risk taking may be affected by the perceived benefit of the activity,[8] differences in risk preferences often result from different perceptions.[9] (For example, entrepreneurs and people who enter crowded markets that offer small chances of financial success tend to be highly optimistic.[10]) Apart from its academic interest, the reasons for differences in risk preferences may have practical consequences. For example, if you are negotiating in a situation where the allocation of risks between the parties is an issue, understanding and addressing the source of the other party's risk preferences may help reach an agreement.[11]

In any event, one cannot, a priori, describe any of these risk preferences as more or less rational than the others. In many situations, risk preferences are as subjective, and hence as *a*rational, as preferences for flavors of ice cream. Sometimes they make perfect sense in terms of your specific goals: If risk seeking behavior seems irrational to you, suppose that you are in Topeka, with no money in your pocket, and eager to take the next flight to New York to attend a friend's birthday party that night. A plane ticket costs $150, and a benefactor offers you a certain $100 or a 0.5 chance of winning $150.

Even if risk preferences often are arational, we will see later in the chapter that they can be affected simply by the way choices are *framed*. In these cases, there is at least cause for concern that the frame-influenced preferences do not always serve an individual's best interests.

---

7. Ann-Renee Blais and Elke U. Weber, *Domain-Specificity and Gender Differences in Decision Making*, 6 Risk Decision and Policy 47 (2001).

8. Hanoch, Joseph Johnson, and Andreas Wilke, *Domain Specificity in Experimental Measures and Participant Recruitment, An Application to Risk-Taking Behavior*, 17 Psychological Science 300 (2006).

9. Elke U. Weber, *Personality and Risk Taking*, *in* International Encyclopedia of the Social and Behavioral Sciences 11274–76 (N. J. Smelser and P. B. Baltes eds., Oxford, UK: Elsevier Science Limited 2001).

10. Arnold Cooper, Carolyn Woo, William Dunkelberg, *Entrepreneurs' Perceived Chances For Success*, Journal of Business Venturing 97–108 (1988); Colin Camerer and Dan Lovallo, Overconfidence and Excess Entry: An Experimental Approach, 89, The American Economic Review 306–318 (1999); Gideon Markman, David Balkin, Robert Baron. *Inventors and new venture formation: The effects of general self-efficacy and regretful thinking*, Entrepreneurship Theory & Practice 149–165 (Winter, 2002).

11. See Elke U. Weber and Christopher Hsee, *Cross-Cultural Differences in Risk Perception, But Cross-Cultural Similarities in Attitudes Towards Perceived Risk*, 44 Management Science 1205 (1998).

> **Policy Problem**
>
> Should policy makers be risk averse, risk seeking, or risk neutral? Does the answer depend on the circumstances and, if so, what might they be?

15.4 THE FRAMING OF RISKY DECISIONS: PROSPECT THEORY REDUX

In Section 14.1 we considered the status quo bias, including the endowment effect, in decisions where risk is not at issue. Here, we return to the same phenomenon in conditions of risk. In addition to the three features of prospect theory noted above—

1. the value function is defined over gains and losses with respect to some *reference point*;
2. individuals are *loss averse* (the slope of the curve for losses is considerable steeper than the slope for gains);
3. both the gain and loss functions display *diminishing sensitivity* as one moves away from the reference point;

—we examine two other features that are relevant to risky choices, particularly:

4. while the utility curve for gains with respect to the status quo is concave (implying *risk aversion*), the utility curve for losses is convex (implying *risk seeking*);
5. individuals overweight very low probabilities and underweight very high probabilities, so that (reversing the phenomenon generally described by the utility function) they tend to be *risk seeking with respect to low probability gains* and *risk averse with respect to unlikely losses.*

The fact that the reference point separating gains and losses for a particular decision is indeterminate and, indeed, manipulable, poses a severe problem for expected utility theory. In what has become a classic experiment, Amos Tversky and Daniel Kahneman gave one group of subjects the following problem (the percentage of responses to each question is shown in parentheses):

> Imagine that the United States is preparing for the outbreak of an unusual virus that is expected to kill 600 people. Two alternative programs to combat the disease have been proposed. Assume that the exact scientific estimates of the consequences of the programs are as follows:
>
> - If Program A is adopted, 200 people will be saved (**72 percent**).

- If Program B is adopted, there is a one-third probability that 600 people will be saved and a two-thirds probability that no people will be saved (**28 percent**).

A second group of subjects was given the same scenario, but these two choices:

- If Program C is adopted, 400 people will die (**22 percent**).
- If Program D is adopted, there is a one-third probability that nobody will die and a two-thirds probability that 600 people will die (**78 percent**).

Notice that Program A is mathematically identical to Program C and that Program B is identical to Program D—the only difference is that the first set of choices is framed in terms of gains (people saved) and the second in terms of losses (people dying). When making the choice in terms of gains, the large majority of subjects were risk averse; when making the choice in terms of losses, an even larger number were risk seeking.[12]

This violates the axiom of *invariance* (Section 12.2.2b)—that the preference between choices should not depend on the manner in which they are described. As Tversky and Kahneman note, "the failure of invariance is both pervasive and robust":

> It is as common among sophisticated respondents as among naïve ones, and it is not eliminated even when the same respondents answer both questions within a few minutes. Respondents confronted with their conflicting answers are typically puzzled. Even after rereading the problems, they still wish to be risk averse in the "lives saved" version; they wish to be risk seeking in the "lives lost" version; and they also wish to obey invariance and give consistent answers in the two versions. In their stubborn appeal, framing effects often resemble perceptual illusions more than computational errors.

15.4.1 Litigation vs. Settlement

In a comprehensive survey of the effect of prospect theory in legal settings, Chris Guthrie notes:[13] "In most lawsuits, plaintiffs choose either to accept a certain settlement from the defendant or to proceed to trial in hopes of obtaining an even more favorable judgment; most defendants, by contrast, must choose either

---

12. Amos Tversky and Daniel Kahneman, *The Framing of Decisions and the Psychology of Choice*, 211 SCIENCE 453 (1981). David Mandel, *Gain-Loss Framing and Choice: Separating Outcome Formulations from Descriptor Formulations*, 85 ORG. BEHAVIOR AND HUMAN DECISION PROCESSES 56 (2001), argues that the formulation of the problem may be ambiguous and that this and other factors may confound the framing effects.

13. Much of the following analysis is based on Chris Guthrie, *Prospect Theory, Risk, Preference, and the Law*, 97 NW. U. L. REV. 1115 (2003).

to pay a certain settlement to the plaintiff or to gamble that further litigation will reduce the amount they must pay. Thus, plaintiffs generally choose between options that appear to represent gains, while defendants generally choose between options that appear to represent losses."

Economic theory predicts that their different perspectives will have no effect on plaintiffs' and defendants' decisions whether to litigate or settle. Given options with the identical expected value, a risk-neutral litigant would be indifferent and a risk-averse litigant would prefer to settle. Overoptimism or the pursuit of nonmonetary values other than wealth (e.g., vengeance, vindication, or stubbornness) might lead to suboptimal decisions to litigate, but theoretically there is no reason to believe that these affect plaintiffs and defendants asymmetrically.

In fact, however, plaintiffs tend to be risk-averse and defendants tend to be risk-seeking. This is suggested by actual settlement patterns[14] and is the robust finding of many experiments. For example, Jeffrey Rachlinski asked students to play the roles of parties in a copyright case.[15] The plaintiffs had a choice between:

- accepting the defendant's $200,000 settlement offer, or
- going to trial with a 50 percent chance of winning $400,000 and a 50 percent chance of winning nothing.

The defendants had a choice between:

- paying the plaintiff $200,000 in settlement, or
- going to trial with a 50 percent chance of losing $400,000 at trial and a 50 percent chance of losing nothing.

Although expected value of all of the options is identical, 77 percent of the plaintiffs preferred settlement, while 69 percent of the defendant chose to go to trial.

In another experiment, participants were assigned the role of the plaintiff or defendant in litigation between a rural bed and breakfast inn (B&B) and an adjacent property owner.[16] The B&B had unintentionally expanded to occupy a small corner of the adjacent property, worth about $50. After unsuccessful negotiations, the property owner sued for an injunction to require the B&B to remove the encroaching structure. The judge can either order the B&B to remove the

14. Jeffrey Rachlinski, *Gains, Losses and the Psychology of Litigation*, 70 So. Cal. L. Rev. 113 (1996); Guthrie, *Prospect Theory, supra*; Russell Korobkin and Chris Guthrie, *Psychology, Economics, and Settlement: A New Look at the Role of the Lawyer*, 76 Texas L. Rev. 77 (1997).

15. Rachlinski, *supra*.

16. Rachlinski, *supra*. Rachlinski did a number of versions of the experiment with different numbers.

structure at considerable cost, or order the adjacent owner to sell the corner of his property for about $50. If the judge orders removal of the structure, then rather than tear it down, the B&B will offer the owner $100,000—an offer that the owner is certain to accept. In other words, depending upon the judge's decision, the plaintiff will win, and the defendant will lose, either $100,000 or $50. The parties are informed that the judge assigned to the case is an adamant defender of property rights who opposes forced sales of land and is very (70 percent) likely to order removal of the buildings. It is now one day before trial. The opposing party is willing to settle for $70,000.

In running this experiment with various stakes and probabilities, 81 percent of the plaintiffs settled, while only 45 percent of the defendants settled. While the defendants were mildly risk seeking, the plaintiffs were highly risk averse.

The reference point from which any decision maker assesses gains and losses is subjective. An experiment by Russell Korobkin and Chris Guthrie shows how a plaintiff's reference point may change in almost identical cases.[17] Participants played the role of plaintiffs, who had been slightly injured and whose cars were totaled in a car accident, and who had a choice between accepting a settlement of $21,000 or going to trial with a 50 percent chance of an award of full damages of $28,000 and a 50 percent chance of receiving only $10,000 (the insurance limit)—an expected value of $19,000. The first group of subjects was informed that $14,000 of the damages were for medical costs that had already been reimbursed by health insurance and the other $14,000 was the full value of their car. The second group was told that $4,000 were for (reimbursed) medical costs and the remaining $24,000 was the value of their car. For subjects in the first group, the settlement reflected a net gain and they were risk averse, overwhelmingly preferring to settle. For subjects in the second group, the settlement represented a loss, and they tended to choose to go to trial.

Not just partisans, but neutrals may be affected by how the issue is framed. Chris Guthrie, Jeffrey Rachlinski, and Andrew Wistrich presented a version of the copyright infringement case described above to judges presiding over settlement conferences, who were asked whether to recommend settlement.[18] They were informed that there was a 50 percent chance that the plaintiff would prevail at trial and win $200,000 and a 50 percent chance that she would not win anything at all—and that it would cost each party $50,000 in attorneys' fees to go to trial.

Half of the judges reviewed the case from the plaintiff's perspective: Should the plaintiff accept defendant's offer to pay the plaintiff $60,000 to settle the case? Those judges thus had a choice between

17. Russell Korobkin and Chris Guthrie, *Psychological Barriers to Litigation Settlement: An Experimental Approach*, 93 MICH. L. REV. 107 (1994).

18. Chris Guthrie, Jeffrey J. Rachlinski, Andrew J. Wistrich, *Inside the Judicial Mind*, 86 CORNELL LAW REVIEW (May 2001).

- a certain $60,000 gain, and
- a 50 percent chance of winning $200,000 judgment less the $50,000 attorneys' fees (EV = $50,000).

The judges who reviewed the case from the defendant's perspective were asked: Should the defendant accede to the plaintiff's demand that it pay $140,000 to settle the case? They saw that the defendant had a choice between

- a certain $140,000 loss or
- a 50 percent chance of a losing a $200,000 judgment minus $50,000 attorneys' fees (EV = $150,000).

In both cases, then, the expected value of settlement was $10,000 greater than the expected value of going to trial. But the plaintiff's options appeared to represent gains (i.e., $60,000 settlement versus $50,000 trial) while the defendant's options appeared to represent losses (i.e., -$140,000 settlement versus -$150,000 trial). Consistent with prospect theory, the researchers found that the framing of decision options influenced the judges' recommendations. Nearly 40 percent of the judges assessing the problem from the plaintiff's perspective indicated that they would recommend settlement to the plaintiff, while only 25 percent of the judges assessing the problem from the defendant's perspective indicated that they would recommend settlement to the defendant. Chris Guthrie suggests:

> judges are likely to advocate settlement more strenuously to plaintiffs than to defendants, even though the experimental evidence suggests that plaintiffs are more likely than defendants to be attracted to settlement in the first place. By urging plaintiffs to accept an amount that is less than appropriate or by failing to urge defendants to pay an appropriate amount, judges may promote unfair settlements that under-compensate plaintiffs and under-deter defendants.

As noted earlier, what someone views as the status quo—and hence the reference point for gains and losses—is entirely subjective. All things being equal, a defendant tends to treat what's in his pocketbook or bank account as an endowment that litigation puts at risk, and the plaintiff views litigation as providing an opportunity to gain something. This perspective on the plaintiff's part depends on her having adjusted to the harm inflicted by the defendant.[19] If the feeling of harm is still highly salient, or if for some other reason the plaintiff still feels the need for revenge, she is more likely to adjust her utility preferences from risk averse to risk seeking.

> Appendix A (Section 15.5) discusses how people's different risk attitudes toward gains and losses can violate the Dominance Axiom.

19. We explored the psychological dynamics of such adjustment in Section 12.1.5.

15.4.2 Targets and Risk-Seeking and Unethical Behavior

Maurice Schweitzer and his colleagues asked students to solve anagrams, check their own work, and reward themselves (in a situation where they were unaware that the experimenters could independently check their results). Participants in one group were just instructed to *do your best* to create as many words as you can; those in a second group were given the *goal* of creating nine words in each round. The *goal* group performed better than the *do your best* group (though the differences were not statistically significant). Although a majority of the goal group reported their achievements honestly, a significant number overstated their achievements. The closer they were to having nine words, the more they were likely to pad their report to achieve the goal.[20]

How does this apply to real-world situations? Chris Guthrie writes:

> An arbitrarily set "target"—for example, a business's quarterly earnings or a law firm associate's minimum billable hours—may serve as a reference point, with the individual executive or lawyer viewing achievements beyond the target as gains, but those below as in the domain of losses. Several commentators, citing examples from the real world, have suggested that the motivation to escape from the domain of losses, especially when one is close to the target, encourages risk-seeking cheating and other forms of ethical misconduct.

By the same token, lawyers' behavior may be influenced by how well they believe the case or transaction is going compared to an assumed baseline. "When things appear to be going well (gains), risky ethical violations will seem unattractive; when things appear to be going poorly (losses), however, those same ethical violations will hold more appeal."[21]

Jeffrey Rachlinski tested this in an experiment where law students played the role of the outside litigation counsel for a pharmaceutical company in a product liability case brought by the parents of a child who had suffered permanent brain damage from a drug.[22] The parents are willing to settle the case for $3 million, but they are unaware that the defendant withheld incriminating documents during discovery. If the lawyers reveal the documents before settlement, the case is likely to cost the defendant considerably more. If they proceed to settlement, there is a reasonable chance that the documents will subsequently be revealed and, if so, that the lawyers will be sanctioned.

---

20. Maurice Schweitzer, Lisa Ordóñez, and Bambi Douma, *Goal Setting as a Motivator of Unethical Behavior*, 47 Academy of Management Journal 422 (2004); Maurice Schweitzer, Lisa, Ordóñez, and Bambi Douma, The Dark Side of Goal Setting: The Role of Goals in Motivating Unethical Decision Making, 47 Academy of Management Proceedings 422 (2002).

21. *Chris Guthrie, Prospect Theory, Risk Preference & the Law*, 97 Northwestern University Law Review 1115, 1140 (2003).

22. Jeffrey J. Rachlinski, *Gains, Losses, and the Psychology of Litigation*, 70 S. Cal. L. Rev. 113, 118 (1996).

Two groups were asked whether they would reveal the documents before going forward with settlement negotiations. The problem was presented to one group in a "gains" frame: The company had expected to have to pay the parents $5 million to settle the case and therefore thought that the case was "going well." The other group was given a "loss" frame: The company had originally expected to pay the parents only $1 million and believed that the case was "going poorly." Only 12.5 percent of the subjects who saw the settlement as a gain chose to settle without disclosing the documents, while 45 percent who saw the settlement as a loss indicated that they would settle with disclosing the documents. By contrast to the risk aversion manifested by those in gains condition, those in the loss condition opted for the riskier—and ethically and legally problematic—course of action rather than face a sure loss.

15.4.3 Low-Probability Gains and Losses

Prospect theory predicts that people overweight very low probabilities and underweight very high probabilities. Correspondingly (and reversing the general phenomenon described above), they tend to be *risk seeking with respect to low probability gains* and *risk averse with respect to unlikely losses.* Chris Guthrie suggests that this explains risk attitudes toward frivolous litigation:[23]

> In frivolous or low-probability litigation, the plaintiff typically chooses between a relatively small settlement amount and a low likelihood of obtaining a much larger amount at trial. Defendants, by contrast, typically must choose either to pay some small settlement or face a low likelihood of having to pay a much larger amount at trial. . . . Decision makers confronted with low-probability gains . . . tend to make risk-seeking decisions, while those confronted with low-probability losses . . . tend to make risk-averse decisions. In short, litigant risk preferences are likely to be reversed in frivolous suits, with plaintiffs relatively more attracted to trial than defendants.

Guthrie assigned law students to play the roles of plaintiffs and defendants in a low-probability litigation. Plaintiffs could choose between a $50 settlement payment or a 1 percent chance at a $5,000 judgment at trial; defendants could either pay a certain $50 settlement to plaintiff or face a 1 percent chance of having to pay a $5,000 judgment at trial.

Although the expected value of the options was identical, 62 percent of the plaintiffs were willing to risk trial, while 84 percent of the defendants chose to settle. "Faced with low-probability gains, plaintiffs appear to make risk-seeking choices unanticipated by the economic theory."

23. Chris Guthrie, *Framing Frivolous Litigation: A Psychological Theory*, 67 University of Chicago Law Review 163 (2000).

Estimating the Probabilities of Rare Events

Suppose that Desmond and Edwina are predicting whether their respective clients will prevail as plaintiff in a civil suit. Desmond has no personal experience with this sort of litigation, but is reliably informed that plaintiffs in this jurisdiction win 10 percent of the time. Edwina handles many such cases as a plaintiff's attorney and wins 10 percent of the time. Who is more likely to predict that her client will win? Consistent with the prospect theory, Desmond will overweight the 10 percent probability in making his prediction. However, Edwina may actually underweight the probability. Her estimate is likely to be affected by the availability of the most recent events in her experience—and, by the nature of probability, the one win out of ten is not likely to be one of the most recent occurrences.[24]

15.4.4 The Certainty Effect

Tversky and Kahneman demonstrated what they call the *certainty effect* with the following experiment.[25]

Subjects were asked to choose between:

A. a sure win of $300, and
B. 80 percent chance to win $450 and 20 percent chance to win nothing.

The large majority chose A, which has a lower expected value than B.

Other subjects were asked to choose between:

C. 25 percent chance to win $300 and 75 percent chance to win nothing, and
D. 20 percent chance to win $450 and 80 percent chance to win nothing.

The large majority of subjects chose D, which has a higher expected value than C.

Note, however, that the relationship between C and D is identical to that between A and B — the probabilities are just reduced fourfold, as shown in Table 15.5.

The greater attraction of A lies in its certainty—in this case the increase in the probability of winning from 0.25 to 1.0 has a greater effect than the increase from 0.2 to 0.8.

The certainty effect was also demonstrated by this problem, given by one of the authors to groups of in-house corporate counsel:

---

24. Elke U. Weber, "Origins and Functions of Risk Perception, Center for the Decision Sciences" (presented at NCI Workshop on Conceptualizing and Measuring Risk Perceptions, February 13–14, 2003), http://dccps.nci.nih.gov/brp/presentations/weber.pdf#search=%22Weber%2C%20Origins%20and%20Functions%20of%20Risk%20Perception%20nci%22.

25. Amos Tversky and Daniel Kahneman, *The Framing of Decisions and the Psychology of Choice*, *supra*.

TABLE 15.5 THE CERTAINTY EFFECT

			EV	% Choosing
A	Sure gain of $300		$300	78%
B	80% chance to win $450	20% chance to win nothing	$360	22%
C	25% chance to win $300	75% chance to win nothing	$75	42%
D	20% chance to win $450	80% chance to win nothing	$90	58%

> A new, damaging computer virus has been detected. A computer consultant, in whom you have complete confidence, informs you that there is a 20% chance that your company-wide computer system will become infected and crash. Your accounting office estimates that the potential damage to the company is somewhere between $1 million and $10 million. How much would you pay the computer consultant to reduce the chances of a crash to 1%? How much additional would you pay to reduce the chances from 1% to 0%?

The large majority of respondents would pay far more—often as much as ten times more—to reduces the chances from 1 percent to 0 percent than for any unit percentage reduction from 20 percent to 1 percent.

Justice Stephen Breyer describes a real-world example arising out of litigation involving cleanup of a toxic waste dump in southern New Hampshire:

> The site was mostly cleaned up. All but one of the private parties had settled. The remaining private party litigated the cost of cleaning up the last little bit, a cost of about $9.3 million to remove a small amount of highly diluted PCBs and "volatile organic compounds" (benzene and gasoline components) by incinerating the dirt. How much extra safety did this $9.3 million buy? The forty-thousand-page record of this ten-year effort indicated (and all the parties seemed to agree) that, without the extra expenditure, the waste dump was clean enough for children playing on the site to eat small amounts of dirt daily for 70 days each year without significant harm. Burning the soil would have made it clean enough for the children to eat small amounts daily for 245 days per year without significant harm. But there were no dirt-eating children playing in the area, for it was a swamp. Nor were dirt-eating children likely to appear there, for future building seemed unlikely. The parties also agreed that at least half of the volatile organic chemicals would likely evaporate by the year 2000. To spend $9.3 million to protect nonexistent dirt-eating children is what I mean by the problem of "the last 10 percent."[26]

26. STEPHEN BREYER, BREAKING THE VICIOUS CIRCLE: Toward Effective Risk Regulation (Cambridge: Harvard University Press, 1995).

At some point, a probability may be so low that people treat it as if it were zero. The vast majority of participants in a study said they would not bother to wear seat belts if the probability of being killed in a car accident was 0.0000025 per trip.[27]

> Appendix B (Section 15.6) discusses the Certainty Effect and Violation of the Independence Axiom.

15.4.5 The Pseudocertainty Effect and Other Violations of the Independence Axiom

Although some manifestations of the certainty effect seem problematic as a matter of public policy, it is hard to characterize the willingness to pay a premium for certainty as irrational if it allows you to sleep better at night. But consider this experiment:

Tversky and Kahneman gave subjects the following two-stage game.

I. In the first stage there is a 75 percent chance to end the game without winning anything, and a 25 percent chance to move into the second stage.
II. If you reach the second stage you have a choice between

E. a sure gain of $300, and
F. 80 percent chance to win $450 and 20 percent chance to win nothing.

There is a one-in-four chance of moving to the second stage, and Table 15.6 shows the expected value of E and F—and also the percent of subjects who made the choices.

TABLE 15.6 THE PSEUDOCERTAINTY EFFECT

			EV	% Choosing
E	Sure win of $300		$75	74%
F	80% chance to win $450	20% chance to win nothing	$90	26%

The expected values of E and F are, respectively, identical to the expected values of C and D in the "certainty effect" example (Section 15.4.4). Note, however, that while the majority of subjects there were risk seeking in

27. JONATHAN BARON, THINKING AND DECIDING 255 (3rd. ed. New York: Cambridge University Press, 2001). The respondents apparently ignored the value of seatbelts in preventing serious injuries.

choosing D, the majority of subjects in the two-stage game made the risk averse choice of E.

Tversky and Kahneman label this phenomenon the *pseudocertainty* effect because an outcome that is actually uncertain is weighted as if it is certain. The framing of probabilities as a two-stage game encourages respondents to apply *cancellation*: the event of failing to reach the second stage is discarded prior to evaluation because it yields the same outcomes in both options.[28] They suggest that the choice between E and F has a greater potential for inducing regret than the choice between C and D.

A simple experiment by Paul Slovic and his colleagues demonstrates how the pseudocertainty effect can affect public health decisions. One group was told that a disease will afflict 20 percent of the population, but that a vaccine will reduce their risk of getting the disease by a half. A second group was told that there are two strains of the same disease, that each will afflict 10 percent of the population, and that a vaccine will entirely eliminate the risk of getting one strain but have no effect on the other. Although each will reduce an individual's risk of getting the disease from 20 percent to 10 percent, many more people (57 percent) in the second group than in the first group (40 percent) said they were willing to be vaccinated.[29]

Tversky and Kahneman replicated the two-stage game described above in these questions given physicians attending a meeting of the California Medical Association:[30]

> In the treatment of tumors there is sometimes a choice between two types of therapies: (i) a radical treatment such as extensive surgery, which involves some risk of imminent death, (ii) a moderate treatment, such as limited surgery or radiation therapy. Each of the following problems describes the possible outcome of two alternative treatments, for three different cases. In considering each case, suppose the patient is a 40-year-old male. Assume that without treatment death is imminent (within a month) and that only one of the treatments can be applied. Please indicate the treatment you would prefer in each case.

---

28. Amos Tversky and Daniel Kahneman, *The Framing of Decisions and the Psychology of Choice, supra.*

29. *See* Paul Slovic Baruch Fischhoff and Sarah Lichtenstein, *Response Mode, Framing, and Information Processing Effects in Risk Assessment, in* NEW DIRECTIONS FOR METHODOLOGY OF SOCIAL AND BEHAVIORAL SCIENCE: THE FRAMING OF QUESTIONS AND THE CONSISTENCY OF RESPONSES 21 (Robin M. Hogarth ed. San Francisco: Jossey-Bass, 1982).

30. *Rational Choice in the Framing of Decisions, in* DANIEL KAHNEMAN AND AMOS TVERSKY, eds. CHOICE, VALUES AND FRAMES 209 (New York: Cambridge University Press, 2000). The order of the cases has been changed to make it parallel to the preceding examples in the text.

CASE 1

Treatment A: certainty of a normal life, with an expected longevity of 18 years. [65%]

Treatment B: 20% chance of imminent death and 80% chance of normal life, with an expected longevity of 30 years. [35%]

CASE 2

Treatment C: 75% chance of imminent death and 25% chance of normal life, with an expected longevity of 18 years. [32%]

Treatment D: 80% chance of imminent death and 20% chance of normal life, with an expected longevity of 30 years. [68%]

CASE 3

Consider a new case where there is a 25% chance that the tumor is treatable and a 75% chance that it is not. If the tumor is not treatable, death is imminent. If the tumor is treatable, the outcomes of the treatment are as follows:

Treatment E: certainty of normal life, with an expected longevity of 18 years. [68%]

Treatment F: 20% Chance of imminent death and 80% chance of normal life, with an expected longevity of 30 years. [32%]

The three cases of this problem correspond, respectively, to the choices of the bets A and B, C and D (Section 15.4.4), and E and F (Section 15.4.5) in the preceding examples, and reveal the same pattern of preferences. The experimenters observe:

> In **case 1**, most respondents make a risk-averse choice in favor of certain survival with reduced longevity. In **case 2**, the moderate treatment no longer ensures survival, and most respondents choose the treatment that offers the higher expected longevity. In particular, 64% of the physicians who chose A in **case 1** selected D in **case 2.** This is another example of the certainty effect.
>
> The comparison of **cases 2 and 3** provides another illustration of pseudocertainty. The cases are identical in terms of the relevant outcomes and their probabilities, but the preferences differ. In particular, 56% of the physicians who chose D in **case 2** selected E in **case 3**. The conditional framing induces people to disregard the event of the tumor's not being treatable because the two treatments are equally ineffective in this case. In this frame, treatment E enjoys the advantage of pseudocertainty: it *appears* to ensure survival, but the assurance is conditional on the treatability of the tumor. In fact, there is only a .25 chance of surviving a month if this option is chosen.

15.5 APPENDIX A

15.5.1 How People's Different Risk Attitudes Toward Gains and Losses Can Violate the Dominance Axiom

The axioms of completeness and dominance in conditions of uncertainty are simply extensions of the axioms described in Section 12.2.2. Suppose a decision maker prefers prospect (i.e., outcome) A to prospect B, and that he has a choice between two lotteries, as shown in Figure 15.10. The first lottery, which we call X, will result in prospect A with probability p, or prospect B with probability 1-p. The second lottery, which we call Y, will result in prospects A or B with probabilities q and 1-q, respectively. To satisfy the dominance axiom, the decision maker will (1) prefer lottery X over lottery Y if and only if $p > q$; and (2) will be indifferent between X and Y if and only if p = q.

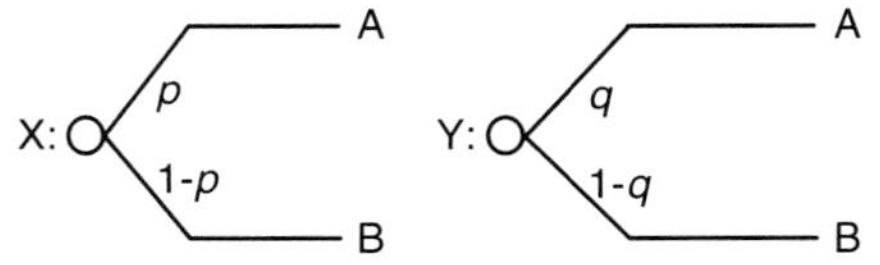

FIGURE 15.10 DOMINANCE IN LOTTERIES.

People's different risk attitudes toward gains and losses can violate the dominance axiom.

Consider the choice between these two lotteries:[31]

E. 25 percent chance to win \$240 and 75 percent chance to lose \$760, and
F. 25 percent chance to win \$250 and 75 percent chance to lose \$750.

When given to a group of subjects, everyone recognizes that F dominates E and chooses F.

Now consider these two pair of concurrent choices.
Choose between:

A. A sure gain of \$240, and
B. 25 percent chance to win \$1000 and 75 percent chance to win nothing.

and
Choose between:

C. Sure loss of \$750, and
D. 75 percent chance to lose \$1000 and 25 percent chance to lose nothing.

31. Daniel Kahneman and Amos Tversky, *Choices, Values, and Frames*, *in* CHOICES, VALUES, AND FRAMES, *supra* at 1.

As shown in Table 15.7, the choice of A and D has precisely the same expected value as E, and the choice of B and C has the same value as F.

However, 73 percent of subjects choose A and D while only 3 percent chose B and C,[32] which dominates A and D: People are risk averse with respect to gains, and risk seeking with respect to losses—and the violation of dominance was stimulated by putting one part of the concurrent choice in the domain of losses and the other in the domain of gains.

TABLE 15.7 SEPARATING THE DOMAINS OF GAINS AND LOSSES

				EV
A & D =	E	25% chance to win $240	75% chance to lose $760	-$510
B & C =	F	25% chance to win $250	75% chance to lose $750	-$500

15.6 Appendix B

15.6.1 The Certainty Effect and Violation of the Independence Axiom

Recall the *independence axiom* (Section 12.2.2.c). In the context of decision making under risk, it is also called the *cancellation*, or *sure thing*, principle. It provides: A decision maker who prefers alternative A to B should continue to prefer A to B even though there is a specified probability that the decision maker will receive neither A nor B, but some other alternative, C.

The French economist, Maurice Allais, noticed that the certainty effect could cause people to violate the independence axiom. Consider this choice:

A. $1,000,000 for sure.
B. A 10 percent chance of receiving $2,5000,000, an 89 percent chance of receiving $1,000,000, and a 1 percent chance of receiving nothing.

Most people choose A despite the fact that B has a considerable higher EV ($1.4 million compared to $1 million).

Now consider this choice

C. An 11 percent chance of receiving $1,000,000 and an 89 percent of receiving nothing.
D. A 10 percent chance of receiving $2,500,000 and a 90 percent chance of receiving nothing.

Most people choose D, which has over twice the EV.

To see why this violates the independence axiom, let's recast the choice in terms of randomly drawing chips out of a bag that contains 89 red,

10 blue, and 1 black chip. The equivalents of A and B, and C and D are shown in Table 15.8.

TABLE 15.8 ALLAIS' PARADOX

	Chips		
	89 Red	1 Black	10 Blue
A	$1 million	$1 million	$1 million
B	$1 million	$0	$2.5 million
C	$0	$1 million	$1 million
D	$0	$0	$2.5 million

Note that choosing the red chip has no effect in the A-B choice; thus, the independence axiom implies that one only need to consider the black and blue chips. By the same token, choosing the red chip has no effect in the C-D choice, and only the black and blue chips need to be considered. And note that, with the red chips excluded, the lottery in A-B is precisely the same as that in C-D.

Thus does the extraordinarily high utility placed on certainty cause a violation of the independence axiom.

16. THE ROLE OF AFFECT IN RISKY DECISIONS

In Chapter 1, we quoted Paul Slovic's observation that virtually everything we experience is accompanied by some sort of affect, ranging from a "faint whisper of emotion" to strong feelings of fear and dread, and that images, marked by positive and negative affective feelings, guide judgment and decision making.[1] This section considers how affect affects people's assessment of risks.

16.1 RISKS AS FEELINGS

George Loewenstein and his colleagues posit a "risks-as-feelings hypothesis"—a model of decision making that incorporates emotions experienced during the decision-making process, as shown in Figure 16.1.[2] They write:

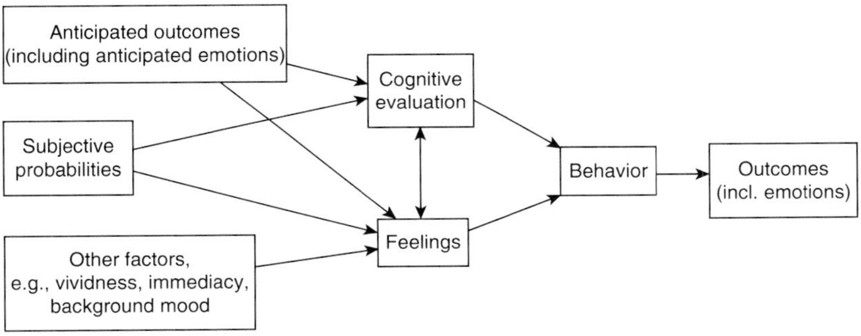

FIGURE 16.1 RISKS AS FEELINGS.

1. "Affect" refers to "the specific quality of 'goodness' or 'badness' (1) experienced, as a feeling state (with or without consciousness) and (2) demarcating a positive or negative quality of a stimulus." Paul Slovic, Melissa Finucane, Ellen Peters, and Donald G. MacGregor, *The Affect Heuristic* [hereafter *Affect Heuristic*], *in* HEURISTICS AND BIASES: THE PSYCHOLOGY OF INTUITIVE JUDGMENT 397–420 (Thomas Gilovich, Dale Griffin, and Daniel Kahneman eds., New York: Cambridge University Press, 2002) [hereafter HEURISTICS AND BIASES].

2. George Loewenstein, Elke Weber, Christopher Hsee, and Ned Welch, *Risk As Feelings*, 127 PSYCH. BULL. 267 (2001).

> The risks-as-feeling hypothesis postulates that responses to risky situations (including decision making) result in part from direct [i.e., System 1] emotional influences, including feelings, such as worry, fear, dread, or anxiety. People . . . evaluate risky alternatives at a cognitive level, as in traditional models, based largely on the probability and desirability of associated consequences. Such cognitive evaluations have affective consequences, and feeling states also exert a reciprocal influence on cognitive evaluations. At the same time, however, feeling states . . . respond to factors, such as the immediacy of a risk, that do not enter into cognitive evaluations of risk and also respond to probabilities and outcome values in a fashion that is different from the way in which these variables enter into cognitive evaluations. Because their determinants are different, emotional reactions to risk can diverge from cognitive evaluations of the same risks. As illustrated by Figure [16.1], behavior is then determined by the interplay between these two, often conflicting, responses, to a situation. . . . Thus feelings may be more than an important input into decision making under uncertainty; they may be necessary and, to a large degree, mediate the connection between cognitive evaluation of risk and risk-related behavior."[3]

Under this model, "affect plays an informational role in decision making—that is, it provides inputs into decision making that help people evaluate alternative courses of action, albeit not always in a normative fashion." Note that Loewenstein et al. use the word *behavior* rather than *decision* in the penultimate box, noting that "many types of emotion-driven risk-related behaviors, ranging from panic reactions (e.g., slamming on the brakes when one skids on the ice) to the agoraphobic individual's inability to leave the house, do not seem to reflect "decisions" in the sense that term is usually used.

Antonio Damasio provides a hypothetical example of the role that negative affect plays in decision making.[4] Using the example of a businessperson deciding whether or not to do a deal with a potentially valuable client who is the archenemy of his best friend, Damasio suggests the complexities of a purely deliberative process:

> Gaining a client may bring immediate reward and also a substantial amount of future reward. How much reward is unknown and so you must estimate its magnitude and rate over time, so that you can pit it against the potential losses among which you must now count the consequences of losing a friendship. Since the latter loss will vary over time, you must also figure its "depreciation" rate! You are, in effect, faced with a complex calculation, set at diverse imaginary epochs, and burdened with the need to compare results of a different nature which somehow much be translated into a common currency for the comparison to make any sense at all. A substantial part of this calculation will

---

3. Minor textual changes throughout.

4. ANTONIO R. DAMASIO, DESCARTES ERROR: EMOTION, REASON AND THE HUMAN BRAIN (New York: HarperCollins, 1995).

depend on the continued generation of yet more imaginary scenarios, built on visual and auditory patterns, among others, and also on the continued generation of verbal narratives which accompany those scenarios, and which are essential to keep the process of logical inference going.[5]

Consciously and systematically processing the myriad representations involved in even this one decision is beyond our cognitive capacity. But Damasio's "somatic marker hypothesis" focuses on the role that these images play before we engage in rational analysis:

> *Before* you apply any kind of cost/benefit analysis . . . and before you reason toward the solution of the problem, something quite important happens. When the bad outcome connected with a given response option comes into mind, however fleetingly, you experience an unpleasant gut feeling. Because the feeling is about the body, I gave the phenomenon the technical term *somatic* state ("soma" is Greek for body); and because it "marks" an image, I called it a *marker*.
>
> . . .
>
> Somatic markers . . . are feelings that have been connected, by learning, to predicted future outcomes of certain scenarios. When a negative somatic marker is juxtaposed to a particular future outcome the combination functions as an alarm bell. When a positive somatic marker is juxtaposed instead, it becomes a beacon of incentive.
>
> [The negative somatic marker] functions as an automated alarm signal which says: "Beware of danger ahead if you choose the option which leads to this outcome." . . . The automated signal protects you against future losses, without further ado, and then allows you to choose from among fewer alternatives. There is still room for using a cost/benefit analysis and proper deductive competence, but only *after* the automated step drastically reduces the number of options.[6]

As Damasio notes, somatic markers may also highlight some options as favorable.[7] While positive markers cannot eliminate options in advance of the rational analytic process, they may play a facilitative role within an intuitive cost-benefit analysis process.

16.1.1 Anxiety as the Shadow of Intelligence[8]

Damasio is a neurologist whose research has focused on patients with damage to the ventromedial region of the frontal lobe of the brain—damage that curtails their emotions or affect but does not compromise intelligence or analytic ability.[9]

---

5. *Id.* at 170.
6. *Id.* at 173–74 (paragraphs rearranged).
7. *Id.* at 174.
8. David H. Barlow, Anxiety and Its Disorders: The Nature and Treatment of Anxiety and Panic (1988) (*quoted in* Loewenstein et al., *supra* note 2).
9. Damasio, *supra* at 193.

His experiments suggest that anxiety may be an important aspect of one's capacity to plan. For example, subjects were given a sum of play money and were asked to repeatedly choose cards from among four decks, which had different risks and payoffs. The subjects had to learn the rules that governed payoffs through trial and error, and the rules were sufficiently complex that they were difficult to learn them with certainty. Two of the decks provided consistent payments but unpredictably required the player to pay the experimenter a very large sum. The other two decks provided smaller payments and unpredictably required the player to pay a smaller amount. The expected value of choosing from the first two decks was smaller than the latter.

Over time, members of a control group learned to avoid the two sets of cards with higher risks and lower expected value. The feeling-impaired subjects continued to choose cards from the risk decks and went bankrupt. Members of the control group hesitated before choosing the risky cards and they exhibited heightened visceral reactions (e.g., change in skin conductance) before making the choice. The feeling-impaired subjects did not hesitate and gave no physiological indications before making the choice.

Loewenstein et al. note that "the lack of an emotional response does not necessarily lead to poor decisions. . . . One could easily design an experiment where the expected value of the high-risk deck (that contains some large losses) is actually higher than that of the low-risk deck. In this case, prefrontal damaged patients would do better in the long run than nonpatients, because the fear in the latter group would hinder them from choosing from the risky but higher expected value deck." Indeed, as we shall see below, emotions can often distort people's perception of or reaction to risk.

Damasio's subjects had brain lesions that left their analytic capacities uncompromised, but impaired their ability to associate emotions with the anticipated consequences of their actions. People with and without similar lesions were given this problem:

> You have abandoned a sinking cruise ship and are in a crowded lifeboat that is dangerously low in the water. If nothing is done it will sink before the rescue boats arrive and everyone will die. However, there is an injured person who will not survive in any case. If you throw that person overboard, the boat will stay afloat and the remaining.

How do you suppose the different groups responded?

See Benedict Carey, *Brain Injury Said to Affect Moral Choices*, New York Times, Mar. 22, 2007. Michael Koenigs et al., *Damage to the Prefrontal Cortex Increases Utilitarian Moral Judgments*, Nature, http://www.nature.com/news/2007/070319/full/070319-9.html.

16.2 THE AVAILABILITY HEURISTIC AND THE ROLE OF VIVIDNESS

Damasio writes that "the action of biological drives, body states, and emotions may be an indispensable foundation for rationality. . . . Rationality is probably shaped and modulated by body signals, even as it performs the most sublime distinctions and acts accordingly."[10] Emotions and reasoning exist in a delicate balance, however, and emotions can sometimes overwhelm reasoning to our detriment. The following pages focus mostly on risks involving human life and safety, where emotions tend to run fairly high.

In Section 9.6 we saw that people often estimate the frequency of events (or their probabilities) based on how easily examples come to mind. We saw that the availability or vividness of events like shark attacks and the 9/11 terrorist attacks affects people's perception of risk. As David Myers notes, such perceptions have behavioral consequences:

> Even before the horrors of September 11th and the ensuing crash at Rockaway Beach, 44 percent of those willing to risk flying told Gallup they felt fearful. . . . After the four crashed airliners, and with threats of more terror to come, cancellations understandably left airlines, travel agencies, and holiday hotels flying into the red.
>
> . . . If we now fly 20 percent less and instead drive half those unflown miles, we will spend 2 percent more time in motor vehicles. This translates into 800 more people dying as passengers and pedestrians. So, in just the next year the terrorists may indirectly kill three times more people on our highways than died on those four fated planes.[11]

A more quotidian example is that purchases of flood and earthquake insurance are high in the aftermath of a natural disaster, but decline as the vividness of the event recedes from memory.

The easier it is to imagine a particular outcome, the more likely its occurrence seems to be. Steven Sherman and his colleagues did an experiment in which students were told about *Hyposcenia-B*, a (fictious) illness that was becoming prevalent on their campus. In the easy-to-imagine scenario, students were told that the disease had concrete symptoms that most of them had probably experienced: low energy level, muscle aches, severe headaches. In the difficult-to-imagine scenario, the symptoms were less concrete: a vague sense of disorientation, malfunctioning nervous system, and inflamed liver. Students given the former scenario thought they were more likely to contract the disease than those given the latter. The experimenters conclude that the effort required to imagine contracting the more difficult-to-imagine symptoms led to a decrease in their availability.[12]

---

10. *Id.* 200.

11. David G. Myers, *Do We Fear the Right Things?*, American Psychological Society Observer (December 2001).

12. Steven J. Sherman et al., *Imagining Can Heighten or Lower the Perceived Likelihood of Contracting a Disease: The Mediating Effect of Ease of Imagery*, *in* Heuristics and Biases, *supra*.

An easily imagined harm can lead people to violate the fundamental principle that a subset cannot be greater than the larger set of which it is a part.[13] A striking example of this is people's stated willingness to pay more for flight insurance for losses resulting from "terrorism" than for flight insurance from all causes (including terrorism).[14] By the same token, in a between-subjects experiment, Eric Johnson and his colleagues asked people how much they would pay for insurance for hospitalization in four different scenarios.[15] The first two groups were respectively asked their willingness to pay (WTP) for hospitalization insurance for any reason, and for any disease or accident. The third group was asked their WTP for insurance for any accident assuming that they already had insurance for disease, and the fourth group was asked their WTP for insurance against any disease assuming that they already had accident insurance. The mean WTP was:

Any reason	$41.53
Any disease or accident	$47.12
Any accident (followed by any disease)	$69.55
Any disease (followed by any accident)	$89.10

Isolating accidents and diseases makes vivid the individual imagine examples of each, and thus leads to an irrational hierarchy of choices. The WTP is more

> All the big money on an accident policy comes from [insuring] railroad accidents. They found out pretty quick, when they began to write accident insurance, that the apparent danger spots, the stops that people think are danger spots, aren't danger spots at all. I mean, people always think a railroad train is a pretty dangerous place to be, . . . but the figures show that not many people get killed, or even hurt, on railroad trains. So on accident policies, they put in a feature that sounds pretty good to the man that buys it, because he's a little worried about train trips, but it doesn't cost the company much, because it knows he's pretty sure to get there safely. They pay double indemnity for railroad accidents.
> —James Cain, Double Indemnity (1936).

13. *Id.* Recall the "Linda" problem in Section 8.2.3, where the representativeness heuristic led to a similar error.

14. *Id.* People's WTP for $100,000 insurance on a trans-Atlantic flight was $14.12 for any act of terrorism, $10.31 for any nonterrorism related mechanical failure, and $12.03 for any reason.

15. Eric J. Johnson, John C. Hershey, and Howard Kunreuther *Framing, Probability Distortions, and Insurance Decisions*, 7 Journal of Risk and Uncertainty, 35–52 (August 1993). Reprinted in: Choices, Values and Frames (Daniel Kahneman and Amos Tversky eds., Cambridge, Eng.: Cambridge University Press, 2000).

strongly correlated with *vividness* than it is with probability—the experimenters' wording "tricked" the subjects into paying more for insurance that was less inclusive.

Many of the same biases—particularly those related to fear—that lead individuals to make poor judgments also affect policy makers. For example, Cass Sunstein notes that many public activities that pose relatively small risks nonetheless engender great public concern because of the biases that promote disproportionate attention to certain types of risks while neglecting others.[16] For example, much of the public fear concerning nuclear power probably stems from its association with memorable events such as Hiroshima, Chernobyl, and Three-Mile Island. Vivid images of the likelihood of a nuclear incident may combine with the invisibility of the risks created by coal-powered electricity to lead policy makers to believe that coal is safer than nuclear.

16.3 OTHER DETERMINANTS OF RESPONSES TO RISKS

16.3.1 The Relative Acceptability of Risks; High Anxiety and Outrage

During the fall of 2002, snipers randomly killed nine people in the Washington, D.C. area, causing widespread fear and the curtailment of outdoor activities by schools and families. The actual increase in residents' risk was very small. (Indeed, Cass Sunstein suggests that "some of the precautionary steps, such as driving to Virginia to purchase gasoline, almost certainly posed risks in excess of those associated with the snipers' attacks."[17]) In commenting on reactions to the Washington, D.C. sniper attacks, *The Economist*, citing Kip Viscusi, noted:

> One of the victims was a child—and parents dramatically overestimate any uncommon threat to their children's lives (such as the risk of kidnapping by a stranger). Similarly, the sniper represents an involuntary risk, not one you would run willingly for a benefit (such as driving too fast to get somewhere). Perhaps people worry less about voluntary risks. Worst of all, the risk is hard to mitigate. You cannot easily change it by changing behavior—like wearing a seat belt. The only way to remove yourself from the sniper's mercy is not to go out at all.

As this suggests, people assign quite different subjective values to risks that have the same probability of resulting in pain, serious injury, or death. Based on the work of Paul Slovic and colleagues, Cass Sunstein and Timur Kuran created

16. Cass R. Sunstein, Laws of Fear: Beyond the Precautionary Principle (New York: Cambridge University Press, 2005). [Hereafter Laws of Fear].

17. *Id* at 69.

a chart of factors that make a risk seem more anxiety-producing or outrageous or more acceptable (see Table 16.1).[18]

TABLE 16.1 AGGRAVATING AND MITIGATING RISK FACTORS

Risk Traits	Aggravating	Mitigating
Familiarity	New	Old
Personal control	Uncontrollable	Controlled
Voluntariness	Involuntary	Voluntary
Media attention	Heavy media coverage	No media coverage
Equity	Unevenly distributed	Evenly distributed
Impact on children	Children at special risk	Children not at risk
Impact on future generations	Future generations at risk	Future generations not at risk
Reversibility	Irreversible	Reversible
Identifiability of victims	Victims known	Victims unknown
Accompanying benefits	Benefits clear	Benefits invisible
Source	Human-generated	Natural origins
Trust in relevant institutions	Low trust in institutions	High trust in institutions
Immediacy of adverse effects	Adverse effects immediate	Adverse effects delayed
Understanding	Mechanisms poorly understood	Mechanisms well understood
Precedents	History of accidents	No past accidents

In the public sphere, the aggravating factors can lead to high levels of concern, or *outrage*. As Dr. Robert Scheuplein, former head of the U.S. Food and Drug Administration's Office of Toxicology, noted: "When risks are perceived to be dread[ful], unfamiliar, uncontrollable by the individual, unfair, involuntary, and potentially catastrophic, they are typically of great public concern, or high outrage. When risks are perceived as voluntary, controllable by the individual,

18. Timur Kuran and Cass R. Sunstein, *Availability Cascades and Risk Regulation*, 51 STANFORD LAW REVIEW 683, 709 (1999).

familiar, equitable, easily reducible, decreasing, and non-catastrophic, they tend to be minimized by the public (or low outrage)."[19]

A study by Peter Sandman and colleagues sought people's reactions to scenarios where the risk was high but outrage was low (radiation in a single-family house caused by naturally occurring radon) and where the risk was low but outrage was high (the sand used to make the concrete foundations for the house had previously been at a storage site for spent nuclear power fuel rods and had been illegally used to make the concrete). Participants reported much greater fear and concern and willingness to take costly remedial action in the low-risk/high outrage case.[20]

16.3.2 Familiarity

Familiar risks, such as driving, engender less dread or outrage than unfamiliar ones, such as the explosion of a nuclear power plant, bioterrorism, or the D.C. snipers' attacks—even when the familiar risks are more likely to eventuate. This may respond to the fact that familiar risks tend to recede to the background and do not gain one's attention. Cass Sunstein suggests that the unacceptability of unfamiliar risks may be a consequence of loss aversion:[21]

> People will be closely attuned to the losses produced by any newly introduced risk, or by any aggravation of existing risks, but far less concerned with the benefits that are foregone as a result of regulation. . . . The opportunity costs of regulation often register little or not at all, whereas the out-of-pocket costs of the activity or substance in question are entirely visible. In fact this is a form of status quo bias. The status quo marks the baseline against which gains and losses are measured, and a loss from the status quo seems much more bad than a gain from the status quo seems good.
>
> . . . [Loss aversion] places a spotlight on the losses introduced by some risk, and downplay[s] the benefits foregone as a result of controls on that risk. . . . Consider the emphasis, in the United States, on the risks of insufficient testing of medicines as compared with the risks of delaying the availability of those medicines. . . . For many people, the possible harms of cloning register more strongly than the potential therapeutic benefits that would be eliminated by a ban on the practice.

---

19. Robert Scheuplein, *Do Pesticides Cause Cancer?*, CONSUMERS' RESEARCH 30–33 (December 1991).

20. Peter M. Sandman, Neil D. Weinstein, and William K. Hallman, *Communications to Reduce Risk Underestimation and Overestimation*, 3 RISK DECISION & POLICY 93 (1998). The "effect of outrage was practically as large as the effect of a 4000-fold difference in risk between the high-risk and low-risk conditions."

21. LAWS OF FEAR 36.

16.3.3 Voluntariness and Controllability[22]

People are more willing to endure risks that they voluntarily assume or over which they believe they have some control. For example, the risks associated with rock-climbing or driving arouse less concern than the risks of an airplane journey, even if the former are greater. Of course, whether or not a risk, such as getting on an airplane, is voluntary is essentially a matter of individual, subjective framing.

16.3.4 (Un)natural Origins

People assume that nature is essentially benign, and find its risks less troubling than those created by human technology. Cass Sunstein suggests that, aided by loss aversion, this creates a bias against innovative technologies and substances:[23]

> Many people fear that any human intervention will create loss from the status quo and that this loss should carry great weight, whereas the gains should be regarded with some suspicion or at least be taken as less weighty. Often loss aversion and a belief in nature's benevolence march hand-in-hand: the status quo forms the baseline or reference state against which to assess deviations. Processes that interfere with nature seem, on the part of many, to be taken as troubling "degradation"—whereas gains or improvements seem, other things being equal, far less significant.

Thus, people believe—often incorrectly—that natural substances are inherently safer than manufactured ones. For example, they overestimate the carcinogenic risk from pesticides and underestimate the risks of natural carcinogens,[24] or overestimate the dangers from genetically modified foods while underestimating those of natural foods.[25]

16.3.5 Omission and Action Biases

In our earlier discussion of regret (Section 14.2), we noted that, in the short run, actions tend to be more salient and more regret-inducing than failures to act. As every first-year law student learns, tort, criminal law, and even constitutional law[26] often distinguish between actions and omissions: the actor who actively

22. These and other factors are analyzed in Paul Slovic, The Perception of Risk (London: Earthscan Publications, 2000) [hereafter, Perception of Risk].

23. Laws of Fear 37.

24. *See* Perception of Risk at 291.

25. *See* James P. Collman, Naturally Dangerous (Sausalito, CA: 2001). Collman writes that organic foods, favored by many people on grounds of safety and health and creating annual revenues of $4.5 billion in the United States alone, are "actually riskier to consume than food grown with synthetic chemicals." (31)

26. *See* Washington v. Glucksberg, 521 US 702 (1997) (distinguishing between right to have life support withdrawn and physician-assisted suicide).

causes a harm is held liable, while someone who fails to prevent a harm usually is not. The distinction is manifested in many moral intuitions as well.[27] Among other things, it reflects the generalization that it is easier to attribute causal responsibility to action than inaction. From childhood, we are taught not to cause direct harm, while the harms of inaction often seem indirect.

But if Hippocrates' mandate, "First, do no harm," captures a preference for inaction where intervention may be counterproductive, the familiar injunction, "Don't just sit there. Do something!" also reflects a strong tendency. Research suggests that people can have both an omission and an action bias, depending on the circumstances and also on individual differences.

In a study modeled on the facts of the DPT vaccine, which causes serious permanent neurological injury in one dose out of 310,000, Ilana Ritov and Jonathan Baron found that many subjects preferred to subject their children to a higher probability of dying from a disease that the vaccine would prevent, than a smaller chance of dying from side-effects of the vaccine.[28] Although a later study by other Terry Connolly and Jochen Reb[29] did not replicate the findings of omission bias with respect to vaccination, they concluded that anticipating regret was nonetheless a significant factor in people's decision whether to vaccinate: "intention to vaccinate was predicted by three measures: the respondent's assessment of the relative seriousness of the disease and the vaccine side-effects; her assessment of the regret she would feel if vaccination turned out badly; and her assessment of the regret she would feel if non-vaccination turned out badly."

A later article by Baron and Ritov documents omission bias in various contexts,[30] but also notes the existence of action bias. As in the case of the soccer goalie's penchant for action described in Section 14.2.2, a decision maker's response may be influenced by what is deemed "normal" behavior under the circumstance. By its nature, a bias in either direction detracts from optimal decision making.

While the unfortunate outcome of an individual decision may result only in personal regret, officials may incur public blame for bad policy decisions. Officials in the Food and Drug Administration might well believe that criticisms for delaying the approval of potentially life-saving drugs are mild compared to the criticism of approving a drug that turns out to be deadly. One can think of

---

27. *See* Cass Sunstein, "Moral Heuristics," University of Chicago Law & Economics, Olin Working Paper No. 180 (2003).

28. Ilana Ritov and Jonathan Baron, *Reluctance to Vaccinate: Omission Bias and Ambiguity*, *in* Behavioral Law and Economics 168 (Cass Sunstein ed., New York: Cambridge University Press, 2000).

29. Terry Connolly and Jochen Reb, *Omission Bias in Vaccination Decisions: Where's the "Omission"? Where's the "Bias?*, 91 Org. Behav. and Human Decision Processes 186–202 (2003).

30. Jonathan Baron and Ilana Ritov, *Omission Bias, Individual Differences, and Normality*, 94 Organizational Behavior and Human Decision Processes 74–85 (2004).

many other instances of omission bias by public officials. But there are also apparent instances of action bias, perhaps including the Bush Administration's decision to invade Iraq after 9/11.

16.3.6 Betrayal Aversion

Betrayal creates a perception of social disorder beyond the particular damage it causes, and harms caused by a violation of trust are accompanied by a particular sense of anger or outrage. As with human agents, we may feel betrayed by *objects* that cause harms of the sort they were intended to guard against, for example, an asthma medicine that constricts one's airway or a sunscreen that causes skin cancer.[31] One of the subjects in the vaccine study just mentioned explained his reluctance to vaccinate in these terms: "I feel that if I vaccinated my kid and he died I would be more responsible for his death than if I hadn't vaccinated him and he died . . ."

And, as in the case of omission bias, people's aversion to the risk of betrayal by a product may lead to seemingly suboptimal decisions. A noteworthy example comes from an experiment in which Jonathan Koehler and Andrew Gershoff gave participants two scenarios involving the role of air bags in fatal car accidents. The betrayal scenario was:

> Suppose that you are offered a choice between two equally priced cars: Car A and Car B. Car A is equipped with Air Bag A. Scientific crash tests indicate that there is a 2% chance that drivers of Car A who are in serious accidents will be killed due to the impact of the crash. Car B is equipped with Air Bag B. Scientific crash tests indicate that there is a 1% chance that drivers of Car B who are in serious accidents will die due to the impact of the crash. However, Car B may kill drivers who would not have died if they were driving Car A instead. Specifically, some drivers of Car B may die due to trauma caused by the force of the air bag deployment. Crash tests indicate that there is an additional one chance in 10,000 (0.01%) that someone who is in a serious accident in Car B will be killed due to air bag trauma.

In the nonbetrayal situation, the risk of death due to air bag deployment was replaced by a risk of death due to toxic fume inhalation from a damaged engine—not a betrayal of the safety device itself.

Participants were asked which car they would prefer and how strong their preference was. Most people in the nonbetrayal situation preferred Car B, which presents roughly half the probability of death (1.01 percent) than Car A (2 percent). However, most participants in the betrayal scenario were willing to double the likelihood of death to avoid betrayal. A typical explanation was, "I'd hate to

31. Jonathan J. Koehler and Andrew Gershoff, *Betrayal Aversion: When Agents of Protection Become Agents of Harm*, 90 Organizational Behavior and Human Decision Processes 244 (2003).

have the air bag that's supposed to save my life be the cause of its termination." The authors consider and reject the possibility that the phenomenon is a result of omission bias, since the participants were forced to actively choose between the two safety devices.

16.3.7 Judgments of Risk and Benefit

The presence or absence of evident benefits may mitigate or aggravate people's fear or outrage over a risk. But there also is evidence that people do not consider risk and benefit separately. Rather, the perception of the risk and benefit of an activity, product, or technology (e.g., alcohol, guns, food coloring, pesticides, nuclear power plants, and vaccines) are not independent but are in fact *inversely correlated*. The relationship seems related to the strength of positive or negative affect associated with that activity. Ali Alhakami and Paul Slovic write that "people base their judgments of an activity or a technology not only on what they *think* about it but also on what they *feel* about it. If they like an activity, they are moved to judge the risks as low and the benefits as high; if they dislike it, they tend to judge the opposite—high risk and low benefit."[32] In addition, "people operate under a strong need for consistency among their beliefs and attitudes. When people view an activity or technology as good, pressure toward consistency would lead them to judge its benefits as high and its risks as low, and vice versa for activities seen as bad."

The phenomenon is not limited to laypersons. When members of the British Toxicological Society were asked to give a quick intuitive affective rating of chemicals (e.g., benzene, aspirin, second-hand smoke) on a good-bad scale and then to judge the risk associated with a *very small exposure* to the chemical, negative affect was correlated with high risk and positive affect with low risk.[33]

Whether through this affective phenomenon or through a more cognitive process, the anxiety or outrage caused by a hazard may dissipate when people become aware of costs of eliminating it. For example, Howard Margolis relates that there was overwhelming popular sentiment for closing New York city schools that contained asbestos, but that once parents had to deal with the real inconveniences of closed schools, the perceived magnitude of the risk diminished.[34] Along the same lines, Cass Sunstein writes that Finland, whose economy depends heavily on Nokia, is not among the countries whose citizens and policy makers are concerned about the health effects of cell phones.[35] He notes

---

32. Ali Alhakami and Paul Slovic, *A Psychological Study of the Inverse Relationship Between Perceived Risk and Perceived Benefit*, 14 Risk Analysis 1085 (1994).

33. *See Affect Heuristic, supra.*

34. Howard Margolis, Dealing with Risk: Why the Public and the Experts Disagree on Environmental Issues 124–125 (Chicago: University of Chicago Press, 1998).

35. Cass Sunstein, Worst-Case Scenarios 219 (Cambridge: Harvard University Press, 2007) [hereafter, Worst Case Scenarios].

that when the U.S. Environmental Protection Agency (EPA) called attention to the toxic risks of a mining town's major industry, the citizens did not respond by taking precautions, but rather by demonizing the EPA.

16.3.8 Cultural Determinants of Perceptions of Risk

We noted earlier that different people may have different risk attitudes, whether as a result of different perceptions of risk, or views of the benefits, or appetites for risk-taking. In a review of Sunstein's *Laws of Fear: Beyond the Precautionary Principle*, Dan Kahan, Paul Slovic, Donald Braman, and John Gastil argue that "culture is prior to facts in societal disputes over risk":[36]

> Normatively, culture might be prior to facts in the sense that cultural values determine what significance individuals attach to the consequences of environmental regulation, gun control, drug criminalization, and the like. But more importantly, culture is *cognitively* prior to facts in the sense that cultural values shape what individuals *believe* the consequences of such policies to be. Individuals selectively credit and dismiss factual claims in a manner that supports their preferred vision of the good society.
>
> The priority of culture to fact is the organizing premise of the "cultural theory of risk." Associated most famously with the work of anthropologist Mary Douglas and political scientist Aaron Wildavsky, the cultural theory of risk links disputes over environmental and technological risks to clusters of values that form competing cultural worldviews—egalitarian, individualistic, and hierarchical. Egalitarians, on this account, are naturally sensitive to environmental hazards, the abatement of which justifies regulating commercial activities that produce social inequality. Individualists, in contrast, predictably dismiss claims of environmental risk as specious, in line with their commitment to the autonomy of markets and other private orderings. Hierarchists are similarly skeptical because they perceive warnings of imminent environmental catastrophe as threatening the competence of social and governmental elites.
>
> Although one can imagine alternative explanations for cultural variation in risk perceptions, cultural cognition offers a distinctively psychometric one. On this view, the impact of cultural worldviews is not an alternative to, but rather a vital component of, the various psychological and social mechanisms that determine perceptions of risk. These mechanisms, cultural cognition asserts, are *endogenous* to culture. That is, the direction in which they point risk perceptions depends on individuals' cultural values. . . .
>
> In sum, individuals adopt stances toward risks that express their commitment to the values integral to their preferred ways of life.

36. Dan M. Kahan, Paul Slovic, Donald Braman, and John Gastil, *Fear of Democracy:A Cultural Evaluation of Sunstein on Risk*, 119 Harv. L. Rev. 1071 (2006).

Kahan, Slovic, et al. criticize Sunstein for, in effect, privileging experts' perceptions of risk over those of laypersons because he believes that laypersons are more prone to the cognitive and affective biases described in this and the preceding chapters. The critics doubt that policies concerning major environmental and other issues involving risk can be adequately addressed only through cost-benefit, or expected value, analysis.

Our own view is that issues of "cultural cognition" do play a role in people's perception of risk and that it is often difficult to separate cognitive and affective biases from an individual's values and tastes in determining his or her risk preferences. However, as Sunstein notes in a response to his critics, most of the risks that we face involve rather quotidian issues rather than divisive cultural and political issues.[37]

16.4 RISK VS. UNCERTAINTY (OR AMBIGUITY)

16.4.1 The Concept and Psychology of Uncertainty

The examples in Chapter 15 and thus far in this chapter deal with known probabilities: Rachlinski's litigants were told that they had a 50 percent chance of winning or losing; the physicians in the medical hypothetical knew the risks of particular treatments. But the probabilities attending most real-world decisions do not come nearly so specified. In many cases, decision makers lack the data needed to make estimates based on frequentist statistics, and are relegated to one-off guesses where not even base rates are well known. Moreover, even when presented with frequentist data, a real-world decision maker may have reason to question their validity because of sample size, bias, collection methods, or other factors.

Drawing on an important paper by Frank Knight,[38] the economic literature distinguishes between a *risk* (known probability) and *uncertainty* (unknown probability). In a review of the literature, the psychologists Deborah Frisch and Jonathan Baron use the word *ambiguity* as a synonym for *uncertainty*, defining ambiguity as the subjective experience of missing information.[39]

Regardless of their risk preferences, people tend to be averse to uncertainty, or ambiguity. Indeed, *Ellsberg's Paradox*[40] demonstrates how uncertainty aversion leads to a violation of the cancellation principle of expected utility theory: a choice between two alternatives should depend only on how those alternatives differ, and not on any factor they have in common.

---

37. Cass Sunstein, *Misfearing*, 119 HARV. L. REV. 1110 (2006).

38. FRANK HYNEMAN KNIGHT, RISK, UNCERTAINTY, AND PROFIT (Boston: Houghton Mifflin, 1921).

39. Deborah Frisch and Jonathan Baron, *Ambiguity and Rationality*, 1 J. BEHAVIORAL DECISION MAKING 149 (1988).

40. The paradox was documented by the economist Daniel Ellsberg. The following text is taken from http://en.wikipedia.org/wiki/Ellsberg_paradox.

Suppose you have an urn containing thirty red balls and sixty other balls that are either black or yellow. You don't know how many black or yellow balls there are, but you know that the total number of black balls plus the total number of yellow equals sixty. The balls are well mixed so that each individual ball is as likely to be drawn as any other. You are now given a choice between two gambles, as shown in Table 16.2a.

TABLE 16.2A ELLSBERG'S PARADOX: GAMBLES A AND B

Gamble A	Gamble B
You receive $100 if you draw a red ball	You receive $100 if you draw a black ball

Also you are given the choice between these two gambles (in a different draw from the same urn), as shown in Table 16.2b.

TABLE 16.2B ELLSBERG'S PARADOX: GAMBLES C AND D

Gamble C	Gamble D
You receive $100 if you draw a red or yellow ball	You receive $100 if you draw a black or yellow ball

Expected utility theory holds that you should prefer Gamble A to Gamble B if, and only if, you believe that drawing a red ball is more likely than drawing a black ball. Thus, there would be no clear preference between the choices if you thought that a red ball was as likely as a black ball. Similarly it follows that you will prefer Gamble C to Gamble D if, and only if, you believe that drawing a red or yellow ball is more likely than drawing a black or yellow ball. If drawing a red ball is more likely than drawing a black ball, then drawing a red or yellow ball is also more likely than drawing a black or yellow ball. So, if you prefer Gamble A to Gamble B, it follows that you will also prefer Gamble C to Gamble D. And, if instead that you prefer Gamble D to Gamble C, it follows that you will also prefer Gamble B to Gamble A. However, most people prefer Gamble A to Gamble B and Gamble D to Gamble C.

Why is this paradoxical—or at least a logical error? A preference for Gamble A to B implies that you believe that there are fewer black balls than red balls – i.e., fewer than 30 black balls, which entails more than thirty yellow balls. A preference for Gamble D to C implies that you believe that there are more black balls than red balls. So a preference for A and D implies that you believe the number of black balls is less than the number of red balls *and* more than the number of red balls.

Most policy and legal decisions must be made in conditions of uncertainty rather than risk. To illustrate the difference in a legal context, consider the difference of a litigant being informed: (1) "Based on a database of jury verdicts and his extensive experience, your lawyer believes that there's a 50 percent chance of a judgment in your favor," or (2) "After much hesitation, your lawyer's best guess is a 50 percent chance; but given the nature of the case, he feels very uneasy about providing you with a number."[41]

In either set of choices, one's best guess is that the probability is 0.5. But (except at low probabilities) most people tend to be averse to the second uncertain, or ambiguous, option. Indeed, people often make different choices in the two situations.[42] For example, given a fifty–fifty chance of winning where the odds are pretty well known, most defendants follow the predictions of prospect theory and incur the risk of litigating. Given the same odds of winning in the uncertainty situation, a majority of defendants manifest ambiguity aversion and choose to settle.[43]

Ambiguity aversion (correctly) predicts that someone making investment decisions from scratch would prefer to buy securities whose recent performance was known rather than unknown. Thus, when experimental subjects were given a choice between:

- the *unambiguous option* of purchasing securities which during the past ninety days had gone up thirty times, down thirty times, and remained the same thirty times, and
- the *ambiguous option* of purchasing securities which had remained the same thirty times in the past ninety days, with no information about what happened the other sixty days,

they opted for the former. But when they were already endowed with the ambiguous option, they preferred to hold onto it rather than exchange it for the unambiguous one.[44]

---

41. *Cf.* Robin Hogarth and Howard Kunreuther, *Decision Making Under Uncertainty: The Effects of Role and Ambiguity*, *in* DECISION MAKING AND LEADERSHIP 189 (Frank Heller, ed., New York: Cambridge University Press, 1992).

42. Noting that even when frequentist statistics cannot produce "objective" probabilities, people often assign subjective probabilities to events, some commentators have questioned whether uncertainty actually exists. WORST-CASE SCENARIOS 159 ff. But when the range of one's subjective estimate of the probability of an event occurring is sufficiently large, assigning a numerical probability seems pointless.

43. Hogarth and Kunreuther, *supra*. It appears that, in making judgments under uncertainty a decision maker anchors on the given probability, but then adjusts the estimate based on imagining other values it might have.

44. Merce Roca, Robin M. Hogarth, and A. John Maule, *Ambiguity Seeking as a Result of the Status Quo Bias*, 32 JOURNAL OF RISK AND UNCERTAINTY 175 (2006).

Ambiguity aversion may be based on several factors:

- in situations of ambiguity, an opponent may have information not available to you;
- because the dispersion of a series of ambiguous gambles is greater than that of a series of gambles with known risks, a series of ambiguous gambles (with the identical missing information) is more volatile that a series of nonambiguous gambles;
- in ambiguous situations, a decision maker might wait and obtain more information; he may regret not having obtained the missing information, or may be blamed by others for not obtaining it.

For these reasons, people may develop a heuristic that disfavors ambiguous gambles.

The availability heuristic may combine with the phenomenon of ambiguity aversion. Referring to the Washington, D.C. snipers, Kip Viscusi suggests that this is a "new sort of risk—and people do not know how to evaluate something they have never seen before. There has never been a serial killer like the sniper before. . . . The sniper has killed randomly at a distance. This means that no one in the Washington area can give any reason why he or she should not be the next victim."[45]

16.4.2 The Principle of Continuity (or Exchange), Maximin, and "Robust Satisficing"

The principle of continuity, an axiom of expected utility theory relevant to decision making under risk is that an individual has some certainty equivalent for any lottery. To put it formally: Suppose A, B, and C are three prospects (possible outcomes), and the decision maker prefers A to B, and prefers B to C. The axiom provides that there must be some probability p such that the decision maker is indifferent between choosing either prospect B with certainty or a lottery in which prospect A occurs with probability p, or prospect C occurs with probability $1-p$. We call this probability p a preference probability, and we call B the certainty equivalent of the A-C lottery.

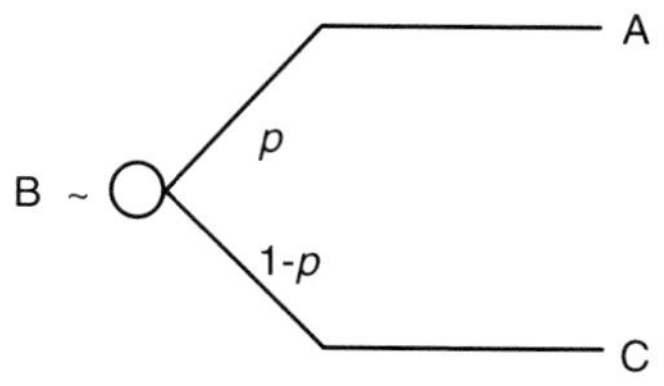

FIGURE 16.2 CERTAINTY EQUIVALENT OF A LOTTERY.

45. THE ECONOMIST, Oct. 19, 2002.

But, citing the writing of Peter Vallentyne, Larry Temkin writes:[46]

> Many reject continuity in cases like the following. Consider three possible outcomes. In B one has a full rich life; in A, a full rich life, with an extra dollar of income; in C, a life of excruciating pain and misery. Vallentyne denies that there is any p such that he ought, rationally, to be indifferent between the prospect of either A with a probability p or C with a probability 1-p.
>
> Examples like Vallentyne's are often thought to trade on our attitudes regarding certainty and risk. But the issue is *not* merely one of certainty versus risk. People do not generally mind risking a certain outcome for a slightly better outcome if the downside risk is small; what they mind is risking a certain outcome for a slightly better one if the downside risk is high. What seems crazy, in Vallentyne's example, is trading the *certainty* of a *full rich life* for the prospect of a *slightly* better one, when doing so means risking—however minimally—a life of pain and misery.

While violating an axiom of expected utility theory, the decision maker in Vallentyne's example may be acting consistently with the principle of *maximin*, which counsels: "choose the policy with the best worst-case outcome." One might think of Pascal's Wager —which addresses a situation of uncertainty or ambiguity rather than of specifiable known risk—in similar terms. Pascal argued against atheism on the ground that even though one couldn't know in advance whether those who believe in God will be rewarded in the afterlife and those who don't will burn perpetually in hell, it was rational to believe since believing had no present costs.

Although the maximin principle captures a strong intuition, it is difficult to know when to apply it. Often, eliminating one worst-case outcome simply reveals another one.[47]

In Section 1.6.2, we introduced the notion of *satisficing*—settling for a good enough rather than optimal outcome when the informational and cognitive costs of making a decision are too high. A recent paper by Yakov Ben Haim, Cliff Dasco, and Barry Schwartz proposes a normative model of *robust satisficing*[48] for decision making in conditions of severe uncertainty. In contrast to expected utility theory, robust satisficing does not seek to maximize expected utility. And in contrast to maximin, robust satisficing does not try to guard against the "worst-case scenario." Rather, it seeks to give the decision maker the best chance of enjoying a good enough outcome.

---

46. Larry S. Temkin, *Weighing Goods: Some Questions and Comments*, 23 PHIL. & PUBLIC AFFAIRS 350 (1994).

47. *See* WORST-CASE SCENARIOS, *supra*.

48. Yakov Ben Haim, Cliff Dasco, and Barry Schwartz, "What Makes a Good Decision? Robust Satisficing as a Normative Standard of Rational Decision Making" (unpublished paper 2009).

Suppose that you are considering a number of entry-level job offers in a large government agency, and that your criteria include (1) salary and other benefits, (2) the quality of city life, (3) whether the work will be interesting and fulfilling, and (4) the quality of support and mentorship you will receive. You can ascertain the first two within a small margin of error, but the latter two are deeply uncertain: they depend on what department or division you will be assigned to and on the particular people you work for, which cannot be known in advance. Ben Haim et al. propose that rather than attempting to determine which decision course will yield the highest expected value, you should identify a threshold of a satisfactory, or "good enough," outcome and choose the job that is most robust to uncertainty—that is most likely to produce a satisfactory outcome. Similarly, robust satisficing would be a useful decision-making strategy for a man presented with a choice of treatments for prostate cancer, which have different chances of curing the cancer and different likely side effects. Even if some of these probabilities can be specified, your prediction of how side effects will affect your future wellbeing fall into the realm of uncertainty.

The mathematics of robust satisficing is pretty complicated—more so than for expected utility. Ben Haim, Dasco, and Schwartz suggest these (satisficing) rules of thumb:

- Ask yourself what you need to achieve in order to be happy or satisfied with the outcome of the decision. . . . Remember that high aspirations are more vulnerable to error than modest ones.
- Distinguish between two very different attributes of each option. One attribute of an option, which we call its nominal outcome, is the estimate of the outcome of that option based on your best data and understanding. . . . The other attribute of an option, called its *robustness,* is the degree of immunity of the outcome to error in your estimates and understanding. The robustness is a nonprobabilistic assessment of immunity to error. Nonetheless, robustness may assess immunity to error in assessments of probabilities. An option may be quite attractive based on your current understanding (good nominal outcome), but may lead to highly undesirable results due to only small errors (low robustness). Alternatively, an option may be both nominally very attractive and very robust to error. Or, an option may nominally be only moderately attractive, but it may be very robust to error. These two attributes—nominal outcome and robustness—are different and not correlated with one another.
- Evaluate the nominal outcome of each option. This is relatively easy, since you can ignore uncertainty and assume that your data and understanding are correct. Rank the options from highest to lowest nominal outcome.
- Evaluate the robustness of each option for the particular quality of outcome that you identified in the first step. This is more difficult, since you must ask:

How wrong can I be and still have the option yield a satisfactory outcome? Listing contingencies (this could go wrong, that could go wrong, etc.) is one approach. . . . Rank the options from highest to lowest robustness.

- Choose the most robust option. If the rankings according to nominal outcome and robustness agree, then the most robust option will also be the nominally most attractive option. If the rankings according to nominal outcome and robustness disagree, then the most robust option may differ from the nominally most attractive option.
- Step back and look carefully at your analysis. Does it make sense? . . . Ask if your thought process fits together coherently, if it uses all relevant information, if it avoids major assumptions or leaps of faith, and if it is free of considerations that are not explicitly included.

16.5 COMPLEXITIES OF EVALUATING RISKS

16.5.1 Evaluability and Framing Redux

Recall the issues of *evaluability* mentioned in Section 13.3.1. Howard Kunreuther and his coauthors did a series of experiments to explore people's sensitivities to significant differences in low probability risks of high consequence events.[49] Participants were asked to assess the relative riskiness of chemical plants that had a 1/100,000, a 1/1 million, or a 1/10 million chance of releasing toxic gases. The questions asked were: (1) How serious a risk would the plant pose to the residents' health and safety? and (2) How close they would be willing to live to the plant?

In the within-subjects group, participants who were asked the questions about all three plants *simultaneously* provided assessments of riskiness commensurate with the probabilities. In other words, the incremental differences in their three responses to the two questions were roughly equal to the incremental differences between the three proposed probabilities. However, in a between-subjects experiment, three separate groups of participants were respectively shown each of the three plants. Here there was no statistically significant difference in their mean risk assessments; the feelings evoked by the images of the power plants overwhelmed the probabilities, and the participants based their risk assessments almost entirely on their emotional responses to the images.[50]

---

49. Howard Kunreuther, Nathan Novemsky, and Daniel Kahneman, *Making Low Probabilities Useful*, 23 J. RISK & UNCERTAINTY 103 (2001).

50. Hypothesizing that the chemical plant risks would be more evaluable if participants were able to compare them to more familiar risks, like a car accident, the experimenters told subjects that the probability of injury in a car accident was 1/6000 per year and asked them to evaluate a 1/650, 1/6300, and 1/68,000 chance of the plant's release of toxics. The differences among the groups were still negligible. However, when subjects

One way in which we evaluate unfamiliar risks is to compare them to risks that are more familiar. Hypothesizing that the chemical plant risks would be more evaluable if people were able to compare them to more familiar risks, like a car accident, the experimenters told participants that the probability of injury in a car accident was 1/6000 per year and asked them to evaluate a 1/650, 1/6300, and 1/68,000 chance of the plant's release of toxics. The differences among the groups were negligible. However, when subjects were given scenarios describing the contexts in which car accidents happened with relatively and low and high probabilities (1/5900 chance of accident on icy mountain roads; 1/66,000 on flat desert highways), the differences in assessing the risks from the plant were significant. The scenarios made the risks more evaluable than the statistics alone. "There needs to be fairly rich context information available for people to be able to judge differences between low probability events. In particular, people need comparisons of risk that are located on the probability scale and evoke people's own feelings of risk."[51]

People sometimes use "natural" levels of risk as a baseline for comparison. For example, in Peter Sandman's study of high outrage/low risk (radon) and low outrage/high risk (nuclear waste) situations described in Section 16.3.1, participants were insensitive to changes in risk levels phrased in terms such as: "For every 1000 people exposed to this level of radiation over a lifetime, 40 more of them would get lung cancer than if they were not exposed." But they were highly sensitive to changes based on normal background radiation, e.g.: "The radiation in your home is 20 times greater than the average outdoor background level." When a risk adds only a very small percentage to normal background, people believe that it is not too serious; when it adds a large multiple of normal background, they conclude that it is quite serious. This point of comparison likely draws on the intuition (noted earlier) that naturally caused conditions are not harmful. The problem, as the experimenters note, is that

> [f]or some hazards, normal background levels are sufficient to constitute a meaningful health risk, and even a small increment would be unwise if it were preventable. For other hazards, the risk due to normal background exposure is negligible, and an exposure many times the background level would

---

were given scenarios describing the contexts in which car accidents happened with relatively and low and high probabilities (1/5900 chance of accident on icy mountain roads; 1/66,000 on flat desert highways), the differences were significant. The scenarios made the risks more evaluable than the statistics alone. "There needs to be fairly rich context information available for people to be able to judge differences between low probability events. In particular, people need comparisons of risk that are located on the probability scale and evoke people's own feelings of risk." Kunreuther, et al., supra.

51. Michael Jones Lee and Graham Loomis, *Private Values and Public Policy*, *in* Elke Weber, Jonathan Baron, and Graham Loomis, Conflict and Tradeoffs in Decision Making 205 (Cambridge, UK: Cambridge University Press, 2001).

still be negligible. Thus, comparisons to background can give misleading impressions contrary to actual risk magnitudes.

A risk can seem greater or smaller based on the *period* during which it is framed. For example, people who are not motivated to wear seat belts to avoid a 0.00001 chance of a serious accident per car trip are more likely to wear one when informed of a 0.33 chance over a fifty-year lifetime of driving.[52]

16.5.2 Cognitive and Affective Processing of Probabilities

In Section 14.6, we mentioned that, when contemplating a harm that instills an affective response (e.g., birds dying because of an oil spill), people may abandon the quantitative evaluation of costs and benefits, and their willingness to pay (WTP) to avoid the harm may become orthogonal to the scope of its harm. More generally, Christopher Hsee and Yuval Rottenstreich note that *valuation by calculation* and *valuation by feeling* can produce quite different results.[53] A person may respond to the same event with one or the other valuation system, depending on how it is framed: consider the difference between statistics about the number of birds at risk and a photo of a bird covered with oil slick.

Jeremy Blumenthal summarizes an interesting line of research indicating that people's affective response to risk may depend on whether the same probability is described with larger or smaller numbers:

> People behave as though certain low-probability events are less probable when represented by equivalent ratios of smaller numbers (1 in 10) than of larger numbers (10 in 100). That is, people saw the likelihood of Event X as greater when the probability was expressed as a 10 in 100 chance than when it was expressed as 1 in 10, and behaved accordingly. Even more striking, . . . despite objective information that Event X had, for instance, a 7 out of 100 chance of occurring versus a 1 in 10 chance, respondents chose and behaved as though the former were more likely. Respondents explained that rationally and objectively, they understood that the likelihood was lower; emotionally and subjectively, however, they felt they had a better chance when the absolute likelihood appeared higher (i.e., 7 chances rather than 1), and thus actually chose as though they had a better chance of obtaining X under those circumstances.[54]

---

52. Paul Slovic, Baruch Fischhoff, and Sara Lichtenstein, *Accident Probabilities and Seat Belt Usage: A Psychological Perspective*, 10 Accident Analysis and Prevention 281 (1978).

53. Christopher K. Hsee and Yuval Rottenstreich, *Music, Pandas, and Muggers: On the Affective Psychology of Value*, 133 J. Experimental Psychol.: Gen. 23, 23–24 (2004).

54. Jeremy A. Blumenthal, *Emotional Paternalism*, 35 Fla. St. U. L. Rev. 1, 23 (2007), *discussing* Veronika Denes-Raj and Seymour Epstein, *Conflict Between Intuitive and Rational Processing: When People Behave Against Their Better Judgment*, 66 J. Personality & Soc. Psychol. 819, 823 (1994); Seymour Epstein and Rosemary Pacini, *Some Basic Issues Regarding Dual-Process Theories from the Perspective of Cognitive-Experiential Self-Theory*, *in*

People also have different perceptions of risks described as *probabilities* or *frequencies*.[55] Paul Slovic and his colleagues asked experienced forensic psychologists and psychiatrists to assess the likelihood that a mental patient would commit an act of violence within six months after being discharged from the hospital.[56] One group of participants was given an expert's prior assessment of the risk of violence phrased in terms of *probabilities*, e.g., "patients similar to Mr. Jones are estimated to have a 20 percent chance of committing an act of violence." Another group was given the same assessment phrased in terms of *relative frequencies*, e.g., "of every one hundred patients similar to Mr. Jones, twenty are estimated to commit an act of violence."

Of those given the data in terms of probabilities, only 21 percent refused to discharge the patient. Of those given the data in terms of relative frequencies, 41 percent refused to discharge the patient. Those given the probabilistic format had relatively benign images of the patient, while those given the frequentistic format conjured up frightening images of violent patients. "These affect-laden images likely induced greater perceptions of risk in responsive to the relative-frequency frames."[57] Along the same lines, a disease that kills 1,286 people out of every 10,000 was judged more dangerous than one that kills 24.14 percent of the population![58]

16.5.3 Worry and Probability Neglect

Given the difficulties of evaluability, people may sometimes ignore probabilities because they are just too difficult to reckon, or (given boundedly rational actors) just not worth their attention. Thus, a study of why people don't insure against large, low-probability losses suggests that the costs of calculating the appropriate premium are too high.[59] And a study of risky business decisions suggests that managers do not even ask for data on the probability of outcomes.[60]

DUAL-PROCESS THEORIES IN SOCIAL PSYCHOLOGY 462 (Shelly Chaiken and Yaacov Trope eds., 1999).

55. Recall the suggestion in Section 8.6.1 that describing events in terms of frequencies rather than probabilities could, under some circumstances, improve individuals' intuitive Bayesian analysis.

56. Slovic, Monahan, and MacGregor, Violence risk assessment and risk communication: The *Effects of Using Actual Cases, Providing Instruction, and Employing Probability Versus Frequency Formats*, 24 LAW HUM BEHAV. 271–96 (2000).

57. *Affect Heuristic, supra.*

58. Kimihiko Yamagishi, *When a 12.86% Mortality Is More Dangerous than 24.14%: Implications for Risk Communication*, 11 APPLIED COGNITIVE PSYCHOLOGY, 495 (1997).

59. Howard Kunreuther and Mark Pauly, *Neglecting Disaster: Why Don't People Insure Against Large Losses*, 28 J. RISK AND UNCERTAINTY 5 (2004).

60. Oswald Hoberet al., *Active Information Search and Complete Information Presentation*, 95 ACTA PSYCHOLOGICA 15 (1997).

Information costs aside, a variety of decisions—from investments to willingness to insure against losses—seem to be based more on a subjective sense of "worry" or "concern" than on a probabilistic assessment of gains and losses.[61] Indeed, in trying to avoid catastrophic risks, such as climate change, people may be prone to what Elke Weber terms "single action bias": being satisfied with taking only one action that mitigates their worry rather than responding with a

Insurance as Protection Against Worry

Boone's older brother, Pete, is orienting Boone for his first day on the job at as an insurance claim adjuster.

> "These are claims," his older brother explained, grabbing a stack of paper-clipped and clamped wads of papers and forms from a bin outside the cubicle marked IN. "Your job is to deny them."
>
> "I see," Boone had said. "You mean, I sort through the claims and deny all the fraudulent ones, right?"
>
> His brother implored heaven for patience with a roll of his eyes, then sighed a gust of wintry disgust. "The fraudulent claims were picked out downstairs by high school graduates and denied three months ago. Anybody can deny a fraudulent claim. You're a college graduate. Your job is to find a way to deny legitimate claims. . . .
>
> "People who file claims believe that money will make them happy and will somehow compensate them for their losses. This idea—that money makes misfortune easier to bear—is an illusion that can only be enjoyed by those who have not suffered an actual loss.
>
> "The most terrifying thing about life is knowing that, at any moment, a freak accident, violence, mayhem, a psychotic break, an addiction, a heart attack, a sexually transmitted disease, cancer, an earthquake, or some other act of God, or worse, can take all of your happiness away from you in the time

61. Elke U. Weber and Christopher Hsee, *Cross-Cultural Differences in Risk Perception, But Cross-Cultural Similarities in Attitudes Towards Perceived Risk*, 44 MANAGEMENT SCIENCE 1205 (1998); Ch. Schade, H. Kunreuther, and K.P. Kaas (2002), "Low-Probability Insurance Decisions: The Role of Concern," Discussion Paper Number 23, SFB 373, Humboldt-Universität zu Berlin/Wharton Risk Center Working Paper Number 02-10-HK, Wharton School, University of Pennsylvania, USA; Paul Slovic, Baruch Fischhoff, and Sarah Lichtenstein, *Facts and Fears: Understanding Perceived Risk*, *in* SOCIETAL RISK ASSESSMENT: HOW SAFE IS SAFE ENOUGH? 181 (R. Schwing and W. A. Albers, Jr., eds., 1980).

it takes you to pick up the phone and get the news. That's why people buy insurance, because they think it will protect them from catastrophes.

"But we are in the insurance business," said Pete. . . . "We *know* there is no protection from catastrophes. No matter what you do, there's always a chance that a catastrophe will come along, tear your heart out of your chest, and rub it in your face.

"When you're crawling on the bathroom floor sick with grief. . ., wondering why God failed to give you the courage to kill yourself, a big check from the insurance company looks like a swatch of wallpaper. You're in a place money can't reach.

"So, insurance only works if catastrophe does *not* strike. . . . We don't sell protection. We sell peace of mind. For a premium, we agree to give the consumer the illusion that money will protect him from every possible foreseeable catastrophe. Once the premium is paid and before catastrophe strikes, the consumer is free to wallow in the illusion that if something terrible happens money will take the sting out of it. When a catastrophe actually occurs, the illusion is shattered and there's nothing to be done but drag yourself out of bed every morning and get on with your life."

"But if what you say is true," asked Boone, "then you are charging people thousands of dollars for . . . an illusion."

"Exactly," said Pete. "Peace of mind. The money is irrelevant. You probably subscribe to the notion that insurance is a way to pool risk and share liability. You think premiums should be based upon risk. Nothing could be more wrong. Premiums should be based upon line thirty-one of your federal tax return, adjusted gross income. Our objective is to charge the insured just enough to make it hurt. We are looking for the financial pain threshold, because only when it hurts does the insured really believe that he is obtaining something of value, and, as I've shown, he is indeed obtaining peace of mind for nothing more than money."

RICHARD DOOLING, WHITE MAN'S GRAVE 25–27 (1994)

set of actions that would more effectively reduce the risk.[62] As Joseph Conrad wrote in *Nostromo*, "Action is consolatory. It is the enemy of thought and the friend of flattering illusions."

62. Elke Weber, *Perception and Expectation of Climate Change: Precondition for Economic and Technological Adaptation*, *in* ENVIRONMENT, ETHICS, AND BEHAVIOR: THE PSYCHOLOGY OF ENVIRONMENTAL VALUATION AND DEGRADATION (M. H. Bazerman, D. M. Messick, A. E. Tenbrunsel, and K. A. Wade-Benzoni eds., 1997).

The stronger the emotions, the more people tend to greatly underweight probabilities or to ignore them altogether and focus only on the horrific, worst case outcome. Cass Sunstein has coined the term *probability neglect* to describe people's departure "from the normative theory of rationality in giving excessive weight to low-probability outcomes when the stakes are high" and giving low-probability outcomes no weight at all when the risks are not vivid.

The phenomenon is illustrated by an experiment, based on an actual problem that faced the Environmental Protection Agency. Sunstein asked law students to indicate their willingness to pay (WTP) to reduce levels of arsenic in drinking water to eliminate

- a cancer risk of 1/1,000,000;
- a cancer risk of 1/100,000;
- a cancer risk of 1/1,000,000 where the cancer was described in vividly gruesome terms;
- a cancer risk of 1/100,000 also described in gruesome terms.

When given the unemotional description, people's WTP increased significantly as the probability of contracting cancer increased. Merely describing the cancer in gruesome terms doubled people's WTP to avoid the 1/1,000,000 risk, but the tenfold increase of gruesome cancer risk did not greatly increase WTP. Sunstein argues that probability neglect does not involve misestimating probabilities based on their vividness or availability. Rather, emotion essentially swamps considerations of probability.[63]

Laypersons' intuitions about toxicology also manifest probability neglect. Nancy Kraus, Torbjörn Malmfors, and Paul Slovic compared the basic attitudes of professionals and laypersons toward toxic risks.[64] A core assumption of toxicology is that "the dose makes the poison," meaning that there is a positive correlation between the size of the dose and the likelihood of harm and that some chemicals that are deadly in high concentrations are harmless in small amounts. However, this view is not shared by the layperson—the "intuitive toxicologist"—who tends to believe that "if large exposures to a chemical are harmful, then small exposures are also harmful." Specifically, laypersons believe:

- any exposure to a toxic chemical makes one likely to suffer adverse health effects;
- any exposure to a carcinogen makes one likely to get cancer;
- the fact of exposure to a pesticide is the critical concern, rather than the amount of exposure;

63. Laws of Fear 77–79, 81.

64. Nancy Kraus, Torbjörn Malmfors, and Paul Slovic, *Intuitive Toxicology: Expert and Lay Judgments of Chemical Risks*, 12 Risk Analysis 215–232 (1992).

- reducing the concentration of a possibly harmful chemical in a city's drinking water would not reduce the danger associated with drinking that water;
- there is no safe level of exposure to a cancer-causing agent.

Although not a majority view, a high percentage of laypersons sampled believed that they should do everything possible to avoid contact with chemicals and chemical products (40.0 percent) and believed that all use of prescription drugs (17.2 percent) and chemicals (29.3 percent) must be risk-free. Thirty percent of laypersons did *not* agree that a 1 in 10 million lifetime risk of cancer from exposure to a chemical was too small to worry about.

The researchers speculate that the concept of *contagion* may account for these attitudes. Anthropologists describe

> the belief, widespread in many cultures, that things that have been in contact with each other may influence each other through transfer of some of their properties via an "essence." Thus, "once in contact, always in contact," even if that contact (exposure) is brief. . . . [E]ven a minute amount of a toxic substance in one's food will be seen as imparting toxicity to the food; any amount of a carcinogenic substance will impart carcinogenicity, and so forth. The "essence of harm" that is contagious is typically referred to as contamination. Being contaminated clearly has an all-or-none quality to it—like being alive or pregnant. . . . This all-or-none quality irrespective of the degree of exposure is evident in the observation by Erikson that: "To be exposed to radiation or other toxins . . . is to be contaminated in some deep and lasting way, to feel dirtied, tainted, corrupted." A contagion or contamination model is obviously very different from the scientist's model of how contact with a chemical induces carcinogenesis or other adverse effects. Further examination of the concepts of contagion and contamination may help us better understand the origins of the public's concerns about very small exposures to chemicals.[65]

The intuitive toxicologist's tendency to view a situation as either safe or unsafe is a form of probability neglect that extends beyond toxics and fear of contagion. Cass Sunstein writes:

> With respect to the decision whether to insure against low-probability hazards, people show bimodal responses. When a risk probability is below a certain threshold, people treat the risk as essentially zero and are willing to pay little or nothing for insurance in the event of loss. But when the risk probability is above a certain level, people are willing to pay a significant amount for insurance, indeed an amount that greatly exceeds the expected value of the risk.

65. Paul Slovic, "If Hormesis Exists . . . Implications for Risk Perception and Communication," http://www.belleonline.com/newsletters/volume7/vol7-1/ifhormesisexists.html. *See also* Paul Rozin and Carol Nemeroff, *Sympathetic Magical Thinking: The Contagion and Similarity "Heuristics," in* HEURISTICS AND BIASES, *supra*.

Such bimodal responses provide further support for the intuitive suggestion that some risks are simply "off-screen," whereas others, statistically not much larger, can come "on-screen" and produce behavioral changes.[66]

The tendency to ignore some low-probability risks is partly due to the difficulty of assessing them. As Sunstein notes, "a decision to disregard low-level risks is far from irrational, even if it is based in whole or in part on emotions; we lack the information that would permit fine-grained risk judgments, and when the probability really is low, it may be sensible to treat it as if it were zero."[67] We may also ignore risks because of our tendency to be unrealistically optimistic—especially about our own futures[68]—and also for peace of mind. As Kai Erickson writes: "One of the bargains men make with one another in order to maintain their sanity is to share an illusion that they are safe, even when the physical evidence in the world around them does not seem to warrant that conclusion."[69]

Preserving sanity through illusion can have its costs, though. Consider the complacency about airline security before September 11, 2001, and the muted reception given the January 31, 2001, report of the U.S. Commission on National Security, co-chaired by former Senators Gary Hart and Warren Rudman, which warned of America's vulnerability to terrorist attacks. The absence of availability may lull people into complacency: What is out of sight is effectively out of mind.[70]

16.5.4 Anchoring and Risk

Given its pervasiveness, it is not surprising that the anchoring phenomenon discussed in Section 10.1 also affects decision making involving risks. In a study of people's WTP to reduce the annual risk of motor vehicle deaths, Michael Jones-Lee and Graham Loomis presented participants with a risk of a certain magnitude and asked if they were willing to pay a particular monetary amount to avoid the risk. If they were willing to pay, the amount was increased in increments until they were unwilling. One group was given the initial amount of £25 and another £75. Not only was the WTP different for the two groups: the minimum WTP for the £75 group was higher than the maximum WTP of the £25 group.[71]

---

66. Cass Sunstein, *Probability Neglect: Emotions, Worst Cases, and Law*, 112 YALE L.J. 61, 75 (2002).

67. *Id.*

68. *See* Section 13.5. Bimodalism in this context may be a close cousin of the certainty effect, discussed above.

69. KAI ERIKSON, EVERYTHING IN ITS PATH: DESTRUCTION OF COMMUNITY IN THE BUFFALO CREEK FLOOD 234 (1976). *See also* George Akerlof and William Dickens, *The Economic Consequences of Cognitive Dissonance*, *in* GEORGE AKERLOF, AN ECONOMIC THEORIST'S BOOK OF TALES 123, 124–28 (1984).

70. Paul Slovic, Baruch Fischhoff, and Sarah Lichtenstein, *Rating the Risks*, 21 Environment 14 (1979).

71. Michael Jones Lee and Graham Loomis, *Private Values and Public Policy*, *supra*.

16.6 COST-BENEFIT ANALYSIS CONCLUDED

The preceding discussions have implications for the practice of cost-benefit analysis surveyed in Section 12.3.

16.6.1 Assessing Risks

The concept of willingness to pay (WTP) assumes not only that individuals are the best judges of their own welfare, but that they are able to assess costs, benefits, and risks. However, we have seen that people may have difficulty estimating the risks of low-probability events (such as a 1/100,000 risk of cancer), and thus that they might underestimate the potential gains of a regulation, yielding a low WTP value.

16.6.2 Not All Risks Are Equal

Most importantly, people do not view all statistically identical risks in the same way. Risks that are uncontrollable, dreaded, and potentially catastrophic produce a much higher WTP to avoid them than other risks.[72] Cass Sunstein notes that "a 1/100,000 risk of dying in a workplace accident might well produce a different WTP from a 1/100,000 risk of dying of cancer from air pollution, from a 1/100,000 risk of dying in an airplane as a result of a terrorist attack, or from a from a 1/100,000 risk of dying as a result of defective snowmobile. [73] He notes:

> Many risks controlled by the EPA [e.g., cancer] are qualitatively different from the workplace risks that EPA has used to generate its value of a statistical life (VSL),[74] and it is possible that the dread of the suffering associated with cancer or AIDS might bring people to project higher WTPs for these illnesses. The "cancer premium"—people seem to have a special fear of cancer and appear willing to pay more to prevent a cancer death than a sudden unanticipated death—might be produced by the "dread" nature of cancer. It is well established that dreaded risks produced special social concern, holding the statistical risks constant.[75]

Similarly, Richard Revesz suggests that "the value of avoiding a death from an involuntary, carcinogenic risk should be estimated as four times as large as the value of avoiding an instantaneous workplace fatality."[76] These potential differences illustrate the weaknesses in basing WPT on revealed preference studies.

---

72. PERCEPTION OF RISK at 291.

73. LAWS OF FEAR 138.

74. *See* Section 12.2.3a.

75. *Id.*; Mark Kelman, "Saving Lives, Saving from Death, Saving from Dying: Reflections on 'Over-valuing' Identifable Victims" (unpublished paper 2008).

76. *See* Richard L. Revesz, *Environmental Regulation, Cost-Benefit Analysis, and the Discounting of Human Lives*, 99 COLUM. L. REV. 941, 962–74 (1999).

Also, as mentioned earlier in this chapter, different people, communities, and age groups value and evaluate different risks differently from one another. Some people "show an intense aversion to risks that others treat with equanimity."[77]

16.6.3 Discounting for Dread

People generally prefer to experience benefits as soon as possible and to defer costs. But we sometimes prefer to hasten experiencing a bad event rather than dread its prospect over a period of time. How should one account for the costs of dread incurred throughout the years between someone's first exposure to an environmental or workplace risk (say, involving a carcinogen) and the ultimate manifestation of the disease? Richard Revesz argues that "any discounting of the adverse consequences of the risk during the latency period needs to be coupled with an *increase* in the estimate of these consequences as a result of dread."[78]

16.6.4 The Uncertain Risks of Catastrophic Harm

Catastrophic harms are ones that create tremendous and possibly irreversible losses for communities or civilizations. The losses may be material—as in the case of various worst-case outcomes of climate change or nuclear warfare, or of nanoparticles or a particle accelerator turning the world into gray goo.[79] Even when not of global magnitude, a community's or nation's economic and social fabric may be destroyed by tsunamis or earthquakes, or a terrorist attack. Because most catastrophic harms have a very small *n*—they occur very infrequently, if at all—their probability of occurrence is not susceptible to frequentist statistical analysis, and even subjectivist estimates are likely to be highly speculative. In other words, decision making concerning catastrophic harms takes place not under conditions of risk but of uncertainty.

Whether cost-benefit analysis (CBA) can adequately or appropriately address uncertain risks of catastrophic harms is a matter of lively and often acrimonious dispute, often centering around environmental issues.[80] Critics of CBA would replace it with a *precautionary principle* (PP), which counsels avoiding any steps that create a risk of harm. For example, the declaration following the 1998 Wingspread Conference on the Precautionary Principle stated: "When an activity raises threats of harm to human health or the environment, precautionary measures should be taken even if some cause and effects relationships are not established scientifically. In this context the proponent of the activity rather than

---

77. *Id.* 131.

78. Richard L. Revesz and Michael A. Livermore, Retaking Rationality: How Cost-Benefit Analysis Can Better Protect the Environment and Our Health 104 (New York: Oxford University Press, 2008).

79. *See, e.g.*, Richard A. Posner, Catastrophe: Risk and Response (2004).http://scholarship.law.cornell.edu/lsrp_papers/50

80. *See generally* Douglas A. Kysar, *It Might Have Been: Risk, Precaution, and Opportunity Costs*, J. Land Use & Envtl. L. 1 (2006).

the public, should bear the burden of proof."[81] There are many other versions of the PP, but they all share the common element that it is worth high social opportunity costs to prevent the possibility of catastrophic harm.

In *Worst-Case Scenarios*, Cass Sunstein undertakes an extensive critique of the PP, arguing that it is extremely vague, prone to biases of the sort described in this book, and likely to be counterproductive to human welfare. Sunstein makes these observations, among others:

- The PP makes a distinction between action and inaction that is at best orthogonal to expected value. For example, the PP is frequently invoked to halt the production of foods using genetically modified organizations, but not to mobilize research and development to prevent a large meteor from hitting the earth.
- The PP is invoked against particularly salient risks, based on the availability heuristic, but not against risks that are not on people's radar screens.
- By virtue of loss aversion, "people will be closely attuned to the potential losses from any newly introduced risk . . ., but far less concerned about future gains they may never see if a current risk is reduced." Consider the barriers to the introduction of new pharmaceuticals, which are on-screen, compared to the illness and death that might be reduced by their introduction, which are off-screen.
- Prohibiting one harm under the PP may create equal or worse harms. For example, in developing countries, bans on DDT have led to increases in malaria, and bans on genetically modified organisms may increase deaths through starvation.

Although Sunstein rejects most formulations of the PP, he proposes what he calls *an irreversible and catastrophic harm principle*, under which "when a harm is irreversible in the sense that restoration is very costly or impossible, special precautions may be justified; . . . it often makes sense to 'buy' an option to preserve future flexibility; and . . . loss of cherished and qualitatively distinctive goods deserve particular attention."[82]

Without delving more deeply into this complex and hotly contested issue, two things are reasonably clear to us. First, that the trade-offs between current benefits and the risk of catastrophic harm cannot be left entirely to experts but, in a democracy, must be the subject of debate and deliberation by legislators informed by diverse civil society organizations. Second, public deliberation should be informed by experts' estimates of the scope and probability of harms, even if they come with large margins of error.

---

81. *Quoted* in WORST-CASE SCENARIOS 124.
82. *Id.* at 189.

CONCLUSION

THE LAWYER AS COGNITIVE COUNSELOR

In concluding **Part 3**, we ask whether lawyers can use the insights of judgment and decision making research to improve their clients' decision making. (We discuss the parallel question for policy makers in **Part 4**.) The difficulties of debiasing even one's own decisions, coupled with the injunction "physician heal thyself," counsels modesty in this enterprise. However, their very distance from their clients' individual decisions may give lawyers a perspective that enables them to see and mitigate biases in others to an extent that they cannot necessarily do for themselves. The hazards of guiding clients' decisions may lie less in lawyers' cognitive biases than in the imposition of their own values.

PERVASIVE BIASES AND THEIR LARGELY INEFFECTUAL REMEDIES[1]

Thus far, we have identified a variety of cognitive biases and heuristics that can lead to incorrect empirical judgments and to decision making that does not maximize an individual's utility. These include:

- the availability heuristic;
- the representativeness heuristic;
- social stereotyping;
- anchoring bias;
- neglect of base rates;
- confirmation bias;
- overconfidence;
- hindsight bias;
- overoptimism;
- self-serving bias
- misforecasting the effects of positive and negative experiences;
- framing effects—particularly the endowment effect and loss aversion;

---

1. *See generally* Scott O. Lilienfeld et al., *Giving Debiasing Away: Can Psychological Research on Correcting Cognitive Errors Promote Human Welfare?*, 4 Perspectives on Psychol. Sci. 390 (2009); Katherine L. Milkman et al., *How Can Decision Making Be Improved?*, 4 Perspectives on Psychol. Sci. 379 (2009); Richard P. Larrick, *Debiasing*, *in* Blackwell Handbook of Judgment and Decision Making 316 (Derek J. Koehler and Nigel Harvey eds., Malden, MA: Blackwell Publishing, 2004).

- difficulties in dealing with too many choices and the framing and grouping of choices;
- difficulties in evaluating and comparing risks.

Along the way, we have occasionally mentioned efforts to debias these phenomena. Here we summarize what is known about debiasing techniques.

Informing people of the biases. Informing decision makers that they are prone to particular biases has little or no effect in most circumstances.[2]

Incentives. The hope is that incentives will reduce error is based on the assumption that they will motivate System 2 analysis and deliberation. But this requires that people have the judgment and decision-making skills that the additional effort will mobilize.[3] While incentives may stimulate the search for additional information, they have little or no effect in mitigating most cognitive biases.[4]

Accountability. As with incentives, accountability to others can only reduce biases if decision makers have the requisite skills. Even then, as we will discuss in Section 19.11, the social pressures of accountability may induce biases of their own.

Considering the alternative. One of the most robust and pervasive debiasing techniques is to consider why one's judgment may be wrong. Hindsight bias can be counteracted by asking people to provide reasons why an event other than the one that actually occurred might have occurred. Overconfidence and the biased assimilation of information can be counteracted by asking people to provide counterarguments for their judgments. And the self-serving bias in litigation can be counteracted by asking parties to write down the weaknesses of their own case.[5] These techniques can sometime backfire, however: if people find it difficult to think of reasons or examples on the other side, it may actually strengthen their prior beliefs.[6]

Representing risks and other matters of likelihood in terms of frequencies rather than probabilities. Under at least some circumstances, people will combine probabilities more accurately when considering likelihoods as frequencies rather than probabilities—for example, that an outcome occurs 25 out of 100 times rather than 25 percent of the time. (See Section 8.6.1).

---

2. *See* Baruch Fischhoff, *Debiasing, in* Daniel Kahneman, Paul Slovic, and Amos Tversky, Judgment Under Uncertainty: Heuristics and Biases 422 (1982).

3. *See* Colin Camerer and Robin Hogarth, *The Effects of Financial Incentives in Experiments: A Review and Capital-Labor-Production Framework,* 19 J. Risk and Uncertainty 7 (1999).

4. Camerer and Hogarth, *supra;* Larrick, *supra.*

5. Linda Babcock, George Loewenstein, and Samuel Issacharoff, *Creating Convergence: Debiasing Biased Litigants,* 22 Law & Social Inquiry 914 (1997).

6. Larrick, *supra.*

Statistical rather than intuitive predictions. We saw in Section 10.5.1 that people tend to rely on intuitive predictions in situations where using a simple linear model would be far more accurate. Of course, the belief that one's own intuition beats a linear model may itself be difficult to debias.

Taking an outsider's perspective. Trying to mentally remove oneself from a particular situation, or viewing it as an example of a broader class of decisions, may reduce people's overconfidence about their knowledge and overoptimism about their likelihood of success.[7]

* * *

In the remainder of this conclusion to **Part 3**, we ask whether a lawyer can help clients avoid the errors of decision making we have just covered. In **Part 4**, and particularly Chapter 18, we acquiesce in the inevitability of people's making such errors, and suggest ways that policy makers can "fight fire with fire" by framing decisions so that uncorrected System 1 processes produce outcomes that are in people's or society's best interests.

THE LAWYER AS COGNITIVE COUNSELOR

About half the practice of a decent lawyer consists in telling would-be clients that they are damned fools and should stop.
— Elihu Root[8]

In both law and medicine, active client or patient participation in decision making is widely accepted as central to good professional practice. This perspective is reflected in both the client-centered, or client autonomy,[9] model of legal counseling, and in the informed consent model of medical decision making.[10]

---

7. Milkman, *supra*.

8. PHILIP C. JESSUP, ELIHU ROOT 133 (New York: Dodd Mead, 1938).

9. The client autonomy model is similar in many respects to the client-centered approach. For a leading defense of client autonomy, *see* MONROE H. FRIEDMAN, UNDERSTANDING LAWYERS' ETHICS (1990).

10. For an account of the development of informed consent as a normative model of doctor-patient decision making, and an extension of that model to the legal counseling relationship, *see* Mark Spiegel, *Lawyering and Client Decisionmaking: Informed Consent and the Legal Profession*, 128 U. PA. L. REV. 41 (1979). For a cognitive limitations critique of the informed consent model of medical decision making, *see* Jon Merz and Baruch Fischhoff, *Informed Consent Does Not Mean Rational Consent*, 11 J. LEGAL MEDICINE 321 (1990). *See also* Donald A. Redelmeier, Paul Rozin, and Daniel Kahneman, *Understanding Patient's Decisions: Cognitive and Emotional Perspectives*, 270 J. OF THE AMERICAN MEDICAL ASSOCIATION 72 (1993) (describing various cognitive biases and heuristics that influence patient's approach to making medical treatment decisions).

According to these models, the professional's task is to present the client or patient with sufficient information about the available options and their reasonably foreseeable outcomes to enable the client or patient to make a fully informed, autonomous choice. It is not the professional's role to make the decision for the client or, on some views, even to tell the client which option she thinks is "best."[11] Clients are presumed to use the information provided by the professional to reach a decision that best serves their interests, as they define and understand them.

There are situations in both legal and public policy decision making where clients not only fully comprehend their own interests, but have already engaged in whatever problem solving is required and have determined what actions they want to take. The lawyer's sole task in these situations may be to implement a decision already made. In many instances, however, the lawyer can usefully act as interlocutor, partner, or guide in identifying and clarifying objectives and determining the best course of action. As former law dean Anthony Kronman writes:

> [O]ften the client's objective is hazy, or in conflict with other objectives, or clear but impetuously conceived. . . . [The lawyer's] job in such cases is to help clarify the client's goal by pointing out ambiguities in its conception and by identifying latent conflicts between it and other of the client's goals. . . . [Indeed, the lawyer's] responsibilities to a client go beyond the preliminary clarification of his goals and include helping him to make a deliberatively wise choice among them. . . . [H]is duty [is] not merely to implement a client's decision . . . but also to help him assess its wisdom through a process of cooperative deliberation. . . .[12]

In recent years, client-centered models have been subjected to what might be termed a cognitive bias critique. The critique proceeds from the observation, based on research of the sort described in the preceding chapters, that people's decision-making skills are deficient in some significant respects. Their judgments about causation and their ability to evaluate risk or predict outcomes are susceptible to a variety of systematic biases. Their preferences are unstable and may be inconsistent, context-dependent, or self-defeating. In short, the processes by which people go about making decisions are flawed in a number of important ways when compared with normative models of decision making derived from statistics, economics, and decision science.

---

11. For a discussion of this issue, *see* David A. Binder, Paul B. Bergman, Susan Price, and Paul R. Tremblay, Lawyers as Counselors: A Client-Centered Approach (Eagan, MN: West. 2nd ed., 2004).

12. Anthony T. Kronman, The Lost Lawyer: Failing Ideals of the Legal Profession 128–129, 131 (New York: Cambridge University Press, 1993).

Legal scholars have begun to apply insights from this research to a wide variety of subjects in law and legal practice.[13] Much of this literature seeks to identify sources of bias that, for example, systematically distort clients' decisions to commence, continue, or settle litigation and that thus lead to suboptimal outcomes in terms of their own interests.[14] The hope is that lawyers can help clients avoid or compensate for these biases and thus make better decisions. In other words, lawyers might add value to client decision making not only by predicting legal outcomes, but also by structuring and improving decision-making processes.

So, for example, Jeffrey Rachlinski observes that by describing settlement offers to clients in ways that counteract framing effects, attorneys can improve outcomes for the clients and for society in general.[15] In an intriguing set of experiments (described below), Russell Korobkin and Chris Guthrie suggest that lawyers are more likely than nonlawyers to apply expected value analysis

---

13. *See, e.g.*, Donald C. Langevoort and Robert K. Rassmussen, *Skewing the Results: The Role of Lawyers in Transmitting Legal Rules*, 5 S. CAL. INTERDISC. L. J. 375 (1997) (using insights from social and cognitive psychology to explain why lawyers might overstate legal risk in counseling business clients); Gary L. Blasi, *What Lawyers Know: Lawyering Expertise, Cognitive Science, and the Functions of Theory*, 45 J. LEGAL EDUC. 313 (1995) (describing the development of legal expertise in terms of cognitive theory and the debiasing of judgment); Jody Armour, *Stereotypes and Prejudice: Helping Legal Decisionmakers Break the Prejudice Habit*, 38 CAL. L. REV. 733 (1995) (applying social cognition theory to the problem of debiasing jury decision making); Donald C. Langevoort, *Where Were the Lawyers? A Behavioral Inquiry into Lawyers' Responsibility for Client's Fraud*, 46 VAND. L. REV. 75 (1993) (applying insights from social psychology and social cognition theory to explain how lawyers may fail to detect client fraud); and Albert J. Moore, *Trial by Schema: Cognitive Filters in the Courtroom*, 37 U.C.L.A. L. REV. 273 (1989) (application of insights from cognitive psychology to trial advocacy).

14. *See, e.g.*, Mark Kelman et. al., *Context-Dependence in Legal Decision Making*, 25 J. LEGAL STUD. 287 (1996) (demonstrating empirically that choice in legal decision-making situations may be influenced by context effects); Jeffrey J. Rachlinski, *Gains, Losses, and the Psychology of Litigation*, 70 S. CAL. L. REV. 113 (1996) (demonstrating how framing effects may influence client decisions to settle or continue litigation); Linda Babock, et al., *Forming Beliefs About Adjudicated Outcomes: Perceptions of Risk and Reservation Values*, 15 INT'L REV. L. AND ECON. 289 (1995) (influence of framing and prior expectancy effects on settlement decision making); Russell Korobkin and Chris Guthrie, *Psychological Barriers to Litigation Settlement: An Experimental Approach*, 93 MICH. L. REV. 107 (1994) (illustrating how framing effects and equity seeking may influence settlement decision making); Russell Korobkin and Chris Guthrie, *Opening Offers and Out of Court Settlement: A Little Moderation May Not Go A Long Way*, 10 OHIO ST. J. ON DISPUTE RESOLUTION I (1994) (anchoring effects and the evaluation of settlement offers); George Loewenstein, et al., *Self-Serving Assessments of Fairness and Pretrial Bargaining*, 22 J. LEGAL STUD. 135 (1993) (demonstrating the effects of overoptimism and other self-serving evaluative biases on settlement decision making).

15. Jeffrey J. Rachlinski, *Gains, Losses, and the Psychology of Litigation*, *supra* at 170–73.

in deciding whether to settle or continue with litigation, and are less likely in such situations to be influenced by certain cognitive biases.

This line of research poses a challenge to the traditional client-centered model of legal counseling: If, at least in certain contexts, lawyers are less likely than clients to be influenced by cognitive biases or the indiscriminate application of simplifying heuristics, does this support introducing a degree of paternalism into normative models of lawyer-client decision making?

Korobkin and Guthrie respond to this question by positing what they refer to as a *cognitive error approach* to legal counseling.[16] Under this approach, the appropriateness of a lawyer's intervention depends on the judgments that underlie the client's decision. As Korobkin and Guthrie state:

> The cognitive error approach to counseling . . . requires the lawyer to assess whether an observed difference between the lawyer's and client's analysis of decision options is due to the client's cognitive error or is merely the manifestation of differences in utility functions. If the difference is due to cognitive error, the lawyer should attempt to change the client's outlook. If the difference is the result of different preference structures, the lawyer should scrupulously avoid any interference.[17]

With this distinction in mind, and with due modesty about lawyers' ability to influence clients' judgments that are based on cognitive biases or affect,[18] let's examine more closely Korobkin and Guthrie's experiments involving the lawyer's role as counselor.[19] They gave laypersons and lawyers these bias-inducing scenarios and asked whether they would settle or go to trial.

- *Anchoring.* A car buyer's suit against the dealer for the purchase of a "lemon," in which the defendant's initial offer of settlement acted either as a high or low anchor for the plaintiff's expectations. (See Section 10.1)

---

16. Russell Korobkin and Chris Guthrie, *Psychology, Economics, and Settlement: A New Look at the Role of the Lawyer*, 76 Texas L. Rev. 77, 129–130 (1977).

17. *Id.* at 130.

18. The modesty implied by the first section of this chapter is supported by Korobkin and Guthrie's efforts to increase settlement rates in the scenarios described in the text that follows. They employed five strategies: (1) informing the client about the psychological factors that might inform her decision, (2) asking the client to consider an opposite or alternative point of view, (3) recommending settlement, (4) giving reasons for the recommendation, and (5) recommending settlement without giving any reasons. All five tended to increase the settlement rate, but not dramatically.

19. The experiments were motivated by the higher rate of settlement of civil cases than predicted by prospect theory. As we have seen, plaintiffs and defendants view litigation from different frames, with defendants tending to be more risk-taking than plaintiffs. Moreover, litigants may have goals besides money, such as vindication, revenge, and justice. The high rate of settlement could nonetheless be explained if *lawyers* did not share the cognitive biases of their clients and if they influenced their clients to settle.

- *Gain/loss framing*. A car accident case in which the identical situation was manipulated so that settlement appeared to the plaintiff either as a gain or a loss. (See Section 14.1)
- *Sympathy*. A suit against a landlord who failed to provide the tenant with heat during an entire winter, in which the landlord either had been willfully indifferent or had a sympathetic excuse (being out of the country on a family emergency). The psychological issue here was not bias, but the participants' sense of justice.[20]

Lawyers tended to settle regardless of the frame. Clients' settlement rates depended on how the issue was framed.

In the lemon case, when the anchor was high (thus creating a high expectation), clients' settlement rates were significantly lower than lawyers'. Since it is not plausible that the client would accord any actual value to this anchor, the lawyers' tendency to ignore the anchor seems unequivocally utility maximizing.

In the accident case, the clients' settlement rates were lower in the loss frame than in the gains frame. This is predicted by prospect theory, as described in Section 14.1. Whether the clients' frame-dependent tendencies produce suboptimal decisions that affect their experienced utility in the long run depends on the interactions of affective forecasting, adaptation, and regret.

And in the heater case, the clients' settlement rates were lower when the landlord had an unsympathetic excuse for not fixing the heater, while the settlement rates for lawyers were the same in both situations. Based on the experimental results and follow-up interviews, Korobkin and Guthrie conclude that the lawyers were single-mindedly focused on monetary expected value and indifferent to the other variables, while some clients wished to maximize a value other than wealth. (See Section 12.1) One certainly cannot characterize a tenant's decision to settle for less out of sympathy as irrational. Yet the lawyer may believe that the client is overvaluing the sympathy discount in terms of his own utility function—say, because the excuse was conveyed in a personal, emotion-laden manner, whose psychological effects will diminish in another week or so.

Korobkin and Guthrie's distinction between a client's errors and utilities echoes David Luban's suggestion in *Paternalism and the Legal Profession*[21] that a lawyer may permissibly compromise client autonomy where the intrusion interferes only with a client's "wants," but not when it would interfere with the expression of a client's "values."[22] Luban defines *values* as those reasons for choosing a particular course of action "with which the agent most closely identifies—those

20. The subjects were informed that it would not affect the outcome of the small claims court trial.

21. David Luban, *Paternalism and the Legal Profession*, 1981 WISCONSIN L. REV. 454 (1981).

22. *Id.* at 474.

that form the core of his personality, that make him who he is."[23] A cognitive error approach to legal counseling is based on the assumption that biases or errors can be distinguished from a client's core preferences or utilities.

To put client-centered counseling in the terms used in this book, we start from the premise that the lawyer's role as counselor is to help a client maximize his or her *utility*—taking into account the broad conception of utility considered in Section 12.1. While the ideal, of course, is to maximize *experienced* utility, lawyers, clients, and indeed all of us, can only forecast the *expected* utility of decisions.

In the simplest case, the lawyer provides the client with information about substantive law and procedure, and makes predictions of the likely consequences of particular courses of actions, based on which the client decides what course of action to pursue. This inevitably requires that the lawyer understand the client's objectives, and sometimes requires working with him to clarify them. The lawyer may also bring to the counseling process decision-making knowledge or tools that not all clients necessarily possess—for example, how to structure a decision process with multiple competing objectives or how to take risk into account when calculating expected value.[24]

Even when only money is at stake, these can be complex matters; consider, for example, quantifying risks, identifying uncertainties and understanding a client's risk tolerance in a particular context. But, as we have seen, subjective utility can encompass a large variety of factors besides money—factors that the client may not be able to specify, let alone predict how they will be affected by a decision. Even relatively simple predictions of expected value are subject to cognitive biases, and as one moves to a broader range of goals the possibilities of bias grow immensely.

What role can the lawyer as counselor play in helping a client navigate these manifold and often hidden shoals? Although not only laypersons but experts as well are subject to biased judgment and decision making, there are several reasons that a lawyer may be able to help a client address errors that the client wouldn't notice himself:

- the lawyer possesses expertise in decision making[25]—especially if he or she has taken a course in problem solving and decision making;
- by virtue of her disinterest, the lawyer can provide the client with a different and neutral perspective in the matter;
- an agent rather than a principal, the lawyer does not have the "endowment" that a client may experience with respect to the status quo;

---

23. *Id.*

24. For example, the subjective linear model described in Section 4.5 and the decision tree described in Section 15.2.2.

25. *See* Russell Korobkin and Chris Guthrie, Psychology, *Economics, and Settlement: A New Look at the Role of the Lawyer*, 76 Texas L. Rev. 77 (1997).

- as a repeat player, the lawyer has the opportunity to get better feedback on recurrent events, and has knowledge about likely outcomes and about clients' satisfaction or dissatisfaction in vindicating certain kinds of interests.

For all of its promise, cognitive counseling cannot escape, and indeed may contribute to, some fundamental dilemmas of the decision-making process described in the preceding chapters. Most notably, if preferences are sometimes constructed in the very process of making a decision, there is a danger that lawyer's preferences may unwittingly influence the client's decision. The very act of communicating information to clients subtly shapes preferences and influences choice.[26] The client may be led, either by the lawyer directly or by the "scripted" nature of the lawyer-client interaction, to value certain aspects of utility at the moment differently than they will be valued in life outside the lawyer's office. Indeed, the lawyer-client interaction may temporarily alter the client's preferences.[27]

Problem: The Case of Elizabeth Fletcher

We end the discussion of the lawyer as counselor with a hypothetical case that illustrates the dilemmas of the counseling relationship in circumstances where deeply held personal values are at stake in situations of risk or uncertainty.

Elizabeth Fletcher is a single woman in her early 40s, who consulted a lawyer after she had been fired from her job as a customer service representative at a regional electrical utility company. The reason given for her termination was excessive absenteeism. Fletcher explained to her lawyer that a year and a half ago she was diagnosed with an autoimmune disease that causes painful and potentially life-threatening inflammation of the joints, muscles, and other organs, including the lining around the lung and the heart. Periods during which the disease is in remission alternate with periods of severe symptoms, requiring Fletcher to miss more work than would an otherwise similarly situated but non-disabled employee. She has also had to miss work because of frequent medical appointments.

Fletcher asked to be allowed to work a flexible schedule as an accommodation under the Americans with Disabilities Act (ADA). While the human resources director offered to help her apply for and obtain social security disability benefits (SSDI), he declined to make this accommodation. After more missed days, the company terminated her employment.

Fletcher has now consulted a lawyer for help in selecting between two possible courses of action. She can either file for SSDI, with the company's cooperation, or she can sue the company under the ADA for failing to accommodate her need for a flexible work schedule. She thought about doing both simultaneously,

26. Steven Ellman, *Lawyers and Clients*, 34 U.C.L.A. L. Rev. 717, 733–53 (1987).

27. William H. Simon, *Lawyer Advice and Client Autonomy: Mrs. Jones' Case*, 50 Maryland L. Rev. 213, 216–17 (1991).

but her lawyer indicates that the law requires her to choose one option or the other.

The lawyer, an expert in disability law, knows that a study by the Commission on Mental and Physical Disability of the American Bar Association[28] indicates that defendants prevail in over 90 percent of litigated ADA cases. Recent amendments to the ADA, providing a broader definition of "disability," may change the estimate somewhat, but the particular facts of Fletcher's case do not seem to distinguish it from others filed under the ADA, so the lawyer sees little reason to adjust significantly the 10 percent base rate of anticipated success. Furthermore, the costs associated with prosecuting the ADA case would be substantial, including filing fees, deposition and expert witness costs, and a contingency fee of 30 percent of any ultimate recovery.

The costs associated with applying for social security disability benefits are much lower and the likelihood of success greater. There is no application fee, and Fletcher could apply without an attorney. Should she have to file an appeal, that could be done for a fraction of the cost associated with civil litigation under the ADA in federal district court. With the employer's cooperation, the probability of having her SSDI application approved are quite high, perhaps 85 percent.

The lawyer tries to provide the data to explain why filing for SSDI has much greater expected value than suing the employer under the ADA. But Fletcher becomes increasingly agitated, and eventually says that, while she accepts that the success rate in ADA cases is low, she is confident that she has a better than average chance of success. Her former employer is a big company. They could easily have put her on a more flexible schedule without having to endure an "undue hardship," which would provide a defense under the ADA. Besides, if she has to rely on Social Security, she feels certain that she will never get better. The very thought of going on "the dole," she explains, makes her feel depressed; it's like acknowledging that her life is over, that she is simply waiting to get worse and die. "If I don't keep fighting, I'll lose the battle with this disease. People with HIV go on SSDI. That's when you know they're on their way out."

One could easily conclude that Elizabeth Fletcher's judgment is distorted—in this case by unrealistic optimism about her chances of winning an ADA suit, and by the seemingly irrational belief that going on Social Security disability insurance has the power to alter the course of her disease. Yet recall Shelley Taylor's research on "positive illusions," in which cancer patients, crime victims, and others who had experienced adverse life events adapted by finding meaning in the adverse experience, by attempting to regain mastery over the negative event

---

28. *See Study Finds Employers Win Most ADA Title I Judicial and Administrative Complaints*, 22 MENTAL AND PHYSICAL DISABILITY LAW REPORTER 403 (May/June 1998) (nationwide rate of defense judgments in ADA Title I cases that went to judgment between 1992 and 1997 was 92.11 percent; rate in Fifth Circuit (highest nationwide) was 98.1 percent, in the Ninth Circuit (lowest nationwide) 83.3 percent). *Id.* at 405.

in particular and over their lives more generally, and by restoring self-esteem through self-enhancing evaluations. (See Section 13.5)

One can understand Fletcher's attraction to litigating the ADA case as a strategy for gaining control and enhancing her self-esteem, even it if involves overoptimism about her own chances of success. Even if her receipt of SSDI benefits does not "objectively" affect her health, Fletcher's *belief* in the causal connection may affect her experienced utility of whatever option she eventually chooses to pursue—and perhaps it will actually come to affect her health as well. On the other hand, if she files the ADA suit, which she has a low chance of winning, she will forego disability benefits at least for the duration of the suit, and reduce her chances for obtaining SSDI for some time thereafter.

How would you counsel Elizabeth Fletcher under the circumstances?

Our own view is that in situations such as these, if the lawyer's personal or professional experience leads him to believe that the client will regret a decision in the long run, it would be irresponsible not to raise his concerns in dialogue with the client—but with sensitivity to the thin lines between dialogue, persuasion, and overbearing influence, and a realization that even raising the question could affect Fletcher's well-being.

PART FOUR

GUIDING AND INFLUENCING DECISIONS

The chapters that follow are concerned mainly with changing people's minds and behavior—and sometimes, conversely, with preventing others from "messing with your mind." As a general introduction to the topic, consider this problem.

Suppose that you are concerned about the rise in obesity among American youth, especially among disadvantaged children. You are concerned about both the health consequences and the economic burdens that will ultimately be imposed on society. Consider these various approaches for promoting healthy behaviors by your target population.

EXTERNAL ENVIRONMENTAL FACTORS

Environmental factors play a significant role in the obesity of poor children. Many children do not eat healthy foods at home because their neighborhoods lack supermarkets or because their working (and often single) parents don't have time to cook. Many children get inadequate exercise because they don't have safe and convenient places to play. Thus, in addition to considering techniques of persuasion and influence, you should consider how to change the external environment, for example, by providing healthier food and more opportunities for exercise in schools, or by supporting organizations such as the Boys & Girls Clubs that provide after-school activities, including sports.

INFORMATION AND PERSUASION

You might try to change the behavior of children by persuading them to eat more healthily. You could do this by informing them about the consequences of obesity and how to follow a healthy diet. These efforts might be aided by labeling foods according to their calories and fat content, though labeling may require legislation. You might try to inform parents in order to affect their behavior with respect to their kids' eating and exercise habits; for example, reducing the time spent in front of the television improves behavior in both dimensions.

INCENTIVES

Economic or other material incentives and disincentives—ranging from cash payments to taxes to threats of punishment—are among the fundamental tools for changing individuals' and organizations' behavior. If we don't want people to speed on the freeway, we levy a fine for speeding. If we want people to borrow more money, we lower interest rates. All other things being equal, people respond to incentives and disincentives as economists would predict, and there is a vast literature on the use of specific kinds incentives and disincentives, ranging from tax policy to criminal punishment.

Several public school systems are experimenting with programs that pay underachieving students for doing well on standardized tests.[1] Might a government agency or nonprofit organization pay kids to maintain a certain weight level? Might this have unintended negative consequences?

PSYCHOLOGY

You might also employ psychological techniques to influence behavior in ways that do not appeal solely to rational considerations—for example, by inducing fear of the consequences of obesity or by appealing, in a positive way, to feelings about being healthy or slim. These messages might be conveyed through various media, by school teachers, in homes and communities, or through counseling programs. Using many of these same techniques, you might try to change the culture of the target population by making healthy lifestyles cool and obesity decidedly uncool. Although this seems more ambitious, it may be the most effective way to change some individual behaviors. (Again, consider whether these strategies might have unintended consequences.)

Two different realms of psychology provide other approaches to changing behavior:

- social psychology, which we'll characterize as *social influence*;
- an amalgam of judgment and decision making (JDM) concepts, which we'll characterize as *framing*.

The social psychology approach to influencing behavior proceeds from the observation that humans are social animals, who are extremely sensitive to signals from and interactions with other people. This has significant adaptive value. More often than not, our personal outcomes depend on the regard in which others hold us, and on their willingness to cooperate with us, promote our interests, and

---

1. http://www.hotchalk.com/mydesk/index.php/the-buzz/418-pay-for-grades-a-controversial-motivation http://www.nytimes.com/2007/06/19/nyregion/19schools.html?_r=1.

assist us in achieving our goals. Our ability to get ahead in life, indeed to survive, depends on social interactions including our impulse to conform to social norms and to obey authority.

The techniques of social influence are designed to change beliefs, attitudes, and behavior through interpersonal interaction[2] through such mechanisms as conformity, obedience, and reciprocity. By contrast, the techniques of framing and persuasion seek to influence beliefs, attitudes, and behavior through the way an issue or choice is presented. These techniques build on the insights of JDM research examined above, including how the number of choices and the way they are presented—for example, as gains or losses—affect decisions. We include in this category what Richard Thaler and Cass Sunstein call "*choice architecture*"—policy makers' use of framing devices to assist individuals in pursuing their own or society's best interests.[3]

Part 4 considers how people's decisions and behavior can be influenced or guided—for better or worse—by individuals or groups.

Chapter 17, *Social Influence*, draws on the realm of social psychology and considers how individuals' behavior is affected by their awareness of and relationships with other people.

Chapter 18, *Influencing Behavior through Cognition*, draws on cognitive psychology, the JDM literature, and behavioral economics. It considers how arguments can be framed to make them more persuasive, how decisions can be unconsciously affected by representations or associations placed in memory shortly before they are made, and how policy makers can use knowledge of the biases described in earlier parts of the book to guide citizens' and consumers' decision making.

Chapter 19, *Improving Group Decision Making*, considers how one can gain the benefits and avoid the pathologies of group decision making, and concludes with a discussion of the effects of accountability on individual and group decision-making performance.

---

2. Susan T. Fiske, Social Beings: A Core Motives Approach to Social Psychology 508 (New York: Wiley, 2004).

3. Richard Thaler and Cass Sunstein, Nudge: Improving Decisions About Health, Wealth, and Happiness (New Haven: Yale University Press, 2008).

17. SOCIAL INFLUENCE

In the spring of 2004, photographs showing U.S. military police torturing and humiliating prisoners at the Abu Ghraib prison in Iraq shocked the American public. Competing explanatory theories quickly filled the news media, personal conversations, Web sites, and blogs. Some attributed the events to a "few bad apples" run amok. Others posited a vast military and CIA plan to use torture systematically as an intelligence tactic. Through this frame, the guards at Abu Ghraib were just scapegoats, taking a fall for following orders. Other people, familiar with Philip Zimbardo's famous "prison study," conducted in the basement of the psychology department at Stanford University in the early 1970s,[1] or with Stanley Milgram's electrical shocks studies conducted a decade earlier, viewed the atrocities at Abu Ghraib differently. To these observers, what happened at Abu Ghraib was a thoroughly predictable product of a particular alignment of social forces that caused ordinary people to do extraordinarily bad things.[2]

The desire to understand the levers of social influence produced much of the most important and interesting social psychological research in the latter half of the twentieth century. Taken as a whole, this research shows that, just as decision making can be impaired through the application of cognitive heuristics that work well most but not all of the time, so can it be impaired by social influence processes that short circuit clear thinking about a particular action or choice. Of course, social influences are not all bad. They conduce to harmony and social order. They sometimes help us take advantage of others' experience and expertise, thereby avoiding costly mistakes. But processes of social influence have downsides: they can induce us to make decisions we later regret.

1. In Zimbardo's study, Stanford undergraduates were assigned the role of either prisoner or guard, in an experiment about role conformity that was expected to last two weeks. Within days, the experiment spun out of control, as "guards" began sexually humiliating and otherwise abusing "prisoners." For Zimbardo's reflections on the similarities between the behavior of his subjects and the Abu Ghraib guards, *see* Philip G. Zimbardo, *Power Turns Good Soldiers into "Bad Apples,"* BOSTON GLOBE, May 9, 2004, Op-Ed.

2. For a thorough treatment of the Stanford prison study and its findings' power in explaining Abu Ghraib, *see* PHILLIP G. ZIMBARDO, THE LUCIFER EFFECT: UNDERSTANDING HOW GOOD PEOPLE TURN EVIL (New York: Random House, 2008).

17.1 CONFORMITY TO GROUP NORMS (SOCIAL PROOF)

Recall Luis Trujillo, the lawyer introduced in Chapter 1. Project his legal career back in time fifteen years, and imagine that he is a brand new lawyer at Cooper & Lytton, a medium-sized Los Angeles law firm specializing in the defense of white collar criminal cases and the civil lawsuits that often accompany them. It is Trujillo's first month in his new job, and he feels utterly at sea. He has to figure out how to dress, how early to arrive at the office and how late to stay, how to behave in meetings with partners, clients, and associates. In writing the briefs he has been assigned to draft, he hasn't quite figured out where to draw the line between vigorous advocacy on the one hand and candor to the tribunal on the other. Asked to respond to discovery requests, he still cannot quite discriminate between a valid objections on the one hand and unethical dilatory tactics on the other. Sitting in on a deposition preparation session with one of the firm's most important clients, Trujillo is deeply concerned; this looks an awful lot like the "witness coaching" he found so distasteful in a Paul Newman movie, *The Verdict*, that he had watched in his law school professional responsibility class. Every day at work, Trujillo's ethical intuitions are challenged, but he is also aware that there is an awful lot about being a lawyer—a good, ethical, but also tough and effective lawyer—that he just doesn't yet understand.

How will the young Luis Trujillo learn to be an ethical but aggressive litigator? In all likelihood, he will observe what the firm's more senior lawyers do, and then he will do the same. Then, as time goes on, he will become a "Cooper & Lytton litigator."

Trujillo would not be alone in looking to the actions of others in his social environment to help him make sense of an uncertain new identity. Much of the time, particularly in novel situations, we do not know how to behave. We only hope that we can figure it out before we make a bad impression or worse. In such situations, we often use the behavior of others like us as a heuristic, a fast and dirty shortcut for figuring out what to do and how to do it.

Social psychologists, such as Robert Cialdini, refer to this phenomenon as "social proof,"[3] others, like Philip Zimbardo and Susan Fiske, as "conformity."[4] Cialdini defines social proof as the tendency to use the actions of similar others to decide on proper behavior for ourselves. In other words, people tend to see behavior as appropriate in a given situation to the degree that they see others performing it. The behavior of others thus serves as "proof" that it is appropriate.

---

3. Robert B. Cialdini, Influence: The Psychology of Persuasion (rev. ed. New York: Quill, 1993).

4. Philip G. Zimbardo, *supra* note 2; Philip G. Zimbardo and Mark R. Lieppe, The Psychology of Attitude Change and Social Influence (New York: McGraw-Hill, 1991); Susan T. Fiske, Social Beings: A Core Motives Approach to Social Psychology (New York: Wiley, 2004).

Zimbardo's definition of conformity runs along the same lines: "a change in a person's belief or behavior in response to real or imagined group pressure, where there is no direct demand for obedience by an authority figure." (By defining the concept in this way, Zimbardo distinguishes *conformity*, discussed here, from *compliance with authority*, discussed later.) While (at least in our society) "conformity" tends to have a negative connotation, "social proof" does not have a positive or negative valance—modeling our behavior on others' can be good or bad, depending on the circumstances.

The best-known empirical illustration of the social conformity effect comes from a now classic study by Solomon Asch. Asch recruited college students to participate in a study that ostensibly concerned visual perception. Subjects were placed in a room in groups of seven and shown a series of two posters. Every time a pair of posters was displayed, the poster on the left had a single line on it (the "standard" line), while the one on the right bore three lines of varying lengths. The single line on the left hand poster was always quite obviously the same size as one of the three lines on the other, as Figure 17.1 shows.

Each time a pair of posters was displayed, subjects were asked to determine which of the lines on the right-hand poster was the same length as the standard line. In every group of seven, six subjects were actually confederates working with the experimenter. The subjects were seated so that five confederates answered before the "real" subject gave his response. (See Figure 17.2.)

At first, the confederates gave the correct answer. But, as the experiment progressed, all six confederates began giving the wrong answers, always with the same ease and assurance with which they had given their earlier, correct answers. In the face of five incorrect answers, 80 percent of Asch's subjects went along with the confederates in at least one trial. In the aggregate, subjects went along

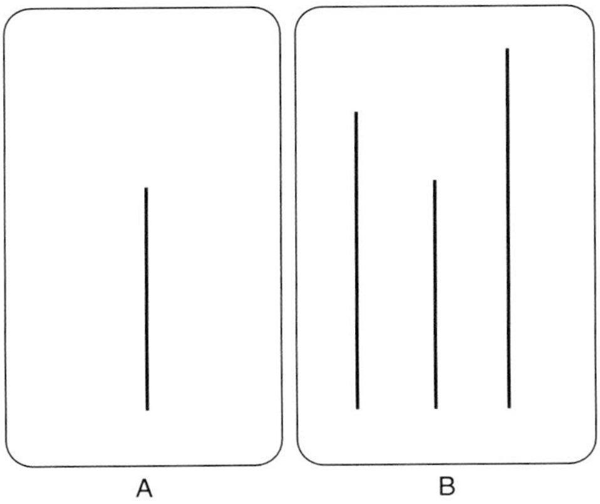

FIGURE 17.1 ASCH'S COMPARATIVE LINES.

FIGURE 17.2 ASCH SUBJECT (CENTER) AND TWO CONFEDERATES.

with the group and gave incorrect responses approximately 30 percent of the time, despite the obviousness of the correct response.[5]

Asch's initial studies generated numerous replications and extensions.[6] In 133 studies, spanning 40 years, the average subject conformed 29 percent of the time. Conformity rates were higher when the stimulus was ambiguous and when confederates and participants were members of the same social reference group. Conformity rates were relatively higher for female than for male subjects, particularly where the object of conformity was gender counterstereotypic, and were also higher in more collectivist cultures.[7]

Research on conformity raises interesting and as yet not fully answered questions. Foremost among these is, when subjects comply in these experiments, are they actually misperceiving the stimulus, or are they simply going along with the group, even though they know that the response they are giving is wrong? Or, is something more complex and nuanced than either one of these two possibilities going on? The best answer appears to be "all of the above."

The earliest evidence that conformity effects can change perception itself emerged from extensions of Muzafer Sherif's conformity experiments in the 1930s, on which Asch's research was based.[8] In his studies, Sherif used a phenomenon known as the "autokinetic effect," the illusion of motion created when one gazes at a stationary point of light. When looking at a point of light and

5. Solomon. E. Asch, *Effects of Group Pressures upon the Modification and Distortion of Judgment*, *in* GROUPS, LEADERSHIP, AND MEN (Harold S. Guetzkow ed., Pittsburgh: Carnegie Press, 1951).

6. For a thorough review, *see* Rod Bond and Peter B. Smith, *Culture and Conformity: A Meta-Analysis of Studies Using Asch's Line Judgment Task*, 119 PSYCHOLOGICAL BULLETIN 111–37 (1996).

7. *Id.* For a focus on intercultural comparisons, *see* Heejung Kim and Hazel R. Markus, *Deviance or Uniqueness, Harmon or Conformity? A Cultural Analysis*, 77 JOURNAL OF PERSONALITY AND SOCIAL PSYCHOLOGY 785–800 (1999).

8. MUZAFER SHERIF, THE PSYCHOLOGY OF SOCIAL NORMS (New York: Harper & Row, 1936).

reporting on its movements by themselves, subjects' reports of how far it moved varied significantly. Some subjects saw small movements, others quite large ones. However, once subjects were placed in groups and listened to each others' reports, their judgments tended to converge. Moreover, subsequent extensions of Sherif's experiments showed that these changes in subjects' perceptions endured. When retested alone, even a year later, subjects whose judgments had been changed by group interactions continued to "see" light movements close to the magnitude of the original group norm.[9]

More recently, brain imaging research suggests that social pressure can actually change people's visual-spatial perception. In a 2005 study using function magnetic resonance imaging (fMRI), Gregory Berns and his colleagues found that, in a spatial judgment task modeled on Asch's paradigm, social conformity shows up in the right intraparietal sulcus, a region of the brain devoted to special perception. Nonconformity, on the other hand, lit up the right amygdala and right caudate nucleus, regions associated with emotional threat.[10]

While some of Asch's subjects reported that they simply went along with the group despite their knowledge that they were giving an incorrect response, many reported that they thought that they must somehow be misunderstanding the nature of the task and conformed for that reason.[11] This suggests that, at least at times, group pressure causes people to reconstrue the meaning of perceptual phenomena, not necessarily the raw perception itself.[12]

At this point, the reader might object that these were just college students being asked about something inconsequential, and wonder whether the phenomenon extends to adults making more consequential decisions. To address these concerns, Stanley Milgram replicated Asch's experiment in the early 1960s. Milgram used adult subjects, who believed that they had been hired to test a new signaling system for jet airliners.[13] His subjects were asked to judge the pitch of a tone in comparison with three others. Like Asch's student subjects, Milgram's adults showed a high rate of conformity to the stated views of an erroneous majority, even though the task on which they were working involved airline safety.

There are, of course, limits on the conformity effect. With respect to the Asch experiments, for example, it is important to remember that almost a third of his

---

9. John H. Rohrer, Jonathan H. Baron, L. Richard Hoffman, and D. V. Swander, *The Stability of Autokinetic Judgments*, 49 JOURNAL OF ABNORMAL AND SOCIAL PSYCHOLOGY 595–97 (1954).

10. Gregory S. Berns, Jonathan Chappelow, Caroline F. Zink, Giuseppi Pagnoni, Megan E. Martin-Skurski, and Jim Richards, *Neurobiological Correlates of Social Conformity and Independence During Mental Rotation*, 58 BIOLOGICAL PSYCHIATRY 245–53 (2005).

11. *See generally* John M. Levine, *Solomon Asch's Legacy for Group Research*, 3 PERSONALITY AND SOCIAL PSYCHOLOGY REVIEW 358–64 (1999).

12. Susan T. Fiske, *supra* note 4, 512.

13. Stanley Milgram, *Nationality and Conformity*, SCIENTIFIC AMERICAN 45–51 (November 1961).

subjects resisted the impulse to conform. Another third resisted more often than they succumbed. Moreover, in follow-up studies, Asch showed that when subjects had at least one ally in dissent rates of conformity plummeted dramatically.[14]

Nonetheless, the conformity effect illustrated by Asch's research has withstood the test of time, both in the lab and in the real world. For example, knowledge about the behavior of peers influences peoples decisions about whether to help in an emergency,[15] pay their taxes,[16] or properly dispose of their trash.[17]

17.1.1 Death by Conformity

One of the most shocking real-world illustrations of the power of social proof unfolded in Queens, New York, in the spring of 1964. One warm March night, a young woman named Kitty Genovese was walking home when she was attacked outside her apartment building by a man wielding a knife. Her violent death did not come quickly or quietly. The attacker set upon Ms. Genovese three separate times over a period of thirty-five minutes, as she screamed for help and twice temporarily escaped his grasp. Thirty-two of her neighbors watched from their apartment windows, without intervening in any way—even to call the police—as Ms. Genovese screamed, struggled, and finally died.

Grappling to understand how such a thing could happen, social psychologists John Darley and Bibb Latané designed a series of experiments in which they "staged" emergencies and observed how the presence of inactive bystanders affected subjects' helping behavior. Over and over again, their results demonstrated the power of social proof. When subjects were alone, they responded to the apparent emergency with much higher rates of intervention than when inactive bystanders were present. Specifically, when people thought they were alone, they helped 85 percent of the time. But when they believed that others were present, and were not intervening, they helped only 31 percent of the time.[18] By 1980, four dozen laboratory and field studies had been conducted testing this "bystander effect."

14. Solomon E. Asch, *Opinions and Social Pressure*, Scientific American 31–35 (November 1955).

15. Bibb Latané and John M. Darley, The Unresponsive Bystander: Why Doesn't He Help? (Englewood Cliffs, NJ: Prentice-Hall, 1970).

16. John T. Scholz, Kathleen M. McGraw, and Marco R. Steenbergen, *Will Taxpayers Ever Like Taxes? Responses to the U.S. Tax Reform Act of 1986*, 13 Journal of Economic Psychology 625–56 (1992).

17. Robert B. Cialdini, Raymond R. Reno, and Carl A. Kallgren, *A Focus Theory of Normative Conduct: Recycling the Concept of Norms to Reduce Littering in Public Places*, 58 Journal of Personality and Social Psychology 1015–26 (1990).

18. Bibb Latané and John M. Darley, The Unresponsive Bystander: Why Doesn't He Help?, *supra* note 15; John M. Darley and Bibb Latané, *Bystander Intervention in Emergencies: Diffusion of Responsibility*, 8 Journal of Personality and Social Psychology 377–83 (1968).

In approximately 90 percent of these, lone bystanders proved more likely to intervene in an apparent emergency than did people in groups.[19]

Social psychologists generally explain these results in the following way: When people witness an apparent emergency, the need for and the appropriateness of intervention are often ambiguous. When people are alone, they will often resolve this ambiguity in favor of intervention. However, when they see other people like themselves idly standing by, they conclude that intervention is inappropriate and stand back.

17.1.2 Social Proof and Professional and Corporate Malfeasance

Many "ethical train wrecks" in law and business can be traced, at least in part, to social proof effects. Consider, for example, the ruin of in-house Enron lawyer Kristina Mordaunt, described by Kurt Eichenwald in his book, *Conspiracy of Fools*.[20] In 2001, Ms. Mordaunt played a minor role in working out "LJM1," one of the shady partnerships (known in accountant-speak as a "special purpose entity") that had been used to manipulate Enron's apparent financial performance and enrich certain Enron executives. LJM1's status as a valid special purpose entity, which accorded it favorable accounting treatment, was highly questionable. But from Mordaunt's point of view, the relevant accounting rules were ambiguous, the deal had been approved by Enron financial officers and accountants, and the executives who had put it together were rising stars in one of the country's best-regarded corporations.

A short time after the her work on LMJ1 was completed, Mordaunt was offhandedly asked by Enron Treasurer, Ben Glisan, Jr., whether she wanted to invest $10,000 in a similar special purpose entity, known by Enron insiders as "Southampton." She ended up investing only $5800, but a few weeks later, when the Southampton deal wound down, she received a return of over a million dollars. Weeks later, her career was ruined, and by the middle of 2002, prosecutors had filed a forfeiture action to seize her home and car.

It is easy—perhaps too easy—to conclude that Mordaunt was a knowing participant in a patently fraudulent scheme who got precisely what she deserved. But Eichenwald suggests an alternative explanation. Caught up in a web of mind-numbingly complex and ambiguous accounting rules, and watching apparently well-respected, successful high-level executives participating in complex transactions like LJM1 and Southampton, Mordaunt could easily have concluded that the deals were legitimate and that she was doing nothing wrong. The "proof" was all around her, in the actions of her superiors and colleagues.

---

19. Bibb Latané and Steve Nida, *Ten Years of Research on Group Size and Helping*, 89 Psychological Bulletin 308–24 (1981).

20. Kurt Eichenwald, Conspiracy of Fools: A True Story (New York: Broadway Books, 2005).

The social proof phenomenon can explain lawyers' passive acquiescence in client misconduct in various legal contexts. For example, Donald C. Langevoort suggests that it can explain attorney inaction in the face of client fraud:

> [A]n attorney who is new to a situation, especially an inexperienced one, is particularly prone to rely on social learning as the basis for constructing a schema. The fact that those more senior and more familiar with the situation are behaving as if there is no problem provides a strong cue. This, indeed, is one explanation for the reduced tendency of people in groups to act heroically, since responsibility is effectively diffused. To this, naturally, must be added the situational pressures on junior members of groups to conform to apparent norms.[21]

17.1.3 More Examples of Social Proof

An impressive volume of empirical research convincingly demonstrates that the information conveyed to people about situational norms has a significant impact on attitudes and behavior.[22]

In one study demonstrating the power of perceived norms, Robert Cialdini and his colleagues placed door-hangers on the front doors of houses in a number of California neighborhoods, encouraging residents to engage in various energy-conserving behaviors. Each of the door-hangers contained one of five message types appealing for energy conservation. The first message type was a simple description of various energy conservation techniques. Other types included messages highlighting the importance of protecting the environment, emphasizing the social benefits flowing from energy conservation, and highlighting the money residents could save through conservation. The final message type informed residents that the majority of their neighbors were already conserving.

Some time later, interviewers went door-to-door and asked residents how much they had engaged in the energy-conserving behaviors that was promoted on the door-hangers; they also requested copies of residents' energy bills, and took readings on outdoor energy meters. The researchers found that households that received the message highlighting that their neighborhood norm was to conserve energy saved significantly more energy than households in any of the other conditions.

Note that the reference group in the descriptive norm message used in this study was other people *in the same neighborhood*. This was a deliberate choice based on the results of a previous study, which showed that people are most

21. Donald C. Langevoort, *Where Were The Lawyers? A Behavioral Inquiry into Lawyers' Responsibility for Clients' Fraud*, 46 VANDERBILT. L. REV. 75, 105–106 (1993).

22. Jessica M. Nolan, Wesley Schultz, Robert B. Cialdini, Noah J. Goldstein, and Vladas Griskevicius, "Normative Social Influence Is Underdetected" (unpublished manuscript 2007).

affected by norms of people who are *similar* to them and groups with which they *identify*.

This category of "similar" others can actually extend to complete strangers, who happen to be (or to have been) in situations similar to our own. For example, Noah Goldstein, Robert Cialdini, and their colleagues found that hotel guests were most likely to participate in a towel reuse program when they were informed that the majority of people who had stayed in the same room had participated in the program.[23] This message was even more effective than one providing the same information about the behavior of people of one's gender, an identity that generally seems more salient than people who happened to have occupied the same hotel room. Goldstein, Cialdini, et al. suggest that when we are deciding how to behave in a particular situation, the social information that is most relevant is how other people behave *in that same situation*.

Descriptive norm information has also been found to affect charitable giving. Rachel Croson and her colleagues collaborated with public radio stations to conduct research during the stations' "pledge drives." In these studies, some listeners who called in to make donations were randomly selected to receive different information regarding donation amounts. For example, before being asked how much money they would like to donate, some listeners were told that another listener had just donated $200. Listeners receiving this information donated, on average, $30 more than callers who were simply asked how much they would like to donate. (The researchers controlled for the anchoring effect.)

In many situations, it is possible to make use of these sorts of techniques without engaging in deception. In the absence of other data, information about one individual can be taken as an indication of the norm. And it is highly likely that radio stations and other organizations that depend on charitable donations can truthfully provide information about at least one generous donor. Moreover, in some cases, such as Cialdini's study of neighborhood energy conservation, many people actually may engage in a desired behavior.

17.1.4 Conformity Effects and the Emergence of Cascades

In recent years, a number of scholars have used the social psychological research on conformity to develop an account of how behavioral norms, viewpoints, and perceptions of risk can spread rapidly through both large and small groups. This account, often referred to as *cascade theory*, offers important insights into the relationship between individual rationality and group behavior. It also helps explain why apparently rational people, who seem to be making independent decisions, might adopt the views of others in their social environment.

---

23. Noah J. Goldstein, Robert B. Cialdini, and Vladas Griskevicius, *A Room with a Viewpoint: Using Normative Appeals to Motivate Environmental Conservation in a Hotel Setting*, 35 JOURNAL OF CONSUMER RESEARCH (2008) (electronically published without page numbers).

Timur Kuran and Cass Sunstein describe three different types of cascades: *informational cascades*, *reputational cascades*, and *availability cascades*, all three of which can derive from conformity-related effects.[24] An *informational cascade* occurs when people with incomplete personal information about a subject base their own beliefs about it on the apparent beliefs of others in their social environment. People's words and actions often convey the impression that they hold a particular belief. Cascade theory posits that in response to such communications, other individuals, who know that they personally lack reliable information on the subject, accept a particular belief simply by virtue of its apparent acceptance by others. Under proper conditions, such a belief, no matter how fanciful, can spread rapidly and widely through a population.

Reputational cascades play a significant role in this process. Even if they doubt the veracity of the belief spreading by means of an informational cascade, people may act and speak as if they believe it to be true. Originally, at least, they do this to earn social approval and avoid social disapproval. Of course, once a person adopts and repeats a belief, even if only to avoid censure, he or she may eventually come to believe it true, if only to reduce the cognitive dissonance that would otherwise result.[25] Reputational cascades can prove very powerful, as direct social pressures to adopt a fast-propagating belief reinforce concerns that deviance would have negative long-term effects on social networks.[26]

Informational and reputational cascades look similar, often co-occur, and drive the same rapid propagation of beliefs. As theoretical constructs, they differ only in their motivation. People participate in an informational cascade primarily because they view adoption of an apparently sound belief held by others as rational, given their own lack of information and the costs associated with independent information search. For this reason, information cascades are also sometimes referred to as "rational herding."[27] In contrast, people participate in reputational cascades to avoid social disapproval, or to enhance their standing in a community.

Informational and reputational cascades sometimes interact with the availability heuristic (Section 9.6) in ways that create what Kuran and Sunstein call an *availability cascade*. In these situations, informational and reputational cascades

24. Timur Kuran and Cass R. Sunstein, *Availability Cascades and Risk Regulation*, 51 Stanford Law Review 683 (1999).

25. Daryl J. Bem, *Self-Perception Theory*, *in* Advances in Experimental Social Psychology 6, 60–61 (Leonard Berkowitz ed., New York: Academic Press, 1972).

26. Michael Klausner, *Corporations, Contracts, and Networks of Contracts*, 81 Virginia Law Review 757 (1995); Marcel Kahan and Michael Klausner, *Path Dependence in Corporate Contracting: Increasing Returns, Herd Behavior and Cognitive Bias*, 74 Washington Law Quarterly 347 (1996).

27. Eric Talley, *Precedential Cascades: An Appraisal*, 73 Southern California Law Review 87 (1999).

result in the frequent repetition of a particular story, trope, or claim. By virtue of its frequent repetition, it becomes increasingly *available*. Through the operation of availability bias, it then seems more plausible and likely. Availability cascades can be accelerated through the work of *availability entrepreneurs*, who fix people's attention on a particular issue, spin that issue in a particular way, and through these processes shape people's perceptions of its nature, importance, and meaning.

Kuran and Sunstein illustrate the cascade effects through various actors' responses to the arguable presence of toxic wastes in a small town. Vivid information about the dangers posed traveled through the community through information cascades. Public officials, who wanted to maintain a good reputation with their constituents, took up the issue and urged action, even though they had little or no knowledge about the actual harms. And some concerned citizens and environmental organizations acted as availability entrepreneurs to intensity and broaden the communications with both groups.

17.1.5 The Strategic Deployment of Social Proof

People sometimes manipulate the impulse toward conformity to achieve their own ends. For example, when a reporter is trying to get an employee to disclose information about confidential events that occurred in her workplace, the reporter may (falsely) tell her that some of her coworkers have already disclosed information about the events. The belief that others have already talked makes the employee's disclosure seem more acceptable and makes her more likely to talk. Reference to the coworkers behavior provides a cue for the employee's appropriate behavior in circumstances in which the proper response is ambiguous.

Form contracts, such as unfavorable provisions in lease agreements or mandatory arbitration agreements, provide similar cues. A tenant or medical patient may say to himself, "There are a lot of people like me signing these types of contracts. This must be the way it's done." Through similar processes, as we discuss in Section 18.6.3.c, default rules may acquire normative power through social proof.

* * *

In summary, people look to the behavior of others in their social environments as a kind of heuristic, applied to resolve uncertainties over what they should think or how they should behave. Other things being equal, tendencies toward social conformity are stronger when people are in novel environments, or where behavioral norms are particularly complex and ambiguous, or where the negative sanctions attached to behavioral deviance are particularly harsh. This tendency to conform our own behavior—and our sense of what is right, normative, or accurate—makes it possible for us to get along with other people, master new roles and environments, and achieve our individual and collective goals. But it can also cause us to behave in ways we later recognize as abhorrent. Unfortunately, that recognition often comes too late.

17.2 OBEDIENCE TO APPARENT AUTHORITY

At the end of World War II, descriptions of Nazi genocide shocked American society and triggered, in academic communities as elsewhere, attempts to explain why so many people collaborated with Hitler's atrocities. In 1950, a group of social scientists led by German exile, Theodor Adorno, provided one explanation in *The Authoritarian Personality*.[28] They posited that certain people possessed particularly rigid personalities, characterized by social conservatism, conformity, authoritarianism, and a strong inclination to obey authority. This personality type, Adorno concluded, was widespread in Germany in the 1930s and '40s and made National Socialism possible.

Building on Adorno's notion that nationality was correlated with conformity and compliance with authority social psychologist Stanley Milgram later set out to demonstrate that the more "contentious" French were less likely to conform in an Asch paradigm than the more "retiring" Scandinavians.[29] After failing to find significant differences between French and Scandinavian subjects, Milgram then designed an experiment to identify the "type of person" who would obey the instructions of an apparent authority figure—even if the instruction was to do something harmful to another person.

In Milgram's now classic study,[30] subjects were asked to play the role of "teacher" by asking questions of a "learner" who was hooked to an instrument that vaguely resembled an electric chair. Upon first entering the laboratory, the subject, or "teacher," assisted an experimenter, dressed in a white lab coat, in strapping the "learner" into the chair and attaching a shocking device to his arm. (See Figure 17.3.)

The "teacher" was then led into an adjacent room and seated in front of a panel with a row of switches on it, each marked with a particular voltage level, ranging from 15 to 450 volts and rising in 15 volt intervals. Under the switches were descriptions of the levels of the shock each would trigger, ranging from "slight shock" to "danger: severe shock." The last two switches were ominously labeled "XXX."

The experimenter then explained to the subject that he should ask the learner a question and, if the learner failed to respond correctly, the subject should administer a shock. Each time the learner failed to respond correctly, the shock to be administered was to increase by 15 volts.

---

28. Theodor W. Adorno, Else Frenkel-Brunswik, Daniel J. Levinson, and R. Nevitt Sanford, The Authoritarian Personality (New York: Harper, 1950).

29. Stanley Milgram, *Nationality and Conformity*, Scientific American 45–51 (November 1961).

30. Stanley Milgram, *Behavioral Study of Obedience*, 67 Journal of Abnormal and Social Psychology, 371–78 (1963).

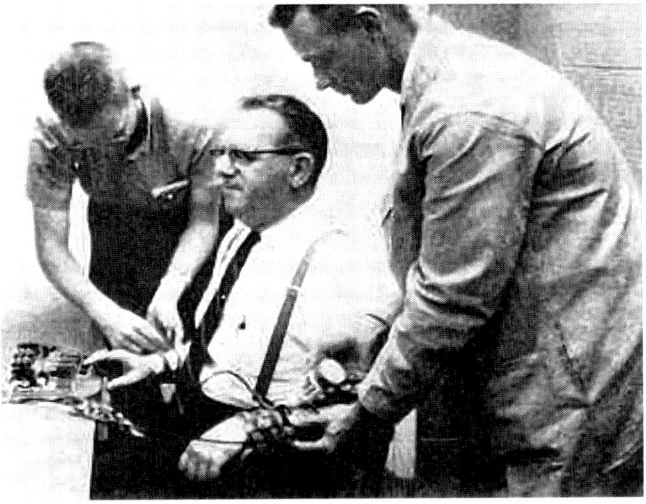

FIGURE 17.3 A SUBJECT (LEFT) ASSISTS EXPERIMENTER IN STRAPPING SHOCKING DEVICE ONTO "LEARNER" IN MILGRAM OBEDIENCE EXPERIMENT AT YALE UNIVERSITY.

Milgram's subjects were not college students. They were adult men from diverse occupational backgrounds who responded to a newspaper advertisement for a study on "learning" to be conducted at Yale University.

Unbeknownst to subjects, the learner was actually a confederate of the experimenter. Prerecorded sounds (e.g., screams, protests) reflecting varying degrees of pain were played, depending on the level of voltage the subject was "applying" to the learner. When the subject indicated a desire to stop either questioning the learner or applying the shock, he was prompted with one of four cues, depending on the nature of the subject's hesitation: "Please continue"; "The experiment

FIGURE 17.4 MILGRAM'S "SHOCK PANEL".

requires that you continue"; "It is absolutely essential that you continue"; or "You have no other choice, you must go on."

Surprisingly, even though they were not coerced or threatened into obeying the experimenter's instructions, nearly 65 percent of the subjects were willing to continue until they had applied what appeared to be life-threatening levels of electricity to those who failed to provide correct answers. Milgram reported that "subjects were observed to sweat, tremble, stutter, bit[e] their lips, groan, and dig their fingernails into their own flesh." Some subjects cried; others burst out into hysterical laughing fits. In post-experiment debriefings, nearly all the subjects reported that they felt that it was wrong to apply the shocks.

Neither Milgram nor any of the social psychologists, psychiatrists, or others he consulted anticipated that people would comply at such high rates, or to so great an extent. And yet, in subsequent replications the results were similar at different locations with different subjects. By the end, Milgram and his associates had run literally thousands of people from a wide cross-section of American society, including postal workers, college students, high school students and teachers, construction workers, college professors, and salespeople. Obedience was the norm. As Milgram concluded, "It is the extreme willingness of adults to go to almost any lengths on the command of an authority that constitutes the chief finding of the study."[31]

Obedience effects are robust across many situations and groups of subjects. However, as is described in greater detail below, subtle changes in the situation can have profound effects on obedience behavior. Individual differences play some role as well.[32] Not surprisingly, authoritarianism[33] sometimes predicts higher levels of obedience. Trust, moral development, and conventionality also show some (albeit weak or inconsistent) effects on obedience levels.[34]

All but one of Milgram's trials included only male subjects, but most of the experimental evidence shows no gender effect on obedience to apparent authority,[35] In the one trial including females, Milgram found no sex differences in obedience rates.[36] Ten of eleven replications found the same result.[37] The one

---

31. *Ibid.*

32. For a review of the literature, *see* Thomas Blass, *Understanding Behavior in the Milgram Obedience Experiment: The Role of Personality, Situations, and Their Interactions*, 60 Journal of Personality and Social Psychology 398–413 (1991).

33. Theodor W. Adorno, Else Frenkel-Brunswik, Daniel J. Levinson, and R. Nevitt Sanford, The Authoritarian Personality (New York: Harper, 1950).

34. *See* Thomas Blass, *The Migram Paradigm after 35 Years: Some Things We Now Know about Obedience to Authority*, 29 Journal of Applied Social Psychology 955–78 (1991).

35. *Ibid.* 968–69.

36. Stanley Milgram, Obedience to Authority: An Experimental View (New York, NY: Harper & Row, 1974).

37. Thomas Blass, *supra* note 34, 968.

exception is an Australian study in which women had significantly lower obedience rates than men.[38]

Other experiments conducted in the 1960s and 1970s demonstrated the power of compliance with authority. For example, in a study of nurses' compliance with physician's orders, an experimental confederate placed a call to a hospital nursing station, falsely identified himself as a hospital physician, and instructed hospital nurses to administer a dangerous dose of an unauthorized drug to a specific hospital patient.[39] Even though the "doctor" was not familiar to them, and even though most nurses would realize that the dosage level was dangerous, 95 percent of the nurses attempted to comply. Experiments aside, it turns out that nurses' and pharmacists' unquestioning compliance with obvious physician errors on prescriptions is a significant cause of medical error.[40]

17.2.1 The Impulse Toward Obedience: Legal and Policy Implications

Research on obedience to authority has important legal and policy implications. Consider, for example, noncustodial searches by police officers. Obedience research suggests that powerful psychological forces are at work in police-citizen encounters, where a pronounced discrepancy usually exists between the status of the detained citizen and the status of the police officer, often accentuated by his uniform. As one commentator has suggested, "Suspects faced with an official request to search may instinctively feel that their options are limited based on a reflexive tendency to obey authority, even when police conduct falls far short of overt coercion."[41]

Police lineup procedures present another example of the policy implications of the psychology of obedience. An officer's instruction to a crime victim to "pick the one who did it," for example, can convey a subtle but powerful message to the victim that they must choose *someone* in the lineup group. Such biased instructions have been shown to increase the frequency of false identifications.[42]

The graphic and perverted display of prisoner abuse at Abu Ghraib prison in Iraq, captured in photographs taken by the soldiers themselves, provides

---

38. Wesley Kilham and Leon Mann, "*Level of Destructive Obedience as a Function of Transmitter and Executant Roles in the Milgram Obedience Paradigm*," JOURNAL OF PERSONALITY AND SOCIAL PSYCHOLOGY, 29 (1974): 696–702.

39. Charles K. Hofling et al., *An Experimental Study in Nurse-Physician Relationships*, 143 JOURNAL OF NERVOUS AND MENTAL DISEASE 171–80 (1966).

40. Neil M. DAVIS and Michael R. COHEN, MEDICATION ERRORS: CAUSES AND PREVENTION (Philadelphia: G. F. Stickley, 1981).

41. Adrian J. Barrio, *Rethinking* Schneckloth v. Bustamonte*: Incorporating Obedience Theory into the Supreme Court's Conception of Voluntary Consent,* UNIVERSITY OF ILLINOIS LAW REVIEW 215 (1997).

42. C. A. Elizabeth Luus and Gary L. Wells, *Eyewitness Identification Confidence, in* ADULT EYEWITNESS TESTIMONY: CURRENT TRENDS AND DEVELOPMENTS (David F. Ross, J. Don Read, and Michael P. Toglia eds., New York: Cambridge University Press, 1994).

troubling evidence of the extent to which obedience can lead us astray. One of the military police who served in Abu Ghraib reported that they were told by superiors, "Use your imagination. Break them. We want them broke by the time we come back."[43] The deadly environment, the pressure for intelligence, and the ambiguity of how they were supposed to "break" the prisoners led to the abuse, torture, and even death of detainees.

17.2.2 Defusing the Impulses Toward Obedience

In sum, we learn from a very early age to obey authority. That is not necessarily a bad thing: society benefits from order. We benefit individually and collectively from the things we learn and the disasters we avoid by doing what those with more knowledge and experience tell us to do. But, like so many rules, the injunction to "obey authority" can be overapplied, particularly in situations that supply powerful cues for compliance. The thought should chill anyone in a subordinate position, especially in an unfamiliar environment.

But despite the powerful pull of obedience, it is possible to defy authority to support one's principles. The abuse at Abu Ghraib continued until Joe Darby, a military policeman on a different assignment at the prison, saw the photographs of the abuse. "It didn't sit right with me," says Darby. He was torn between loyalty to his friends and the moral offensiveness of the acts, which "violated everything I personally believed." After three days of weighing the competing demands, he reported the photographs.[44]

Consider Hugh Thompson, a helicopter pilot whose regiment perpetrated the My Lai Massacre in Vietnam. With all of his comrades—including his superior officers—shooting villagers and looting huts, Hugh Thompson got out of his helicopter, stood in the line of fire between his fellow soldiers and a house where wounded Vietnamese civilians were seeking refuge, and told his fellow soldiers to cease fire.[45]

Darby's and Thompson's experiences remind us that although the forces that compel us to obey authority are strong, people can and do stand up to authority even when the consequences are grave. But it is also incredibly difficult to do. To control the unthinking impulse to obey authority, we need to understand its dynamics. Insights come from a number of sources, some of them in Milgram's experiments themselves.

Milgram conducted a total of nineteen variations of his basic experimental design. Under some conditions, rates of compliance dropped from the original 63 percent baseline, and under others, they increased. Rates of compliance rose when subjects first watched peers administering the shocks (showing the

---

43. Phillip C. Zimbardo, The Lucifer Effect: Understanding How Good People Turn Evil, *supra* note 3, 352.

44. *Id.* at 330.

45. *Id.* at 474.

interactive relationship between compliance and conformity effects). Rates of compliance were highest when subjects were high school students and the experiment was conducted by lab-coated experimenters on the grounds of Princeton University. Compliance rates dropped precipitously when another subject rebelled. Contradictory instructions by two experimenters, having instructions given by an ordinary person rather than a white-lab-coated experimenter, placing the subject in close proximity to and/or visual contact with the "learner," and allowing subjects to choose the level of shock they would administer, all decreased compliance rates significantly.

As numerous social psychologists have observed, certain structural features of the situation Milgram constructed made it particularly powerful in eliciting high rates of compliance. At the beginning of the session, the procedure was explained to subjects. By agreeing to participate, they implicitly consented to following the instructions. The intensity of the shocks increased gradually, 15 "volts" at a time. Having given a shock of just slightly less intensity than the one they were now being asked to administer made it more difficult for subjects to refuse. (See Section 17.3 on consistency and commitment.) When subjects did object, the experimenter's icy responses "You have no choice," The experiment requires that you continue," or "You have no other choice, you *must* go on," left open no "disobedience channel" through which subjects could exit without "making a scene." Most people don't like to make a scene.

Imagine, as social psychologist Lee Ross suggested, that there had been a large red button on the shock generator panel in front of Milgram's subjects labeled, "Stop the Experiment." How would that have affected compliance rates? So far as we know, the experiment has not been done, but our intuitions support Ross's suggestion that the presence of such a button would have served as a *channel factor* for disobedience and would have reduced compliance.[46]

Milgram concluded that the impulse toward obedience is "a deeply ingrained tendency, indeed a prepotent impulse overriding training in ethics, sympathy, and social conduct."[47] Robert Cialdini suggests that the rule, "obey legitimate authority figures," functions as a heuristic, or rule of thumb, that people use to decide how to act when conditions are ambiguous. He proposes that the heuristic is automatically activated when features of the social environment provide cues to its applicability.[48]

---

46. Lee Ross, *Situationist Perspectives on the Obedience Experiments,* 33 CONTEMPORARY PSYCHOLOGY 101–04 (1988).

47. Stanley Milgram, *Behavioral Study of Obedience, supra* note 30.

48. Robert B. CIALDINI, INFLUENCE: THE PSYCHOLOGY OF PERSUASION, *supra* note 3. Robert B. Cialdini, *Compliance Principles of Compliance Professionals: Psychologists of Necessity, in* SOCIAL INFLUENCE FROM THE ONTARIO SYMPOSIUM 5 165–84 (Mark P. Zanna, James M. Olson, and C. P. Herman eds., Hillsdale, NJ: Erlbaum, 1987).

This way of understanding Milgram's results suggests several approaches to inoculating oneself against automatic obedience. Psychologists Philip Zimbardo and Michael Lieppe suggest:[49]

- remain engaged with alternate systems of authority, such as a those deriving from your religious, spiritual, political, or philosophical commitments;
- trust your intuition when you find yourself thinking, "something is wrong here";
- when in doubt, seek out a knowledgeable—but independent—person to give you an "obedience check";
- mentally rehearse disobedience strategies and techniques for various situations;
- be particularly vigilant when you notice people using euphemisms to describe harmful behaviors or the people they harm;
- don't expect not to suffer adverse consequences when refusing to obey an authority figure—rather, consider the worst case scenario and act on that possibility;
- chose carefully the organizations and situations in which you place yourself, because it's all too easy to overestimate your powers to resist.

17.3 CONSISTENCY AND THE ESCALATION OF COMMITMENT

In Section 14.3 we discussed various factors that lead people to take "sunk costs" into account when making decisions about the future. We continue that discussion here, focusing more on social determinants.

Once we have taken a position, whether through an activity or communication, we tend to behave in a manner consistent with that position and to accede to requests that are consistent with it. Why people might act this way is no mystery: the social costs of changing one's mind or of otherwise appearing inconsistent can be steep.

17.3.1 The Foot in the Door

How might one persuade residents of Palo Alto, California, to place large, ugly "Drive Safely" signs on their tidy front lawns? When Jonathan Freedman and Scott Fraser asked Palo Alto homeowners to let them place an enormous, tacky, hand-painted sign on their front lawns, only 16.7 percent agreed. But in the experimental condition, in which homeowners had agreed two weeks earlier to place a three-inch sign with the same message on their front lawns, 76 percent acceded to the request.[50]

---

49. PHILIP. G. ZIMBARDO AND MARK R. LIEPPE, *supra* note 4, 75 (1991).

50. Jonathan L. Freedman and Scott C. Fraser, *Compliance Without Pressure: The Foot-in-the-Door Technique,* 4 JOURNAL OF PERSONALITY AND SOCIAL PSYCHOLOGY 195 (1966).

The key to this *foot-in-the-door technique* is that compliance with the first request causes the target to *think of himself* in a way that makes him more likely to accede to the second through a process of *self-attribution*.[51] That is, by freely agreeing to perform and then performing the first action, the foot-in-the-door target comes to view himself as "the kind of person" who would do things of that kind or support the position expressed by the first action.

Fundraisers use the foot-in-the-door technique all the time, which is why your graduate school will try to get you to make a donation, no matter how small, before you have earned your first dollar as a lawyer or policy professional—perhaps even while you are still paying tuition. Lawyers and investigators use the technique, too, for example, when they are trying to persuade reluctant witnesses to discuss a case with them. Later, perhaps even in the same case, a mediator may use the technique in an attempt to help the parties reach a settlement.

Police officers use the foot-in-the-door technique when dealing with suspects. For instance, a police officer may ask permission to enter a residence "just to talk" (first request). Once inside, and after some friendly conversation, she may then ask for consent to conduct a search (bigger second request). One can readily see from this example how various social influence factors, in this case both obedience to authority and the consistency and commitment tendency, could work together to amplify compliance.

17.3.2 The Low-Ball Technique

The tendency toward consistency and commitment can work in other ways to induce compliance in the unwary. After a person has made a tentative agreement, say, to settle a case for a specific amount, or to accept a job offer on particular terms, she will tend to follow through with that agreement even if the terms of the deal are subsequently made less favorable to her. Social psychologists (and car salespeople) refer to the phenomenon as the "low-ball effect."

The best-known experimental demonstration of the low-ball effect comes from a study by Robert Cialdini conducted in the late 1970s. In one condition, Cialdini asked students enrolled in an introductory psychology class if they would be willing to participate in a study "on thinking processes" to be held at 7:00 a.m. Only 24 percent agreed. A different group from the same class was simply asked if they would participate in a study of "thinking processes," with no time specified; 56 percent agreed. Cialdini and his associates then told these students that the study would start at 7:00 a.m. None reneged, despite having the opportunity to do so.[52]

---

51. Donald R. Gorassini and James M. Olson, *Does Self-Perception Change Explain the Foot-in-the-Door Effect?*, 69 Journal of Personality and Social Psychology 91 (1995).

52. Robert B. Cialdini, John T. Cacioppo, Rodney Bassett, and Geoffrey A. Miller, *Low-Ball Procedure or Producing Compliance: Commitment then Cost*, 36 Journal of Personality and Social Psychology 463–76 (1978).

As Richard Birke and Craig Fox have observed, foot-in-the-door, low-ball, and other aspects of the consistency and commitment tendency often converge in affecting the parties' behavior in mediations.[53] First, mediators often begin by inducing the parties to commit to a general statement of principles, or an aspiration. Once the mediator has this foot in the door, she is more likely to induce party compliance with later, more substantial requests. The low-ball technique also often comes into play, as Birke and Fox note. Once the parties have invested significant time and energy into crafting a tentative agreement, they can often be induced to agree to last-minute modifications, even if they make the deal less beneficial to them.

17.3.3 The Irrational Escalation of Commitment

Many situations provide fertile ground for the *irrational escalation of commitment*. These include decisions facing bank officers, who must decide whether to loan more money to a defaulting client or write off the loan; lawyers and clients deciding whether to settle a suit or continue its litigation; and managers deciding whether to fire an employee or invest additional resources in helping him improve.[54] All these situations have a common structure. First, they involve a continuing course of action toward a desired end with periodic opportunities for exit. Second, at some point along the way, some loss or cost is incurred, making achievement of the goal less likely, or more costly than previously anticipated. Third, despite this initial cost or loss, ultimate success is still possible, although it would require the investment of additional resources. Finally, withdrawal from the situation would impose an immediate loss or cost, in contrast with the eventual success that perseverance could theoretically bring.

As business administration professors Barry Staw and Jerry Ross explain, "escalation situations can be defined as predicaments where costs are suffered in a course of action, where there is an opportunity to withdraw or persist, and where the consequences of persistence and withdrawal are uncertain."[55]

The escalation cycle begins when a questionable or negative outcome—the loss of an initial motion to dismiss a lawsuit, for example—has been experienced. At that point, the actors (e.g., a litigation defendant and his lawyer) must reexamine their commitment to the original course of action (i.e., defending the suit) and decide whether to withdraw (i.e., settle on terms less favorable than

---

53. R. Birke and C. R. Fox, *Psychological Principles in Negotiating Civil Settlements*, 1 Harvard Negotiation Law Review 61 (1999).

54. Barry M. Staw, Sigal G. Barsade, and Kenneth W. Koput, *Escalation at the Credit Window: A Longitudinal Study of Bank Executives' Recognition and Write-off of Problem Loans*, 82 Journal of Applied Psychology 130–42 (1997).

55. Barry M. Staw and Jerry Ross, *Understanding Behavior In Escalation Situations, in* Psychological Dimensions of Organizational Behavior 206–13 (Barry M. Staw ed., 3rd ed. Upper Saddle River, NJ: Pearson Prentice Hall, 2004).

previously deemed acceptable), or press forward (i.e., undertake discovery and prepare for summary judgment and/or trial). In making this assessment, the lawyer-client team will balance the perceived utility of continuing in the current course of action (litigation) against the perceived utility of exit (settling) and decide whether or not to recommit and invest additional resources.

A substantial amount of research has demonstrated that people and organizations tend to escalate their commitment to a failing course of action beyond rational levels.[56] Additional research has illuminated the particular conditions under which such irrational escalation of commitment is most likely to occur.[57]

Why Cases Don't Settle Early and Often

Although the vast majority of civil cases settle, they often settle very late, after enormous amounts of money have been spent on pleadings, discovery, and motion practice.[58] There are, of course, many reasons for this, including the asymmetrical valuation of losses and gains, the financial incentives motivating lawyers who bill by the hour, the persistence of information asymmetries between the parties, and the various cognitive distortions that comprise what was referred to in Section 14.3 as the *sunk costs fallacy*. But the escalation of commitment likely also plays a role in keeping cases from settling optimally.

Explanatory accounts of escalation tend to cluster around four sets of factors that conduce to its occurrence. Barry M. Staw and Jerry Ross classify these as: (1) project determinants; (2) psychological determinants; (3) social determinants; and (4) and organizational determinants.

With respect to *project determinants*, some projects by their very nature entail a long delay between investment and payoff, with setbacks and revenue shortfalls reasonably expected along the way. Research and development projects are one example. Civil litigation is another. Decision making about projects such as these is particularly vulnerable to escalation effects because of the expected delay between expenditures and the resulting benefits. Because of the long time horizon, initial losses or shortfalls do not raise alarms, and organizations are unlikely

56. *See* Max Bazerman, Judgment in Managerial Decision Making (5th ed., New York: Wiley, 2002) for a review.

57. Barry M. Staw and Jerry Ross, *Behavior in Escalation Situations: Antecedents, Prototypes, and Solutions*, *in* Research in Organizational Behavior (Barry M. Staw and Larry L. Cummings eds., Greenwill, CT: JAI Press, 1987); Joel Brockner and Jerry Z. Rubin, Entrapment in Escalating Conflicts (New York: Springer-Verlag, 1985).

58. Samuel R. Gross and Kent D. Syverud, *Getting to No: A Study of Settlement Negotiations and the Selection of Cases for Trial*, 90 Michigan Law Review 319–93 (1991).

to alter course.[59] Other projects may conduce toward escalation of commitment because they have little or no salvage value, or because they involve very high closing costs if abandoned mid-stream.[60]

We described in earlier chapters many of the cognitive biases constituting the major *psychological determinants* of irrational escalation of commitment. Primary among these is confirmation bias, through which people preferentially seek and then overweight evidence supporting their prior beliefs and ignore or rationalize evidence opposing them. Other psychological factors include the power of intermittent reinforcement,[61] ego-enhancing bias,[62] belief perseverance,[63] the desire to avoid regret and negative self-attribution.[64]

Organizational determinants of suboptimal escalation include the absence of a clearly defined exit strategy, past failure to hedge against the possibility that the chosen strategy would fail, and whether the decision to escalate or withdraw is made by the same or different people than those who made the original decision to invest or reinvest.[65] The strength of the escalation tendency may also depend on whether the purpose of the project in question is closely tied to the values or purposes of the organization that has undertaken it,[66] or on factors as banal as whether the administrative resources needed to formulate and effectuate an exit strategy are readily available.

Of greatest relevance to this section, however, are the *social determinants* of escalation, as these relate most closely to the consistency and commitment tendency

---

59. Barry M. Staw and Jerry Ross, *Behavior in Escalation Situations: Antecedents, Prototypes, and Solutions, supra* note 57; John Platt, *Social Traps*, 28 AMERICAN PSYCHOLOGIST 642–43 (1973).

60. Gregory B. Northcroft and Gerrit Wolf, *Dollars, Sense, and Sunk Costs: A Life Cycle Model of Resource Allocation Decisions*, 9 ACADEMY OF MANAGEMENT REVIEW 225–34 (1984).

61. Barry M. Staw and Jerry Ross, *Behavior in Escalation Situations: Antecedents, Prototypes, and Solutions, supra* note 57; John Platt, *Social Traps, supra* note 59.

62. Barry M. Staw, *Knee-Deep in the Big Muddy: A Study of Escalating Commitment to a Chosen Course of Action*, 16 ORGANIZATIONAL BEHAVIOR AND HUMAN PERFORMANCE 27–44 (1976); Max Bazerman, R.I. Beekum, and F. D. Schoorman, *Performance Evaluation in a Dynamic Context: A Laboratory Study of the Impact of Prior Commitment to the Ratee*, 67 Journal of Applied Psychology 873–876 (1982).

63. RICHARD E. NISBETT AND LEE ROSS, HUMAN INFERENCE: STRATEGIES AND SHORTCOMINGS OF SOCIAL JUDGMENT (Englewood Hills, NJ: Prentice-Hall, 1980).

64. Barry M. Staw and Jerry Ross, *Behavior in Escalation Situations: Antecedents, Prototypes, and Solutions, supra* note 57.

65. *Ibid.*

66. Lynn G. Zucker, *Organizations as Institutions, in* RESEARCH IN THE SOCIOLOGY OF ORGANIZATIONS 2, 53–111 (Samuel B. Bacharach ed., Greenwich, CT: JAI Press, 1981); Paul S. Goodman, Max Bazerman, and Edward Conlon, *Institutionalization of Planned Organizational Change, in* RESEARCH IN ORGANIZATIONAL BEHAVIOR: VOL. 2, 215–46 (Barry M. Staw and Lynn L. Cummings eds., Greenwich, CT: JAI Press, 1980).

described earlier in this section. In an escalation situation, certain social determinants function to increase the perceived utility of recommitment to an ongoing course of action, while others tend to decrease the perceived utility of exit.

Consider in this regard decisions between two options: settling an ongoing lawsuit on disappointing terms, or continuing to litigate. Even after significant monetary losses or strategic setbacks, lawyers and clients will be pushed toward recommitment by social norms of perseverance, to which innumerable sayings like "keep on keepin' on," "venceremos," "against all odds," and "dare to struggle, dare to win" bear witness. This norm of perseverance is reinforced by media representations of successful lawsuits and the lawyer-heroes that litigated them. Think, for example, how bleak the prospects looked for the plaintiffs portrayed in the movies *Erin Brockovich* and *The Verdict*, and recall how glorious were their eventual victories.

Just as perseverance norms and scripts may inflate the perceived utility of recommitment, so other factors may diminish the perceived utility of withdrawal. Lawyers are notoriously competitive, and the litigation process seldom turns adversaries into friends. A litigant or his lawyer may want to persevere if only to deny the opponent the savor of success. To the extent that the litigation has been acrimonious (and it often is), any existing sense of rivalry be amplified.

If a party or his lawyer has taken a public position on a dispute, pressures to escalate commitment may be intensified even further. Public statements of commitment powerfully bind people to a course of action, particularly when actions taken in connection with it are unambiguous and freely undertaken.[67]

In sum, the consistency and commitment tendency, combined with other psychological forces and situational factors, conduces toward the irrational escalation of commitment to a questionable or failing course of action. As with other systematic biases and tendencies toward misjudgment, it is possible to reduce—though probably not eliminate—the escalation syndrome. Staw and Ross, for example, make the following suggestions:

- When an ongoing course of action has led to unexpected losses or setbacks and a decision regarding recommitment or exit must be made, involve new decision makers who were not responsible for the original decision to commit.
- Hedge possible losses on one project with other opportunities for gain.
- Provide organizational support for decision makers to reverse course, and lower the personal costs of an exit decision.
- In situations where irrational escalation is a possibility, provide decision makers with unambiguous feedback, preferably gathered and presented by people with minimal connection to the original decision.

67. Barry M. Staw and Jerry Ross, *Behavior in Escalation Situations: Antecedents, Prototypes, and Solutions*, *supra* note 57; Gerald R. Salancik, *Commitment and the Control of Organizational Behavior and Belief*, *in* New Directions in Organizational Behavior 1–54 (Barry M. Staw and Gerald R. Salancik eds., 1977).

- Calculate the costs and make a plan for closing at the outset of the project.

17.4 LIKING

We tend to like those who like us. We tend to keep track of "credits and debits" with people we are not close to, but are less likely to do so for those we like a lot. We tend to credit views expressed by people we like and discredit views expressed by people we dislike. We prefer to say "yes" to those we like. For these and other reasons, "liking" can impair our judgments and make us more susceptible to influence.[68] Several factors promote liking, including: familiarity, similarity, cooperation, compliments, and physical attractiveness.[69]

17.4.1 Familiarity

All else being equal, we tend to like people and things that are more, rather than less, familiar. As the late Stanford psychologist Robert Zajonc demonstrated, mere exposure to an initially neutral or favorable stimulus enhances its evaluation.[70] So, for example, people express greater liking of, and express higher levels of agreement with, people whose faces they have encountered frequently, even in subliminal exposures.[71] These sorts of exposure effects appear to be even stronger in the real world than they are in the laboratory.[72]

---

68. A study described in Section 17.5 leaves open the question of how effective liking is in gaining compliance. Dennis T. Regan, *Effects of a Favor and Liking on Compliance,* 7 Journal of Experimental Pscyhology 627–39 (1971). Liking for a male confederate was manipulated (i.e., the subject overheard him behave in either a "pleasant" or "nasty" way to someone with whom he was speaking on the phone), and the participants received a soft drink (a favor) from either the confederate, or from the experimenter, or received no favor at all. The confederate then asked the participants to purchase some raffle tickets. Regan found that the favor strongly increased compliance with the request, but he did not find a similar effect for liking. However, he cautioned that "[i]t would not be warranted to conclude, on the basis of the manipulation used in this study, that liking does not generally affect compliance." *Id.* at 635.

69. Different social psychologists proffer slightly different taxonomies. Ours represents a combination of Robert Cialdini's and Susan Fiskes'. *See* Robert Cialdini, Influence: Science and Practice 136–53 (3rd ed. New York: HarperCollins, 1993) and Susan T. Fiske, Social Beings, *supra* note 4, 257–276.

70. Robert. B. Zajonc, *Attitudinal Effects of Mere Exposure,* 9 Journal of Personality and Social Psychology 1–27 (1968).

71. Robert F. Bornstein, Dean R. Leone, and Donna J. Galley, *The Generalizability of Subliminal Mere Exposure Effects: Influence of Stimuli Perceived without Awareness on Social Behavior,* 53 Journal of Personality and Social Psychology 1070–79 (1987).

72. Robert F. Bornstein, *Exposure and Affect: Overview and Meta-Analysis of Research 1968–1987,* 106 Psychological Bulletin 265–89 (1989).

17.4.2 Similarity

Not surprisingly, we tend to like those who share our cultures, values, and beliefs more than we like people who don't. Common notions that "opposites attract" notwithstanding, the vast weight of social psychological evidence supports the proposition that people are preferentially attracted to and are more satisfied with their interactions with people whose attitudes, interests, and personalities are similar to their own.[73] With respect to the effect of attitude similarity on liking, proportions are critical. "If a person only agrees with us on twelve out of twenty-four topics, he or she is not liked as much as another who agrees with us on four out of six topics."[74]

The similarity principle has obvious legal policy implications, as various empirical researchers have demonstrated. In one such study, mock jurors who perceived a defendant as sharing many of their beliefs and attitudes were less inclined to find him guilty and were more inclined toward leniency in sentencing.[75] Results like these have obvious implications for jury selection, judicial qualifications, and legal advocacy.[76]

17.4.3 Reciprocity and Cooperation

As Susan Fiske observes, "Next to similarity, reciprocity is the most powerful predictor of attraction."[77] Cooperative interdependence is a powerful engine of good feeling.

These observations have obvious implications for the practice of law—or politics. To the extent that cooperation engenders liking, lawyers and politicians often induce good feeling, and from good feeling, compliance, by behaving in a cooperative way towards others. Contrary to the popular belief that a successful negotiator is one who ruthlessly intimidates and exploits her counterparts, a cooperative relationship can be more effective for achieving mutually beneficial and equitable outcomes.[78] Moreover, studies of lawyers as negotiators have

---

73. Ellen Berscheid and Harry T. Reis, *Attraction and Close Relationships, in* HANDBOOK OF SOCIAL PSYCHOLOGY 193–281 (Daniel. T. Gilbert, Susan T. Fiske, and Gardner Lindzey eds., 4th ed. New York: McGraw-Hill, 1988).

74. CURT BARTOL AND ANNE BARTOL, PSYCHOLOGY AND LAW: THEORY, RESEARCH AND APPLICATION, 3d EDITION (Florence, KY: Wadsworth Publishing, 2004)

75. William Griffitt and Thomas Jackson, *Simulated Jury Decisions: The Influence of Jury-Defendant Attitude Similarity-Dissimilarity,* 1 SOCIAL BEHAVIOR AND PERSONALITY (1973).

76. CURT BARTOL AND ANNE BARTOL, PSYCHOLOGY AND LAW: RESEARCH AND APPLICATION, *supra* note 75.

77. Susan T. Fiske, *supra* note 4, 270.

78. *See* Richard Birke and Craig R. Fox, *Psychological Principles in Negotiating Civil Settlements,* 1 HARVARD NEGOTIATION AND LAW REVIEW 1–57 (1999); Max H. Bazerman and Margaret A. Neale, *The Role of Fairness Considerations and Relationships in a Judgmental Perspective of Negotiation, in* BARRIERS TO CONFLICT RESOLUTION (Robert H. Mnookin,

shown that those who are cooperative are perceived by others as more effective, on average, than lawyers who are not.[79]

17.4.4 Compliments

In the psychological literature, the use of compliments is classified under "ingratiation tactics." Ingratiation tactics are a class of strategic behaviors that are designed to elicit liking from the target.[80] The use of compliments to engender liking is an artful skill, for if the tactic "becomes obvious to a target (entirely transparent) [it] is likely to fail miserably at increasing a target's liking for the ingratiator," and may even be counterproductive. To avoid transparency, for example, a low-status person who can obviously gain from successful ingratiation may do best to compliment a high-status person in an indirect manner, such as by telling a third person what they like about the high-status person in a way that allows the high-status person to "overhear" the compliment.[81]

17.4.5 Physical Attractiveness

Attractive people have advantages in social interaction. Physical attractiveness operates as a powerful "halo effect," influencing people's judgments of other people's talent, kindness, honesty, and intelligence, among other traits.[82]

Many studies examining the effects of defendant attractiveness on verdicts have found attractiveness to be associated with leniency in mock criminal cases.[83] These laboratory experiments are complimented by field studies showing

---

Lee Ross, Kenneth J. Arrow, and Amos Tversky, eds., Stanford, CA: Stanford Center on Conflict and Negotiation, 1995), 86–107.

79. *See* Gerald R. Williams, Legal Negotiation and Settlement 19 (St. Paul, Minnesota: West Publishing, 1983).

80. Other ingratiation tactics include opinion conformity, rendering favors, self-deprecation, and modesty. *See* Randall A. Gordon, *Impact of Ingratiation on Judgments and Evaluations: A Meta-Analytic Investigation*, 54 Journal of Personality and Social Psychology 71 (1996).

81. However: "Developing a relationship takes time and must progress at its own pace. In fact, pursuing friendliness as an influence tactic usually requires that the relationship between the agent and the target already be in place before the request is made so the relationship can be used effectively. If the agent tries to cultivate a relationship very quickly and to use it simply as a vehicle in which to lodge the influence request, it is likely that the target will see the friendliness gestures as superficial and insincere, a perception that will raise the target's defensiveness rather than lower it." Roy J. Lewicki, Joseph A. Litterer, John W. Minton and David M. Saunders, Negotiation 316 (McGraw Hill, 1994).

82. Alice H. Eagly, Richard D. Ashmore, Mona G. Makhijani, and Laura C. Longo, *What Is Beautiful Is Good: A Meta-Analytic Review of Research on the Physical Attractiveness Stereotype*, 110 Psychological Bulletin 109–28 (1990).

83. *See* Michael G. Efran, *The Effect of Physical Appearance on the Judgment of Guilt, Interpersonal Attraction, and Severity of Recommended Punishment in a Simulated Jury Task*, 8 Journal of Research in Personality 45–53 (1974) (finding that attractive female

that, when other variables are controlled for, less physically attractive defendants generally receive more severe sentences.[84] In the civil litigation context as well, the evidence that physically attractive individuals experience better legal outcomes is both compelling and disturbing.[85]

Similar effects have been found in the context of hiring, voting, and helping behavior. In all three contexts, decision makers seem unaware of the effect of physical attractiveness on their judgment.[86]

Some qualifications to the case for physical attraction effects are in order here. First, although physical attractiveness powerfully influences people's judgments of others, notions of attractiveness—and the extent of their impact on person judgment—vary cross-culturally. For example, Chinese immigrants to Canada did not show the effect in a study by Karen K. Dion, A. Won-Ping Pak, and Kenneth L. Dion.[87] In a Taiwanese study, the effect of attractiveness was moderated by Western value orientation (perhaps showing the independent effect of familiarity).[88]

Second, people who score higher in measures of self-consciousness show stronger effects of physical attractiveness on their judgments than do people

defendants were less likely than unattractive female defendants to be found guilty by, and receive lighter sentences from, male jurors); Martin F. Kaplan and Gwen D. Kemmerick, *Juror Judgment as Information Integration: Combining Evidential and Non-evidential Information*, 30 JOURNAL OF PERSONALITY AND SOCIAL PSYCHOLOGY 493 (1974); Gloria Leventhal and Ronald Krate, *Physical Attractiveness and Severity of Sentencing*, 40 PSYCHOL. REP. 315, 315–17 (1977) (finding that mock jurors recommended shorter sentences for physically attractive defendants than for physically unattractive defendants, regardless of juror's gender, defendant's gender, or seriousness of offense); John E. Stewart, II, *Defendant's Attractiveness as a Factor in the Outcome of Criminal Trials: An Observational Study*, 10 J. APPLIED SOC. PSYCHOL. 348 (1980); Wayne Weiten, *The Attraction-Leniency Effect in Jury Research: An Examination of External Validity*, 10 J. APPLIED SOC. PSYCHOL. 340 (1980).

84. *See, for example*, J. E. Stewart II, *Defendant's Attractiveness as a Factor in the Outcome of Criminal Trials: An Observational Study*, 10 JOURNAL OF APPLIED SOCIAL PSYCHOLOGY 348–61 (1980).

85. For a literature review, *see* A. Chris Downs and Phillip M. Lyons, *Natural Observations of the Links Between Attractiveness and Initial Legal Judgments*, 17 PERSONALITY AND SOCIAL PSYCHOLOGY BULLETIN 541–47 (1990).

86. The studies are collected in Robert B. Cialdini, *supra* note 3, 141–42.

87. Karen K. Dion, A. Won-Ping Pak, and Kenneth L. Dion, *Stereotypic Physical Attractiveness: A Sociocultural Perspective*, 21 JOURNAL OF CROSS-CULTURAL PSYCHOLOGY 158–79 (1990).

88. David R. Shaffer, Nicole Crepaz, and Chien-Ru Sun, *Physical Attractiveness Stereotyping in Cross-Cultural Perspective: Similarities and Differences Between Americans and Taiwanese*, 31 JOURNAL OF CROSS-CULTURAL PSYCHOLOGY 557–82 (2000).

who score lower.[89] This suggests that liking based on physical attractiveness is mediated by the salience of motives toward self-enhancement.

These caveats aside, existing experimental evidence—in both the laboratory and the field—suggests that physical attractiveness is a significant determinant of liking, which in turn has a powerful effect on judgment and choice.

17.5 RECIPROCITY

Our social inclination to reciprocate makes us prone to accede to requests from people who have done favors for us—even when the favors were uninvited and trivial and the subsequent requests are substantial. To inoculate themselves against this tendency, some lawyers, for example, will refuse even the slightest favor from an opposing counsel, even if it is as trivial as the opponent's paying for their cup of coffee at the downstairs Starbucks. We also tend to reciprocate concessions. If we have refused an initial request, we are more likely than we would be otherwise to accede to a subsequent, smaller request by the same person. So, beware if an opponent asks you for a patently unreasonable extension of time, followed up by a more measured request.

Our tendency to reciprocate is a well-studied phenomenon. In the early 1970s, for example, Dennis T. Regan set out to determine which of two factors—liking, or prior receipt of a favor—would most powerfully influence people's compliance with a request. Prior receipt of a favor won hands down. Subjects were far more willing to buy raffle tickets from a confederate they had heard behave badly on the phone, but who had given them a free Coke, than subjects who had heard the confederate behave kindly on the phone but from whom they had not received a free Coke. Across all conditions, receipt of the favor had a significant effect on compliance. The effect of liking, on the other hand, proved quite weak.[90]

Elaborating on the Regan study, Mark Whately and his associates sought to determine whether the strength of the reciprocity norm would be affected by a person's belief that his compliance with a request would become publicly known. Whateley placed participants, together with a confederate, in a situation where they thought they would be evaluating art for a study on aesthetic judgment. During a break in the evaluations, the confederate left and returned either with a small bag of candy (the "favor") for the subject or empty-handed. When the evaluations were over, all participants received a written request from the confederate to pledge a donation to a charity.

---

89. Mark Snyder, Ellen Berscheid, and Peter Glick, *Focusing on the Exterior and the Interior: Two Investigations of the Initiation of Personal Relationships*, 48 Journal of Personality and Social Psychology 1427–39 (1985).

90. Dennis T. Regan, *Effects of a Favor and Liking on Compliance*, 7 Journal of Experimental Social Psychology 627–39 (1971).

In one condition, subjects were led to believe that the confederate would know whether they made a pledge (the public compliance condition). In another (the private compliance condition), subjects were led to believe that the confederate would not. The presence of the favor increased compliance in both public and private conditions. That is, people receiving an unsolicited favor were more likely to comply with subsequent requests from the person doing the initial favor, regardless of whether the compliance was public or private. But subjects in the public compliance condition donated significantly more money than did those in the private compliance condition.[91]

We reciprocate concessions as well as favors, as demonstrated by research on what Robert Cialdini calls the *door-in-the-face technique*. The basic insight here is that a person is more likely to induce compliance with a request for a small favor if she asks for a more extreme favor first. The technique works as follows: the persuader presents the target with a significant request, something she knows the target will turn down (the door in the face). Then, after the target refuses, the persuader makes the smaller request, the one she was actually interested in all along. Viewing the second request as a concession on the persuader's part, the target feels compelled to accede.

In the classic study of this door-in-the-face effect, Cialdini and his associates asked college students who were walking across campus if they would be willing to accompany a group of juvenile offenders on a day trip to the zoo.[92] Only seventeen percent said "yes." In a second condition, students were first presented with a more extreme request: would they be willing to spend two hours a week for two years as unpaid counselors to juvenile offenders? After refusing this extreme request, subjects in this second condition were asked to take part in the zoo trip. Fifty percent agreed so to do.

The door-in-the-face technique prompts action—not merely a verbal agreement to act. For example, researchers investigated whether door-in-the-face victims who had agreed to work for two unpaid hours in a community mental-health agency actually showed up to perform their duties as promised.[93] The tactic of starting with a larger request (to volunteer for two hours of work per week in the agency for at least two years) produced more verbal agreement to the smaller retreat request (76 percent) as compared to the tactic of asking for the smaller request alone (29 percent). Even more remarkable was the rate of follow-through.

---

91. Mark A. Whately, J. Matthew Webster, Richard H. Smith, and Adele Rhodes, *The Effect of a Favor on Public and Private Compliance: How Internalized Is the Norm of Reciprocity?*, 21 Basic and Applied Social Psychology 251 (1999).

92. Robert B. Cialdini et al., *Reciprocal Concessions Procedure for Inducing Compliance: The Door-in-the-Face Technique*, 31 Journal of Personality and Social Psychology 206 (1999).

93. *Ibid.*

Subjects in the door-in-the-face condition showed up at a rate of 85 percent, as compared to 50 percent of subjects in the control condition.

A reader might wonder whether the door-in-the-face technique merely results from a (cognitive) contrast effect. After all, a person might be more willing to accede to a second, more modest request simply because it looks smaller in comparison with the earlier, more extreme request. But Cialdini's studies suggest that the phenomenon results from reciprocal concession giving. Merely exposing subjects to an extreme request did not increase the likelihood of compliance. Compliance with the second request must be construed as a *concession* on the part of the requester.

The strategic offering of favors and its cousin, the door-in-the-face technique, are deployed by lawyers and politicians all the time. Be wary, then, when you are presented with a favor, no matter how trivial, or when you are presented with serial offers or requests. By doing you a favor, the requester will have triggered in you an inclination to reciprocate in kind, whether or not it is in your or your client's interest to do so. When someone asks you for a favor and you turn it down, consider whether the requester could have reasonably foreseen your refusal to comply. If so, and if your refusal is followed by a second, less extreme request, you may want to give yourself some time to consider before responding. The extra time should buffer the pressure to comply, and allow you to think more rationally about whether it is really in your client's interest to accede.

17.6 CONCLUSION

Humans are social animals—we care a great deal about what other people think of us. There is nothing irrational in this. More often than not, our personal outcomes depend on the regard in which others hold us, and on their willingness to cooperate, promote our interests, and assist us in achieving our goals. It should come as no surprise, then, that processes of social influence play a major role in shaping behavior.

Social influence processes affect the work of lawyers and policy makers in significant ways. For this reason, it is important to understand them. Lawyers can affirmatively use influence mechanisms to enhance their persuasiveness when advocating on behalf of their clients. On the defensive front, lawyers can use their knowledge of social influence to guard against situations in which third parties may subtly attempt to alter their attitudes, or explain to clients ways in which others might attempt to influence them to act against their own best interests. The ability to recognize and react intelligently to various sources of social influence makes the difference between being at their mercy and resisting their appeal.

Policy makers, too, must understand and be able to use the levers of social influence. Policy initiatives, no matter how well intended or otherwise sound, may founder if they fail to take such forces as social proof into account. Conversely, the achievement of policy goals may be dramatically enhanced though the skilled deployment of the tendency toward consistency and commitment, or liking, or the triggering of norm cascades. Social influence is integral to persuasion, and persuasion—both to effecting it and resisting it.

The various cognitive processes mediating message processing, persuasion, and behavioral choice can be either *systematic* or *heuristic* in nature.[94] Systematic processing is a System II function—motivated, deliberate, conscious, and demanding of cognitive resources. Heuristic processing is a System I phenomenon, which can function automatically, with little awareness, and requiring only minimal cognitive effort. In some situations, a person might apply a quick persuasion rule, such as "believe the authority," or "if everyone else thinks it's right, it must be," instead of carefully analyzing a message's merit. Various factors, such as the listener's level of distraction[95] or the message's relevance to the listener[96] play a role in determining which type of processing, systematic or heuristic, occurs. Similar processes—either systematic or heuristic, mediate behavioral choice.

As this discussion suggests, social influence factors function in much the same way as other mental heuristics. In a message and choice-saturated world, shortcuts are essential. And given the social worlds in which we live, cooperation with and at times deference to others is both rational and effective. But, like all heuristics, social influences can lead us into errors, so we should strive to understand and seek to control their effects.

---

94. Shelly Chaiken, *The Heuristic Model of Persuasion*, *in* SOCIAL INFLUENCE: THE ONTARIO SYMPOSIUM VOL. 5, 3–39 (Mark P. Zanna, James M. Olson, and C. P. Herman eds., Hillsdale, N.J.: Erlbaum, 1987); John T. Cacioppo, Richard E. Petty, Chuan Feng Kao, and Regina Rodriguez, *Central and Peripheral Routes to Persuasion: An Individual Difference Perspective*, 51 JOURNAL OF PERSONALITY AND SOCIAL PSYCHOLOGY 1032–43 (1986).

95. Richard. E. Petty, Gary L. Wells, and Timothy C. Brock, *Distraction Can Enhance or Reduce Yielding to Propaganda: Thought Disruption versus Effort Justification*, 34 JOURNAL OF PERSONALITY AND SOCIAL PSYCHOLOGY 874–84 (1976).

96. Richard E. Petty, John T. Cacioppo, and Rachel Goldman, *Personal Involvement as a Determinant of Argument Based Persuasion*, 41 JOURNAL OF PERSONALITY AND SOCIAL PSYCHOLOGY 847–55 (1981).

18. INFLUENCING BEHAVIOR THROUGH COGNITION

This chapter asks how lawyers and policy makers can influence decision making by citizens, consumers, legislators, judges, and other officials through approaches that are mediated by people's judgment and perception rather than social influence. We begin with *argument*, the paradigmatic form of persuasion, and then turn to *priming*, and end by considering how policy makers can influence citizens' and consumers' behavior by *framing* the context for their choices.

18.1 PERSUASION THROUGH ARGUMENT

The chances are that readers of this book—whether students, lawyers, or policy makers—spend much of their time making and listening to arguments based on reason and evidence. But arguments can be more or less persuasive independent of their merits. Paradoxically, to ensure that meritorious arguments prevail, it often helps to use communication techniques that have nothing to do with the merits.

The study of persuasive argument dates back at least to Aristotle's *Rhetoric*. Our focus here is on the psychology of persuasion, in which argument is sometimes modeled as a multistage process:[1]

1. *Exposure* to the message.
2. *Attention* to the message.
3. *Comprehension* of the message.
4. *Acceptance* of the message's conclusion.
5. *Memory* of the message or its conclusion.
6. *Action* based on the message.

Much of the psychological research on rhetoric focuses on how communicators can increase recipients' comprehension, acceptance, and memory of the message. For example, in their popular book, *Made to Stick: Why Some Ideas Survive and*

1. Carl I. Hovland, Arthur A. Lumsdaine, and Fred. D. Sheffield, Studies in Social Psychology in World War II, Vol. 3: Experiments in Mass Communication (Princeton, NJ: Princeton University Press, 1949); Carl I. Hovland, Irving L. Janis, and Harold H. Kelly, Communication and Persuasion (New Haven, CT: Yale University Press, 1953); Carl I. Hovland ed., Order of Presentation in Persuasion (New Haven, CT: Yale University Press, 1957).

Others Die, Chip and Dan Heath provide a practical guide to making arguments memorable and influential.[2]

Simplicity. Simplicity is not about dumbing down ideas or using sound bites; rather it is about prioritizing. Because people have limited attention, it is often best to focus on a single, core message. Adding secondary points and unnecessary detail can detract from the impact of a message. Heath and Heath suggest that the ideal of simplicity is a message that gets at the core of the idea you are trying to convey and includes nothing else. For example, Bill Clinton's campaign advisor, James Carville, developed the communication strategy captured by the phrase: "It's the economy, stupid." This meant that Clinton's campaign speeches would focus almost exclusively on the economy. As Carville put it, "There has to be message triage. If you say three things, you don't say anything."

Unexpectedness. Hearing things that are unexpected often leads to curiosity, a state that increases our interest in and the attention we pay to a topic or question.[3] Heath and Heath argue that this often leads to extra thinking, which helps make ideas stick in our memories. Describing your idea in terms that are counterintuitive or surprising can be a good way to make a message stick.

Heath and Heath describe the example of Nordstrom, a department store known for its excellent customer service. In order to maintain this reputation, managers must impress on their employees how much they value good service. Rather than just giving speeches about "the importance of customer service," managers give examples of past instances of outstanding service by Nordstrom employees. Because they were surprising, examples such as ironing a shirt for a customer who needed it for a meeting that afternoon and cheerfully gift-wrapping clothing a customer bought at Macy's, got the message across effectively.

Concreteness. There is a tendency, especially when we have a lot of knowledge about a topic, to communicate ideas in abstract terms. But abstract ideas are difficult for nonexperts to understand and are easily misconstrued even by experts. The Nordstrom example described above is also an example of the power of concreteness. If managers just told employees that they should "go above and beyond what it expected," that would leave a lot of room for interpretation and probably wouldn't leave a lasting impression. Providing concrete examples of the good service makes clear exactly what is expected.

Credibility. The traditional way to establish credibility is to have credentials—for example, advanced training or a degree. But people can sometimes establish credibility by alternative means. Heath and Heath refer to "testable credentials," in which listeners are asked to evaluate the credibility of a contention for themselves. During a presidential debate with Jimmy Carter, Ronald Regan asked the rhetorical

---

2. Chip Heath and Dan Heath, Made to Stick: Why Some Ideas Survive and Others Die (New York: Random House, 2007).

3. George Loewenstein, *The Psychology of Curiosity: A Review and Reinterpretation*, 116 Psychological Bulletin 75–98 (1994).

question: "Are you better off now than you were four years ago?" Rather than argue directly that the economy had worsened during Carter's tenure, he asked the audience to test the proposition for themselves.

Emotionality. Research on charitable giving has shown that people donate more money in response to appeals that focus on a single, identifiable victim than they do when appeals cite statistics reflecting mass-scale suffering.[4] Researchers who study this phenomenon proffer the following explanation for it: learning about a single victim evokes emotion, whereas learning about statistics shifts people into a more analytical frame of mind that suppresses emotion. Emotion is the motivational engine that drives people to respond to messages involving appeals for charitable donations. Focusing on analytical themes undermines messages intended to promote charitable giving.[5]

In his book, *The Political Brain*, psychologist Drew Westen makes a similar contention about political appeals. He argues that political messages based on rational, emotion-free arguments fail to have much effect on voters. Because people's decisions are often guided primarily by emotion and rationalized after the fact, attempts to persuade are more likely to resonate with voters if they focus on deeply held values and principles that tend to evoke emotion.[6]

Stories. Stories help ideas stick. They give coherence to a message and, because we find them entertaining and engrossing, they capture our attention better than a simple list of facts. Also, unlike more direct persuasive messages, stories tend not to put the audience in an evaluative frame of mind. Rather, people tend to empathize with the story's protagonist and to be less critical of the underlying message.

A study by Nancy Pennington and Reid Hastie found that when participants judged evidence in a hypothetical criminal trial, they were more likely to render a verdict for the side that presented evidence in an order that made it easy to construct a story of the events in question.[7] Recall our discussion, in Section 8.3, of the power of narrative. While arguments can establish formal or abstract truths, stories are better at convincing people of the verisimilitude of a point because stories make a point seem *representative* of reality. Recall that people use the representativeness heuristic to make judgments about the likelihood that

4. Deborah A. Small, George Loewenstein, and Paul Slovic, *Sympathy and Callousness: Affect and Deliberations in Donation Decisions*, 102 ORGANIZATIONAL BEHAVIOR AND HUMAN DECISION PROCESSES 143–53 (2007).

5. George Loewenstein and Deborah A. Small, *The Scarecrow and the Tin Man: The Vicissitudes of Human Sympathy and Caring*, 11 REVIEW OF GENERAL PSYCHOLOGY 112 (2007).

6. DREW WESTEN, THE EMOTIONAL BRAIN: THE ROLE OF EMOTION IN DECIDING THE FATE OF THE NATION (Public Affairs, New York, 2007).

7. Nancy Pennington and Reid Hastie, *Explanation-Based Decision Making: Effects of Memory Structure on Judgment*;14 JOURNAL OF EXPERIMENTAL PSYCHOLOGY: LEARNING, MEMORY, & COGNITION 521–33 (1988).

something is true. Persuasion often consists less of convincing others of the logic of your argument than of having them replace their narrative construction of reality with your own.[8]

The distinction between judgment and decision making under so-called System I and System II, made throughout this book, applies no less to a recipient's processing of communications. The processes can be either *heuristic* or *systematic* in nature.[9] Heuristic message processing is a System I function, while systematic message processing is System II. The study of rhetoric since Aristotle has shown how effective persuasion can work through both systems. Which of Heath and Heath's observations relate to System I processing, and which to System II? Recall from Chapter 17 how social influence heuristics, such as "believe an authority," or "if everyone else thinks it's right, it must be," can substitute for analyzing a message on its merits.

18.2 FRAMING ARGUMENTS IN TERMS OF GAINS AND LOSSES

Recall the now familiar S-shaped curve of Prospect Theory of Figure 14.1, and recall that losses from a reference point loom larger than gains. Because the reference point is essentially subjective, even arbitrary, a strategic communicator may try to get her audience to adopt a reference point that will influence attitudes in the direction she wants. Consider these experiments.

George Quattrone and Amos Tversky conducted an experiment asked participants to imagine that a hypothetical country had dedicated $100 million to reducing crime by unemployed immigrant youths. They were asked to allocate the $100 million between two groups of equal size, Alphans and Betans.

Half the participants were told that, by the age of twenty-five, 3.7 percent of Alphans and 1.2 percent of Betans had criminal records, while the other half were told that, by the age of twenty-five, 96.3 percent of Alphans and 98.8 percent of Betans had *no* criminal record. The participants had to determine whether to give a little bit more to the Alphans, or a lot more to the Alphans—the group with the higher rate of criminality. Objectively, the two groups were given identical information, but the information in the second condition was framed in terms of a *lack* of criminality instead of criminality.

---

8. Jerome Bruner, Making Stories: Law, Literature, Life (New York: Farrar, Straus, & Giroux, 2002).

9. Shelly Chaiken, *The Heuristic Model of Persuasion, in* Social Influence: The Ontario Symposium Vol. 5, 3–39 (Mark P. Zanna, James M. Olson, and C. Peter Herman eds., Hillsdale, NJ, 1987). Lawrence Erlbaum et al., *Central And Peripheral Routes to Persuasion: An Individual Difference Perspective,* 51 Journal of Personality and Social Psychology 1032–43 (1986).

In the "criminality" frame (3.7 percent Alphans versus 1.2 percent Betans) participants allocated more of the money to the Alphans than in the noncriminality framing (96.3 percent versus 98.8 percent). Quattrone and Tversky attributed this to what they call the "ratio-difference principle." In the criminality frame, Alphans are perceived as three times more criminal as Betans; but they are seen as only slightly less noncriminal than the Betans under the noncriminality frame. This is a result of diminishing sensitivity, shown in the S-shaped prospect theory curve as one moves away from the reference point. According to the ratio-difference principle, "the impact of any fixed positive difference between two amounts increases with their ratio."[10] In other words, the difference between 3.7 percent and 1.2 percent seems bigger than a difference between 98.8 percent and 96.3 percent because the ratio of the first pair is much bigger than that of the second pair. Our sensitivity to differences in objective numbers like crime rates is an approximate function of the ratio associated with that difference.

In another experiment, Quattrone and Tversky found that whether an economic indicator was described as the *unemployment* rate or the *employment* rate had a significant impact on how concerned people seemed about a 5 percent worsening of it. People weighed the difference between 5 percent and 10 percent unemployment much more heavily than the difference between 95 percent and 90 percent employment. Indeed, descriptive statistics of the sort used in these experiments are common in discussions about public policy, and this research suggests that subtle differences in framing can affect how much people approve (or disapprove) of a policy, irrespective of its actual impact.

18.3 LINGUISTIC FORM

Heath and Heath describe how messages can be shaped at a macro level to make them more persuasive. Recent research by other scholars suggests that subtle manipulations of language can affect the meaning that recipients take from a message.

18.3.1 Agentive vs. Passive

Caitlin Fausey and Lera Boroditsky studied the effects of how an accident is described on how blame for that accident is assigned.[11] Specifically, they were interested in the difference between reactions to agentive and nonagentive descriptions of the same event. Agentive language specifically mentions an agent (e.g., Dave broke the vase), while nonagentive language does not (e.g., the vase broke).

10. George Quattrone and Amos Tversky, *Contrasting Rational and Psychological Analyses of Political Choice*, 82 APSR 719–36 (1988).

11. Caitlin M. Fausey, Neil, Snider, Lera Boroditsky (in prep). Speaking of Accidents: *"He did it"* invites more punishment than *"It happened."*

Both are common and sound natural in English, and they are generally considered to be equivalent ways to say the same thing. Consider, for example, the following story:

> Mrs. Smith and her friends were finishing a lovely dinner at their favorite restaurant. After they settled the bill, they decided to head to a nearby café for coffee and dessert. Mrs. Smith followed her friends and as she stood up, *she flopped* her napkin on the centerpiece candle. *She had ignited* the napkin! As Mrs. Smith reached to grab the napkin, *she toppled* the candle and *ignited* the whole tablecloth, too! As she jumped back, *she overturned* the table and *ignited* the carpet as well. Hearing her desperate cries, the restaurant staff hurried over and heroically managed to put the fire out before anyone got hurt.
>
> Contrast this story:
>
> Mrs. Smith and her friends were finishing a lovely dinner at their favorite restaurant. After they settled the bill, they decided to head to a nearby café for coffee and dessert. Mrs. Smith followed her friends and as she stood up, her *napkin flopped* on the centerpiece candle. The *napkin had ignited!* As Mrs. Smith reached to grab the napkin, *the candle toppled* and the whole *tablecloth ignited,* too! As she jumped back, the *table overturned* and the *carpet ignited* as well. Hearing her desperate cries, the restaurant staff hurried over and heroically managed to put the fire out before anyone got hurt.

Fausey and Boroditsky found that people who read the former, agentive version of the story assigned significantly more blame for the fire to Mrs. Smith. When asked how much of the $1500 in total damages from the fire Mrs. Smith should have to pay, participants who read the agentive version, on average, said she should have to pay $935, while those who read the nonagentive version said, on average, $689 (i.e., less than half the total amount).

The implications of this research for the courtroom are apparent. Outside the courtroom, policy makers and other actors sometimes try to blunt criticism by using the passive, "*mistakes were made.*" In an interview on CBS's *60 Minutes,* Marine Staff Sgt. Frank Wuterich, who was charged with eighteen counts of murder after the squad he was leading killed twenty-four civilians in apparent response to the death of one of their fellow marines, said "I am completely sorry that *that happened.*" Note that the research described above deals with cases in which the passive voice is used by a third party. A perpetrator's use of the nonagentive form may trigger a cynical response both in courtrooms and in the court of public opinion.

18.3.2 Verbs and Causal Inference

Along similar lines, Dutch psychologists Gun Semin and Christianne De Poot have found that the specific type of verb you use to ask a question can have an important effect on the answers you receive.[12] They distinguish between "verbs of action" (such as to help, to push, to cheat, etc.) and "verbs of state" (such as to respect, to dislike, to love). Semin and De Poot's research shows that questions about action verbs tend to yield answers that focus on the sentence *subject*, while the answers to questions about state verbs tend to focus on the sentence *object*. So, if I ask you "Why do you think John helped David," you will tend to answer by telling me something about John that explains his helping behavior. On other hand, if I ask you "Why do you think John likes David," your answers will likely refer to something about David that makes him likeable.

At first this might not seem to be the kind of thing that is subject to easy manipulation: action verbs and state verbs tend not to be interchangeable. It is hard to imagine a defense lawyer asking her client to explain to the jury why he "disliked" the person he assaulted instead of why he "attacked" the victim. As Semin and De Poot point out, though, once we know the effect of these verbs, other elements of a sentence are susceptible to customization. For example, we sometimes have a choice about whom to use as the subject and whom to use as the object of a sentence. Imagine, for example, a rape case in which it is undisputed that the victim and the defendant danced together before the alleged crime. Knowing that *to dance* is an action verb and that answers to action verbs tend to focus causal explanations on the object of a sentence, a defense attorney might prefer to ask the victim whether *she* danced with the defendant rather than whether *the defendant* danced with her.

18.3.3 The Power of Nouns

We sometimes have the option not to use a verb at all to describe behavior. Gregory Walton and Mahzarin Banaji have examined the different effects of describing behavior using a verb or a noun.[13] For example, a person who "plays the piano" can also be referred to as a "pianist," and someone who "runs a lot" might be called a "runner." In one experiment, Walton and Banaji provided behavioral descriptions of fictional people using either the verb form (e.g., Jennifer eats a lot of chocolate) or the noun form (Jennifer is a chocolate-eater). They found that people tended to think the behavior reflected stronger, more stable preferences when the noun form was used than when the verb form was used.

---

12. Gün R. Semin and Christianne J. De Poot, *The Question-Answer Paradigm: You Might Regret Not Noticing How a Question Is Worded*, 54 JOURNAL OF PERSONALITY AND SOCIAL PSYCHOLOGY 558–68 (1997).

13. Gregory M. Walton and Mahzarin R. Banaji, *Being What You Say: The Effect of Essentialist Linguistic Labels on Preferences*, 22 SOCIAL COGNITION 193–213 (2004). This paper was inspired by the following paper examining a similar difference in children: Susan A. Gelman and Gail D. Heyman, *Carrot-Eaters and Creature-Believers: The Effects of Lexicalization on Children's Inferences About Social Categories*, 10 PSYCHOLOGICAL SCIENCE 489–93 (1999).

Banaji and Walton then wondered if the same thing would happen when people were being asked to think about their own behavior. Under the guise that they were conducting a handwriting study, they had participants write out a behavioral tendency or preference of their own, using either the noun of the verb form. If a person said he liked Coke, he was either asked to write "I am a Coke-drinker" or "I drink a lot of Coke" three times in his "natural handwriting." They found similar effects. People who had written about their own behavioral preferences using the noun form tended to say that those preferences were stronger than if they had used the verb form.

In subsequent research, Christopher Bryan, Gregory Walton, and Carol Dweck investigated whether a similar manipulation might affect not only people's attitudes about products but important behavioral decisions such as whether or not to vote in a presidential election.[14] The day before the 2008 presidential election, they asked people who were eligible to vote but not yet registered to complete a questionnaire about their "attitudes about voting and the electoral process." In that questionnaire, people were either asked questions like "How important is it to you to *vote* in the upcoming election" or "How important is it to you to *be a voter* in the upcoming election." After the election, the researchers used official records to determine whether participants had turned up at the polls.

It turned out that participants who had completed the questionnaire about their attitudes about "being a voter" were more likely to have voted than participants who had answered questions about "voting." The fact that such a seemingly minuscule manipulation can have an effect on the decision to vote in a presidential election—behavior that one would expect to be determined by motives such as a sense of civic duty or interest in the outcome—suggests that this subtle difference may have significant implications.

Where do these nouns get their power? The answer is not yet completely clear, but researchers agree that the use of a noun to refer to a preference or behavior invokes the idea of essentialism. This is the folk notion that a person (or object) has some fundamental essence that makes her what she is and determines her attitudes, thoughts, and behaviors.[15] It may be that, when a characteristic is described in the noun form, the implication is that this is a central aspect of that person's self. It is conceivable that this affects even our perceptions of our own characteristics and behavior.

---

14. Christopher J. Bryan, Mark R. Lepper, and Carol S. Dweck, "Voting versus Being a Voter: The Effect of a Subtle Linguistic Manipulation on Voting Behavior" (unpublished data, Stanford University 2005).

15. Dale Miller and Deborah Prentice, *Some Consequences of a Belief in Group Essence: The Category Divide Hypothesis, in* Deborah Prentice and Dale Miller eds., CULTURAL DIVIDES: UNDERSTANDING AND OVERCOMING GROUP CONFLICT 213–238 (New York: Russell Sage Foundation, 1999).

18.3.4 The Power of Metaphors

Most people think of a metaphor as a rhetorical device by which we explain one concept, often an unfamiliar one, in terms of another, more familiar concept. This has the effect of highlighting the properties of the former that it shares with the latter. Linguist George Lakoff argues that our choice of metaphors can change the way we think about a concept or issue.[16] According to Lakoff, we use metaphors to understand and experience many of the most important and familiar concepts in our lives. He argues that many of these concepts, such as *love, the mind,* or *ideas,* are too abstract and complex for us to understand directly. Instead, we understand them through the lenses of other familiar concepts that are more tangible and clearly defined.

Think, for example, about the concept of *ideas.* Lakoff argues that we talk about ideas in terms of more concrete concepts. For example, the metaphor *ideas are commodities* is evident in the following phrases: "He won't *buy* that," "it's important how you *package* your ideas," and "your ideas don't have a chance in the *intellectual marketplace.*" Similarly, the metaphor *ideas are food* is evident in: "all this paper has in it are *raw facts, half-baked ideas, and warmed-over theories,*" "there are too many facts here for me to *digest* them all," and "there's a theory you can really *sink your teeth into.*"

One reason that there are often numerous different metaphors available for the same concept is that most important concepts are complex and multifaceted. Each metaphor highlights some aspects of our experience and hides others. For example, the metaphor, *ideas are commodities,* highlights the fact that we often want to convince others of our ideas, using the similarity between that experience and the experience of buying or using a commodity. Meanwhile, the metaphor *ideas are food* highlights the fact that, once we learn about an idea, it becomes a part of who we are and, in some sense, makes us stronger intellectually—a phenomenon comparable to the absorption of nutrients when we consume food. Importantly, our choice of metaphor affects how we think about ideas. For example, using the *ideas are commodities* metaphor is likely to focus our attention on how our ideas are perceived by *others,* while the *ideas are food* metaphor focuses our thinking on the value of ideas to *us.*

The fact that metaphors structure how we understand and experience a concept means that they also have the power to shape our actions. Think about the commonly used metaphor *argument is war* (exemplified in such phrases as "that *position* is *indefensible*" and "he *shot down* my argument"). Lakoff asserts that this metaphor structures the way we engage in argument. For example, if instead of *argument is war,* we used an *argument is exchange* metaphor, we might feel less of a need to *defend* our position and *attack* the positions of those who disagree with us.

16. George Lakoff and Mark Johnson, Metaphors We Live By (Chicago: University of Chicago Press, 1980).

To recap, according to Lakoff:

- We often understand the abstract and complex concepts in our lives better if they are presented in concrete terms.
- A number of different metaphors often are available to help us understand a given concept.
- Each metaphor highlights particular aspects of that concept and hides others.
- The metaphor we use to think about a concept affects how we experience that concept and behave with respect to it.

While empirical evidence is still lacking, these points suggest that our choice of a particular metaphor may influence people's thinking and behavior; it could mean the difference between a public that favors and opposes a policy. Take, for example, the phrase *tax relief*. This phrase is often used by Republicans and others seeking reductions in most taxes. The word *relief* invokes a metaphor of taxes as an affliction.[17] As Lakoff points out, we have a script about afflictions that includes a notion of the reliever as a hero; those who oppose relief are seen as villains. The use of the metaphor, *taxes are an affliction*, influences our thinking about taxes and is likely to have an effect on the popularity of tax cuts. A big part of the power of such framing lies in its subtlety; the phrase *tax relief* is a perfectly reasonable way to describe reductions in taxes. It highlights an aspect of taxes that almost everyone experiences: it is unpleasant to pay them. At the same time, though, it hides another aspect of taxes that many people also experience: we appreciate the programs they make possible.

Another example is the debate about the legality of abortion. Lakoff points out that referring to an "embryo" or a "fetus" has very different implications from referring to a "baby." The terms "embryo" and "fetus" frame the discussion through the medical domain, and the question becomes one about whether or not women should be allowed to make unfettered medical decisions. The term "baby," on the other hand, places the debate in the moral domain, making the question one about whether or not unborn babies should be protected by the law.

Discussing politics more broadly, Lakoff has suggested that the metaphor of the community or nation as a "family" plays a central role in our thinking. He argues that two different family models help to determine our political sensibilities. Associated with conservative thinking is the authoritarian, rule-bound family that rewards or punishes on the basis of perceived merit, while liberal thinking derives from the more nurturing, forgiving, family that provides resources as a function of need rather than merit.[18] Because most people endorse

---

17. George Lakoff, Don't Think of an Elephant! Know Your Values and Frame the Debate (White River Junction, VT: Chelsea Green, 2004).

18. George Lakoff, Moral Politics: How Liberals and Conservatives Think (Chicago: University of Chicago Press, 1996).

both models to some extent, it may be possible to influence people's policy opinions by invoking the relevant family model in political appeals.

18.4 FROM INCLINATION TO ACTION: CHANNEL FACTORS

Even when people understand and agree with communications that call for action, they do not necessarily take the next step and act on them. People may have an inclination to act, but if their intended behavior has no available outlet, then they may be less likely to do so. For example, researchers found that the best predictor of whether people would show up at a health clinic was not their attitudes about health and medicine, but how far they were from the clinic.[19] *Channel factors* are simply ways of structuring a situation to increase the likelihood that the recipient of a communication will act on it.

Consider this example:[20] Robert Leventhal and his colleagues were studying the effects of fear on the likelihood that people would get a tetanus shot. They found that when conveying the risk of tetanus, a fear-inducing appeal made people change their attitudes in favor of getting the shot significantly more than a neutral informational appeal. Nevertheless, even with this attitude, only 3 percent of participants followed up and got inoculated against tetanus. Strikingly, the simple act of giving participants a map and instructing them to select a particular time when they would go to get inoculated raised this percentage to 28 percent.

By the same token, sales of war bonds improved during World War II when the government arranged for the bonds to be sold at workplaces rather than at banks and post offices.[21] In sum, people may have every intention to act in a certain way, but if they don't have a "channel" for their behavior, their intention may never be carried out.

18.5 PRIMING

Priming involves the automatic influence of exposure to environmental cues on people's judgment, decision making, and behavior. Cues as subtle as the presence of particular objects may implicitly communicate meanings and norms, thereby guiding one's behavior in situations that are novel or ambiguous (and in

19. Berenice E. Van Dort and Rudolf H. Moos, *Distance and the Utilization of a Student Health Center*, 24 JOURNAL OF AMERICAN COLLEGE HEALTH ASSOCIATION 159–62 (1976).

20. Howard Leventhal, Robert Singer, and Susan Jones, *Effects of Fear and Specificity of Recommendation upon Attitudes and Behavior*, 2 JOURNAL OF PERSONALITY AND SOCIAL PSYCHOLOGY 20–29 (1965).

21. Dorwin Cartwright, *Some Principles of Mass Persuasion: Selected Findings of Research on the Sale of U.S. War Bonds*, 2 HUMAN RELATIONS 253 (1949).

which people are therefore more susceptible to suggestion about what the relevant norms are). In Section 11.3, we described how the priming of particular schemas can influence people's perceptions of and behavior toward members of stereotyped groups. Here we broaden the discussion to other forms of judgment and decision making.

Recall the "Ultimatum Game," described in Section 12.1.2, in which one participant is asked to propose a division of a fixed sum of money that a second participant can either accept or reject.[22] Would priming participants with cues that invoked a business environment lead them to behave in a more competitive, cut-throat manner, consistent with a business stereotype? Researchers asked some participants to play the ultimatum game seated in front of a large desk on which a briefcase, an executive-style silver pen, and a black-leather portfolio had been placed. For other participants, a backpack replaced the briefcase, a cardboard box replaced the executive portfolio, and the participants were given a standard wooden pencil instead of an executive pen. It turned out that participants in the business-objects condition proposed significantly less generous divisions of the money than participants in the second condition.

The result of the research on the ultimatum game is important because it suggests that random and seemingly irrelevant features of our environments can serve as primes and have a significant influence on our behavior. Perhaps the most striking demonstration of the significance of implicit priming effects is a study by Jonah Berger and his colleagues that suggests that the polling place in which people vote (e.g., church, school, or firehouse) may influence how they vote. Berger et al. analyzed data from Arizona's 2000 general election and found that people who cast their votes in schoolhouses were more likely than others to vote to raise taxes to support education.[23] This study suggests that subtle environmental cues can influence decisions on consequential issues even in complex real-world environments.

In Section 1.5.2 we introduced the concept of social scripts that define appropriate behavior for ourselves and others, including public officials. People often have recourse to alternative scripts, and priming can affect which alternative someone applies to a given situation. For example, Thomas Gilovich presented participants with a hypothetical foreign conflict and asked whether the United

22. Aaron C. Kay, S. Christian Wheeler, John A. Bargh, and Lee Ross, *Material Priming: The Influence of Mundane Physical Objects on Situational Construal and Competitive Behavioral Choice*, 95 Organizational Behavior and Human Decision Processes 83–96 (2004).

23. Jonah Berger, Marc Meredith, and S. Christian Wheeler, "Can Where People Vote Influence How They Vote? The Influence of Polling Location Type on Voting Behavior" (2006) Stanford Graduate School of Business Research Paper, No. 1926. The researchers controlled for the voters' political views, demographics, and whether or not they lived near schools.

States should intervene militarily.[24] He found that superficial similarities between the hypothetical conflict and either World War II or the Vietnam War—for example, whether refugees were fleeing on trains or in small boats—affected whether participants were likely to recommend military intervention. Those primed with similarities to World War II applied the "Munich" script and favored an early show of military strength, while those primed with similarities to "Vietnam" tended to avoid a military commitment for fear that it could lead to a quagmire.

While the Gilovich study involved priming specific historical scripts, other research has shown that it is possible to prime broad ideological schemas that influence people's views on specific policy issues.[25] One element of the conservative schema is the endorsement of notions of meritocracy in which success is seen as the product of hard work, wise decision making, self-discipline, and other aspects of personal merit. The liberal schema, by contrast, includes the notion that success may in large measure be a matter of good fortune, social advantage, the help one receives from others, and other factors independent of personal merit.[26]

Students at Stanford University were asked to write a brief essay describing how they got into Stanford; they were instructed either to focus on the role of "hard work, self-discipline, and wise decisions" or of "chance, opportunity, and help from others" in getting them where they were. Participants were then asked to indicate their views on a number of controversial policy proposals such as the creation of a universal guaranteed health care system and the implementation of a flat income tax. Those who had written the essay focusing on hard work and personal merit expressed more conservative views than those who had focused on good fortune and help from others. Most people hold aspects of both liberal and conservative schemas, and it seems that priming can affect which one is active at a given time, with potentially important effects on their judgments.

One common way to prime participants in the laboratory is to have them solve word puzzles, where the words may either be neutral or designed to influence the participants' behavior. For example, before being asked to play a resource management game in which they fished from a lake with limited stock,

---

24. Thomas Gilovich, *Seeing the Past in the Present: The Effects of Associations to Familiar Events on Judgments and Decisions,* 40 JOURNAL OF PERSONALITY AND SOCIAL PSYCHOLOGY 797–808 (1981).

25. Christopher J. Bryan, Carol S. Dweck, Lee Ross, Aaron C. Kay, and Natalia Mislavsky, "Ideological Mindsets: A Demonstration of Political Malleability" (2006) (manuscript submitted for publication).

26. JAMES R. KLUEGEL AND ELIOT R. SMITH, BELIEFS ABOUT INEQUALITY: AMERICANS' VIEWS OF WHAT IS AND WHAT OUGHT TO BE (New York: Aldine deGruyter, 1986); Irwin Katz and R. Glen Hass, *Racial Ambivalence and American Value Conflict: Correlation and Priming Studies of Dual Cognitive Structures,* 55 J. PERS. SOC. PSYCHOL. 893–905 (1988); Robert E. Lane, *The Fear of Equality,* 53 AM. POLIT. SCI. REV. 35–51 (1959).

participants worked on an unrelated puzzle that had either cooperation-related words (dependable, helpful, support, reasonable, honest, cooperative, fair, friendly, tolerant, and share) or neutral words (salad, umbrella, city, gasoline, wet, purposeful, switch, lead, mountain, and zebra).[27] Members of the first group were more likely to act cooperatively, taking fewer fish, than the second—though not as much so as the members of a third group, who were explicitly asked to set the goal: "I will cooperate as much as possible." Similar experiments indicate that priming may improve people's achievement, their persistence in the face of obstacles, and the likelihood that they will resume a task that has been interrupted.[28]

Because its effects decay quickly, priming seems most applicable to irreversible one-time decisions where the agent can manipulate the context immediately before the decision is made. For better or (likely) worse, voting seems a prime candidate.

How might a policy maker prime drivers to exercise caution in dangerous places on highways?

18.6 INFLUENCING AND GUIDING CITIZENS' DECISION MAKING

The question we just asked implies that policy makers can use their knowledge about the techniques of social and cognitive influence to help citizens act in their own best interests or in the interests of society. Of course, policy makers' use of such techniques raises core normative questions about the obligations of liberal democratic governments to their citizens, who have heterogeneous values and goals and diverse views about how to achieve them. But although liberal democracy implies a presumption favoring autonomy, most political theorists hold that citizens' autonomy may sometimes be limited for the benefit of the greater society and many hold that their choices may be (paternalistically) limited for the benefit of individuals themselves.

18.6.1 Counseling Citizens about Risks: When Better Information Doesn't Necessarily Lead to Better Choices

Respect for individuals' autonomy implies a preference for governments providing citizens and consumers with information about choices rather than restricting their choices. And it is a tenet of rational decision making that accurate information about the consequences of behavior, including the probability of good or bad outcomes, will lead to better decisions.

27. John A. Bargh, Peter M. Gollwitzer, Annette Y. Lee-Chai, Kimberly. Barndollar, and Roman Troetschel, *The Automated Will: Nonconscious Activation and Pursuit of Behavioral Goals*, 81 JOURNAL OF PERSONALITY AND SOCIAL PSYCHOLOGY 1014–27 (2001).

28. *Id.*

However, we have seen people often have considerable difficulty in understanding quantitative information about risks. Kip Viscusi and Wesley Magat conducted a study that showed that consumers respond to the format of warning labels on household items (bleach, drain openers) in ways that diverge from expected utility.[29] In the absence of vivid information about a low probability risk, consumers may treat the risk as zero, but "when a risk information program forces them to focus on the probability that some rare injury will occur, they may treat the probability as if it were higher than its objective value because of the cognitive difficulties in making risky choices when the probabilities are extremely low."[30]

If people's judgments of risk generally move in the direction of univocal new information about risk, what happens when they receive conflicting information, with one source asserting that the risk is high and another that it is low? In a different experiment, Viscusi asked participants to rate the risk of cancer from airborne pollutants where (1) two government studies disagreed whether the risk was high or low; (2) two industry studies disagreed with each other; and (3) government and industry studies were in disagreement. Except in the government versus government disagreement, participants treated the high risk information as being more informative—whether the government study showed a higher risk than the industry study or vice versa.[31]

Viscusi notes that "symmetry is not violated because a particular information source's credibility is more consequential. Rather, it is the divergence of judgments from different sources that largely accounts for the differing information weights . . . [People] devote excessive attention to the worst case scenarios." Prescriptively, he suggests that consensus risk estimates are likely to be processed more accurately than multiple risk assessments. "There may be considerable advantage to focusing the risk communication effort on the mean risk not the risk assessment range. Particular care should be taken with respect to the worst case scenarios. In practice, the distortions in risk beliefs due to the worst case scenarios may be even greater than found here since these experiments presented low risk and high risk estimates symmetrically. In contrast, the media and advocacy groups often highlight the worst case scenarios, which will tend to intensify the kinds of biases observed here."

Cass Sunstein cautions that simply by disclosing low probability risks—e.g., "this food is genetically modified" or "this water contains 5 parts per billion of arsenic" (a very small amount)—labeling is likely to "greatly alarm people, causing various kinds of harms, without giving them any useful information at all.

---

29. KIP VISCUSI AND WELSEY A. MAGAT, LEARNING ABOUT RISK: CONSUMER AND WORKER RESPONSES TO HAZARD INFORMATION (Cambridge: Harvard University Press, 1987).

30. *Id.* at 128.

31. W. Kip Viscusi, *Alarmist Decisions with Divergent Risk Information,* 107 THE ECONOMIC JOURNAL 1657 (1997).

If people neglect probability, they may fix, or fixate, on the bad outcome, in a way that will cause anxiety and distress but without altering behavior or even improving understanding. Sunstein suggests that it might be possible to tell people not only about the risk but also about the *meaning* of the probability information—for example, by comparing a risk to others encountered in ordinary life." But, he asks, "if the risk is low, and of the sort that usually do not trouble sensible human beings, is it really important to force disclosure of facts that will predictably cause high levels of alarm?"[32]

The problem is that the very discussion of a low-probability risk leads people to imagine or visualize the worst case—even if the discussion consists mostly of trustworthy assurances that the likelihood of harm really is infinitesimal. Emphasizing the low probability that the risk will eventuate is a lame strategy against affect-laded imagery. Of course, there's another potential problem as well: "People may attempt to deal with their fear by refusing to think about the risk at all."[33]

18.6.2 When Incentives Are Counterproductive

In the introduction to Part 4, we mentioned the idea of paying students to maintain an appropriate weight or improve their grades. Skeptics of this approach might be concerned that external incentives will undermine people's long-term motivations in both spheres. Indeed, traditional economic incentives sometimes backfire and have the opposite of the effect they are designed to have. This usually happens because people are already motivated by some nonmaterial incentive (like guilt or a sense of civic duty) to engage in the behavior the incentives are designed to encourage. Introducing an economic incentive can change the way people think about that behavior, resulting in what psychologists refer to as the *overjustification effect.*

James Heyman and Dan Ariely conducted a series of studies suggesting that when you want someone to perform a minor task, you might be wiser to ask the person for a "favor" than to offer to pay him or her.[34] In one experiment, people asked to perform a menial task put less effort into it when offered 50 cents than when offered no payment at all. Heyman and Ariely explain that the introduction of payment invokes people's schema for monetary exchanges rather than the schema for a "social market." Interestingly, offering a small "gift" (like a piece of candy) as compensation does not invoke a monetary exchange schema unless you tell the recipient how much it is worth.

---

32. Cass R. Sunstein, Laws of Fear: Beyond the Precautionary Principle 61 (Cambridge: Cambridge University Press, 2005).

33. Andrew Caplin, *Fear as a Policy Instrument, in* Time and Decision: Economic and Psychological Perspectives on Intertemporal Choice (George Loewenstein, Daniel Read, and Roy Baumeister eds., New York: Russell Sage, 2003) 441, 443.

34. James Heyman and Dan Ariely, *Effort for Payment: A Tale of Two Markets,* 15 Psychological Science 787–93 (2004).

Uri Gneezy and Aldo Rustichini examined the effect of introducing a small fine to discourage a nuisance behavior.[35] They conducted a study in ten day-care centers in Haifa, Israel. The day-care centers all operate from seven-thirty in the morning until four in the afternoon, but teachers regularly have to stay past four because some parents were late picking up their children. The researchers arranged for some of the day-care centers to introduce a small fine (equivalent to approximately one eighth the amount of a parking ticket) each time a parent was more than ten minutes late. Surprisingly, the effect of the fine was to *increase* the number of late-arriving parents in those day-care centers. After several weeks of fines and increased rates of lateness, those centers that had introduced fines eliminated them, but to no avail. The rate of lateness in those centers remained at the same high level they were at under the fine system.

The researchers hypothesize that before the implementation of the fines, parents had been operating with the understanding that teachers who stayed late to watch over their children were doing so out of generosity, and therefore that the parents should avoid imposing on them. The introduction of a fine, however, was interpreted as a price for the service of staying late. Once this occurred, parents thought of the service as a commodity that they could buy as often as was convenient. The researchers further theorize that rates of lateness stayed high when the fines were removed because the service continued to be seen as a commodity—only now it was a commodity with a price of zero.

Other research shows that even large incentives can sometimes be counterproductive.[36] Researchers went door-to-door in Switzerland asking residents if they would be willing to accept a nuclear waste dump in their town. Although residents were obviously apprehensive about the idea, approximately half of the people polled said they would accept the dump. They presumably did this out of a sense of civic responsibility; the dumps have to go somewhere after all. Other residents were asked the same question but told that if they accepted the dump in their neighborhood, they would be compensated with the equivalent of approximately six weeks' pay each year. The rate of acceptance dropped to half the rate when no compensation was offered. Residents may have been willing to accept a certain level of risk out of a sense of civic responsibility, but being paid to risk their health was a losing proposition.

The common theme in these examples is that the introduction of economic incentives into transactions that are governed by social norms changes the way those transactions are understood by the people involved. In short, relying on economic incentives to influence behavior that is governed by nonmaterial motives sometimes can backfire.

---

35. Uri Gneezy and Aldo Rustichini, *A Fine Is a Price*, 24 JOURNAL OF LEGAL STUDIES 1–17 (2000).

36. Bruno S. Frey and Felix Oberholzer-Gee, *The Cost of Price Incentives: An Empirical Analysis of Motivation Crowding Out*, 87 AMERICAN ECONOMIC REVIEW 746–55 (1997).

18.6.3 Framing Citizens' Choices and Other Aspects of Choice Architecture[37]

Albert Einstein once said, "We can't solve problems by using the same kind of thinking we used when we created them." However, it is possible that the unconscious mental system can, in fact, do just that. In recent years, researchers have proposed a new general strategy for improving biased decision making that leverages our automatic cognitive processes and turns them to our advantage. Rather than trying to change a decision maker's thinking from System 1 to System 2 in situations where System 1 processing is known to frequently result in biased decisions, this strategy tries to change the environment so that System 1 thinking will lead to good results."[38]

Humans are prone to many errors that can be reduced by mechanical design. Just consider the devices in a modern car that turn on the headlights at dusk, turn them off when you leave the car, warn you if a seatbelt is not fastened, and keep you from losing the gas tank cap. Consider ATMs that require you to remove the card before getting cash, or the packaging of birth control pills in twenty-eight numbered compartments. Policy makers can be more or less intrusive in efforts to prevent such errors. For example, there was a brief time in which you couldn't start a car unless the seatbelts were buckled; now, the car merely emits loud beeps—an intentionally annoying way of providing information.

This book has focused on biases in perception and decision making rather than on mechanical errors—though issues of attention are pervasive in both. In *Nudge: Improving Decisions About Health, Wealth, and Happiness*, Richard Thaler and Cass Sunstein describe a number of methods for counteracting biases and other limitations of bounded rationality in individuals' decision making. Their overall approach, which they term *choice architecture*, rests on the two fundamental premises that individuals' behavior and choices are subject to predictable errors and that it is legitimate for policy makers (*choice architects*) to structure choices and communicate information to citizens and consumers to help them avoid these errors.

Thaler and Sunstein style the political philosophy underlying choice architecture as *libertarian paternalism*.[39] Since there is no way *not* to frame a decision, they argue, decision frames should be intentionally designed to encourage enlightened, self-interested behavior—for example, default enrollment in a retirement plan rather than an employee's having to take active steps to enroll.

---

37. Much of this section is based on RICHARD THALER AND CASS SUNSTEIN, NUDGE: IMPROVING DECISIONS ABOUT HEALTH, WEALTH, AND HAPPINESS (New Haven: Yale University Press, 2008).

38. Katherine L. Milkman et al., *How Can Decision Making Be Improved?*, 4 PERSPECTIVES ON PSYCHOL. SCI. 379 (2009).

39. For an earlier version of this argument, *see* Richard H. Thaler and Cass R. Sunstein, *Libertarian Paternalism*, 93 AM. ECON. REV. 175 (2003); CHRISTINE JOLLS AND CASS SUNSTEIN, DEBIASING THROUGH LAW (2005); Christine Jolls, Cass Sunstein, and Richard Thaler, *A Behavioral Approach to Law and Economics*, 50 STANFORD LAW REVIEW 1471 (1998).

If it seems ironic that some of these interventions themselves take advantage of biases, such as the status quo bias, at least they "nudge" people toward enlightened self-interested or other prosocial behavior. That's the paternalistic aspect of libertarian paternalism. The libertarian aspect is that citizens and consumers are free to reject the nudge if they so desire—that's the difference between a nudge and a shove.

As with other techniques of influence examined in this and the preceding chapter, the techniques of nudging are orthogonal to the ends for which they are used. Thaler and Sunstein give an example of Carolyn, who can determine how food is set out in the cafeterias of a large school system. Without restricting students' choices, the order in which foods are placed, whether they are at eye level, and other display variables, can have a large effect on what the students eat. Carolyn might arrange the food:

- to encourage healthy choices that make the students better off;
- to facilitate students' choosing the items that they would probably choose anyway;
- to maximize profits to the cafeteria;
- to maximize bribes from food suppliers to Carolyn; or
- randomly.

All but the last are instances of choice architecture, though the third and fourth do not fit the rubric of libertarian paternalism.

We begin with an example (*not* from *Nudge)* of how framing behavior in terms of gains or losses may affect health, and then turn to the major categories of Thaler and Sunstein's nudges.

18.6.3.a Framing Health Behaviors as Gains or Losses Research by Alex Rothman and Peter Salovey shows the effect of framing appeals to engage in healthy behavior in terms either of gains or losses. Which frame is more effective depends on the type of behavior we seek to encourage. Rothman and Salovey distinguish between three types of health behavior: (1) *detection behaviors,* such as getting a mammogram or a colonoscopy, where the goal is to detect a health problem early so it can be addressed, (2) *prevention behaviors,* like wearing sunscreen or using condoms, where the goal is to avoid heath problems in the first place, and (3) *recuperative behavior,* or getting treatment for an existing condition.

They argue that detection behaviors are likely to be seen as risky, not because they actually pose a risk to a person's health, but because detection behaviors expose us to the short-term risk of getting scary news about our health. Because people tend to be risk-seeking in the domain of losses (Section 15.4), loss-framed appeals, which emphasize the potential *cost* of failing to detect a problem early, are the best way to get people to engage in detection behavior.[40] Gain-framed

40. Sara M. Banks et al., *The Effects of Message Framing on Mammography Utilization,* 14 Health Psychology 178–84 (1995).

appeals that emphasize the potential health benefits of early detection are likely to be less effective. Because people tend to be risk-averse in the domain of gains, such frames are likely to make people want to avoid the risk of scary news associated with detection.

In contrast, prevention behaviors such as wearing sunscreen or using condoms are perceived as safe. In fact, not performing such behaviors is generally seen as the risky option. Because people tend to be risk-seeking in the domain of losses, loss-framed appeals, like warning people of the potential *costs* of unprotected sun exposure, might actually make people *more* likely to take the risk of not wearing sunscreen. Instead, it is preferable to use gain-framed appeals, like emphasizing the *benefits* of wearing sunscreen, to encourage this type of nonrisky behavior.[41]

Similar to prevention behaviors, recuperative behaviors (i.e., obtaining treatment for an existing condition) are usually seen as nonrisky. Therefore, as with prevention behavior, Rothman and Salovey find that loss-framed appeals—such as those that emphasize the potential *costs* of failing to obtain treatment—tend to be counterproductive because they are more likely encourage risk-seeking attitudes. Gain-framed appeals that focus on the health *benefits* of treatment are preferable.

18.6.3.b Providing Feedback and "Mapping" Choices to Experienced Utility Simply making people more aware of the relationship between an action and its consequences can shape behavior. For example, the environmental costs of people's actions are rarely salient. But the display in the Toyota Prius, which shows drivers their momentary gas mileage, may affect their acceleration and speed. Thaler and Sunstein describe a device called the Ambient Orb, which changes color when home energy use rises above a certain level; people who began using this device decreased their energy usage by 40 percent.

The information provided consumers as a basis for evaluating and choosing among options is often obscure, with different options often being described with different metrics. The problem will be familiar to readers who have shopped for cell phone providers or cable TV packages. Thaler and Sunstein suggest that a good choice architecture makes information about relevant dimensions of each option salient.

Consider the advantage of displays that show supermarket shoppers the cost per unit of different brands of the same item, or the advantage of giving purchasers of home mortgages a comparison of lenders' fee structures and interest rates. Thaler and Sunstein suggest that consumers would make better choices if credit card lenders were required to report a summary of fees and interest rates on a

---

41. Alexander J. Rothman, Peter Salovey, Carol Antone, Kelli Keough, and Christina D. Martin, *The Influence of Message Framing on Intentions to Perform Health Behaviors*, 29 Journal of Experimental Social Psychology 408–33 (1993).

standardized form. They generalize this approach to a regulatory scheme called RECAP—**R**ecord, **E**valuate, and **C**ompare **A**lternative **P**rices.

There are other approaches to mapping as well. Federal regulations require car dealers to display a car's mileage per gallon. Richard Larrick and Jack Soll have proposed the alternative of gallons consumed per (say) 100 miles, arguing that miles per gallon (MPG) leads consumers to underestimate the gains in fuel savings from even a slightly more efficient car. For example, most people rank an improvement from 34 to 50 MPG as saving more gas over 10,000 miles than an improvement from 18 to 28 MPG, even though the latter saves twice as much gas.[42] People tend not make this error when presented with fuel efficiency expressed in gallons used per 100 miles.[43]

18.6.3.c Setting Default Options In Germany, only 12 percent of people are registered to donate their organs upon their death, while in Austria, 99 percent of people are registered. It is less likely that cultural differences account for this difference than defaults. Austrians are automatically registered as organ donors but may "opt out" and become unregistered at any time. Germans, by contrast, are unregistered by default, but may "opt in" and register as donors if they wish.

The power of the default option may result from a number of factors:

- the status quo bias and loss aversion;
- inertia, laziness, and procrastination (the "yeah, whatever" heuristic);
- people's belief that a default represents policy makers' or peers' sound judgment (social proof).

Sunstein and Thaler argue that policy makers should be intentional in determining which option to designate as the default. They might select the default that represents their best guess of individual preferences—for example, enrolling Medicare recipients in a prescription drug plan that maximizes savings on the most commonly used drugs—or that maximizes the welfare of society—for example, consent to organ donation.

In keeping with the libertarian part of libertarian paternalism, Thaler and Sunstein require that defaults be easy to change based on an individual's preference. But the better designed the choice architecture, the less necessary this becomes. In fact, if the default is based on sound objective analysis, citizens should be cautious about dismissing the default.

18.6.3.d Simplifying and Structuring Complex Choices We have seen that large decision sets can demotivate choice or lead people to use simplifying strategies that lead to suboptimal choices. Yet policy makers' restriction of choices may infringe the liberty of people who know they want something not included

42. Going from 34 to 50 MPG saves 94 gallons; but going from 18 to 28 MPG saves 198 gallons.

43. 20 Science 1593–94 (June 2008). DOI: 10.1126/science.1154983.

in the choice set. Thaler and Sunstein suggest the middle ground of simplifying and structuring choice sets.

Consider the challenge of sorting through all the options for Medicare Plan D prescription drug plans. Each plan contains information about all the different drugs it covers at what rate and with what copayments. The challenge of sorting through all the plans to find the right coverage would confound even a well-informed person. But a computer program could recommend a smaller set of options based on the prescriptions a particular individual uses most.

Large choice sets can be made easier to navigate by grouping options. For example, some investment funds, rather than provide customers with a list of funds in alphabetical order, group them by risk level (low, moderate, high) and portfolio composition (primarily stocks, primarily bonds). Without limiting the number of options available, this approach can limit the number of options that people *actually* consider.

People could also be given the option of delegating their decision to an expert, for example in choosing among 401(k) retirement plans. Delegation to an expert could even be made the default choice.

18.6.3.e Making Incentives Salient For incentives to be effective in shaping people's behavior, they must be noticeable and salient. But the effects of decisions often are delayed or difficult to imagine. Consider a family choosing whether to purchase a car or rely on alternative means of transportation. The costs of owning and operating a car may far exceed the costs of the alternatives. But the financial shock of purchasing a car occurs only once, while one feels the pain of losing money every time one pays a bus fare, or rents a car, or watches the meter on a taxi. Recall from our discussion of prospect theory that losses are more upsetting when segregated rather than integrated. (See Section 14.4) By the same token, *anticipating* myriad cab fares and rental car fees may feel more salient than the single loss of the price of purchasing a car. Perhaps making the installment payments and operating costs of the car equally salient would help level the playing field.

Prospect theory also suggests that several small incentives are likely to affect behavior more than would one large incentive. Receiving a year-long $100-per-month subsidy after buying a hybrid car might increase hybrid purchases more than providing a single payment of $1200—and would almost surely lead to more of an increase than discounting the car purchase by $1200. Hefty fines for speeding that are only occasionally enforced are probably less effective at reducing speeding than moderate fines that are frequently enforced.

18.6.3.f Criticisms of Libertarian Paternalism The effectiveness of choice architecture is an empirical question that is highly dependent on the contexts in which its techniques are applied. We expect that, over time, social scientists will develop useful generalizations about what works, what doesn't, and why. But as policy makers continue to explore the techniques of choice architecture, it is worth noting some recurring concerns about its underlying political premise, libertarian paternalism.

- Libertarian paternalism is an insidious use of government power because, by not regulating conduct directly, it does not mobilize the same sort of focused opposition as hard regulatory policies. *But* if there is no "neutral" way to structure a choice, policy makers might as well choose frames and defaults that are most likely to achieve citizens' interests or, where there is no apparent conflict, the public interest. In any event, a democratic government should be transparent to its citizens about its use of choice architecture.
- Libertarian paternalism encourages citizens' passivity and manipulates their choices rather than seeking to educate them to be better decision makers. *But* the literature on debiasing is not optimistic about the possibilities for countering biases, and the pervasiveness of bounded rationality means that even very thoughtful individuals will make many decisions by default.
- Choice architects are subject to their own biases and to corruption, partiality, and narrow-mindedness. Choice architecture offers the same opportunities for influence by special interests as any regulation. *But* the deliberative decision making that underlies good policies provide safeguards against biases. (Though, to refer back to the first criticism, choice architecture may embody tacit assumptions that would be more readily exposed in the contest over non-libertarian regulations.[44])
- Policy makers' choice of defaults, or even about what information to provide individuals, may assume an unjustified homogeneity of interests. Maybe there are individuals who would genuinely prefer to have more cash today than to save for retirement. When Thaler and Sunstein argue that governments should inform parents' choices of schools, they focus on information about educational achievement, but some parents may be more concerned about social or religious values. *But* as long as it isn't onerous to override the defaults, why shouldn't policy makers choose defaults that they believe to be in individuals' or society's best interests? And if governments do not provide all the information people need to make a decision based on their own interests, they have access other sources of information.
- Although choice architects endeavor to protect citizens' liberty in pursuing their diverse values and goals, the fact that goals are often constructed in the very process of decision making undercuts its implicit distinction between people's ends and their means for achieving them. Mark Kelman argues that efforts to assist citizens in pursuing their own values tend to

---

44. For example, there is an asymmetry between the defaults involving organ donation, with some individuals believing that the practice violates religious imperatives.

embody policy makers' implicit theory of the "good society."[45] *But* there are plenty of instances where people's bounded rationality and biases pretty clearly result in bad decisions in terms of interests that were not constructed on the spot.

There are no simple solutions to these problems of choice architecture. But Thaler and Sunstein offer an alternative to defaults that may obviate some of them and improve people's decision-making processes: *mandated choice.* Suppose that you can't obtain a driver's license without specifying whether or not you wish to be an organ donor if you are in a fatal accident. Suppose that an employer cannot hire you until you have specified what, if any, retirement savings plan you want to enroll in. Mandated choice doesn't work in all circumstances, and it doesn't obviate the inevitability of framing—consider Carolyn's cafeteria. But, when it is feasible, it nudges citizens to deliberate about important choices rather than nudging the choice in a particular direction—perhaps the ideal sort of libertarian paternalism in a deliberative democracy.

---

45. Mark G. Kelman, The Heuristics Debate: Its Nature and Its Implications for Law and Policy (Oxford University Press, forthcoming 2010); Mark Kelman, *Hedonic Psychology and the Ambiguities of "Welfare,"* 33 Phil. & Pub. Aff. 391, 395–97 (2005).

19. GROUP DECISION MAKING AND THE EFFECTS OF ACCOUNTABILITY ON DECISION QUALITY

Many if not most important decisions by policy makers and lawyers are made in group settings. For example, as Luis Trujillo and Christine Lamm deal with the problem at Terra Nueva, they will involve teams of colleagues and experts and work with other groups of stakeholders. Sometimes they will just seek advice; sometimes the group will have the authority to make decisions. This is characteristic of decision making in the private and nonprofit sectors as well as governments, and in private as well as public institutions. In situations like these, social dynamics within the decision-making group can exert a powerful effect on decision quality.

This chapter explores a variety of questions relating to the performance of small decision-making groups. Do groups outperform their individual members and, if so, when? What are the most common sources of dysfunction in decision-making groups, and how can their effects be minimized? Are there ways in which a group can be constituted, or its work structured, to set the stage for optimal group decision making? We conclude by considering how a decision maker's accountability to others—for individual as well as group decisions—can affect decisions for better or worse.

19.1 THINKING ABOUT GROUP DECISION MAKING

In a classic 1975 article entitled *Suppose We Took Groups Seriously*, Harvard Business School professor Harold J. Leavitt asserted that small groups, rather than individuals, should be the "building blocks" for organizations simply because groups perform better than individuals working alone.[1] Leavitt suggested that people perform better in groups for three reasons:

1. the group setting satisfies their need for social belonging;
2. groups are more creative than individuals; and
3. (most pertinent to our present inquiry) groups can pool the decision-relevant information possessed by some, but not all, group members and because members can correct each other's errors.

1. Harold J. Leavitt, *Suppose We Took Groups Seriously*, *in* Man and Work in Society 67–77 (Eugene L. Cass and Frederick G. Zimmer eds., New York: Van Nostrand Reinhold, 1975).

In any event, Leavitt observed, small groups will form within organizations as a result of natural patterns of human social interaction. Given the inevitability of groups, it is best to manage them in ways that will maximize their effectiveness. Leavitt's faith in the power of groups spread rapidly and became the received wisdom in popular and academic thinking about business and government administration.

At about the same time, the social psychologist Irving L. Janis published a book on the perils of group decision making. In an expanded 1982 edition entitled *Groupthink*,[2] Janis sought to explain government decision-making disasters, such as the failure to anticipate the Japanese attack on Pearl Harbor, the decisions to escalate the war in Vietnam, the Bay of Pigs invasion, and the Watergate cover-up.

The basic idea of Janis's "groupthink" hypothesis was that highly cohesive decision-making groups have a strong tendency to suppress their members' independent thinking and to converge too quickly on poor-quality decisions. The drive to avoid intragroup conflict prevents rigorous evaluation of competing alternatives. Divergent perspectives and theory-disconfirming information are suppressed in favor of supportive opinions and theory-confirming views. Buckling under the overt and covert social pressure, even those group members who harbored serious private reservations about the group's preferred choice do not express them and acquiesce in the decision. Janis also described a few successful policy decisions, including President John F. Kennedy's response to the Cuban Missile Crisis and the development of the Marshall Plan after World War II, in which the decision-making process did not appear to be infected with these dynamics.

Three decades of research tell a more nuanced and complex story than either Leavitt's rosy or Janis's pessimistic account. Groups can add value to a decision-making process, but they can also run it off the rails. Small groups often make better decisions than their average member would make alone, but they seldom outperform their best members.[3] Small groups fall prey to virtually all of the cognitive biases that plague individual decision makers and sometimes actually amplify the effects of those biases. Moreover, deliberation, which commentators like Leavitt credit with improving the effectiveness of group decision making, can actually introduce additional sources of error into the process.

Most of this chapter will focus on decision making by groups whose members *interact* with each other. As a prelude, however, it is useful to contrast the

---

2. Irving L. Janis, Victims of Groupthink: A Psychological Study of Foreign Policy Decisions and Fiascos (Boston: Houghton Mifflin, 1972); Irving L. Janis, Groupthink: Psychological Studies of Policy Decisions and Fiascos (Boston: Houghton Mifflin, 1982).

3. Gayle W. Hill, *Group versus Individual Performance: Are N + 1 Heads Better than One?*, 91 Psychological Bulletin 519–39 (1983).

aggregation of judgments about an issue made by individuals who do *not* interact—in effect, a *statistical* or *nominal group*.

19.2 AGGREGATION WITHOUT GROUP PROCESS: THE WISDOM OF CROWDS

In a phenomenon that James Surowiecki has termed the "wisdom of crowds," combining a sufficient number of diverse and independent judgments often yields a better outcome than the judgment of any isolated person, no matter how smart or well informed he or she might be.[4] The result requires that four conditions be met:

1. The "group" must reflect a *diversity* of skills, opinions, information, and perspectives.
2. Each member's judgment must be *independent* from the others. That is, an individual's knowledge and opinions cannot be influenced by the knowledge and opinions of other group members.
3. The members must make and report their "sincere" judgments rather than skewing them for strategic purposes.
4. The decision maker needs a mechanism for *aggregating* the individual judgments to turn large numbers of private judgments into a single one.

An early example of a statistical group is a 1906 experiment by Sir Francis Galton, a proponent of eugenics who—to put it mildly—had little regard for the common person's potential as a decision maker. Because of his interest in breeding, Galton was attending the West England Fat Stock and Poultry Exhibition. Its organizers had devised a game in which fairgoers were asked to guess the butchered and dressed weight of a particularly fat ox. Eight hundred people—farmers, butchers, and random fairgoers, tried their luck that day.

Galton did not expect them to perform particularly well. Indeed he wrote, ". . . like those clerks and others who have no expert knowledge of horses, but who bet on races, guided by newspapers, friends, and their own fancies . . . [t]he average competitor was probably as well fitted for making a just estimate of the dressed weight of the ox, as an average voter is of judging the merits of most political issues on which he votes."[5]

At the end of the fair, Galton conducted some statistical tests on the 787 contest entries. He correctly anticipated that most participants' guesses would be way off the mark, with only a small minority coming close to the beast's actual

---

4. James Surowiecki, The Wisdom of Crowds: Why the Many Are Smarter than the Few and How Collective Wisdom Shapes Business, Economies, Societies, and Nations (New York: Doubleday, 2004).

5. *Id.* xii.

dressed weight. However, the *average* of the estimates, 1,197 pounds, turned out to be only one pound less than the weight of the ox when slaughtered and dressed.

The power of statistical averaging illustrated by Galton's experience derives from a law known as the Condorcet Jury Theorem.[6] Here's how the theorem works: Suppose that a number of people are independently answering a yes or no question, and that the probability that each individual will answer the question correctly is at least somewhat greater than 50 percent. Then the probability that a majority of group members will answer the question correctly increases as the size of the group increases. If the answers are not binary, but are spread over a continuous range, Condorcet's theorem predicts that the average answer will more closely approximate the correct answer as the size of the group increases. (If the probability that each individual member will decide correctly is *less* than 50 percent, the probability that a majority will answer correctly approaches *zero*.)

Over half a century ago, Friedrich Hayek observed that aggregated knowledge is crucial for providing information to the market.[7] Yet the mechanisms for systematically accumulating and organizing information from dispersed individuals (other than through revealed preferences exhibited by their participation in the market) were largely unexplored until the late 1990s, when Caltech and Hewlett-Packard Laboratories undertook an innovative experiment to implement an Information Aggregation Mechanism within the corporation.

Kay-Yut Chen, a scientist at Hewlett-Packard Laboratories (HP) in Palo Alto, California, and Charles R. Plott, a professor of economics and political science at Caltech, experimented with internal "securities markets" to improve product sales forecasting.[8] They selected a small number of employees from different parts of HP's business operations and different geographical regions. Some employees had information about clients, others about pricing strategies, others about competitors' strategies and products. Participants were given an initial portfolio of securities (created for the experiment) with each security associated with one of ten different levels of HP sales, and were allowed to buy and sell securities associated with these levels. To make money, participants had to accurately predict the level of sales HP would experience three months in the future. If participants accurately did so (by holding securities within that range), they

6. Marquis de Condorcet, *Essai sur l'application de l'analysé à la probabilité de decisions rendues à la pluralité des voix* (I. McLean and F. Hewitt trans., Paris: L'imprimerie Royale, 1785); McLennan A, "Consequences of the Condorcet Jury Theorem for beneficial information aggregation by rational agents," *American Political Science Review* 92, (1998): 413–18.

7. Friedrich A. Hayek, Individualism and economic order (Chicago: University of Chicago Press, 1948).

8. Kay-Yut Chen and Charles Plott, "Information Aggregation Mechanisms: Concept, Design, and Implementation for a Sales Forecasting Problem," 2002, http://www.hss.caltech.edu/SSPapers/wp1131.pdf.

would receive a payoff, but they would receive nothing for securities held at any other level.[9]

Chen's and Plott's futures market consistently yielded better marketing forecasts than did HP's official predictions, arrived at through deliberation by the company's sales forecasting experts.[10] Why? Because it provided an effective mechanism for aggregating the specialized knowledge of an independent and diverse group of people, and because the participants had no reason to strategically distort their predictions.

It is this efficient aggregation of decentralized, privately held information that makes projects like the Iowa Electronic Markets (IEM) so interesting. IEM is a small-scale futures market where interested individuals make contracts based on their own predictions of economic and political events, such as elections. In 2008, for example, individuals could make contracts based on whether Barack Obama or John McCain would win the U.S. Presidential election. The market is operated by faculty at the University of Iowa's Henry B. Tippie College of Business; the results routinely outperform polls and surveys in predicting electoral outcomes.[11] A similar idea is the Hollywood Stock Exchange (HSX), which allows people to place wagers on movie box office returns, Oscar results, and other film-related events.[12] HSX produces surprisingly accurate predictions, demonstrating the power of markets to aggregate the information dispersed over a large population of independent actors.[13]

* * *

Decision makers must often forecast future events in order to assess the advantages and disadvantages of alternative courses of action. These examples suggest that information markets can sometimes do a better job than experts. But it is often not feasible to use statistical groups, and the responsibility falls on

---

9. To ensure that participants had no knowledge of each others' identities or of the aggregated results until the experiment was over, thus limting the effects of influence on their trading decisions, participants drew only on their personal, privately held information, general information available from HP, and the patterns of trade they observed other participants making online (based on anonymous ID numbers). Access to information was therefore limited to a web-based trading system.

10. Kay-Yut Chen and Charles Plott, "Information Aggregation Mechanisms: Concept, Design, and Implementation for a Sales Forecasting Problem," 2002, http://www.hss.caltech.edu/SSPapers/wp1131.pdf.

11. Iowa Electronic Markets Web site, operated by the University of Iowa Henry B. Tippie College of Business http://www.biz.uiowa.edu/iem/.

12. Hollywood Stock Exchange Web site, http://www.hsx.com/about/whatishsx.htm.

13. James Surowiecki, The Wisdom of Crowds: Why the Many are Smarter than the Few and How Collective Wisdom Shapes Business, Economies, Societies, and Nations 20 (New York: Doubleday, 2004); Cass. R. Sunstein, *Group Judgments: Deliberation, Statistical Means, and Information Markets*, 80 New York University Law Review 962–1049 (2005).

actual face-to-face groups. Also, as illustrated in the previous chapters of this book, most decision making involves far more than estimating and forecasting—situations to which application of the "wisdom of crowds" is at least untested, if not problematic.

The remainder of this chapter considers the determinants of good decision making in actual, interactive groups: diversity, independences, candor, and an ability to aggregate information, among other things.

19.3 GROUPTHINK

Irving Janis defined *groupthink* as the tendency of highly cohesive decision-making groups to converge too quickly on a bad decision.[14] The core claim of the *groupthink hypothesis* is that certain antecedent conditions can lead decision-making groups to employ defective processes, which lead to poor policy outcomes.[15]

As background for understanding the groupthink hypotheses, recall the model of fully deliberative decision making introduced in Section 4.5. As Figure 19.1 illustrates, a fully deliberative process comprises both divergent and convergent elements. *Divergent* thinking predominates early in the process, as one frames and reframes the problem, identifies the full complement of decision-relevant goals and objectives, and generates a range of alternative courses of action. Later in the process, these various alternatives are systematically evaluated to determine what outcomes—both intended and unintended—they might produce. This is largely *convergent* thinking, characterized by an analytic evidence-based appraisal of the likely positive and negative consequences of each possible course of action. The process looks something like the one shown in Figure 19.1.

By contrast, groupthink is characterized by the group's reaching premature convergence without adequate analysis—all in the interest of achieving concurrence within the group. As a result, the problem is inadequately framed, objectives are underspecified, and an initially preferred course of action is inadequately scrutinized, while potential competing alternatives are too rapidly rejected or are left

---

14. Irving L. Janis, *Groupthink*, 5 PSYCHOLOGY TODAY 43–46, 74–76 (1971); IRVING L. JANIS, VICTIMS OF GROUPTHINK: A PSYCHOLOGICAL STUDY OF FOREIGN POLICY DECISIONS AND FIASCOS (Boston: Houghton Mifflin, 1972); IRVING L. JANIS, GROUPTHINK: PSYCHOLOGICAL STUDIES OF POLICY DECISIONS AND FIASCOS (Boston: Houghton Mifflin, 1982); IRVING L. JANIS, CRUCIAL DECISIONS: LEADERSHIP IN POLICYMAKING AND CRISIS MANAGEMENT (New York: Free Press, 1989); IRVING L. JANIS AND LEON MANN, DECISION MAKING: A PSYCHOLOGICAL ANALYSIS OF CONFLICT, CHOICE AND COMMITMENT (New York: Free Press, 1977).

15. Robert S. Baron, *So Right It's Wrong: Groupthink and the Ubiquitous Nature of Polarized Group Decision Making, in* ADVANCES IN EXPERIMENTAL SOCIAL PSYCHOLOGY 37, 219 (Mark P. Zanna, ed., San Diego, CA: Elsevier Academic Press, 2005); Mark Schafer and Scott Crichlow, *Antecedents of Groupthink*, 40 JOURNAL OF CONFLICT RESOLUTION 415–35 (1996).

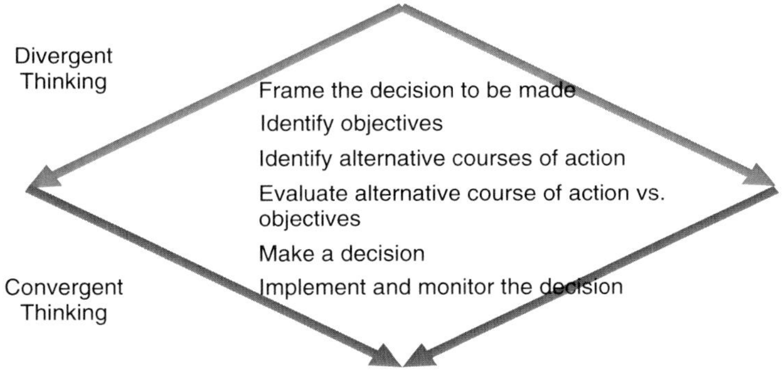

FIGURE 19.1 DIVERGENT AND CONVERGENT ELEMENTS IN DELIBERATIVE DECISION MAKING.

unidentified altogether. Rather than resembling a diamond, decision making under conditions of groupthink looks more like the process shown in Figure 19.2.

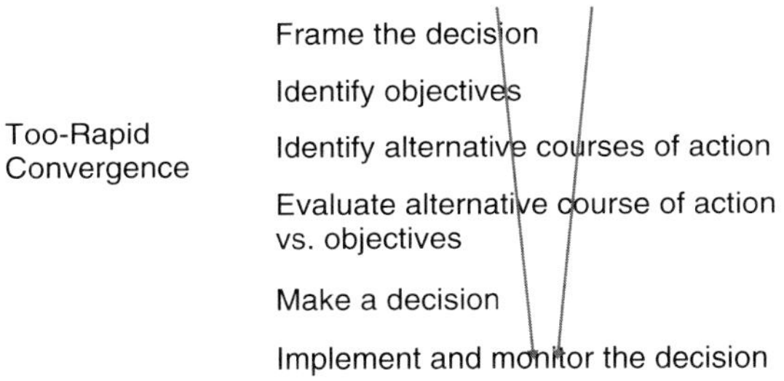

FIGURE 19.2 GROUPTHINK'S CONVERGENT PROCESSES.

From his examination of selected policy fiascos and successes, Janis identified four sets of attributes characterizing groupthink.

1. groupthink symptoms;
2. decision-making characteristics;
3. antecedents; and
4. remedial interventions.

We review the first three here and will return to the last in Section 19.8.

19.3.1 Groupthink Symptoms and Decision-Making Characteristics

The core symptoms of groupthink consist of:

- overestimation of the group's skill, power, and morality;
- close-mindedness; and
- pressure toward uniformity

In Janis's view, a group that has fallen prey to the groupthink syndrome tends to have an exaggerated view of its skills, knowledge, power, and moral righteousness.

Misgivings and dissenting viewpoints are quickly discounted, as are cautionary admonitions from outsiders, if they are allowed to penetrate the group's boundaries at all. The competence, strength, and reasonableness of the group's real or imagined adversaries are underestimated; those adversaries are reduced to stereotypes, and often dismissed as "evil" or as "weak and stupid."[16]

But the most significant symptoms of groupthink fall into the third category: pressures toward uniformity. In groupthink situations, a favored course of action emerges early in the decision-making process, often because it is, or is believed to be, the option favored by the group's leader. Group members who harbor doubts about the emerging consensus feel inhibited from expressing them, creating an illusion of unanimity. Group members who do voice doubts are subjected to subtle or overt forms of social pressure, disparagement, or reprisal, often through the efforts of "mindguards"—group members who police the group's thinking.

Under these circumstances, divergent elements of the formal decision-making process are given short shrift, leading to underidentification of goals and objectives and an unduly limited set of options. Additionally, in generating or evaluating alternative courses of action, the group conducts an inadequate information search, fails to take advantage of expert knowledge, and looks for information that confirms the preferred course of action. The group fails to conduct a thorough comparison of the available alternatives, fails fully to assess the risks attending the preferred course of action, and fails to develop contingency plans.

As a result, groupthink neutralizes what would otherwise be advantages provided by group decision making. Diversity of perspectives is squandered and members' specialized expertise neutralized. The potential that a group has for generating more ideas and for bringing more information to bear on the decision-making process goes unrealized.

19.3.2 Groupthink Antecedents

Groupthink is primarily a disorder of highly *cohesive* groups. However, cohesiveness alone is not sufficient. Janis thought that factors such as the group's insulation, the presence of partisanship, directive group leadership, and ideological homogeneity among group members all made groupthink more likely to emerge. Janis proposed that common contextual antecedents included high levels of external pressure and internal stress, which could be exacerbated by the experience of recent failure or by the problem's complexity and "high stakes." He posited that, when accompanied by other situational and contextual antecedents, high group cohesion was a strong predictor of the groupthink syndrome.

---

16. Irving L. Janis, Groupthink: Psychological Studies of Policy Decisions and Fiascos 197 (Boston: Houghton Mifflin, 1982).

19.3.3 Empirical Perspectives on the Groupthink Framework

Janis's own analysis of the groupthink hypothesis was based largely on case studies of policy decisions selected because of their (mostly bad) outcomes. Even if one could control for the myriad factors involved in these complex decisions, it would be difficult to draw conclusions about correlation, let alone causation. Thirty years of subsequent research has not provided strong empirical evidence of the link between the posited antecedents to the groupthink phenomenon.[17] Here is a brief summary of what's known about the groupthink hypothesis today.

- Reanalyses of Janis's case studies have confirmed that structural and procedural organizational defects predict the groupthink syndrome, but have not determined that group cohesiveness and provocative situational contexts predict the syndrome.[18]
- Analyses of other policy fiascos—including the Ford Motor Company's decision to produce the Edsel, price fixing in the electrical industry, the Challenger space shuttle launch decision, and the Iran-Contra fiasco—have found present many of the groupthink antecedents, symptoms, and decision process characteristics.[19]
- Some researchers argue that the groupthink hypothesis is so complex and incorporates so many variables that, unless it is broken up into its component parts, it cannot possibly be validated empirically.[20]
- It has proved difficult to recreate the groupthink antecedents (genuine in-group cohesion, meaningful threat, group insulation, homogeneity of

---

17. Robert S. Baron, *supra*.

18. Philip E. Tetlock et al., *Assessing Political Group Dynamics: A Test of the Groupthink Model*, 63 Journal of Personality and Social Psychology 403–25 (1992). McCauley (1989) also found no support for the predictive value of group cohesion, although he did find significant predictive value for insulation, promotional leadership, and in-group homogeneity. The studies that do exist focus primarily on the groupthink antecedents, attempting to determine whether groupthink symptoms emerge if, and only if, particular antecedent variables are present.

19. Richard C. Huseman and Russell W. Driver, *Groupthink: Implications for Small Group Decision Making in Business*, in Readings in Organizational Behavior 100–10 (Richard C. Huseman and Anne Carroll eds., Boston, MA: Allyn and Bacon, 1979); Thomas R. Hensley and Glen W. Griffin, *Victims of Groupthink: The Kent State University Board of Trustees and the 1977 Gymnasium Controversy*, 31 Journal of Conflict Resolution 203–26 (1986); James Esser and Joanne Lindoerfer, *Groupthink and the Space Shuttle Challenger Accident: Toward a Quantitative Case Analysis*, 2 Journal of Behavioral Decision Making 167–77 (1989); Paul t'Hart, *Irving L. Janis' Victims of Groupthink*, 12 Political Psychology 247–78 (1991); Gregory Moorhead et al., *Group Decision Fiascoes Continue: Space Shuttle Challenger and a Revised Groupthink Framework*, 44 Human Relations 539–50 (1991).

20. Robert S. Baron, *supra*.

values) in laboratory settings.[21] Those laboratory studies that have been done generally do not support Janis' notion that group cohesiveness is the most important antecedent predictor of groupthink.[22]

We turn our attention to some discrete pathologies of group decision making.

19.4 THE COMMON KNOWLEDGE EFFECT

In Chapter 1, we introduced Jack Serrano, a client of attorney Luis Trujillo's who owns Terra Nueva, a low-income housing development. Recall that a group of Serrano's Terra Nueva tenants were about to file a class action lawsuit against him, claiming that foam insulation used in building their apartments was making them sick.

Imagine that the lawsuit is filed and that the lawyer representing the Terra Nueva plaintiffs convenes a meeting to discuss the litigation with representatives from some advocacy groups. Those present include an organizer from the United Electrical Workers and activists from East Los Angeles Tenants United and L.A. Consumers' Action, along with representatives of the Terra Nueva plaintiffs and the newly formed Terra Nueva Tenant's Union. The main purpose of the meeting is to allow representatives from the various groups to discuss how the litigation could be used to focus attention on the many toxic-exposure–related problems facing low-income residents in Southern California. More specifically, the participants want to explore whether similar suits should be filed against other developers and low-income housing operators in the area.

All of the individuals present at the meeting are familiar with the allegations made in the Terra Nueva lawsuit. They have all read the media coverage, including the articles putting the Terra Nueva situation in the larger context of toxic residential insulation cases being filed across the country. But only the organizer from the United Electrical Workers is aware that exposure to toxic chemicals in the semiconductor plants, in which some of the tenants work, could cause similar symptoms.

Imagine also that shortly after the suit is filed, Luis Trujillo, two of his firm's associates, and a paralegal are meeting with an epidemiologist with knowledge

21. *Id.*; James Esser, *Alive and Well After 25 years: A Review of Groupthink Research*, 73 Organizational Behavior and Human Decision Processes 116–41 (1998).

22. Matie L. Flowers, *A Laboratory Test of Some Implications of Janis's Groupthink Hypothesis*, 35 Journal of Personality and Social Psychology 888–96 (1977); Eugene M. Fodor and Timothy Smith, *The Power Motive as an Influence on Group Decision Making*, 42 Journal of Personality and Social Psychology 178–85 (1982); Michael R. Callaway and James K. Esser, *Groupthink: Effects of Cohesiveness and Problem-Solving Procedures on Group Decision Making*, 12 Social Behavior and Personality 157–64 (1984).

of "sick building syndrome" and a professor of toxicology from a local university. The purpose of the meeting is to develop a litigation strategy for the defense. Collectively, the six people present have a great deal of relevant knowledge—- about the Terra Nueva residents, about the potential harmful health effects of foam insulation and other building materials, about disease cluster analysis, and about the litigation of toxic exposure cases. But one piece of information is known only to the paralegal who happens to have family ties to some of the Terra Nueva residents: that some of the residents work in a shipyard where they are exposed to solvents and other hazardous materials that could cause the symptoms the tenants are complaining about.

Thus, one participant in each group has a unique piece of information that points to a possible cause of the Terra Nueva tenants' symptoms, other than the foam insulation in their apartments. This information could make an enormous difference to the strategies the group formulates.

Group decision making has the potential benefit of aggregating the knowledge of diverse members.[23] But realizing this benefit requires that group members who possess unshared information—information not known by other members—recall it and actually share it with the group, and that the group combine the shared information to make its decision. Will the participant share the unique information with the rest of the group?

Unfortunately, group deliberations often focus on shared rather than unshared information.[24] The so-called "common knowledge effect"[25] biases group decision making in the direction supported by shared information. Even when group members with unshared information recall it and share it with the group, it tends not to be optimally considered in subsequent group deliberation.[26]

23. Amiram Vinokur and Eugene Burnetein, *The Effects of Partially Shared Persuasive Arguments on Group Induced Shifts: A Group Problem Solving Approach*, 29 Journal of Personality and Social Psychology 305–15 (1974).

24. James R. Larson et al., *Discussion of Shared and Unshared Information in Decision Making Groups*, 67 Journal of Personality and Social Psychology 446–61 (1994); Garold Stasser and Dennis Stewart, *Discovery of Hidden Profiles by Decision Making Groups: Solving a Problem versus Making a Judgment*, 63 Journal of Personality and Social Psychology 426–34 (1992); Garold Stasser and William Titus, *Pooling of Unshared Information in Group Decision Making: Biased Information Sampling During Discussion*, 48 Journal of Personality and Social Psychology 1467 (1985).

25. Daniel Gigone and Reid Hastie, *The Common Knowledge Effect: Information Sharing and Group Judgment*, 65 Journal of Personality and Social Psychology 959–74 (1993). The phenomenon is also called the "common information sampling bias." Gwen M. Wittenbaum and Garold Stasser, *Management of Information in Small Groups*, *in* What's Social About Social Cognition? Research on Socially Shared Cognition in Small Groups 3–28 (Judith L. Nye and Aaron M. Brower eds., Thousand Oaks, CA: Sage, 1996).

26. Gigone and Hastie, *supra*.

19.4.1 Research on the Common Knowledge Effect: The "Hidden Profile" Paradigm

In the mid-1980s, Garold Stasser and William Titus asked randomly selected groups of people to make a decision about which of three candidates for a particular position was the most qualified.[27] All relevant information about the three candidates was provided to all members of the control group (the shared information condition). In the aggregate, the information strongly supported Candidate A, and the control group tended to choose that candidate by wide margins.

In the experimental condition, the negative information about the "best qualified candidate" (the one most frequently chosen by the control group) was shared, while positive information about that candidate was divided among group members. If all of the information possessed by all group members had been aggregated, Candidate A's superiority over Candidates B and C would be readily apparent. However, in their deliberations, the experimental group members were far more likely to bring up and discuss shared information. As a result, they were unable to uncover the "hidden profile" that made Candidate A's superiority so apparent to the control group.[28]

Stasser and Titus's results have been replicated in a variety of experimental contexts[29] to yield these robust generalizations: small group deliberation relies

---

27. Garold Stasser and William Titus, *Pooling of Unshared Information in Group Decision Making: Biased Information Sampling During Discussion*, 48 Journal of Personality and Social Psychology 1467 (1985); Garold Stasser and William Titus, *Hidden Profiles: A Brief History*, 14 Psychological Inquiry 304 (2003).

28. *See* Garold Stasser and William Titus, *Hidden Profiles: A Brief History*, 14 Psychological Inquiry 304 (2003).

29. Gwen M. Wittenbaum and Jonathan M. Bowman, *A Social Validation Explanation for Mutual Enhancement*, 40 Journal of Experimental Social Psychology 169–84 (2004); Gwen M. Wittenbaum, Anne P. Hubbell, and Connie Zuckerman, *Mutual Enhancement: Toward an Understanding of the Collective Preference for Shared Information*, 77 Journal of Personality and Social Psychology 967–78 (1999); Janice R. Kelly and Steven J. Karau, *Group Decision Making: The Effects of Initial Preferences and Time Pressure*, 25 Personality and Social Psychology Bulletin 1342–54 (1999); Garold Stasser, Sandra Vaughn, and Dennis Stewart, *Pooling Unshared Information: The Benefits of Knowing How Access to Information Is Distributed Among Group Members*, 82 Organizational Behavior and Human Decision Processes 102–16 (2000); Jennifer R. Winquist and James R. Larson, *Information Pooling: When It Impacts Group Decision Making*, 74 Journal of Personality and Social Psychology 371–77 (1998); James R. Larson, Pennie G. Foster-Fishma, and Timothy M. Franz, *Leadership Style and the Discussion of Shared and Unshared Information in Decision Making Groups*, 24 Personality and Social Psychology Bulletin 482–95 (1998); James R. Larson et al., *Diagnosing Groups: The Pooling, Management, and Impact of Shared and Unshared Case Information in Team-based Medical Decision Making*, 75 Journal of Personality and Social Psychology 93–108 (1998); Gwen M. Wittenbaum, *Information Sampling in Decision Making Groups: The Impact of*

most heavily on completely shared information, and information known by a majority of group members has some effect. However, information known by only one or few members tends to not be shared or, when it is, tends not to have as much effect as common information.[30]

The strength of the common knowledge effect appears to be a function of several main variables, including:

- The group's familiarity with the decision domain. Unshared information is accorded the least weight in situations where group members are familiar with the subject matter to which the decision pertains.[31]
- Verifiability of the unshared information. Unshared information that is objectively verifiable is used more than unshared information that is not.
- The number of group members who possess the information. The more group members who possess a piece of unshared information, the more weight it is given.[32]

Members Task-Relevant Status, 29 SMALL GROUP RESEARCH 57–84 (1998); Garold Stasser and Gwen M. Wittenbaum, *The Reevaluation of Information During Group Discussion*, 1 GROUP PROCESSES & INTERGROUP RELATIONS 21–34 (1998); Dennis Stewart and Garold Stasser, *Expert Role Assignment and Information Sampling During Collective Recall and Decision Making*, 69 JOURNAL OF PERSONALITY AND SOCIAL PSYCHOLOGY 619–28 (1995); James R. Larson, Pennie G. Foster-Fishman, and Christopher B. Keys, *Discussion of Shared and Unshared Information in Decision Making Groups*, 67 JOURNAL OF PERSONALITY AND SOCIAL PSYCHOLOGY 446–61 (1994); Daniel Gigone and Reid Hastie, *The Common Knowledge Effect: Information Sharing and Group Judgment*, 65 JOURNAL OF PERSONALITY AND SOCIAL PSYCHOLOGY 959–74 (1993); Daniel Gigone and Reid Hastie, *The Impact of Information on Group Judgment: A Model and Computer Simulation*, *in* UNDERSTANDING GROUP BEHAVIOR: VOL. I. CONSENSUAL ACTION BY SMALL GROUPS (Erich H. White and James H. Davis eds., Hillsdale, NJ: Erlbaum, 1996); Garold Stasser and Dennis Stewart, *Discovery of Hidden Profiles by Decision Making Groups: Solving a Problem versus Making a Judgment*, 63 JOURNAL OF PERSONALITY AND SOCIAL PSYCHOLOGY 426–34 (1992); Garold Stasser, Laurie A. Taylor, and Coleen Hanna, *Information Sampling in Structured and Unstructured Discussions of Three- and Six-Person Groups*, 57 JOURNAL OF PERSONALITY AND SOCIAL PSYCHOLOGY 67–78 (1989); Garold Stasser and William Titus, *Effects of Information Load and Percentage of Common Information on the Dissemination of Unique Information During Group Discussion*, 53 JOURNAL OF PERSONALITY AND SOCIAL PSYCHOLOGY 81–93 (1987).

30. Craig D. Parks and Rebecca Cowlin, *Acceptance of Uncommon Information into Group Discussion When That Information Is or Is Not Demonstable*, 66 ORGANIZATIONAL BEHAVIOR AND HUMAN DECISION PROCESSES 307–15 (1996).

31. *Id.*

32. *Id.*

- Contextual factors. Time pressure increases reliance on common information,[33] as does an increase in the decision's apparent importance and group members' sense of accountability for it.[34]

19.4.2 Causal Accounts of the Common Knowledge Effect

A number of causal theories have been advanced to explain the common knowledge effect. These include:

- The Probabilistic Information Sampling Account;
- The Confirmation Bias Account;
- The Social Validation Account;
- The Mutual Enhancement Account;
- The Social Identity Formation Account;
- The Conversational Norms Account.

There is no reason to believe that they are mutually exclusive.

Probabilistic sampling. The essence of the common knowledge effect is that the probability that a particular item of information will be used in group deliberation is a function of the number of group members who possess the information before discussion begins. The earliest explanation for the effect was simply that, as a matter of basic sampling theory, the more group members who possess a piece of decision-relevant information ex ante, the higher the probability that it will be recalled by at least one group member and mentioned during group discussion.[35]

But this information sampling account was unable to account for some aspects of the common knowledge effect. Specifically, even when group members possessing unshared information shared it with the group, it was not subsequently

---

33. Steven J. Karau and Janie R. Kelly, *The Effects of Time Scarcity and Time Abundance on Group Performance Quality and Interaction Process*, 28 JOURNAL OF EXPERIMENTAL SOCIAL PSYCHOLOGY 542–71 (1992).

34. James R. Larson, Pennie G. Foster-Fishman, and Christopher B. Keys, *Discussion of Shared and Unshared Information in Decision Making Groups*, 67 JOURNAL OF PERSONALITY AND SOCIAL PSYCHOLOGY 446–61 (1994); Dennis Stewart, Robert S. Billings, and Garold Stasser, *Accountability and the Discussion of Unshared, Critical Information in Decision Making Groups*, 2 GROUP DYNAMICS 18–23 (1998).

35. Garold Stasser and William Titus, *Effects of Information Load and Percentage of Common Information on the Dissemination of Unique Information During Group Discussion*, 53 JOURNAL OF PERSONALITY AND SOCIAL PSYCHOLOGY 81–93 (1987); James R Larson, Pennie G. Foster-Fishman, and Christopher B. Keys, *Discussion of Shared and Unshared Information in Decision Making Groups*, 67 JOURNAL OF PERSONALITY AND SOCIAL PSYCHOLOGY 446–61 (1994); Garold Stasser, *Information Salience and the Discovery of Hidden Profiles by Decision-Making Groups: A Thought Experiment*, 52 ORGANIZATIONAL BEHAVIOR AND HUMAN DECISION PROCESSES 5156–81 (1992).

mentioned in discussion as frequently as commonly held information, and it received less weight than common information in making the decision.

Confirmation bias. In Section 10.3, we described the bias under which people tend to overweight information that confirms their initial hypothesis and underweight information that would tend to disconfirm it. This bias has been offered as a partial explanation for the common knowledge effect.

Group members often come to the meeting with some decision-relevant information and an ex ante preference for a particular decision. To the extent that more individual group members base their initial preferences on common pieces of information, the distribution of ex ante preferences will be skewed in the direction the information supports. Newly acquired information will be assimilated in a confirmatory direction,[36] resulting in the shared information being mentioned more frequently and weighted more heavily than unshared information.[37]

Social validation and mutual enhancement. In group decision-making situations, participants are often concerned about their task competence. This concern is exacerbated when the subject matter relevant to the decision is unfamiliar, the decision is very important, or group members feel a high level of accountability for the outcome. As a result, participants are constantly trying to assess the appropriateness and accuracy of their thoughts, arguments, and opinions; they are worried about how their competence will be assessed, both by themselves and by others.

Social comparison processes play a significant role in people's monitoring of the accuracy and appropriateness of their thoughts, as the Asch experiments, described in Section 17.1, illustrated so vividly. The importance, relevance, even the accuracy of shared information can be validated through a process of social comparison. As any particular group member hears others mentioning, crediting, and relying upon information she too possess, she feels more secure in mentioning, crediting, and relying on that information as well. Because unshared information cannot be so easily validated, mentioning, crediting, or using it in arguing for a position is more socially risky.[38] Indeed, experiments by Gwen

---

36. Barry M. Staw, *The Escalation of Commitment: An Update and Appraisal, in* Organizational Decision Making—Cambridge Series on Judgment and Decision Making 191–215 (Zur Shapira ed., New York: Cambridge University Press, 1997).

37. Daniel Gigone and Reid Hastie, *The Common Knowledge Effect: Information Sharing and Group Judgment*, 65 Journal of Personality and Social Psychology 959–74 (1993); Jennifer R. Winquist and James R. Larson, *Information Pooling: When It Impacts Group Decision Making*, 74 Journal of Personality and Social Psychology 371–77 (1998).

38. Gwen M. Wittenbaum., Anne P. Hubbell, and Connie Zuckerman, *Mutual Enhancement: Toward an Understanding of the Collective Preference for Shared Information*, 77 Journal of Personality and Social Psychology 967–78 (1999); Gwen M. Wittenbaum and Ernest S. Park, *The Collective Preference for Shared Information*, 10 Current Directions in Psychological Science 172–75 (2001).

Wittenbaum and her collaborators indicate that the discussion of shared information leads people both to feel more like a "group" and to feel better about that group.[39]

Conversational norms. As every good lawyer and politician knows, effective communicators tailor their messages to what they believe to be the knowledge, background, and expectations of their audience. By creating a "cognitive common ground," one makes the message both more comprehensible and more persuasive to the communicator.

This phenomenon may play a role in the common knowledge effect. If I am a member of a group, and want to make a point, I may begin by mentioning information that is believed by others in the group. If group members follow the rhetorical axiom, "begin your remarks by mentioning facts you know others believe true," they will mention shared information more frequently than unshared information.[40] In this way, the common knowledge effect can result from the operation of a simple conversational norm.

19.4.3 Reducing the Bias in Favor of Shared Information: What Works, What Doesn't, What Makes Things Worse?

Empirical research on the conditions that exacerbate or ameliorate the common knowledge effect has yielded two generalizations.

First, forewarning people that they may have relevant information that other group members may not possess has no effect.[41] Nor does instructing group members not to come to judgments about the best course of action before all information possessed by group members is surfaced.[42]

---

39. Gwen M. Wittenbaum and Jonathan M. Bowman, *A Social Validation Explanation for Mutual Enhancement,* 40 Journal of Experimental Social Psychology 169–84 (2004); Gwen M. Wittenbaum, Anne P. Hubbell, and Colleen Zuckerman, *Mutual Enhancement: Toward an Understanding of the Collective Preference for Shared Information,* 77 Journal of Personality and Social Psychology 967–78 (1999). *See also* Michael A. Hogg, *Social Identity and the Sovereignty of the Group: A Psychology of Belonging, in* Individual Self, Relational Self, Collective Self 123–43 (Constantine Sedikides and Marilyn B. Brewer eds., Philadelphia, PA: Psychology Press/Taylor & Francis, 2001).

40. Herbert H. Clark and Susan E. Brennan, *Grounding in Communication, in* Perspectives on Socially Shared Cognition 127–49 (Lauren Resnick, John Levine, and Stephanie D. Teasley eds., Washington, DC: American Psychological Association, 1991); Gwen M. Wittenbaum and Jonathan M. Bowman, *A Social Validation Explanation for Mutual Enhancement,* 40 Journal of Experimental Social Psychology 169–84 (2004).

41. Garold Stasser, Sandra I. Vaughan, and Dennis D. Stewart, *Pooling Unshared Information: The Benefits of Knowing How Access to Information Is Distributed Among Group Members,* 82 Organizational Behavior and Human Decision Processes 102–16 (2000).

42. R. Scott Tindale et al., *Shared Cognition in Small Groups, in* Blackwell Handbook of Social Psychology: Group Processes 1–30 (Michael A. Hogg and R. Scott Tindale eds., Malden, MA: Blackwell Publishers, 2001).

Second, placing a decision-making group under time pressure, or increasing the stakes and group members' sense of their accountability for the ultimate outcome, exacerbates the effect. These conditions seem to make group members more risk averse. Using shared information is less risky than using unshared information and bolsters the group's confidence in its decision.[43]

But certain measures tend to reduce the common knowledge effect:

- Framing the task as a "problem to be solved," implying that it has a "correct" answer.[44]
- *Publicly* assigning roles to different group members the responsibility to supply information on a particular decision-relevant topic.[45]
- Extending the time for discussion, which results in the use of more unshared information.[46]
- Increasing the number of options from which the group can choose, and explicitly listing those options.[47]
- Providing an objective source of verification of unshared information. (Objectively and authoritatively shared information gets treated the same as originally shared information, suggesting that sharedness is often used as a proxy for reliability.[48])

---

43. Steven J. Karau and Janice R. Kelly, *The Effects of Time Scarcity and Time Abundance on Group Performance Quality and Interaction Process*, 28 Journal of Experimental Social Psychology 542–71 (1992); James R. Larson, Pennie G. Foster-Fishman, and Christopher B. Keys, *Discussion of Shared and Unshared Information in Decision Making Groups*, 67 Journal of Personality and Social Psychology 446–61 (1994); Dennis D. Stewart, Robert S. Billings, and Garold Stasser, *Accountability and the Discussion of Unshared, Critical Information in Decision Making Groups*, 2 Group Dynamics 18–23 (1998).

44. Garold Stasser and Dennis Stewart, *Discovery of Hidden Profiles by Decision Making Groups: Solving a Problem versus Making a Judgment*, 63 Journal of Personality and Social Psychology 426–34 (1992).

45. Dennis Stewart and Garold Stasser, *Expert Role Assignment and Information Sampling During Collective Recall and Decision Making*, 69 Journal of Personality and Social Psychology 619–28 (1995); Garold Stasser, Sandra I. Vaughan, and Dennis D. Stewart, *Pooling Unshared Information: The Benefits of Knowing How Access to Information Is Distributed Among Group Members*, 82 Organizational Behavior and Human Decision Processes 102–16 (2000).

46. James R. Larson, Pennie G. Foster-Fishman, and Christopher B. Keys, *Discussion of Shared and Unshared Information in Decision Making Groups*, 67 Journal of Personality and Social Psychology 446–61 (1994); Craig D. Parks and Rebecca Cowlin, *Group Discussion as Affected by Number of Alternatives and by a Time Limit*, 62 Organizational Behavior and Human Decision Processes 267–75 (1995).

47. Craig D. Parks and Rebecca Cowlin, *Group Discussion as Affected by Number of Alternatives and by a Time Limit*, 62 Organizational Behavior and Human Decision Processes 267–75 (1995).

48. Craig D. Parks and Rebecca Cowlin, *Acceptance of Uncommon Information into Group Discussion When That Information Is or Is Not Demonstrable*, 66 Organizational Behavior and Human Decision Processes 307–15 (1996).

- Finally, as we will discuss, using "nominal" groups, through methods like the "stepladder" or Delphi techniques, can help reduce the bias toward shared information.

19.5 GROUP POLARIZATION

Consider again the Terra Nueva lawsuit, and the efforts of community and consumer activists to use it to mobilize other community groups to take actions relating to toxic exposure-related harms. Imagine that going into the meeting described above, representatives from East Los Angeles Tenants United (ELATU), L.A. Consumers' Action (LACA), and the Terra Nueva Tenants' Union are enthusiastic about filing similar suits elsewhere. But the organizer from the United Electrical Workers (UEW) is more cautious. She wants to see how the Terra Nueva suit unfolds before allocating more union resources to similar initiatives—in part, because she thinks that toxic chemicals, rather than the foam insulation, might be causing the Terra Nueva tenants' health problems. Suppose that the plaintiffs' lawyers have learned about this possibility as well, and that they share her concern about taking action in other communities, which at this point seems a risky strategy.

Assuming that the UEW representative and the lawyers make their knowledge and views known to the rest of the group, what do you think will happen during this meeting? As different strategy options are discussed, will the UEW representative's and lawyers' concerns moderate the enthusiasm for expanding the litigation strategy with which the other organizations came into the meeting? Or will deliberation simply embolden participants to take broader actions than they might have decided on alone?

Your intuition might be that deliberation would tend to temper the judgment of a group's most extreme members on either side and draw the group toward a middle ground.[49] But it turns out that rather than moderating the views of the community organizers, the group may be pulled toward their more extreme views.[50] Group discussion tends to magnify differences within the group and enhance the position of those whose views initially predominate.

In an early experiment involving what has come to be called *group polarization*,[51] James Stoner presented participants with hypothetical problems involving a

---

49. *See* RUPERT BROWN, GROUP PROCESSES (2d ed. Malden, MA: Blackwell Publishing, 2000).

50. Cass R. Sunstein, *The Law of Group Polarization*, 10 JOURNAL OF POLITICAL PHILOSOPHY 175–95 (2002).

51. Serge Moscovici and Marisa Zavalloni, *The Group as a Polarizer of Attitudes*, 12 JOURNAL OF PERSONALITY AND SOCIAL PSYCHOLOGY 125–35 (1969); David G. Myers and

choice between cautious and risky courses of action. After making tentative decisions on their own, the participants were placed in groups and asked to reach a unanimous decision. When participants' median position before discussion was risk seeking, group deliberation led to a "risky shift,"[52] in which decisions were riskier than their individual prediscussion choices. Subsequent studies have shown that "cautious" shifts occur when the predominant view of the individual participants is risk averse.[53] (In addition to the group's tending to shift to one extreme or another, individual members internalize the group's position and tend to hold it after the discussion has ended.[54])

Group polarization is not restricted to shifts in risk preference. For example, David Myers demonstrated that groups of moderately pro-feminist women subjects became more strongly pro-feminist following discussion of feminist ideas.[55] Jurors are affected by group polarization in awarding damages.[56] And Cass Sunstein and his colleagues recently demonstrated that circuit court judges' ideological tendencies are amplified when they sit on panels consisting of judges appointed by presidents from the same political party. Republican appointees show an increased tendency to vote in a stereotypically conservative fashion when they are accompanied by two other Republican appointees, while

---

Helmut Lamm, *The Group Polarization Phenomenon*, 83 PSYCHOLOGICAL BULLETIN 602–27 (1976); Daniel J. Isenberg, *Group Polarization: A Critical Review and Meta-Analysis*, 50 JOURNAL OF PERSONALITY AND SOCIAL PSYCHOLOGY 1141–51 (1986); Cass R. Sunstein, *The Law of Group Polarization*, 10 Journal of Political Philosophy 175–95 (2002).

52. James A. F. Stoner, *Risky and Cautious Shifts in Group Decisions: The Influence of Widely Held Values*, 4 JOURNAL OF EXPERIMENTAL AND SOCIAL PSYCHOLOGY 442–59 (1968). James A. F. Stoner, "A Comparison of Individual and Group Decisions Including Risk" (unpublished thesis, Massachusetts Institute of Technology, School of Management, Cambridge, MA).

53. Serge Moscovici and Marisa Zavalloni, *The Group as a Polarizer of Attitudes*, 12 JOURNAL OF PERSONALITY AND SOCIAL PSYCHOLOGY 125–35 (1969); Willem Doise, *Intergroup Relations and Polarization in Individual and Collective Judgments*, 12 JOURNAL OF PERSONALITY & SOCIAL PSYCHOLOGY 136–43 (1969).

54. Michael A. Wallach, Nathan Kogan, and Daryl J. Ben, *Group Influence on Individual Risk Taking*, 65 JOURNAL OF ABNORMAL AND SOCIAL PSYCHOLOGY 75–86 (1962). *See also* Joel Cooper, Kimberly A. Kelly, and Kimberlee Weaver, *Attitudes, Norms, and Social Groups*, *in* BLACKWELL HANDBOOK OF SOCIAL PSYCHOLOGY: GROUP PROCESSES 259–82 (Michael. A. Hogg and R. Scott Tindale eds., Malden, MA: Blackwell Publishers 2001); Johannes A. Zuber, Helmut W. Crott, and Joachim Werner, *Choice Shift and Group Polarization: An Analysis of the Status of Arguments and Social Decision Schemes*, 62 JOURNAL OF PERSONALITY AND SOCIAL PSYCHOLOGY 50–61 (1992).

55. David G. Myers, *Discussion-Induced Attitude Polarization*, 28 HUMAN RELATIONS 699–712 (1975).

56. David Schkade, Cass Sunstein, and Daniel Kahneman, *Deliberating About Dollars*, 100 COLUMBIA LAW REVIEW 1139–75 (2000).

Democratic appointees show the same effect in the opposite direction when accompanied by their co-partisans.[57]

19.5.1 What Causes Group Polarization?

Causal accounts of group polarization divide into two broad categories, one centering on social forces, the other on cognitive or informational processes.

19.5.1.a Social Comparison and Social Identity Maintenance There are three related theories here. One builds on the fact that people generally want to be viewed well by others. In order to present themselves in a socially desirable light, they constantly monitor others' reactions to determine how to adjust their self-presentation. As group members see how others view the issue under discussion, they tend to present themselves to be congruent with the perceived emerging trend. Indeed, to be "distinct" from their peers in the socially valued direction they often go "one step further" in the direction of increasingly extreme positions.[58] Seen in this way, group polarization can be understood as a type of bandwagon effect.[59]

Second, people generally see themselves and like to be seen by others as moderate, and initially express positions that may be more moderate than their true beliefs. But after being exposed to others having their own viewpoints, people become disinhibited from expressing more extreme views and they become more confident of those views. Robert Baron and his colleagues demonstrated that discussion with like-minded people can move individuals to more extreme positions solely by virtue of this *social corroboration* effect.[60]

A third account of polarization, *social identity*, concerns the relationship of the group to others outside the group. As group members begin interacting with each other, they collectively begin to identify the characteristics, behaviors, and norms that differentiate their group from other groups. To differentiate their

---

57. Cass R. Sunstein, David Schkade, and Lisa M. Ellman, *Ideological Voting on Federal Courts of Appeals: A Preliminary Investigation*, 90 Virginia Law Review 301–55 (2004). Similar polarization effects in panel and individual judicial decision making was found three decades earlier by Walker and Main. Thomas G. Walker and Eleanor C. Main, *Choice Shifts in Political Decisionmaking: Federal Judges and Civil Liberties Cases*, 3 Journal of Applied Social Psychology 39–48 (1973).

58. Robert S. Baron and Gard Roper, *Reaffirmation of Social Comparison Views of Choice Shifts: Averaging and Extremity Effects in an Autokinetic Situation*, 33 Journal of Personality and Social Psychology 521–30 (1976); Daniel J. Isenberg, *Group Polarization: A Critical Review and Meta-Analysis*, 50 Journal of Personality and Social Psychology 1141–51 (1986); Joel Cooper, Kimberly A. Kelly, and Kimberlee Weaver, *Attitudes, Norms, and Social Groups*, *in* Blackwell Handbook of Social psychology: Group Processes 259–82 (Michael A. Hogg and R. Scott Tindale eds., Malden, MA: Blackwell Publishers, 2001).

59. John C. Turner, Social Influence (Pacific Grove, CA: Brooks/Cole, 1991).

60. Robert S. Baron et al., *Social Corroboration and Opinion Extremity*, 32 Journal of Experimental Social Psychology 537–60 (1996).

group from others, members attribute more extremity to their own group than is objectively the case; they distinguish their group from others by accentuating the perceived distance between their group norm and the norms they attribute to out-groups.[61] Group members then conform their own behaviors, norms, and self-conceptions to their group's.[62] Polarization thus occurs through a process of contrast with other groups within a specific social context.[63]

The social accounts of group polarization are not mutually exclusive. Indeed, each incorporates theoretical elements of the other and experimental research supports all of them.[64]

19.5.1.b Cognitive/Informational Accounts of Group Polarization A second set of theories focuses on cognitive rather than social explanations for group polarization. The *persuasive argument theory* builds on the observation that, before group discussion of an issue begins, a member will usually have formulated an initial position and formulated arguments favoring his position. The group discussion exposes the participant to new arguments that support or detract from his initial position. The phenomenon of *confirmation bias* suggests that the participant will find new information and arguments that support his initial position more persuasive than information and arguments that oppose it. As a purely statistical phenomenon, this predicts group polarization, in much the same way

---

61. Diane Mackie, *Social Identification Effects in Group Polarization*, 50 Journal of Personality and Social Psychology 720–28 (1986).

62. John C. Turner, *Toward a Cognitive Redefinition of the Social Group*, *in* Social Identity and Intergroup Relations 15–40 (Henri Tajfel ed., Cambridge, UK: Cambridge University Press, 1982); John C. Turner, *Social Categorization and the Self-Concept: A Social Cognitive Theory of Group Behavior*, *in* Advances in Group Processes 2, 77–122 (Edward J. Lawler ed., Greenwich, CT: JAI, 1991); Diane Mackie, *Social Identification Effects in Group Polarization*, 50 Journal of Personality and Social Psychology 720–28 (1986); Michael A. Hogg, John C. Turner, and Barbara Davidson, *Polarized Norms and Social Frames of Reference: A Test of the Self-Categorization Theory of Group Polarization*, 11 Basic and Applied Social Psychology 77–100 (1990).

63. Michael A. Hogg, John C. Turner, and Barbara Davidson, *Polarized Norms and Social Frames of Reference: A Test of the Self-Categorization Theory of Group Polarization*, 11 Basic and Applied Social Psychology 77–100 (1990); Craig McGarty et al., *Group Polarization as Conformity to the Prototypical Group Member*, 31 British Journal of Personality and Social Psychology 1–19 (1992). This social identity account is supported by experimental evidence showing that the context in which a deliberating group is embedded influences the extent and the direction of group polarization. Specifically, if a deliberating group is embedded with outgroups at one or another pole of an attitudinal continuum, the group will polarize away from the direction in which those outgroups lean. This is consistent with the operation of the in-group/outgroup contrast effect that lies at the center of the social identity account.

64. Gary Stasser and Beth Dietz-Uhler, *Collective Choice, Judgment, and Problem Solving*, *in* Blackwell Handbook of Social Psychology: Group Processes 31–55 (Michael A. Hogg and R. Scott Tindale eds., Malden, MA: Blackwell Publishers, 2001).

as probabilistic sampling theory predicted the common information effect discussed earlier in Section 19.4.2.[65]

Another cognitive account of group polarization understands group interaction as an exercise in *rationale construction* rather than information collection. This model posits that people bring to a discussion their ex ante preferences and that interaction calls upon them to explain these to other group members. As people explain their positions, they gain confidence in them, whether or not they are accurate. Indeed, as Chip Heath and Richard Gonzalez have shown, interaction with others increases confidence in, but not the accuracy of, judgments.[66] A related causal theory draws on the *effects of repeated expression*: polarization occurs as people repeat their own arguments and are repeatedly exposed to particular arguments, evidence, or expressions of a conclusion by like-minded others.[67]

19.5.2 Reducing the Tendency Toward Group Polarization

There has been very little research directly testing the effectiveness of particular interventions in reducing group polarization. However, some inferences can be drawn from research on the contextual factors that tend to reduce or exacerbate the effect:[68]

- Polarization is moderated by heterogeneity of initial opinions within a deliberating group.
- As with groupthink, polarization is exacerbated where the group is an ideologically cohering, high-solidarity entity.

---

65. Eugene Burnstein and Amiram Vinokur, *What a Person Thinks upon Learning He Has Chosen Differently from Others: Nice Evidence for the Persuasive Arguments Explanation of Choice Shifts*, 11 Journal of Experimental Social Psychology 412–26 (1975); Eugene Burnstein and Amiram Vinokur, *Persuasive Argumentation and Social Persuasion as Determinants of Attitude Polarization*, 13 Journal of Experimental Social Psychology 315–32 (1977); Markus Brauer, Charles M. Jud, and Melissa D. Gliner, *The Effects of Repeated Expressions on Attitude Polarization During Group Discussions*, 68 Journal of Personality and Social Psychology 1014–29 (1995).

66. Chip Heath and Richard Gonzalez, *Interaction with Others Increases Decision Confidence but Not Decision Quality: Evidence Against Information Collection Views of Interactive Decisionmaking*, 61 Organizational Behavior and Human Decision Processes 305 (1995).

67. Markus Brauer, Charles M. Jud, and Melissa D. Gliner, *The Effects of Repeated Expressions on Attitude Polarization During Group Discussions*, 68 Journal of Personality and Social Psychology 1014–29 (1995).

68. Harris Bernstein, *Persuasion as Argument Processing*, *in* Group Decisionmaking (Hermann Brandstatter, James H. Davis, and Gisela Stocker-Kreichgauer eds., London: Academic Press, 1982); Rupert Brown, Group Processes (2d ed. Malden, MA: Blackwell Publishing, 2000); Cass Sunstein, *Deliberative Trouble? Why Groups Go to Extremes*, 110 Yale Law Journal 72–119 (2000).

- Groups that work together over a sustained period of time, making numerous similar decisions, may get feedback on the quality of those decisions, which may moderate overconfidence and lead to more effective use of information in subsequent decision making.
- Polarization is moderated where a group is subject to external shocks (e.g., losing an election, being sued, experiencing a severe policy failure) or where the group must temper its preferences to preserve its prestige with external constituencies.
- Polarization can be reduced by increasing decision-making independence through mechanisms like the Delphi technique (Section 19.8.4), and through norms and facilitation that encourage open-mindedness, the inclusion of minority perspectives, and evidence-based decision making.[69]

19.6 STRATEGIC PARTICIPATION IN GROUP DECISION MAKING

Group members' concerns about their relations with others in the group play a significant role in the pathologies of group decision making. Individual group members may have interests that differ from those of their colleagues. So, for example, in a meeting to help a company's managers decide whether to settle or litigate an employment discrimination case, the lawyer may be concerned to maintain the impression that she is "on their side" even as she attempts to impress upon them the nature of the exposure to risk that they face. She may also want to convey a gender counter-stereotypical "toughness" that she hopes will instill confidence in her competence as a vigorous advocate.

Other participants in the decision-making process may have their own sets of competing processing goals. The manager who made the now-challenged decision may seek to save face, preventing his colleagues from concluding that he made a mistake or otherwise acted imprudently. Yet another group member may simply want to create a good impression and be viewed as a "team player." And all (or almost all) of the group members will be attempting to maintain a certain level of social harmony, both during and after the decision making process.

In other words, the goal of making a "good" decision is only one of the items on members' individual and collective agendas. The susceptibility of a group to decision-making errors will depend in substantial measure on these often hidden competing motivations.

---

69. Tom Postmes, Russell Spears, and Sezgin Cihangir, *Quality of Decisionmaking and Group Norms*, 80 Journal of Personality and Social Psychology 918–30 (2001).

19.7 THE SUSCEPTIBILITY OF GROUPS TO BIASES AND HEURISTICS

Earlier in the book, we described a variety of biases and heuristics that systematically distort individuals' judgment and decision making. Despite some hopes to the contrary,[70] groups are not less susceptible to these phenomena than individuals, and in some circumstances are more so.

Overconfidence. As we saw in Section 10.4, individuals often are overconfident in the accuracy of their own judgment. It turns out that groups don't do better—even when even they appoint a "devil's advocate" or explicitly consider reasons why their estimates might be wrong—and may actually be more overconfident.[71] Group overconfidence may result from the group polarization effect.[72] Persuasive argument theory[73] suggests that if (as often happens) group members enter the group discussion with an overconfident orientation, they will make more confidence-inducing than caution-supporting arguments, thus skewing overall group opinion in an optimistic direction. Second, social comparison processes may come into play, as group members offer overconfident outlooks on the subject of group discussion so as to demonstrate loyalty and commitment to the project, and to assure that they compare favorably in this regard with other group members.[74]

Confirmation bias. Small deliberating groups, no less than individuals, fall prey to the tendency to overweight information that confirms a prior position, theory, or attitude and to underweight information that would tend to disconfirm it. Groups manifest a preference for information that confirms individual members' prediscussion preferences. The more social support for their views participants anticipated from an upcoming group discussion, the more preference they showed for confirming information.[75] For both laypeople and

70. George P. Huber, Managerial Decision Making (Glenview, IL: Scott Foresman, 1980).

71. Scott Plous, *A Comparison of Strategies for Reducing Interval Overconfidence in Group Judgments*, 80 Journal of Applied Psychology 443–54 (1995).

72. Roger Buehler, Deanna Messervey, and Dale Griffin, *Collaborative Planning and Prediction: Does Group Discussion Affect Optimistic Biases in Time Estimation?*, 91 Organizational Behavior and Human Decision Processes 47–63 (2005).

73. Amiram Vinokur and Eugene Burnetein, *The Effects of Partially Shared Persuasive Arguments on Group Induced Shifts: A Group Problem Solving Approach*, 29 Journal of Personality and Social Psychology 305–15 (1974).

74. Daniel Kahneman and Dan Lovallo, *Timid Choices and Bold Forecasts: A Cognitive Perspective on Risk Taking*, 39 Management Science 17–31 (1993).

75. Bozena Zdaniuk and John M. Levine, *Anticipated Interaction and Thought Generation: The Role of Faction Size*, 36 British Journal of Social Psychology 201–18 (1996). On a related matter, group discussion may attenuate or eliminate the theory-perseverance effect, in which people retain a belief in the functional relationship between two variables even after evidence for any such relationship has been discredited. Edward F.

groups of experts making decisions within their areas of expertise (say, business managers making economic decisions), the more homogeneous the members' preferences, the stronger the effect.[76] Only when the deliberating group is reasonably balanced on the issue in question does confirmation bias diminish.

Various judgmental errors. The little research that exists provides no clear picture about the relative susceptibility of individuals and groups to the availability and representativeness heuristics.[77] Group discussion seems to amplify conjunction errors when the individual members' susceptibility to conjunction bias is high, and to attenuate the errors when it is low.[78] Group interaction does not appear to attenuate base rate neglect and may, indeed, increase it.[79] The evidence on groups' proneness to hindsight bias is equivocal.[80] Deliberating groups appear to be even more prone to unrealistic optimism than individuals;[81] this may result from the same informational, social comparison, and social identity management processes mentioned in connection with group polarization.[82]

Wright and Scott D. Christie, "The Impact of Group Discussion on the Theory-Perseverance Effect" (unpublished manuscript, St. Francis Xavier University, Department of Psychology, Antigonish, NS). Craig A. Anderson, *Inoculation and Counterexplanation: Debiasing Techniques in the Perseverance of Social Theories*, 1 SOCIAL COGNITION 126–39 (1982).

76. Stefan Schulz-Hardt et al., *Biased Information Search in Group Decisionmaking*, 78 JOURNAL OF PERSONALITY AND SOCIAL PSYCHOLOGY 655–69 (2000).

77. Mark F. Stasson et al., *Group Consensus Processes on Cognitive Bias Tasks: A Social Decision Scheme Approach*, 30 JAPANESE PSYCHOLOGICAL RESEARCH 68–77 (1988).

78. R. Scott Tindale, Susan Sheffey, and Joseph Filkins, "Conjunction Errors by Individuals and Groups" (paper presented at the meetings of the Society for Judgment and Decisionmaking, New Orleans, LA, 1990); R. Scott et al., "An Attempt to Reduce Conjunction Errors in Decision-Making Groups" (paper presented at the annual meeting of the Society for Judgment and Decisionmaking, Washington, DC, 1993). Other researchers obtained mixed results in studies testing susceptibility to other types of representativeness biases, finding bias amplification in some contexts, but not others. Mark F. Stasson et al., *Group Consensus Processes on Cognitive Bias Tasks: A Social Decision Scheme Approach*, 30 JAPANESE PSYCHOLOGICAL RESEARCH 68–77 (1988).

79. Linda Argote, Mark A. Seabright, and Linda Dyer, *Individual versus Group Use of Base-Rate and Individuating Information*, 38 ORGANIZATIONAL BEHAVIOR AND HUMAN DECISION PROCESSES 65–75 (1986); Linda Argote, Rukmini Devadas, and Nancy Melone, *The Base-Rate Fallacy: Contrasting Processes and Outcomes of Group and Individual Judgment*, 48 ORGANIZATIONAL BEHAVIOR AND HUMAN DECISION PROCESSES 296–311 (1990); R. Scott Tindale, *Decision Errors Made by Individuals and Groups*, *in* N. JOHN CASTELLAN JR. (ed.), INDIVIDUAL AND GROUP DECISION MAKING: CURRENT ISSUES 109–24 (Hillsdale, NJ, England: Lawrence Erlbaum Associates, Inc., 1993).

80. Dagmar Stahlberg et al., *We Knew It All Along: Hindsight Bias in Groups*, 63 ORGANIZATIONAL BEHAVIOR AND HUMAN DECISION PROCESSES 46–58 (1995).

81. Roger Buehler, Deanna Messervey, and Dale Griffin, *Collaborative Planning and Prediction: Does Group Discussion Affect Optimistic Biases in Time Estimation?*, 91 ORGANIZATIONAL BEHAVIOR AND HUMAN DECISION PROCESSES 47–63 (2005).

82. *Id.*

Gain/loss framing effects and other departures from expected utility theory. The research on group susceptibility to framing effects shows mixed results. One study found that group discussion amplified the asymmetrical treatment of potential losses and gains,[83] while another found that group discussion attenuated framing bias.[84] Yet another found bias when the outcome had been framed by individual group members as a loss or a gain *before* group discussion began; but framing bias was attenuated if the outcome was not framed until after group discussion began, or if it was reframed in the course of the discussion.[85] The research does not suggest any robust generalizations about gain/loss framing or, consistency with expected utility theory more generally.[86]

Escalation of commitment. Some research suggests that small groups are, if anything, more prone than individuals to escalate commitment to a failing course of action.[87] This should not be surprising, since the escalation of commitment is caused, at least in part, by the desire to appear consistent to others,[88] and since group polarization could readily contribute to escalation. However, other research found no difference between individuals and groups in the amounts of resources they were willing to invest in a failing endeavor.[89]

The fundamental attribution error. Curiously, group discussion appears to attenuate susceptibility to the fundamental attribution error—the tendency to

---

83. Timothy W. McGuire, Sara Kiesler, and Judith Siegel, *Group and Computer-Mediated Discussion Effects in Risk Decisionmaking*, 52 JOURNAL OF PERSONALITY AND SOCIAL PSYCHOLOGY 917–30 (1987).

84. Margaret A. Neale et al., *"Choice Shift" Effects in Group Decisions: A Decision Bias Perspective*, 2 INTERNATIONAL JOURNAL OF SMALL GROUP RESEARCH 33–42 (1986).

85. Paul W. Paese, Mary Bieser, and Mark E. Tubbs, *Framing Effects and Choice Shifts in Group Decisionmaking*, 56 ORGANIZATIONAL BEHAVIOR AND HUMAN DECISION PROCESSES 149–65 (1993).

86. Norbert L. Kerr, Robert J. MacCoun, and Geoffrey P. Kramer, *Bias in Judgment: Comparing Individuals and Groups*, 103 PSYCHOLOGICAL REVIEW 687–719 (1996); John C. Mowen and James W. Gentry, *Investigation of the Preference-Reversal Phenomenon in a New Product Introduction Task*, 65 JOURNAL OF APPLIED PSYCHOLOGY 715–22 (1980); John Bone, John Hey, and John Suckling, *Are Groups More (or Less) Consistent than Individuals?*, 8 JOURNAL OF RISK AND UNCERTAINTY 63–81 (1999).

87. Glen Whyte, *Escalating Commitment in Individual and Group Decisionmaking*, 54 ORGANIZATIONAL BEHAVIOR AND HUMAN DECISION PROCESSES 430 (1993).

88. Barry Staw and Jerry *Ross, Behavior in Escalation Situations: Antecedents, Prototypes, and Solutions, in* RESEARCH IN ORGANIZATIONAL BEHAVIOR (Larry L. Cummings and Barry Staw eds., Greenwich: CT: JAI Press, 1987).

89. Max H. Bazerman, Toni Giuliano and Allan Appelman, *Escalation of Commitment in Individual and Group Decisionmaking*, 33 ORGANIZATIONAL BEHAVIOR AND HUMAN PERFORMANCE 141–52 (1984).

over-attribute people's behavior to dispositional factors and under-attribute it to situational variables.[90]

19.8 IMPROVING GROUP DECISION MAKING

This section considers several approaches to reducing the pathologies that can infect group decision making. These include measures suggested by Irving Janis and his collaborators to prevent groupthink and other forms of premature convergence, and two mechanisms—the "stepladder" and Delphi techniques—that can be used to maximize the constructive contribution of each member to a decision-making group.

19.8.1 Preventing Groupthink

Janis's ultimate goal was to develop strategies for improving government decision making. To this end, he suggested a set of remedial measures that could prevent the emergence of groupthink and facilitate what he referred to as *vigilant appraisal*, or *vigilant decision making*.[91]

Vigilant appraisal looks a great deal like the optimal, or full, formal model of decision making introduced in Section 1.4.1. It entails:

- a careful specification of all relevant goals and objectives, not only those immediately identified by the group's leadership;
- extensive and unbiased search for and use of relevant information;
- careful, critical consideration of a range of alternative courses of action;
- the development of contingency plans.

Janis's remedial measures are all designed to break down the tendency of a highly cohesive group to function as a single social and psychological entity.[92] They require that the group be guided by an open, nondirective leader who takes tangible steps to foster divergent and critical thinking, and who not only tolerates, but encourages, contrarian thinking and dissent.

To facilitate vigilant appraisal, the leader must adopt a neutral role, refraining from directly endorsing or covertly signaling support for a particular choice. He or she must encourage the expression of minority viewpoints, ensure that input

90. Edward F. Wright and Gary L. Wells, *Does Group Discussion Attenuate the Dispositional Bias?*, 15 JOURNAL OF APPLIED PSYCHOLOGY 531–46 (1985).

91. IRVING L. JANIS, GROUPTHINK: PSYCHOLOGICAL STUDIES OF POLICY DECISIONS AND FIASCOS (Boston, MA: Houghton Mifflin, 1982); Irving L. Janis and Leon Mann, *Cognitive Complexity in* INTERNATIONAL DECISIONMAKING, IN PSYCHOLOGY AND SOCIAL POLICY 33–49 (Peter Suedfeld and Philip Tetlock eds., Washington, DC: Hemisphere Publishing Corp., 1992).

92. ALEXANDER S. HASLAM, PSYCHOLOGY IN ORGANIZATIONS: THE SOCIAL IDENTITY APPROACH (London, UK & Thousand Oaks, CA: Sage Publications, 2001).

is obtained from experts outside the group, and even appoint formal *devil's advocates* to aggressively question any emerging consensus. As Clark McCauley has described the leader's task, "If groupthink is a disease of insufficient search for information, alternatives, and modes of failure, the cure is better search procedures: impartial leadership that encourages airing of doubts and objections in the group and encourages search for information and evaluation from sources outside the group, procedural norms supporting systematic consideration of alternatives, 'second-chance' meetings after preliminary consensus, and special attention to the motives and communications of threatening competitors."[93]

Janis' specific suggestions for enhancing vigilant decision making include the following:

1. The leader should be impartial and should not state or even imply preferences or expectations about the decision at the outset.
2. The leader should assign the role of critical evaluator to each member, encouraging all participants to vigorously air objections and doubts.
3. Periodically, the group should be broken up into smaller subgroups, under different leaders, to work on the same question. Then the groups should be brought back together to compare perspectives and discuss differences.
4. Periodically, each group member should discuss the subject under deliberation with trusted associates who are not in the decision-making group, and report back to the group their ideas and reactions.
5. Experts and qualified colleagues who are not members of the decision-making group should periodically be invited to attend group meetings and challenge the views of the group's members.
6. At each meeting devoted to the discussion of policy alternatives, at least one member should be assigned the role of devil's advocate.
7. Whenever the issue being discussed involves relations with a rival organization, nation, or other collectivity, ample time should be allocated to constructing varying conceptions of the rival's intentions.
8. After the group reaches a preliminary consensus about the best decision, the leader should conduct a "second chance" meeting at which group members are instructed to express, as forcefully and persuasively as they can, all of their doubts about the preliminary consensus, and to reconsider the entire problem before making a final choice.

93. Clark McCauley, *Group Dynamics in Janis's Theory of Groupthink: Backward and Forward*, 73 Organizational Behavior and Human Decision Processes 142–62 (1998).

19.8.2 Preventing Premature Convergence: Devil's Advocacy and Dialectical Inquiry

One of the most common structures for group-based strategic decision making is an "expert approach," where a group of individuals, selected for their presumed expertise, present and seek consensus for a single recommended course of action.[94] This procedure invites premature convergence.

Devil's advocacy is one way to inhibit premature convergence. After a plan is proposed by an individual or subgroup, another individual or subgroup attempts to identify everything wrong with the plan The larger group then uses this critique to improve or replace the original proposal.[95] Problem-solving groups that use devil's advocacy have been shown to generate a wider range of alternative courses of action than do conventional deliberating groups.[96] Janis cites President John F. Kennedy's handling of the Cuban Missile Crisis as an example of successful use of devil's advocacy. During those critical days in October 1962, President Kennedy assigned his brother, Attorney General Robert F. Kennedy, the role of devil's advocate with the task of aggressively challenging the assumptions and analysis underlying any emerging consensus. Devil's advocacy is not without its limitations: for example, if group members view the devil's advocate as being insincere, they may ignore his critique.

In *dialectical inquiry*, the entire group plays the role of devil's advocate. After identifying and discussing an initial plan, the entire group develops a "counterplan." There follows a structured debate, in which those responsible for making an ultimate decision hear arguments for and against the plan and the counterplan, with the possibility that yet another plan may emerge.

Devil's advocacy and dialectical inquiry can be used in face-to-face decision-making groups, or can be incorporated into computer-mediated group processes. Because they permit anonymity, computer-mediated processes reduce the effects of social status,[97] reduce social pressures from dominant group members, and inhibit social conformity effects more generally. However, anonymity can lead to

---

94. Richard Mason, *A Dialectical Approach to Strategic Planning*, 15 MANAGEMENT SCIENCE B403–B411 (1969).

95. Joseph S. Valacich and Charles Schwenk, *Devil's Advocacy and Dialectical Inquiry Effects on Face-to-Face and Computer-Mediated Group Decisionmaking*, 63 ORGANIZATIONAL BEHAVIOR AND HUMAN DECISION PROCESSES 158–73 (1995).

96. Charles Schwenk, *Effects of Planning Aids and Presentation Media on Performance and Affective Responses in Strategic Decisionmaking*, 30 MANAGEMENT SCIENCE 263–72 (1984).

97. Caryn Christenson and Ann Abbott, *Team Medial Decisionmaking, in* DECISIONMAKING IN HEALTH CARE 267 (Gretchen Chapman and Frank Sonnenberg eds., New York: Cambridge University Press, 2000).

incivility, create dissention, and injure morale.[98] Computer-mediated groups can create a sense of alienation, and lead to dissatisfaction with the process.[99] And groups that use computer-mediated devil's advocacy tend to have difficulty reaching agreement.[100]

19.8.3 The Stepladder Technique

Many of the dysfunctions of small decision-making groups result from social processes that interfere with the group's ability to fully utilize the potential contribution of all of its members. The group may be dominated by particularly aggressive individuals who stifle input from others in the group.[101] Some group members may engage in social loafing, depriving the group of their potential contribution.[102] Social pressures and social conformity effects may cause group members to withhold valuable information, opinions, or perspectives.[103]

In the 1990s, Steven Rogelberg and his colleagues developed a procedure known as the *stepladder technique* to minimize the impact of these negative dynamics on group deliberation.[104] The stepladder technique structures the entry of individuals into a decision-making group so as to maximize their independence from other group members and highlight their uniquely held information, opinions, ideas, and perspectives.

Before entering the discussion, each member is presented with the group's task and sufficient time to think about it alone. After the first two members discuss the problem, new members join the group one at a time. When entering the group, each new member must present his or her preliminary solution to the problem before hearing what the other group members think. Then the group discusses the problem before another new member enters. No final decision is

98. Joseph S. Valacich and Charles Schwenk, *Devil's Advocacy and Dialectical Inquiry Effects on Face-to-Face and Computer-Mediated Group Decisionmaking*, 63 Organizational Behavior and Human Decision Processes 158–73 (1995).

99. Leonard M. Jessup, Terry Connolly, and Jolene Galegher, *The Effects of Anonymity on Group Process in an Idea-Generating Task*, 14 MIS Quarterly 313–21 (1990).

100. Joseph S. Valacich and Charles Schwenk, *Devil's Advocacy and Dialectical Inquiry Effects on Face-to-Face and Computer-Mediated Group Decisionmaking*, 63 Organizational Behavior and Human Decision Processes 158–73 (1995).

101. Dennis Falk and David W. Johnson, *The Effects of Perspective-Taking and Egocentrism on Problem Solving in Heterogeneous and Homogeneous Groups*, 102 Journal of Social Psychology 63–72 (1977).

102. Bibb Latane, Kipling Williams, and Stephen Harkins, *Many Hands Make Light the Work: The Causes and Consequences of Social Loafing*, 37 Journal of Personality and Social Psychology 822–32 (1979).

103. David Johnson and Frank Johnson, Joining Together: Group Theory and Group Skills (Engelwood Cliffs, NJ: Prentice-Hall, 1987).

104. Steven G. Rogelberg, Janet L. Barnes-Farrell, and Charles A. Lowe, *The Stepladder Technique: An Alternative Group Structure Facilitating Effective Group Decisionmaking*, 77 Journal of Applied Technology 730–37 (1992).

made until all group members have been incorporated into the group in this manner.

The stepladder technique tends to improve a group's decision performance. Stepladder groups outperformed both their average and best member more often than conventional deliberating groups.

19.8.4 Generating and Evaluating Alternatives with Nominal Groups: The Delphi Technique

As described in Section 19.2, the members of a "nominal group" work alone to solve a problem and their individual solutions are then aggregated. In some situations, nominal groups are more effective than either individuals or interactive groups. For example, nominal groups tend to outperform face-to-face groups in brainstorming tasks, where the goal is to generate lots of ideas and eventually improve on them.[105]

The *Delphi Technique* is a well-known form of nominal group brainstorming.[106] A coordinator transmits questions to group members. Working alone, the members transmit their responses to the coordinator, who assembles the information and generates additional information requests. Suppose, for example, that a humanitarian relief nongovernmental organization (NGO) is deciding what precautions to take in a conflict-ridden country in which its workers are in physical danger, or whether to pull out altogether. The coordinator states the problem, and asks each participant to generate as many ideas as possible for dealing with the issue. The coordinator then asks for comments on their strengths and weaknesses, and asks for refinements and new ideas. The process continues, with eventual resolution either through the emergence of a consensus or through voting.

19.9 AVOIDING "PREDICTABLE SURPRISES"

The discussion so far has focused on groups coming to conclusions about issues recognized as requiring a decision. But organizations may have impediments to even recognizing the need for a decision. They can become trapped in a particular mindset, and be unable or unwilling to adjust to a changing reality.

---

105. Norbert L. Kerr and R. Scott Tindale, *Group Performance and Decisionmaking*, 55 Annual Review of Psychology 623–55 (2004); Brian Mullen, Craig Johnson, and Eduardo Salas, *Productivity Loss in Brainstorming Groups: A Meta-Analytic Integration*, 115 Psychological Bulletin 210–27 (1991).

106. Gene Rowe and George Wright, *Expert Opinions in Forecasting: The Role of the Delphi Technique*, *in* Principles of Forecasting 125–44 (J. Scott Armstrong ed., Norwell, MA: Kluwer Academic Publishers, 2001).

Without delving into the large field of organizational behavior, we summarize Max Bazerman's and Michael Watkins' study of "predictable surprises"—instances in which entire organizations failed to recognize impending crises and correct their behavior in order to avert them, despite "prior awareness of all of the information necessary to anticipate the events and their consequences."[107]

Bazerman and Watkins describe six basic characteristics that lead to predictable surprises:

1. People know that a problem exists that would not solve itself. (For example, Enron and Arthur Andersen managers knew that not having independent consultants and auditors would lead to conflicts of interests.)
2. People recognize that the problem is getting worse over time, but do not respond adequately. (For example, global warming is widely recognized to be an impending crisis, but the nations of the world have yet to make it a top priority.)
3. Fixing the problem is costly, while the benefits of action are delayed. (For example, investing in alternative sources of energy requires a large upfront investment, while the rewards may not accrue until many years into the future.)
4. Along the same lines, fixing the problem will incur a certain cost in order to prevent an uncertain outcome. (For example, investing in security for ports and chemical plants has little incentive for leaders, since they are answerable for the high costs, but get no credit for the absence of a catastrophe.)
5. Needed changes do not occur because of the tendency to maintain the status quo. (For example, reducing the national debt may require reductions and/or equalization of Americans' standards of living.)
6. A "vocal minority benefits from inaction and is motivated to subvert the actions of leaders for their own private benefit." (For example, the U.S. auto industry fought hard to prevent increased fuel efficiency standards which they believe would be costly for them to meet.)

Bazerman and Watkins suggest a three-part model to help avoid predictable surprises. Their "RPM" model consists of: **R**ecognizing the problem, making it a **P**riority, and **M**obilizing a response.

First, recognizing a problem requires an effortful process that helps prevent groups from collectively falling prey to the tendency to see what they expect or want to see, just as individuals often do. For instance, setting clear performance thresholds helps groups recognize when a strategy is failing, thus triggering a reevaluation that might otherwise have been neglected.

---

107. Max H. Bazerman and Michael D. Watkins, Predictable Surprises: The Disasters You Should Have Seen Coming, and How to Prevent Them: Leadership for the Common Good (Boston, MA: Harvard Business Press, 2004).

Second, once it identifies potential problems, an organization must prioritize them. The authors suggest assigning an advocate to focus on a particular problem and to give that person a strong voice in the organization. This helps to ensure that as long as the problem has a committed and consistent advocate, it cannot be easily ignored.

Finally, once a potential problem has been recognized and made a priority, the organization must mobilize to confront it. Here the authors suggest strategies, such as effective coalition-building, to ensure that various actors are working toward the same ends.

19.10 OPTIMIZING GROUP DECISION MAKING

For all of the hazards described in the preceding pages, group decision making is inevitable. In an increasingly complex world, many problems cannot be adequately addressed by a single individual with limited knowledge and cognitive capacity. Groups can pool knowledge, information, and experience. They can divide a complex task into multiple components. And groups have the potential to correct members' errors, to reduce decision variability, and moderate individual idiosyncrasies. Moreover, participation in making decisions can increase people's motivation and sense of commitment, and can enhance the perceived legitimacy of whatever course of action is chosen.

Rupert Brown noted, "[T]he question is not . . . how we can dispense with group decision making, but how we can capitalize on its advantages while circumventing its defects."[108] The key to answering his question lies in assembling a decision-making group whose members bring diverse knowledge sets, skills, and perspectives to the task, and then utilizing the potential unique contribution of each member. The independence of group members must be preserved, so that they can, in fact, make their diverse contributions. This requires addressing pressures toward social conformity, power imbalances, and members' needs to maintain their social position. The decision-making process must be designed to ensure that the group considers a broad range of alternative options before converging on a decision. And, where the group is to persist over time and make repeated decisions, mechanisms must be designed to aggregate and re-present information to enable the group and its members to receive feedback and learn from experience.

Lawyers and policy makers regularly serve as the leaders of decision-making groups. The leader's role is key in harnessing the power of groups and in preventing the pitfalls that attend group decision making. Understanding the

---

108. Rupert Brown, Group Processes (2d ed. Malden, MA: Blackwell Publishing, 2000).

dynamics of group decision making is essential for good policy making in an increasingly complex world".

19.11 THE EFFECTS OF ACCOUNTABILITY ON INDIVIDUAL AND GROUP DECISION-MAKING PERFORMANCE

The preceding discussion has focused on the interaction of decision makers with other people. But knowledge that one will be required to justify one's decision to others may influence one's decision, even without any actual interaction with one's audience. Mere anticipation of others' reactions may cause decision makers to change their approach to the problem.

Accountability has become a popular concept in business, politics, and elsewhere, but its effects are not always clearly understood. Received wisdom tells us that that a decision maker's accountability to others improves the quality of the decision. Though this sometimes is true, accountability can also lead to poorer decision making. This section summarizes the literature on the effects of accountability.[109]

All other things being equal, accountability is likely to reduce error and bias in contexts in which, for whatever reasons, people tend to make mistakes that they could prevent with extra attention or effort. For example, the expectation that they will have to justify their decision leads people to think more carefully and logically, and not to be satisfied with using unarticulated criteria or unsubstantiated empirical judgments to arrive at answers. Moreover, accountability makes people more likely to identify their own sources of bias, because of the need to justify themselves to others who do not necessarily view the decision with the same biases.

But, like other social phenomenon, the benefits of accountability depend on a number of factors, and holding a decision maker accountable can sometimes be counterproductive. Like other social phenomena, the benefits of accountability depend on a number of factors, such as:

- *Whether the views of the audience are known or unknown.* Decision makers who know the views of the audience to whom they are accountable tend to conform decisions to gain the audience's favor. For example, officials awarding financial aid who did not need to justify their decisions to students tended to award aid based on recipients' needs; accountable officials tried to please all applicants by giving something to everyone. When the audience's views are unknown, decision makers tend to engage

109. This section is based largely on the excellent review essay by Jennifer S. Lerner and Philip E. Tetlock, *Accounting for the Effects of Accountability*, 125 PSYCHOLOGICAL BULLETIN 225 (1999).

in *preemptive self-criticism*, anticipating how the decision would be viewed from various perspectives.

- *Whether one is accountable for the quality of the decision process or the decision's substantive outcome.* For example, a foundation could hold its program officers accountable for the success of their grants each year, or it could focus instead on whether the program officers were making thoughtful, informed outcome-focused decisions. Ultimately, the proof of a good process is in its outcomes; but this may take many years. A program officer who is held accountable only for outcomes may be afraid to take appropriate risks in making grants since, even if the risks are well-considered in terms of expected value, they could still fail and lead to a bad outcome. On the whole, accountability for the process tends to improve the decision's accuracy and calibration while accountability for outcome can reduce decision quality.

Even when accountability has the potential to improve decision making, it does not necessarily attenuate all biases, and may actually amplify some. In a review of the experimental literature, Jennifer Lerner and Philip Tetlock concluded that "accountability attenuated biases to the extent that (a) suboptimal performance resulted from lack of self-critical attention to the judgment process and (b) improvement required no special training in formal decision rules, only greater attention to the information provided."

Accountability may actually lead to poorer decision making when a biased choice seems the easiest to justify. For example, decision makers may anticipate less criticism of a decision if they choose the middle ground between two extreme values (see Section 14.5.3.b) or if they take into account all of the information presented, including irrelevant information that reduces diagnosticity (see Section 8.5.3).

Finally, it should be noted that in some situations where accountability detracts from the quality of a decision, the decision maker may actually be pursuing other goals—for example, a politician may wish to satisfy members of her political base, or members of a group may wish to manage their relationships with each other at the expense of full deliberation of a wide range of available policy alternatives.

20. CONCLUSION
Learning from Experience

In Section 1.7, we inquired into the nature of expertise—particularly the ways that experts integrate deliberative and intuitive processes into their judgments and decisions. And much of the book has been designed to provide the academic foundation for lawyers and policy makers to develop their own professional expertise in problem solving and decision making. This concluding chapter outlines what we hope you have learned in the classroom, and asks how you can develop and hone your expertise beyond the classroom.

20.1 LEARNING IN THE CLASSROOM: THE FOUNDATIONS OF PROBLEM-SOLVING EXPERTISE

The core analytic attributes that underlie problem-solving and decision-making expertise include:

- clarity about interests and objectives—your own, your clients', and your constituents';
- creativity in considering a problem in alternative frames;
- creativity in generating plausible alternative solutions that solve the problem and best satisfy the interests at stake;
- strategic planning—the ability to chart a course from wherever you are to a satisfactory solution;
- creativity and rigor in analyzing correlation and causation—creativity in developing hypotheses and methods for testing them, and rigor in applying the tests.

This book introduces some basic concepts and techniques for problem solving and decision making, including:

- A deliberative process checklist—essential for novices and often useful even for experts.
- Statistics, which provide a formal approach to hypothesis testing. Statistics is the empiricist's most fundamental tool, and an honest policy maker's best friend.
- Expected utility theory, which provides a formal approach to decision making, and a couple of easy-to-use tools: the subjective linear model for value-based decision making and decision trees for decision making under risk. Whatever its limits, expected utility theory sets a baseline for rational choice—strong enough as to require a justification for departures from it.

We have also devoted much attention to errors that attend intuitive decision making—the so called "heuristics and biases" research agenda in the field of judgment and decision making (JDM) and the insights of its offspring, behavioral economics. And we have described methods for helping avoid these errors, to the limited extent possible. Beyond the core domain of JDM, we have also looked at the dynamics of social influence in the belief that lawyers and policy makers are called upon both to influence others and to protect clients and citizens from pernicious influence.[1]

How does the academic study of these matters bear on your development of *expertise* as lawyers and policy makers? Expertise depends as much on intuition as analysis. Yet, as the JDM and social psychology literature demonstrate, intuition is extremely vulnerable to biases, framing, and influence. How—as the JDM scholar Robin Hogarth asked—does one educate intuition?

The scientific method and statistics play important roles in the process. They suggest that even when one-off intuitive judgments must be made rapidly on the spot, they should be tested in retrospect—in aggregate, where possible—so you can see how well you fared and learn how to improve. The scientific method and statistics help you avoid some of the recurrent errors that we have examined. They press us to seek disconfirming evidence: a contingency table requires you to fill in the cells where there is *no* result. Statistics counter the availability and representativeness heuristics by treating sample size as an essential determinant of statistical significance. It counters overconfidence by requiring that statistical hypothesis testing state the acceptable margin of error.

We believe that developing the systematic habits of thought inherent in deliberative decision making improves subsequent problem solving done at the intuitive end of the spectrum, or at least facilitates reflective monitoring of intuitive judgments. We find a compelling parallel in Constantin Stanislavski's description of an actor's preparation:[2]

> One cannot always create subconsciously and with inspiration. No such genius exists in the world. Therefore our art teaches us first of all to create consciously and rightly, because that will best prepare the way for the blossoming of the subconscious, which is inspiration. The more you have of conscious creative moments in your role, the more chance you will have of a flow of inspiration.

20.2 LEARNING FROM EXPERIENCE

Gary Blasi, from whom we borrowed our protagonist, Luis Trujillo, says that he "has acquired a significant body of knowledge—about opposing lawyers, about

---

1. Robin Hogarth, Educating Intuition (Chicago: University of Chicago Press, 2001).

2. Constantin Stanislavski, An Actor Prepares 15 (Elizabeth Reynolds Hapgood trans., New York: Routledge, 1989).

trial judges, about the likely consequences of certain actions—from his many previous interactions with other lawyers, other judges." It would be more accurate to say that Trujillo, like any other professional, has had the *opportunity* to gain this knowledge. For example, while Trujillo's observation (in Chapter 1) about the judge's reception to motions for summary judgment may well be correct, it may also be based on a few vivid personal experiences or on settled wisdom with little empirical foundation.

While experience is inevitable, learning from experience is not. The last item in our deliberative checklist in Section 1.4.1 included monitoring the outcome of the decision in order to learn from it. As Gary Klein writes, experts learn from experience in several ways:

- They engage in reflective practice, so that each opportunity for practice has a goal and evaluation criterion.
- They compile an extensive experience bank.
- They obtain feedback that is accurate, diagnostic, and reasonably timely.
- They review experiences to derive new insights and learn from mistakes.

Personal characteristics play a role as well. Mark Kelman writes:

> People who might be described as "open-minded" rather than dogmatic, especially in the sense that they accept the possibility that their own thinking is fallible and that they feel obliged to evaluate the quality of arguments without much regard to their predispositions about how an issue ought to be resolved, are less prone to make many of the errors that . . . researchers have identified as "biases." If one wants to get a quick, intuitive feel for the sorts of dispositions one might be trying to measure here, think about how two subjects might answer the questions: "People should always take into consideration evidence that goes against their own beliefs" and "No one can talk me out of something that I know is right."[3]

The ability to learn from experience depends not only on the expert's personal qualities and stance toward learning, but on the learning environment in which he or she works. Learning requires reliable feedback and requires using that feedback advertently. Robin Hogarth distinguishes *kind* learning structures, in which people receive good feedback, from *wicked* environments, in which feedback can be misleading.[4] Determinants of the quality of the learning environment include the ratio of relevant to irrelevant or random feedback, and how exacting or lenient the system is with respect to incorrect judgments.[5] With respect to the speed and systematicity of feedback, consider the difference

3. Mark G. Kelman, The Heuristics Debate: Its Nature and Its Implications for Law and Policy (Oxford University Press, forthcoming 2010), *citing* Keith Stanovich, Who Is Rational? (Mahwah, NJ: Lawrence Erlbaum 1999).

4. Hogarth, *supra* at 98.

5. *Id.* 88–89.

between a meteorologist predicting tomorrow's weather and one predicting changes in climate as a result of global warming.

Recurring to Section 8.5, you can think about learning from experience in terms of Bayesian updating. You start with a set of beliefs—the prior probability—based on what you have learned in school, through mentorship, prior experience, and hunches. Experience provides new data, based on which you revise your beliefs. A kind learning environment provides highly diagnostic feedback.

Unfortunately, the learning environments for many lawyers and policy makers tend toward the wicked. Granted that a lawyer who specializes in handling a limited number of issues—say, disability or personal injury claims—has many opportunities to get feedback, most lawyers deal with a pretty wide variety of situations. Because of the large number of exogenous variables affecting most policy decisions, the frequent disconnect between a good process and a good outcome, and the delay in learning what the outcome actually was, policy makers often get no useful feedback at all.

20.2.1 The Focused Feedback of Mentorship

An expert's mentorship of a novice provides a "kind" learning environment in which the novice engages in practice with the expert's feedback and corrections. One of the most reflective and eloquent descriptions of the acquisition of expertise is Mark Twain's account of becoming a riverboat pilot under the tutelage of the experienced pilot, Horace Bixby. In *Life on the Mississippi*, Mark Twain writes:[6]

> It was plain that I had got to learn the shape of the river in all the different ways that could be thought of—upside down, wrong end first, inside out, fore-and-aft, and thrortships,—and then know what to do on gray nights when it hadn't any shape at all. So I set about it. In the course of time I began to get the best of this knotty lesson, and my self-complacency moved to the front once more. Mr. Bixby was all fixed, and ready to start it from the rear again. He opened on me after this fashion—
>
> "How much water did we have in the middle crossing at Hole-in-the-Wall, trip before last?
>
> I considered this an outrage. I said—
>
> "Every trip, down and up, the leadsmen are singing through that tangled place for three quarters of an hour on a stretch. How do you reckon I can remember such a mess as that?"
>
> "My boy, you've got to remember it. You've got to remember the exact spot and the exact marks the boat lay in when we had the shoalest water, in every one of the five hundred shoal places between St. Louis and New Orleans; and

6. Mark Twain, Life on the Mississippi 57–64 (New York: Penguin Classics, 1883: 1962).

you mustn't get the shoal soundings and marks of one trip mixed up with the shoal soundings and marks of another, either, for they're not often twice alike. You must keep them separate." . . .

[Twain sees what he believes to be a dangerous reef, and Bixby orders him to run over it.]

As it disappeared under our bows, I held my breath; but we slid over it like oil.

"Now don't you see the difference? It wasn't anything but a *wind* reef. The wind does that."

"So I see. But it is exactly like a bluff reef. How am I ever going to tell them apart?"

"I can't tell you. It is an instinct. By and by you will just naturally *know* one from the other, but you never will be able to explain why or how you know them apart."

It turned out to be true. The fact of the water, in time, became a wonderful book—a book that was a dead language to the uneducated passenger, but which told its mind to me without reserve, delivering its most cherished secrets as clear as if it uttered them with a voice.

20.2.2 After Mentorship: Learning from Mistakes

Experience is a great teacher but the tuition is high.

Some professions provide structured peer learning opportunities even after the mentorship phase; the morbidity and mortality conferences at hospitals are paradigmatic. To a large extent, however, professionals' continuing learning must come from their own reflections on experience. This is certainly true of much lawyering and policy making. So how do we revise our views based on experience? And particularly, how do we learn from mistakes?

In earlier chapters we saw that once people have committed to a course of action, there arise psychological barriers to changing that course. Beliefs, once formed, have a way of sticking, even in the face of evidence that they are mistaken.

Recognizing the mistakes and biases of others is often very easy. It may be obvious that Jim is far too optimistic about his investment portfolio, or that Anne may have fallen prey to the availability heuristic in deciding that driving across the country is safer than flying. Recognizing mistakes in our own reasoning, however, can be much more difficult. Building on Lee Ross's concept of *naïve realism* (Section 9.8), Emily Pronin, Thomas Gilovich, and Lee Ross have coined the term *bias blind spot* to describe people's readiness to see others' biases while believing that their own thinking is relatively bias-free.[7]

---

7. Emily Pronin, Thomas Gilovich, and Lee Ross, *Objectivity in the Eye of the Beholder: Divergent Perceptions of Bias in Self Versus Others*, 111 Psychological Review 781–99 (2004).

In concluding the book, let us review some common ways in which biases hinder learning from experience.

Confirmation biases. As we saw in Section 10.3, people tend to seek out evidence that supports their existing (or preferred) hypothesis and avoid looking for evidence that contradicts it. Closely related is the *biased assimilation* of evidence—our tendency to view evidence that favors our beliefs more favorably and less critically than evidence that challenges them. *Belief perseverance* is a cousin of these phenomena. Once we have formed an initial belief about any fact or value, we tend to process new information in light of our belief. If we have accumulated a network of supporting beliefs, it can become extremely difficult to reverse course, even when new evidence suggests that it would be reasonable to do so.

What Jerome Bruner and his colleagues have termed the "thirst for confirming redundancy"[8] has motivational as well as cognitive roots. We get invested—sometimes literally—in our own ideas and practice. The possibility of their being wrong can be a blow to our pocketbooks as well as our egos and reputations.

Poor feedback mechanisms. Learning from mistakes depends on feedback. Sometimes it is difficult to get feedback just because the data are not available, or not available quickly or in sufficient quantity or in a form conducive to learning. We are also prone to *distortions in acquiring data*—because of stress, schemas, and expectations—and to *distortions in retention and retrieval*—because of intervening events or just plain forgetting. We tend *not to notice omissions* (the dog that didn't bark in the nighttime). If these are largely cognitive phenomena, there's a strong motivational one as well: *avoiding feedback to minimize regret.*

Under- and over-generalization. Data are often presented in ways that make it difficult to generalize, to connect the dots. On the flip side, we readily overgeneralize, seeing relationships where none exist. This results from basic statistical errors—misunderstandings of probability, randomness, independence, sample size, regression to the mean—exacerbated by the illusion of control and the availability heuristic.

The flipside of the illusion of control is the *self-fulfilling prophecy*, where our empirical judgment actually affects the outcome. An example is the "Pygmalion" effect, where students who are predicted to perform better actually do so. There's a story about a nineteenth-century physician who didn't wash his hands between examining patients for a particular infectious disease and was therefore very good in predicting that the next patient he examined would have the disease.

Hindsight bias—the erroneous belief that we "knew it all along"— is also a barrier to learning from experience. Because many decisions are made in conditions of uncertainty about the outcomes, and because improving our

8. Jerome Bruner, Jacqueline Goodnow, and George Austin, A Study of Thinking (New York: Wiley, 1956).

decision-making prowess often depends on improving our predictions, each time we think that we "knew it all along" we lose an opportunity to improve.

Blame-avoidance strategies provide tremendous barriers to learning from experience. The phenomenon known as *attribution bias* leads us to attribute success to our ability and our failures to bad luck, our good deeds to our superior character and our bad deeds to compelling circumstances."[9] As the Duke of Wellington is said to have quipped, "victory has a thousand fathers; defeat is an orphan."

Defensiveness. Even if you don't kill the messenger, acting *defensively* will at least signal him not to bring you bad news again. We know a few people who are genuinely nondefensive—who will accept a criticism with dispassion or even invite it. Here's an alternative for those of us who don't have this quality: Whatever your inner feelings when someone criticizes you, *act* nondefensively. Not only will you get a lot more information that way, but you may actually become less instinctively defensive.

* * *

The overarching hypothesis of this book is that academic study can lay the foundation for developing expertise in problem solving, decision making, and professional judgment on the job. If many aspects of this hypothesis remain to be tested, it nonetheless seems like a pretty good bet. At very least we hope that you have learned something interesting about human behavior, including your own.

---

9. Lee Ross, *The Intuitive Psychologist and His Shortcomings: Distortions in the Attribution Process*, *in* L. Berkowitz (ed.), Advances in Experimental Social Psychology (Vol. 10) 173–220. (New York: Academic Press, 1977).

INDEX

Figures, notes, and tables are indicated by f, n, and t following the page numbers.